Individuals with Profound Disabilities

Individuals with Profound Disabilities

Instructional and Assistive Strategies

Les Sternberg
Editor

pro·ed
8700 Shoal Creek Boulevard
Austin, Texas 78757

pro·ed

© 1994 by PRO-ED, Inc.
8700 Shoal Creek Boulevard
Austin, Texas 78757-6897

Library of Congress Cataloging-in-Publication Data

Individuals with profound disabilities : instructional and assistive
    strategies / Les Sternberg, editor.
        p.   cm.
    Includes bibliographical references and index.
    ISBN 0-89079-557-6
        1. Handicapped—Education—United States.   2. Handicapped—
    Services for—United States.   I. Sternberg, Les.
    LC 4031.I53   1994
    371.91′0973—dc20   93-40705
                                                                    CIP

Production Manager: Alan Grimes
Production Coordinator: Adrienne Booth
Art Director: Lori Kopp
Reprints Buyer: Alicia Woods
Editor: Debra Berman
Editorial Assistant: Claudette Landry

Printed in the United States of America

1 2 3 4 5 6 7 8 9 10   98 97 96 95 94

In everyone's life sometimes the inner light goes out and bursts again into flame by an encounter with another human being. We should all be grateful for other people who rekindle our spirit.

Albert Schweitzer

This book is dedicated to the memory of Tom Haring.

Contents

Preface

The main impetus for this book was dissatisfaction. In 1982, Gary Adams and I edited a text called *Educating Severely and Profoundly Handi-capped Students* (published by Aspen). In 1988, I edited a second edition of that text entitled *Educating Students with Severe or Profound Handicaps* (published by PRO-ED). I must admit that these two efforts were monumental for me, for I told everyone after I completed my graduate studies that I would never get involved in authoring or editing a book because I never wanted to "reinvent the wheel." In producing these two texts, I convinced myself that I had not. But when each text was finally finished and available to the public, I came to share the same feelings of inadequacy that many authors and editors have experienced. Could I have better organized the material? Did I leave out anything, especially something that more appro-priately expressed my philosophy and beliefs? Should I have been more focused? These feelings started the day I received my advance copy.

During the spring of 1991, while drafting notes for a class that was using the 1988 text, I had an overwhelming feeling to try once again. But this time I was going to do it differently. This time I was going to solicit opinions from those who were familiar with the text and ask them how I ought to go about completing a revision. After sending out a survey both to those individuals who had used the text in course instruction and to those who had used the text as a resource, I found that the general perception was that the 1988 text was not focused enough. The consensus was to create a text that dealt only with individuals with profound disabilities; to excise consideration of topics that applied more to individuals with severe disabilities; and to expand cover-age of topics that would assist teacher trainers, researchers, and practition-ers who are dealing with or specializing in concerns of individuals with profound disabilities.

With help from others (many of whom are contributors to this text), I set about to design a new effort. I believe that this current text is more focused and has less content that one might describe as pertaining only to individuals with lesser degrees of disability. Of course, I would like to think that this effort will be considered *the* defining work by all of those who are involved with individuals with profound disabilities. Unfortunately, my personal philosophy and paranoia, as well as the reality of constant change, will ensure that this will never happen. It seems to have taken me an awfully long time to realize that the worth of texts of this nature should be measured only by the degree of change that they produce.

In the 1988 text, I spoke about the "virtue of ignorance," a concept coined by Seymour Sarason. Those possessing this virtue understand that we *may* have some short-term solutions to current problems experienced by individuals with profound disabilities, and that new problem constructs will likely force us not only to modify what once was but to abandon prior positions as well.

Those possessing the virtue of ignorance can admit that all of the answers are not known today and, most assuredly, will not be known tomorrow. We might be uncomfortable admitting that problems of individuals with profound disabilities are not finite and simple, but to do anything else will lead us to ignore a perplexity that forces continuous improvement.

I guess I'm still dissatisfied.

L. S.

Acknowledgments

I have been involved in a number of writing and editing tasks over the past few years, but I must admit that this current effort was my most difficult. I had been forewarned by many of my colleagues that choosing higher education administration as a career path would necessitate that I put my professional interests on the back burner. Given my personal nature, I took that as a challenge. To those colleagues who are taking the time to read the acknowledgment section of this text, you were right. But I have still been able to keep a small fire burning with the help of some very special people.

I would first like to thank Norene Daly who persuaded me to continue up the administrative stepladder, and then provided guidance as to how not to get hung up. She knew that these time-saving techniques would afford me the opportunity to not completely lose sight of my personal and professional agenda regarding individuals with profound disabilities.

To all of the contributors to the text, I owe a debt of gratitude not only for their written work but for the time they took to communicate their own agendas to me. These conversations helped to crystalize my own thoughts and positions.

To our office's administrative assistant, Katy Rice, and office secretaries, Debbie Graf and Heidi Eichorn, for their patience in refining tables and figures, reading some sections of my drafts, and asking pertinent questions such as "Can't you say this more simplistically?"

And finally to my wife Jean, my sons Bill and Matthew, and my daughters Karen and Katie, for their patience with my compulsive behavior, their constant efforts to make me change, and their humor along the way.

Part I

General Concerns

Individuals with Profound Disabilities: Definitions, Characteristics, and Conceptual Framework

LES STERNBERG

T he debate as to who are individuals with profound disabilities has tended to overshadow consideration of what educational or training efforts should be used with them. This situation has been caused, in part, by a lack of definition of the population and by educators' lack of exposure to them as individuals. It has also been caused by the tendency of many in the educational community to espouse curriculum and intervention practices as being appropriate regardless of any issues or concerns that might be idiosyncratic to a population. Specifically, two predominant issues have emerged: whether individuals with profound disabilities exhibit similar needs to those whose disabilities differ significantly in terms of type and degree, and whether techniques used with the latter group can effectively meet the needs of the former group.

Within the framework of this text (further clarification will follow), individuals with profound disabilities include those who experience, what has been termed until recently, profound mental retardation. Individuals with this type and degree of impairment have a greater likelihood than those from other populations to have accompanying sensory and/or physical disabilities, as well as significant medical problems.

Given the new definition of mental retardation adopted by the American Association on Mental Retardation (Luckasson et al., 1992), degrees of mental disability (e.g., mild, moderate, severe, profound) are no longer posited. Rather, mental retardation is viewed within the framework of the type or level of support that might be needed to address specific needs. Within this definition, four dimensions are used to describe an individual: intellectual functioning and adaptive skills, psychological and emotional considerations, physical health and etiology of the condition, and current and optimal environments. Once a comprehensive description of the individual's strengths and weaknesses is provided, the pattern and intensity of necessary support is determined. Four levels of intensity are possible: intermittent (as needed), limited (time-limited but more concentrated than intermittent), extensive (regular involvement, as in a daily regimen, over a long-term basis), and pervasive (constant and high-intensity involvement). Meeting the needs of individuals with profound disabilities will likely require a pervasive level of support.

Knowing who comprises this population is only a first step in addressing the needs of individuals who are profoundly disabled. In that considerable differences of opinion exist as to who these individuals are (Logan, Alberto, Kana, & Waylor, 1991), it should not be surprising that the history of training or educational services for them has been extremely brief. Definitional problems notwithstanding, this brevity is due primarily to the fact that the types and severity of the disabilities represented by this population are of such a degree that many professionals once had extreme difficulty conceiving of any benefit that might accrue to this group through educational or training efforts. This conception, in turn, led to a prevailing attitude among many individuals that any research involving education or training directed toward this population, aside from being extremely time-consuming, would likely produce limited dividends. Without any substantive research base documenting that changes or gains could be obtained through specific interventions, therefore, the overall attitude of educational or training stagnation persisted (Sternberg, 1988).

The past few years, however, have witnessed a significant change in this situation. Professionals have revisited issues related to the relevance of various initiatives directed toward individuals with profound disabilities, with a concomitant increased emphasis on educational and training research. Although still very limited, the research base has been expanding. Even though many of the findings from these research efforts are somewhat equivocal, certain positive outcomes have been found.

These research findings, however, were not the predominant causes for change but rather resulted from the change itself. Professionals have redirected their efforts because various philosophical and ethical viewpoints, originally conceived of in application to individuals with lesser degrees of disability, have become initiatives for change for individuals with profound disabilities as well. These viewpoints cover such issues as equal access to and efficacy of services, deinstitutionalization, integration, and improved quality of life. Although discussions and debate have continued related to drawing distinctions between those who might benefit from education or training and those who might not, the principle of zero exclusion has tended to obviate the distinction (Dussault, 1989).

DEFINING THE POPULATION

To provide a clearer picture of what is and will continue to be involved with research and practice pertaining to individuals with profound disabilities, in this section, I discuss in more detail the characteristics of this population. As is typically found in consideration of individuals with disabilities, general definitions are often posited to serve as a framework within which needs and characteristics can be discussed. The area of profound disabilities is no exception, although the degree of effort in defining the population has certainly been less than definitional efforts directed toward other areas of handicapping condition (Lorr & Rotatori, 1985).

A definition can serve a number of purposes. First, it can provide guidance in relation to eligibility of services. Second, it can assist in administrative decision making (e.g., placement for service and specification of general program goals). Third, it can provide direction in terms of assessment and delineation of specific services.

Historically, individuals with profound disabilities have been subsumed under general definitions of individuals termed severely disabled or severely–profoundly disabled. Many of these definitions have served limited purposes. For example, those definitions that have relied on exclusion (e.g., describing the group as one that simply does not belong to other identified categories or one that needs services beyond those typically offered) have provided almost no clarification regarding assessment and practice. Definitions that have delineated categories for eligibility (e.g., deafness and blindness), without specifying service or educational needs, have often led to intervention decisions based solely upon the presence of a label. Likewise, psychometric definitions (e.g., those specifying scores from some measure) have tended not to delineate the specific needs of individuals.

Perhaps the major problem with these definitions, however, is the assumption that the characteristics and needs of individuals with profound disabilities are similar to those characteristics and needs of individuals with severe disabilities. This was understandable given the fact that many members of the former group were likely to be found in extremely segregated settings, which for all intents and purposes produced an "out of sight, out of mind" condition. Especially over the past decade, however, deinstitutionalization and integration efforts have afforded more professionals and families to experience the differences. Also, as stated earlier, not only are these differences significant, but they have subsequently led to the questioning of the relevance and utility for individuals with profound disabilities of various educational or training models and practices designed for individuals with severe disabilities (Green, Canipe, Way, & Reid, 1986).

Attempts have been made to more adequately differentiate individuals with profound disabilities from those with lesser degrees of disability. A number of these attempts have involved descriptions of the general behavioral characteristics of individuals with profound disabilities, with emphases on behavioral excesses and deficits (Guess et al., 1988; Landesman-Dwyer & Sackett, 1978; Rainforth, 1982). As Logan et al. (1991) pointed out, however, many of these descriptions conflict or overlap, thereby creating confusion as to what individuals constitute the group termed *profoundly disabled*. Also, without placement of these characteristics into a developmental or comparative perspective, critical information is lost (e.g., expectations of the individual; meaning and relevance of specific behavioral excesses).

Sternberg (1988), using a developmental framework, attempted to provide separate definitions for *students* with severe disabilities and those with profound disabilities. The definitions for both groups were similar in that they (a) expressed the need to have individuals identified as members of a legally defined category of handicapping condition; (b) focused on specific areas of functioning within which an individual would have to display a significant developmental discrepancy and ceiling level; and (c) described the type of educational structure that might be necessary for the provision of services. The following suggested definition for individuals with profound disabilities represents a slight modification of the one Sternberg proposed in 1988:

> An individual with profound disabilities is one who (a) is eligible to receive services under one or more legally defined categories of handicapping conditions; (b) exhibits profound developmental discrepancies in all five of the following behavioral–content areas: cognition, communication, social skills development, motor–mobility, and activities of daily living (self-help skills); and (c) requires a service structure with continuous monitoring and observation.

The basic differences between the group classified as profoundly disabled and the group classified as severely disabled relate to the number of areas of functioning affected and the degree of effect on those areas. To classify an individual as profoundly disabled, one must demonstrate that all five areas of functioning are affected (vs. only a majority of areas for those classified as severely disabled) and that the individual exhibits a developmental discrepancy of no more than one-fourth of chronological-age expectancy (one-half of expectancy for those classified as severely disabled). This definition also posits a developmental ceiling of 2 years of age for each area of functioning (6 years of age for those classified as severely disabled). If the individual functions above that level, the individual cannot be classified as profoundly disabled.

In terms of needed educational or service structure, Sternberg (1988) indicated that more restrictive structures would likely be necessary for individuals with profound disabilities. In his description, a wide range of placements were possible, including segregated programs in completely segregated facilities. Due to various initiatives regarding movement into more integrated and normalized settings, and the success that these initiatives have shown, the recommended range should be more limited in favor of less restrictiveness. For example, within the school arena, the range would likely be from segregated classrooms to fully integrated classrooms, with both on regular school campuses. Within the home and community environments, the range would likely be from cluster arrangement living facilities as the most restrictive placement to fully integrated community-based facilities and programs as the least restrictive. Since Sternberg's (1988) book, a wider range of support options have become available for people with profound disabilities.

The major intent of the definitions posited by Sternberg (1988) was two-fold: (1) to provide a type of operational distinction between individuals with severe disabilities and those with profound disabilities, and (2) to clarify what developmental repertoire might be used to describe individuals who were profoundly disabled. Although considered rather restrictive at the time, the definition of individuals with profound disabilities may not be representative or restrictive enough by current standards. Although a range of performance is specified in the definition, the overall developmental discrepancy and ceiling levels may not adequately describe a considerable segment of the population of individuals with profound disabilities that is currently presenting itself. These individuals are portraying developmental discrepancies and ceiling levels that are considerably lower than the upper range of discrepancy levels initially used to distinguish them from individuals with severe disabilities.

Readjusting the upper limits downward to more adequately describe individuals with profound disabilities (e.g., a developmental discrepancy representing a 10% level of performance with a ceiling of 1 year of age) would certainly be feasible if the individuals then excluded would more appropriately fall within the definition of severe disabilities. This becomes a matter of expectations and implications—expectations of performance level and type, and implications for the use of various educational and training strategies. Many professionals have now drawn distinctions between individuals with profound disabilities and individuals with severe disabilities because the expectations and implications for each are different. These differences are related not only to one's capability for independent functioning but also to the utility of specific educational or training models and methods.

Some data indicate that differences exist in performance between subgroups of individuals who have been classified as profoundly disabled (Hotte, Monroe, Philbrook, & Scarlata, 1984). Additional data are needed, however, to determine whether these differences are sufficient to assume that expectations of and implications for any "higher functioning" subgroup are the same as those related to individuals with severe disabilities.

Due to the questions raised above, and the lack of a sufficient data base, the following discussion of characteristics of individuals with profound disabilities assumes a recommended developmental ceiling of approximately 24 months of age.

CHARACTERISTICS

Although one might expect a group that typifies some extreme level of functioning to comprise members who are rather similar, this is certainly not the case for individuals who are profoundly disabled. The heterogeneity of conditions within this group makes a delineation of specific characteristics rather difficult. If one accepts the premises, however, that (a) the presence of a significant cognitive impairment is common to the group and (b) a certain ceiling level of performance can be used as an inclusion designator, it is possible to describe types and ranges of developmental characteristics for the population. The major purpose of the section that follows is to give the reader a general idea of what characteristics might typically be displayed by individuals who are classified as profoundly disabled. The five areas of functioning employed in Sternberg's (1988) definition are used as the framework for a discussion of these characteristics.

A number of cautions are in order. First, one should not assume that a depiction of developmental characteristics is meant to imply that individuals with profound disabilities necessarily follow the same developmental progression as individuals who are nondisabled. As Hogg and Sebba (1987) pointed out, "that framework offers us a context in which to observe and question, a framework which would otherwise be lacking, and a context in which the presence or absence of deviancy can be considered" (p. 23). Second, such a depiction is not meant to imply that individuals who are profoundly disabled will display equal levels of discrepancy across all areas of functioning. Third, when multiple handicapping conditions are present, characteristics within each area will likely reflect the effects of central nervous system (CNS) dysfunction and sensory or physical disabilities (see Chapter 3). Fourth, an interactive effect is likely between areas such that functioning within one area will interact with and affect functioning within another. Fifth, a discussion of developmental characteristics does not preclude the potential use of functional models of services delivery or expectations of functional types of behaviors for many individuals with profound disabilities.

Cognitive Characteristics

The presence of a cognitive impairment affects both the manner in which and the degree to which an individual interacts with the environment, as well as the impact that the environment has on that individual. In terms of extremely depressed levels of functioning, it is not uncommon to find individuals with profound disabilities who are totally *unresponsive to the external environment* (see the discussion of persistent vegetative state in Chapter 3). Their *behavioral repertoire may be reflexive* in nature. If movement is possible, *movements may not be in response to external stimulation.*

At a somewhat higher level of functioning, some individuals may exhibit *changes in behavior as a result of aural, visual, tactile, or olfactory stimulation. Repetitive bodily movements* (e.g., self-stimulation) may be exhibited where a physical disability does not preclude the possibility of the individual's making more intricate movements. Some individuals may begin to exhibit *anticipatory behaviors* when placed in certain positions (e.g., preparation for feeding). If a significant visual or auditory impairment is not obvious, *eye–ear coordinating movement* may be displayed. If the presence of a physical disability does not adversely affect range of motion of the arms or use of the hands, *reaching for objects or persons* and *grasping objects* may be observed. The individual may *demonstrate familiarity with certain objects* by manipulating them over time in the same fashion.

Some individuals with profound disabilities may exhibit even higher level cognitive behaviors, including *chaining behaviors to intentionally obtain objects* and *demonstrating knowledge that objects can cause specific actions* (e.g., grabbing a person's hand to reactivate a blender). Also included may be a preliminary *understanding of differences in size* (e.g., initial interaction with small objects leads to appropriate hand and finger movements, whereas initial interaction with large objects produces appropriate arm and body movements). *Interacting or playing with objects in new and different ways* and *functionally using varieties of nonfeeding and nondressing items* (e.g., comb) may also be exhibited. Typically, individuals who exhibit these types of behaviors also demonstrate various forms of *trial-and-error problem-solving behavior.*

Behaviors that are exemplars of the highest level of cognitive functioning for individuals who are profoundly disabled are those that indicate a more advanced grasp of representational skills. These include *solving practical problems without first engaging in trial-and-error practices, using objects to represent other objects, demonstrating an understanding that pictures can represent objects,* and *remembering after a protracted period of time where an object was left,* even though the object was not left in its customary place.

Communication Characteristics

In that communication skills are precursors to the development of language skills, they have both receptive and expressive components. As with language skills, receptive and expressive communication behaviors often develop in a type of parallel fashion.

Receptive communication characteristics

For individuals who are not deaf, the lowest level of receptive communication is likely to be exhibited through some type of *startle response to loud, sudden noises.* If physical movement is being displayed, *movement may cease in reaction to some noise produced artificially* (e.g., a bell). Later in development, one might observe a *cessation of movement in response to a voice.* Higher development might be assumed when *gross body movement is initiated in reaction to a voice. Localization of a speaker* (e.g., through head or eye movement) may be exhibited if not prevented by the presence of a physical disability or if the individual is not placed in a position that interferes with the production of the behavior. The individual may *more actively participate in a movement or motion that is begun and continued by another* who is in close physical contact.

At a somewhat higher level of functioning, an individual who is profoundly disabled might *demonstrate understanding of simple tactile and verbal signals* (e.g., someone tugs the individual's arm, which leads him or her to display approach behavior). The individual might *imitate familiar movements or sounds produced by another.* Also, the individual might *stop movement or an activity when his or her name is called or when "no" is spoken.* Some individuals might *exhibit appropriate behaviors when another provides a gesture indicating the action to be performed.* More sophisticated representational skills are assumed when individuals *begin to anticipate routine events when shown an object that is associated with the event.* Also, an individual might *comply to certain simple actions based upon verbal requests* (e.g., "open mouth").

More involved receptive communication behaviors include *demonstrating understanding of gesture–object relationships,* where the gesture indicates how the object is used; *identifying familiar objects when those objects are referred to through the use of formal language;* and *responding appropriately to inhibitory words* (e.g., "stop," "wait") *and to two- or three-word commands or requests.* Behaviors that are exemplars of the highest level of receptive communication functioning for individuals who are profoundly disabled involve even more sophistication. For example, an individual might *carry out multiple-step commands, demonstrate understanding of a distinction in pronouns,* and *exhibit discrimination and matching skills in choice-making situations.*

Expressive communication characteristics

Although intention cannot be assumed at extremely low levels of functioning, certain behaviors that are considered potential expressive communication skills might be obvious. These include *crying, turning one's eyes to a person's face,* and, somewhat later, *vocalizing other than crying.* When a familiar person is talking, an individual who is profoundly disabled might *smile* or *vocalize.* Intentional expressive skills are indicated when an individual exhibits *undifferentiated communication,* where one behavior means a number of different things. In addition, intentional expressive skills can be assumed when the individual *provides a motoric or vocal indication that a person in physical contact should continue movement or activity.* Some individuals might exhibit *spontaneous vocal sounds to indicate either the initiation or continuation of socialization activities.*

Self-initiated simple gestures or noncrying vocalizations to express wants or needs might be exhibited. If speech sounds are possible, an individual might display some types of *echolalic syllable (nonword) speech.* As indices of a somewhat higher level of functioning, individuals might display *gestures or vocalizations that are meaningful to them and a few others but used only in specific contexts or environments* (e.g., using a nonformal bathroom gesture, but only at home). These gestures might become more refined as an individual *uses gestures when asking for objects, with the gesture indicating how the object can be used.* An individual might begin to *vocalize or exhibit an appropriate gesture in protest of something that he or she wishes not to do.*

The highest level of expressive communication skill development is indicated by the individual's beginning to *use more formal language means in place of gestures to express wants and needs.* Although gestures might still be used, these *gestures begin to represent objects or activities* rather than what one might do with objects or in the activities. *Combinations of words or gestures* become more likely, and an individual might be able to *specify the relationships between pictures and what they represent.*

Social Skills Characteristics

Within the social skills domain, indices of extremely depressed performance would be obvious when individuals are *unable to exhibit appropriate and observable reactions to pleasant and unpleasant stimuli.* These reactions might be followed by *increasing or decreasing activity levels based upon visual or tactile contact with objects.* In terms of person-to-person interaction, individuals with profound disabilities might *react to direct attention by moving, vocalizing, or smiling.*

At a somewhat higher level, an individual might *respond to social approach* and *display continued interest in persons who are present.* An individual may begin to *recognize familiar people* (e.g., produce the same type of sound or movement when a specific person is present), *begin to discriminate strangers,* and *attempt to solicit adult attention through eye contact, vocalizing, and/or smiling.* This solicitation may be followed by *more pronounced efforts at seeking reactions from others.* Attempts at gaining social approval may become apparent (e.g., continuing a behavior that produced smiles from others).

An individual might begin to *cooperate in social interactions that are initiated by others* (e.g., self-care routines). *Self-initiated interactions with other people* might be apparent if the individual begins to offer objects, imitates an action, or initiates a routine. A more sophisticated level of social skills development is indicated when an individual who is profoundly disabled begins to *more actively use objects to establish social interactions and relationships with people.* Also, the individual may begin to develop an awareness of the importance of these objects in social control as he or she *begins to claim and defend ownership of personal items.*

Motor–Mobility Characteristics

For the sake of adequate description, a differentiation between fine-motor characteristics, gross-motor characteristics, and mobility characteristics is necessary. Fine-motor characteristics refer to the use of hands and arms, where arm use is for the expressed purpose of facilitating hand use (e.g., extension movements for grasping to occur). Gross-motor characteristics refer to those motor behaviors used in postural control (e.g., being able to hold one's head, trunk, and/or arms in a stable position). Mobility characterisics refer to those behaviors that must be committed when an individual wishes to change position in space. An individual's capacity to exhibit all of the aforementioned categories of behaviors is based in large part on the intactness of the motoric system.

Fine-motor characteristics

The ability to demonstrate a voluntary grasp is one of the hallmarks of fine-motor development. Although the presence of a significant physical or visual disability affects such development, exemplars of various developmental levels of grasps are likely to be found in the population of individuals who are profoundly disabled. At the most depressed level, *no motility of hands or arms would be obvious.* If motility is possible, an individual might exhibit a *palmar grasp reflex,* where the entire palmar surface of the hands and fingers is used. This reflex may be reduced if more voluntary and digital grasps develop. For example, the palmar reflex grasp might change to a *radial palmar grasp* (where the individual uses only the radial [near forearm] half of the palm including the thumb and index finger) and *scissor grasp* (use of the hollowed surface between the thumb and the index finger). An individual might exhibit a *preliminary pincer grasp* (use of tip of the index finger with the hollowed surface between this finger and the thumb). This might be followed by *pointing-to-touch,* but the individual is unable to grasp an object. A more *fully articulated pincer grasp* might be observed, where an individual uses only the tips of both the index finger and the thumb.

Other fine-motor exemplars might be evident. *Reaching to touch one's hand with the other hand while looking at the first hand* is a behavior that is exhibited even by individuals who are blind. This might be followed by *more extensive hand playing* and *reaching and touching objects using symmetrical arm and hand movements.*

Gross-motor characteristics

The type and degree of postural control can be observed within a number of different bodily positions. In the prone position (i.e., front part of the body lying upon the ground), an individual with profound disabilities *may not be able to lift his or her head.* Some individuals may be *able to lift their heads briefly without the use of elbows or hands.* A transition period may be exhibited when an individual *uses elbows with arms spread out to the side to lift his or her head.* This might then be modified to a position where the individual is *able to lift and hold his or her head upward while bearing weight on opened hands and extended arms.* In this position, some individuals may begin to *bring their knees under their abdomen* and then *support their bodies on extended arms and knees.*

An individual's ability to demonstrate sitting-up and standing behavior is also dependent upon postural control. Some individuals with profound disabilities *will not be able to assume a sitting-up position.* Others *will be able to assume a sitting-up position but only with support* through external means (e.g., another person or equipment) or internal means (e.g., leaning on one's own arms). Those individuals who are *able to assume independent sitting* may be able to exhibit a transition to standing-up and, possibly, walking behavior.

Mobility characteristics

Type and degree of mobility can also be observed within a number of different positions. In the prone position, an individual with profound disabilities might *not exhibit any movement.* Another individual might *exhibit mobility in the prone position through arm and leg movements,* but the movement may appear to be haphazard. Some individuals might *display intentional forward movement on the stomach through movement of the arms and/or legs.* This may eventually lead to *creeping and crawling on all fours.*

Another type of mobility has to do with *rolling from prone to supine* (on the back) or *supine to prone.* Again, some individuals with profound disabilities may not exhibit these skills. If the ability is expressed, individuals with profound disabilities will likely exhibit different ways in which the mobility is achieved (e.g., rotating or not rotating the hips).

Self-Help Skills Characteristics

A number of areas are included within the general category of self-help skills or activities of daily living. In relation to individuals who are profoundly disabled, the four that typically receive the most attention are eating, toileting, dressing, and personal grooming. These categories are most often related to concepts of independent functioning. It is important to realize that, even though significant deficits are obvious, through methods of partial participation, considerably higher levels of functioning might be developed with many individuals with profound disabilities (see Chapter 10).

Eating skills characteristics

For individuals with profound disabilities who are able to receive food products orally, a range of eating skills are obvious, from *being totally dependent on others to initiate and complete a feeding routine* to *being able to finger feed* to *independently using a cup and spoon for self-feeding.* Many individuals with profound disabilities, especially due to the presence of medical conditions or physical disabilities, present significant problems related to what types of food products they may ingest. If the individual is on a type of liquefied or semi-solid food diet, once food substances are placed near the lips, he or she may *exhibit a continuous sucking behavior* to bring food into the mouth. If more solid types of food are permitted, an individual may *exhibit limited chewing skills and limited ability to move food within the mouth.*

Toileting skills characteristics

As with eating skills, individuals with profound disabilities exhibit a range of toileting skills. What skills an individual exhibits are related, in large part, to whether any significant physical or medical conditions exist. It is highly likely, however, that individuals with profound disabilities *will be unable to exhibit total, independent toileting.* Some may display precursors to assisted toileting, such as *an awareness of being wet or soiled, a regular pattern of urination or bowel movements,* and *the ability to remain dry for extended periods of time.* Some individuals may *be able to follow and be successful through use of an artificial toileting routine* (i.e., being toileted after a fixed amount of time transpires) *or a natural schedule* (i.e., being toileted based upon the passage of typical or natural events).

Dressing skills characteristics

Although different types of clothing and assistive aids affect the type and degree of dressing skills exhibited, as a rule, individuals with profound disabilities who are physically capable of displaying requisite behaviors *will be unable to fully execute dressing and undressing behaviors.* Some individuals may *participate in or cooperate with various dressing and undressing routines* initiated by another. As a rule, individuals will tend to display *more advanced undressing than dressing skills.*

Grooming skills characteristics

Individuals with profound disabilities will likely *require assistance in washing and drying hands and face, brushing teeth, and brushing hair.* As with dressing and undressing skills, some individuals will *participate or show active cooperation when grooming skills are initiated by another.* In certain respects, the degree of participation or cooperation will be based upon how invasive an individual with profound disabilities perceives the grooming skill to be.

Other Behavioral Characteristics

Aside from the range of characteristics and behavioral deficits described above, individuals with profound disabilities often display other characteristics that are not as easily described within a content-based developmental framework. Many of these behaviors fall under the category of behavioral excesses and include *stereotypy* (ritualistic and repetitive behaviors that apparently are purposeless), high rates and intensity of *self-stimulatory behavior* (a subset of stereotypy in which movements are reinforced by perceptual consequences produced by the behavior), and *self-injurious behavior*. Although depressed cognitive functioning has often been used as the mediator for the presence of certain types of behavioral deficits and excesses, attempts have been made to relate some behavioral excesses to the intent or functions they might serve (Carr & Durand, 1985; Donnellan, Mirenda, Mesaros, & Fassbender, 1984). Most recently, the role of behavior state and arousal in individuals' behavioral repertoires has come under increased scrutiny (Guess & Carr, 1991; Guess et al., 1990; Richards & Sternberg, 1992; Sternberg & Richards, 1989). The implication of these investigations and discussions has become rather crucial to educational programming and training efforts for some individuals with profound disabilities (see Chapter 4). In addition, this population demonstrates a myriad of sensory and health characteristics (see Chapters 3 and 8).

All of the above descriptions serve to reiterate the fact that behaviors of individuals with profound disabilities are not only heterogeneous but also extremely complex. This complexity and heterogeneity make consideration and discussion of suggested practices rather difficult.

A CONCEPTUAL FRAMEWORK

It has become increasingly apparent that the behaviors exhibited by individuals with profound disabilities must be looked upon from a considerably larger perspective than simply the behaviors in and of themselves. With this in mind, a conceptual framework needs to be posited within which these behaviors can be both understood and dealt with.

One such framework, proposed by Sternberg (1988), was based upon a vertical umbrella model wherein various components related to the education of individuals with severe or profound disabilities were addressed. With a refocusing of application concerns to only individuals with profound disabilities, this model is still of use (see Figure 1.1).

Within the umbrella model, general areas are considered from a supraordinate to subordinate basis. These areas are interactive and constitute predominant concerns or components for understanding and delivering appropriate services to individuals with profound disabilities. The overriding umbrella is the individual's environment. Environments that are both internal and external to individuals with profound disabilities must be considered. Internal environments are represented, in part, by biobehavioral state and arousal levels. External environments are represented by the individual's school, home, and community, and by the people who provide services within those situations.

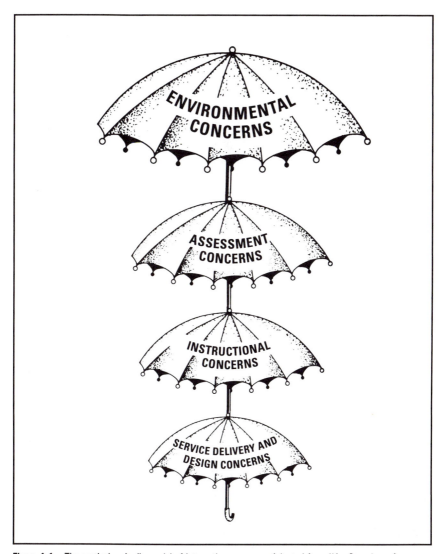

Figure 1.1.   The vertical umbrella model of interactive concerns. Adapted from "An Overview of Educational Concerns for Students with Severe and Profound Handicaps" in *Educating Students with Severe or Profound Handicaps* (2nd ed., p. 10) by L. Sternberg (Ed.), 1988, Austin, TX: PRO-ED. Copyright 1988 by PRO-ED, Inc. Adapted by permission.

Below the environmental concerns umbrella is one dealing with assessment. The placement of this umbrella below the environmental umbrella indicates that assessment must take into account both the internal and the external environmental constraints and conditions to which individuals with profound disabilities are exposed. Assessment likely includes how aspects of an individual's internal environment might affect reactions to external environmental components (e.g., awareness to and benefits from types of interventions). Ecological assessment is completed relative to external environmental concerns.

The third umbrella is devoted to instructional concerns. For individuals with profound disabilities, issues related to acquisition of behaviors to remedy precursor behavioral deficits (e.g., awareness, attending behaviors) as well as control of behavioral excesses must be considered. Both educational tactics and behavior management concerns are included in this area. The position of this umbrella in the model dictates that guidance for both acquisition and control matters must stem from assessment data, and that these data must be considered within the context of the individual's internal and external environments.

The last umbrella deals with concerns related to services design and delivery. Considerations within this area include both direct and related services, such as special health care needs and curriculum–services models and interventions. Inherent in this umbrella's placement in the overall structure is consideration of services delivery within the contexts of behavioral acquisition and control, services that are based on appropriate assessment data, and services that relate to the total environment within which an individual finds himself or herself.

The placement of these umbrellas does not dictate an order of importance. The vertical umbrella model provides a framework for understanding what parameters are likely to affect individuals with profound disabilities and what services are likely to be most appropriate. Given the integrated nature of concerns, the model also provides an avenue through which needs and services can be viewed from an integrated rather than piecemeal fashion.

CONCLUSION

The knowledge base that is required for determining the most appropriate education and training practices for individuals with profound disabilities is dependent in large measure on whether we as professionals are sensitive to these individuals' needs. This sensitivity is somewhat difficult to assume when the presence of a profound disability prevents an individual from expressing those needs. Even with the very short history of educational and training initiatives geared toward individuals who are profoundly disabled, this situation has created significant controversy. Do we use models of practice and interventions that have proven to be worthwhile when applied to individuals with lesser degrees of disability? Do we use "what if" scenarios in hopes that our conceptions of another's needs are accurate and appropriate? Should we modify these models and practices, and to what degree? Or do we discard models and practices in favor of developing group-specific initiatives? Hopefully, time and consistent effort will provide the answers; however, for a reasonable start, we must admit that we do not know.

REFERENCES

Carr, E. G., & Durand, V. M. (1985). Reducing behavior problems through functional communication training. *Journal of Applied Behavior Analysis, 13,* 101–117.

Donnellan, A. M., Mirenda, P. L., Mesaros, R. A., & Fassbender, L. L. (1984). Analyzing the communicative functions of aberrant behavior. *Journal of The Association for Persons with Severe Handicaps, 9,* 201–212.

Dussault, W. (1989). Is a policy of exclusion based upon severity of disability legally defensible? In F. Brown & D. H. Lehr (Eds.), *Persons with profound disabilities: Issues and practices* (pp. 43–59). Baltimore: Brookes.

Green, C. W., Canipe, V. S., Way, P. J., & Reid, D. H. (1986). Improving the functional utility and effectiveness of classroom services for students with profound multiple handicaps. *Journal of The Association for Persons with Severe Handicaps, 11,* 162–170.

Guess, D., & Carr, E. (1991). Emergence and maintenance of stereotypy and self-injury. *American Journal on Mental Retardation, 96,* 299–319.

Guess, D., Siegel-Causey, E., Roberts, S., Rues, J., Thompson, B., & Siegel-Causey, D. (1990). Assessment and analysis of behavior state and related variables among students with profoundly handicapping conditions. *Journal of The Association for Persons with Severe Handicaps, 15,* 211–230.

Guess, D., Mulligan-Ault, M., Roberts, S., Struth, J., Siegel-Causey, E., Thompson, B., Bronicki, J., & Guy, B. (1988). Implications of bio-behavioral states for the education and treatment of students with the most profoundly handicapping conditions. *Journal of The Association for Persons with Severe Handicaps, 13,* 163–174.

Hogg, J., & Sebba, J. (1987). *Profound retardation and multiple impairment* (Vol. 1). Rockville, MD: Aspen.

Hotte, R. A., Monroe, H. S., Philbrook, D. L., & Scarlata, R. W. (1984). Programming for persons with profound mental retardation: A three year retrospective study. *Mental Retardation, 22,* 75–78.

Landesman-Dwyer, S., & Sackett, G. P. (1978). Behavioral changes in nonambulatory, profoundly mentally retarded individuals. In C. E. Meyers (Ed.), *Quality of life in severely and profoundly mentally retarded people: Research foundations for improvement* (Monograph of the American Association on Mental Deficiency, No. 3, pp. 55–144). Washington, DC: American Association on Mental Deficiency.

Logan, K., Alberto, P., Kana, T., & Waylor, T. (1991). *Who are students with profound disabilities? A data based description.* Paper presented at The Association for Persons with Severe Handicaps national conference, Washington, DC.

Lorr, C., & Rotatori, A. F. (1985). Who are the severely and profoundly handicapped? In A. F. Rotatori, J. O. Schwenn, & R. A. Fox (Eds.), *Assessing severely and profoundly handicapped individuals* (pp. 38–48). Springfield, IL: Thomas.

Luckasson, R., Coulter, D., Polloway, E. A., Reiss, S., Schalock, R. L., Snell, M. E., Spitalnick, D. M., & Stark, J. A. (1992). *Mental retardation: Definition, classification, and systems of supports*. Washington, DC: American Association on Mental Retardation.

Rainforth, B. (1982). Biobehavioral state and orienting: Implications for educating profoundly retarded students. *Journal of The Association for the Severely Handicapped, 6,* 33–37.

Richards, S., & Sternberg, L. (1992). A preliminary analysis of environmental variables affecting the observed biobehavioural states of individuals with profound handicaps. *Journal of Mental Deficiency Research, 36,* 403–414.

Sternberg, L. (1988). An overview of educational concerns for students with severe or profound handicaps. In L. Sternberg (Ed.), *Educating students with severe or profound handicaps* (pp. 3–13). Austin, TX: PRO-ED.

Sternberg, L., & Richards, S. (1989). Assessing levels of state and arousal in individuals with profound handicaps: A research integration. *Journal of Mental Deficiency Research, 33,* 381–387.

Chapter 2

Creating Environments that Support and Enhance the Lives of All Participants

LUCILLE ZEPH

Like the ideas of normalization, deinstitutionalization, conservatism, or liberalism, the educability hypothesis is powered (or dismissed) by the conception one has of what human beings ought to be like and what opportunities they ought to have. (Blatt, 1987, p. 58)

While the broader population of persons categorized as having severe disabilities has benefited over the past 10 years from a great deal of attention from researchers, policymakers, and practitioners, there is a question as to whether persons with profound disabilities have shared in these benefits (Sailor, Gee, Goetz, & Graham, 1988). During this period, people with severe disabilities have increasingly moved to less restrictive, community-based living (Braddock, Hemp, Fujiura, Bachelder, & Mitchell, 1990; Hayden, Lakin, Hill, Bruininks, & Chen, 1992), educational environments (Stainback, Stainback, & Forest, 1989), and work settings (Rusch, Chadsey-Rusch, & Johnson, 1991). Nonetheless, people with profound disabilities are still most likely to be exempted from these progressive trends (Brown, Davis, Richards, & Kelly, 1989). Although individual cases of successful community inclusion can be documented for people with profound disabilities, these cases are not representative of the majority of children and adults with profound disabilities who continue to reside in institutions, nursing homes, intermediate care facilities for persons with mental retardation, and other congregate living situations (Hayden et al., 1992; Klein, 1992). These individuals continue to attend segregated schools and classrooms (Geiger & Schilit, 1988) and, for the most part, remain ineligible for employment opportunities (see Chapter 14). In short, despite the great progress in recent years in the fields of mental retardation and severe disabilities, the lives of the majority of people with profound disabilities have not changed a great deal.

Despite the lack of significant change in the quality of life for persons with the most complex needs, there are indications that the winds of change are upon us. One of the most telling changes is the recent redefinition of mental retardation adopted by the American Association on Mental Retardation (AAMR) (Luckasson et al., 1992). As described in Chapter 1, individuals with profound disabilities typically have been considered to have a primary disabling condition of mental retardation. The new AAMR definition effectively eliminates levels of mental retardation. It focuses on establishing a diagnosis of mental retardation and identifying the levels of support that the person requires across each aspect of life. This approach creates an emphasis on the individual supports required by the person to ensure the independence/interdependence, productivity, and integration of the person across all aspects of life. For those who would have chosen to eliminate the concept of mental retardation as a means of describing anyone, the new definition may be dismissed as hair-splitting semantics. Nonetheless, it is a clear indication that even in the most established realms of the field, people are beginning to question the traditional perceptions of persons with mental retardation. This questioning, and the acceptance that a person's environment either supports or impedes his or her independence/interdependence, contributions, and inclusion, will directly affect the quality of life for persons with profound disabilities.

Given the present realities of the lives of people with profound disabilities, in this chapter, I identify the characteristics of desirable environments for persons who experience these disabilities. Although some of the identified characteristics may be fully realized only in inclusive environments, others can be created in almost any environment. However, the purpose of this chapter is not to provide ways to improve segregated environments *in lieu of* creating inclusive ones. It is rather to suggest that physical placement is but one aspect of an inclusive environment, and that other characteristics may either support or interfere with the overall quality of a person's life. In this chapter, I propose ways to improve the quality of life for persons with profound disabilities regardless of the restrictiveness of their environments. The rationale for this approach stems from a belief that real change in the realities of persons with profound disabilities can happen by improving the ways in which their personal care, social relationships, communication, and emotional needs are met *today*. These changes can be made *immediately* by those family members and others providing direct supports, and are not dependent upon major changes that are controlled by bureaucracies. It should be noted, however, that such accommodations by no means relieve each of us from the ultimate responsibility to create systemic change that will result in inclusive communities for all persons regardless of perceived abilities or disabilities.

DEVELOPING ENVIRONMENTS BASED UPON DESIRED OUTCOMES

One approach to determining appropriate characteristics of environments for people is to consider what outcomes are considered desirable as a result of their involvement in that environment. At first, this might seem to be an easy task. That perception, however, may be the very reason why things have not significantly changed for persons with profound disabilities over the recent past. For example, programs that are currently available may exist because they *are* consistent with the outcomes society envisions for people with profound disabilities. If this is the case, one requisite aspect of identifying desirable outcomes for this population is to confront the difficulties society has in envisioning alternative futures for people whose needs appear overwhelming. Therefore, the first step in the development of environments that lead to an improved quality of life for persons with profound disabilities may be to affect the way in which others perceive them. People who have been labeled as having profound disabilities must be seen as unique and complex individuals with a full range of human needs and desires. When those who are providing supports and services see people with profound disabilities as "fully human," it is likely that the outcomes they determine to be desirable for the people they serve will be similar to those they consider desirable for themselves.

A basis for determining quality of life indicators for persons with developmental disabilities in North America may be traced to Wolfensberger's (1972) concept of normalization, and to his subsequent arguments that the true measure of quality of life for persons with developmental disabilities is being perceived in valued ways by other community members (Wolfensberger 1983, 1991). Building on the normalization concept, others have attempted to refine the definition of quality of life for persons with developmental disabilities (Kibele, 1988; Kozleski & Sands, 1992; Vogelsberg, 1990). What becomes clear in these efforts is that we cannot approach success in our definitions until we are able to perceive people with disabilities as full-fledged human beings with the same needs as others (Kunc, 1992). Once people with even the most severe disabilities are accepted as fully human, issues related to quality of life and desirable outcomes become much easier to determine and confront.

Abraham Maslow provided a framework for considering human needs (Kunc, 1992). He conceptualized these needs as falling within a five-level hierarchy, with the most basic needs at the base. Maslow proposed that lower level needs would have to be met before higher levels could be attained. Maslow's hierarchy includes *physiological needs* (food, water, shelter); *safety needs* (security, freedom from fear); *belonging* (friendship, family, partner); *self-esteem needs* (achievement, recognition, mastery); and *self-actualization* (creativity, inner fulfillment). Maslow's hierarchy allows us to move the discussion of quality of life beyond the typical correlation of placement in community settings with improved quality of life, to the more complex consideration of quality of life regardless of where one lives, attends school, works, or plays. Although one can argue that integrated settings are essential to the achievement of desirable outcomes for persons with disabilities, placement in integrated environments without attention to meeting human needs is not enough to result in the achievement of desirable outcomes.

If we accept that quality of life must be determined by outcome measures that are based upon human needs, the remaining issue becomes one of how to go about measuring whether programs and supports for people with profound disabilities are meeting their human needs. Certainly, the most appropriate and direct approach is to assess the perceptions of the person directly. Procedures currently exist for directly assessing quality of life for persons without disabilities (Kozleski & Sands, 1992) and for people with less severe disabilities (Hoover, Wheeler, & Reetz, 1992). These procedures usually involve the use of interviews or questionnaires that focus on personal satisfaction. The limited communication of most persons with profound disabilities, however, seems to make these direct approaches difficult if not impossible. However, other nonverbal means of assessing personal satisfaction of quality of life have been suggested. These include observing–assessing a variety of possible indicators of emotion, such as level of activity or involvement; facial expressions; and measures related to biobehavioral state, such as heart rate, blood pressure, or galvanic skin response (Evans & Scotti, 1989; see Chapter 4). The use of more direct methods in the evaluation of satisfaction of persons with profound disabilities may assist in assessing the impact of supports on quality of life more accurately than can procedures that rely solely on indirect measures, such as interviews with support providers and family members. Although indirect measures provide insights into the perceptions of key individuals in the lives of persons with profound disabilities, they may provide more information about the ways in which the person is perceived by others than about the person's satisfaction with the supports and services being evaluated.

Another aspect of assessing quality of life is the evaluation of the quality of the programs serving the person. In inclusive settings, it is most appropriate to use quality indicators that are generic to all persons served by that provider. For example, Strully and Strully (1992) provided a parent's perspective on evaluating the quality of inclusive educational programs. They offered three areas for parents to consider when measuring quality: the welcoming of students into all aspects of school life; opportunities for peer interactions and the development of friendships; and a curriculum that expands a student's knowledge, skills, and awareness. In the future, this approach may prove useful in designing program evaluations for other inclusive environments.

ENVIRONMENTAL CHARACTERISTICS

In this section, I identify the major characteristics of environments that combine to determine the quality of life for those sharing the environment. Included are consideration of physical characteristics, learning and participation characteristics, and social characteristics.

Physical Characteristics

One of the most basic issues related to the physical characteristics of environments is that of accessibility. Because people with profound disabilities are likely to have physical, communication, and sensory impairments, they are often barred from participation in activities across all aspects of life due to issues of physical access. This remains true despite the mandates of Section 504 of the *Rehabilitation Act of 1973* (Public Law [PL] 93-112, 1973) and the *Americans with Disabilities Act* (ADA) (PL 101-336, 1990). Individuals with disabilities still find themselves routinely excluded from schools, restaurants, churches, libraries, public services, and recreational activities due to physical barriers. Whether physical barriers continue to exist due to ignorance, insensitivity, or fiscal limitations, they have a detrimental effect on the ability of persons with profound disabilities to be included in their communities. Simple oversights, such as a lack of curb cuts, can become overwhelming obstacles to persons with profound disabilities and to those providing supports to them. In addition, lack of attention to physical accessibility may reflect even greater attitudinal barriers.

Although physical barriers to access are the most obvious, more subtle environmental barriers include the lack of access to support services (e.g., communication therapy) or programs (e.g., vocational training) on the basis of the perceived inability of an individual to benefit from them. Similar barriers based upon perception exist in medically related supports, including the provision of glasses or contact lenses, hearing aids, and corrective surgeries for cosmetic or improved functional purposes. As one physician stated in a personal conversation, when refusing to place ear tubes to drain fluid and improve hearing in a young child with profound disabilities, "Not being able to hear is the least of his problems."

Whereas laws and regulations can mandate particular aspects of access to persons with significant disabilities, attitudes and acceptance cannot be legislated. Therefore, it is up to those of us who work to improve the quality of life for persons with profound disabilities to question our own perceptions of the gifts and capacities of each individual, and to provide supports in a manner that are truly respectful of the dignity inherent in each human being.

One area that holds great potential in facilitating quality of life changes for persons with profound disabilities and adaptability to the environment is assistive technology. Here again, gaining access to such equipment for an individual is often full of barriers. Garner and Campbell (1987) have identified obstacles to the optimal use of assistive technology. These include the prohibitive costs of the devices, the lack of expertise in understanding and using the devices, the lack of resources to design and adapt devices, and the lack of understanding of the need for personal choice in the selection and use of a device. Dunn (1991) suggested that particular attention be given to preventing assistive technology and adaptations from becoming an end unto themselves, rather than a means to greater natural participation and opportunity for personal choice.

Learning and Participation Characteristics

For years, persons with profound disabilities were considered unable to learn and, therefore, incapable of benefiting from educational opportunities and experiences (Orelove & Sobsey, 1991). Even after the passage of the *Education for All Handicapped Children's Act* (EHA) (PL 94-142, 1975), the issue of educability of students with profound disabilities continued to be argued in the courts (Dussault, 1989; Orelove & Sobsey, 1991). The EHA was reauthorized by Congress in 1990 as the *Individuals with Disabilities Education Act* (IDEA) (PL 101-476, 1990). IDEA continues to mandate the education of all students, regardless of the severity of their disabilities. Whereas the primary issue for many years was *whether* to educate students with profound disabilities, that question has been replaced by those of *where* and *how* to educate students with profound disabilities. From the late 1980s to the present time, educators and families have made progress in ensuring that *all* students are educated in regular schools and classrooms (Stainback et al., 1989; Villa, Thousand, Stainback, & Stainback, 1992). The results of this inclusion have been measured in terms of the outcomes related to others in the process, including the attitudes of teachers and administrators and the educational impact on typical peers (Evans, Salisbury, Palombaro, Berryman, & Hollowood, 1992; Peck, Donaldson, & Pezzoli, 1990; Rainforth, 1992; Salisbury, Palombaro, & Hollowood, 1993). Other outcomes, such as effect on the quality of student Individualized Education Programs (IEPs), have also been considered (Hunt & Farron-Davis, 1992). Little attention, however, has been given to studying the outcomes of inclusive education on the quality of life of students with profound disabilities (Sailor et al., 1988).

For the past 4 years, LEARNS (Local Education for All in Regular Neighborhood Schools), Maine's statewide project for inclusive schools, has been monitoring the outcomes of students with profound disabilities who have been included in their local schools and regular classrooms. Many of the students live in a pediatric intermediate care facility for persons with mental retardation, whereas others live in foster homes or with their families. As these students have been followed, some of the most notable changes that have been observed have been in their apparent change in affect; their motivation to remain involved in educational and recreational activities; and, on the most basic level, their ability to remain awake and aware for longer periods of the day. Future evaluations for these and similar students throughout the country must be designed in such a way as to document these outcomes, and to identify ways in which various environmental characteristics might contribute to or interfere with improved quality of life for all participants.

In addition to the question of *where* to educate students with the most complex needs, professionals continue to grapple with the question of how to educate them. Orelove and Sobsey (1991) provided a review of the research on instructional formats and suggested areas for future research in this area. Some of the most interesting and challenging research will likely focus on issues related to motivation, responsiveness, and initiation on the part of the student. Because many students with profound disabilities have limited ability to control movements, they are often assumed to be unable to initiate routines or activities due to limitations in their central nervous system (see Chapter 3); this often leads to the perception that the lack of initiation is within the student and, therefore, beyond the reach of the educator. Absence of initiation, in fact, may be the result of poor student motivation or insensitivity of educators and others to the student's subtle behaviors. Upon close examination, many persons with profound disabilities *do* initiate. The initiation may be to engage another person in interaction by crying, or to prolong or prevent an activity through gross body movement. Regardless of the form, these initiations are often overlooked, deliberately ignored, or in some cases targeted as behaviors to be eliminated (Guess & Siegel-Causey, 1985).

Although some persons with profound disabilities may not evidence initiation, most do initiate in some way. The challenge to those providing supports to all students with profound disabilities is to become aware of these students' most basic initiations and to become sensitive to each individual's behavior state (Guess et al., 1988; Guess et al., 1991; Guess et al., 1993; Guy, Guess, & Mulligan-Ault, 1993; Richards & Sternberg, 1992, 1993; Sternberg & Richards, 1989; see Chapter 4). One way to accomplish this end is to spend a week actively documenting anything the individual appears to initiate. A list might be kept in a convenient place and all initiations noted. With this type of documentation, one can more easily determine how a student might initiate through the use of sounds, movements, and changes in state and affect. As these observations are noted, they will likely have a positive impact on staff as they begin to realize that the individual is responding differentially to various elements of the environment and the people in it.

Once any initiations are noted, it becomes easier to determine varying responses to the environment that reflect the person's preferences. As preferences are observed, it becomes clearer as to how the environment should be arranged to reflect those preferences. As individuals with profound disabilities begin to realize that the preferences they exhibit are understood and respected, they may begin to understand for the first time that they have an ability to control the environment (Guess & Siegel-Causey, 1985; Reichle, York, & Eynon, 1989). This awareness can be the basis for the development of choice-making skills for the person. The acquisition of choice-making skills can enable those supporting the person to create environments that are based upon that person's needs, preferences, and desires (Guess, Benson, & Siegel-Causey, 1985; Houghton, Bronicki, & Guess, 1987; Shevin & Klein, 1984; Zeph, 1984).

Participation in a variety of ordinary activities that comprise most of our lives may enable persons with profound disabilities to become familiar with the natural rhythms and routines of daily life. Although there may be few, if any, activities in which such individuals may engage independently, most activities can involve individuals through the use of *partial participation* (Baumgart et al., 1982). Partial participation involves allowing the person to participate in any aspect of an activity by having someone else provide various supports. Typically, the support provided to a person is physical and involves the use of hand-over-hand assistance to the person with disabilities. This allows these individuals to participate in activities that might otherwise be done for (or to) them. This approach to partial participation may allow the person to participate in an activity, but it does not ensure that the person has any control over the situation. In fact, the person may be a passive participant or be coerced into participating in an activity in which he or she has no interest.

Another way to interpret partial participation is to define the person's participation as first choosing the activity and then determining how the activity will be carried out. This interpretation of partial participation places as much control as possible in the hands of persons with profound disabilities. A more comprehensive look at partial participation options can be seen in Chapter 10.

One of the most common features identified as contributing to the quality of life of persons with and without disabilities is that of control. We tend to view people with the most complex needs as vulnerable and in need of constant supervision. This supervision often translates into control rather than support (Klein, 1992). Although the need for support for people who are vulnerable must be recognized, a characteristic of desirable environments is that people receive the supports that *they* require and desire, not those determined by service providers and regulatory agencies. In situations where people have things done to them rather than for them, the issue of control is obvious. A more subtle form of control, however, involves who is in control of determining what supports will be provided for an individual, and how those supports will be implemented. In terms of desirable outcomes, the issue becomes whether the person receiving the support is satisfied with the type of support and the manner in which it is delivered. Being in control does not mean being able to do it all oneself, but rather determining the ways and means it will be done. The challenge for those providing supports to persons with profound disabilities is how to determine what the individual wants. For those individuals with little or no means of communicating, the challenge may seem impossible to meet.

Communication is the transfer of information through which an individual can affect the behavior of others. It requires a sender, a message, and a receiver. When a person sends a message that is not understood or is ignored, the communication effort is not successful. Most of us respond to a variety of verbal and nonverbal messages throughout the day. We consider the ability to communicate a fundamental aspect of our humanness, and would likely feel devastated if we were to lose it. For persons with profound disabilities, effective communication has often been considered to be beyond their capabilities. If we do not believe that a person has the capacity to formulate a message, then we are not likely to look for one. Therefore, efforts at communication may be discouraged because, even when the person sends a message, it is not received as it was intended. Recently, however, facilitated communication has been found to help many individuals communicate (see Chapter 7). Facilitated communication is a method of providing physical and emotional support to a person who cannot speak, and assisting the person to communicate through pointing to letters on a letter board or keyboard (Biklen, 1990). The method was originally developed in Australia by Rosemary Crossley, who first used it with Annie, a young woman who lived in an institution and who was considered to be profoundly mentally retarded. Although there are several striking aspects to the story of Rosemary and Annie, the most haunting is the fact that Annie had spent several years in the institution sending messages to people who did not recognize her attempts to communicate (Crossley & McDonald, 1980). Similar situations have been described by other people who have gained the ability to communicate after years of not being heard (Sienkiewicz-Mercer & Kaplan, 1989).

These stories lead back to the question of perception. If communication is viewed as a critical element of humanness, it is important to focus on communication as a "can do" ability of people with profound disabilities. Unfortunately, expectations are often influenced by the labels ascribed to people and to the limitations attributed to the labels. Through broadening our perception of the human potential of people, regardless of their labels, we can begin to open ourselves to phenomena that we have missed in the past. If we believe that all people have the need and the capacity to communicate, if provided an appropriate vehicle, then we have a clear responsibility to be alert to and enable the communication efforts of people with profound disabilities. Once again, these communications may be demonstrations of preferences, which, if noted and respected, may be used to assist the person in indicating choices and learning that he or she can exert power and control over the environment (Reichle et al., 1989; Williams, 1991).

Social Characteristics

The concept of creating circles of friends or support circles (Perske, 1988; Stainback et al., 1989) continues to gain success and acceptance as a critical element in the lives of persons with disabilities and their families. However, for a support circle to be successful, the person must be perceived as a full-fledged human being. In the past, people with profound disabilities were surrounded by several professionals and paraprofessionals, all of whom were paid to be with them. Although good and caring relationships may develop between paid staff and persons with disabilities, the relationships depend upon the continued employment of the paid staff persons. When a paid support person leaves a job, or even experiences a change in service shift, the relationship typically suffers and may end. Once again, this situation establishes a need for environments that are inclusive.

An inclusive environment is one with a capacity to reach out and embrace each member regardless of differing needs and abilities, thereby creating a true sense of community (McKnight, 1987). The ability to reach out is an essential one for persons with profound disabilities, because they may be unable to initiate membership independently. In addition, they do not automatically assume that membership is open to them. Because most community members do not have experience interacting with persons with profound disabilities, the responsibility to initiate and nurture the person's entry into the environment may fall to those who provide services and supports. Once in the environment, the person who is paid to provide supports must extend invitations to other community members to provide natural supports, and to facilitate opportunities to form relationships between the person with disabilities and other members of the community (Forest & Pearpoint, 1992). An inclusive environment encourages respect and understanding among its members. It provides opportunities for persons to interact with and support one another in a climate where diversity is recognized and celebrated (Sapon-Shevin, 1992; Stainback et al., 1989) and where membership is shared in a manner that creates friendships, networks, and associations (O'Brien & O'Brien, 1992).

PERSONNEL

The key to creating appropriate supportive environments for individuals with profound handicaps rests with those who will assume the responsibility of providing those supports. In the following sections, I consider crucial concerns related to that involvement.

Attitudes

The nature of the supports necessary to enable persons with complex and multiple needs to participate in their lives requires direct, hands-on interaction. This level of physical support can easily move from support to control. Because people with disabilities who are able to communicate directly indicate that maintaining control is essential to a desirable quality of life, it is imperative that people providing direct supports understand their supportive role. This is particularly difficult when the attitude of the support person is that the person receiving the support is incapable of establishing preferences, making choices, or determining what he or she wants and needs. Therefore, although skills and knowledge are important in preparing people to provide supports to persons with profound disabilities, a support person's attitudes will ultimately determine how his or her skills and knowledge will affect the quality of life of the individual being served. If a support person has a respectful attitude toward the individual being served, then he or she will find ways to learn whatever is essential to support that person, or will assist the person in finding someone else to provide for that particular need. This behavior is common in families who, prior to the arrival of a family member with profound disabilities, had little or no knowledge of the complexities of providing support. Nonetheless, parents and other family members must and do quickly learn how to provide a wide variety of support services.

Attitudes of those providing support to a person with complex needs will ultimately determine the quality of life for that person. As people with significant disabilities tell their stories, they discuss their relationships with others and describe how those relationships have affected their lives (Nolan, 1988; Sienkiewicz-Mercer & Kaplan, 1989; Snow, 1989). Support personnel must begin to ask the question "How can we help?" directly to the person with disabilities (Lovett, 1991), and then follow that person's lead and direction. No substitute exists for directly posing the question. Also, those providing support must understand that, although they may disagree with the choices expressed by the person, they have a responsibility to interpret the choice to others as presented, and to be respectful of the person and his or her choices.

Personnel Preparation and Staff Development

Much attention has been directed toward identifying the skills and knowledge necessary for educators of students with severe disabilities. For a long time, the assumption was that those providing education for students with profound disabilities needed the same skills and knowledge as those providing the same type of services to students with lesser degrees of disability. Recent research by Thompson and Guess (1989) has brought this assumption into question. They surveyed teachers of students with profound disabilities who had graduated from personnel preparation programs in the area of severe disabilities. They asked the teachers what they had been taught and how that compared with what they did in their educational programs. Most teachers noted that, although they had been trained in programs that emphasized state-of-the-art, behaviorally oriented, and functional skill programming, they used an eclectic approach with their students. They indicated that students with profound disabilities presented a different set of characteristics and challenges, and what was accepted as best practice for students with severe disabilities fell short in meeting the complex needs of their students. The functional approach to skill development left teachers of students with profound disabilities frustrated in identifying the appropriate curricula for their students.

Although little attention has been given to the training needs of persons providing supports to adults with profound disabilities, the findings are likely to be similar. In fact, anyone who provides staff development to those providing supports to people with profound disabilities knows that the participants often comment that the techniques being presented are not appropriate for the individuals with whom they work. Most of the time, they are assured that the content is generalizable to persons with profound disabilities. Guess and Thompson (1991) advocated that personnel being prepared to work with students with profound disabilities be provided with choices and options in theories and strategies as part of their training. They asserted that, by doing so, professors would be upholding the tenets of higher education as well as producing professionals who are capable of continuing to advance the field through questioning and creative problem solving.

Team Models

Although the use of teams has been the accepted means of providing services to people with profound disabilities for at least 20 years, the nature and function of teams continue to evolve to accommodate concepts of inclusion and interdependence (Dunn, 1991). As persons with profound disabilities have moved from medical and institutional settings, the teams serving them have become less clinical and more collaborative. Present models include transdisciplinary models of assessment and delivery of integrated therapy services (Dunn, 1991; see Chapter 11), and the use of person-centered planning processes that focus on identifying the capacities, gifts, and talents of the individual. Person-centered planning has been instituted in schools through the McGill Action Planning System (MAPS) process (Vandercook, York, & Forest, 1989) and personal futures planning typically used in community settings (Green-McGowan, 1987; Mount & Zwernik, 1988; O'Brien, 1990). The common elements in each of these models include broadening the team to include the person with disabilities, friends, and others who support and understand the person; listening to what the person has to say; and identifying ways to assist the individual in achieving what he or she wants and needs (Racino & Walker, 1993). For persons with profound disabilities, it is essential that the team focus on identifying *who* the person really is through identifying personal characteristics, capacities, and gifts. To accomplish these ends, teams must include those who know the person well and who are most likely to be able to interpret the person's communication.

Creating Positive Work Environments

It is difficult for someone who feels oppressed and devalued to be kind, sensitive, and caring in his or her work. People who work directly with persons with disabilities often are the lowest paid and have the least power in their organizations. As agencies attempt to invert the structure of relationships and power for people with disabilities, they must also find ways to empower and support their staff (Racino, 1993; Walker & Racino, 1993). Thus, administrators and supervisors must be willing to share power as well as responsibility with direct care and support staff. Relationships that develop between people with disabilities and support staff must be respected. Supervisors often use support staff interchangeably, without considering the emotional and social bonds that develop between people. This dehumanization of staff persons creates a climate where relationships and human needs are devalued and the sense of community is violated. Under such circumstances, it is difficult for the staff to see the value of inclusive community for the people they support.

CONCLUSION

The creation of environments that enhance the quality of life of people with profound disabilities depends upon our ability to recognize and respond to the full range of their human needs. This means we must get beyond the traditional focus on the obvious physical, health, and safety needs of this complex group of individuals and begin to address each individual's need to belong, need for self-esteem, and need for self-actualization. This requires a move beyond a deficit-oriented view of persons with disabilities, to a perspective that encourages us to discover the capacities, gifts, and talents of each individual. In doing so, we not only will move the field forward, but also will open ourselves to experiencing true relationships with people who face and overcome incredible challenges on a daily basis—people who choose each day to go on and give us another chance to *see* them for the persons whom they are.

We are a capable society. We will create the futures that we choose to create for persons with profound disabilities. The responsibility is upon us to create environments that will result in futures that are desirable to them.

REFERENCES

Baumgart, D., Brown, L., Pumpian, I., Nisbet, J., Ford, A., Sweet, M., Messina, R., & Schroeder, J. (1982). Principle of partial participation and individualized adaptations in educational programs for severely handicapped students. *Journal of The Association for the Severely Handicapped, 7*, 17–27.

Biklen, D. (1990). Communication unbound: Autism and praxis. *Harvard Education Review, 60*(3), 291–314.

Blatt, B. (1987). *The conquest of mental retardation.* Austin, TX: PRO-ED.

Braddock, D., Hemp, R., Fujiura, G., Bachelder, L., & Mitchell, D. (1990). *The state of the states in developmental disabilities.* Baltimore: Brookes.

Brown, F., Davis, R., Richards, M., & Kelly, K. (1989). Residential services for adults with profound disabilities. In F. Brown & D. Lehr (Eds.), *Persons with profound disabilities: Issues and practices* (pp. 295–331). Baltimore: Brookes.

Crossley, R., & McDonald, A. (1980). *Annie's coming out.* New York: Penguin.

Dunn, W. (1991). Integrated related services. In L. Meyer, C. Peck, & L. Brown (Eds.), *Critical issues in the lives of people with severe disabilities* (pp. 353–377). Baltimore: Brookes.

Dussault, W. L. (1989). Is a policy of exclusion based upon severity of disability legally defensible? In F. Brown & D. Lehr (Eds.), *Persons with profound disabilities: Issues and practices* (pp. 43–60). Baltimore: Brookes.

Evans, I. M., Salisbury, C., Palombaro, M., Berryman, J., & Hollowood, T. (1992). Peer interactions and social acceptance of elementary age children with severe disabilities in an inclusive school. *Journal of The Association for Persons with Severe Handicaps, 7,* 205–212.

Evans, I. M., & Scotti, J. R. (1989). Defining meaningful outcomes for persons with profound disabilities. In F. Brown & D. Lehr (Eds.), *Persons with profound disabilities: Issues and practices* (pp. 83–107). Baltimore: Brookes.

Forest, M., & Pearpoint, J. (1992). Families, friends, and circles. In J. Nisbet (Ed.), *Natural supports in school, at work, and in the community for people with severe disabilities* (pp. 65–86). Baltimore: Brookes.

Garner, J., & Campbell, P. (1987). Technology for persons with severe disabilities: Practical and ethical considerations. *Journal of Special Education, 21,* 122–132.

Geiger, W., & Schilit, J. (1988). Providing appropriate educational environments. In L. Sternberg (Ed.), *Educating students with severe or profound handicaps* (2nd ed., pp. 17–51). Austin, TX: PRO-ED.

Green-McGowan, K. (1987). *Functional life planning for persons with complex needs.* Peachtree City, GA: KMG Seminars.

Guess, D., Benson, H., & Siegel-Causey, E. (1985). Concepts and issues related to choice-making and autonomy among persons with severe disabilities. *Journal of The Association for Persons with Severe Handicaps, 10,* 79–86.

Guess, D., Mulligan-Ault, M., Roberts, S., Struth, J., Siegel-Causey, E., Thompson, B., Bronicki, G. J. B., & Guy, B. (1988). Implications of bio-behavioral states for the education and treatment of students with the most profoundly handicapping conditions. *Journal of The Association for Persons with Severe Handicaps, 13,* 163–174.

Guess, D., Roberts, S., Siegel-Causey, E., Ault, M. M., Guy, B., Thompson, B., & Rues, J. (1991). Investigations into the state behaviors of students with severe and profound handicapping conditions. *Monograph of the special education department–severely handicapped area.* Lawrence: University of Kansas.

Guess, D., & Siegel-Causey, E. (1985). Behavioral control and education of severely handicapped students: Who's doing what to whom? and why? In D. Bricker & J. Filler (Eds.), *Serving students with severe mental retardation: From theory to practice* (pp. 230–244). Reston, VA: Council for Exceptional Children.

Guess, D., Siegel-Causey, E., Roberts, S., Guy, B., Mulligan-Ault, M., & Rues, J. (1993). Analysis of state organizational patterns among students with profound disabilities. *Journal of The Association for Persons with Severe Handicaps, 18,* 93–108.

Guess, D., & Thompson, B. (1991). Preparation of personnel to educate students with severe and multiple disabilities: A time for change? In L. Meyer, C. Peck, & L. Brown (Eds.), *Critical issues in the lives of people with severe disabilities* (pp. 391–398). Baltimore: Brookes.

Guy, B., Guess, D., & Mulligan-Ault, M. (1993). Classroom procedures for the measurement of behavior state among students with profound disabilities. *Journal of The Association for Persons with Severe Handicaps, 18,* 52–60.

Hayden, M. F., Lakin, K. C., Hill, B. K., Bruininks, R. H., & Chen, T. H. (1992). Placement practices in specialized foster homes and small group homes for persons with mental retardation. *Mental Retardation, 30,* 53–61.

Hoover, J. H., Wheeler, J. J., & Reetz, L. J. (1992). Development of a leisure satisfaction scale for use with adolescents and adults with mental retardation: Initial findings. *Education and Training in Mental Retardation, 27,* 153–160.

Houghton, J., Bronicki, G. J. B., & Guess, J. (1987). Opportunities to express preferences and make choices among students with severe disabilities in classroom settings. *Journal of The Association for Persons with Severe Handicaps, 12,* 18–27.

Hunt, P., & Farron-Davis, F. (1992). A preliminary investigation of IEP quality and content associated with placement in general education versus special education classes. *Journal of The Association for Persons with Severe Handicaps, 17,* 247–253.

Kibele, A. (1988). Occupational therapy's role in improving quality of life for persons with cerebral palsy. *American Journal of Occupational Therapy, 43,* 371–377.

Klein, J. (1992). Get me the hell out of here: Supporting people with disabilities to live in their own homes. In J. Nisbet (Ed.), *Natural supports in school, at work, and in the community for people with severe disabilities* (pp. 277–339). Baltimore: Brookes.

Kozleski, E. B., & Sands, D. J. (1992). The yardstick of social validity: Evaluating quality of life as perceived by adults without disabilities. *Education and Training in Mental Retardation, 27,* 119–131.

Kunc, N. (1992). The need to belong: Rediscovering Maslow's hierarchy of needs. In R. Villa, J. Thousand, W. Stainback, & S. Stainback (Eds.), *Restructuring for caring and effective education* (pp. 25–39). Baltimore: Brookes.

Lovett, H. (1991). Empowerment and choices. In L. Meyer, C. Peck, & L. Brown (Eds.), *Critical issues in the lives of people with severe disabilities* (pp. 625–626). Baltimore: Brookes.

Luckasson, R., Coulter, D., Polloway, E. A., Reiss, S., Schalock, R. L., Snell, M. E., Spitalnick, D. M., & Stark, J. A. (1992). *Mental retardation: Definition, classification, and systems of support.* Washington, DC: American Association on Mental Retardation.

McKnight, J. (1987). Regenerating community. *Social Policy, 17*(3), 54–58.

Mount, B., & Zwernik, K. (1988). *It's never to early, it's never to late: A booklet about futures planning.* St. Paul, MN: DD Case Management Project, Metropolitan Council.

Nolan, C. (1988). *Under the eye of the clock.* London: Pan Books.

O'Brien, J. (Ed.). (1990, October). *Effective self advocacy: Empowering people with disabilities to speak for themselves.* Minneapolis: Institute on Community Integration, Research and Training Center on Community Living.

O'Brien, J., & O'Brien, C. L. (1992). Members of each other: Perspectives on social support for people with severe disabilities. In J. Nisbet (Ed.), *Natural supports in school, at work, and in the community for people with severe disabilities.* Baltimore: Brookes.

Orelove, F., & Sobsey, D. (1991), *Educating children with multiple disabilities: A transdisciplinary approach* (2nd ed.). Baltimore: Brookes.

Peck, C., Donaldson, J., & Pezzoli, M. (1990). Some benefits non-handicapped adolescents perceive for themselves from their relationships with peers who have severe handicaps. *Journal of The Association for Persons with Severe Handicaps, 15,* 241–249.

Perske, R. (1988). *Circles of friends: People with disabilities and their friends enrich the lives of one another.* Nashville: Abingdon Press.

Public Law 93-112. (1973). *Rehabilitation Act of 1973,* sec. 504.

Public Law 94-142. (1975). *Education for All Handicapped Children Act of 1975,* 20 U.S.C. secs. 1401–1461.

Public Law 101-336. (1990). *The Americans with Disabilities Act of 1990.* 42 U.S.C., 12101.

Public Law 101-476. (1990). *Individuals with Disabilities Education Act,* 20 U.S.C., Chapter 33.

Racino, J. A. (1993). "There if you need and want them": Changing roles of support organizations. In J. A. Racino, P. Walker, S. O'Connor, & S. Taylor (Eds.), *Housing, support, and community: Choices and strategies for adults with disabilities* (pp. 107–136). Baltimore: Brookes.

Racino, J. A., & Walker, P. (1993). "Whose life is it anyway?": Life planning, choices, and decision making. In J. A. Racino, P. Walker, S. O'Connor, & S. Taylor (Eds.), *Housing, support, and community: Choices and strategies for adults with disabilities* (pp. 57–80). Baltimore: Brookes.

Rainforth, B. (1992). *The effects of full inclusion on regular education teachers* (final report to the California Research Institute). Binghamton, NY: Center for Research on Social and Educational Equity, State University of New York.

Reichle, J., York, J., & Eynon, D. (1989). Influence of indicating preferences for initiating, maintaining, and terminating interactions. In F. Brown & D. Lehr (Eds.), *Persons with profound disabilities: Issues and practices* (pp. 191–211). Baltimore: Brookes.

Richards, S. B., & Sternberg, L. (1992). A preliminary analysis of environmental variables affecting the observed biobehavioral states of individuals with profound handicaps. *Journal of Intellectual Disability Research, 36,* 403–414.

Richards, S. B., & Sternberg, L. (1993). Corroborating previous findings: Laying stepping stones in the analysis of biobehavioral states in students with profound disabilities. *Education and Training in Mental Retardation, 28,* 262–268.

Rusch, F., Chadsey-Rusch, J., & Johnson, J. R. (1991). Supported employment: Emerging opportunities for employment integration. In L. Meyer, C. Peck, & L. Brown (Eds.), *Critical issues in the lives of people with severe disabilities* (pp. 145–171). Baltimore: Brookes.

Sailor, W., Gee, K., Goetz, L., & Graham, N. (1988). Progress in educating students with the most severe disabilities: Is there any? *Journal of The Association for Persons with Severe Handicaps, 13,* 87–99.

Salisbury, C., Palombaro, M., & Hollowood, T. (1993). On the nature and change of an inclusive elementary school. *Journal of The Association for Persons with Severe Handicaps, 18,* 75–84.

Sapon-Shevin, M. (1992). Celebrating diversity, creating community: Curriculum that honors and builds on differences. In S. Stainback & W. Stainback (Eds.), *Curriculum considerations in inclusive classrooms: Facilitating learning for all students* (pp. 19–36). Baltimore: Brookes.

Shevin, M., & Klein, N. (1984). The importance of choicemaking skills for students with severe disabilities. *Journal of The Association for Persons with Severe Handicaps, 9,* 159–166.

Sienkiewicz-Mercer, R., & Kaplan, S. (1989). *I raise my eyes to say yes: A memoir.* Boston: Houghton-Mifflin.

Snow, J. (1989). Systems of support: A new vision. In S. Stainback, W. Stainback, & M. Forest (Eds.), *Educating all students in the mainstream of regular education* (pp. 221–231). Baltimore: Brookes.

Stainback, S., Stainback, W., & Forest, M. (Eds.). (1989). *Educating all students in the mainstream of regular education.* Baltimore: Brookes.

Sternberg, L., & Richards, S. (1989). Assessing levels of state and arousal in individuals with profound handicaps: A research integration. *Journal of Mental Deficiency Research, 33,* 381–387.

Strully, J., & Strully, C. (1992). The struggle toward inclusion and the fulfillment of friendship. In J. Nisbet (Ed.), *Natural supports in school, at work, and in the community for people with severe disabilities* (pp. 165–178). Baltimore: Brookes.

Thompson, B., & Guess, D. (1989). Students who experience the most profound disabilities: Teacher perspectives. In F. Brown & D. Lehr (Eds.), *Persons with profound disabilities: Issues and practices* (pp. 3–41). Baltimore: Brookes.

Vandercook, T., York, J., & Forest, M. (1989). The McGill Action Planning System (MAPS): A strategy for building the vision. *Journal of The Association for Persons with Severe Handicaps, 14,* 205–215.

Villa, R., Thousand, J., Stainback, W., & Stainback, S. (Eds.). (1992). *Restructuring for caring and effective education.* Baltimore: Brookes.

Vogelsberg, T. (1990). Supported employment in Pennsylvania. In F. Rusch (Ed.), *Supported employment: Models, methods, and issues* (pp. 45–63). DeKalb, IL: Sycamore.

Walker, P., & Racino, J. A. (1993). "Being with people": Support and support strategies. In J. A. Racino, P. Walker, S. O'Connor, & S. Taylor (Eds.), *Housing, support, and community: Choices and strategies for adults with disabilities* (pp. 81–106). Baltimore: Brookes.

Williams, R. (1991). Choices, communication, and control. In L. Meyer, C. Peck, & L. Brown (Eds.), *Critical issues in the lives of people with severe disabilities* (pp. 543–544). Baltimore: Brookes.

Wolfensberger, W. (1972). *The principle of normalization in human services.* Toronto, Canada: National Institute on Mental Retardation.

Wolfensberger, W. (1983). Social role valorization: A proposed new term for the principle of normalization. *Mental Retardation, 21,* 234–239.

Wolfensberger, W. (1991). *A brief introduction to social role valorization as a high-order concept for structuring human services.* Syracuse, NY: Training Institute for Human Services Planning, Leadership and Change Agency, Syracuse University.

Zeph, L. (1984). *The model of CHOICE: A curriculum framework for incorporating choice-making into programs serving students with severe handicaps.* Paper presented at the Eleventh Annual Conference of The Association for Persons with Severe Handicaps, Chicago.

Chapter 3

Biomedical Conditions: Types, Causes, and Results

DAVID L. COULTER

In Chapter 1, a definition and accompanying range of characteristics were used to describe individuals with profound disabilities. Using these criteria, it becomes rather obvious that the presence of a brain disorder is the only condition that will account for the existence of a profound disability. To have a more in-depth understanding of this population, therefore, one needs to examine brain development and various biomedical disorders of the brain that can cause or result in profound disabilities. These brain disorders are sometimes associated with other biomedical conditions (e.g., bone, heart, or kidney problems) that may affect the life functioning of the individual with profound disabilities. Assessment of health care needs and delivery of health services to respond to these associated biomedical concerns are considered in Chapter 8.

Brain disorders occur as the result of one or the other of the following processes:

1. Abnormal brain development from the beginning of the formation of the brain (*brain dysgenesis*)
2. Adverse influences that alter the structure and/or function of a brain that had developed normally up to that point in time (*brain damage*)

This is an important conceptual distinction. Brain dysgenesis means that the brain never develops in a typical way; in this case, observed brain functions reflect atypical patterns of development. Brain damage means that the brain developed normally up to a certain point; in this case, some prior elements indicative of typical patterns of development may persist along with the abnormal patterns caused by the damaging event. Educators and therapists should expect that individuals with brain dysgenesis may differ in some important ways from individuals with brain damage.

Another important distinction concerns the extent of brain abnormality. Two broad categories are recognized:

1. *Focal* abnormalities, which involve only one part or several parts of the brain, while other unaffected parts of the brain may be fairly normal

2. *Diffuse* abnormalities, which involve all of the brain, so that no part of the brain is normal

The developing brain has the ability to respond to functional deficits by reorganizing itself in an attempt to restore function. This ability to reorganize is what is commonly termed *plasticity*. In general, normal parts of the brain undergo reorganization to take over the functions of abnormal parts of the brain. It follows that plasticity is more likely to occur in the setting of focal abnormalities, when some parts of the brain are relatively unaffected by the cause of the profound disability. Diffuse abnormalities, on the other hand, are less likely to permit much plasticity to occur because no relatively unaffected parts of the brain exist to take over the absent functions.

In either situation, the opportunities for plasticity are limited by the individual's age, because the ability to reorganize decreases with age. Therefore, educators and therapists are likely to see the greatest functional improvement in relatively young individuals with focal brain abnormalities. Functional improvement may also occur in older individuals and in those with diffuse brain abnormalities, but one should expect the results to be more limited.

Understanding the causes of profound disabilities requires a consideration of how the brain develops normally, as well as how it may develop abnormally (brain dysgenesis) or be affected by acquired insults (brain damage). In this chapter, I first review normal brain development and consider ways in which the brain may develop abnormally in persons with profound disabilities. I then discuss the more common categories of identifiable brain disorders that may result in profound disabilities. Some evidence of the relative frequencies of these categories of brain disorders are presented. I conclude the chapter with a description of the most profound degree of disability. This category is termed the *vegetative state* and is the result of the most extreme type of brain disorder.

NORMAL AND ABNORMAL BRAIN DEVELOPMENT

The field of human development studies has often been influenced by the "nature versus nurture" controversy. Some consider human development to be the result of a genetically programmed sequence of events that is determined entirely by the information contained in genes (the *nature* point of view). Others consider human development to be the result of the effects of the nurturing environment on a relatively "blank slate" of developmental potential that is present at birth (the *nurture* point of view). It is now generally recognized that neither of these extreme positions is entirely correct. In fact, human development reflects the interaction between genetic programs or influences contained within our genes with a variety of environmental influences that are present from intrauterine life throughout childhood. This process can be understood by considering the metaphor of building a house. The blueprint contains all of the information needed to build the house. How this blueprint is implemented—how the house is actually built—is determined by the quality of the materials and the skill with which the construction is done. No matter how good the blueprint may be, a poor builder using poor materials will build a house that does not function very well. On the other hand, a good builder using good materials can improve on a poor blueprint and build a house that functions better than might have been expected. In the end, it is the interaction between the blueprint (the information contained in the genes) and the construction process (the intrauterine environment and the nurturing environment during childhood) that will determine how well the individual functions.

We do not have a clear picture of the genetic information that determines brain development. We can certainly assume that genes do control some aspects of brain development, because abnormal brain development occurs commonly in some well-defined genetic disorders. This is particularly likely to occur when there are abnormalities of all or part of entire chromosomes. Chromosomal abnormalities undoubtedly affect hundreds or thousands of individual genes, so it is hard to separate out the effect of individual genes that may control brain development. Nonetheless, individual genes for brain development may very well exist. Animal studies suggest that some genes that affect brain development may "turn on" early in fetal life, exert their effect on brain development, and then "turn off" long before the individual is born. Because the gene is inactive after birth, it may be very difficult to detect its presence after birth. Thus, our inability to detect these abnormal genes in human subjects at this time does not necessarily mean that they are not present or that they did not have an important effect on brain development. We can expect that future research will define these genetic influences more clearly and perhaps someday allow us to detect their presence in affected individuals with profound disabilities.

Understanding the Transmission of Information

The "unit" or essential component of brain development is the nerve cell or *neuron*. The neuron is unique because it has the potential to assume a linear structure that will permit passage of information from one end to the other. The primordial neuron is round or globular in shape, but it very quickly begins to change by extending processes outward from the body of the neuron. These processes are also called *growth cones* to indicate their shape and function, since the growth of the neuron is determined by what happens to these processes. Very early in brain development, these growth cones extend outward to make contact with other neurons. Specific chemicals (called *growth factors*) that are present in fetal brain tissue may determine the direction taken by these growth cones and the resulting connections with other neurons. If a successful connection is made, the neuron also has the ability to move in the direction of this contact. In time, a network of connections is established between each neuron and a multitude of other neurons. The growth cones become refined into two types of processes: *axons* and *dendrites*. These processes permit the passage of information from one end of the neuron to the other: Dendrites convey information to the body of the neuron, whereas axons convey information away from the body of the neuron.

Information is transmitted across neurons through the contacts that have been made between them. These contacts are known as *synapses*. Functional activity at the synapse—information transfer from one neuron to another—promotes the survival of both neurons. Nonfunctional synapses are eliminated. Indeed, entire neurons may be eliminated during the process of normal brain development. Considerable evidence exists for an excess of neurons and synapses early in development. A relatively large group of neurons compete to make successful functional contact with the intended target. Unsuccessful neurons die, while successful neurons form the basis of a network of connections between different parts of the brain. The magnitude of this competition is surprising. As many as 30% to 75% of the original pool of competing neurons may die during this process of building a functional network of connections.

Abnormalities in the Process

Apparently, the process of building a functional network of connections in the brain is complicated and involves many steps. Each of these steps may reflect separate genetic influences, and there are many opportunities for the process to go awry. Table 3.1 lists some possible abnormalities in this process that could result in profound disabilities. Evidence for the existence of these abnormalities comes from animal studies and from careful pathological studies of human brain tissue obtained after death from individuals with profound disabilities. Most of these abnormalities cannot be detected during life, so their presence in individuals with profound disabilities can only be suspected at the present time. Additional information on normal and abnormal brain development can be found in several texts (Coulter, 1988; Jacobson, 1991; Purves & Lichtman, 1985).

One often encounters individuals with profound disabilities for whom no apparent cause of their disabilities can be identified. Typically, these are individuals who were the product of an uncomplicated pregnancy, labor, and delivery; who did not suffer any significant adverse events (brain damage) after birth; and who have had an extensive medical evaluation that did not identify any known disorder. Nonetheless, there is no doubt that they have profound disabilities and, therefore, must have a serious brain disorder. Most of the abnormalities of brain development listed in Table 3.1 would not be detectable by any medical test, so any of them could be present in these individuals. This is an important realization for educators and therapists who may be puzzled by the apparent lack of a cause for these profound disabilities. There *is* a cause, and it is almost certainly related to abnormal brain development beginning during fetal life. Furthermore, abnormalities of brain development (brain dysgenesis), such as those listed in Table 3.1, are usually very extensive and involve most or all of the brain. Thus, educators and therapists can reasonably assume that the cause of profound disabilities in individuals for whom no cause has been identified is related to diffuse brain dysgenesis involving the abnormal formation of connections between neurons during fetal life.

TABLE 3.1. Possible Causes of Profound Handicaps

- Insufficient sprouting of growth cones by the neuron
- Absence or deficiency of growth factors in the brain
- Failure of the neuron to establish contacts with other neurons
- Migration of the neuron to the wrong position in the brain
- Excessive or inappropriate cell death
- Lack of specificity of connections between neurons
- Inadequate activity at the synapses between neurons
- Defects in development or function of other supporting cells (neuroglia) in the brain

Of course, there are other individuals with profound disabilities whose medical evaluation does demonstrate some evidence of abnormal brain development. These abnormalities are usually detected by some type of brain imaging study, such as computed tomography (CT scan) or magnetic resonance imaging (MRI scan). The more common types of abnormalities that can be detected during life are described below under "Disorders of Brain Development." Several points concerning individuals with these detectable abnormalities of brain development should be recognized:

1. They may also have abnormal connections between neurons, such as those listed in Table 3.1.

2. Some detectable brain abnormalities occur because of the presence of an identifiable genetic disorder; therefore, a genetic evaluation of these individuals is always warranted.

3. The detectable brain abnormality may have occurred for no obvious reason (negative genetic evaluation), in which case it represents a sufficient cause in and of itself for the profound disability.

For the most part, the extent of the detectable abnormality of brain development is related to the severity of the individual's disabilities. As noted above, abnormalities affecting only one side or one part of the brain may be less severe than abnormalities affecting all of the brain. This fact is considered further when these detectable brain abnormalities are described below.

IDENTIFIABLE CAUSES OF PROFOUND HANDICAPS

The causes of profound disabilities can be divided into three broad groups, based on the time in an individual's life when a particular cause affects brain development:

1. *Prenatal:* events occurring during fetal life from conception to birth.

2. *Perinatal:* events during the birth process and in the first few weeks after birth.

3. *Postnatal:* events occurring during infancy and childhood.

Within each of these time periods, several categories of causes are recognized. These categories are outlined in Table 3.2.

TABLE 3.2. Categories of Causes of Brain Disorders in Persons with Profound Disabilities

Prenatal onset
  Chromosomal disorders
  Syndrome disorders
  Inborn errors of metabolism
  Disorders of brain development
  Environmental Influences

Perinatal onset
  Intrauterine disorders
  Neonatal disorders

Postnatal onset
  Head injuries
  Infections
  Degenerative disorders
  Seizure disorders
  Toxic or metabolic disorders
  Environmental deprivation

In the following discussion, I describe some examples of specific brain disorders in each of these categories. One should keep in mind that many more known causes exist and more are being identified every day. A more complete discussion of the process of evaluating, identifying, and classifying the cause of profound disabilities (intended primarily for physicians) can be found elsewhere (Luckasson et al., 1992).

Prenatal Causes

Chromosomal disorders

Humans have 23 pairs of chromosomes, including one pair comprising the sex chromosomes X and Y. All of the chromosomes together contain approximately 100,000 genes, so each chromosome contains thousands of individual genes. Abnormalities can occur when there is an excess or a deficiency of this chromosomal material. An excess occurs when there are three or more copies of all or part of a chromosome. When three copies are present, the condition is known as a *trisomy*. A deficiency occurs when all or part of a chromosome is absent. When part of a chromosome is absent, the condition is known as a *deletion*. The most common chromosomal disorder associated with mental retardation is Down syndrome, or trisomy 21, but this rarely results in the presence of a profound disability. Chromosomal disorders that are more likely to result in profound disabilities include trisomy 18 or deletion of part of chromosome 5. Individuals with these disorders often have a recognizable disorder of brain development. Because hundreds or thousands of genes may be involved in these chromosomal disorders, affected individuals often have abnormal development of other organs such as the heart or kidney. They usually have some alteration in physical growth and appearance (dysmorphic facial features) such that their facial characteristics differ considerably from those of other individuals. The dysmorphic facial features may be as obvious as a cleft lip or as subtle as altered size or placement of the ears. Certainly, the presence of a chromosomal disorder should be suspected when an individual with profound disabilities "looks different" and has evidence of abnormalities in one or more internal organs.

Occasionally, individuals appear to have a chromosomal disorder, but a test performed in the past indicated that the chromosomes were normal. New techniques developed in recent years may not have been used during the original diagnostic procedure conducted with these individuals. It is possible that, if the test were repeated using these new techniques (e.g., high-resolution banding), a chromosomal disorder might be identified. The importance of searching for a chromosomal disorder in these individuals is that the disorder might occur again in the family. If a specific chromosomal disorder is identified in an affected individual, tests can be done on other family members (or on unborn fetuses) to see if the same disorder is present.

Syndrome disorders

A *syndrome* is a constellation or collection of abnormal features that tend to occur together more often than one would expect by chance. Some syndromes have a known genetic basis and presumably reflect the presence of a single abnormal gene. Other recognized syndromes have no apparent genetic basis at this time. Thousands of syndromes have been identified that describe constellations of a wide variety of features, but most of these syndromes do not result in profound disabilities. A relatively well-known syndrome that sometimes results in profound disabilities is Bourneville syndrome, also known as tuberous sclerosis. The genetic basis of this syndrome has been identified, and it is classified as an *autosomal dominant disorder*. This means that every child of an affected individual has a 50% chance of having the syndrome. The gene for tuberous sclerosis is present in approximately 1 of every 10,000 births, which is approximately the same frequency as that for phenylketonuria (see next section entitled "Inborn Errors of Metabolism"). Many individuals with tuberous sclerosis do not have profound disabilities, but some do. The syndrome can be recognized by finding evidence in a CT or MRI scan of multiple areas of abnormal brain development (called tubers) in the brain. Other characteristic features include abnormal skin findings (acne-like bumps on the face, called adenoma sebaceum, and multiple, small white spots on the skin), benign tumors of the heart muscle, and cysts or tumors of the kidney.

Educators and therapists may suspect the presence of a syndrome disorder whenever there is a family history of other affected individuals, or when an individual with profound disabilities has several unusual physical features. Because new syndromes are being recognized all the time, the fact that a syndrome disorder was not recognized in the past does not necessarily mean that one does not exist. A clinical geneticist is the professional most likely to be aware of this new information and most able to make a diagnosis of a syndrome disorder.

Inborn errors of metabolism

An inborn error of metabolism is an abnormality in some biochemical pathway that may result in an excess or deficiency of some chemical in the body. Excessive amounts of some chemicals may be toxic to the developing brain, whereas deficiencies of other chemicals may result in abnormal functioning of critical biochemical pathways in the neuron. Most inborn errors of metabolism are caused by the presence of two copies of a single abnormal gene and are classified as *autosomal recessive disorders.* This means that both parents must carry a single copy of the abnormal gene (called the heterozygous or carrier state), but a child is affected only if the individual inherits the same abnormal gene from both parents (called the homozygous state). Most individuals with inborn errors of metabolism do not have a detectable abnormality of brain development and do not have any abnormal physical features. Indeed, they may look fairly normal at birth. One of the most well-known inborn errors of metabolism that can result in profound disabilities is phenylketonuria (PKU). In PKU, there is an excess of a group of chemicals called phenylketones. The buildup of toxic amounts of phenylketones, and thus the occurrence of profound disabilities, can be prevented by appropriate dietary management from birth and throughout childhood. Profound disabilities often resulted before the technique of dietary management of phenylketonuria was developed.

There are few ways for educators and therapists to suspect the presence of an inborn error of metabolism. Some of these disorders result in excretion of chemicals in the urine that have an unusual odor, so the presence of such an odor might raise the question of an inborn error of metabolism. Most of these disorders, however, do not produce a typical odor in the urine. Identification of an inborn error of metabolism requires the performance of special blood and/or urine tests by professionals who specialize in this area. Certainly, if no apparent cause can be identified in an individual with profound disabilities, an evaluation for a possible inborn error of metabolism is appropriate.

Disorders of brain development

Several types of abnormalities, including the detectable abnormalities mentioned above, can be recognized as disorders of brain development. A number of predominant disorders reflect the manner in which the nervous system itself has developed.

The nervous system initially forms by folding of the primordial flat plate of neural tissue into a tube. The rostral or "head" end of the neural tube ultimately forms the brain. Abnormalities of this process are called *neural tube defects*. An extreme form of neural tube defect occurs when the rostral end fails to develop, resulting in a fatal condition called *anencephaly*. In this case, the cerebral and cerebellar hemispheres are usually undeveloped. A less extreme form of neural tube defect occurs when the folding process is incomplete and some of the neural tissue is left outside the body. If this happens at the rostral end, some neural tissue protrudes visibly from the head, a condition known as an *encephalocele*. Individuals born with an encephalocele often have profound disabilities. If incomplete folding of the neural tube occurs along the spine, the condition is known as *spina bifida* or *myelomeningocele*. Most individuals with spina bifida, however, do not have profound disabilities.

Once the rostral end of the neural tube has closed, formation of the brain begins. *Brain formation defects* reflect abnormalities in this process. Many types of brain formation defects vary in their severity. *Holoprosencephaly* describes incomplete separation of the two sides of the brain and may involve fusion of all or only a part of the two sides. *Lissencephaly* describes incomplete development of the surface of the brain, which results in a smooth surface of all or a part of the brain. Less severe abnormalities of formation of the brain surface are also recognized, including *pachygyria* (unusually thick convolutions of the cerebral cortex) and *microgyria* (abnormal narrowness of the cerebral convolutions). *Heterotopias* are a type of neuronal migration defect in which a collection of neurons is located in the wrong place in the brain. Most individuals with the more severe types of these defects have profound disabilities. As noted above, some of them also have genetic or chromosomal disorders that are the ultimate cause of the brain formation defect.

In that brain formation defects are not visible, educators and therapists will not be able to specifically ascertain their presence in most cases. They are detectable, however, by CT or MRI scanning. If no cause of a profound disability is apparent, it is appropriate to recommend scanning procedures to discover the brain defect that might be responsible for the existence of the disabling condition. MRI scanning is the preferred technique for identifying these abnormalities, because CT scanning may fail to detect some of the defects.

Environmental influences

The metaphor of building a house that was presented earlier implied that adverse influences could occur during the process of brain development. Some of these influences can occur during fetal life. For example, exposure of the mother to radiation or maternal ingestion of a variety of drugs or alcohol can result in harmful effects on the child (e.g., fetal alcohol syndrome). Some maternal illnesses during pregnancy (e.g., rubella) can also affect the fetus. Some of these adverse influences may be detectable shortly after the child is born, but often the history of the pregnancy provides a good indication of their effect on fetal brain development. The spectrum of outcomes in this category is very broad and typically reflects the timing, amount, and duration of exposure to the adverse influence during fetal life. Generally, the most severe outcomes (including profound disabilities) occur when the adverse influence is present during the first few months of a pregnancy.

Perinatal Causes

Two categories of perinatal disorders are recognized: intrauterine disorders and neonatal disorders. The occurrence of these disorders is fairly obvious from the history of the labor, delivery, and infant's experiences immediately after birth. Perinatal disorders represent conditions in which the brain developed normally throughout fetal life and was then damaged by some event during the perinatal period. In terms of the distinction outlined earlier in this chapter, prenatal disorders are forms of brain dysgenesis, whereas the perinatal disorders described in this section (as well as the postnatal disorders described below) fall within the category of brain damage. As a general rule, perinatal disorders that are severe enough to result in substantial cognitive limitations (IQ below 50) also result in a motor disability (e.g., cerebral palsy). Individuals with a very low IQ who do not have cerebral palsy almost always have some type of prenatal disorder (brain dysgenesis) as the cause of their disabilities.

Intrauterine disorders

Abnormalities of the birth process can result in significant brain damage and lead to the occurrence of a profound disability. These abnormalities include extreme prematurity, separation of the placenta during labor, and birth asphyxia (lack of oxygen to the fetus during labor and delivery). Because the brain developed normally up to this point, the head circumference (a measure of brain growth) is normal at birth. In that brain damage at birth results in reduced brain growth afterward, the head circumference is often abnormally small when the child is a year old or more. Documentation of a normal head circumference at birth and a small head circumference during childhood is strong supporting evidence for the presence of significant brain damage in a child with a history of an intrauterine disorder.

Neonatal disorders

Many disorders may occur in the neonatal period (defined as the first 4 weeks of life after birth) and subsequently result in the presence of a profound disability. Twenty-five to 35% of all premature infants will have bleeding into the brain, the severity of which may vary from minimal to very extensive. Extensive bleeding may also result in *hydrocephalus* (an excessive accumulation of fluid within the central part of the brain). Even though medical advances have improved the prognosis for infants with brain hemorrhage, infants with the most extensive hemorrhages (who often have hydrocephalus) may have profound disabilities.

Brain infections during the neonatal period may also cause extensive brain damage and result in profound disabilities. These infections may be caused by bacteria (e.g., Escherischia coli or group B Streptococcus) or viruses (e.g., herpes simplex or cytomegalovirus). Infection with the human immunodeficiency virus (HIV) may also occur at birth but does not usually cause brain damage until later in life.

Postnatal Disorders

Head injuries

Head injuries during childhood may result in profound disabilities if the brain damage is extensive and severe. Mild head injuries (cerebral concussion) will not result in profound disabilities, and focal injuries (skull fractures and cerebral contusions) will result in profound disabilities only if there is also diffuse brain injury. The existence of a profound disability after a head injury usually means that a condition called *diffuse axonal injury* has occurred. This is damage to the networks of connections between neurons and can be very extensive and severe. Recovery of function can continue to occur for several years after the injury. Current research does not support the idea that children are more likely than adults to recover after a head injury.

Infections

Meningitis (inflammation of the membranes of the brain or spinal cord) and *encephalitis* (inflammation of the brain) during childhood can cause sufficient brain damage to result in profound disabilities. Infection from a variety of bacteria, viruses, and parasites is possible; the specific cause is usually obvious from the individual's history.

Educators and therapists should be aware that infection with HIV can also result in profound disabilities. If the child's mother is infected with HIV, the child has approximately a 30% chance of also being infected. Children who received transfusions with blood or blood products before 1985 (including most older children with hemophilia) may also be infected with HIV. An infected child may appear quite healthy for as long as several years. HIV infection can affect any part of the body, including the brain. Progressive brain involvement with HIV is manifested as a loss of previously acquired skills, which ultimately results in profound disabilities. Whenever a child who has (or is at risk for having) HIV infection loses previously acquired skills or has profound disabilities, progressive brain involvement with HIV should be suspected.

Degenerative disorders

Although many degenerative disorders are caused by the presence of an abnormal gene, they are discussed as postnatal disorders because the brain usually develops normally until some point during childhood when the disorder first begins to manifest itself. These disorders may begin insidiously, with gradual loss of previously acquired skills, and progress to a state of profound disabilities. Many degenerative disorders have been identified, but none of them are common. One of the most widely recognized degenerative disorders is Tay-Sachs disease. In this disease, the gene for a particular enzyme (hexosaminidase A) is absent in neurons and results in the gradual accumulation of a chemical (GM2 ganglioside) within the neuron. Over time, this damages the neuron to the point that it can no longer function normally. As more and more neurons become affected, the individual becomes severely cognitively impaired, blind, and paralyzed, and has frequent seizures. The condition is not treatable and is ultimately fatal.

Another degenerative disorder that is not known to have a genetic basis at this time is Rett syndrome. This condition affects only girls, but the reason for this is not clear. Girls with this disorder are the product of a normal pregnancy and are normal at birth and throughout most of the first year of life. During the second year of life, they begin to lose previously acquired language, motor, and social skills, and exhibit an unusual form of stereotypic hand movement that resembles hand-wringing. Usually, seizures begin at this time. The degenerative process may progress to the point that the child has profound disabilities. Although the degenerative process usually stabilizes or stops progressing during childhood, it may begin again in adolescence. Affected individuals may survive into adulthood with profound disabilities. Educators and therapists should be aware of Rett syndrome and suspect it when girls exhibit the typical clinical course and the characteristic hand-wringing movements.

Seizure disorders

Many individuals with profound disabilities have seizures, but the seizures are rarely the cause of their profound disabilities. One fairly obvious situation in which seizures can cause profound disabilities is when a child experiences a very prolonged episode of continuous, severe, convulsive seizure activity (called *status epilepticus*) lasting for several hours. Fortunately, this is a rare occurrence, and most seizures do not cause brain damage.

One type of seizure disorder that is often associated with profound disabilities is called *infantile spasms*. Most children with infantile spasms have a brain disorder (e.g., tuberous sclerosis) that is the cause of both the seizures and the profound disabilities. Some children, however, show a completely normal history prior to the onset of the spasms. Extensive evaluation reveals no evidence of any brain disorder or other condition that might have caused their problems. These children may also develop profound disabilities, and the only apparent causative agent in such cases is the history of infantile spasms.

Toxic or metabolic disorders

Some disorders are caused by intoxications or severe biochemical disturbances during childhood. Lead poisoning is one form of intoxication that can cause brain damage but that does not usually result in profound disabilities. The metabolic disturbance that most often causes profound disabilities is *anoxia* or lack of oxygen for more than a few minutes. Near-drowning (often from unsupervised immersion in a backyard swimming pool) is a tragically common cause of anoxia in young children. Various congenital or acquired disorders of the heart or lungs can cause cardiopulmonary arrest and also result in severe anoxia. Whatever the cause, anoxia resulting in lack of oxygen to the brain for more than a few minutes can produce severe brain damage and result in profound disabilities.

Environmental deprivation

Environmental deprivation can cause a variety of disabilities but does not usually result in profound disabilities. I include it as a category because the most severe forms of deprivation could potentially produce sufficient brain damage to result in profound disabilities. Examples of such severe deprivation might include the experiences of infants who grew up in orphanages in Romania or the extreme malnutrition experienced by children in Somalia. It must be stressed that only these extremely severe forms of deprivation are likely to result in profound disabilities. Environmental deprivation should not be deemed the cause of profound disabilities simply because no other cause is apparent and the child's environment was suboptimal in some respect.

EPIDEMIOLOGY OF BRAIN DISORDERS CAUSING PROFOUND HANDICAPS

Severe cognitive limitation (IQ below 50) affects approximately 0.4% of the population. Although many of these individuals do not have profound disabilities, it is reasonable to conclude that all individuals with profound disabilities are included within this number. Thus, examining the relative frequencies of the categories of causes of severe cognitive limitation can provide a rough estimate of the relative frequencies of the categories of causes of profound disabilities (see Table 3.3). Most likely, however, these prevalence figures underrepresent the true category proportions for individuals with profound disabilities.

The information presented in Table 3.3 is based on McLaren and Bryson's (1987) review of 10 epidemiological studies of the causes of severe

TABLE 3.3. Estimated Epidemiology of Brain Disorders Causing Profound Disabilities

Category		Relative Frequency[a]
Prenatal onset		62.5
Chromosomal disorders	27.0	
Syndrome disorders and inborn errors of metabolism	8.8	
Disorders of brain development	20.8	
Environmental influences	5.9	
Perinatal onset		12.8
Intrauterine disorders	9.0	
Neonatal disorders	3.8	
Postnatal onset		9.7
Head injuries	6.2	
Other disorders	3.5	
Unknown cause		15.0

[a]Percentage of all cases of profound disabilities.
Based on data from "Review of Recent Epidemiological Studies of Mental Retardation: Prevalence, Related Disorders and Etiology" by J. McLaren and S. E. Bryson, 1987, *American Journal of Mental Retardation, 92,* 243–254.

cognitive limitation. The table lists the percentage of all cases that can be attributed to each of the various categories of causes. Two points are readily apparent from inspection of Table 3.3. First, prenatal disorders are much more common causes of profound disabilities than either perinatal or post-natal disorders. Second, no identifiable cause is apparent in almost one sixth of cases. As noted above, these cases with no apparent cause may well have a prenatal disorder of brain development affecting connections between neurons. Thus, the information in Table 3.3 suggests that prenatal brain dysgenesis in some form probably accounts for the majority of cases of profound disabilities, and perinatal or postnatal brain damage accounts for a minority of cases.

THE PERSISTENT VEGETATIVE STATE (PVS)

The most debilitating form of profound disabilities is seen in individuals who are in a vegetative state. A *vegetative state* is defined as a condition in which the person's eyes are open and the person appears to be awake, but there is no evidence of consciousness. The person does not exhibit or demonstrate any voluntary behaviors, although involuntary and reflexive behaviors may occur. *Involuntary behaviors* include blinking in reaction to light or noise, wandering eye movements, alerting to painful stimuli, grunting or groan-ing, self-quieting (hand to mouth), crying or grimacing to painful stimuli, postural reflexes, and autonomic reactions (gagging, coughing, chewing, swal-lowing). *Voluntary behaviors* include exemplars such as turning to visual or auditory stimuli, following complex visual stimuli with the eyes, alerting to social stimuli (voice), social smiling and vocalization, cuddling to com-forting interaction, and choosing discrete interactive behaviors (e.g., prefer-ring one specific type of interaction over another). Elicitation of many of these responses depends on the child's state, so the child should be in an optimal state to elicit voluntary behaviors (see Chapter 4). Voluntary behav-iors must be exhibited consistently to be considered evidence of conscious-ness. If repeated examinations conducted when the child is in an optimal state fail to elicit consistent performance of any of these voluntary behaviors, then the child may be in a vegetative state (Coulter, 1990).

Educators and therapists may occasionally encounter children who seem to fit this description of a vegetative state. The diagnosis of a vegetative state should be made only by a qualified neurologist, who can also help to define the prognosis. The vegetative state is not always persistent or permanent, and some children do eventually become conscious (exhibit voluntary behav-iors). As a general rule, a child over the age of 2 years who has been in a vegetative state for more than a year is not likely to become conscious. These issues related to both children and adults have been discussed extensively by the multispecialty Task Force on Medical Aspects of the Persistent Vegetative State (in press).

The epidemiology of the vegetative state in children is not known. Recently, Ashwal, Eyman, Call, and Schneider (1992) reviewed data in the Client Development Evaluation Report (CDER) for approximately 100,000 children with developmental disabilities residing in California. They identified 1,183 children who met their criteria for the vegetative state. Forty percent of these children were living at home, and the rest were in some form of residential care. They did not examine these children personally, so their data should be considered only a rough estimate of the frequency of the vegetative state in children. Nonetheless, their report does suggest that educators and therapists can expect to see children in a vegetative state from time to time.

The issue of treatment and management of children in a vegetative state is beyond the scope of this chapter. Suffice it to say that there are strong and differing opinions regarding the ethics of treatment, especially in relation to the impact of treatment on an individual's quality of life. Like all children with profound disabilities, however, it is important to consider children in a vegetative state as people first, and they should be considered as valued persons who deserve whatever treatment is indicated. Defining indications for treatment and the appropriate intervention strategies will certainly be a continuing challenge for those who care for people with profound disabilities.

CONCLUSION

In this chapter, I have presented an overview of biomedical conditions that might lead to the presence or development of a profound disabling condition. Although some type of brain disorder accounts for all cases of profound disabilities, given the intricacy of the brain itself, the pinpointing of a disorder–condition match is an ongoing challenge. However, determining causes of conditions can never be looked upon as an end in and of itself. Such determinations can be of enormous assistance not only in prevention efforts, but also in determining appropriate methods for both short-term and long-term interventions.

REFERENCES

Ashwal, S., Eyman, R. K., Call, T. L., & Schneider, S. (1992). Life expectancy of children in the persistent vegetative state. *Annals of Neurology, 32,* 454.

Coulter, D. L. (1988). The neurology of mental retardation. In F. J. Menolascino & J. A. Stark (Eds.), *Preventive and curative intervention in mental retardation* (pp. 113–152). Baltimore: Brookes.

Coulter, D. L. (1990). Is the vegetative state recognizable in infants? *Medical Ethics for the Physician, 5*(2), 13–14.

Jacobson, M. (1991). *Developmental neurobiology* (3rd ed.). New York: Plenum Press.

Luckasson, R., Coulter, D. L., Polloway, E. A., Reiss, S., Schalock, R. L., Snell, M. E., Spitalnik, D. M., & Stark, J. A. (1992). *Mental retardation: Definition, classification and systems of supports.* Washington, DC: American Association on Mental Retardation.

McLaren, J., & Bryson, S. E. (1987). Review of recent epidemiological studies of mental retardation: Prevalence, related disorders and etiology. *American Journal on Mental Retardation, 92,* 243–254.

Purves, D., & Lichtman, J. W. (1985). *Principles of neural development.* Sunderland, MA: Sinauer Associates.

Task Force on Medical Aspects of the Persistent Vegetative State. (in press). Medical aspects of the persistent vegetative state. *New England Journal of Medicine.*

Part II

General Strategies and Designs

Chapter 4

Assessing Levels of State and Arousal

STEPHEN RICHARDS and LES STERNBERG

Historically, some researchers and educators have questioned the educability of students with profound disabilities (see discussions by Noonan, Brown, Mulligan, & Rettig, 1982; Noonan & Reese, 1984). In part, this doubt may be due to the basic intent of prior education efforts. Traditionally, educators have focused on developing and measuring skill acquisition (e.g., communication skills). Measurement of progress in individuals with profound disabilities frequently involved the use of methods developed for and used with individuals with severe disabilities (Sailor, Gee, Goetz, & Graham, 1988); however, this has presented several problems. First, skill acquisition in individuals with profound disabilities is typically slower than in other populations (Sternberg, 1988). Second, instability in day-to-day skill performance is not uncommon (Switzky, Haywood, & Rotatori, 1982). Third, as Rainforth (1982) noted, students with profound disabilities may be relatively unresponsive to other persons, as well as to the environmental stimuli intended to elicit behavior, thereby reducing the quantity of behaviors that might be displayed and subsequently measured. Given these problems, it is not surprising that practitioners have questioned how progress is monitored with individuals who have profound disabilities (Sailor et al., 1988). Simeonsson, Huntington, and Parse (1980) questioned whether appropriate child outcomes have been identified for assessment and suggested that state analysis might be an important area for investigation.

More recently, researchers and educators concerned with the needs of individuals with profound disabilities have turned their attention toward the investigation of biobehavioral state assessment as a potentially useful direction. State assessment has been used in infant research and intervention for a number of years. Special educators have revised and modified the techniques used by infant researchers and applied those techniques to individuals with profound disabilities. Although the number of published studies related to this latter group is relatively small, the results indicate there is promise for devising new assessment and intervention strategies based on biobehavioral state analysis.

In this chapter, we discuss the theoretical foundations for state assessment. As a basis for these foundations, we review early research with normal infants, as well as studies that included infants who were at risk for or had known disabilities. In addition, we explore recent research that specifically includes state assessment with the target population. This body of research not only suggests potential interventions but also future avenues for investigation.

AROUSAL AND STATE THEORY

Wolff (1959) described the states of neonates as falling into six types: regular sleep, irregular sleep, drowsiness, alert–inactivity, alert–activity, and crying. Of considerable importance were Wolff's efforts to quantify differences in these states. He primarily relied on rates of respiration to distinguish between sleep states, although he also examined the frequency of startles and the average interval between startles as added indicators of sleep states. Wolff also used various stimulating events during waking periods of neonates in an attempt to quantify (a) specific response differences during waking states and (b) response differences based on type and level of stimulation.

Wolff suggested that a child's ability to attend briefly during alert–inactivity states was the result of an interplay between "neural excitation" and "sensory threshold." More specifically, whether a response occurred and whether there was an increase or decrease in activity were dependent primarily on an infant's inner state of need and only secondarily on the quality and intensity of stimulation.

Prechtl (1974) reviewed research based on Wolff's earlier findings. He stressed that there were various weaknesses in state research. First, states had been descriptively categorized and, although this was convenient, it also led to the use of varied selection criteria and rating scales. Second, the use of behavioral descriptors tended to lead to a circular interpretation of state; that is, a researcher might describe the state being observed, attach a label to that state, and then proceed to interpret the meaning of any behavior observed (or not observed) to the presence or absence of that state. This circular interpretation occurred because the behavioral characteristics used to describe states had been (and continue to be) relatively stable over time.

Prechtl's own research explored the use of state criteria that could be observed and/or physiologically measured—that is, eyes opened or closed, rate of respiration, gross movements, and crying vocalizations. He further explored the use of these four "physiologic vectors" to differentiate between various states. Prechtl found that he could identify two sleep and three waking states based on the four vectors. Prechtl avoided attaching labels to those states but rather referred to them as States 1–5. He also pointed out that within-state trends in respiratory or heart rate occurred, yet the qualitative aspect of the state did not appear to change. In other words, these states appeared to be autonomous and independent of one another. They were also interspersed with brief transitory periods in which the person moved, vocalized, and so on, but these periods did not represent distinct states in and of themselves. Prechtl's assertion that States 1–5 were purely descriptive rather than interpretive is understandable given his use of physiologic as well as observational data.

Prechtl (1974) reviewed research concerning the effects of various types and levels of stimulation on the states of neonates. A number of responses to stimulation were observed, and Prechtl suggested that some stimulus events could induce a change of state (e.g., vestibular stimulation could reduce crying). As Prechtl noted,

> We have to suppose mechanisms which switch on, maintain and switch off a state, set the gate for the next following state to occur and so forth. We neither know where to locate these mechanisms, nor what kind they are. External conditions have a modulating effect on these mechanisms but the regulation of state cycles is a fundamental function of the nervous system. (p. 210)

Rainforth (1982) noted that arousal theory was the precursor to state theory among professionals concerned with neonatal behavior. As Rainforth stated, "Arousal theory put infants at the mercy of the environment" (p. 34). Arousal theorists asserted that a child's level of arousal was the result of the level of stimulation available; that is, sleep was the result of low levels of stimulation, and the movement from wakefulness to agitated states, such as crying, was the result of ever-increasing levels of stimulation. Although both arousal and state theorists have recognized the same basic continuum of observed states (see Figure 4.1), they differ in opinion as to why these states (or arousal levels) have been observed.

By the mid-1970s, researchers had amassed considerable evidence that, although states were not independent of the level of stimulation, they did serve to "control" that stimulation (Rainforth, 1982). Brazelton (1978) asserted that biobehavioral states were presumed to be the mediators of incoming stimuli and served as the internal mechanism by which the child

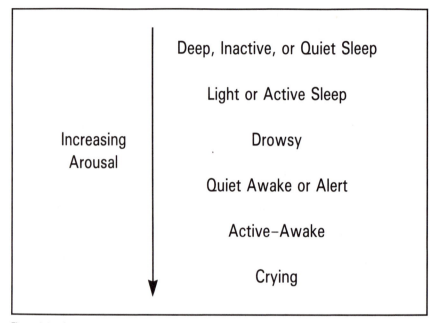

Figure 4.1. Continuum of states used by infant researchers.

could regulate receptivity to stimulation. In other words, the child's central nervous system (CNS) functioned in such a way as to decrease or increase physiological and/or psychological level of arousal in order to access and respond to stimulation. This would also include CNS functioning to shut out or defend against stimulation.

What is of considerable importance from an educational perspective is that researchers have identified a state of calm, alert arousal that, when achieved, creates a condition of greatest receptivity to environmental stimulation (Rainforth, 1982). The achievement of such a state may be necessary for optimal learning to occur (Brazelton, 1978). This level of arousal in neonates is associated with the exhibition of an orienting response.

Orienting responses are integrally related to biobehavioral states during or in which learning is presumed to occur (Rainforth, 1982). Orienting responses refer to physiologic changes (e.g., heart rate change) that are reflected in visually observable behaviors (e.g., the turning of one's head toward sounds, people, and objects). They also refer to attempts to respond to environmental stimuli (Guess et al., 1988; Rainforth, 1982). The measurement of orienting responses has served as a means to measure how different levels and types of stimulation impact on state.

OBSERVATIONAL STUDIES INVOLVING INFANTS AND AT-RISK POPULATIONS

Biobehavioral state research has been conducted with both normal and at-risk populations (Als, Tronick, Lester, & Brazelton, 1977; Brazelton, 1973). These researchers proceeded on the assumption that CNS disorganization would be reflected in the observed states of infants.

The *Brazelton Neonatal Behavioral Assessment Scale* (BNBAS) (Brazelton, 1973) was specifically designed to assess the CNS organization of newborns. Six states were included on the scale and were specified as operating from least to highest level of arousal: *deep sleep, light sleep, drowsy, alert, active,* and *crying.* In a similar vein to Brazelton, Campos and Brackbill (1973) identified six biobehavioral states: *quiet sleep, active sleep, drowsiness, quiet awake, active awake,* and *crying awake.* The continua not only are similar, but serve as a consistent frame of reference for more recent infant research.

In administering the BNBAS, an assessment specialist provides a variety of environmental stimuli (e.g., rattle, light, pull-to-sit, undressing) and records the child's subsequent responses. Recording sheets from the second edition of the BNBAS are included in Figures 4.2 and 4.3. Various items on the scale are administered when appropriate states are displayed, and the exhibited changes in the child are recorded (Sostek, 1978). Specifically, the examiner observes motor responses, skin color, hand–mouth coordination, and irritability, consolability, cuddliness, and self-quieting. The examiner also measures the child's orienting responses to stimuli (Sostek, 1978). Als, Tronick, Adamson, and Brazelton (1976) posited that, when a child's CNS is compromised, that child will likely exhibit state patterns that differ from those of children with uncompromised central nervous systems. A number of researchers have confirmed this hypothesis.

Soule, Standley, Copans, and Davis (1974) compared BNBAS scores of babies born to mothers with drug addiction with those of full-term infants with no known source of compromise of their CNS. These researchers found significant differences in state patterns between the groups. They also found that a child's state changes were useful for following the effectiveness of the course of treatment. For example, if a child moved from a crying state to a calm state after having been swaddled, it was logical to assume that swaddling had a beneficial effect (Soule et al., 1974). This study served as a clear example of how the observed states of infants could serve a communicative function during infants' interactions with caregivers.

Als et al. (1976) compared the state patterns of malnourished children with those of full-term, normal weight babies. These researchers found that, although the overall state organization of the two groups did not differ significantly, the group of malnourished children consistently exhibited problems

Behavioral and Neurological Assessment Scale

Infant's name		Date	Hour
Sex	Age	Born	
Mother's age	Father's age	Father's S.E.S.	
Examiner(s)		Apparent race	
Conditions of examination:		Place of examination	
Birthweight		Date of examination	
Time examined		Length	
Time last fed		Head circ.	
Type of delivery		Type of feeding	
Length of labor		Apgar	
Type, amount and timing of medication given mother		Birth order	
		Anesthesia?	
		Abnormalities of labor	

Initial state: observe 2 minutes

1	2	3	4	5	6
deep	light	drowsy	alert	active	crying

Predominant states (mark two)

1	2	3	4	5	6

Elicited Responses

	O*	L	M	H	A†	Descriptive paragraph (optional)				
Plantar grasp		1	2	3		Attractive	0	1	2	3
Hand grasp		1	2	3		Interfering variables	0	1	2	3
Ankle clonus		1	2	3		Need for stimulation	0	1	2	3
Babinski		1	2	3						
Standing		1	2	3		What activity does he use to quiet self?				
Automatic walking		1	2	3		hand to mouth				
Placing		1	2	3		sucking with nothing in mouth				
Incurvation		1	2	3		locking onto visual or auditory stimuli				
Crawling		1	2	3		postural changes				
Glabella		1	2	3		state change for no observable reason				
Tonic deviation of head and eyes		1	2	3						
Nystagmus		1	2	3		COMMENTS:				
Tonic neck reflex		1	2	3						
Moro		1	2	3						
Rooting (intensity)		1	2	3						
Sucking (intensity)		1	2	3						
Passive movement		1	2	3						
Arms R		1	2	3						
L		1	2	3						
Legs R		1	2	3						
L		1	2	3						

O* = response not elicited (omitted)
A† = asymmetry

Figure 4.2. Recording sheet from *Neonatal Assessment Scale.* From *Neonatal Assessment Scale* (2nd ed.) by T. Brazelton, 1984, Philadelphia: Spastics International Medical Publications, J. B. Lippincott. Reprinted with permission.

5. Orientation response-inanimate visual (4 and 5)
1   Does not focus on or follow stimulus.
2   Stills with stimulus and brightens.
3   Stills, focuses on stimulus when presented, little spontaneous interest, brief following.
4   Stills, focuses on stimulus, following for 30° arc, jerky movements.
5   Focuses and follows with eyes horizontally for at least a 30° arc. Smooth movement, loses stimulus but finds it again.
6   Follows for two 30° arcs with eyes and head. Eye movements are smooth.
7   Follows with eyes and head at least 60° horizontally, maybe briefly vertically, partly continuous movement, loses stimulus occasionally, head turns to follow.
8   Follows with eyes and head 60° horizontally and 30° vertically.
9   Focuses on stimulus and follows with smooth, continuous head movement horizontally, vertically, and follows in a circular path for a 180° arc.

6. Orientation response-inanimate auditory (4 and 5)
1   No reaction.
2   Respiratory change or blink only.
3   General quieting as well as blinking and respiratory changes.
4   Stills, brightens, no attempt to locate source.
5   Shifting of eyes to sound, stills and brightens.
6   Alerting and shifting of eyes and head turns to source.
7   Alerting, head turns to stimulus, and search with eyes.
8   Alerting prolonged, head and eyes turn to stimulus repeatedly (3 out of 4 times).
9   Turning and alerting to stimulus presented on both sides on every presentation of stimulus (4 out of 4 times).

7. Orientation—inanimate visual and auditory (4 and 5)
1   Does not focus on or follow stimulus.
2   Stills with stimulus and brightens.
3   Stills, focuses on stimulus when presented, little spontaneous interest, brief following.
4   Stills, focuses on stimulus, following for 30° arc, jerky movements.
5   Focuses and follows with eyes horizontally for at least a 30° arc. Smooth movement, loses stimulus but finds it again.
6   Follows for two 30° arcs with eyes and head. Eye movements are smooth.
7   Follows with eyes and head at least 60° horizontally, maybe briefly vertically, partly continuous movement, loses stimulus occasionally, head turns to follow.
8   Follows with eyes and head 60° horizontally and 30° vertically.
9   Focuses on stimulus and follows with smooth, continuous head movement horizontally, vertically, and follows in a circular path for a 180° arc.

8. Orientation-animate visual (4 and 5)
1   Does not focus on or follow stimulus.
2   Stills with stimulus and brightens.
3   Stills, focuses on stimulus when presented, little spontaneous interest, brief following.
4   Stills, focuses on stimulus, follows for 30° arc, jerky movements.
5   Focuses and follows with eyes for at least a 30° arc. Smooth movement, loses stimulus but finds it again.
6   Follows for two 30° arcs with eyes and head. Eye movements are smooth.
7   Follows with eyes and head at least 60° horizontally, maybe briefly vertically, partly continuous movement, loses stimulus occasionally, head turns to follow.
8   Follows with eyes and head 60° horizontally and 30° vertically.
9   Focuses on stimulus and follows with smooth, continuous head movement horizontally, vertically, and follows in a circular path for a 180° arc.

9. Orientation-animate auditory (4 and 5)
1   No reaction.
2   Respiratory change or blink only.
3   General quieting as well as blinking and respiratory changes.
4   Stills, brightens, no attempt to locate source.
5   Shifting of eyes to sound, stills and brightens.
6   Alerting and shifting of eyes and head turns to source.
7   Alerting, head turns to stimulus, and search with eyes.
8   Alerting prolonged, head and eyes turn to stimulus repeatedly (3 out of 4 times).
9   Turning and alerting to stimulus presented on both sides on every presentation of stimulus (4 out of 4 times).

Figure 4.3. Example recording sheet from *Neonatal Assessment Scale*. From *Neonatal Assessment Scale* (2nd ed.) by T. Brazelton, 1984, Philadelphia: Spastics International Medical Publications, J. B. Lippincott. Reprinted with permission.

related to interactive processes and physiological organization. Als et al. noted that, occasionally, the malnourished babies appeared overwhelmed by the environment. This gave the examiners the impression that the babies were experiencing physical stress or a desire to be left alone. The researchers concluded that the children apparently could not easily muster the energy to cry or shift to sleep states to shut out stimulation. These same babies could and did achieve alert states, but their orienting responses were poorer and slower than those of the babies in the comparison group. This suggested to Als et al. that the effort required to achieve the alert state left the malnourished children with a diminished capacity to benefit maximally from achieving this state. Once the state was achieved, the energy required to process incoming information was lessened, thereby retarding their orienting responses. In follow-ups, these researchers reported that the malnourished children continued to appear to be easily overstimulated. In addition, their sleeping and eating habits were less predictable than those of babies in the comparison group. Als et al. concluded that, while the entire continuum of states may be displayed, the intrastate behaviors of subgroups of children can be comparatively inferior. Furthermore, they noted that the diminished quality of the malnourished children's state behaviors may have negatively impacted on the parent–child interactions they experienced.

Jackson (1974) conducted a study that was critical in establishing the validity of observing overt behaviors in lieu of measuring physiologic responses. Jackson found that the heart rate of infants changed predictably with changes in stimulus intensity. The change in heart rate also occurred with the simultaneous exhibition of orienting responses and reflexes that served as a defensive mechanism. Perhaps equally important from the results of these observations was the generation of the hypothesis that a level of stimulation might exist when orienting responses are elicited and defensive responses are not. Brown, Leavitt, and Graham (1977) and Campos and Brackbill (1973) obtained results consistent with those of Jackson (1974). These researchers found that heart rate decreased with observed orienting responses and increased with responses that could be categorized as defensive.

BIOBEHAVIORAL STATES AND THE EFFECTS OF ENVIRONMENTAL STIMULATION

Other investigators have been interested in how differing degrees and types of stimulation influence an individual's state. These studies are important in that they established one of the foundations for exploring the interaction of environmental variables with the biobehavioral state variable.

Brackbill (1971) examined the effects of increasing stimulation on the states of infants. Various sensory modalities (e.g., visual, auditory) were continuously stimulated. Brackbill noted that this stimulation appeared to have a differential effect on the states of infants. The more extreme states on the continuum (i.e., quiet sleep and crying) were most affected. For example, Brackbill found that, with continuous stimulation of several modalities, sleep actually increased. This suggested that a level of increased stimulation might occur at which arousal is actually depressed. An interesting finding was that similar results were obtained with one infant with anencephaly included in the study.

Barnett and Lodge (1967) included a group of infants with developmental retardation along with infants who were developing normally in a study examining evoked response characteristics. These researchers were interested in comparing the responsiveness of the two groups to environmental stimulation. They found that, compared with the normal infants, the infants with developmental retardation demonstrated slower or late responses. The authors suggested that these response differences were more related to the regulation of sensory input than to the reception of sensory input. In other words, they hypothesized that responses of the infants with developmental retardation were affected by a less organized arousal level rather than any sensory deficit stemming from their disabilities.

Similar to Barnett and Lodge, Bradley-Johnson and Travers (1979) found that infants with mental retardation were not as receptive to moderate levels of stimulation as were babies who were developing normally. Although heart rate changes were similar in the two groups, the researchers found that the changes were less pronounced in the group of infants with retardation. These authors conjectured that less pronounced heart rate changes might indicate fewer orienting responses; this would adversely affect level of acquired cognitive stimulation and development.

In an earlier study, Moskowitz and Lohmann (1970) found that infants with Down syndrome required more intense levels of auditory stimulation before exhibiting an orienting response than did infants without a known disability. Additionally, the infants with Down syndrome tended to show more physiologic involvement in their orienting responses, perhaps suggesting further difficulty in organizing states and the exhibition of orienting responses.

As a group, the aforementioned studies illuminate the fact that quantitative differences exist between groups of infants with developmental difficulties versus those without. These early studies also established the importance of arousal, states, and orienting responses to promoting interaction between the environment and the individual. There is a presumption that the quiet alert state and its corresponding orienting responses are necessary to growth and development, and are the precursors to more complex attending behaviors necessary for more "intentional" learning. The infant literature also serves to establish that some relationship exists between the level and type of stimulation received and the exhibited states of young children. It is necessary, therefore, to examine how this body of knowledge has been applied and expanded through studies involving individuals with profound disabilities.

STUDIES RELATED TO INDIVIDUALS WITH PROFOUND DISABILITIES

In an early study related to biobehavioral state research, Landesman-Dwyer and Sackett (1978) examined the influence of environmental stimulation on behavior change in individuals with profound disabilities. The dependent variables in this study were sleep–wake patterns and low, moderate, or high levels of activity while awake. The study included 16 individuals, all of whom resided in an institution. The subjects were assigned to an experimental or a control group, where the control group received the ordinary care and services provided at the facility. The experimental group received stimulation through interacting with toys, enticing objects, and peers, as well as by being placed in an upright sitting position. The researchers noted that a majority of individuals in the experimental group increased activity level (e.g., became more interactive) and developed more predictable sleep–wake patterns. They also reported an increase in "looking behaviors," which might be interpreted as orienting responses. Although sleep–wake patterns became more predictable, it is interesting to note that the actual amount of time spent sleeping did not change significantly. Two individuals in the experimental group experienced no change in sleep–wake patterns. No significant changes from baseline levels in either sleep–wake patterns or in activity levels were noted for the control group.

Several important implications arise from this study. Landesman-Dwyer and Sackett (1978) demonstrated that, with most of their experimental subjects, both animate and inanimate environmental stimulation was associated with positive changes in overall state patterns. In addition, positioning proved to be an important variable in the study in regards to its effects on increasing orienting responses and interactive behaviors. The fact that the amount of sleep did not significantly change, but sleep–wake patterns did, lends support to the notion that state is internally organized and regulated at least partially in response to environmental events. Seemingly conflicting results were those associated with the two individuals in the experimental group whose sleep–wake patterns did not change. The data from these two subjects, however, might still lend support to the premise that state is internally regulated. For example, one can hypothesize that state is so internally regulated in some individuals as to make the encouragement of state change a more difficult matter.

It should also be recognized that Landesman-Dwyer and Sackett (1978) did not find that their methods produced overall differences in levels of sleep in members of the experimental group. This might suggest that, at least in the short term, fairly regular lengths of time must be spent in particular states. A further implication is that, although an alert state is optimal for learning, it may be very necessary for individuals to spend substantial periods of time in other states as well. Certainly, this would seem apparent regarding sleep states.

Some of the same issues dealt with in Landesman-Dwyer and Sackett's (1978) study have been explored more recently by other researchers concerned with improving education for individuals with profound disabilities. Rainforth (1982) outlined a research agenda pertaining to the investigation of biobehavioral states and orienting responses in students with profound disabilities. More specifically, the following questions were posed:

1. Is it possible to identify state cycle patterns for individuals with profound mental retardation, and, if so, would these patterns vary among groups with different developmental ages?

2. Is it possible to alter the state of individuals with profound retardation in the direction of an optimal orienting response (e.g., quiet alert)?

3. Is it possible to observe and measure baseline orienting responses for individuals with profound disabilities, and, if so, would these baseline levels vary with developmental age or individual behavioral characteristics?

4. Would stimulation of one sensory system produce optimal benefits for eliciting orienting responses?

Rainforth's agenda was a broad and ambitious one. Fortunately, a few researchers have attempted to explore the answers to the above questions. By no means have all avenues of investigation been exhausted; however, the studies discussed in the following sections do represent a promising start.

Defining and Measuring Biobehavioral States

Guess et al. (1988) reported on two studies designed to develop an instrument for reliably measuring the biobehavioral states of individuals with profound disabilities. In their first study, these researchers used a momentary time sampling procedure that produced reliable results, but the information obtained appeared to be insufficient to draw any definitive conclusions (Guess et al., 1988). The observers looked up at the end of 10-second intervals and recorded the state of the individual under study. Unfortunately, this did not necessarily result in the recording of the state that was predominant during the interval. The second study used an interval recording method as well, but this time raters recorded the state that predominated during the entire 10-second interval. This method was also reliable and, in addition, provided more information. In these two studies, state was the only variable recorded.

Guess et al. (1988) used a state continuum derived from those used by researchers studying infants. Although similar states were observed in students with profound disabilities as in infants who were developing normally, additional states were observed in the target population (Guess et al., 1988). Epilepsy among the students studied required the designation of a seizure state. The occurrence of high rates of self-stimulatory behavior in some individuals necessitated that this behavior be reflected in a state designation. Finally, a daze state was observed in which there was wakefulness with no apparent interaction with or receptivity to the environment. Guess et al. (1990) amended the Guess et al. (1988) state designations to include nine states (see Table 4.1).

Sternberg and Richards (1989) proposed a research program and potential state designations that, like those of Guess et al. (1988), stressed the need for developing a reliable instrument as well as exploring the interaction of state with environmental variables. Richards and Sternberg (1992) conducted a preliminary investigation involving individuals with profound disabilities using somewhat different state designations and a different recording procedure than those employed by Guess et al. (1988) and Guess et al. (1990). The state designations used by these researchers are included in Table 4.2.

Richards and Sternberg (1992) recorded both state and co-occurring environmental variables in this study. They used an interval recording procedure whereby the arousal/orienting state or the state closest to that along the continuum depicted in Table 4.2 was recorded if it was observed at any point during an interval. The co-occurring environmental variables were recorded in the same fashion. Although this method did not necessarily result in the recording of the state that predominated the interval, it did result in the recording of interactions between environmental variables and orienting responses. For example, if at the end of an interval, a staff member were to call the student's name and the student were to turn her head to look at the staff member, this would have resulted in both the recording of the staff member's attempt to interact and the resulting orienting response of the student.

A study conducted by Green, Canipe, Gardner, and Reid (1990) provided another assessment paradigm that could be used to describe the state and

TABLE 4.1. Definitions of Behavioral State

S¹/Asleep-Inactive: Persons's eyes are closed. Respiration is relatively slow and regular. Body tone is relaxed. Exhibits little motor activity (e.g., startle, mouthing, brief limb or body movements) or no motor activity.

S²/Asleep-Active: Person's eyes are closed and body tone is relaxed. Respiration is generally uneven. Sporadic movements (tossing and turning, head and limb twitching) may occur but muscle tone generally low between movements. Person may exhibit rapid eye movements (REM). Other behavior may include occasional facial expressions (smiles, grimaces, frowns) and/or vocalizations (sighs, grunting, gurgling) and/or thumb and/or finger sucking.

DR/Drowsy: Person's eyes are either open and eyelids appear "heavy" or eyes are opening and closing repeatedly. Vocalizations may occur.

DA/Daze: Nonorientation to visual, auditory, or tactile stimuli predominates. If person's vision is intact, eyes are open and appear glassy, dull, and immobile. Motor movements are infrequent but are nonorienting in nature (brief limb or body movements, startles). Respiration is regular. Few or no vocalizations occur.

A¹/Awake Inactive-Alert: Persons's eyes are open and some active visual or auditory orientation, focusing, or tracking is displayed (orienting/focusing on stimuli, turning head, eyes looking toward stimuli, or following stimuli). Eyes may be closed *with* displays of orientation (smiling, leaning toward/away, head turning). Nonorienting motor movements may occur (brief limb or body movements, startles). Demonstrates regular respiration. Vocalizations may occur.

A²/Awake Active-Alert: Person engages/interacts by making contact with a person or objects. If person's vision is intact, eyes are open, bright, and shiny. Visual, auditory, or tactile interactive patterns are exhibited with distinct fine- and/or gross-motor movements. Body movements to avoid stimuli or interaction (e.g., pulling away from someone, turning head away from spoon) are considered inter-active. Vocalizations in direct response to verbalized questions are also interactive.

A²/S/Awake-Active/Self-Stimulatory: Person exhibits behaviors that are self-stimulatory or stereotypical (idiosyncratic, repetitive rhythmic movements of body or body parts). Movements may include repetitive touching of any body part (two or more times in 5-second interval) or any repetitive limb movement that is not reflexive (e.g., headweaving, rocking, mouthing hand or objects, teeth grinding, rubbing hands, banging objects).

C/A/Crying/Agitated: Person may exhibit intense vocalizing, crying, or screaming. Grimacing and/or frowning may occur with or without intense vocalizations or crying. Self-injurious behavior possible. Respiration may be irregular and eyes may be open or closed. Overall increased tension in body tone with accompanying agitation behaviors (intense vocalizing, facial expressions, crying).

Seizures: If a seizure occurs within any 10-second observation period, a large S is drawn inside the data box.

TABLE 4.2. State Designations

Seizure:	A seizure occurs within the interval.
Asleep:	Eyes are closed but rapid eye movements may be present; there may be some jerky movements; there may be some vocalization; student is not responsive to environment. Eyelids appear to flutter or are "heavy" in that student appears to be nodding off or "fighting sleep"; there may be some vocalization.
No Orienting:	Student's eyes are opened but there is no eye movement; eyes do not appear focused; motor movements may appear jerky (e.g., startle response) or are slight and not purposeful; vocalizations may occur.
Agitated:	Student is awake and may be crying or screaming or otherwise vocalizing in a manner indicating discomfort or anger. Student may exhibit facial or physical gestures indicating distress (e.g., grimacing, self-abuse).
Arousal/Unclear:	Student's eyes are opened but are not clearly focused; there may be voluntary gross- or fine-motor movement but not movements purposefully interactive with any object or other person in the environment; there may be vocalization; there is no visual or auditory tracking; there is no orienting to clear environmental stimuli.
Arousal/Orienting:	Student's eyes are opened and focused; there may be fine- and/or gross-motor movements toward interaction with clear environmental stimuli; there may be visual or auditory tracking of environmental stimuli; changes in facial expressions (not of an agitated nature) in response to environmental stimuli; vocalizations in response to environmental stimuli.

From "Corroborating Previous Findings: Laying Stepping Stones in the Analysis of Biobehavioral States in Students with Profound Disabilities" by S. Richards and L. Sternberg, 1993, *Education and Training in Mental Retardation, 28*, p. 264. Copyright 1993 by the Council for Exceptional Children. Reprinted with permission.

arousal levels of individuals with profound disabilities. Their method included a time sampling procedure whereby the observed state of the individual was recorded every 30 minutes across 5½ hours of a day. These researchers used three alertness levels: asleep, drowsy, and awake. They further categorized the awake state into five separate types: nonalert/nonactive, alert/nonactive, alert/active/purposeful, alert/active/nonpurposeful, and agitated. These categories were differentiated based on eye position and movement, occurrence or nonoccurrence of purposeful gross-motor movement, and the presence or absence and type of vocalization exhibited (Green et al., 1990).

It is apparent from the above discussion that a variety of methods currently exist for both defining and recording observed states in individuals with profound disabilities. It is also clear that any particular method may offer advantages over other methods, but is also likely to yield disadvantages. For example, Guess et al. (1988) used a method that likely results in a better portrayal of overall time spent in various states; however, it may not capture all shifts in state that are potentially important (at least as defined by the occurrence of orienting responses that may be short in duration). The method used by Richards and Sternberg (1992) resulted in the recording of such shifts, but may not have always reflected the overall time spent in particular states. The method used by Green et al. (1990) may not have achieved either of the above results, but did allow for long periods of recording with less manpower.

Guy, Guess, and Ault (1993) compared results from two different data sets obtained from observations of the same students. One data set included 30 intervals over a 5-minute period and was collected by classroom teachers. The other data set included 60 intervals collected over a 10-minute period and was collected by research staff. In addition, the research staff collected data on more occasions (sessions) than did the teachers. The overall purpose of the study was to determine if the differences in length of the observation period and/or the actual number of observation periods would result in different state profiles on the same subject(s). In fact, there were no differences in the data distributions from the different measurement procedures, suggesting that a shorter and less frequent observation method (i.e., 5-minute samples taken for 20 observation periods) may be sufficient to determine students' state profiles. Guy et al. stressed, however, that comparing different profiles using different recording procedures across studies might prove problematic. It should also be noted that the observed students included those that spent the larger percentage of time in sleep, drowse, and daze states. Richards (1990) and Richards and Sternberg (1992) also used 5-minute observation sessions, but the length of intervals differed from those of Guy et al.

Because no particular method of state measurement appears to have been developed that is clearly better in all respects than any other, it is important to continue to conduct research that might ultimately yield such a method. For the present time, it would probably be safe to assume that 5-minute observation periods taken across all days of the week, including samplings of behavior during both mornings and afternoons, would be sufficient to obtain an overall state profile of any particular individual (Guy et al., 1993; Richards, 1990).

With the establishment of reliable methods for observing states, researchers have turned to measuring state cycles and patterns. Based on previous research (Landesman-Dwyer & Sackett, 1978), there appeared to be no conclusive answer to Rainforth's question concerning whether state cycles could be identified and, if so, whether they would vary among groups.

State Cycles and Patterns

Guess et al. (1990) reported on a study that examined the state cycle patterns in 50 students with severe, profound, and multiple disabling conditions. After the observations of these students had been completed, the researchers characterized students' overall profiles as being (a) alert and interactive, (b) alert and not interactive, (c) agitated, (d) self-stimulatory, (e) drowsy or dazed, or (f) sleeping. According to the researchers, students' individual and group profiles were determined based on percentage of time observed in each of the nine state categories (as listed in Table 4.1).

Guess et al. (1990) then tested for differences between their profile groups. Each group did not necessarily differ significantly in overall profile from every other group; however, more than a sufficient number of differences were exhibited to justify the identification of profile groups. In addition, more precise labels for each group and respective descriptors from an analysis of results were developed. The groups and their respective descriptors are included in Table 4.3. Guess et al. concluded that, as a group, the students included in their study spent a large percentage of time (42%) in nonalert states. This suggested that most of the students were probably not attaining the presumably more optimal states for learning.

Green et al. (1990) investigated the state cycles of three individuals with profound disabilities. The researchers found no obvious cyclical patterns in any of the individuals studied prior to the implementation of experimental conditions comprising three different educational interventions.

TABLE 4.3. Behavior State Profile Groups

Impaired Alert-Response Relationship: This group spent the largest percentage of time in the awake inactive–alert and awake active–alert states, with more than 20% of the observed states falling in the awake active–alert category.

Impaired Responsiveness: This group spent a large percentage of time in the awake inactive–alert and awake active–alert states, but less than 20% of time was spent in the latter and at least 55% of time was spent in the former.

Impaired Alertness due to Excessive Self-Stimulation and Crying/Agitation: This group was the second largest group. Less than 75% of time was spent in the awake active–alert and awake inactive–alert states. They were observed more often in the awake active–self-stimulatory and crying/agitated states than in sleep, drowsy, or daze states.

Impaired Alertness due to Excessive Sleeping, Drowsiness, and Daze: This was the largest group. These students spent less than 75% of time in awake active–alert and awake inactive–alert states but were observed more often in the asleep–inactive, asleep–active, drowsy, and daze states than in crying/agitated or self-stimulatory states.

Undifferentiated: This was the smallest group. These students spent less than 75% of time in any of the state ranges as outlined for any other group. These students exhibited a wide range of states.

Adapted from *Investigations into the State Behaviors of Students with Severe and Profound Handicapping Conditions* by D. Guess et al., 1991, Lawrence: University of Kansas, Department of Special Education.

Richards (1990) and Richards and Sternberg (1992) also investigated the cycles of occurrences of state in individuals with profound disabilities. These researchers, using the partial interval recording system discussed previously, compared the occurrence of the state recorded in each interval with the state occurring in the prior interval. They found the relationships between the prior and the present states to be significant in two different studies. For example, Richards (1990) found that, in 81% of the intervals, the state currently being exhibited did not change from the previous state. This certainly suggested that, across relatively short time periods (i.e., from one 20-second interval to the next over 5 minutes of observation), these individuals' states tended to remain the same. Furthermore, Richards and Sternberg (1993) found some similarities between the profiles of the five subjects included in one of their studies and those identified by Guess et al. (1990; see Table 4.3). Although specific comparisons were not possible given differences in both recording procedures and state definitions, it was of interest that individuals in the Richards and Sternberg study spent very similar proportions of time in states similar to those identified by Guess et al. In other words, there were individuals who were primarily aroused and orienting, aroused but not orienting, or sleeping or not aroused, and observed states were distributed relatively evenly across categories. The majority of observations indicated that these students were awake, but as a group were not in the optimal state for learning (arousal/orienting).

Guess et al. (1991) extensively examined state cycle patterns in students with profound disabilities across 5-hour observation periods. They found no evidence that the individuals in their study exhibited cycles that were only temporally based; that is, particular states did not occur purely in accordance with the passage of time. Interestingly, they did find that overall *rates* of change in state tended to exceed 20 seconds by documenting that state type did not typically change until 20 or more seconds had elapsed. The findings of Richards (1990) and Richards and Sternberg (1992) appear to be consistent with these findings; that is, given the 20-second recording intervals used in these two studies, state did not tend to change from one interval to the next across over 80% of the comparisons between present and prior state.

Guess et al. (1991) also found some evidence in their data to support the premise that, when state does change, it may change in a somewhat predictable sequence or pattern. For example, Guess et al. (1991) noted that their awake inactive–alert state tended to precede other states, including awake active–alert states as well as states indicative of decreased arousal (e.g., sleep or drowsy states). Sleep and drowsy states were also found to be interactive.

The importance of the findings of all the above researchers is not to be overlooked. Landesman-Dwyer and Sackett's (1978) earlier research that suggested that activity levels might be alterable in some individuals and less so in others has yet to be fully understood or investigated. Attempting to establish whether states are possibly cyclical, change sequentially, are of predictable duration, occur in predictable proportions, or occur in predictable sequences is extremely critical to supporting or rejecting these hypotheses. Landesman-Dwyer and Sackett noted that activity levels did increase during certain periods of intervention for most of their experimental subjects; however, the proportion of time spent sleeping did not change for most of these subjects even though cycles of sleep did become more predictable. Nevertheless, for two of the subjects, no significant change in activity levels or the cycles of sleep were noted. Therefore, it remains to be established whether it is possible to change the overall proportion of time spent in states that are, for all intents and purposes, less optimal for learning.

In addition, it has been posited that the state of an individual can be encouraged toward alertness and orienting from states that are presumably less optimal for learning. Whether these changes may be sequential along the state continuum is as yet unknown, but such a possibility certainly exists (Guess et al., 1991). Whether there are certain environmental variables that may be manipulated to encourage such changes has been examined by some researchers.

Investigation of Environmental Variables and State

Richards (1990) and Richards and Sternberg (1992) investigated the relationships between various environmental variables and the observed states of five and seven individuals, respectively, with profound mental and multiple physical disabilities. In the Richards and Sternberg (1992) study, five environmental variables were simultaneously recorded along with the observed biobehavioral states of students with profound disabilities in a regular public school. The variables included the following: (a) grouping of the students (i.e., alone, with one or more peers, with one or more peers and a staff member, or the student only with one or more staff members); (b) type of stimulation available (i.e., no stimulus activity, gustatory–olfactory, auditory available to everyone in the class, auditory available primarily to the observed student, visual–motor, tactile, kinesthetic, or a combination of two or more of the previous types); (c) position of the student (i.e., sitting, standing, supine, prone, side-lying, or a changing position); (d) type of cue delivered to the observed student (i.e., no cue, verbal, touch, or a combination of verbal and touch cues); and (e) proximity of staff (i.e., distant, close, or in physical contact with the observed student). These variables were selected based on those used in Landesman-Dwyer and Sackett's (1978) study (grouping, position), infant research (auditory and visual stimulation), and typical instructional variables (type of stimulation, type of cue, degree of physical contact). The results indicated that all of the environmental variables could be reliably observed. Type of stimulation was the only variable that appeared to require alteration in order to obtain more specific information. As a result of the use of a radio, phonograph, or tape player in the classroom during most of the intervals in the study, the type of stimulation recorded was almost exclusively a combination. Additionally, it was concluded from the infant literature and the results of this study, that other types of stimulation might be effectively recorded as either visual, auditory, or some combination.

With these revisions, Richards (1990) conducted a similar study involving five students with profound disabilities. Although the study began with the same seven students discussed in Richards and Sternberg's (1992) report, one of these individuals died and another had surgery requiring an extended absence from school. An eighth student identified for use in both studies moved prior to the conduct of the study.

In both studies, relationships between environmental variables and the biobehavioral state variable were examined to determine how these variables might have co-occurred. Subsequently, possible influences of the classroom on the students' biobehavioral states (and vice versa) were explored. For example, it was found that when a student was grouped with a staff member(s), the student exhibited an alert state more often than when alone or grouped only with a peer.

The type of stimulation provided did not appear to be particularly important to the arousal level of students in these studies. More specifically, because auditory stimulation from a radio, phonograph, or tape player was available during virtually every interval recorded, it was not possible to discern its impact on state. Although infant researchers have speculated that continuous stimulation may depress arousal, insufficient numbers of observations occurred when such stimulation was not available to posit any reasonable conclusions in this study. The type of individual-specific stimulation (i.e., visual, auditory, or some combination of these stimuli) did not appear to co-occur with state in unequivocal patterns. Although students were exhibiting orienting responses more often when such stimulation was available than when not, it was not clear whether the stimulating activity might have impacted the state of the individual. When staff were present, orienting responses were more frequent, thereby increasing the association between the occurrence of alert states and the presence of stimulating activities. When staff were not present, however, the presence of such activities was less clearly associated with orienting responses. Therefore, when students were left alone with a presumably enticing object or other stimulation to serve as encouragement for them to interact, the students did not necessarily do so.

The position of the student and its relationship to state appeared to be predictable. The least desirable position for the occurrence of alert states appeared to be the supine position. A predictable relationship was also discovered in regards to environmental cues. When students were verbally or physically cued to make a physical or vocal response, the students also were more likely to exhibit an orienting response. A no cue condition was more closely associated with no orienting.

When the proximity of staff to students was examined in relation to biobehavioral state, a similar pattern to that of the grouping and cue variables emerged. This variable was included because a staff member could be with an individual or group of students, but still not deliver a cue to elicit a response. A staff member could also be distant from a student (more than two arm's lengths) and still deliver a verbal cue. A closer look at the data revealed that, when staff were close to or in contact with students, the students were also more likely to exhibit an alert state. A further analysis revealed that, even when physical contact was not intended to elicit a response from a student (e.g., a staff member was holding a student in her lap but with no particular response expected from the student), the student still tended to be exhibiting orienting responses more often than not. Separately recorded variables—the day of the week and the time of day—appeared not to be particularly significant in their relationships with students' states.

The results of the two above studies may be summarized as follows. First, contact with staff appeared important in the occurrence of orienting responses. Second, the presence of continuous stimulation did not increase arousal, but it could not be demonstrated that such stimulation decreased arousal. Third, the position of the student affected exhibition of orienting responses. The immediate implication was that an individual should be positioned so that both physical and performance benefits (i.e., emission of orienting responses) could accrue to the student. Fourth, the day of the week and the time of day appeared to be unrelated to the exhibition of students' biobehavioral states. Finally, the provision of stimulating activities, apart from staff guidance or interaction, was not associated with increased exhibition of orienting responses.

The two studies suggested that biobehavioral states and environmental variables did co-occur in potentially important patterns in a small group of individuals with profound disabilities. Although the external validity of these studies is clearly limited, their usefulness lies as much in what they do not indicate as in what they do. The area of biobehavioral state research has great potential, but relatively few studies have been conducted from which definitive information may be derived. Therefore, research efforts must be continued to more clearly delineate the practical applications of biobehavioral state assessment.

IMPLICATIONS FOR INTERVENTION

Despite the relatively small number of studies and the limited data bases, there are implications for the use of biobehavioral state assessment, especially regarding interventions to modify states and develop orienting responses. It is important for the reader to realize, however, that these database limitations necessitate that the suggestions described below be dealt with cautiously.

Guess et al. (1993) provided a number of recommendations based on several studies conducted over the past few years. First, these investigators speculated that undesirable state organizational patterns (i.e., inordinate time spent in nonalert states) might become entrenched over a long period of time. They suggested, therefore, that interventions might start for some individuals in the neonatal intensive care unit (NICU). Drawing upon a syntactic theory model advocated by Als (1982, 1986; cited in Guess et al., 1993), Guess et al. suggested that the NICU environment be altered to promote stabilization and integration of neurophysiological and developmental functions, which would include biobehavioral state. Like many early childhood specialists, Guess et al. (1993) recommended strongly for the use of parents as early interventionists.

Second, Guess et al. (1993) suggested that a significant emphasis in early intervention programs should be on the development of multiple responses that extend and enhance the individual's ability to interact with the environment. These researchers suggested that such an emphasis could increase the time spent in alert states and decrease the possibility of the emergence of less desirable state organization patterns. Guess et al. recognized that educators currently lack sufficient procedures to impact on the development of such responses to the degree one would hope. They did, however, offer suggestions for improving Individualized Education Program (IEP) goals and objectives that might facilitate movement in such a direction. For example, they recommended that IEP objectives be developed to increase overall duration of desirable states and, in particular, adaptive responsiveness (i.e., inactive–alert and active–alert states). In addition, Guess et al. suggested that the use of augmentative devices, opportunities for interactions with nondisabled peers, and attention to nonsymbolic communication be encouraged.

Clearly, further exploration into how educational environments might be altered to promote such increases is needed. Richards (1990) has offered a number of instructional guidelines. Given that students when left alone were much less likely to display alert states, he suggested that small group instruction might be both useful and more efficient for delivering staff attention to students than would be one-to-one instruction. In both Richards's (1990) and Richards and Sternberg's (1992) studies, the interaction of staff members appeared very important in eliciting orienting responses. Therefore, the practice of leaving a student alone with an enticing object or activity to presumably occupy the student's attention might be a relatively unproductive practice.

Another important instructional guideline relates to the scheduling of staff. During observation periods, Richards (1990) found that students were interacting with staff less than 50% of the time. This was partially due to the demands of the typical classroom, including responsibilities related to meal preparation and eating, laundry, and paperwork. Richards suggested that teachers might examine how staff schedules for meals and other duties might be arranged to decrease the amount of time staff are not available to interact with students. Also, teachers might carefully consider what typical staff duties might involve student helpers to increase interaction and to provide exposure to functional educational activities.

A common practice in classrooms for students with multiple disabilities is the regular positioning and repositioning of students to promote better health and increase opportunities for interaction. It has been advocated frequently that no more time be spent in the supine position than is necessary for health reasons. Richards (1990) found that the supine position was the least desirable for the display of orienting responses. He suggested, therefore, that both health *and* performance requisites be integrated within any positioning program established for a student.

The use of an audio device to produce music or talk in a classroom throughout the day was of unknown impact (Richards, 1990). This practice appears to conflict with infant research that suggests that the more modalities and the more continuous stimulation, the more arousal will be depressed (Brackbill, 1971). Richards suggested that teachers who provide such auditory stimulation may wish to evaluate the effects of such stimulation on the overall alertness of students in their classrooms.

The use of cues, and in particular touch of any kind, appeared to be associated with orienting responses (Richards, 1990; Richards & Sternberg, 1992). Touch may be a critical factor in eliciting orienting responses from students. Of some interest was the finding that touch did not necessarily have to be intended to elicit a specific motor response from students. Touch in and of itself appeared to be useful in working with students with multiple disabilities.

Both Richards (1990) and Guess et al. (1993) suggested that intraindividual variables (e.g., medication levels, diagnosed medical conditions) be examined more fully to develop understanding of their impact on state. For example, Guess et al. (1993) found that dietary and medication changes can have significant impact on the alertness of students with disabilities.

RESEARCH IMPLICATIONS

As noted previously, one of the major problems in outlining specific suggestions for classroom applications is the need for further applied and theoretical research. A number of suggestions for research have been tendered. Sternberg and Richards (1989) suggested that the dependent versus independent variable relationship between state and environmental variables be explored. Given issues regarding internal versus external control of behavior state, paradigm shifts might be warranted. For example, Richards (1990) noted that at times students appeared to react to the environment (e.g., displaying orienting responses and increased alertness in response to staff interaction) while at other times the staff appeared to react to a student's state (e.g., a change from asleep to awake, leading staff to begin talking to the student). Therefore, a student's state may at times be a dependent variable (former case) and at other times an independent variable (latter case).

Guess et al. (1991) noted that additional studies need to be conducted to investigate the temporal nature of state cycles and patterns. Although the results of their study were illuminating, they stressed that the relatively limited observation period may not have captured cycles or patterns that emerged across a 24-hour period or across days and even weeks.

Richards (1990) and Guess et al. (1991) stressed the need to examine state as a quality of life variable. It was noted in the infant literature (Als et al., 1977) that state could be used to judge the effectiveness of certain interventions with children born with compromised central nervous systems. In a similar vein, increases or decreases in arousal and alert states might be used as indicators of the effectiveness of educational interventions. Guess et al. (1993) clearly perceived this possibility as well, as they suggested that such increases be used as objectives on students' IEPs.

Sternberg and Richards (1989) and Guess et al. (1988) asserted that there is an obvious need to increase the data bases and the number of studies concerned with state assessment. Guess et al. (1993) strongly recommended that longitudinal research be conducted to examine both intraindividual and environmental variables that both influence the patterns of state organization and can enhance or maintain preferred states and orienting responses. For example, these researchers recommended that in-depth analyses be conducted to determine what conditions might produce high occurrences of self-injury or stereotypic behavior (as behavioral exemplars of state regulation), as well as what variables might tend to contribute to an overall depression of arousal and alertness in this population versus their nondisabled peers. Guess et al. (1993) also suggested that these and other research analyses could lead to the development of a "massive" intervention model that would include many possible combinations of variables that might impact on the state patterns of students. Guess et al. noted that nutritional and medical interventions, positioning, adaptive and augmentative devices, and new instructional procedures were but a few of the possibilities that might be researched. Advocating for the worthwhile nature of such investigations, Richards (1990) inferred that such comprehensive analyses would likely be time-consuming and difficult, given the large number of environmental variables that might be investigated. Such investigations are imperative, however, if one is to determine whether the overall time spent in particular states might be changed, if the sequence of state changes might be exploited, or if state change patterns might be altered to encourage the achievement of alert and orienting states.

Finally, it is important that researchers and classroom teachers collaborate to develop state measurement systems that accurately reflect state organization that are of practical use in the classroom. These systems should be easy to administer so that they are minimally intrusive on instructional time (Guy et al., 1993).

CONCLUSION

In a relatively short number of years, the knowledge of biobehavioral states in students with multiple disabilities has expanded and, perhaps more importantly, led toward new directions of investigation. Although to the practitioner, much of this discussion may seem esoteric, biobehavioral state analysis very possibly represents one of the most important areas of research in the area of profound disabilities.

Over the years, relatively little has been done in the way of developing instructional and assessment procedures specifically for use with students with profound disabilities. It has not been uncommon for teachers of this population to lament their students' lack of progress. What may well be at the root of the problem is not so much that progress will not or does not occur, but that educators have not developed instruments that are sensitive to and that accurately reflect relatively subtle changes in behavior. The use of biobehavioral state assessment is a promising development toward this end.

REFERENCES

Als, H., Tronick, E., Adamson, L., & Brazelton, T. B. (1976). The behavior of the full-term but underweight newborn. *Developmental Medicine and Child Neurology, 18,* 590–602.

Als, H., Tronick, E., Lester, B. M., & Brazelton, T. B. (1977). The Brazelton Neonatal Behavioral Assessment Scale. *Journal of Abnormal Child Psychology, 5*, 215–231.

Barnett, A. B., & Lodge, A. (1967). Click-evoked EEG responses in normal and developmentally retarded infants. *Nature, 214,* 252–255.

Brackbill, Y. (1971). Cumulative effects of continuous stimulation on arousal level of infants. *Child Development, 42,* 17–26.

Bradley-Johnson, S., & Travers, R. M. W. (1979). Cardiac change of retarded and nonretarded infants to an auditory signal. *American Journal of Mental Deficiency, 83,* 631–636.

Brazelton, T. B. (1973). *Brazelton Neonatal Behavioral Assessment Scale.* Philadelphia: Lippincott.

Brazelton, T. B. (1978). Introduction. In A. J. Sameroff (Ed.), *Monographs of The Society for Research in Child Development* (pp. 1–13). Chicago: University of Chicago.

Brazelton, T. (1984). *Neonatal Assessment Scale* (2nd ed.). Philadelphia: Lippincott.

Brown, J. W., Leavitt, L. A., & Graham, F. K. (1977). Response to auditory stimuli in 6- and 9-week-old human infants. *Developmental Psychobiology, 10,* 255–265.

Campos, J. J., & Brackbill, Y. (1973). Infant state: Relationship to heart rate, behavioral response and response decrements. *Developmental Psychobiology, 10,* 9–19.

Green, C., Canipe, V., Gardner, S., & Reid, D. (1990). *A behavior analysis of the (non)existence of biobehavioral states among persons with profound multiple handicaps.* Paper presented at annual conference of The Association for Persons with Severe Handicaps, Chicago.

Guess, D., Mulligan-Ault, M., Roberts, S., Struth, J., Siegel-Causey, E., Thompson, B., Bronicki, G. J. B., & Guy, B. (1988). Implications of biobehavioral states for the education and treatment of students with the most profoundly handicapping conditions. *Journal of The Association for Persons with Severe Handicaps, 13,* 163–174.

Guess, D., Roberts, S., Siegel-Causey, E., Ault, M. M., Guy, B., Thompson, B., & Rues, J. (1993). Analysis of behavior state conditions and associated variables among students with profound handicaps. *American Journal on Mental Retardation, 97,* 634–653.

Guess, D., Roberts, S., Siegel-Causey, E., Mulligan-Ault, M., Guy, B., Thompson, B., Rues, J., & Siegel-Causey, D. (1991). *Investigations into the state behaviors of students with severe and profound handicapping conditions.* Lawrence: University of Kansas.

Guess, D., Siegel-Causey, E., Roberts, S., Rues, J., Thompson, B., & Siegel-Causey, D. (1990). Assessment and analysis of behavior state and related variables among students with profoundly handicapping conditions. *Journal of The Association for Persons with Severe Handicaps, 15,* 211–230.

Guy, B., Guess, D., & Ault, M. M. (1993). Classroom procedures for the measurement of behavior state among students with profound disabilities. *Journal of The Association for Persons with Severe Handicaps, 18,* 52–60.

Jackson, J. C. (1974). Amplitude and habituation of the orienting reflex as a function of stimulus intensity. *Psychophysiology, 11,* 647–649.

Landesman-Dwyer, S., & Sackett, G. (1978). Behavioral changes in nonambulatory profoundly mentally retarded individuals. In C. E. Meyers (Ed.), *Quality of life in severely and profoundly mentally retarded people: Research foundations for improvement* (pp. 55–144). Washington, DC: American Association on Mental Deficiency.

Moskowitz, H., & Lohmann, W. (1970). Auditory threshold for evoking an orienting reflex in Mongoloid patients. *Perceptual and Motor Skills, 31,* 879–882.

Noonan, M. J., Brown, F., Mulligan, M., & Rettig, M. A. (1982). Educability of severely handicapped persons: Both sides of the issue. *Journal of The Association for the Severely Handicapped, 7,* 3–12.

Noonan, M. J., & Reese, R. M. (1984). Educability: Public policy and the role of research. *Journal of The Association for Persons with Severe Handicaps, 9,* 8–15.

Prechtl, H. F. R. (1974). The behavioural states of the newborn infant (a review). *Brain Research, 76,* 185–212.

Rainforth, B. (1982). Biobehavioral state and orienting: Implications for educating profoundly retarded students. *Journal of The Association for the Severely Handicapped, 6,* 33–37.

Richards, S. B. (1990). *An analysis of environmental variables affecting the observed biobehavioral states of individuals with profound handicaps.* Boca Raton: Florida Atlantic University.

Richards, S. B., & Sternberg, L. (1992). A preliminary analysis of environmental variables affecting the observed biobehavioural states of individuals with profound handicaps. *Journal of Intellectual Disability Research, 36,* 403–414.

Richards, S. B., & Sternberg, L. (1993). Corroborating previous findings: Laying stepping stones in the analysis of biobehavioral states in students with profound disabilities. *Education and Training in Mental Retardation, 28,* 262–268.

Sailor, W., Gee, K., Goetz, L., & Graham, N. (1988). Progress in educating students with the most severe disabilities: Is there any? *Journal of The Association for Persons with Severe Handicaps, 13,* 87–99.

Simeonsson, R. J., Huntington, G. S., & Parse, S. A. (1980). Assessment of children with severe handicaps: Multiple problems—multivariate goals. *Journal of The Association for the Severely Handicapped, 5,* 55–72.

Sostek, A. M. (1978). The Brazelton Neonatal Behavioral Assessment Scale. In O. K. Buros (Ed.), *The eighth mental measurements yearbook.* Highland Park, NJ: Gryphon Press.

Soule, A. B., Standley, K., Copans, S., & Davis, M. (1974). Clinical uses of the Brazelton Neonatal Scale. *Pediatrics, 54,* 583–586.

Sternberg, L. (1988). An overview of educational concerns for students with severe or profound handicaps. In L. Sternberg (Ed.), *Educating students with severe or profound handicaps* (pp. 3–13). Austin, TX: PRO-ED.

Sternberg, L., & Richards, S. (1989). Assessing levels of state and arousal in individuals with profound handicaps: A research integration. *Journal of Mental Deficiency Research, 33,* 381–387.

Switzky, H. N., Haywood, H. C., & Rotatori, A. F. (1982). Who are the severely and profoundly retarded? *Education and Training of the Mentally Retarded, 17,* 268–272.

Wolff, P. H. (1959). Observations on newborn infants. *Psychosomatic Medicine, 21,* 110–118.

Chapter 5

Behavioral Interventions: Issues and Practices

LES STERNBERG and RONALD L. TAYLOR

Behavioral analysis represents the predominant method through which researchers and practitioners have attempted to change behaviors of individuals with disabilities. Given the acute or chronic biomedical conditions experienced by individuals with profound disabilities, a more recent trend has been to integrate behavioral analysis with biomedical information for this group. This emphasis on the use of *behavioral medicine* points out the need not only to treat the disorder but also to promote health (Luiselli, 1989). Without a clear understanding of the relationship between the presence of biomedical conditions and the presence (or absence) of specific types of behavior, the efficacy of any intervention may be questioned.

The overt behaviors of individuals with profound disabilities can typically be described as representing two general classes: *behavioral deficits,* which are desired behaviors that do not occur at an acceptable level or rate, and *behavioral excesses,* which are undesirable behaviors that occur too frequently. With individuals with profound disabilities, behavioral deficits can be conceptualized within the framework of two areas: precursor thresholds and adaptive behaviors. *Precursor thresholds* include arousal, awareness, orienting, and responsiveness. They are considered requisite to the display of all behaviors. Unless an individual with profound disabilities displays threshold levels for skill acquisition and performance, significant skill development will not likely be possible. *Adaptive behaviors* are those that, when acquired and performed successfully, assist the individual to become more independent and better able to adapt to a variety of appropriate environments. Typically, these behaviors include social skills related to appropriate interactions, interpersonal skills, and social-communicative behaviors. They also include other skills related to independent living (e.g., personal hygiene).

Issues Concerning Behavioral Deficits

Extremely limited research has been conducted in the area of establishing precursor thresholds with individuals with profound disabilities. This may be due, in part, to the necessity to address certain preliminary factors. For example, prior to attempting to establish threshold levels, one must first have a clear definition of the threshold type and an acceptable manner in which the threshold type can be measured (see Chapter 4). Given the characteristics of the population classified as profoundly disabled, however, this area is receiving more and more attention (Guess et al., 1988; Guess et al., 1990; Richards & Sternberg, 1992; Sternberg & Richards, 1989).

Social skills development in individuals with profound disabilities has received more attention. Reid, Phillips, and Green (1991) provided a comprehensive review of effects of behavioral interventions on the teaching of skills to this population. Whereas early research efforts tended to focus on whether behavioral interventions could merely effect a change in behavior, Reid et al. wished to document more recent efforts in which behavioral interventions were designed to teach "meaningful" skills. In this case, meaningful skills were defined as those that would provide some immediate function within one or more domains (e.g., self-help). The review indicates that more recent efforts have indeed been directed toward the development of these meaningful skills, albeit some have emphasized a positive change in quality of life rather than a specific function.

Overall, Reid et al.'s (1991) findings were not encouraging. Although they found behavior change evident, of the 39 studies that met their inclusion criteria, only two demonstrated conclusively that individuals with profound disabilities could acquire meaningful skills (Wacker, Berg, Wiggins, Muldoon, & Cavanaugh, 1985; Wacker, Wiggins, Fowler, & Berg, 1988). This lack of positive results, however, is likely due to limitations of instrumentation and technology rather than to limitations of the individuals themselves. In fact, Reid et al. pointed out that the vast majority of research efforts have suffered from significant inadequacies, including limited sampling of behavior, limited length of intervention sessions, and limited attempts at transfer, generalization, or maintenance. They also stressed that the sheer number of attempts was certainly insufficient to conclude whether an appropriate teaching technology now exists for this population or whether the present technology has been effectively used. Certainly, this is an area that deserves considerable exploration.

Reid et al. (1991) suggested a number of avenues to follow to deal with the issues involved in teaching skills to individuals with profound disabilities. First, they emphasized that effective behavioral assessment protocols should be established. These should include analyses pertaining to controlled body movements of the individual, types of environmental stimuli to which the individual responds, and biobehavioral states. Second, they recommended that more varied behavioral interventions should be attempted, as prior attempts have been extremely limited in terms of type of intervention. Third, they suggested that traditional behavioral interventions should be expanded to include those that combine behavioral applications and neuromotor approaches and treatment programs. Fourth, they emphasized that the outcomes of behavioral interventions should look beyond the development of traditional independent or adaptive skills. Instead, for some individuals with profound disabilities, outcomes should be directed toward maintaining current behaviors, preventing regression, and providing enjoyment to the individual. As an example of this last goal, Realon (1990) successfully trained two adults with profound disabilities to select their own leisure activities.

Issues Concerning Behavioral Excesses

Behavioral excesses usually refer to *aberrant behaviors*. For the most part, these behaviors are considered extremely abnormal and are often very disturbing to others (Gaylord-Ross, 1980). Such behaviors can be directed to the self (e.g., self-stimulation, self-injury) or to others (e.g., biting). An individual's type and level of aberrant behavior can affect his or her ability to acquire and display various social skills. When individuals with profound disabilities exhibit excessive aberrant behaviors, those behaviors interfere with their ability to attend to relevant aspects of social skills training situations (LaGrow & Repp, 1984).

A number of related issues have been raised concerning behavioral excesses. The first has to do with whether the behavior serves or has the potential to serve some function (Iwata, Vollmer, & Zarcone, 1990; Lennox & Miltenberger, 1989; O'Neill, Horner, Albin, Sprague, & Storey, 1990; Repp & Singh, 1990; Wacker, Northup, & Cooper, 1992). If a function can be determined, it is likely that the behavior may not be viewed in a purely negative light (Evans & Meyer, 1985). Certainly, the use of functional analyses has become a benchmark of behavioral interventions (Luiselli, Matson, & Singh, 1992), and functional analyses have demonstrated that certain behavioral excesses of individuals with severe or profound disabilities may serve communicative purposes (Reichle & Wacker, 1993).

The second issue has to do with how the behavioral excess may be an example of and/or interact with one's internal system of regulating stimulation. In regards to this issue, differences of opinion exist concerning the applicability of interventions to the behavior change of certain individuals who are profoundly disabled. For the most part, these individuals are those who purportedly do not present state levels conducive to potential operant effects.

These individuals and the issue of applicability of behavioral interventions are discussed later in this chapter.

MODELS FOR BEHAVIOR CHANGE PROGRAMS

The behavioral school has been at the forefront in terms of suggested and researched applications for skills development and behavior change for individuals with whom there are few questions as to potential utility. For this group, however, questions remain regarding efficiency and efficacy (Reid et al., 1991). Nevertheless, there is support for the use of a modified or revised behavioral technology. What appears to be needed is a *systems approach* in which, at a minimum, both behavioral deficits and excesses are dealt with simultaneously. A number of approaches provide such model system frameworks for establishing behavior change programs. Two of these are discussed in the following sections.[1]

Evans and Meyer

Evans and Meyer (1985) provided a comprehensive and detailed decision-making system for selecting an appropriate behavior change strategy for behavior excesses. In their system, two conditions must be met before determining what type of behavior change program might be necessary.

The first is a *functional analysis* of the behavior. This involves determining if any environmental events are currently acting to "cause" the behavior. This analysis usually takes the form of systematically charting events that precede (*before events* or *antecedents*) and immediately follow (*after events* or *consequences*) the behavior. The observer then looks for consistencies that can probably account for the behavior. For example, a child might begin self-abuse incidents each time a certain adult comes in close proximity (an antecedent "cause") or display more self-abuse as a result of someone's telling him or her to stop the incident each time it occurs (a consequence "cause"). A functional analysis can provide direction in choosing a specific behavior change strategy. It also is an effective tool to generate ideas concerning the *intent* (function), if any, of the behavior. A number of researchers (Carr & Durand, 1985; Donnellan, Mirenda, Mesaros, & Fassbender,

---

1. Next two sections from "Systems and Procedures for Managing Behavior" by L. Sternberg and R. L. Taylor in *Educating Students with Severe or Profound Handicaps* (2nd ed., pp. 159–169) by L. Sternberg (Ed.), 1988, Austin, TX: PRO-ED. Copyright 1988 by PRO-ED, Inc. Reprinted with permission.

1984; Durand & Carr, 1985; Iwata, Dorsey, Slifer, Baumann, & Richman, 1982) have developed comprehensive functional analysis schemes to determine whether certain types of aberrant behaviors actually serve functional purposes (e.g., when self-injurious behavior is used intentionally to communicate a desire for or against physical or social interaction).

Evans and Meyer cautioned that, in certain situations, consistencies may be difficult to establish. This is especially the case when certain environmental events might be hard to observe. Examples would be antecedent *setting events,* where an environmental event that took place considerably before the behavior occurrence affects the behavior, and consequent *intrinsic reinforcers,* where the behavior continues to occur because of its self-reinforcing quality (e.g., self-stimulation).

Functional analysis can also prove extremely worthwhile in helping set up programs for social skills training, especially in regard to antecedent effects on social skills development. Renzaglia and Bates (1983) reviewed potential antecedent factors that can be used to increase social skills. These include expanding the environmental opportunities for increased interaction between students with disabilities and their peers without disabilities, changing the quality of materials with which students with disabilities are required to interact, and more carefully controlling the types of prompts and prompt sequences used with students.

The second major condition that must be met before a behavior change program is formalized is *prioritizing the behaviors that should be changed.* As Evans and Meyer (1985) pointed out, a person with significant disabilities very rarely exhibits only one behavior excess. What is necessary is to determine how serious the behavior actually is, for this will determine whether and what type of an intervention plan will be followed. Although there are many types of systems for determining the severity of behavior excesses, Evans and Meyer provided a number of categories of behavior excesses:

- Behaviors in urgent need of reduction due to their potential for self-harm (e.g., self-abuse)

- Behaviors that are a concern to others in that they most probably will be used to hurt others (e.g., aggressive acts)

- Behaviors that may negatively affect one's adjustment to people and environments (e.g., excessive self-stimulation behavior in public)

- Behaviors incompatible with or that prevent more positive behavior (e.g., when self-stimulation may prevent on-task behavior)

- Behaviors that, if changed, could increase functionality for the individual in more than one way (e.g., increasing appropriate toothbrushing skills so as to prevent tooth decay and afford the individual a better appearance)

- Behaviors that, if changed, assist the teacher in more easily carrying out his or her instruction (e.g., decreasing masturbation so that the student will more appropriately interact with objects during instructional episodes)

These categories of behavior are associated with priority levels: Behaviors that are life threatening are Level I, behaviors that are potentially harmful to others are Level II, and all other behaviors are Level III.

Evans and Meyer refer practitioners to a decision-making procedure (flow chart) for designing and implementing behavior change programs. The crux of most of the suggested procedures is the concept of *positive alternatives*. This implies that one can decrease a behavior excess by providing intervention or instruction toward developing a more positive behavior. Often this positive alternative will serve the same function as the inappropriate behavior. Emphasis, then, is on the development of this alternative, especially in that it will typically be reinforced because it is behavior preferred and desired by others. Evans and Meyer do not, however, preclude the possibility of using *negative consequences* (punishment) for behavior excesses. They typically recommend that, if at all possible, such consequences be delivered for a very short time with the positive alternative reinforced simultaneously. They discuss alternatives in the event simultaneous programming is not possible.

Sternberg and Schilit

Sternberg and Schilit (1986) also provided a system for developing behavior change programs for social skills training and aberrant behavior reduction. The purpose of their model is three-fold: (1) to provide descriptions of specific consequent behavioral strategies and everyday examples of how those strategies might be used; (2) to describe a decision-making process for identifying what type of behavioral strategy with which to start; and (3) to outline a procedure of what to do if a technique does not seem to be working.

The system describes prerequisites to the establishment of any behavior change program, including

- A concise and accurate description of the behavior one wishes to change and a determination of whether the desire is to increase or decrease the behavior (for the purpose of communication to others)

- A functional analysis of the behavior, including a determination of the intent, if any, of the behavior

- A measure of the degree or level of the behavior (requires knowledge of various types of observation strategies and corresponding data collection systems)

Sternberg and Schilit recommended that, when one is at the point of selecting a consequent behavioral technique, the "flow" of behavioral options be outlined. This outline is necessary so that the practitioner can see the options that might be available for dealing with any targeted behavior. A range of behavioral options is provided based on the concept that the least intrusive (least restrictive) technique should always be opted for initially; that is, the selected procedure should be as *natural, non-disruptive, and non-aversive* as possible to the student and to others. Also, any other technique considered as a result of the student's not reaching the criterion should proceed from less restrictive to more restrictive.

Figure 5.1 is a summary of some options, with their progression based on a *hypothetical* sequence of least to most restrictive. The techniques are general classes or categories of procedures, and headings above each column indicate the basic intent of their implementation (i.e., to reduce or increase behavior).

Following is a brief description of each procedure type specified in Figure 5.1. Suggestions or guidelines concerning implementation are also provided.

Positive Reinforcement. This is one technique to use when the intent is to increase a behavior. If the student displays the behavior, he or she receives something that has the potential to increase the probability the behavior will occur again. However, one can never assume that something is reinforcing or a reinforcer; it can be deemed reinforcing only if, as a result of its application, the behavior increases.

Response Differentiation. This procedure is used to teach a new behavior. It is used only if one is sure that the student can actually produce the behavior but does not because the behavior is "hidden" or masked by other behaviors. Using this technique, the student receives reinforcement only when he or she commits the correct behavior, but not when the student either produces the target behavior with other behaviors or produces only the other behaviors.

Shaping. This procedure is also used to teach a new behavior. In this case, however, the student has never displayed the targeted

Increase	Increase	Reduce	Reduce	Reduce	Reduce	Increase	Reduce	Reduce	Reduce
Positive reinforcement	DRH	Extinction	DRO	Contingent observation	Response cost	Negative reinforcement	Positive practice	Over correction	Positive punishment
Teach new behaviors			DRI		Exclusion time-out			Seclusion time-out	
Response differentiation			DRL						
Shaping									
Maintenance									
Scheduling									

Least Restrictive → **Most Restrictive**

Figure 5.1. Hypothetical sequence of least to most restrictive behavioral techniques. DRH = differential reinforcement of high rates of behavior. DRO = differential reinforcement of other behaviors. DRI = differential reinforcement of incompatible behaviors. DRL = differential reinforcement of low rates of behavior. From "Systems and Procedures for Managing Behavior" in *Educating Students with Severe or Profound Handicaps* (2nd ed., p. 163) by L. Sternberg (Ed.), 1988, Austin, TX: PRO-ED. Copyright 1988 by PRO-ED, Inc. Adapted by permission.

behavior. In shaping, one typically breaks down immediate expectations of behavior. Instead of the student's being expected to display the entire targeted behavior, he or she is expected to demonstrate only a small predetermined part or step. If it is displayed, a reinforcer is delivered. Slowly, expectations are increased, and reinforcers are delivered based on the demonstration of improved performance.

Scheduling. This procedure is used to maintain a behavior once the student has shown it consistently. In this procedure, reinforcement delivery changes from continuous to more intermittent. Reinforcers are not delivered each time the student commits the behavior. The student must eventually understand that he or she will receive a reinforcer only intermittently because this is a more natural way that reinforcers are delivered and obtained.

Differential Reinforcement of High Rates of Behavior (DRH). This procedure is used to increase behaviors. With a DRH technique, the intent is to have the student display behaviors *more rapidly.* Both rate behaviors (e.g., number of vocalizations within a prescribed amount of time) and behaviors that should be exhibited before a certain amount of time has elapsed (e.g., initiating) can be considered potential targets for DRH procedures.

Extinction. This procedure is used to reduce behaviors. It is based on the assumption that, if the student desires attention, he or she will reduce inappropriate behavior if the behavior is ignored. As a rule, extinction is employed when there is evidence that the target behavior has received prior attention, thereby causing its continued occurrence.

Differential Reinforcement of Other Behaviors (DRO). This procedure is used to reduce a behavior. In this procedure, *all* other behaviors *except* the one targeted for reduction are reinforced usually at specific predetermined points in time or after predetermined durations (as long as the target behavior is not occurring or has not occurred). Using this procedure, one is usually interested in reducing only *one* behavior and is not concerned about reinforcing any other behavior the student might display.

Differential Reinforcement of Incompatible Behaviors (DRI). This procedure is used to reduce a behavior. In this case, only behaviors that are opposite to (or incompatible with) the targeted behavior are reinforced according to the same type of time frames used in the DRO procedure. This procedure is often used as an alternative to the DRO technique. One is willing to accept only certain behaviors to reinforce (those that are incompatible with the targeted behavior) rather than merely any other behavior.

Differential Reinforcement of Low Rates of Behavior (DRL). This procedure is used to reduce behavior. The assumption is that certain behaviors are "allowable" if they occur at low rates. As implied, the targets for this procedure are typically behaviors that are occurring at too high a rate (e.g., inappropriate vocalizations) or that occur too quickly (e.g., behaviors that are used to terminate an activity that should be continued for a longer period of time).

Contingent Observation. This procedure is used to reduce behavior. If the student displays an inappropriate behavior, he or she is moved to another area of the classroom to observe other students' behaviors that are appropriate and that receive reinforcement.

Response Cost. This procedure is used to reduce behavior. In this case, something that is reinforcing to the student is taken away as a result of the display of the inappropriate behavior.

Exclusion Time-Out. This procedure is used to reduce a behavior. If a student displayed an inappropriate behavior, he or she would be removed from the immediate situation but remain in the same room. The student is not permitted either to observe or participate in the classroom activities but may hear what is going on. This time-out procedure is based on the assumption that if a potential reinforcer is removed (e.g., the teacher's attention or the attention of the class), the inappropriate behavior will decrease.

Negative Reinforcement. This procedure is used to increase a behavior. It is based on the premise that if an unpleasant situation or stimulus is removed from the student when he or she exhibits an appropriate behavior, then that behavior will increase.

Positive Practice. This procedure is typically used to reduce a behavior. If a student displays an inappropriate behavior, the student "overpractices" a behavior considered by others to be more appropriate or preferable. Therefore, this procedure can also be viewed as one that promotes development of positive, alternative behaviors.

Overcorrection. This procedure is used to reduce a behavior. It can be used with inappropriate behaviors that disrupt the environment. As the name implies, in overcorrection, one typically requires the student not only to correct what he or she has done wrong to the environment but to "overcorrect" it. Usually, positive practice accompanies this technique.

Seclusion Time-Out. This procedure is used to reduce a behavior. In this method, if a student displays an inappropriate behavior, he or she is removed from the situation and placed in a truly isolated area. While in seclusion, the student interacts with no one and cannot observe or hear anything going on in the classroom. This procedure is based on the assumption that, if a potential reinforcer is removed (e.g., the teacher's attention or the attention of the class), the inappropriate behavior will decrease.

Positive Punishment (Contingent Application of an Aversive). This procedure is used to reduce behavior. If the student displays an inappropriate behavior, one administers an unpleasant or aversive event or stimulus to the student. As with positive reinforcement, one cannot assume that something is punishing to a student. If behavior decreases as a result of the stimulus being applied, the stimulus can be considered punishing.

Sternberg and Schilit noted that some of these techniques may not be appropriate for certain students. For example, a time-out procedure would have limited, if any, positive effect on a student with considerable self-stimulatory behavior, or on a student whose overall awareness behavior was severely limited.

Merely knowing that certain techniques are less restrictive than others does not necessarily dictate which specific procedure should be used. Sternberg and Schilit provided a decision-making framework for determining which procedure to start with, as well as which procedure to opt for in the event the student is not making progress. These decisions are typically based on accurate and representational data concerning the present level of the behavior, one's expectations of the behavior once a procedure is implemented, and the effect the disabling condition might have on the range of options (e.g., it would probably be impossible to use contingent observation or an exclusion time-out procedure for a student who is both deaf and blind).

Sternberg and Schilit's model does differ in a number of respects from Evans and Meyer's approach in regard to behavior excesses. Principally, these differences involve the assumption that reductive procedures may have to be used at the initial intervention stage (rather than attempting the positive alternatives procedure as a first step) and that the full range of reductive procedures may be necessary. However, and as described previously, Sternberg and Schilit cautioned that any reductive procedure will produce diminishing returns if positive alternatives are not quickly provided.

RESULTS OF PREVIOUS INVESTIGATIONS

As noted previously, the choice of which behaviors to change first requires systematic prioritizing. Consistent with Evans and Meyer's (1985) model, Level I behaviors are those that have typically been the target of most behavior change programs. As a result, the vast majority of the research literature pertaining to the management of social behaviors has been concerned with attempts to eliminate or reduce *socially inappropriate, maladaptive, or aberrant behaviors.* Furthermore, the major portion of that body of literature has focused on attempts to decrease *self-injurious behavior* (SIB). This attention is due to the fact that engaging in SIB is potentially life threatening.

The prevalence of SIB is relatively high among individuals with profound retardation. Griffin, Williams, Stark, Altmeyer, and Mason (1986), for example, reported the results of a statewide survey regarding the prevalence of SIB among the institutionalized mentally retarded population. They found that approximately 14% of the individuals engaged in SIB and of that percentage almost 90% were individuals with severe or profound retardation. Similarly, Lapierre and Reesal (1986) noted that the rate of SIB correlates directly with the degree of mental retardation—the greater the degree of retardation, the higher the incidence of SIB. Clearly, SIB is a major concern for professionals who work with individuals with profound retardation and is also an important area for research.

Several approaches have been used to reduce SIB. These include the use of differential reinforcement techniques (either alone or in combination with other approaches), overcorrection, the use of aversives, the use of medication, sensory stimulation, restraint procedures, and facial screening. Several issues emerge regarding the choice of which approach to use. One issue relates to ethical considerations. This topic has been debated in the professional literature, primarily related to whether aversives should be used for reductive purposes. Evans and Meyer (1985) and LaVigna and Donnellan (1986) have argued against the use of aversive interventions for SIB; however, Favell, Azrin, et al. (1982) suggested that such treatments are appropriate for certain types of SIB.

Another issue has to do with choosing the intervention based on the purported cause of the SIB. Carr and Durand (1985) noted four potential "motivating conditions" to consider when designing intervention techniques for reducing SIB. These were social attention, tangible consequences, escape from aversive situations, and sensory consequences. If, for example, a student's SIB was considered the result of social attention, extinction might be the treatment of choice. Alternatively, if the SIB was thought to be a method to produce sensory stimulation for an individual, then providing other, more appropriate methods of stimulation might be suggested. Such an approach to determine treatments implies that a functional analysis of the SIB be conducted. Unfortunately, such functional analyses are not predominant in the professional literature. Repp, Singh, Olinger, and Olson (1990) noted that most studies are based on the technology of applied behavior analysis rather than the functional analysis of behavior. In other words, most treatment choices are more philosophically based than functionally based.

Interventions for SIB

A number of procedures have been used to reduce or eliminate SIB of individuals with profound disabilities. In the following sections, we review the effectiveness of these various procedures. For the most part, the targeted group for these procedures has been individuals with profound mental retardation.

Differential reinforcement

Differential reinforcement procedures include DRO, DRI, and DRA (differential reinforcement of alternative behavior, where a specific behavior is targeted for increase). The research literature regarding the use of DRO to reduce SIB is generally positive. Lockwood and Bourland (1982) found that reinforcement for toy play decreased SIB in two nonambulatory young adults with profound mental retardation. Similarly, Favell, McGimsey, and Schell (1982) found that reinforcement for appropriate toy play reduced SIB in six individuals with profound disabilities. Interestingly, they noted that, when the toys were presented without external reinforcement, the SIB decreased but was replaced by self-stimulation with the toys. Heidorn and Jensen (1984) found that DRO was effective when used to reduce forehead gouging, and Conrin, Pennypacker, Johnston, and Rust (1982) reported that DRO was successful in decreasing rumination in two individuals with profound retardation. However, some researchers (e.g., Rapoff, Altman, & Christophersen, 1980) found that DRO was ineffective in reducing SIB.

Azrin, Besalel, Jamner, and Caputo (1988), in comparing several components of a treatment paradigm, found that DRI was one of the most effective treatments for the subjects in their study. They also noted that the treatment was rapid, although greater training time was necessary compared with other treatments, such as the use of aversives. Smith (1987) found that differential reinforcement was effective in decreasing pica behavior in an adult with profound mental retardation. Mulick, Schroeder, and Rojahn (1980a) also compared various types of treatment and found that DRI resulted in the most significant lowering of the rates of SIB (i.e., rumination). Interestingly, the rumination was most frequent during extinction and DRO. Donnelly and Olczak (1990) found that DRI (using gum chewing) was highly effective in reducing pica to near-zero levels in two adults.

In a review of over 20 years of research on the use of differential reinforcement with individuals with severe or profound retardation, O'Brien and Repp (1990) reported that the highest reinforcer efficacy was from the use of vibration, olfactory stimulation, and edibles. Procedures using social reinforcers were not as effective with this population. They pointed out the need to discover ways to program better generalization and to discover more potent reinforcers.

Differential reinforcement procedures have also been used in combination with other types of procedures to provide effective treatment for SIB. For example, Wesolowski and Zawlocki (1982) found that auditory time-out and overcorrection, when used in combination with DRO, were the most effective methods of decreasing eye gouging in two young blind girls with profound retardation. Caulier and Ferretti (1980) reported that a mild slap in combination with DRA was more effective in treating SIB than either DRA or the slap used alone.

Many procedures have been reported using differential reinforcement procedures in combination with restraint. For example, Saloviita (1988) and Konarski and Johnson (1989) found that DRA and brief restraint were helpful in decreasing head banging and hand and arm biting. Similarly, Underwood, Figueroa, Thyer, and Nzeocha (1989) found that DRI and interruption were successful in decreasing head hitting and scratching. Another combination that has been reported is the use of differential reinforcement with protective equipment (Neufeld & Fantuzzo, 1987).

Overcorrection

When research on overcorrection first appeared in the professional literature, many felt it would be the most effective and appropriate procedure to reduce SIB and other negative behaviors. Gorman-Smith and Matson (1985) conducted a meta-analysis of selected research on SIB and found that overcorrection procedures were used more than any other approach. The popularity of overcorrection was probably due to the claim that it combined the reduction of inappropriate behaviors with the "educative" aspects of training appropriate behaviors (positive practice). Unfortunately, the research on overcorrection is somewhat equivocal concerning its effectiveness. Perhaps as a result of the inconsistent results, research on overcorrection procedures has decreased in recent years.

Although many studies have supported the use of overcorrection, particularly regarding its short-term effectiveness, others have found general problems in using the procedure. These problems include the development of negative side effects and the lack of generalization and maintenance of treatment effects (Carter & Ward, 1987). On the positive side, Singh, Dawson, and Gregory (1980) found that overcorrection was helpful in reducing the jaw hitting of a girl with profound retardation. Similarly, Halpern and Andrasik (1986) noted that the procedure was effective in decreasing head banging in a 23-year-old individual with profound retardation. They also noted that follow-up data indicated long-term effectiveness of the overcorrection procedure.

In another study, Duker and Seys (1983) compared the effectiveness of overcorrection with extinction and found overcorrection to be superior. They also reported that (a) long-term maintenance was obtained in five of their six subjects, (b) the effectiveness of the overcorrection seemed to be greater for behaviors that occurred infrequently, and (c) the procedure in general was very time-consuming. Barton and LaGrow (1983) also reported the reduction of SIBs of three individuals who were deaf–blind, and that the treatment gains were maintained at follow-up.

Other data, however, suggest that overcorrection is not as effective in reducing SIB as other procedures and/or that the effects of overcorrection are not generalized or maintained over time. Gorman-Smith and Matson (1985), for example, found in their meta-analysis of the SIB literature that, even though overcorrection was the most frequently used procedure, it was not the most effective. In one study, Rapoff et al. (1980) found that overcorrection was not effective in reducing SIB. In another, Singh and Bakker (1984) found that overcorrection was not as effective as restraint in decreasing pica. Some studies have also reported that overcorrection *increased* the frequency of SIB (e.g., Holburn & Dougher, 1985). Other studies (Agosta, Close, Hops, & Rusch, 1980; Czyzewski, Barrera, & Sulzer-Azaroff, 1982) found that, whereas overcorrection was effective in the short term, the results did not generalize or were not maintained over time.

The issues of generalization and maintenance of treatment effects of overcorrection were addressed by Foxx and Livesay (1984). They examined overcorrection programs over a 10-year period and concluded that maintenance seemed to be related to the level of retardation, with lower functioning individuals demonstrating fewer maintenance effects. They also noted that, because of the complexity of the procedures and the subsequent time involvement, overcorrection programs were frequently reinstated after the initial treatment phase. Their suggestion was to build in generalization components in the initial treatment and to keep the overcorrection programs as short as possible.

Use of aversives

As noted previously, the ethical use of aversives has been a source of recent debate even though the majority of the literature supports the notion that the use of aversives is successful in reducing SIB. Furthermore, it seems that the success of the program, in part, is due to the intensity of the aversive. Durand (1982) found, for instance, that mild aversives were not successful in reducing the SIB of an adolescent with profound mental retardation. On the other hand, Singh et al. (1980) found that the use of ammonia was successful in reducing face hitting. Similarly, Rapoff et al. (1980) noted that the use of ammonia was the most effective among several approaches, including DRO and overcorrection, in reducing SIB.

Another aversive that has proven effective is the use of water mist. Dorsey, Iwata, Ong, and McSween (1980) found that spraying water into the face was effective in reducing a variety of SIBs. Furthermore, pairing of the water mist with a verbal cue allowed the subsequent use of the verbal cue alone to reduce the SIB. Bailey, Pokrzywinski, and Bryant (1983) also found that the use of water mist reduced SIB and noted no physical side effects or avoidance behaviors after its use. Singh, Watson, and Winton (1986), however, reported mixed results when attempts were made to reduce SIB by using water mist. Food-related SIBs, including pica and rumination, have been decreased using alum (Beukelman & Rogers, 1984), lemon juice, Tabasco sauce (Marholin, Luiselli, Robinson, & Lott, 1980; Paisey & Whitney, 1989), and verbal reprimands (Paniagua, Braverman, & Capriotti, 1986).

Physical activity has also been used contingently as an aversive to reduce SIB. Borreson (1980) found that forcing a 22-year-old man with profound retardation to run when he engaged in SIB reduced that behavior and resulted in positive side effects, such as increased smiling. Finally, in one study (Bates & Smeltzer, 1982), electroconvulsive therapy was used to control SIB. It should be noted, however, that the SIB under investigation was of a life-threatening nature.

In a 20-year review of punishment to decrease a variety of behaviors, including SIB, Matson and Taras (1989) reported the results of almost 400 studies. Among their findings and conclusions were the following:

- Painful stimuli were used largely with children under 10 years of age.

- Overcorrection was the most frequently used nonpainful approach.

- DRO was the most frequently used positive approach.
- Positive methods had greater long-term effects than aversives.
- Studies having follow-up had significant maintenance of treatment gains.
- Based upon short- and long-term effects and additional considerations, electric shock should never be used.
- Misrepresentation and misunderstanding of procedures are evident.
- Much research is needed in the area of aversives.

Gast and Wolery (1987) indicated that, given the current research base for the use of nonpunitive alternatives, it may very well be necessary to use extreme aversives. They cautioned, however, that such use must be predicated on four points: (1) that a least intrusive to most intrusive behavior paradigm be adopted if the behavior is not life threatening to the individual or others; (2) that movement from a less intrusive to more intrusive procedure be based on available data; (3) that punishment can be rendered as a first choice if the behavior is life threatening (and if there is no data base to indicate that a less intrusive procedure may be successful); and (4) when punishment is indicated, that levels of punishment should also follow a less intrusive to more intrusive pattern if data support that such movement is possible and efficacious.

Use of medication

Another approach that has been used in an attempt to eliminate SIB is medication. For example, Singh and Winton (1984) compared the effects of Tegretol, Mellaril, and Largactil on the reduction of face rubbing in a 15-year-old male with profound retardation. They found that only Mellaril reduced the SIB. Durand (1982) combined the use of mild punishment with haloperidol and reported that, whereas neither was effective in reducing SIB when used independently, dramatic reduction occurred when they were used in combination.

A large number of studies, however, have reported nonsignificant results regarding the use of drugs to decrease SIB. For example, Szymanski, Kedesdy, Sulkes, Cutler, and Stevens-Orr (1987) reported no measurable decrease in a variety of SIBs when naltrexone, an oral opiate antagonist, was administered. Similarly, Kars, Briekema, Flandesman-van Grideren, Verhoeren, and VanRee (1990) reported that naltrexone was effective in only two of five individuals with profound retardation. It also appears that many of the studies investigating the efficacy of pharmacologic agents lack appropriate control. For example, Ruedrich, Grush, and Wilson (1990), in a review of the literature on the use of beta-blockers to decrease SIB, concluded that more controlled, double-blind studies need to be conducted. Similarly, Singh and Millichamp (1984, 1985), in their reviews of the effects of medication, noted the need for more controlled studies. In addition, they reported the following:

- Overall, the efficacy of drug therapy is not promising.

- Tranquilizers were the most often prescribed drugs.

- The use of stimulants and antipsychotics resulted in nonsignificant results.

- The use of antimanics (e.g., lithium) effectively reduced SIB but had severe side effects.

- More research is needed on the effects of taking the drugs over long periods of time, as well as the effects of withdrawing from the drugs.

Sensory stimulation

Several forms of sensory stimulation have been used to decrease SIB. These have been used both contingently as a type of reinforcer or noncontingently as a "substitute" for the SIB. Barmann (1980), for example, used a vibrator to eliminate the rumination and hand mouthing behaviors of a 6-year-old boy with profound retardation. Similarly, Taylor and Chamove (1986) used a vibrator and a flashing red light alternately to determine their reductive effect on head hitting in a 24-year-old woman. They reported a significant reduction using both forms of stimulation, with the visual stimulation being slightly more effective.

Vestibular stimulation has also been used successfully. Dura, Mulick, and Hammer (1988) reported that it was effective in reducing a variety of SIBs in a nonambulatory adolescent with profound retardation. Wells and Smith (1983) combined noncontingent vestibular and tactile stimulation to decrease SIB in four subjects. Other types of stimulation have included transcutaneous nerve stimulation (Linn, Rojahn, Helsel, & Dixon, 1988), which resulted in reduction of self-biting but not finger gouging, and alternate sensory activities using toys (Favell, McGimsey, & Schell, 1982), which resulted in a decrease of SIB in six subjects. Murphy (1982) reviewed the existing literature on sensory reinforcement techniques and found support for the use of these approaches. He also noted several advantages of these techniques over others. Advantages included ease of delivery, a slow rate of satiation, unlimited variability, and the availability of automated equipment that can be used.

Restraint procedures

Another approach to decreasing SIB is the use of procedures that actually impede or interfere with the SIB. These include *physical restraint* and the *use of protective equipment.* In general, physical restraint procedures have been found to be effective in decreasing SIB. Furthermore, it appears that restraint for brief periods is more effective than for long periods (Singh, Dawson, & Manning, 1981; Winton & Singh, 1983). Hamad, Isley, and Lowry (1983) used a mechanical restraint device to decrease SIB in an adult living in an institution. They also paired the restraint with a differential reinforcement procedure and response incompatibilty and were able to fade the use of restraint.

The effect of using protective equipment to reduce SIB is somewhat unclear. Parrish, Aguerrevere, Dorsey, and Iwata (1980) reported that the use of a protective helmet with a shield caused a rapid decrease in head banging behavior. Conversely, Mace and Knight (1986) found that contingent staff attention for non-SIB was effective and that their subject engaged in less SIB when a protective helmet was not worn. Mulick, Schroeder, and Rojahn (1980b) used both physical restraint and protective equipment and reported that the procedures eliminated the SIBs but also decreased social interactions in three individuals with profound retardation.

Facial or visual screening

Another technique used to decrease SIB is facial screening. This involves the placement of an opaque screen (usually a bib) over the individual's face when the SIB occurs. Lutzker and Wesch (1983) reviewed the literature on facial screening and noted that it was a harmless yet effective method for decreasing SIB. A variation of this approach is visual screening, in which only the eyes are covered briefly. Blankenship and Lamberts (1989) reported the successful use of visual screening to significantly reduce a variety of SIBs. Watson, Singh, and Winton (1986), in fact, found visual screening to be more effective than facial screening. Similarly, Winton, Singh, and Dawson (1984) found that facial screening was more effective when combined with visual blocking (screening) than when used alone.

Other approaches

Many other techniques have been successfully used to reduce SIB. These include food satiation for rumination (Clauser & Scibak, 1990; Rast, Johnston, Allen, & Drum, 1985) and food satiation in combination with time-out (Borreson & Anderson, 1982; Davis, Wieseler, & Hanzel, 1980). Others have included functional language communication (Bird, Dores, Moniz, &

Robinson, 1989), social isolation in a padded room (Rose, Sloop, & Baker, 1980), change in nutrition (Gedye, 1990), and negative reinforcement (Steege et al., 1990).

Summary of SIB Literature

To determine the efficacy of the intervention procedures for reducing SIB of individuals with profound retardation, we conducted a quantitative analysis of the research literature. In addition, we were interested in determining which variables (e.g., sex, age) were related to intervention efficacy.

Articles focusing on the self-injurious behavior of individuals with profound retardation between the years 1980 and 1990 were located. Computer searches using Psychlit and ERIC were conducted, as well as a manual search of *Index Medicus*. The searches were then cross-referenced with a number of journals and textbooks concerned with SIB. A total of 142 journal studies were located that dealt with the SIB of individuals with severe or profound mental retardation. A total of 295 subjects were described as subjects of interventions, with 172 being classified as profoundly mentally retarded. Only those studies that dealt with this latter group were analyzed.

SIB was defined as repeated nonaccidental behavior that was initiated by the individual and that directly resulted in physical injury to that individual (Jones, 1987). Over 18 types of SIB were included, although we later collapsed these into four major categories because of small frequencies for some intervention types. The four categories were combination, eating SIB (including ruminative vomiting and pica), head insults, and abuse (including biting, hitting, scratching, picking, and/or gouging). A coding sheet was developed to collect and code the data for each subject. A variety of demographic and environmental variables were coded, as well as the efficacy of the intervention of each subject. Efficacy was defined using the criteria specified by Lundervold and Bourland (1988); that is, efficacy of intervention was specified as the mean of percentage of decrease in SIB from baseline to treatment. The three levels of efficacy used by Lundervold and Bourland were 0%–49%, 50%–74%, or 75% and higher. The percentage of improvement was calculated for those subjects for whom the percentage was not reported.

The initial step for data analysis was to determine the frequency of occurrence of each variable type within each variable category. Cross-tabulations were conducted between (a) type of intervention and other variable categories and (b) the efficacy variable and other variable categories. Correlations were then calculated to determine the degree of relationship between (a) intervention and other variable categories and (b) efficacy and other variable categories.

A number of significant results were found. In terms of interventions, the data indicated a higher than expected frequency of punishment being used with females. This gender bias was described by Scotti, Evans, Meyer, and Walker (1991), who hypothesized that these types of techniques are used because of the perception that female subjects will be less likely to exhibit counteraggressive behavior. In addition, the data indicated that a higher than expected frequency of drug interventions was evident in studies conducted between 1986 and 1990, with a commensurate lower than expected frequency of drug intervention studies conducted between 1980 and 1985. This finding is somewhat surprising, given the research base that indicates that many drug interventions produce equivocal results.

Other noteworthy findings related to efficacy of the studies. First, there were higher than expected efficacy ratings for studies whose subjects experienced sensory disabilities and where interventions were confined to only one environmental setting. These data appear to indicate that both sensory and environmental limitations can have a beneficial effect on the success of an SIB intervention. Second, interventions with school-aged subjects had higher than expected efficacy ratings than those interventions with adults. This result supports the often-cited premise that the earlier in one's life one is exposed to interventions, the greater the likelihood that benefits will be realized. Finally, higher than expected efficacy ratings were found in studies done between 1980 and 1985, with lower than expected efficacy ratings for studies done between 1986 and 1990. Further research is needed to determine whether efficacy has decreased due to changes in targeted behaviors (e.g., a research focus on more intractable types of SIB from 1986 to 1990), dramatic shifts in intervention emphases (e.g., overcorrection to drug interventions), or changes in subject profiles or characteristics.

Stereotypy

Another behavior displayed by this population that is frequently targeted for an intervention program is stereotypy. Stereotypic behavior can be defined as ritualistic, repetitive behavior that essentially is purposeless. The definition, however, is not as clear-cut as that of SIB (Jones, 1987). In fact, it could be argued that SIB and stereotypy are in the same general class of behaviors (see the following section entitled "A Conceptual Model of Behavioral Excesses"). Indeed, the intervention approaches that have been used are similar for both SIB and stereotypy.

Several techniques have been reported to be effective in decreasing stereotypy. These include contingent sensory reinforcement (Case-Holden & Hupp, 1989), auditory feedback (Christopher & Lewis, 1984), and ambulation training (Strawbridge, Drnach, Sisson, & Van Hasselt, 1989). Others include DRO alone (Wieseler, Hanson, Chamberlain, & Thompson, 1988) and DRO with response interruption (Barton & Lagrow, 1983). Also reported to be effective have been visual screening (McGonigle, Duncan, Cordisco, & Barrett, 1982) and the use of flexible arm splints (Ball, Datta, Rios, & Constantine, 1985).

Consistent with the trend in the literature reported about SIB, the use of medication has increased in recent years as a method of intervention for stereotypy. Also consistent with the SIB literature, the results are not conclusive that drugs such as haloperidol or thioridazine are effective in reducing stereotypic behavior (Aman, Teehan, White, Turbott, & Vaithianathan, 1989; Aman & White, 1988; Millichamp & Singh, 1987).

A CONCEPTUAL MODEL OF BEHAVIORAL EXCESSES

As discussed earlier in the chapter, there are individuals with profound disabilities for whom behavioral interventions appear not to have an effect. For the most part, the concern is with those individuals who exhibit behavioral excesses. Guess and Carr (1991) presented a model to explain this situation. They viewed many cases of stereotypic or self-injurious behavior as being either repetitious or rhythmic in nature. Given these characteristics, and the fact that these behaviors are often resistant to change in individuals with profound disabilities, the authors posited that these behaviors may be a direct reflection of an individual's behavior state.

Their model can be conceived of as a "downward extension" of a two-factor theoretical perspective used to account for the presence of stereotypy or self-injurious behavior. These two factors are described as *operant control* and *homeostasis*. Stereotypy or self-injurious behavior that is accounted for by the operant control factor implies that the behavior is learned or maintained through the application of behavioral principles (e.g., positive or negative reinforcement). Stereotypy or self-injurious behavior that is accounted for by the homeostatic factor implies that the behavior is directly related to the present level of stimulation being experienced by the individual. When the stimulation emanates from external sources, the homeostatic process is one in which the display of stereotypy or self-injury is purposefully displayed by the individual and intended to produce a more acceptable level in the stimulation itself.

The third factor that Guess and Carr (1991) added relates to the *internal regulation of behavior state*. Although the adaptive nature of operant or homeostatic stereotypy and self-injurious behavior can be more easily determined, Guess and Carr indicated that such may not be the case for behaviors that are accounted for by internal regulation. They also emphasized the point that behaviors that are internally regulated behavior state conditions will likely not be affected by external environmental events.

According to Guess and Carr (1991), all three factors can likely be placed within a movement framework. Homeostasis can serve as a transition stage between internal regulation and operant control. Specifically, homeostasis can be viewed as a type of lower level controlling mechanism (e.g., of arousal). Once this mechanism is acquired by the individual, it can be extended as a method to control others via the display of stereotypic or self-injurious behavior (e.g., an individual exhibiting self-injurious behavior to escape from an unpleasant situation). This capability would stem from the effect of operant procedures. Guess and Carr also pointed out that movement might occur in a reverse direction. For example, in situations of extreme environmental deprivation, individuals who would be capable of homeostatic control instead might display stereotypy as an internally regulated behavior state condition. This reverse movement might be described as a regression to an earlier, less demanding situation or stage. They also stated that there might be some forms of self-injury that bypass homeostasis, proceeding directly from internal behavior state regulation to operant control.

Applying the theory to more practical implications, Guess and Carr (1991) noted that the three-factor model could have extreme utility in the areas of assessment and intervention. If, as they pointed out, rhythmic self-injurious behavior and stereotypy are adaptive, it would not be appropriate to merely consider them as targets for reduction. Rather, one would first use an assessment paradigm to determine which factor (internal regulation, homeostasis, or operant control) appeared to account for the presence of the behavior. For example, if no relationship appeared to exist between the behavior and the level of stimulation or reinforcing contingencies, one might infer that the behavior was an exemplar of internal regulation of behavior state.

Guess and Carr (1991) viewed interventions primarily from the standpoint of prevention of stereotypy and self-injurious behavior. They deemed it especially crucial to deal effectively with these behaviors at the internal regulation or homeostatic levels before there was significant involvement at the operant level. This is due to the premise that, once these behaviors reach the operant level, they are often extremely difficult to reduce or eliminate. As a starting point, Guess and Carr presented a case for the existence of an inverse relationship between stereotypy and motor development; that is, stereotypy decreases when there is an increased development of motor skills. Although a direct functional connection has not been proven, some hypothesize that stereotypy itself must play a significant role in motor development. Guess and Carr emphasized the need to become attuned to this potential, especially as it relates to an assessed finding that stereotypy or self-injurious behavior appears to be an internally regulated behavior state condition of an individual. In this case, they suggested that interventions should be conducted to enhance or increase the current motor repertoire of that individual. If assessment data indicated that the stereotypy or self-injurious behavior was accounted for by homeostasis, Guess and Carr recommended that the emphasis in interventions be on those attempts to create a more balanced environment in terms of stimulation to the individual.

Another suggestion of Guess and Carr (1991) is that stereotypy can lead to the emergence of self-injurious behavior. One example might be a situation in which the individual displays stereotypy to deal with an overstimulating environment (homeostasis). If the characteristics of the environment were not changed, the individual might alter the stereotypy into behaviors that were of the self-injurious type. If these behaviors were then consequated by another person (e.g., the environment was immediately made less stimulating), the individual might continue to display this self-injury as a "learned" behavior (operant control).

According to Guess and Carr (1991), it is also important to develop interventions with self-injurious behavior that take into account the homeostatic versus operant control paradigms. Although much has been said concerning the possible operant or communicative function of self-injurious behavior (Cipani, 1990; Neel & Billingsley, 1989), certain instances of self-injurious behavior may reflect the active use of homeostasis. In these cases, attempts at behavioral control through the use of operant techniques would likely not be successful.

As with any theoretical perspective, Guess and Carr's (1991) model has both supporters and critics. Baumeister (1991) agreed with their overall theoretical thrust, although he emphasized that much more needed to be done regarding the infusion of neurological, pharmacologic, and biomedical parameters into the understanding of what leads to and maintains stereotypy and self-injury. Mulick and Meinhold (1991) and Lovaas and Smith (1991) expressed rather serious reservations about the model. Criticisms ranged from the premise that all stereotypy and self-injury can be understood from a purely operant perspective to the point that operationalizing the proposed model could lead to interventions that have limited functional utility.

CONCLUSION

Regardless of the disagreements that exist concerning the use of behavioral analysis, some appropriate directives can be posited. It is paramount that, prior to the design and implementation of any intervention, consideration must first be given to the overall ramifications of the potential outcome of any application. Practitioners can no longer be content with considering only whether a proposed intervention will decrease a behavioral excess or increase a behavioral deficit. In-depth attention should be paid to other matters. First, the concepts of excess and deficit should be defined in direct relation to the individual exhibiting or not exhibiting the behavior. Second, the function that a behavior serves for the individual should be extended beyond the framework of what one might observe as a function to what one might conceptualize or hypothesize as a function.

It is also important to consider the relevance of behavioral analysis to instructional and other assistive endeavors. One of the predominant criticisms of the use of behavioral approaches, especially for intractable types of behavior, has been that the techniques tended to focus only on a targeted behavior, and did not take into account how the changed behavior might impact or be integrated with other important behaviors. Evans and Meyer (1985) pointed out a number of crucial considerations for designing and implementing behavior change programs for students so that impact and integration concerns could be addressed. First, the program must be designed so as to take into account each student's Individualized Education Program. By doing so, emphasis can be placed not only on the targeted behavior but also on collateral behaviors that are worthy of attention. Extending the educational paradigm to adults with profound disabilities would necessitate a careful analysis of individuals' habilitation programs. Second, one must never lose sight of the social and empirical validity of what one is trying to accomplish. *Social validity* refers to how important other people think the targeted behavior is and how acceptable the method to change that behavior is considered. This is especially crucial in regard to the selection of an aversive technique as the intervention of choice, an issue that has been discussed earlier. *Empirical validity* refers to the actual measures that ultimately prove a change will make a difference. If social and empirical validity are not established for change programs for individuals with profound disabilities, the direction of any behavior change program will be suspect. Even though the worth of a behavioral approach is often judged through evaluation data, Evans and Meyer (1985) stated that any evaluation system should never take precedence over the meaning and ramificatons of all behavior change:

> As an *evaluation* approach, the charting of individual responses leaves much to be desired. It will not answer the question of whether the change documented is clinically or educationally significant; it will not answer the question of what other collateral effects (good or bad) have taken place; it will not answer the question of whether the intervention strategy itself was appropriate, humane, and in keeping with philosophical or legal assumptions regarding the handicapped child's right. (p. 161)

REFERENCES

Agosta, J., Close, D., Hops, H., & Rusch, F. (1980). Treatment of self-injurious behavior through overcorrection procedures. *Journal of The Association for the Severely Handicapped, 5,* 5–12.

Aman, M. G., Teehan, C. J., White, A. J., Turbott, S. H., & Vaithianathan, C. (1989). Haloperidol treatment with chronically medicated residents: Dose effects on clinical behavior and reinforcement contingencies. *American Journal on Mental Retardation, 93,* 452–460.

Aman, M. G., & White, A. J. (1988). Thioridazine dose effects with reference to stereotypic behavior in mentally retarded residents. *Journal of Autism and Developmental Disorders, 18,* 355–366.

Azrin, N. H., Besalel, V. A., Jamner, J. P., & Caputo, J. N. (1988). Comparative study of behavioral methods of treating severe self-injury. *Behavioral Residential Treatment, 3,* 119–152.

Bailey, S., Pokrzywinski, J., & Bryant, L. (1983). Using water mist to reduce self-injurious and stereotypic behavior. *Applied Research in Mental Retardation, 4,* 229–241.

Ball, T. S., Datta, P., Rios, M., & Constantine, C. (1985). Flexible arm splints in the control of a Lesch–Nyhan victim's finger biting and a profoundly retarded client's finger sucking. *Journal of Autism and Developmental Disorders, 15,* 177–184.

Barmann, B. C. (1980). Use of contingent vibration in the treatment of self-stimulatory hand-mouthing and ruminative vomiting behavior. *Journal of Behavior Theory and Experimental Psychiatry, 11,* 307–311.

Barton, L., & LaGrow, S. (1983). Reducing self-injurious and aggressive behavior in deaf–blind persons through overcorrection. *Journal of Visual Impairment and Blindness, 77,* 421–424.

Bates, W., & Smeltzer, D. (1982). Electroconvulsive treatment of psychotic self-injurious behavior in a patient with severe mild retardation. *American Journal of Psychiatry, 139,* 1355–1356.

Baumeister, A. A. (1991). Expanded theories of stereotypy and self-injurious responding: Commentary on "Emergence and maintenance of stereotypy and self-injury." *American Journal on Mental Retardation, 96,* 321–323.

Beukelman, F., & Rogers, J. (1984). Noncontingent use of alum in the reduction of rumination. *Psychology in the Schools, 21,* 500–503.

Bird, F., Dores, P. A., Moniz, D., & Robinson, J. (1989). Reducing severe aggressive and self-injurious behavior with functional communication training. *American Journal on Mental Retardation, 94,* 37–48.

Blankenship, M. D., & Lamberts, F. (1989). Helmet restraint and visual screening as treatment for self-injurious behavior in persons who have profound mental retardation. *Behavioral Residential Treatment, 4,* 253–265.

Borreson, P. (1980). The elimination of a self-injurious avoidance response through a forced running consequence. *Mental Retardation, 18,* 73–77.

Borreson, P. M., & Anderson, J. L. (1982). The elimination of chronic rumination through a combination of procedures. *Mental Retardation, 20,* 34–38.

Carr, E. G., & Durand, V. M. (1985). Reducing behavior problems through functional communication training. *Journal of Applied Behavioral Analysis, 18,* 111–126.

Carter, M., & Ward, J. (1987). The use of overcorrection to suppress self-injurious behavior. *Australia and New Zealand Journal of Developmental Disabilities, 13,* 227–242.

Case-Holden, V., & Hupp, S. C. (1989). Reducing stereotypic hand-mouthing of a child with severe/profound retardation. *Journal of Early Intervention, 13,* 165–172.

Caulier, A. R., & Ferretti, R. P. (1980). Stereotyped behavior, alternative behavior and collateral effects: A comparison of four intervention procedures. *Journal of Mental Deficiency Research, 24,* 219–236.

Christopher, R., & Lewis, B. (1984). The effects of auditory tempo changes on rates of stereotypic behavior in handicapped children. *Mental Retardation and Learning Disability Bulletin, 12*(2), 105–114.

Cipani, E. (1990). The communicative function hypothesis: An operant behavior perspective. *Journal of Behavior Therapy and Experimental Psychiatry, 21,* 239–247.

Clauser, B., & Scibak, J. W. (1990). Direct and generalized effects of food satiation in reducing rumination. *Research in Developmental Disabilities, 11,* 23–36.

Conrin, J., Pennypacker, H. S., Johnston, J., & Rust, J. (1982). Differential reinforcement of other behaviors to treat chronic rumination of mental retardates. *Journal of Behavioral Theory and Experimental Psychiatry, 13,* 325–329.

Czyzewski, M., Barrera, R., & Sulzer-Azaroff, B. (1982). An abbreviated overcorrection program to reduce self-stimulatory behaviors. *Journal of Behavior Therapy and Experimental Psychiatry. 13,* 55–62.

Davis, N. B., Wieseler, A., & Hanzel, T. E. (1980). Contingent music in management of rumination and out-of-seat behavior in a profoundly mentally retarded institutionalized male. *Mental Retardation, 18,* 43–44.

Donnellan, A. M., Mirenda, P. L., Mesaros, R. A., & Fassbender, L. L. (1984). Analyzing the communicative functions of aberrant behavior. *Journal of The Association for Persons with Severe Handicaps, 9,* 210–212.

Donnelly, D. R., & Olczak, P. V. (1990). The effect of differential reinforcement of incompatible behavior (DRI) on pica for cigarettes in persons with intellectual disability. *Behavior Modification, 14,* 81–97.

Dorsey, M. F., Iwata, B. A., Ong, P., & McSween, T. E. (1980). Treatment of self-injurious behavior using a water mist: Initial response suppression and generalization. *Journal of Applied Behavior Analysis, 13,* 343–354.

Duker, P., & Seys, D. (1983). Symposium on behavior modification treatments: II. Long-term follow up effects of extinction and overcorrection procedures with severely retarded individuals. *British Journal of Mental Subnormality, 29,* 74–80.

Dura, J. R., Mulick, J. A., & Hammer, D. (1988). Rapid clinical evaluation of sensory integration therapy for self-injurious behavior. *Mental Retardation, 26,* 83–87.

Durand, M. (1982). A behavioral/pharmacological intervention for the treatment of severe self-injurious behavior. *Journal of Autism and Developmental Disorders, 12,* 243–251.

Durand, V. M., & Carr, E. G. (1985). Self-injurious behavior: Motivating conditions and guidelines for treatment. *School Psychology Review, 14,* 171–176.

Evans, I. M., & Meyer, L. H. (1985). *An educative approach to behavior problems: A practical decision model for interventions with severely handicapped learners.* Baltimore: Brookes.

Favell, J. E., Azrin, N. H., Baumeister, A., Carr, E. G., Dorsey, M. F., Forehand, R., Foxx, R. M., Lovaas, O. I., Rincover, A., Risley, T. R., Romanczyk, R. G., Russo, D. C., Schroeder, J. R., & Solnick, J. V. (1982). The treatment of self-injurious behavior. *Behavior Therapy, 13,* 529–554.

Favell, J., McGimsey, J., & Schell, R. (1982). Treatment of self-injury by providing alternative sensory activities. *Analysis and Intervention in Developmental Disabilities, 2,* 83–104.

Foxx, R., & Livesay, J. (1984). Maintenance of response suppression following overcorrection: A 10-year retrospective examination of eight cases. *Analysis and Intervention in Developmental Disabilities, 4,* 65–79.

Gast, D. L., & Wolery, M. (1987). Severe maladaptive behaviors. In M. E. Snell (Ed.), *Systematic instruction of persons with severe handicaps* (3rd ed., pp. 300–332). Columbus, OH: Merrill.

Gaylord-Ross, R. (1980). A decision model for the treatment of aberrant behavior in applied settings. In W. Sailor, B. Wilcox, & L. Brown (Eds.), *Methods of instruction for severely handicapped students* (pp. 135–158). Baltimore: Brookes.

Gedye, A. (1990). Dietary increase in serotonin reduces self-injurious behavior in a Down syndrome adult. *Journal of Mental Deficiency Research, 39,* 195–203.

Gorman-Smith, D., & Matson, J. (1985). A review of treatment research for self-injurious and stereotyped responding. *Journal of Mental Deficiency Research, 29,* 295–308.

Griffin, J. C., Williams, D. E., Stark, M. T., Altmeyer, B. K., & Mason, M. (1986). Self-injurious behavior: A state wide prevalence survey of the extent and circumstances. *Applied Research in Mental Retardation, 7,* 105–116.

Guess, D., & Carr, E. (1991). Emergence and maintenance of stereotypy and self-injury. *American Journal on Mental Retardation, 96,* 299–319.

Guess, D., Mulligan-Ault, M., Roberts, S., Struth, J., Siegel-Causey, E., Thompson, B., Bronicki, J., & Guy, B. (1988). Implications of bio-behavioral states for the education and treatment of students with the most profoundly handicapping conditions. *Journal of The Association for Persons with Severe Handicaps, 13,* 163–174.

Guess, D., Siegel-Causey, E., Roberts, S., Rues, J., Thompson, B., & Siegel-Causey, D. (1990). Assessment and analysis of behavior state and related variables among students with profoundly handicapping conditions. *Journal of The Association for Persons with Severe Handicaps, 15,* 211–130.

Halpern, L., & Andrasik, F. (1986). The immediate and long-term effectiveness of overcorrection in treating self-injurious behavior in a mentally retarded adult. *Applied Research in Mental Retardation, 7,* 59–65.

Hamad, C. E., Isley, E., & Lowry, M. (1983). The use of mechanical restraint and response incompatibility to modify self-injurious behavior: A case study. *Mental Retardation, 21,* 213–217.

Heidorn, S., & Jensen, C. (1984). Generalization and maintenance of the reduction of self-injurious behavior maintained by two types of reinforcement. *Behavior Research and Therapy, 22,* 581–586.

Holburn, C. S., & Dougher, M. J. (1985). Behavior attempts to eliminate air-swallowing in two profoundly mentally retarded clients. *American Journal of Mental Deficiency, 89,* 524–536.

Iwata, B. A., Dorsey, M. F., Slifer, K. J., Baumann, K. E., & Richman, G. S. (1982). Toward a functional analysis of self-injury. *Analysis and Intervention in Developmental Disabilities, 2*(3), 3–20.

Iwata, B., Vollmer, T., & Zarcone, J. (1990). The experimental (functional) analysis of behavior disorders: Methodology, applications, and limitations. In A. Repp & N. Singh (Eds.), *Perspectives on the use of nonaversive and aversive interventions for persons with developmental disabilities* (pp. 301–330). Sycamore, IL: Sycamore Publishing.

Jones, R. (1987). The relationship between stereotyped and self-injurious behavior. *British Journal of Medical Psychology, 60,* 267–289.

Kars, H., Briekema, W., Flandesman-van Grideren, G. I., Verhoeren, W. M. A., & VanRee, J. M. (1990). Naltrexone atenuates self-injurious behavior in mentally retarded subjects. *Biological Psychiatry, 27,* 741–746.

Konarski, E. A., & Johnson, M. (1989). The use of brief restraint plus reinforcement to treat self-injurious behavior. *Behavioral Residential Treatment, 4*(1), 45–52.

LaGrow, S. J., & Repp, A. C. (1984). Stereotypic responding: A review of intervention research. *American Journal of Mental Deficiency, 88,* 595–609.

Lapierre, Y. D., & Reesal, R. (1986). Pharmacologic management of aggressivity and self-mutilation in the mentally retarded. *Psychiatric Perspectives on Mental Retardation, 9,* 745–754.

LaVigna, G. W., & Donnellan, A. M. (1986). *Alternatives to punishment: Solving behavior problems with non-aversive strategies.* New York: Irvington.

Lennox, D., & Miltenberger, R. (1989). Conducting a functional assessment of problem behavior in applied settings. *Journal of The Association for Persons with Severe Handicaps, 14,* 304–311.

Linn, D. M., Rojahn, J., Helsel, W. J., & Dixon, J. (1988). Accute effects of transcutaneous electric nerve stimulation on self-injurious behavior. *Journal of the Multihandicapped Person, 1*(2), 105–109.

Lockwood, K., & Bourland, G. (1982). Reduction of self-injurious behaviors by reinforcement and toy use. *Mental Retardation, 20,* 169–173.

Lovaas, O. I., & Smith, T. (1991). There is more to operant theory and practice: Comment on Guess and Carr. *American Journal on Mental Retardation, 96,* 324–327.

Luiselli, J. K. (1989). Behavioral medicine, behavior therapy, and developmental disabilities. In J. K. Luiselli (Ed.), *Behavioral medicine and developmental disabilities* (pp. 1–20). New York: Springer-Verlag.

Luiselli, J. K., Matson, J. L., & Singh, N. N. (1992). *Self-injurious behavior: Analysis, assessment, and treatment.* New York: Springer-Verlag.

Lundervold, D., & Bourland, G. (1988). Quantitative analysis of treatment of aggression, self-injury, and property destruction. *Behavior Modification, 12,* 590–617.

Lutzker, J., & Wesch, D. (1983). Facial screening: History and critical review. *Australia and New Zealand Journal of Developmental Disabilities, 9,* 209–223.

Mace, F. C., & Knight, D. (1986). Functional analysis and treatment of severe pica. *Journal of Applied Behavorial Analysis, 19,* 411–416.

Marholin, D., Luiselli, J., Robinson, M., & Lott, I. (1980). Response-contingent taste aversion in treating chronic ruminative vomiting of institutionalized profoundly retarded children. *Journal of Mental Deficiency Research, 24,* 47–56.

Matson, J. L., & Taras, M. E. (1989). A 20 year review of punishment and alternate methods to treat problem behaviors in developmentally delayed persons. *Research in Developmental Disabilities, 10,* 85–104.

McGonigle, J. J., Duncan, D., Cordisco, L., & Barrett, R. (1982). Visual screening: An alternative method for reducing stereotypic behaviors. *Journal of Applied Behavior Analysis, 15,* 461–467.

Millichamp, C. J., & Singh, N. N. (1987). The effects of intermittent drug therapy on stereotypy and collateral behaviors of mentally retarded persons. *Research in Developmental Disabilities, 8,* 213–227.

Mulick, J. A., & Meinhold, P. M. (1991). Evaluating models for the emergence and maintenance of stereotypy and self-injury. *American Journal on Mental Retardation, 96,* 327–333.

Mulick, J. A., Schroeder, S. R., & Rojahn, J. (1980a). Chronic ruminative vomiting: A comparison of four treatment procedures. *Journal of Autism and Developmental Disorders, 10,* 203–213.

Mulick, J. A., Schroeder, S. R., & Rojahn, J. (1980b). Ecological assessment of self-protective devices in three profoundly retarded adults. *Journal of Autism and Developmental Disorders, 10,* 59–66.

Murphy, G. (1982). Sensory reinforcement in the mentally handicapped and autistic child: A review. *Journal of Autism and Developmental Disorders, 12,* 265–278.

Neel, R. S., & Billingsley, F. F. (1989). *Impact: A functional curriculum handbook for students with moderate to severe disabilities.* Baltimore: Brookes.

Neufeld, A., & Fantuzzo, J. W. (1987). Treatment of severe self-injurious behavior by the mentally retarded using the bubble helmet and differential reinforcement procedures. *Journal of Behavior Therapy and Experimental Psychiatry, 18,* 127–136.

O'Brien, S., & Repp, A. C. (1990). Reinforcement-based reductive procedures: A review of 20 years of their use with persons with severe or profound retardation. *Journal of The Association for Persons with Severe Handicaps, 15,* 148–159.

O'Neill, R. E., Horner, R. H., Albin, R. W., Sprague, J., & Storey, K. (1990). *Functional analysis of problem behavior: A practical assessment guide.* Sycamore, IL: Sycamore Publishing.

Paisey, T. J., & Whitney, R. B. (1989). A long-term case study of analysis, response suppression, and treatment maintenance involving life-threating pica. *Behavioral Residential Treatment, 4*(3), 191–211.

Paniagua, F., Braverman, C., & Capriotti, R. (1986). Use of a treatment package in the management of a profoundly mentally retarded girl's pica and self-injury. *Journal of Behavior Therapy and Experimental Psychiatry, 16,* 159–168.

Parrish, J. M., Aguerrevere, L., Dorsey, M. G., & Iwata, B. A. (1980). The effects of protective equipment on self-injurious behavior. *The Behavior Therapist, 3,* 28–29.

Rapoff, M., Altman, K., & Christophersen, E. (1980). Suppression of self-injurious behavior: Determining the least restrictive alternative. *Journal of Mental Deficiency Research, 24,* 37–46.

Rast, A., Johnston, J. M., Allen, J. E., & Drum, C. (1985). Effects of nutritional and mechanical properties of food on ruminative behavior. *Journal of the Experimental Analysis of Behavior, 44,* 195–206.

Realon, R. (1990). The effects of making choices on engagement levels with persons who are profoundly multiply handicapped. *Education and Training in Mental Retardation, 25,* 299–305.

Reichle, J., & Wacker, D. P. (1993). *Communicative approaches to the management of challenging behavior.* Baltimore: Brookes.

Reid, D. H., Phillips, J. F., & Green, C. W. (1991). Teaching persons with profound multiple handicaps: A review of the effects of behavioral research. *Journal of Applied Behavior Analysis, 24,* 319–336.

Renzaglia, A. M., & Bates, P. (1983). Socially appropriate behavior. In M. E. Snell (Ed.), *Systematic instruction of the moderately and severely handicapped* (2nd ed., pp. 314–356). Columbus, OH: Merrill.

Repp, A. C., & Singh, N. (1990). *Perspectives on the use of nonaversive and aversive interventions for persons with developmental disabilities.* Sycamore, IL: Sycamore Publishing.

Repp, A. C., Singh, N. N., Olinger, E., & Olson, D. R. (1990). The use of functional analysis to test causes of self-injurious behavior: Rationale, current status, and future directions. *Journal of Mental Deficiency Research, 34,* 95–105.

Richards, S. B., & Sternberg, L. (1992). A preliminary analysis of environmental variables affecting the observed biobehavioural states of individuals with profound handicaps. *Journal of Intellectual Disability Research, 36,* 403–414.

Rose, V., Sloop, W., & Baker, P. (1980). Elimination of chronic self-injurious behavior by withdrawal of staff attention. *Psychological Reports, 4,* 327–330.

Ruedrich, S. L., Grush, L., & Wilson, J. (1990). Beta adrenergic blocking medications for aggressive or self-injurious mentally retarded persons. *American Journal on Mental Retardation, 95,* 110–119.

Saloviita, T. (1988). Elimination of self-injurious behavior by brief physical restraint and DRA. *Scandinavian Journal of Behavior Therapy, 17*(1), 55–63.

Scotti, J. R., Evans, I. M., Meyer, L. H., & Walker, P. (1991). A meta-analysis of intervention research with problem behavior: Treatment validity and standards of practice. *American Journal on Mental Retardation, 96,* 233–256.

Singh, N. N., & Bakker, L. (1984). Suppression of pica by overcorrection and physical restraint: A comparative analysis. *Journal of Autism and Developmental Disorders, 14,* 331–341.

Singh, N. N., Dawson, M., & Gregory, M. (1980). Self-injury in the profoundly retarded: Clinically significant versus therapeutic control. *Journal of Mental Deficiency Research, 24,* 87–97.

Singh, N. N., Dawson, M., & Manning, P. (1981). The effects of physical restraint on self-injurious behavior. *Journal of Mental Deficiency Research, 25,* 206–216.

Singh, N. N., & Millichamp, C. J. (1984). Effects of medication on the self-injurious behavior of mentally retarded persons. *Psychiatric Aspects of Mental Retardation Resources, 3*(4), 13–16.

Singh, N. N., & Millichamp, C. J. (1985). Pharmacological treatment of self-injurious behavior in mentally retarded persons. *Journal of Autism and Developmental Disorders, 15,* 257–262.

Singh, N. N., Watson, J. E., & Winton, A. S. (1986). Treating self-injury: Water mist spray versus facial screening or forced arm exercise. *Journal of Applied Behavior Analysis, 19,* 403–410.

Singh, N. N., & Winton, A. S. (1984). Behavioral monitoring of pharmacological interventions for self-injury. *Applied Research in Mental Retardation, 5,* 161–170.

Smith, M. D. (1987). Treatment of pica in an adult disabled by autism by differential reinforcement of incompatible behavior. *Journal of Behavior Theories and Experimental Psychiatry, 18,* 285–288.

Steege, M. W., Wacker, D. P., Cigrand, K. C., Berg, W. K., Novak, C. G., Reimers, T. M., Sasso, G. M., & DeRadd, A. (1990). Use of negative reinforcement in the treatment of self-injurious behavior. *Journal of Applied Behavioral Analysis, 23,* 459–467.

Sternberg, L., & Richards, S. (1989). Assessing levels of state and arousal in individuals with profound handicaps: A research integration. *Journal of Mental Deficiency Research, 33,* 381–387.

Sternberg, L., & Schilit, J. (1986). *Behavioral guidelines manual: Programs for students with profound handicaps.* Ft. Lauderdale, FL: Broward County Public Schools.

Strawbridge, L. A., Drnach, M., Sisson, L., & Van Hasselt, V. (1989). Behavior therapy combined with physical therapy to promote walker use by a child with multiple handicaps. *Education and Training in Mental Retardation, 24,* 239–247.

Szymanski, L., Kedesdy, J., Sulkes, S., Cutler, A., & Stevens-Orr, P. (1987). Naltrexone in treatment of self-injurious behavior: A clinical study. *Research in Developmental Disabilities, 8,* 179–190.

Taylor, C. R., & Chamove, A. S. (1986). Vibrator or visual stimulation reduces self-injury. *Australia and New Zealand Journal of Development Disabilities, 12,* 243–248.

Underwood, L. A., Figueroa, R. G., Thyer, B. A., & Nzeocha, A. (1989). Interruption and DRI in the treatment of self-injurious behavior among mentally retarded and autistic self-restrainers. *Behavior Modification, 13,* 471–481.

Wacker, D. P., Berg, W. K., Wiggins, B., Muldoon, M., & Cavanaugh, J. (1985). Evaluation of reinforcer preferences for profoundly handicapped students. *Journal of Applied Behavior Analysis, 18,* 173–178.

Wacker, D., Northup, J., & Cooper, L. (1992). Behavioral assessment. In D. Greydanus & M. Wolraich (Eds.), *Behavioral pediatrics* (pp. 57–68). New York: Springer-Verlag.

Wacker, D. P., Wiggins, B., Fowler, M., & Berg, W. K. (1988). Training students with profound or multiple handicaps to make requests via microswitches. *Journal of Applied Behavior Analysis, 21,* 331–343.

Watson, J., Singh, N. N., & Winton, A. S. (1986). Suppressive effects of visual and facial screening on self-injurious finger-sucking. *American Journal of Mental Deficiency, 90,* 526–534.

Wells, M., & Smith, D. (1983). Reduction of self-injurious behavior of mentally retarded persons using sensory-integrative techniques. *American Journal of Mental Deficiency, 87,* 664–666.

Wesolowski, M. D., & Zawlocki, R. J. (1982). The differential effects of procedures to eliminate an injurious self-stimulatory behavior (digit-ocular sign) in blind retarded twins. *Behavior Therapy, 13,* 334–345.

Wieseler, N. A., Hanson, R., Chamberlain, T., & Thompson, T. (1988). Stereotypic behavior of mentally retarded adults adjunctive to a positive reinforcement schedule. *Research in Developmental Disabilities, 9,* 393–403.

Winton, A., & Singh, N. (1983). Suppression of pica using brief duration physical restraint. *Journal of Mental Deficiency Research, 27,* 93–103.

Winton, A., Singh, N., & Dawson, M. (1984). Effects of facial screening and blindfold on self-injurious behavior. *Applied Research in Mental Retardation, 5,* 29–42.

Chapter 6

Providing Support for Sensory, Postural, and Movement Needs

BONNIE L. UTLEY

The present system of service provision for individuals with disabilities and their families is based on a series of categories established by local, state, and federal governing bodies. These categories exist primarily for the purpose of fiscal accountability. A parallel system of categorization serves to guide professional preparation and certification, as well as to provide a description of the individuals served. This system permits the continued development and implementation of an empirical base to underlie service provision. Although efforts are under way to minimize those aspects of categorization and labeling that are a hindrance to more inclusive practices (e.g., the redefinition and reclassification of mental retardation [Luckasson et al., 1992]; see Chapter 1), it may still be appropriate to provide a description of a population group for whom particular procedures are intended. The individuals for whom information in this chapter may be appropriate are those whose *functional abilities* are indicative of a severe to profound range of cognitive disability, and who may have any combination of additional sensory, physical, and emotional disabilities.

Throughout this chapter, the reader is encouraged to heed the advice given in Chapter 2: to view *all* individuals as having untapped potential, to be sensitive to the substantial impact that confinement to non-normalized environments has on the potential for full development, and to defer judgment on what a person can (or cannot) do until the opportunity for full participation in more inclusive school, home, and community activities for everyone is realized. In addition, the reader is advised to speak with the students served with the expectation that what is said is, in fact, understood.

Needs that Arise from Sensory Disabilities

Estimates of the prevalence of sensory disabilities in individuals with severe to profound cognitive disabilities are tentative at best. Multiple factors contribute to the lack of certainty regarding the approximate numbers of individuals with sensory disabilities, including inconsistent acceptance of various definitions (Dantona, 1986; Jacobson & Janicki, 1985), differences in sampling procedures (Fredericks & Baldwin, 1987), and ongoing dissatisfaction with assessment procedures (Guess & Siegel-Causey, 1988). Sobsey and Wolf-Schein (1991), however, emphasized that, regardless of which estimate is most valid, it is clear that disabilities in vision and/or hearing occur many times more frequently among individuals with severe to profound disabilities than in the general population. They stated that "approximately one child with multiple disabilities in five can be expected to have impaired hearing, and two in five can be expected to have impaired vision" (p. 121).

Impairments in vision

The severity of sensory loss varies tremendously across the population. Visual impairments have multiple causes, including structural defects (i.e., one or more structures of the eye fail to receive visual images in the normal way); an inability of the visual pathway to transmit images; and the inability of the brain to organize, interpret, and store visual input. Examples of common structural defects include *refractive errors* (i.e., the failure of visual images to come to a focus point directly on the retina) and impairment of binocular vision. *Binocular single vision,* also referred to as *fusion,* is the ability of the brain to fuse the slightly different images received and transmitted by the two eyes into one single, clear image that includes the dimension of depth perception. An example of damage to the visual pathway is *hemianopsia* (i.e., loss of vision in one half of the visual field in one or both eyes) due to damage in that part of the pathway that transmits information from one half of each eye. In addition to the causes of visual impairment described earlier, manifestations of damage to the brain also can limit the ability of the visual system to receive and transmit visual images. An example is *nystagmus* (i.e., an involuntary movement of the eyes in either a rotary, horizontal, or vertical direction).

Impairments in audition

Impairments in audition are typically characterized as being conductive, sensorineural, or mixed. *Conductive losses* are due to structural defects in the outer and middle ear which prevent sound from being received, amplified, and transmitted to the inner ear. *Sensorineural losses* are those in which one or more of the highly sophisticated structures of the inner ear are defective, thereby limiting the ability of the auditory system to detect the full range of sound frequencies (i.e., pitch, measured in hertz [Hz]) and intensities (i.e., loudness, measured in decibels [dB]). Sensorineural losses are also characterized by distortion in sound reception and, in some people, an abnormal growth of loudness termed *recruitment*. The presence of distortion and/or recruitment complicates the fitting and functional use of hearing aids for many people with sensorineural losses. Finally, impairment in audition may also result from defects in the auditory pathway and/or in the areas of the brain where auditory information is received, interpreted, and stored.

Needs that Arise from Disorders in Posture and Movement

According to Campbell (1989), many individuals who are identified as having profound disabilities experience limitations in posture and movement. *Posture* may be described as the ability to maintain a stable position in space that serves as the foundation for controlled movement. *Movement* is the ability to engage in motor behavior that is coordinated, controlled, and accurate.

Concomitant with disorders in posture and movement are difficulties with the maintenance of balance, not only in standing but in sitting as well. Many individuals with disorders in posture and movement are unable to move parts of the body selectively (e.g., to reach to the side and down in an attempt to retrieve a fallen toy) and may also lack *trunk rotation* (i.e., segmental movement around the body axis). An example of trunk rotation in sitting is a slight turn of the shoulders to one side while the base of support—the pelvis and buttocks—remain stable. An individual without trunk rotation is more likely to move the trunk as a single unit (i.e., "log rolling").

The presence of these characteristics may limit the ability of an individual to search for objects and people in the surrounding environment, and may also result in disruptions to the coordinated use of sensory and motor skills in tandem. For example, an individual without good balance, trunk rotation, or the ability to engage in isolated arm movements may be unable to localize to the voice of a playmate, reach a book that is offered during library time, or visually track a ball as it moves down the soccer field during recess. Significant limitations in normal posture and movement may also contribute to the development of secondary health problems, such as respiratory difficulties, contractures and deformities, and skin breakdown (see Chapter 8).

Although few students with severe physical disabilities may ever acquire the traditional motor milestones of independent sitting, standing, and walking, ongoing intervention in the form of handling techniques to promote development and/or maintenance of motor skills is recommended. Additional program components include *therapeutic positioning* (i.e., the selection of overall body positions that promote beneficial muscle length, improve breathing, and provide weight-bearing as recommended) and *functional adaptations* (i.e., the use of equipment that permits supported performance of certain postures, such as sitting or switch interfaces, that permit interaction with the physical and/or social world in the absence of coordinated arm and hand function).

The Need for Teamwork

The sensory and physical needs of individuals with profound disabilities are such that neither educators nor a single representative of a related service discipline (e.g., occupational therapy, audiology, speech–language pathology, nursing) singularly possesses all the information and skills necessary to meet the varied needs of these individuals. Instead, the contributions of a *team* of professionals, who represent a range of disciplines, are considered both necessary and desirable to ensure that individuals with profound disabilities are able to access the full range of educational opportunities guaranteed under Public Law 101-476 (1990), the Individuals with Disabilities Education Act (IDEA).

Historically, the first teams were *multidisciplinary* (i.e., professionals with expertise in different disciplines evaluated and worked with a client individually). This approach was originally designed to meet the needs of people served in medical settings (Hart, 1977). Over time, a second model of team functioning emerged, which was termed *interdisciplinary*. The interdisciplinary team also included evaluations completed individually; however, a formal system of communication and assignment of a "case manager" were established to reduce fragmentation of services (McCormick & Goldman, 1979). Of more recent origin, the *transdisciplinary* team model evolved as a way for professionals to share important disciplinary knowledge and skills across traditional disciplinary boundaries (Hutchison, 1978). This model emerged in recognition of the fact that functioning in everyday routines requires individuals to perform sensorimotor and cognitive *and* communication skills in clusters (Rainforth, York, & MacDonald, 1992). The transdisciplinary model, through an emphasis on sharing discipline-specific knowledge and skills, was an attempt to promote more consistency in meeting the multiple needs of persons with severe and profound disabilities in the areas of health, motor skills, sensory skills, and communication. Additionally, it was hoped that the integration of discipline-specific knowledge and skills throughout the school day would permit more longitudinal implementation of specialized strategies, and result in greater therapeutic benefit.

The transdisciplinary approach provided a new model of who provides therapeutic services to individuals with profound disabilities. Typically, however, descriptions of this model fail to provide guidelines regarding *where* and in *what* context services should be tendered. Initially, transdisciplinary services were characterized by parents, teachers, and other service providers becoming "pseudo-therapists," implementing methods associated with various disciplines irrespective of context (Rainforth et al., 1992). In a parallel development, an approach that addressed the context for delivering therapy evolved as well. This approach was referred to as "integrated therapy" (Sternat, Messina, Nietupski, Lyon, & Brown, 1977). Proponents of integrated therapy emphasized that services should be delivered in functional contexts (i.e., when and where a person would naturally use a skill, rather than in isolation from ongoing demands in everyday home, school, and community environments). This approach complements the transdisciplinary model both philosophically and programmatically.

Another characteristic of the transdisciplinary team model is the use of an indirect model of service provision. Indirect service may be described as a form of intervention during which team members teach, consult with, and directly supervise other team members so the team members receiving supervision can implement educationally and therapeutically appropriate activities (Association for Retarded Citizens/Minnesota, 1989, pp. 3–4). This form of intervention is in contrast to direct service, in which hands-on interaction between professionals and students occurs. Proponents of the transdisciplinary model do not, however, presume that professionals stop providing direct service. In fact, rarely would professionals be effective consultants unless they maintained direct, hands-on contact with people who have disabilities (Orelove & Sobsey, 1991; York, Rainforth, & Giangreco, 1990). An important element of this model is that team members work closely with one another so that the educational and related service goals of each student can be integrated within multiple activities conducted in a variety of settings. The transdisciplinary model requires that the traditional roles practiced by educators and related service providers become more flexible to permit a combination of direct and indirect service provision.

Although a group of professionals may label themselves a team, Hutchison (1978), an originator of the transdisciplinary model, stated that "calling a small group of people a team does not make them so" (p. 70). Clearly, a fundamental aspect of optimal team functioning is mutual understanding of and respect for the skills and knowledge of each individual member (Orelove & Sobsey, 1991). It is with this spirit of collaboration that the remainder of this chapter will proceed. For more in-depth information on the transdisciplinary team model and collaboration, see Orelove and Sobsey (1991), Thousand and Villa (1992), and Utley (1992).

The Need to Implement Partial Participation

The manifestations of multiple disabilities may result in individuals who have little or no purposeful movement. For this reason, the assessment and intervention procedures described in this chapter reflect the *partial participation principle* (Baumgart et al., 1982; see Chapter 2). Adherence to the partial participation principle requires acceptance of the following assumptions: (a) that there are no prerequisite skills that individuals must possess prior to initiation of instruction on a particular skill or task, and (b) that instruction on component parts of a task is valuable even if there is little reason to expect that the student will ever achieve complete independence on that same task.

The use of the partial participation principle is implied, implicitly or explicitly, throughout the assessment and intervention procedures recommended in this chapter. Small steps toward independence are encouraged and expected. This expectation of maximum participation is reflected in two ways within the suggested assessment and intervention strategies. The first is the exacting degree of task analysis that is revealed in some of the procedures. For example, for some students with virtually no voluntary movement, an initial level of participation may simply be the exhibition of a critical developmental skill (e.g., active visual fixation on a washcloth as the student is assisted to use the washcloth during a grooming task). The second way through which a high expectation of participation is communicated is the general recommendation that service providers use language or communication input that is both informative and grammatically correct throughout the teaching and learning process, and that the context of assessment and intervention be viewed as interactive. The assessment and intervention procedures should be conducted in a way that encourages meaningful interaction to emerge. Therefore, pauses at appropriate intervals should be part of the interactive nature of the assessment and intervention procedures. In addition, the service provider should be attentive to each individual's attempts to communicate (and reciprocate to those communicative attempts) throughout the day.

FUNCTIONAL ASSESSMENT AND INTERVENTION FOR VISUAL IMPAIRMENTS

To be functional, vision assessment should be completed on multiple aspects of visual functioning. Typically, most sets of assessment procedures begin with gross measures of visual functioning, such as pupillary constriction and the blink reflex. Although assessment of these aspects of visual functioning may be important, particularly for those students with complex health care needs, the data yielded from these assessments do not lead directly to specific guidelines regarding the provision of instruction (e.g., where on a wheelchair tray a spoon should be placed to increase the probability that the student will be able to reach and grasp the spoon). Indeed, information on gross structural measures do not lead to intervention, per se, as these behaviors are not *teachable*. For this reason (and additional reasons of efficiency), it may be important to begin vision assessment with those procedures that focus on higher level visual skills, with progression to subsequent measures only if an individual does poorly on the initial assessment procedures. This method of organizing assessment serves as the basis for the model summarized here and that is described more fully in Utley, Nelson, and Ferrell (1990). This assessment model is designed to assist teams of professionals to answer the following questions:

1. Is the student able to locate materials visually that are used in a variety of typical instructional activities?

2. Is the student able to engage in simple visual–motor behaviors (e.g., tracking) and use his or her eyes and hands together to reach, grasp, transport, and release objects?

3. Is the student able to use both eyes together?

4. Is the student able to detect objects and/or people outside of his or her direct line of vision?

5. Is the student able to use vision as a way to gather information about his or her environment?

In addition to establishing an organizational structure for assessment, it is also important to define "levels" of assessment. Gathering precise information regarding an individual's ability to engage in specific visual behaviors can be a time-consuming process. For this reason, it may be important to conduct an abbreviated level of functional vision assessment that will permit team members to identify those individuals for whom more in-depth measures may be needed to answer specific questions regarding visual and visual–motor skills. The preliminary level of assessment may be conceptualized as a *screening* measure. The preliminary measure in this model is termed the Assessment Overview (see Appendix 6A). This overview corresponds, in terms of organization, to the questions listed above. Each section of the overview contains three or more items that summarize information regarding an individual's ability to engage in specific visual and visual–motor responses.

The use of the partial participation principle (Baumgart et al., 1982) is exemplified in Section 2 of the Assessment Overview (Visual–Motor), specifically with regard to the use of visual and upper extremity skills completed in tandem (e.g., visually directed reach). Each visual–motor dyad assessed in this section is described in two parallel assessment items. The first item is used to record the performance of a visual–motor behavior as completed by an individual with near-normal upper extremity function (e.g., "Watches an object as he or she reaches for that object"). The second item is used for those individuals who lack upper extremity function, and for whom only the performance of the visual component of the task is assessed (e.g., "Watches an object as an adult physically assists him or her [partially or fully] to reach toward that object"). An individual's ability to engage in the visual component of a task is observed even under conditions when the motor behavior is prompted fully by a peer or adult.

As mentioned earlier, the sequence of procedures described here differs somewhat from that of other materials developed for a similar purpose. These procedures reflect a "test-down" approach. An important question that must be answered for most individuals with profound disabilities is whether there is a sufficient amount of functional vision for these individuals to respond to peers, adults, and the presence of functional, age-appropriate instructional materials found in typical classroom and community environments. Screening data obtained from the Assessment Overview are designed to answer this question. If the answer to the question is "yes," and the individual has moderate to good head control with some degree of head–neck flexion, as well as the ability to look to both sides, it may not be necessary to conduct additional vision assessment procedures. If the answer is "no," more in-depth assessment procedures are required. The remainder of this section describes a comprehensive assessment model that can be implemented to determine level of functional vision. Copies of the suggested procedures are found in the form of tables within the text and appendices at the end of the chapter, depending on the depth and breadth of the content of each section.

Localization Acuity

This procedure is designed to provide information regarding whether an individual is able to respond visually to functional, age-appropriate materials within a variety of home, school, and community environments. The procedures require identification of a series of objects that fall into six size categories, ranging from small objects (¼ to 1 inch) to objects that are between 8 and 10 inches in size.

As described in Appendix 6B ("A Model to Assess Localization Acuity"), a localization acuity assessment is designed to be conducted in two stages:

(1) in a series of several short sessions consisting of multiple trials with the objects positioned on a typical "work" surface (tabletop, wheelchair tray, etc.) and (2) in one or more functional, natural contexts to refine the results of the data collected earlier. The information yielded through completion of this measure is limited to knowledge of an individual's ability to respond visually within a framework that is defined by the length of the individual's arms and the width of his or her shoulders. Although these parameters are helpful to guide presentation of materials within this framework, it is also of interest to know how large an object should be for presentation in group instruction (often conducted at distances of approximately 2 to 4 feet), as well as for travel in the school and community. To meet this need, Tables 6B.3 and 6B.4 in the concluding section of Appendix 6B provide information regarding guidelines for the sizes of objects that may be needed for a particular individual to respond to objects at various other distances.

Visual–Motor Behaviors

This section of the model includes two distinct measures. The first provides the framework for assessing tracking, scanning, and gaze shift. The second provides the framework for assessing visually directed upper extremity functions (i.e., reaching, grasping, and manipulating).

The first measure in this section (Visual–Motor Part I) requires that assessment be carried out in the context of functional, daily routines during which these visual–motor skills may be likely to occur naturally. Conducting assessment in this manner requires generation of multiple "visual–motor" task analyses, in which each visual and visual–motor skill required for participation in a task is articulated in a step-by-step progression. In addition, the motor components of the task are analyzed by using a rule that states that each topographical change in movement necessitates a new step. The definitions of visual and visual–motor behaviors that comprise some of the steps in a visual–motor task analysis are found in Table 6.1. A sample visual–motor task analysis for the domestic skill of wiping a table is shown in Figure 6.1.

Assessment of visual and visual–motor skills within the context in which they are likely to occur leads naturally to intervention on those skills the individual is lacking. It should be noted, however, that conducting assessment in natural contexts is, in itself, a form of intervention. Many individuals with whom these procedures were field-tested showed increasing ability to track, scan, and shift gaze from one object to another on assessment sessions conducted over time. Structuring the assessment to be conducted in a highly interactive, potentially meaningful, and positive social context may result in poor test–retest reliability; however, a higher degree of validity may be obtained.

TABLE 6.1. Definitions and Examples of Some Visual and Visual–Motor Behaviors

Fixation

Definition:	Active alignment of the visual axis on a stationary object.
Example:	Looking at a toothbrush while reaching to pick it up.

Orientation and mobility

Definition:	Orientation refers to the skills needed to establish one's position in space, and relationships to all other significant objects and persons in one's environment. Mobility means the ability to navigate safely from one's present fixed position to a desired position in another part of the environment.
Example:	Orientation—Facing in the appropriate direction.
	Mobility—Avoiding obstacles when walking from one place to another.

Scanning

Definition:	Visually searching for a particular object or person among a display of various visual stimuli.
Example:	Visually locating a ball among a display of several toys.

Tracking

Definition:	Visually following a moving stimulus.
Example:	Watching a person walk across the room.

Gaze shift

Definition:	Shifting visual attention and fixation from one point to another.
Example:	Fixating on one food item, then another, when given a choice between two foods.

The second measure in this section (Visual–Motor Part II) serves as the framework for measuring the highly dynamic visual and visual–motor processes that occur as an individual localizes on an object visually, and then seeks to reach and explore that object. Unlike Visual–Motor Part I, this procedure is designed to be conducted in a more tightly controlled environment. Figure 6.2 shows a data sheet for assessment of visually directed reach and grasp, as well as an explanation of the symbols on the form. This assessment is to be completed using many of the same procedures described in Appendix 6B for localization acuity. Whereas the objects used for the localization acuity measure were drawn from multiple sources, high-preference objects are presented in Visual–Motor Part II to obtain the best possible indication of an individual's ability to use his or her hands and eyes together. Another difference between the completion of Visual–Motor Part II and the localization acuity measure is that each "trial" of presentation in the former is much more lengthy. The multiple visual and visual–motor behaviors that occur in response to presentation of objects for manipulation occur in rapid succession. For this reason, completion of the recording form for each trial

Task Analysis

Student _____

Date _____

Domain: Domestic Skills

Activity: Wiping a Tabletop with a Wet Sponge

		Legend:	V	= Visual Skill
			M	= Motor Skill
			V/O	= Orientation
			V/F	= Fixation
			V/S	= Scanning
			V/T	= Tracking

_____ V/O 1. Looks at teacher when he or she attempts to obtain student's attention.

_____ V/F 2A. (For students who understand spoken language.) Looks at teacher's face when teacher says, "It's time to clean the table. We're going to the sink to get the sponge."

_____ V/F 2B. (For students who understand manual language.) Looks at teacher's hand when he or she signs the above message.

_____ V/F 2C. (For students who understand pictorial representations.) Looks at picture(s) that represent the above message when the teacher points to that (those) picture(s).

_____ V/OM 3. Looks toward sink while teacher pushes wheelchair.

_____ V/OM 4. Faces appropriate direction when positioned at sink.

_____ V/S 5. Visually locates faucet.

_____ M 6. Reaches and touches faucet.

_____ M 7. Turns water on.

_____ V/S 8. Visually locates sponge.

_____ M 9. Reaches and touches sponge.

_____ M 10. Picks up sponge.

_____ M 11. Places sponge under water.

_____ V/T 12. Visually follows sponge from sink to water.

_____ M 13. Releases sponge onto sink.

_____ V/F 14. Looks at sponge when releasing sponge onto sink.

_____ V/S 15. Visually relocates faucet.

_____ M 16. Reaches and touches faucet.

_____ M 17. Turns water off.

_____ V/S 18. Visually relocates sponge.

_____ M 19. Reaches and touches sponge.

_____ V/OM 20. Looks toward table while teacher pushes wheelchair.

_____ V/OM 21. Faces in appropriate direction before beginning to wipe table.

_____ V/F 22. Looks at table.

_____ M 23. Reaches out with sponge and makes contact with table.

_____ M 24. Wipes table.

_____ V/T 25. Visually follows sponge while wiping table.

_____ V/OM 26. Looks at other side of table while teacher or peer moves wheelchair to opposite side of table.

(continued)

Figure 6.1. Sample visual–motor task analysis for the task of wiping a table.

_____	M	27.	Maintains grasp on sponge.
_____	M	28.	Reaches out with sponge and makes contact with table.
_____	V / OM	29.	Looks at table when contact is made.
_____	M	30.	Wipes table.
_____	V / T	31.	Visually follows sponge while wiping table.
_____	V / OM	32.	Looks toward sink.
_____	M	33.	Holds sponge.
_____	M	34.	Releases sponge onto sink.

$$\frac{\text{Total Visual Skills}}{18} = \frac{}{18} = \underline{}\%$$

$$\frac{\text{Total Motor Skills}}{16} = \frac{}{16} = \underline{}\%$$

Record an X to the left of the visual skills that need to be practiced, based on the student's performance on this visual–motor task analysis.

_____ Orientation/Mobility
_____ Fixation
_____ Scanning
_____ Tracking

Figure 6.1. *Continued.*

is delayed until the individual has completed localizing the object visually and attempted to reach and grasp that object.

The Visual–Motor Part II assessment permits service providers to capture the optimal combination of head position and eye position for an individual with both sensory and physical disabilities. This measure is particularly appropriate for those students for whom the balance of therapeutic needs and other programmatic considerations must be determined by the team. For example, this procedure is helpful as a guide for teams that engage in decision making regarding the design of a direct-selection communication system in which an individual is expected to indicate choices, answer questions, or express needs (e.g., by selecting outputs/symbols arrayed on a rigid board placed on a work surface or wheelchair tray). These data also may be useful in determining the area on a work surface that is most accessible to an individual student, both visually *and* motorically. More specifically, an individual may have asymmetrical distribution of tone (e.g., high tone on one side of the body and low tone on the other) and may respond better physically to

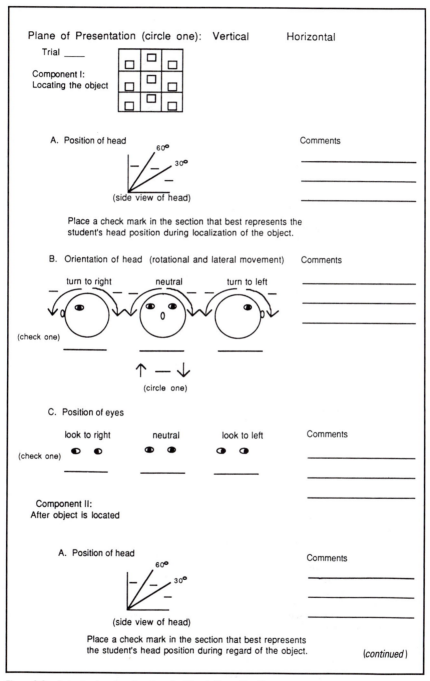

Figure 6.2. Data sheet and explanations for Visual–Motor Part II.

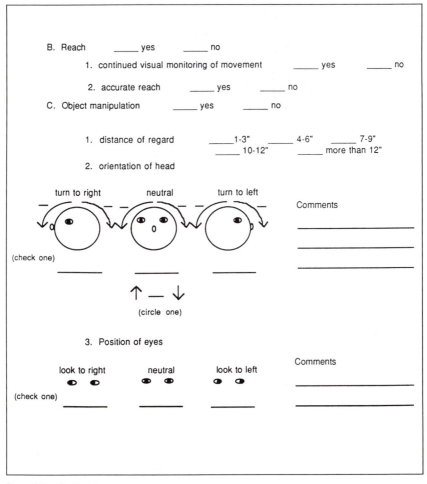

Figure 6.2. *Continued*

Explanation: This data sheet should be duplicated so there is one copy for each trial of presentation. Begin completing the data sheet by indicating whether the assessment is done with objects presented on a vertical or horizontal plane. As you prepare to conduct a trial, place the trial number on the line next to the outline of the presentation grid; then place a check mark in the small square that represents where on the work surface the object is presented for that trial.

In A, place a check mark in the quadrant that best represents the location of the student's head as he or she attempts to locate the object.

In B, first determine whether the head is in midline or turned to a lateral side. Place a check mark below the face symbol that best represents the student's facial orientation to the object. On the same face symbol, place an additional check mark near the appropriate arrow if the student rotates his or her head as well (i.e., moves the head in such a way as to bring one ear close to the shoulder on the same side). Finally, circle the arrow that best represents whether the student's head is neutral, or whether the chin is elevated (i.e., head/neck extended) or flexed.

In C, place a check mark under the face symbol that best represents the position of the student's eyes as he or she attempts to locate the object visually.

objects placed on one half of the work surface that would not require movement across midline. However, this same student may have multiple visual disabilities that require that he or she be permitted to turn and lower his or her head to better view the work surface. The use of trunk restraints may prevent the individual from using naturally occurring compensatory postural adjustments that permit maximum use of visual abilities. For this student, completion of the assessment, both with and without upper trunk restraints, permits the team to use empirical data to design an individualized presentation area on the work surface. A sample outcome of this decision-making process would be that, for those tasks that require the most precise visual and visual–motor skills, the trunk restraint would be loosened to permit the student to hold his or her upper trunk and head in a particular way to regard the work surface. However, to avoid promoting increased tone, the objects would be positioned to only one lateral side of the trunk.

Although this measure is highly reliable, the form used to record the data is somewhat complicated. Service providers who are somewhat unfamiliar with data collection procedures should practice this procedure on a friend or colleague prior to attempting the measure in a classroom context.

Binocular Vision

Strabismus, the most common cause of decreased binocularity, may occur for a number of reasons. It results in an inability to use both eyes together to produce a single, clear image with all of the qualities related to the perception of depth. In addition to depth perception, binocular vision also provides an extensive visual field (approximately 180 degrees), and the images transmitted by both eyes compensate for the naturally occurring blind spot that results at the point where the head of the optic nerve is located at the back of each eye. The structure of the human visual system is such that uncorrected strabismus may result in a condition termed *amblyopia ex anopsia.* This condition occurs when the central nervous system suppresses the messages that arise from the deviating eye (or the eye producing the less clear image), because images that are too dissimilar cannot be fused into a single clear image. Over time, the vision in the eye that produces the less clear image diminishes.

Although the lack of binocular vision may not be a particularly severe visual impairment for persons without other disabilities, the implications of this type of vision loss in a person who also has significant dysfunction in posture and movement are much more significant. In the event that amblyopia develops, an individual with strabismus must essentially function with only one eye. Individuals without additional disabilities may learn to compensate for this condition by learning scanning strategies that compensate for the reduced visual field. However, the individual who lacks head control and is positioned in a wheelchair or other form of adapted equipment that limits the head position to midline orientation only, may be limited to approximately half of the expected visual field and may be unaware of peers or adults approaching from one lateral side of the body. This same individual may also be able to access visually only one half of the work surface, wheelchair tray, or play area in front of him or her. Finally, when positioned in side-lying, this individual may have the "good" eye buried in the supporting surface of the equipment (e.g., side-lyer, pillows), and may respond poorly to toys, instructional materials, or people who are in proximity to the individual in this position. Clearly, it is important for service providers to understand the implications of strabismus and make the adaptations necessary to enable these individuals to benefit from visual input.

Information regarding the presence of strabismus is available from two sources: an individual's medical records and functional vision assessment. Poor performance on one or both of the visual–motor measures described earlier may suggest that an individual lacks binocular vision. Information may also be obtained from two additional assessment measures. The first is termed the Cover Test. This test is designed to be carried out in a tightly controlled situation and requires the use of high-preference materials. The procedures for conducting the Cover Test are found in Table 6.2. A data sheet that can be used to record the outcomes of the assessment is found in Figure 6.3.

The second measure designed to provide information regarding the presence of binocular vision is termed Accomodative Convergence. This measure requires that a service provider position a high-preference object approximately 18 inches from the individual's face at midline and nose-tip level. An attempt is made to have the individual orient to the object, and localize or fixate on the object. The object is then moved toward the individual's face slowly enough to be nonthreatening, but quickly enough to promote continued fixation. At some point, the student's visual fixation will shift away from the object. The service provider should record the distance from the individual's face at which fixation ceases, and also describe if the individual turns his or her head laterally to watch the object approach with one eye, shuts his or her eyes, pushes the object out of the way, or blinks. Another possibility is that the individual will regard the object until a certain point (measured in inches), and then one or both eyes will roll laterally to either the nose or temple.

The measure is repeated at least five times over several days. If the individual stops looking at the approaching object at the same point during the majority of the trials, the service provider can infer that objects should not be presented closer than that distance if optimal visual regard is to occur. Additional behaviors to be recorded include whether one or both eyes con-

TABLE 6.2. Procedures for Conducting the Cover Test

Purpose: To permit determination of a student's eye preference.

Materials:
1. Hand-held occluder or unlined index card
2. Preferred object

Steps:
1. With your nondominant hand, position a preferred object at the student's midline and level with the tip of his or her nose. The object should be held 12–16 inches from the student's face.
2. Attempt to gain the student's fixation on the object. Shake or tap the object if necessary. It is acceptable for the student to hold the object jointly with you as long as the object is not moved from the position described in Step 1.
3. Immediately following fixation, introduce the occluder in front of one of the student's eyes as indicated on the data sheet (Figure 6.3). The occluder should be no more than 3–4 inches in front of the student's eye.
4. *Simultaneous* with occlusion of the designated eye, observe the other eye for a rolling movement. You may also observe a number of other, more overt student responses.
5. Repeat Steps 1–4 for the number of trials indicated on the data sheet. Please note the random order in which one eye is occluded.

Student Response:

The student may engage in any or all of the following responses:
1. The *unoccluded* eye may roll in any direction. A rolling movement may indicate that binocular vision is weak and that the *occluded* eye is dominant. In this case, blocking the view of the preferred object by the dominant eye disrupts the coordinated use of both eyes together.
2. The student may simply move his or her head around the occluder to maintain his or her view of the object. This response may (or may not) have the same implications as Item 1 above.
3. The student may push the occluder out of his or her line of sight. This response also may (or may not) have the same implications as Item 1 above.
4. The student may not respond following introduction of the occluder. This may mean that the *unoccluded* eye is dominant.

There is no ''correct'' response to introduction of the occluder. What may occur, however, is a particular pattern of student responses that differ as a function of which eye is occluded. Such a pattern *may* indicate the student's visual functioning is essentially monocular.

---

verge (i.e., roll nasally) as the object approaches, and whether the pupils constrict (i.e., become smaller) as the object approaches. Both convergence and pupillary constriction are observable behaviors that suggest that the individual's accommodative system is functioning to at least some degree.

Accommodation is that feature of the visual system that permits objects of different sizes, presented at different distances, to be viewed clearly. Although accommodation occurs primarily through changes in the shape or thickness of the lens of the eye (which is not externally observable), changes in accommodation to near objects is also accompanied by convergence and pupillary constriction. These data are important, as accommodation to near

Student: _____

Directions: Place a check mark in the column that best describes the student's response. If the student fails to respond to introduction of the occluder, place a check mark under the column titled "No Response." Check marks recorded in the "No Response" column are not counted when summing the total number of student responses.

Student Response

Occlude Observe	Unoccluded Eye Rolls	Head moves to avoid introduction of the occluder	Occluder is pushed out of line of sight	Other	No Response
1. R L					
2. L R					
3. R L					
4. R L					
5. L R					
6. R L					
7. L R					
8. L R					
9. R L					
10. L R					

Total Student Responses to occlusion of the:

    Right Eye (Trials 1, 3, 4, 6, & 9) _____ (If 4 or more responses are recorded, right eye may be dominant).

    Left Eye (Trials 2, 5, 7, 8, & 10) _____ (If 4 or more responses are recorded, left eye may be dominant).

Figure 6.3. Data sheet used to record the outcomes of the Cover Test.

objects is necessary for an object to be viewed clearly. Although changes that occur during accomodation are structural, the stimulus for accommodation to occur is cognitive. Changes in the accommodative system occur in response to a shift in concentration or attention to a particular object. For this reason, it is important to use high-preference objects to conduct this assessment *and* to present programming (with accompanying instructional materials) that is meaningful for the individual. A data sheet to record Accommodative Convergence is found in Figure 6.4.

Peripheral Visual Field

A complete description of visual fields includes an individual's ability to regard objects that are located (a) centrally (i.e., more or less at midline and at arm's reach), (b) above eye level (i.e., superior field), (c) below eye level (i.e., inferior field), and (d) to either side (i.e., lateral fields). The localization acuity measure described earlier provides a measure of central field, in addition to information regarding an individual's ability to use detail vision. In fact, poor performance on this early measure is often related to impairments in the central field in addition to, or in lieu of, a problem with detail vision.

	Distance (in inches) at which student ceases to regard object	Student Response (see code)	Accommodation (Place a check mark if the response occurs)	
			Convergence	Pupillary Constriction
Trial 1		A B C D Comments _____		
Trial 2		A B C D Comments _____		
Trial 3		A B C D Comments _____		
Trial 4		A B C D Comments _____		
Trial 5		A B C D Comments _____		

Code for Student Response:
A — Student's eyes close
B — One eye rolls nasally or temporally (indicate which eye and direction of deviation)
C — Student turns head to watch object approach with one eye (indicate which eye was used)
D — Other _____

Figure 6.4. Data sheet used to record assessment of Accommodative Convergence.

Measurements of peripheral fields are most functional when undertaken in natural contexts. An individual's ability to respond to both *static* stimuli (those that are not moving) and *dynamic* (moving) stimuli should be examined. Assessment should be carried out in an individualized fashion across a range of classroom and community environments. For example, measurement of an individual's peripheral visual responses may be taken in a kitchen during home living class. The environmental stimuli might include cabinets that overhang the sink area (a functional measure of superior field), a waste receptacle (a measure of inferior field), and an aisle between the table and counter (a measure of lateral fields).

Measures of peripheral field are not, however, limited to those individuals who are ambulatory. Even individuals who are not yet independent in wheelchair mobility may be assessed and receive intervention on the functional use of peripheral vision. This is done through implementation of the partial participation principle described earlier. For example, a service provider may combine responses from three areas of development within a natural routine: (1) communication, (2) sensory skills, and (3) orientation and mobility. A sample set of responses might consist of the following:

1. The service provider indicates to the individual that movement to the sink area in the kitchen is about to occur. A pause is provided for the individual to acknowledge the initiation in some way (e.g., through grasping an object cue that serves as a three-dimensional symbol for the activity).

2. The service provider requests that the individual orient his or her head in the direction of the sink (i.e., demonstration of an early orientation skill).

3. On their way to the sink, the service provider begins to direct the individual's wheelchair too close to a table on one side of the table–counter aisle. The service provider observes the individual closely for an indication that he or she is aware of the objects in the lateral field. If the individual exhibits awareness, the service provider praises the individual and records the functional use of information regarding the lateral visual field. If no awareness is observed, the service provider may pause and ask questions such as "Am I going the right way? What do you need? Help?"

For many individuals with profound disabilities, long histories of passive treatment by caregivers may have prevented the development of the functional use of peripheral vision. For these individuals, it may be necessary to present multiple opportunities for visual stimuli to be perceived as meaningful before assessment in this area becomes valid (i.e., to permit determination of whether the individual lacks sufficient peripheral vision or whether the person is simply unresponsive to visual stimuli). The fact that assessment is done in the same way as intervention (i.e., in the context of naturally occurring routines and as part of commonsense sequences of basic skills) makes this task less problematic.

Basic Visual Processes

As mentioned earlier, the assessment and intervention model described is organized in a test-down fashion. For this reason, assessment on the most basic visual skills is delayed until a service provider determines that an individual has done poorly on all earlier measures and questions whether the individual is able to benefit from even the most salient visual input. At this point, two simple measures are completed: pupillary constriction and the blink reflex. Completing these measures is also appropriate for those students who have seizure activity and/or a shunt to control hydrocephalus. For learners who have these medical conditions, service providers need to know each individual's particular visual characteristics. These data serve as baseline measures of pupillary functioning and provide a reference point for assessing medical complications that may arise.

Pupillary constriction is assessed through precise observation of the change in pupil size that occurs in response to rapid and dramatic changes of illumination in the environment. To assess pupillary constriction, the service provider should be positioned in such a way that he or she can observe a learner's eyes (i.e., be within 12–18 inches of the student, and on the same "plane"). The immediate environment should be dimly lit. The service provider should activate a large and bright light source (e.g., a table lamp, window shade, or overhead light) and watch for a sudden decrease in the size of the learner's pupils. The change in size should occur within 1–3 seconds of the change in illumination. The service provider should conduct this assessment several times over the course of a few days to see if the changes that occur (or fail to occur) are consistent. It is also helpful to observe the pupil size of other people in the environment under the same illumination levels to determine their initial pupil size. Again, this may serve as a baseline measure against which the pupil size of the learner to be assessed is evaluated. Eye color may determine, at least in part, the typical pupil size for learners in a variety of environments (e.g., individuals with blue eyes may have a somewhat different pupil size than someone with brown eyes under the same lighting conditions). For this reason, when determining a standard for assessing "normal" pupil size, select a person whose eye color is the same as that of the learner being assessed.

Failure of the pupils to constrict may suggest reduced capacity to respond to visual input. Unequal constriction in the two eyes may suggest asymmetrical vision. In the latter situation, if these data are similar to those obtained in the Cover Test (i.e., the least favored eye constricts less) and in Accommodative Convergence (i.e., the head turns to regard the approaching object with only one eye), modifications may be warranted in materials presentation, approaching of the individual for social interaction, and overall body positioning for instruction.

The blink reflex occurs in response to various stimuli, including loud noises, the sudden passage of air over the cornea of the eye, and the approach of a "threatening" target. To assess the blink reflex, the service provider may move his or her hand toward the face of the individual with the fingers apart to minimize the airflow. The movement must stop approximately 4 inches from the individual's face. Those students who may be frightened by this procedure, or who may have an adverse reaction in terms of muscle tone, may be positioned in supported supine (i.e., back-lying), and the service provider's hand may be introduced from one lateral side in a slow-moving arc over the individual's face at a height of approximately 4 inches. The implications of a failure to blink are twofold. The first implication is similar to the outcomes of failure to demonstrate pupillary constriction (i.e., the person may have diminished visual capacity in one or both eyes). The second implication is that the individual may be receiving inadequate cleansing and lubrication of the eye, which is one of the functions of blinking. A persistent failure to blink upon presentation of a threatening stimulus should be followed by a simple measure of the individual's blink rate when he or she is involved in a task or at rest. Failure to achieve a blink rate equal to or greater than two blinks per minute is a reason to pursue the opinion of a medical professional regarding the need for artificial lubrication of the eyes.

FUNCTIONAL ASSESSMENT AND INTERVENTION FOR AUDITION

Assessment of audition is much more complicated than assessment of vision because visual behaviors are more observable to service providers. Two service providers can observe the visual behaviors of an individual and determine, with a high degree of agreement, that the individual is looking at a particular person or object, as well as whether one or both eyes are being used. Measures of convergence and eye movements are also highly reliable. In contrast, functional measures of audition for individuals without expressive language, and whose receptive language status is unknown, present a challenge to service providers and medical professionals. Observable responses to sound stimuli are limited to a *localization response,* in which an individual turns his or her head and looks in the direction of a sound source presented to one lateral side of the body, or a variety of other behaviors, such as eye widening, an increase or decrease in activity level, or a startle. Although these responses are helpful to determine whether the individual responds to some sound stimuli, these responses are often observed in the presence of sound stimuli whose spectral characteristics (i.e., the range and number of sound frequencies that are generated within a particular sound source) and intensities are unknown. Additionally, it is difficult for service providers to determine *interaural differences* (i.e., whether hearing levels are approximately equal in both ears) because sounds greater than approximately 60 dB presented to one lateral half of the head may travel through the skull to be detected by the ear on the opposite side of the head.

Auditory assessment requires the expertise of professionals who typically are not represented on teams that serve students with profound disabilities. For this reason, the reader is encouraged to review background information regarding auditory assessment, including descriptions of ear structures and the processes that comprise audition (Cleeland, 1984; Kenworthy, 1982; Sobsey & Wolf-Schein, 1991).

Auditory assessment procedures are typically organized into those termed *objective* (i.e., tests that measure involuntary responses to acoustic stimuli and that can be conducted without active involvement of the student) and those termed *behavioral* (i.e., tests that measure overt responses to sound stimuli). As described earlier, an individualized profile of a person's ability to respond to specific sound frequencies at a range of intensities is necessary to determine whether speech is the preferred input mode. This information is also necessary to determine what adjustments are required for those students who will benefit from amplification should a hearing loss be detected. An individualized profile of a person's hearing (including differences in hearing between the two ears) can be developed only in the environment of a soundproof booth, in which precise control over the presentation of sound stimuli at various frequencies and intensities can be implemented. This test must be administered with headphones for the results to be the most meaningful, as this arrangement permits the presentation of sound stimuli to be isolated to one ear at a time. For these reasons, it is imperative that students who fail to show consistent responses to sound stimuli be prepared to participate in formal behavioral testing so that team members can act with confidence in the selection of a communication system for that student.

This section is devoted to three components of classroom-based hearing assessment procedures. The first component is a simple method of conducting a classroom-based screening to determine a student's responses to the presentation of a range of functional, meaningful sound sources. The second component is a description of procedures that may be coordinated through other team members (e.g., a speech-language pathologist, an audiologist, the school nurse). The third component is a classroom-based approach to preparing a student to participate in more formal hearing evaluations (Goetz, Utley, Gee, Baldwin, & Sailor, 1979).

Classroom-Based Informal Screening

The screening measure described in this section is intended for use with those students who are nonverbal and do not yet demonstrate sufficient receptive language (e.g., consistent direction following) to provide evidence that they can hear. The first step required to implement this procedure is to select a set of common, functional objects that generate sound. The service provider presents these objects to both lateral sides of the student's body (and out of view), while carefully observing the student's responses to those sound sources in the first few seconds that immediately follow presentation. The objects that are selected and the location of observation should be meaningful to the student and be contextually correct.

Sample sound sources include a variety of musical instruments (e.g., maracas, a triangle, a drum) that may be presented within the context of music class; the sounds of stacking plates and/or cutlery being placed on a tabletop or cafeteria tray in the lunchroom; and the sounds of balls bouncing and/or the coach's whistle being blown on the soccer field or in the gym. The sound sources should be positioned in such a way that the student being assessed has no visual cue that indicates when presentation is about to occur. Functionally, this means that the sound source should be activated to one lateral half of the student's body, just slightly to the posterior of the student's ear. Presentation to a particular lateral side of the body should be randomized on successive trials so the student does not learn to anticipate where a particular sound source may originate. In addition, presentation to a lateral side of the body and to the posterior of the student's ear will prevent peripheral visual cues from being used to determine the presentation of the sound source.

Because it is necessary to present sound stimuli out of the student's view, it is sometimes difficult for a service provider to both activate the sound source and observe the student for a response. For this reason, it may be helpful for the service provider to coordinate this assessment with other adults in the environment (e.g., the gym and music teachers) or enlist the aid of a peer, parent, or volunteer to provide assistance during the assessment. The assistant can present the sound source or indicate to the service provider when contextual presentation is about to occur.

As mentioned earlier, a range of possible responses may occur immediately following presentation of the sound source that suggest that the student heard the sound. These responses are listed in Figure 6.5 on a completed, sample data sheet.

This screening procedure should be completed in multiple environments with a range of meaningful sound sources over several days. Assessment should be conducted only when the student is free from any indications of an upper respiratory infection (this may produce fluid in the middle ear and temporarily suppress hearing acuity). Also, the external ear should be examined and determined to be clean (i.e., the ear canal should be free of cerumen or "earwax").

Name ___Taylor S.___   Date ___12/17/93___

	Right or Left Side	Sound Stimulus	Student Response(s)					
			Eye blink or movement	Localization	Change in Activity	Change in Expression	Other	No Response
1.	R	Maracas			√			
2.	L	Triangle	√					
3.	L	Drum					√ startle	
4.	R	Peers Singing		√				
5.	L	Piano	√					
6.	R	Drum			√			
7.	R	Peers Singing		√				
8.	L	Maracas			√			
9.	R	Drum			√			
10.	L	Piano	√					
TOTALS			3	2	4	0	1	0

Total trials on which responses to sound were observed 10
Total responses to right side 5 to left side 5

Comments: _Taylor seemed most interested in locating her peers during the chorus time._

Figure 6.5. Sample completed data sheet that may be used to collect auditory data from classroom-based informal screening.

Coordination of Assessment Through Team Participation

A number of procedures may be accomplished through the expertise of parents or other team members that may provide helpful information regarding the likelihood that a student can hear. Some of these procedures may be conducted in the school setting, and others must be conducted in medical settings. All of these procedures are considered objective tests. As discussed earlier, the use of objective hearing tests involves measurement of involuntary responses to acoustic stimuli, and can be conducted without active participation on the part of the student being tested.

One procedure, termed *impedance audiometry,* is designed to measure the capability of the peripheral auditory system to transmit sound to the inner ear. Impedance audiometry does not permit a team to determine a student's response to particular sound frequencies and/or intensities; therefore, it is not helpful for recommending and/or fitting amplification. The procedures may be useful for students with profound disabilities, however, because they can be conducted without active participation on the part of the student. In addition, they are particularly useful for detecting conductive losses that may be amenable to medical and/or surgical intervention.

Impedance audiometry consists of three separate tests that rely on the use of an *electroacoustic bridge.* The bridge consists of a headset with an earphone for one ear (through which sound is delivered) and a probe from which measurements are obtained from the other ear. This assessment comprises the following three subtests:

1. *Tympanometry:* In this subtest, the relative mobility and integrity of the eardrum (tympanic membrane) is assessed. Excessive stiffness or looseness in the eardrum may have a direct effect on the transmission of sound waves to the middle ear. The results of this test are charted on a graph called a *tympanogram* (Goetz et al., 1979). The graphs produced as a result of a tympanogram adhere to one of several particular curves, or may be flat. The graphs are interpreted to reflect specific disorders in the peripheral auditory system. A tympanogram can be conducted and interpreted by an audiologist, speech-language pathologist, or pediatrician. If indicated, these individuals can make the appropriate referral for follow-up. For those situations in which the team may not include an audiologist, a parent can request that a child's pediatrician conduct the procedure as part of a routine office visit.

2. *Static Compliance:* This subtest also permits assessment of the mobility of the middle ear system, but does so in the absence of a sound source. As with tympanometry, the purpose of this measure is to detect abnormal stiffness in the peripheral auditory system that may indicate a particular pathology. The outcomes of this procedure are complicated by the fact that there is a broad range of what is considered normal, which limits the use of this procedure if conducted as a single subtest.

3. *Acoustic Reflex Threshold:* This subtest evaluates the hearing level at which the protective mechanism in the middle ear, termed the *acoustic reflex,* is activated. Activation of this reflex occurs in response to loud sounds (typically equal to or greater than 90 dB). Activation of this reflex results in the rotation of the stapes (one of the sound-conductive bones in the middle ear) away from the oval window and the pulling in of the eardrum. These actions prevent transmission of sound sources that are dangerously loud from being transmitted to the inner ear. The presence of the reflex indicates that the student heard the sound, as the occurrence of the reflex is mediated by the perception of loudness (Goetz et al., 1979).

The results of any one of the three subtests, when used alone, have relatively little validity. However, when the results of all three are considered together, a substantial amount of information can be obtained. Although the use of these procedures requires only that an individual remain quiet for a brief period of time, and permit that a probe be inserted in the ear for less than a 1-minute period, these measures are rarely used to provide even preliminary information to team members and parents regarding the presence (or absence) of hearing in a particular student. Although these measures are insufficient to allow determination of specific frequencies or intensities that may constitute a particular student's degree of hearing, they may be considered a starting point to guide decision making regarding the potential availability of hearing as a sensory input mode.

A final objective hearing test that may be coordinated through the team is brainstem evoked response audiometry (BSER). The use of BSER permits measurement of changes that occur in electrical brain wave activity in response to the presentation of controlled auditory stimuli, typically a series of "clicks." The use of this test requires that a student lie motionless for approximately 30 minutes, and tolerate the attachment of electrodes to the scalp. Students who are incapable of demonstrating this level of willing cooperation may be given a drug that makes them sleepy, or receive a general anesthetic. There are several drawbacks to the use of BSER, including (a) the expense of administering the procedure, (b) the limited availability of the equipment and expertise to conduct and interpret the procedure, and (c) a slight degree of risk from the use of an anesthetic. Nonetheless, the use of this procedure may provide information to service providers and parents regarding the availability of hearing as an input mode for a particular student.

Classroom-Based Preparation for Formal Testing

A third component to assessment of hearing for students with profound disabilities is to prepare them for participation in a more formal behavioral hearing test, in which overt behavioral responses to auditory stimuli are used.

The reader is encouraged to obtain a copy of the manual titled *Auditory Assessment and Programming for Severely Handicapped and Deaf–Blind Students* (Goetz et al., 1979) for detailed information on two procedures that may be used for this purpose. The manual is available from the headquarters of The Association for Persons with Severe Handicaps in Seattle, Washington. Although this manual was developed over a decade ago, it remains a useful source of step-by-step information to prepare students for participation in behavioral testing.

Two procedures described in the manual are used to prepare students for participation in behavioral testing. Both procedures rely on sophisticated strategies that systematically transfer control of a selected student response from a light stimulus to a sound stimulus. The procedures are based on the work of Touchette (1971) and others who perfected stimulus control transfer techniques with students who demonstrate a range of abilities. Although these procedures are time-consuming (e.g., a student may require up to 4 months to acquire the discrimination that is required), the data obtained from implementation of these procedures is invaluable in making one of the most important decisions that a team will ever confront: selection of a communication system that either does or does not depend upon sound as an input mode.

The first of the two procedures (*visually reinforced localization*) requires only that a student be able to turn his or her head slightly from side to side, and that there be light projection available. The second program (*operant motor response*) requires a reach and touch response and some detail vision (i.e., the ability to locate an object visually on a work surface, as well as the ability to reach and touch that object). The use of either of these two procedures permits a student to participate in formal audiometric testing, as the equipment used is completely portable and can be transported to the soundproof booth used by a pediatric audiologist. The level of discrimination can be reestablished in that setting, followed by use of the precise frequencies and intensities that enable the audiologist to determine the exact degree of hearing loss that may be present. These data can then be used as the basis to recommend or withhold amplification, and to fit hearing aids in an individualized manner.

The outcomes of formal testing may suggest whether a particular student has a hearing loss, as well as whether that student might benefit from amplification. Regardless of these outcomes, it becomes necessary to conduct follow-up to ensure that the student is able to respond functionally to a range of meaningful sound stimuli in school and nonschool environments. To do so requires that a number of meaningful sound sources be identified and that these sources be integrated into ongoing functional activities. Some examples include the use of the student's name and other meaningful verbalizations; stimuli that signal the beginning and end of class periods (e.g., bells or other tones broadcast within a school building at predetermined intervals throughout the school day); and other sounds that are associated with meaningful activities, such as the voices of other children at recess, desks closing, or chairs being moved across the floor to communicate the beginning or end of an activity. These sounds should become the cues that are paired with other antecedent stimuli within a student's communication system that can be used to set the occasion for a student to make a particular response.

For example, a program might be designed for a student that requires that he or she move from a back-lying to a side-lying position as the first step to meet a mobility goal. This program might begin with the adult or peer calling the student's name to one lateral side of the student's head (e.g., "Larry, look over here"). A brief latency period would likely follow this cue. If the student failed to respond to the initial statement, the phrase might be repeated with an additional auditory cue (e.g., tapping the floor, clapping hands) and/or visual cue (e.g., waving or gesturing to move in the desired direction). After the student turned his head in the desired direction, the teacher and/or peer might say, "Hi Larry, roll over so we can play the xylophone," as the physical prompts to initiate the rolling movement were presented. After Larry engaged in the appropriate level of response on the rolling movement, a number of additional responses might be prompted to occur, such as reaching and touching the xylophone mallet, visually locating the xylophone, and using a visually directed reach to activate the xylophone. Social skills (e.g., shaking hands) might also occur in this instructional context. Progress though the sequence of skills in the task would be dependent upon Larry's response to the specific auditory stimuli that were presented within the sequence. Initially it might be necessary to gently guide Larry's head to the left or right in response to calling his name, with fading of the prompt occurring over time. Additional examples of functional localization can be found in Goetz et al. (1979).

ASSESSMENT AND INTERVENTION FOR DISORDERS IN POSTURE AND MOVEMENT

Many students with profound disabilities exhibit significant disorders in posture and movement. The nature of these disorders is such that assessment and intervention requires careful coordination between multiple team members. The initial forms of assessment that serve as the basis for the design of instruction are specific to the disciplines of occupational and physical therapy. To a somewhat lesser degree, the discipline of speech–language pathology is involved. These discipline-specific assessments consist of measures of *muscle tone* (i.e., the degree of stiffness in the muscles); *range of motion* (i.e., the ability to move parts of the body through a series of movements around the joints); the presence or absence of *reflex activity* (i.e., whether primitive or abnormal reflexes exist that may require that particular orientations in space be promoted for maximum function); and the extent to which a student has acquired the *motor milestones* that are typical for his or her chronological age. This background information serves as the basis for the contributions that these team members may make to the development of the student's overall educational program.

After these discipline-specific assessments are completed, an additional series of measures may be made, in conjunction with teachers and parents, to determine what specific aspects of the professional roles of related service providers may be needed to support the student's educational program (e.g., equipment design and adaptations; "hands-on" contact to reduce deformity, discomfort, or pain; etc.). The most important of these measures is participation of related service providers in the ecological inventory process during which therapists may evaluate the need for appropriate seating, mobility goals, equipment adaptations, or specific hands-on strategies to maximize the student's abilities in each of the subenvironments and activities in which the student participates during the school day (see Chapter 10). Following these measures, the team must decide which of the various related service functions (e.g., equipment adaptations) are needed to enhance the student's ability to benefit from special education. Additionally, decisions can be made regarding whether those functions may be provided indirectly or directly. As stated earlier, although a particular student may receive primarily indirect service from a particular discipline (e.g., consultative services), that related service representative needs to maintain at least limited hands-on contact for the purposes of program evaluation and problem solving. In addition, continued involvement is necessary in the event that a particular adaptation or strategy fails to achieve the desired outcome.

Although related service recommendations must be individualized for each student, some guidelines may assist team members to better serve students with disorders in posture and movement. These guidelines may help team members improve the health and comfort of the students they serve, as well as maximize participation of these students in functional activities. In the following sections, these guidelines are divided into those addressing therapeutic positioning and those addressing handling.

Therapeutic Positioning

The term *therapeutic positioning* refers to the overall body position used to promote maximum student participation in a particular activity, the position of instructional materials used in the activity, and the position of peers and adults during the activity. The most frequent overall body positions include sitting, standing (accomplished for many students through the use of adapted equipment, such as a prone stander), and three positions on the floor or other horizontal surface including side-lying, back-lying (i.e., supine), and stomach-lying (i.e., prone).

The first and foremost recommendation regarding the selection of an overall body position is that the position selected for the student be matched with the task to be performed. As the team designs adaptations that are likely to enhance a student's ability to participate in most forms of independent activity, three aspects of positioning should be considered: (1) the position selected should reflect the practical and movement demands of the task, (2) the body must be balanced in the position, and (3) the coordinated movement required to perform the task must be possible in that position (Rainforth & York, 1991).

Of equal importance is sensitivity to the social implications of selecting a particular position. For example, although there may be a compelling reason to use a floor sitter that promotes proper hip formation for a particular student, the use of the floor sitter should be reserved for those times of the school day during which peers who are nondisabled also sit on the floor (e.g., library, story time, free play). The social implications of having a student with a physical disorder positioned on a different plane from his or her peers may not only create an unnecessary emphasis on "differences," but also reduce the opportunities for social interaction that may otherwise occur more readily if students were in greater plane proximity to one another. A general guideline for participation in an activity is for students with disabilities to be positioned in ways that are the most similar to those of their peers who are not disabled. Ideas include having the student stand for doing dishes or other activities of daily living, sit for periods of instruction, and adopt a variety of floor positions (e.g., prone over a wedge) for more casual activities during the day. The medical implications of positioning—that is, the prevention of pain and/or the reduction of deformity—mandate that the team jointly determine each student's daily schedule to ensure that the student's therapeutic needs are met regardless of setting.

A final consideration in overall body positioning is that a particular position that is selected for therapeutic reasons not contradict another educational need for that same student. For example, it may be necessary for a particular student to spend time in side-lying to help ameliorate difficulties in breathing due to excessive tightness of the chest muscles. That same student may also have a significant degree of strabismus that has resulted in the student's being able to use only one eye functionally. Care must be taken to schedule side-lying in such a way that either the side selected for weight bearing does not result in the good eye's being "buried" in the side-lyer, or that this position be used at those times during which the demands on the student for use of vision are at a minimum (e.g., music appreciation). Another example concerns the frequent use of adapted seating that includes straps, cushions, or harnesses that hold the trunk in an exaggerated upright posture. Although important for therapeutic reasons, this position may limit the ability of a student with a visual impairment from adjusting his or her posture to regard an object of interest more closely. Joint assessment and scheduling by multiple team members is necessary so that therapeutic positioning supports, not restricts, a student's ability to participate fully in an instructional activity.

A second positioning consideration is that instructional materials be positioned in ways that enable the student to access those materials both visually and physically. As described above, the team must schedule instruction in ways that permit that all of a student's needs be met over the course of the school day. For example, students who may lack complete head control may be transported in an adapted wheelchair with the seat-in-space angle tilted so the student is in a semi-reclining position. Although this position may help stabilize the student's head during a bumpy bus ride, many service providers leave the wheelchair at this angle during school hours as well. Clearly, students positioned in this way may be able to view only the upper walls and ceiling in the rooms in which they spend their time. Although a particular student may not yet be able to hold his or her head in a full upright posture for significant periods of time, the team may design wheelchair adaptations (e.g., head and/or neck supports, a strap to be placed gently around the student's forehead) or recommend that external support (e.g., an adult or peer gently holding the student's head in the upright position) be used for those periods of the school day in which it is of particular importance that the student be able to view the blackboard, the teacher, or other relevant classroom or instructional materials.

An additional team consideration regarding the position of materials is the design and position of the wheelchair tray, which should enable the student to view and touch materials related to a particular task. For example, a wheelchair tray or other adaptation (e.g., a small wooden easel to be placed on the tray) could be devised so that the plane of presentation is at a 30- to 45-degree angle to the student's trunk, as opposed to being horizontal and parallel to the student's lap. A student may also benefit from having the location of a set of instructional materials shifted to one lateral half of the body (i.e., to either the left or the right side of midline). This is appropriate for those students who may not be able to see a display that extends across both sides of midline and/or who may not be able to reach the full display if it extends to both sides of midline.

The third and final consideration for therapeutic positioning is the relative location of peers and adults during interaction and instruction. Students who lack a full field of vision and/or who lack full movement to both lateral sides of the body may benefit from being approached predominantly from one side. Of additional benefit is being positioned in a group in such a way that the more functional side of the body is oriented to the remainder of the class. Again, the appropriate side for a particular student can be determined through joint assessment of vision and movement by multiple team members working in partnership with one another. There will be some students whose need in a particular area (e.g., vision) contradicts a need in another area (e.g., movement), but this can be addressed through joint scheduling and thoughtful decision making regarding which area of need should be a priority during a particular activity. Finally, the adult, the student, and his or her peers should be on the same plane as much as possible to avoid having the student look up or down to obtain face-to-face regard. Such movement of the head up or down may produce unwanted reflex activity and/or an increase in abnormal muscle tone.

Handling

The term *handling* may be used to describe the techniques that are used to improve a particular student's disorders in posture and movement. Rainforth and York (1991) described the goals of handling as

1. To elicit more normal muscle tone.

2. To facilitate more upright positions with normal posture.

3. To facilitate normal movement patterns, including:
   a. Automatic movements that maintain balance.
   b. Locomotion for independent mobility.
   c. Arm and hand movements for task performance.
   d. Oral movements for eating and speech. (p. 83)

As with all other aspects of service provision for students with disorders in posture and movement, team members must confer with one another to make decisions jointly regarding which strategies are appropriate for individual students.

Service providers are encouraged to address three considerations in the design of handling procedures for students with profound disabilities: (1) the importance of integrating essential sensory skills (e.g., fixation, localization) into handling procedures designed to promote arm and hand movements; (2) sensitivity to the impact of "demand" situations; and (3) systematic fading of physical assistance as students begin to engage in more purposeful, goal-directed movement over time. Each of these considerations is discussed in more detail below.

Integration of essential sensory skills

Campbell (1987) defined essential skills as "simple forms of behavior which are important in and of themselves, but that also provide the basis for elaborated (and more complex) forms of behavior" (p. 163). For students with profound disabilities, many of whom fail to demonstrate the ability to act on their environments, it is important to develop task sequences that promote the use of available sensory skills, in the context of basic motor behaviors, to achieve environmental control. Careful assessment is critical to provide information to the team regarding whether binocular vision is present and, if only one eye has usable vision, what location in space should be used to implement strategies that may assist the student to acquire these important developmental milestones. Clearly, from a Piagetian framework, students labeled profoundly disabled are at the sensorimotor stage of development. Interventions for these students must incorporate elements of both sensory input and motor output.

Sensitivity to demand situations

Intervention for students with profound disabilities should reflect attention to two aspects of traditional demand situations that are often component parts of systematic instructional strategies. The first is the fact that traditional systematic instructional strategies, based on the principles and practices of applied behavior analysis, rely on the service provider to present an antecedent cue (e.g., "Roxanne, touch the toy"), followed by a brief latency period during which the student is expected to respond. Failure to respond may result in the service provider's employing a second component of systematic instruction: moving through a prompt hierarchy to help occasion the appropriate behavior (see Chapter 9). However, students with profound disabilities may be ill equipped to participate in traditional systematic instructional formats due to minimal levels of receptive language (which may preclude understanding of the direction), as well as undeveloped acquisition of cause–effect relationships. Additionally, some students with disorders in posture and movement show a reduced ability to engage in voluntary movement when placed in demand situations. Particular patterns of neurological disorder may compromise a student's ability to coordinate intentionality and movement.

For these reasons, many students may benefit from an *expanded antecedent event* (i.e., a set of stimuli that are presented *prior* to when the student is expected to respond). This expanded antecedent event consists of a full physical assist through the desired movement pattern after the appropriate sensory stimulus has been provided. The service provider also activates the consequent event, which has been selected for the student in the particular instructional context. Immediately after presentation of this expanded antecedent event, a more traditional form of antecedent stimulus is presented, during which the student is expected to make a small, but active response to the instructional situation. The expanded antecedent event described above may be thought of as an opportunity to "rehearse" or "practice" the desired movements while the service provider supplies the guidance to prevent errors. This strategy also permits the student to match the sensation of the movement with the verbal description of the movement (which reduces the demand nature of the situation), as well as to experience the temporal relationship of the antecedent, behavior, and consequence. This approach differs markedly from those situations in which adults *act on* children but do not expect children to act on their environments in return. An example of the expanded antecedent event (described as a "practice trial") is described more fully in Table 6.3 for a visually directed reach and grasp program. The data sheet for the program is show in Figure 6.6.

Fading physical assistance from handling procedures

The provision of expanded antecedent events as described above has many advantages, but has a disadvantage as well. This disadvantage is the possibility that a student will become dependent upon the full physical assistance and fail to make the transition to more goal-directed, voluntary movements over time. To lessen this possibility, three approaches to program design are recommended. These approaches may be described conceptually as *backward shaping procedures*. The procedures are technically termed shaping because only a single response is the target of instruction. The procedures are termed backward because the student is initially expected to engage in only the last segment of the response, with more and more of the response expected over time.

Backward shaping may occur along three dimensions: distance, time, and location of physical assistance. Distance-based instruction is appropriate for building those responses that involve movement in space. Examples include a reach response or movement from one location to another in a teaching and learning environment using a particular form of mobility (e.g., rolling, crawling). Distance-based instruction begins with a precise analysis of the movement, where it is broken down into steps ranging from as small as ½ inch (for a reaching program) to 1 foot (for a crawling program). The precise application of the handling procedures designed to assist the student make the movement response is described as well. This description may consist of preprogram procedures, such as relaxation or gentle pressure on the weight-bearing joints. Again, the appropriate sensory input mode is selected. Each opportunity to engage in the desired movement begins with presentation of the sensory cue, followed by the application of the designated

TABLE 6.3. Procedures for Testing Visually Directed Reach for Students who Are Nonambulatory with Limited or No Voluntary Arm Movement

Setting:

1. An area of the classroom with the learner facing away from the windows.
2. Normal light levels.
3. Student should be in his or her wheelchair or positioned in an upright or tilted position, with support as necessary.
4. Teacher should be positioned directly in front of the student, so that the student's eyes can be observed.

Materials:

1. Object that is large enough for the student to see (preferably, an object that the student enjoys).
2. Wheelchair tray, tabletop, etc., that can be used for presentation of the object. The surface can be flat or tilted depending on the degree of head control exhibited by the student. *NOTE:* It may be necessary to use a head strap to support the student's head if the surface supporting the object is flat, or to use Velcro to attach the object to the wheelchair tray if it is tilted.
3. Data sheet.

Steps:

1. Conduct one "practice trial" to familiarize the student with the expectations for his or her behavior, the movement pattern to be used, and the consequence for his or her attempt. The practice trial comprises the following:
   a. Attempt to gain the student's attention or facial orientation. Use a verbal cue (e.g., "Name" or "Ready") or other direction or command words usually used in the classroom to obtain attention. Gain the student's attention first on his or her right hand and then on the object to be touched.
   b. Present the object in front of the student at his or her arm's length and at midline unless previous assessment procedures have indicated otherwise.
   c. Request that the student reach for the object (e.g., "Arnold, touch the truck"). Use verbal and signed or tactile cues as appropriate.
   d. Physically guide the student through reaching and touching the object. *NOTE:* Provide the least amount of physical assistance necessary for the student to make contact with the object.
   e. Activate the object and provide verbal and/or signed approval.
   f. Immediately reposition the student's hand and/or arm and the object to be touched. The hand should be approximately 10 inches from the object. THIS COMPLETES THE PRACTICE TRIAL. NOW FOLLOW THE SAME PROCEDURES WITHOUT PROVIDING PHYSICAL ASSISTANCE AS OUTLINED IN STEPS 2 THROUGH 7.
2. Attempt to gain the student's attention or facial orientation. Use a verbal cue (e.g., "Name" or "Ready") or other direction or command words usually used in the classroom to obtain attention. Gain the student's attention first on his or her right hand and then on the object to be touched.
3. The object should be located approximately 10 inches from the student's hand.
4. Request that the student reach for the object (e.g., "Arnold, touch the truck"). Use verbal and signed or tactile cues as appropriate.
5. Allow a latency period of up to 3 seconds.
6. Observe and record the following (see Figure 6.6):
   • Voluntary arm movement (any observable movement)
   • Approximate distance of reach (in inches)
   • Contact with the object (yes or no)

(continued)

TABLE 6.3. *Continued*

- Fixation in the right eye (yes or no)
- Fixation in the left eye (yes or no)
- Fixation in both eyes (yes or no)
- Sustained fixation in one or both eyes if student does make a voluntary arm movement, whether or not the movement is sufficient to make contact with the object (yes or no)

7. Provide verbal and/or signed approval, activation of the object, and other forms of potential positive reinforcement for any movement, fixation, etc. Make the verbal approval descriptive (e.g., "Good, you looked! Next time touch the ball too!" "Great, you are really trying to touch that toy!").
8. Repeat Steps 2 through 7 for a total of five trials. Then repeat the entire procedure, beginning with the practice trial, requiring the student to use his or her left arm in an effort to measure left upper extremity movement and left eye movements.
9. Repeat the entire set of procedures on 3 separate days.

Response:

1. The series of responses to be recorded is outlined below, along with specific criteria for recording occurrence or nonoccurrence of each response.
   a. *Response:* Voluntary arm movement
      A plus mark is recorded if any movement in the target upper extremity is observed. The movement may be lateral or even in the opposite direction from the location of the object.
      OR
   b. *Response:* Approximate distance of reach
      A plus mark is recorded in the cell adjacent to the approximate number of inches moved.
      OR
   c. *Response:* Contact with the object
      A plus mark is recorded if the target upper extremity touches the object.
2. *Response:* Fixation in right eye
   A plus mark is recorded if the student regards the object with his or her right eye. A fleeting glance is acceptable. The student may adopt a particular head position during regard of the object. If so, describe the position in the space marked "comments."
3. *Response:* Fixation in left eye
   Repeat above, substituting *left* for right.
4. *Response:* Fixation in both eyes
   A plus mark is recorded if the student regards the object with both eyes simultaneously. For credit to be given on this item, both eyes must be in the same relative location (e.g., if the student is looking straight ahead, both eyes should be slightly to the nasal side).
5. *Response:* Sustained fixation
   A plus mark is recorded if the student sustains regard of the object as the movement is made.

Recording the Data:

1. Use the data sheet to record the data.
2. If the session is split into several time periods during the day, indicate that information on the data sheet. Time of day, changing light conditions, and hunger may have an effect on attention and the outcome of assessment.
3. If a noise or other event occurs in the classroom simultaneous with presentation of your cue to touch the object, repeat the trial.

Indicate which upper extremity is
being assessed: Left_____ Right_____ Date_____

Series of Responses	Trial 1	Trial 2	Trial 3	Trial 4	Trial 5	Totals
1a. Voluntary arm movement (any observable movement)						
or						
1b. Approximate distance of reach						
1-3"						
4-7"						
8-9"						
or						
1c. Contact with the object (10" of movement)						
2. Fixation: Right eye						
3. Fixation: Left eye						
4. Fixation: Both eyes						
5. Sustained fixation (fixation plus simultaneous movement)						

Comments:

Figure 6.6. Data sheet used to record student participation in a visually directed reach and grasp program.

handling procedures. The consequence is provided as well. The student is
then returned to the original starting position, the sensory cue is repeated,
and the handling procedures are again provided *but only to the point designated in the first step in the program.* For example, if the distance a particular student must move to access a toy or food item is 10 inches, the handling
procedure is applied to promote movement for the first 9½ inches. The student is expected to make the last ½-inch movement. This level of assistance

is provided for approximately 7–10 days, based on the assumption that the student may have about 15 opportunities per day to engage in this movement response in a variety of instructional contexts (e.g., free play, opening exercises, library, mealtime and other activities of daily living). The service provider systematically reduces the amount of the handling procedure that is applied to 9 inches, then 8½ inches, and so on. The program described in Table 6.3 is an example of a distance-based, backward shaping program.

The second dimension along which backward shaping may occur is time. Many of the goals for students with disorders in posture and movement consist of motor milestones, such as head-erect behavior, upright sitting, tall kneeling, and so on. Time-based motor milestones may be analyzed to reflect steps ranging from as short as 1 second to as long as 10 minutes. Again, the appropriate sensory stimulus is selected, the appropriate handling procedures to promote the particular milestone are determined and described, and the procedure is implemented in a backward fashion. For example, it may be decided that a student may benefit from an increased degree of head-erect behavior. The student may be unable to hold her head erect except for momentary periods of time at the beginning of the program. The team has decided that this particular student should learn to hold her head erect in supported sitting, because her chronological age and particular pattern of abnormal tone contraindicate working on head control in prone. The initial goal for the student is to hold her head erect for 10 seconds. The service provider selects the appropriate sensory stimulus (e.g., a computer station where the student will partially participate in playing a game with her peers) and provides the handling procedure designed to promote head-erect behavior (e.g., the service provider gently moves the student's head into upright, and strokes the back of the student's neck with the fingertips). The service provider, through gentle support at the base of the student's head, holds the student's head upright for 9 seconds. During this time, the student is encouraged to look at the screen while a peer takes a turn activating the game. The service provider says softly during the 9-second period, "Good Cheryl, you are holding up your head so you can see the game." The service provider then gradually removes the support after 9 seconds and says, "Cheryl, hold up your head yourself for a bit." If Cheryl maintains her head erect for the 1-second period, she is praised and the support is then reintroduced so she does not experience the discomfort of having her head fall to one side, the front, or the back. She then receives instruction on a visually directed reach and grasp program to take her turn at the game. It is important to note, however, that her head would be supported fully during this latter instructional procedure so she could work on her vision skills and arm movements, and not have to hold her head erect as well.

Finally, more traditional fading procedures (e.g., a most to least intrusive prompt hierarchy of physical assistance; see Chapter 9) may also be conceptualized as occurring in a backward shaping sequence. These procedures typically involve systematic removal of various forms of physical assistance, usually moving from providing full physical support of an upper extremity (or other body part) to progressively less support over time. A typical example is a gradual shift in the location of the service provider's hands (e.g., the service provider may support a student's arm fully during the initial stage of teaching, and then move support to the level of the student's wrist, then forearm, elbow, etc.). These strategies may, in fact, be combined with the other backward shaping procedures described above to best meet the needs of students with profound disabilities.

CONCLUSION

Students with profound disabilities often exhibit sensory impairments in addition to disorders in posture and movement. The combined impact of these disabilities requires assessment and intervention that address both areas of need. Careful teamwork is necessary to ensure that all needs are met, and that students' overall educational experiences reflect a balance between their sensory and their physical needs. A precise level of analysis is necessary for these students to acquire a foundation of essential skills. Only through attention to both sensory input and movement output can students with profound disabilities participate maximally in the full range of home, school, and community environments that is every student's birthright.

ACKNOWLEDGMENT

Development of much of the content of this chapter was supported by two grants awarded to the University of Pittsburgh from the Office of Special Education and Rehabilitative Services of the United States Department of Education. The first and primary source of support was Grant No. G00873039888, a nondirected demonstration project for children and youth with severe disabilities. The second source was Grant No. H086L00006, funded under the program related to the application of innovative practices. The information contained in this chapter does not necessarily reflect the views or policies of the Department of Education and no official endorsement by the Department should be inferred.

Assessment Overview

Section 1. Localization Acuity (Near Point)

Instructions: For this section, the teacher needs to occlude the student's vision for a few seconds while the preferred object is positioned. A suggested way to occlude the student's vision is to hold a record album, mirror, or magazine 3–4 inches in front of his or her face. Remember to inform the student that you will block his or her vision temporarily and introduce the occluder gradually.

1. Looks at preferred object presented on a horizontal plane (e.g., tabletop, desk, or wheelchair tray) at a distance of approximately 15 inches from his or her face and at midline.	__ Yes __ No __ Unsure Comments: _____ _____
2. Looks at preferred object presented on a horizontal plane (e.g., tabletop, desk, or wheelchair tray) at a distance of approximately 15 inches from his or her face and to the right of midline.	__ Yes __ No __ Unsure Comments: _____ _____
3. Looks at preferred object presented on a horizontal plane (e.g., tabletop, desk, or wheelchair tray) at a distance of approximately 15 inches from his or her face and to the left of midline.	__ Yes __ No __ Unsure Comments: _____ _____

Total: _____ Yes _____ No _____ Unsure

Follow-up: If any item is checked "no" or "unsure," conduct an in-depth assessment of the student's localization acuity.

(continued)

Appendix 6A (*continued*)

Section 2. Visual–Motor

1. Gaze shift	
a. Looks at a preferred object when presented with that object (placed to the left of midline) and another object (placed to the right of midline). Both objects should be located within arm's length.	a. __ Yes __ No __ Unsure Comments: _____ _____
b. Looks at preferred object when presented with that object (placed to the right of midline) and another object (placed to the left of midline). Both objects should be located within arm's length.	b. __ Yes __ No __ Unsure Comments: _____ _____
2. Tracking Watches an object or person located at a distance of 3–5 feet move laterally from one location to another.	__ Yes __ No __ Unsure Comments: _____ _____
3. Scanning Visually locates a preferred object among a display of objects.	__ Yes __ No __ Unsure Comments: _____ _____

(*continued*)

Appendix 6A (*continued*)

4a. Visually directed reach (independent) Watches an object as he or she reaches for that object. — — — — — or — — — — — 4b. Visually directed reach (partial participation) Watches an object as an adult physically assists him or her (partially or fully) to reach toward that object.	__ Yes __ No __ Unsure Comments: _____ _____
5a. Visually directed grasp (independent) Looks at an object as he or she picks it up. — — — — — or — — — — — 5b. Visually directed grasp (partial participation) Looks at an object as an adult physically assists him or her (partially or fully) to pick up that object.	__ Yes __ No __ Unsure Comments: _____ _____
6a. Visually directed transport (independent) Watches an object as he or she moves it through space. — — — — — or — — — — — 6b. Visually directed transport (partial participation) Watches an object as an adult physically assists him or her (partially or fully) to move that object through space.	__ Yes __ No __ Unsure Comments: _____ _____

(*continued*)

Appendix 6A (*continued*)

7a. Visually directed release (independent) Watches an object as he or she places it into a container. — — — — — or — — — — — 7b. Visually directed release (partial participation) Watches an object as an adult physically assists him or her (partially or fully) to place it into a container.	__ Yes __ No __ Unsure Comments: _____ _____

Total: __ Yes   __ No   __ Unsure

Follow-up: If the combined total of items checked "no" or "unsure" surpasses the total number of items checked "yes," conduct an in-depth assessment of the student's visual–motor behavior.

Section 3. Binocular Vision

1. Looks at preferred object within arm's length and at midline with head in a neutral position and both eyes oriented symmetrically.	__ Yes __ No __ Unsure Comments: _____ _____
2. Looks at preferred object presented within arm's length and left of midline with head in a neutral position and both eyes oriented symmetrically.	__ Yes __ No __ Unsure Comments: _____ _____
3. Looks at preferred object presented within arm's length and right of midline with head in a neutral position and both eyes oriented symmetrically.	__ Yes __ No __ Unsure Comments: _____ _____

(*continued*)

Appendix 6A (*continued*)

4. Looks at preferred object presented at midline as it is moved forward from a distance of 18 inches to within 8 inches of the face, with head in a neutral position and both eyes oriented symmetrically.	__ Yes __ No __ Unsure Comments: _____ _____

Total: __ Yes   __ No   __ Unsure

Follow-up: If any of the items are checked "no" or "unsure," conduct an in-depth assessment of the student's use of visual information from one or both eyes.

Section 4. Peripheral Visual Field

1. Looks at someone standing perpendicular to the right side at eye level and an appropriate social distance. (No auditory cues should be used.)	__ Yes __ No __ Unsure Comments: _____ _____
2. Looks at someone standing perpendicular to the left side at eye level and an appropriate social distance. (No auditory cues should be used.)	__ Yes __ No __ Unsure Comments: _____ _____
3.* Looks at an object (e.g., large ball, scooter, wastebasket) located on the floor approximately 3–4 feet from the lower extremities and to the right of midline.	__ Yes __ No __ Unsure Comments: _____ _____
4.* Looks at an object (e.g., large ball, scooter, wastebasket) located on the floor approximately 3–4 feet from the lower extremities and to the left of midline.	__ Yes __ No __ Unsure Comments: _____ _____

*Note: The student should be seated in an upright position for these items. External support to achieve a neutral head position with the chin slightly flexed should be provided with straps, a collar, or physical support from an adult.

(*continued*)

Appendix 6A (*continued*)

5. Looks at an obstruction (e.g., cabinet, coat rack) located approximately 3 inches above eye level, 1–2 feet away from the head, and to the right of midline.	__ Yes __ No __ Unsure Comments: _____ _____
6. Looks at an obstruction (e.g., cabinet, coat rack) located approximately 3 inches above eye level, 1–2 feet away from the head, and to the left of midline.	__ Yes __ No __ Unsure Comments: _____ _____

Total: __ Yes   __ No   __ Unsure

Follow-up: If any of the items are checked "no" or "unsure," conduct a comprehensive assessment of the student's visual field.

Section 5. Use of Vision to Obtain Information About the Environment

1. Looks at familiar person or preferred object presented at midline and	
a. At a distance of 18 feet or more.	a. __ Yes __ No __ Unsure
b. At a distance of 10 feet.	b. __ Yes __ No __ Unsure
c. At a distance of 3 feet.	c. __ Yes __ No __ Unsure
d. At a distance of the student's arm length.	d. __ Yes __ No __ Unsure
e. At a distance of 13–15 inches.	e. __ Yes __ No __ Unsure Comments: _____ _____

(*continued*)

Appendix 6A (*continued*)

2. Looks at preferred object when that object is presented within 3–5 feet of the student and	
a. To the left of midline.	a. __ Yes __ No __ Unsure
b. To the right of midline.	b. __ Yes __ No __ Unsure
	Comments: _____
	_____
3. Responds when darkened area is illuminated. (Sample responses are an eye blink, startle response, and/or looking in the direction of the light source.)	a. __ Yes __ No __ Unsure Comments: _____ _____

Total: __ Yes __ No __ Unsure

Criterion for Pass/Fail: A total of six (6) "yes" responses must be recorded to pass Section 5.

Pass: __ Yes __No

A Model to Assess Localization Acuity

Introduction

The purpose of this model is to give service providers information regarding a student's ability to locate materials visually that are used in a variety of typical instructional activities. Please note that the title of this section describes the model as an assessment of *localization* acuity as opposed to *discrimination* acuity. The data from implementation of these procedures permit service providers to know only that a particular student can locate objects visually from a range of size categories, at three distances (all within the length of the student's arm), and in three locations (midline, left, and right) within an area that is defined by the width of the student's shoulders. This framework was selected because the majority of instructional tasks require a student to use his or her vision (either alone or in combination with a number of upper extremity functions) within this limited area. It is not possible to determine from these procedures whether a student can discriminate visually between two or more objects that are present at the same time in this work space.

This model is designed for implementation in two stages: (1) in a massed practice format so that a substantial amount of data can be obtained quickly and (2) in a follow-up procedure designed to occur in one or more natural instructional contexts (e.g., a vending machine task, a toothbrushing task). An additional component of this model contains information regarding extrapolation of the results obtained here to objects and settings beyond those that were used during the assessment processes.

Audience

This procedure is appropriate for implementation with all students, even those who may have quite limited vision. A student needs only to make a visual response; no motor responses are required. A positive visual response (defined later) to even a limited number of objects at various locations gives service providers information regarding the most appropriate location in space for presentation of instructional materials. This is true even for those students who may not yet be able to reach and/or touch those same objects. In the latter case, the guidelines derived through implementation of these procedures provide direction regarding the level of partial participation appropriate for a particular student. For some students, a visual response alone (e.g., momentary fixation in the direction of a washcloth) may be the first step to achieving competence (and more independence) in a grooming task.

STAGE 1: MASSED TRIAL PRESENTATION

Procedures

Materials

Implementation of this assessment procedure requires the use of a range of functional materials that fall into six size categories. The largest objects to be used should be 8–10 inches at the largest dimension (i.e., height or width); the smallest should be ¼–¾ inch at the largest dimension. The service provider should also select a box of some sort (e.g., plastic tool box, tackle box) to organize and store the materials. A large flat object to be used as an occluder is also required. The occluder will be used to block the student's view of the work surface temporarily while the service provider positions the functional object to be regarded visually. Suggestions for the occluder include a record album, a mirror, and a large magazine or book. Table 6B.1 provides sample materials to be used for this assessment procedure.

Preparation

Measure the following distances from the student's eyes and mark the distances on a piece of poster board or on the work surface itself (e.g., wheelchair tray, tabletop) with small pieces of tape or a washable marking pen. Please note that the distances should be measured from the student's eyes with the head held in the most typical or comfortable position.

- 15 inches
- 18 inches

TABLE 6B.1. Sample Objects to Be Used During Assessment of Localization Acuity

Object Size	Description
8–10 inches	Book/magazine/comic book, radio, article of clothing, record album, writing tablet
6–7 inches	Toothbrush, toothpaste, hairbrush, comb, pen/pencil/marker, small doll, "action" toy
4–5 inches	Bar of soap, cassette tape, stapler, package of tissues, deck of playing cards, wallet, watch, bracelet, crayon
2–3 inches	Small toys, battery, assembly parts (e.g., parts of pens, flashlights), Chapstick tube
1 inch	Paper clip, stamp/sticker, puzzle piece, quarter, game piece (e.g., bingo chip), "super" ball
¼–¾ inch	Penny, dime, stamp/sticker, assembly parts (e.g., nuts, bolts), cap of toothpaste or Chapstick tube

- 21–24 inches (depending on the length of the student's arms and the size of the work surface)

Measures should be made at the student's midline and approximately 6 inches to either side of midline. The lateral measures typically result in a presentation "grid" that forms an arc. Figure 6B.1 illustrates a sample presentation grid.

Presentation of objects

The object selected for presentation, the location for presentation (i.e., midline, left, or right), and the distance of presentation (i.e., 15, 18, or 21–24 inches) should all be determined randomly. In other words, the service provider should *not* complete all trials of the 8- to 10-inch object size category at the 15-inch distance to the student's right side in succession. Instead, various object sizes and locations for presentation should be used.

The service provider may want to assemble the objects and complete the data sheet indicating which objects have been selected from each size category prior to conducting the assessment session. A copy of the data sheet is found in Figure 6B.2. The service provider should refer to the data sheet while reading the remainder of the steps to be followed in conducting this assessment procedure. The remaining steps are as follows:

1. Refer to the data sheet for an indication of an object that represents a particular size category (e.g., 6–7 inches) and determine which location and distance will be used for the first trial of the assessment session.

2. Place the object on the work surface in front of the student. *Note that the object should be positioned on the work surface in the*

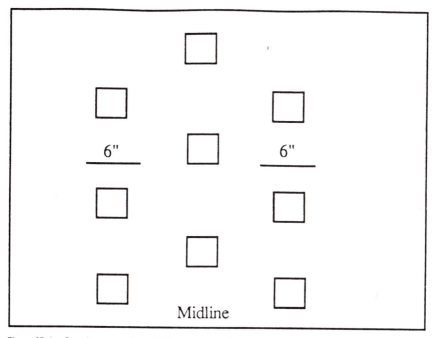

Figure 6B.1. Sample presentation grid illustrating locations of functional objects.

plane (vertical or horizontal) that represents the way the object is used functionally. For example, a pencil is held vertically when it is used, but also is commonly viewed placed horizontally on a work surface. Either plane of presentation is appropriate for a pencil. However, a stapler is rarely viewed held in a vertical position, but instead is typically seen resting on a work surface. Only the horizontal plane is appropriate for presentation of the stapler.

3. Provide "experience" with the object. This process, which takes approximately 45–60 seconds, requires you to demonstrate the function of the object while simultaneously describing (verbally and in sign language, if appropriate) what the object is and how it is used. Physical assistance should be used (if necessary) so the student may participate in the demonstration. For example, assume the object is a marking pen. You may show the marking pen to the student, remove the lid, and demonstrate making marks on a piece of paper. You should communicate with the student during this demonstration regarding the name of the object and what it is used for ("This is a marking pen; it can be

Localization Acuity: Massed Trial Data Sheet

Student_____   Date_____

Block 1

		8-10" ____ + -		21-24"	
		6-7" ____ + -		# Correct ____	
8-10" ____ + -		6-7" ____ + -	8-10" ____ + -	% Correct ____	
8-10" ____ + -		4-5" ____ + -	8-10" ____ + -		
6-7" ____ + -		4-5" ____ + -	6-7" ____ + -		
4-5" ____ + -		2-3" ____ + -	6-7" ____ + -	8-10" ____ # ____	
4-5" ____ + -		1" ____ + -	4-5" ____ + -	6-7" ____ # ____	
2-3" ____ + -		1" ____ + -	2-3" ____ + -	4-5" ____ # ____	
2-3" ____ + -		1/4"-	2-3" ____ + -	2-3" ____ # ____	
1" ____ + -		3/4" ____ + -	1" ____ + -	1" ____ # ____	
1" ____ + -		1/4-	1/4"-	1/4	
1/4-		3/4" ____ + -	3/4" ____ + -	3/4" ____ # ____	
3/4" ____ + -			1/4-3/4" ____ + -		

Block 2

		8-10" ____ + -		18"	
		8-10" ____ + -		# Correct ____	
8-10" ____ + -		6-7" ____ + -	8-10" ____ + -	% Correct ____	
6-7" ____ + -		6-7" ____ + -	8-10" ____ + -		
6-7" ____ + -		4-5" ____ + -	6-7" ____ + -		
4-5" ____ + -		4-5" ____ + -	4-5" ____ + -	8-10" ____ # ____	
4-5" ____ + -		2-3" ____ + -	2-3" ____ + -	6-7" ____ # ____	
2-3" ____ + -		2-3" ____ + -	2-3" ____ + -	4-5" ____ # ____	
1" ____ + -		1" ____ + -	1" ____ + -	2-3" ____ # ____	
1" ____ + -		1/4-	1" ____ + -	1" ____ # ____	
1/4"-		3/4" ____ + -	1/4"-	1/4	
3/4" ____ + -			3/4" ____ + -	3/4" ____ # ____	
1/4"-			1/4"-		
3/4" ____ + -			3/4" ____ + -		

Block 3

		8-10" ____ + -		15"	
		6-7" ____ + -		# Correct ____	
8-10" ____ + -		6-7" ____ + -	8-10" ____ + -	% Correct ____	
8-10" ____ + -		4-5" ____ + -	8-10" ____ + -		
6-7" ____ + -		2-3" ____ + -	6-7" ____ + -		
4-5" ____ + -		2-3" ____ + -	6-7" ____ + -	8-10" ____ # ____	
4-5" ____ + -		1" ____ + -	4-5" ____ + -	6-7" ____ # ____	
2-3" ____ + -		1" ____ + -	4-5" ____ + -	4-5" ____ # ____	
2-3" ____ + -		1/4"-	2-3" ____ + -	2-3" ____ # ____	
1" ____ + -		3/4" ____ + -	1" ____ + -	1" ____ # ____	
1/4"-		1/4-	1" ____ + -	1/4"-	
3/4" ____ + -		3/4" ____ + -	1/4"-	3/4" ____ # ____	
1/4"-			3/4" ____ + -		
3/4" ____ + -					

Position: right	Position: midline	Position: left	
# Correct ____	# Correct ____	# Correct ____	
% Correct ____	% Correct ____	% Correct ____	

Figure 6B.2. Data sheet used for Stage 1 of localization acuity assessment.

used to make marks on a piece of paper. See how it works? Now you try it.") Let the student perform the function of the object too. Experience with the object should occur across as much of the work surface as appropriate (i.e., demonstration of object function should occur across an arc from the student's right side, across midline, to his or her left side, and at distances ranging from 15 to 24 inches). This will promote visual regard of the object throughout a broad visual field.

4. Remove the object from the student's view.

5. Position the occluder in the student's line of sight, between the student's face and the viewing distance (and location) designated

on the data sheet. Remember to communicate to the student what you are doing. For example, say "I am putting the record album here for you to look at while I hide the marker."

6. Remove the occluder and ask the student to look at or "find" the object.

7. Observe the student to determine whether he or she looks at the object. *Allow no more than 5 seconds for the student to respond.*

8. If the individual fails to respond visually to the object, provide a second cue "to look." The second cue should be supplemented with auditory input (e.g., tapping the object gently on the edge of the sink) and/or movement of the object (e.g., waving the object back and forth in a small arc approximately three times). If the individual still fails to respond to the object visually, go on to the next step. The student should be allowed to manipulate the object for a few seconds (including demonstrating the function of the object) while you record the student's response (correct or incorrect) and select the next object for presentation.

9. If the student responds correctly during presentation of the first object of a particular size category (e.g., 8–10 inches) in a particular location (e.g., 15 inches from the student and to the left of midline), there is no need to present additional objects of that size category at that same location. However, if there is an error response, a long latency between removal of the occluder and the student's response, or a question regarding the reliable occurrence of the student's response, then additional objects from that size category should be presented.

Recording the data

After presentation of the object, circle the plus sign (+) for a correct response and a minus sign (–) for an incorrect response. If the individual responds to the object only after the cue "to look" is supplemented with auditory and/or movement of the object, record a minus sign and add an "A" or "M" adjacent to the minus sign.

Student responses

The following are definitions of potential student responses:

1. A *correct response* is defined as looking at the object with one or both eyes for a period of time ranging from a momentary glance to several seconds of fixation.

2. An *incorrect response* may consist of either general inattentiveness to the work surface and object or an attempt to locate the object tactually without facial orientation in the direction of the work surface and object.

Summarizing the data

Note that the data sheet is constructed so that data can be analyzed in two ways. First, the number of correct student responses for the positions at midline, left, and right can be computed by simply adding in a downward direction the number of trials scored as correct. The figure is entered in the fourth and final row found at the bottom of the data sheet. A separate score is computed for each of the three columns on the data sheet. This figure collapses the data from multiple size categories *and* distances of presentation. The percentage correct is computed by dividing that sum by 30. This figure provides information as to whether a student functions better (visually) to a particular lateral side (left or right) or at midline. An example of a completed data sheet with the student's performance summarized *downward* is shown in Figure 6B.3. In this example, a student's ability to respond visually to objects on the left side is highlighted.

Second, the data can be summarized to determine a particular student's ability to respond visually within each of the three distances of presentation: 15, 18, or 21–24 inches. It is possible to summarize the student's *overall* performance at each of the three distances by adding the total number of correct responses *across* the three columns of the data sheet and recording those data in the fourth and final column in the space provided. This figure collapses the data from multiple size categories and in all three positions relative to the student: left, midline, and right. This figure can be converted to a percentage by dividing the sum for each row by 30. It is also possible to determine the total number of correct responses for each separate category of object size (e.g., 6–7 inches) within each distance of presentation as well. A maximum number of five responses can be made to objects of each size category at each distance. This figure can be converted to a percentage by adding the total number of correct responses for each size category and dividing by 5. *Note: Remember that additional objects of a size category are presented to a student at a particular distance* only *if the student fails to respond to the first object of that size category. If the student responds to presentation of the first object of a size category at a particular distance, the student is assumed to have "passed" that size category.*

An example of a data sheet that illustrates how well a student responds visually to objects at various distances of presentation (e.g., 15 inches) is found in Figure 6B.4. Using the 15-inch summary square as an example, it can be seen that both *total* student responses to objects at that distance

Localization Acuity: Massed Trial Data Sheet

Student __Michelle__   Date _____ 2-19-93

Block 1

8-10" flashlight + -	8-10" ___ + -	6-7" h. brush + -	4-5" cassette + -	4-5" ___ + -
2-3" chapstick + -	2-3" den. floss + -	1" nickel + -	1" paper clip + -	1/4"-3/4" nut/bolt + -

8-10" book + -	6-7" pen + -
6-7" ___ + -	4-5" soap + -
4-5" ___ + -	2-3" plax + -
1" puzzle + -	1" quarter + -
1/4"-3/4" dime + -	1/4"-3/4" sticker + -

8-10" radio + -	8-10" ___ + -
6-7" comb + -	6-7" ___ + -
4-5" cards + -	2-3" battery + -
2-3" toy + -	1" paper clip + -
1/4"-3/4" stamp + -	1/4"-3/4" plax lid + -

21-24"
Correct _____
% Correct _____

size	#	%
8-10"	___	___
6-7"	___	___
4-5"	___	___
2-3"	___	___
1"	___	___
1/4"-3/4"	___	___

Block 2

8-10" magazine + -	6-7" toy + -
6-7" ___ + -	4-5" cards + -
4-5" ___ + -	2-3" battery + -
1" quarter + -	1" puzzle + -
1/4"-3/4" sticker + -	1/4"-3/4" plax lid + -

8-10" radio + -	8-10" ___ + -
6-7" t. brush + -	6-7" ___ + -
4-5" cassette + -	4-5" ___ + -
2-3" chapstick + -	2-3" plax + -
1" nickel + -	1/4"-3/4" stamp + -

8-10" flashlight + -	8-10" ___ + -
6-7" pen + -	4-5" soap + -
2-3" den. floss + -	2-3" key ring + -
1" paper clip + -	1" quarter + -
1/4-3/4" dime + -	1/4"-3/4" nut/bolt + -

18"
Correct _____
% Correct _____

size	#	%
8-10"	___	___
6-7"	___	___
4-5"	___	___
2-3"	___	___
1"	___	___
1/4"-3/4"	___	___

Block 3

8-10" book + -	6-7" ___ + -
6-7" comb + -	4-5" soap + -
4-5" ___ + -	2-3" toy + -
2-3" plax + -	1" puzzle + -
1/4"-3/4" dime + -	1/4"-3/4" nut/bolt + -

8-10" radio + -	6-7" h. brush + -
6-7" ___ + -	4-5" cards + -
2-3" key ring + -	2-3" den. floss + -
1" marker lid + -	1" paper clip + -
1/4"-3/4" sticker + -	1/4"-3/4" plax lid + -

8-10" magazine + -	8-10" ___ + -
6-7" toy + -	6-7" ___ + -
4-5" cassette + -	4-5" ___ + -
2-3" chapstick + -	1" nickel + -
1" puzzle + -	1/4"-3/4" stamp + -

15"
Correct _____
% Correct _____

size	#	%
8-10"	___	___
6-7"	___	___
4-5"	___	___
2-3"	___	___
1"	___	___
1/4"-3/4"	___	___

Position: right	Position: midline	Position: left
# Correct 24	# Correct 20	# Correct 21
% Correct 80	% Correct 67	% Correct 70

Figure 6B.3. Sample completed data sheet illustrating summary of performance according to position (i.e., left, midline, right).

can be determined (e.g., 80%) and total correct responses to objects of each size category (e.g., the student did well with the majority of objects from the middle and large size categories at the 15-inch distance, but did less well with very small objects).

Interpreting the data

At this point in the assessment process, the service provider can decide whether the student is able to respond visually to a range of objects from

Localization Acuity: Massed Trial Data Sheet

Student __Michelle__   Date _____2-19-93_____

		8-10"	book	+ -				21-24"			
		6-7"	pen	+ -				# Correct	20		
8-10"	flashlight	6-7"	-	+ -	8-10"	radio	+ -	% Correct	67		
8-10"	-	4-5"	soap	+ -	8-10"	-	+ -				
6-7"	h. brush	4-5"	-	+ -	6-7"	comb	+ -				
4-5"	cassette	2-3"	plax	+ -	6-7"	-	+ -	8-10"	# 5	% 100	
4-5"	-	1"	puzzle	+ -	4-5"	cards	+ -	6-7"	# 5	% 100	
2-3"	chapstick	1"	quarter	+ -	2-3"	battery	+ -	4-5"	# 5	% 100	
2-3"	den. floss	1/4-			2-3"	toy	+ -	2-3"	# 2	% 40	
1"	nickel	3/4"	dime	+ -	1"	paper clip	+ -	1"	# 2	% 40	
1"	paper clip	1/4-			1/4-			1/4			
1/4-		3/4"	sticker	+ -	3/4"	stamp	+ -	3/4"	# 1	% 20	
3/4"	nut/bolt				1/4-						
					3/4"	plax lid	+ -				
		8-10"	radio	+ -				18"			
		8-10"	-	+ -				# Correct	21		
8-10"	magazine	6-7"	t. brush	+ -	8-10"	flashlight	+ -	% Correct	70		
6-7"	toy	6-7"	-	+ -	8-10"	-	+ -				
6-7"	-	4-5"	cassette	+ -	6-7"	pen	+ -				
4-5"	cards	4-5"	-	+ -	4-5"	soap	+ -	8-10"	# 5	% 100	
4-5"	-	2-3"	chapstick	+ -	2-3"	den. floss	+ -	6-7"	# 5	% 100	
2-3"	battery	2-3"	plax	+ -	2-3"	key ring	+ -	4-5"	# 5	% 100	
1"	quarter	1"	nickel	+ -	1"	paper clip	+ -	2-3"	# 2	% 40	
1"	puzzle	1/4-			1"	quarter	+ -	1"	# 1	% 20	
1/4-		3/4"	stamp	+ -	1/4-			1/4			
3/4"	sticker				3/4"	dime	+ -	3/4"	# 2	% 40	
1/4-					1/4-						
3/4"	plax lid				3/4"	nut/bolt	+ -				
		8-10"	radio	+ -				15"			
		6-7"	h. brush	+ -				# Correct	24		
8-10"	book	6-7"	-	+ -	8-10"	magazine	+ -	% Correct	80		
6-7"	-	4-5"	cards	+ -	8-10"	-	+ -				
6-7"	comb	2-3"	key ring	+ -	6-7"	toy	+ -				
4-5"	soap	2-3"	den. floss	+ -	6-7"	-	+ -	8-10"	# 5	% 100	
4-5"	-	1"	marker lid	+ -	4-5"	cassette	+ -	6-7"	# 5	% 100	
2-3"	toy	1"	paper clip	+ -	4-5"	-	+ -	4-5"	# 5	% 100	
2-3"	plax	1/4-			2-3"	chapstick	+ -	2-3"	# 5	% 100	
1"	puzzle	3/4"	sticker	+ -	1"	nickel	+ -	1"	# 3	% 60	
1/4-		1/4-			1"	puzzle	+ -	1/4-			
3/4"	dime	3/4"	plax lid ·	+ -	1/4-			3/4"	# 1	% 20	
1/4-					3/4"	stamp	+ -				
3/4"	nut//bolt										
Position: right		Position: midline			Position: left						
# Correct	_____	# Correct	_____		# Correct	_____					
% Correct	_____	% Correct	_____		% Correct	_____					

Figure 6B.4. Sample completed data sheet illustrating summary of performance according to object size and distance of presentation.

a set of size categories at each of several distances and locations relative to the body. A criterion of 20 out of 30 correct responses (67%) for each of the summary sections of the data sheet (the scores in both the fourth column and the fourth row of the data sheet) is suggested. Student performance at or above this criterion may give service providers some confidence that the student is able to see a range of objects sufficiently well to participate in routine activities conducted within the distances used during this assessment procedure. If the student fails to achieve a 67% criterion in one or more summary squares on the data sheet, it is recommended that additional assessment be carried out using objects representative of the sizes missed during the massed trial presentation. Follow-up assessment is carried out in one or more natural instructional contexts. The procedures for follow-up assessment are described below.

STAGE 2: ASSESSMENT IN THE NATURAL CONTEXT

Procedures

Materials

Follow-up assessment in the natural context requires selection of one or more activities that are (or can be) a routine part of the student's school day. An activity selected for follow-up should be comprehensive in scope (i.e., consist of multiple steps that incorporate use of instructional materials that range in both size and distance of presentation). *The instructional materials to be used during follow-up assessment should represent both the size categories and distances of presentation to which the individual responded poorly during the massed trial presentation.* Three follow-up activities were used during validation of these materials: (a) a toothbrushing activity, (b) a grooming activity, and (c) a vending machine activity. The 27-step task analysis for the grooming activity is found in Table 6B.2; the data sheet for the grooming activity is in Figure 6B.5. Please note that these three activities were selected as being representative of those experienced by many students with severe disabilities in a range of settings. The task analysis and data sheet provided are examples only. A service provider who is interested in systematic assessment of a student's ability to respond visually to a particular set of materials in a specific task (e.g., food preparation, dusting) should use that particular setting and selection of materials as the framework for conducting follow-up assessment. A blank data sheet that includes the framework for presentation of various instructional materials at three distances and at the individual's midline, left, and right sides for use in an activity other than the ones described here is found in Figure 6B.6.

Preparation

Following selection of the natural context to serve as the setting for follow-up assessment, the training environment itself (e.g., a bathroom for the grooming or toothbrushing tasks; a student or staff lounge for the vending

TABLE 6B.2. Sample Visual–Motor Task Analysis for Use in the Natural Context of Grooming

1. **The student looks at the adult's face when she tells the student that it is time to brush her teeth and brush her hair. (8–10 inches)**

2. The adult wheels the student to the restroom (if necessary), or uses the appropriate form of assistance to relocate to the grooming environment. **The student looks at the symbol for "women" on the restroom door. (1 inch)**

3. **The student looks at the sign with the word "women." (4–5 inches)**

4. The adult places the tube of toothpaste on the sink (or opens the door of the storage cabinet where the toothpaste is stored, if appropriate). **The student looks at the tube of toothpaste before the adult assists her in reaching for and picking up the tube. (6–7 inches).** The adult assists the student in removing the lid from the tube of toothpaste.

5. The adult places the toothbrush on the sink (or redirects the student to the storage cabinet, if appropriate). **The student looks at the toothbrush before the adult assists her in reaching for and picking up the toothbrush. (6–7 inches)** The adult assists the student in squeezing the toothpaste onto the toothbrush, and then releasing the tube of toothpaste onto the sink.

6. The adult helps the student brush her teeth, rinse the toothbrush, and release the toothbrush onto the sink. **The student looks at the tube of toothpaste before the adult assists her in reaching for, and picking up the tube. (6–7 inches)**

7. **The student looks at the lid of the toothpaste before the adult assists her in reaching for and picking up the lid. (¼–¾ inch)** The adult assists the student in replacing the lid onto the tube and releasing the tube onto the sink (or back into the storage cabinet, if appropriate).

8. **The student looks at the container of dental floss before the adult assists her in reaching for and picking up the container. (2–3 inches)** The adult removes the dental floss from the container and explains its use to the student.

9. The adult places a bottle of mouthwash on the sink. **The student looks at the bottle before the adult assists her in reaching for and picking up the bottle. (4–5 inches)**

10. **The student looks at the lid of the mouthwash bottle before the adult assists her in opening the bottle. (¼–¾ inch)**

11. The adult pours a small amount of mouthwash into a cup and adds water. **The student looks at the cup before the adult assists her in reaching for and grasping the cup. (4–5 inches)** The adult assists the student in drinking the mouthwash mixture.

12. **The student looks at the lid of the mouthwash before the adult assists her in replacing it onto the bottle. (¼–¾ inch)**

13. The adult places a basket, or makeup bag, which contains grooming items, onto the sink. **The student looks at the bag before the adult assists her in reaching for and picking up the bag. (6–7 inches)**

14. The adult takes a hairbrush from the bag and places it on the sink. **The student looks at the brush before the adult assists her in reaching for and picking up the brush. (6–7 inches)**

15. The adult places a mirror in front of the student (or makes sure the student is positioned in such a way as to view the mirror on the wall). **The student looks at her reflection in the mirror while the adult assists her in brushing her hair. (8–10 inches)**

16. The adult removes a tube of Chapstick, lip gloss, or lipstick from the makeup bag and places it on the sink. **The student looks at the lip treatment before the adult assists her in reaching for and picking up the tube. (2–3 inches)**

(continued)

TABLE 6B.2. *Continued*

17. The adult displays the lid of the lip treatment, covering the rest of the tube with his or her hand. **The student looks at the lid before the adult assists in reaching for and removing the lid from the tube. (¼–¾ inch)**

18. The adult assists the student in applying the lip treatment to her lips, then places the lid on the sink. **The student looks at the lid before the adult assists her in reaching for and picking up the lid. (¼–¾ inch)** The adult assists the student in replacing the lid onto the tube.

19. The adult removes a tube of hand lotion from the makeup bag and places it on the sink. **The student looks at the tube of lotion before the adult assists her in reaching for and picking up the tube. (2–3 inches)**

20. The adult displays the lid of the tube by covering up the rest of the tube with his or her hand. **The student looks at the lid before the adult assists her in removing it from the tube. (1 inch)**

21. The adult then applies some lotion to the student's hands and places the lid on the sink. **The student looks at the lid before the adult assists her in reaching for and picking up the lid. (1 inch)**

22. The adult assists the student in replacing the lid onto the tube, and places the tube on the sink. **The student looks at the tube of lotion before the adult assists her in reaching for and picking up the tube. (2–3 inches)** The adult then assists her in reaching for and putting away the tube of lotion.

23. The adult places the tube of lip treatment on the sink. **The student looks at the tube of lip treatment before the adult assists her in reaching for and putting away the tube. (2–3 inches)**

24. The adult places the container of dental floss on the sink. **The student looks at the container before the adult assists her in reaching for and putting away the dental floss container. (2–3 inches)**

25. The adult places a penny on the sink as one of the choices for a reward. **The student looks at the penny. (¼–¾ inch)**

26. The adult places a sticker on the sink as one of the choices for a reward. **The student looks at the sticker. (¼–¾ inch)**

27. The adult then places a nickel on the sink as the third choice for a reward. **The student looks at the nickel and then makes her choice. (¼–¾ inch)**

machine task) should be analyzed. The analysis will reveal where materials should be placed (e.g., on a sink or counter top) to permit assessment of the individual's responses to objects to which he or she failed to respond visually during the massed trial presentation. For example, an individual may have failed to respond visually to objects from the ¼- to ¾-inch size category at presentation distances of 18 and 21–24 inches during the massed trial presentation. The toothbrushing task may be selected for follow-up assessment because it is an Individualized Education Program objective for the individual. Environmental analysis of the bathroom used for toothbrushing may reveal that small objects, such as the lid of the toothpaste tube, the spool of dental floss, and the lid of the mouthwash bottle (all within the target size category), may be positioned on the edge of the sink so the individual's responses to those objects may be assessed within a natural context.

Follow-up assessment in the natural context is used to determine if the outcomes of the massed trial presentation are valid. Given that functional

Natural Context Validity Check Grooming Sequence

Student_____   Date_____

			21-24 inches

10. (1/4-3/4) Looks at lid of mouthwash before opening the bottle.
 	
    +   -
14. (6-7") Looks at hairbrush.
    +   -
20. (1") Looks at lid of lotion before opening the tube.
    +   -
22. (2-3") Looks at tube of lotion before putting it away.
    +   -
	18. (1/4-3/4") Looks at lid of vaseline before replacing it onto tube.
	
	    + -
		2. (1") Looks at symbol for women.
		    + -
		13. (6-7") Looks at bag.
		    + -
		19. (2-3") Looks at tube of lotion.
		    + -
		27. (1/4-3/4") Looks at nickel when choosing reward.
		    + -
			# Correct _____
			% Correct _____
			
			8-10" ____ # ____
			6-7" ____ # ____
			4-5" ____ # ____
			2-3" ____ # ____
			1" ____ # ____
			1/4
			3/4" ____ # ____

21. (1") Looks at lid of lotion tube before replacing it onto tube.
 	
    +   -
	16. (2-3") Looks at vaseline.
	    + -
	17. (1/4-3/4") Looks at lid of vaseline before opening tube.
	    + -
	26. (1") Looks at sticker when choosing reward.
	    + -
		17. (1/4-3/4") Looks at mouthwash lid.
		    + -
		24. (2-3") Looks at dental floss when putting container away.
		    +
			18"
			# Correct _____
			% Correct _____
			
			8-10" ____ # ____
			6-7" ____ # ____
			4-5" ____ # ____
			2-3" ____ # ____
			1" ____ 4 ____
			1/4
			3/4" ____ # ____

1. (8-10") Looks at adult's face.
    +   -
4. (6-7") Looks at tube of toothpaste.
    +   -
7. (1/4-3/4") Looks at toothpaste lid.
    +   -
8. (2-3") Looks at container of dental floss.
    +   -
9. (4-5") Looks at bottle of mouthwash.
    +   -
	5. (6-7") Looks at toothbrush.
	    + -
	11. (4-5") Looks at cup.
	    + -
	15. (8-10") Looks at reflection in mirror.
	    + -
		3. (4-5") Looks at the sign for "women".
		    + -
		6. (6-7") Looks at tube of toothpaste.
		    + -
		23. (2-3") Looks at vaseline when putting tube away.
		    + -
		8. (1/4-3/4") Looks at penny when choosing reward.
		    + -
			15"
			# Correct _____
			% Correct _____
			
			8-10" ____ # ____
			6-7" ____ # ____
			4-5" ____ # ____
			2-3" ____ # ____
			1" ____ # ____
			1/4
			3/4" ____ # ____
			
			TOTALS:
			8-10" ____ # ____
			6-7" ____ # ____
			4-5" ____ # ____

Position: right #_____ %_____	Position: midline #_____ %_____	Position: left #_____ %_____	2-3" ____ # ____ 1" ____ # ____ 1/4 3/4" ____ # ____

Figure 6B.5. Data sheet for use with grooming sequence.

vision comprises two components (i.e., sufficient "structural" capability to receive and transmit visual information, as well as sufficient cognitive ability to interpret, integrate, and store visual messages), the natural context assessment may be viewed as using the individual's familiarity with the activity as contributing to visual functioning in that setting. The final draft of the localization acuity measures were field-tested with five individuals. In all instances, the data obtained in the follow-up settings reflected better visual functioning in the natural context. Project staff considered suggesting that all localization acuity data be collected in the natural context; however, it was determined that such a recommendation may make data collection too time-consuming. In no instance did the data collected in the natural context contradict the data collected in the massed trial presentation. The follow-up data simply revealed that the final determination of an individual's best visual

Localization Acuity: Natural Context Data Sheet

Student_____   Date_____

8-10" Step#_____	8-10" Step#_____	8-10" Step#_____	21-24"
Object_____ + -	Object_____ + -	Object_____ + -	# Correct _____
6-7" Step#_____	6-7" Step#_____	6-7" Step#_____	% Correct _____
Object_____ + -	Object_____ + -	Object_____ + -	
4-5" Step#_____	4-5" Step#_____	4-5" Step#_____	8-10" _____ # _____
Object_____ + -	Object_____ + -	Object_____ + -	6-7" _____ # _____
2-3" Step#_____	2-3" Step#_____	2-3" Step#_____	4-5" _____ # _____
Object_____ + -	Object_____ + -	Object_____ + -	2-3" _____ # _____
1" Step#_____	1" Step#_____	1" Step#_____	1" _____ # _____
Object_____ + -	Object_____ + -	Object_____ + -	1/4
1/4-	1/4-	1/4-	3/4" _____ # _____
3/4" Step#_____	3/4" Step#_____	3/4" Step#_____	
Object_____ + -	Object_____ + -	Object_____ + -	
8-10" Step#_____	8-10" Step#_____	8-10" Step#_____	18"
Object_____ + -	Object_____ + -	Object_____ + -	# Correct _____
6-7" Step#_____	6-7" Step#_____	6-7" Step#_____	% Correct _____
Object_____ + -	Object_____ + -	Object_____ + -	
4-5" Step#_____	4-5" Step#_____	4-5" Step#_____	8-10" _____ # _____
Object_____ + -	Object_____ + -	Object_____ + -	6-7" _____ # _____
2-3" Step#_____	2-3" Step#_____	2-3" Step#_____	4-5" _____ # _____
Object_____ + -	Object_____ + -	Object_____ + -	2-3" _____ # _____
1" Step#_____	1" Step#_____	1" Step#_____	1" _____ # _____
Object_____ + -	Object_____ + -	Object_____ + -	1/4
1/4-	1/4-	1/4-	3/4" _____ # _____
3/4" Step#_____	3/4" Step#_____	3/4" Step#_____	
Object_____ + -	Object_____ + -	Object_____ + -	
8-10" Step#_____	8-10" Step#_____	8-10" Step#_____	15"
Object_____ + -	Object_____ + -	Object_____ + -	# Correct _____
6-7" Step#_____	6-7" Step#_____	6-7" Step#_____	% Correct _____
Object_____ + -	Object_____ + -	Object_____ + -	
4-5" Step#_____	4-5" Step#_____	4-5" Step#_____	8-10" _____ # _____
Object_____ + -	Object_____ + -	Object_____ + -	6-7" _____ # _____
2-3" Step#_____	2-3" Step#_____	2-3" Step#_____	4-5" _____ # _____
Object_____ + -	Object_____ + -	Object_____ + -	2-3" _____ # _____
1" Step#_____	1" Step#_____	1" Step#_____	1" _____ # _____
Object_____ + -	Object_____ + -	Object_____ + -	1/4
1/4-	1/4-	1/4-	3/4" _____ # _____
3/4" Step#_____	3/4" Step#_____	3/4" Step#_____	
Object_____ + -	Object_____ + -	Object_____ + -	
Position: right	Position: midline	Position: left	
# correct_____	# correct_____	# correct_____	
% correct_____	% correct_____	% correct_____	

Figure 6B.6. Blank data sheet for use with follow-up activities in the natural context.

performance can be more accurately determined in the context of natural, familiar routines.

The final aspect of preparation for follow-up assessment is to ensure that the activity and setting are familiar to the individual. Following environmental analysis (with subsequent determination of the objects to be used for presentation, as well as the distance of presentation for each object), it is recommended that the individual be provided with three instructional sessions on the activity. The appropriate level of prompts and participation should be determined individually. Each step, including the specific steps that focus on visual and visual–motor skills, should be cued and include positive consequences as appropriate. However, no data are collected during this set of instructional sessions. These sessions are used to provide the individual with sufficient experience with the setting, materials, and expectations for performance. Follow-up data to be used for the purpose of decision making and program planning are collected on the fourth presentation of the task.

Presentation of objects

As stated earlier, the object size categories selected for presentation, the location of presentation (i.e., the individual's midline, left, or right), and the distance of presentation (i.e., 15, 18, or 21–24 inches) should be determined on the basis of data collected during the massed trial presentation. Although the activity to be conducted in the natural context may include multiple objects, locations, and distances of presentation, the number of trials during which data specific to an individual's visual responses are collected *is limited* to those object sizes, locations, and distances of presentation that proved problematic for the individual during massed trial presentation.

It is recommended that the data sheet be prepared in advance of the assessment session. Refer to the sample data sheet from the grooming sequence for an example of how the data sheet may be prepared. Note that the grooming activity data sheet reflects the specific environmental conditions available to project staff during the field-test and is not necessarily intended for general use. After the data sheet is prepared, the follow-up assessment session is implemented. The service provider should refer to the task analysis of the follow-up activity to determine which steps require the individual to engage in a visual response to an object of a particular size, location, or distance that is of interest. (Project staff indicated those steps with boldface print.) Instruction on all other steps does not need to yield data for the purpose of determining an individual's localization acuity. As progress through the task analysis is made and as each target step is reached, the service provider should follow the steps (listed below in the form of a task analysis) to complete the follow-up session.

1. Place the object at the designated distance and location relative to the individual's midline.

2. Cue the individual to look at the object. (It is assumed that the appropriate form of communication is used during all interactions with the individual.)

3. Observe the individual to determine whether he or she looks at the object. *Allow no more than 5 seconds for the student to respond.* The individual should be permitted (and should, in fact, be encouraged) to manipulate the object in accordance with the response specified on the next step in the task analysis.

4. If the individual fails to respond visually to the object, provide a second cue "to look." The second cue should be supplemented

with auditory input (e.g., tapping the object gently on the edge of the sink) and/or movement of the object (e.g., waving the object back and forth in a small arc approximately three times). If the individual still fails to respond to the object visually, proceed to the next step of the task analysis.

Recording the data

After presentation of the object, circle the plus sign (+) for a correct response and a minus sign (−) for an incorrect response. If the individual responds to the object only after the cue "to look" is supplemented with auditory and/or movement of the object, record a minus sign and add an "A" or "M" adjacent to the minus sign. Visual responses that are limited to those occasions when auditory and/or movement input is provided is an important aspect of an individual's behavior in terms of instructional decision making.

Student responses

The following are definitions of potential student responses:

1. A correct response is defined as looking at the object with one or both eyes for a period of time ranging from a momentary glance to several seconds of fixation.

2. An incorrect response may consist of either general inattentiveness to the work surface and object or an attempt to locate the object tactually without facial orientation in the direction of the work surface and object.

Summarizing the data

Please note that the natural context data sheet is constructed in the same way as the massed presentation data sheet. This arrangement permits data to be analyzed in two ways. The number of correct student responses for the positions at midline, left, and right can be computed by adding the number of trials scored as "correct" downward. This figure collapses the data from multiple size categories *and* distances of presentation and provides information as to whether a student functions better (visually) to a particular lateral side (left or right) or at midline.

The data can also be summarized to determine a particular individual's ability to respond visually within each of the three distances of presentation (15, 18, or 21–24 inches). It is possible to summarize the student's *overall* performance at each of the three distances by adding the total number of correct responses across the three columns of the data sheet and recording those data in the fourth and final column in the space provided. This figure collapses the data from multiple size categories and in all three positions relative to the individual (left, midline, and right). It is also possible to determine the total number of correct responses for each separate category of object size (e.g., 6–7 inches) within each distance of presentation. Unlike the data yielded in the massed presentation session, however, it is unlikely that a sufficient number of trials with objects of each size will occur during a single session conducted in the natural context. If a service provider has a concern regarding an individual's visual response to objects of a particular size category, additional sessions in the natural context can be conducted so that data from multiple sessions can be combined to address that concern with the benefit of data.

Interpreting the data

At this point, the service provider can decide whether the student is able to respond visually to a range of objects from a set of size categories at each of several distances and locations relative to the body. In the massed trial presentation, a criterion of 20 out of 30 correct responses (67%) for each of the summary sections of the data sheet (the scores in both the fourth column and the fourth row of the data sheet) was suggested. Student performance at or above this criterion may give service providers some confidence that the student is able to see a range of objects sufficiently well to participate in routine activities conducted within the distances used during this assessment procedure. If the student failed to achieve a 67% criterion in one or more summary squares on the data sheet, it was recommended that follow-up assessment be carried out using objects representative of the sizes missed during the massed trial presentation. The results of the follow-up assessment may simply confirm the results from the earlier assessment, or some improvements in localization acuity may be seen in the natural context. In the former case, the service provider can act with even more confidence regarding selection of instructional materials. In the latter case, the service provider may want to provide instruction in the natural context for several sessions before determining that a particular set of instructional materials is appropriate (or inappropriate) for a particular individual.

EXTRAPOLATION OF THE DATA

Data collected during both stages of localization acuity assessment can be extrapolated so that a service provider can *estimate* what size an object should be to ensure that a particular individual will be able to see that object at a range of distance beyond those used during the assessment sessions. *These data are estimates only.* A variety of visual impairments (e.g., severe myopia) may limit the application of these procedures for some individuals. Nonetheless, some service providers may find these guidelines helpful in program planning. It should also be noted that motivational factors (rather than functional vision) may limit an individual's response to objects presented at a distance beyond arm's length.

The procedures described in the following tables are selected for use depending on the best localization acuity achieved by a particular individual during the two stages of assessment. Refer to Table 6B.3 for individuals who are able to respond visually to objects between ¼ inch and 3 inches. Refer to Table 6B.4 for individuals whose best localization acuity is between 4 inches and 10 inches.

TABLE 6B.3.   Steps Used to Determine Estimated Object Size for Presentation at Distances Other than Those Used for the Localization Acuity Assessment (Rounded to the Nearest Half Inch)

Note. This table is used for those students whose best performance during massed trial presentation was to objects between ¼ inch and 3 inches in size.

Steps

1. From summary data obtained through massed trial presentation, determine the smallest object that was seen easily by the student at the farthest distance.

2. Circle the presentation distance under the appropriate column heading:

	¼ – ¾" Object Presented at			1" Object Presented at			2–3" Object Presented at		
	21–24"	18"	15"	21–24"	18"	15"	21–24"	18"	15"

3. Find the desired distance for presentation in Column 1 below.

4. Using the presentation distance circled above as your reference point, move downward in that column to the row that is equivalent to the desired presentation distance identified in Step 3.

5. The number that intersects the values identified in Steps 3 and 4 is the *estimated* object size suggested for presentation at that distance.

	21–24"	18"	15"	21–24"	18"	15"	21–24"	18"	15"
21–26 in.	1	1.5	1.5	1.5	1.5	2	4	4.5	5.5
27–28 in.	1	1.5	1.5	1.5	1.5	2	4.5	5	6
29–30 in.	1	1.5	1.5	1.5	1.5	2	4.5	5.5	6.5
31–32 in.	1.5	1.5	2	2	2	2.5	5	5.5	6.5
33–34 in.	1.5	1.5	2	2	2	2.5	5	5.5	7
35–36 in.	1.5	1.5	2	2	2	2.5	5.5	6.5	7.5
37–38 in.	1.5	1.5	2	2	2	2.5	5.5	6.5	8
39–40 in.	1.5	2	2	2	2	3	6	7	8
41–42 in.	1.5	2	2	2	2.5	3	6.5	7.5	8.5
43–44 in.	2	2	2.5	2.5	2.5	3	6.5	7.5	9
45–46 in.	2	2	2.5	2.5	2.5	3	6.5	8	9.5
47–48 in.	2	2	2.5	2.5	3	3.5	7	8	10
49–50 in.	2	2	2.5	2.5	3	3.5	7.5	8.5	10
51–52 in.	2	2.5	2.5	2.5	3	3.5	7.5	9	10.5
53–54 in.	2	2.5	2.5	2.5	3	3.5	8	9.5	11
55–56 in.	2	2.5	3	3	3	4	8	9.5	11.5
57–58 in.	2	2.5	3	3	3.5	4	8.5	10	12
5 ft.	2	2.5	3	3	3.5	4	9	10.5	12.5
10 ft.	4.5	5	5.5	5.5	6.5	8	17.5	20.5	24.5

TABLE 6B.4. Steps Used to Determine Estimated Object Size for Presentation at Distances Other than Those Used for the Localization Acuity Assessment (Rounded to the Nearest Half Inch)

Note. This table is used for those students whose best performance during massed trial presentation was to objects between 4 inches and 10 inches in size.

Steps

1. From summary data obtained through massed trial presentation, determine the smallest object that was seen easily by the student at the farthest distance.

2. Circle the presentation distance under the appropriate column heading:

4–5″ Object Presented at			6–7″ Object Presented at			8–10″ Object Presented at		
21–24″	18″	15″	21–24″	18″	15″	21–24″	18″	15″

3. Find the desired distance for presentation in Column 1 below.

4. Using the presentation distance circled above as your reference point, move downward in that column to the row that is equivalent to the desired presentation distance identified in Step 3.

5. The number that intersects the values identified in Steps 3 and 4 is the *estimated* object size suggested for presentation at that distance.

	21–24″	18″	15″	21–24″	18″	15″	21–24″	18″	15″
21–26 in.	6.5	7.5	9	9.5	11	12.5	12.5	14.5	17.5
27–28 in.	7	8	9.5	10.5	12	13.5	13.5	15.5	19
29–30 in.	7.5	8.5	10.5	10.5	12.5	14	14.5	15.5	19
31–32 in.	8	9	11	11	12.5	15	15.5	18	21.5
33–34 in.	8.5	9.5	11.5	11.5	13.5	16	16.5	19	23
35–36 in.	9	10.5	12.5	12	14	17	17.5	20	24
37–38 in.	9.5	11	13	13.5	15	18	18.5	21.5	25.5
39–40 in.	10	11.5	13.5	13.5	16	19	19.5	22.5	27
41–42 in.	10.5	12	14	14	16.5	20	20	23.5	28
43–44 in.	10.5	12.5	15	15	17.5	21	21	25	29.5
45–46 in.	11	13	15.5	15.5	18	21.5	22	25.5	31
47–48 in.	11.5	13.5	16	16.5	19	22.5	23	27	32
49–50 in.	12	14	17	17	20	23.5	24	28	33.5
51–52 in.	12.5	14.5	18	18	20.5	24.5	25	29	35
53–54 in.	13	15.5	18.5	18.5	21	25.5	26	30	36
55–56 in.	13.5	16	19	19	22	26.5	27	31.5	37.5
57–58 in.	14.5	16.5	20	20	23	28	28.5	33	39.5
5 ft.	14.5	17	20.5	20.5	23.5	28	28.5	33.5	40
10 ft.	29	33.5	40.5	40	47	56	57	66.5	80

REFERENCES

Association for Retarded Citizens/Minnesota. (1989). *A parent's guide to obtaining occupational and physical therapy services in the public schools.* Minneapolis: Author.

Baumgart, D., Brown, L., Pumpian, I., Nisbet, J., Ford, A., Sweet, M., Messina, R., & Schroeder, J. (1982). Principle of partial participation and individualized adaptations in educational programs for severely handicapped students. *Journal of The Association for the Severely Handicapped, 7,* 17–27.

Campbell, P. H. (1987). Integrated programming for students with multiple handicaps. In L. Goetz, D. Guess, & K. Stremel-Campbell (Eds.), *Innovative program design for individuals with dual sensory impairments* (pp. 159–191). Baltimore: Brookes.

Campbell, P. H. (1989). Dysfunction in posture and movement in individuals with profound disabilities: Issues and practice. In F. Brown & D. H. Lehr (Eds.), *Persons with profound disabilities: Issues and practices* (pp. 163–190). Baltimore: Brookes.

Cleeland, L. K. (1984). Function of the auditory system in speech and language development. In R. H. Hull & K. I. Dilka (Eds.), *The hearing-impaired child in school* (pp. 7–19). Orlando, FL: Grune and Stratton.

Dantona, R. (1986). Implications of demographic data for planning services for deaf–blind children and adults. In D. Ellis (Ed.), *Sensory impairments in mentally handicapped people* (pp. 69–82). San Diego: College Hill.

Fredericks, H. D. B., & Baldwin, V. A. (1987). Individuals with sensory impairments: Who are they? How are they educated? In L. Goetz, D., Guess, & K. Stremel-Campbell (Eds.), *Innovative program design for individuals with dual sensory impairments* (pp. 3–14). Baltimore: Brookes.

Goetz, L., Utley, B., Gee, K., Baldwin, M., & Sailor, W. (1979). *Auditory assessment and programming for severely handicapped and deaf–blind students.* Seattle: The Association for Persons with Severe Handicaps.

Guess, D., & Siegel-Causey, E. (1988). Students with severe and multiple disabilities. In E. L. Meyen & T. M. Skrtic (Eds.), *Exceptional children and youth: An introduction* (pp. 293–320). Denver: Love Publishing.

Hart, V. (1977). The use of many disciplines with the severely and profoundly handicapped. In E. Sontag, J. Smith, & N. Certo (Eds.), *Educational programming for the severely and profoundly handicapped* (pp. 391–396). Reston, VA: The Council for Exceptional Children.

Hutchison, D. J. (1978). The transdisciplinary approach. In J. B. Curry & K. K. Peppe (Eds.), *Mental retardation: Nursing approaches to care* (pp. 65–74). St. Louis: Mosby.

Jacobson, J. W., & Janicki, M. P. (1985). Functional and health status characteristics of persons with severe handicaps in New York State. *Journal of The Association for Persons with Severe Handicaps, 10,* 51–60.

Kenworthy, O. T. (1982). Integration of assessment and management processes: Audiology as an educational program. In B. Campbell & V. Baldwin (Eds.), *Severely handicapped hearing impaired students: Strengthening service delivery* (pp. 47–77). Baltimore: Brookes.

Luckasson, R., Coulter, D., Polloway, E. A., Reiss, S., Schalock, R. L., Snell, M. E., Spitalnick, D. M., & Stark, J. A. (1992). *Mental retardation: Definition, classification and systems of support.* Washington, DC: American Association on Mental Retardation.

McCormick, L., & Goldman, R. (1979). The transdisciplinary model: Implications for service delivery and personnel preparation for the severely and profoundly handicapped. *AAESPH Review, 4*(2), 152–161.

Orelove, F. P., & Sobsey, D. (1991). Designing transdisciplinary systems. In F. P. Orelove & D. Sobsey (Eds.), *Educating children with multiple disabilities: A transdisciplinary approach* (2nd ed., pp. 1–33). Baltimore: Brookes.

Public Law 101-476. (1990). *Individuals with Disabilities Education Act,* 20 U.S.C., Chapter 33.

Rainforth, B., & York, J. (1991). Handling and positioning. In F. P. Orelove & D. Sobsey (Eds.), *Educating children with multiple disabilities: A transdisciplinary approach* (pp. 79–119). Baltimore: Brookes.

Rainforth, B., York, J., & MacDonald, C. (1992). *Collaborative teams for students with severe disabilities: Integrating therapy and educational services.* Baltimore: Brookes.

Sobsey, D., & Wolf-Schein, E. G. (1991). Sensory impairments. In F. P. Orelove & D. Sobsey (Eds.), *Educating children with multiple disabilities: A transdisciplinary approach* (2nd ed., pp. 199–254). Baltimore: Brookes.

Sternat, J., Messina, R., Nietupski, J., Lyon, S., & Brown, L. (1977). Occupational and physical therapy services for severely handicapped students: Toward a naturalized public school service delivery model. In E. Sontag, J. Smith, & N. Certo (Eds.), *Educational programming for the severely and profoundly handicapped* (pp. 263–278). Reston, VA: The Council for Exceptional Children.

Thousand, J. S., & Villa, R. A. (1992). Collaborative teams: A powerful tool in school restructuring. In R. A. Villa, J. S. Thousand, W. Stainback, & S. Stainback (Eds.), *Restructuring for caring and effective education* (pp. 73–108). Baltimore: Brookes.

Touchette, P. E. (1971). Transfer of stimulus control: Measuring the moment of transfer. *Journal of the Experimental Analysis of Behavior, 15,* 347–354.

Utley, B. L. (1992). Facilitating and measuring the team process within more inclusive educational settings. In L. Kupper (Ed.), *Proceedings of the Second National Symposium on Effective Communication for Children and Youth with Severe Disabilities: A vision for the future* (pp. 59–83). McLean, VA: Interstate Research Associates.

Utley, B. L., Nelson, G. L., & Ferrell, D. (1990). *Classroom-based vision assessment for students with multiple disabilities.* Pittsburgh: University of Pittsburgh, Institute for Practice and Research in Education.

York, J., Rainforth, B., & Giangreco, M. (1990). Transdisciplinary teamwork and integrated therapy: Clarifying the misconceptions. *Pediatric Physical Therapy, 2*(2), 73–79.

Chapter 7

Communication and Language Development

ROBIN ALVARES and LES STERNBERG

Individuals with profound disabilities will likely experience significant problems related to communication skill development. Adding to their problems are long-held assumptions concerning what constitutes communication. For example, when asked to define communication, many people envision speech or sign language as the primary exemplars. However, especially with individuals with profound disabilities, the entire concept of communication has to be reconfigured. Although some individuals with profound disabilities may be able to display appropriate speech and sign language behaviors, many will be unable to do so. Thus, the concept of communication needs to be separated from that of specific communicative behaviors (i.e., language).

Communication can best be defined as the transmission of information or ideas from one individual to another. Language is one form of communication that is symbolic and conventional. Language is considered symbolic because it is representational; its communicative components (e.g., words, signs) stand for objects, actions, and concepts that may or may not have any physical representation. The abstract nature of language allows individuals to communicate about subjects that are not present in the immediate environment, that might have happened in the past or could happen in the future. Language is considered conventional because the symbols used and the rules that govern its structure and use are tacitly agreed to by a community; these rules vary as a function of geographical region, ethnicity, and social status. Formal language structures are those that are generative in nature; that is, a finite number of symbols can be used to make an infinite number of statements.

Communication can occur without the use of a formal language system. For example, by extending one's foot, the communicative message "tie my shoe" might be delivered. Pushing away the hand of someone offering food might convey the message "I don't want any more." These are nonlanguage or nonverbal forms of communication. These forms often emerge in infants without disabilities, and serve as precursors to the use of a formal language system. They also provide the foundation for later language learning. For individuals with profound disabilities, cognitive, sensory, and motoric deficits often limit communicative behaviors to nonverbal and nonlanguage modes exclusively. What is important to realize, however, is that these individuals may still use these nonverbal means to express a wide range of choices, preferences, and feelings.

BASIC CONCEPTS OF COMMUNICATION DEVELOPMENT

For an individual to be able to communicate, he or she must have some connection with the social world. The asocial individual is unlikely to ever fully participate in or appreciate communication, because communicaton is a social act. To interface social aspects with communicative behaviors, the individual must realize a number of accomplishments. The first is an awareness that he or she is separate from the environment. The individual must know the boundaries of the environment. For example, if an individual with profound disabilities immediately mouths objects, continually manipulates objects close to the body, or never varies the manner in which he or she interacts with objects, the individual probably does not comprehend that the object is separate from himself or herself. The realization of separation of self from the environment is crucial to the acquisition and display of two additional accomplishments: the ability to communicate and the understanding that there are things in the environment about which to communicate and people with whom to communicate. Active interaction with people and objects helps the individual to learn specific aspects related to people and familiar events. Later, these aspects can be used as representations for objects, persons, and events.

In the past 20 years, there has been an increased understanding of how infants without disabilities learn to communicate within the context of social interactions with their caregivers. Bates (1976) provided a developmental model that has come to represent both a theoretical and a methodological foundation for many past and present intervention efforts. In her view, communication develops through various phases, but individuals do not merely acquire one phase before they begin another. Instead, the phases appear to meld as one phase naturally leads to the next.

The earliest phase of communication, termed *perlocutionary,* does not really appear to be communicative in the typical sense. In this phase, the individual exhibits various behaviors that are viewed and reacted to by others as communicative. For example, the child may gurgle for apparently no reason, yet an attending adult may talk back as though the child were communicating. In the early stages of this phase, a child may exhibit only primitive reflexes in reaction to various stimuli. Toward the middle of this stage, a child might exhibit a movement after an enjoyable interplay has taken place. It would appear to an observer that the child moved out of desire to continue the interaction. However, in both of these cases, direct communicative intent or meaning by the child cannot be inferred but rather is generated by one who is attending to the child. Toward the latter part of the perlocutionary stage, intent begins to develop.

During the second phase, termed *illocutionary,* communicative intent is generated by the child. During the early stages of this phase, the child might make very general types of requests. For example, the child might grasp a toy and wave it in front of an individual. The intent is to get assistance, but the specific type of assistance is not clear. Therefore, at this level, *clear* intent is still generated by another. During the latter stages of this phase, more refinement of specific communicative intent takes place. Pointing and other gestures begin to develop. The child might display the object to an adult *and* point to a part of the object with which he or she needs assistance. Regardless of the stage in this phase, most of the child's communication is tied to whether the objects or desired events are present in the immediate environment; if not present, the child will most likely not communicate about them.

The last communication phase, termed *locutionary,* involves formal language accomplishments. During this phase, the child begins to use conventional words and/or signs. These words or signs are truly representational or symbolic in nature in that the objects, people, or events being referred to do not have to be present in the immediate environment.

Aside from social-interactive factors, cognitive competence has also been shown to affect or account for communication skills acquisition and demonstration (Bates, Benigni, Bretherton, Camaioni, & Volterra, 1977; Lobato, Barrera, & Feldman, 1981). The ability to process information (cognitive competence) has been viewed as directly associated with whether an individual can develop specific communication skills. Although theorists agree somewhat regarding the *general* level of cognitive competence that might be necessary for various communication skills to be acquired, such is not the case for the specific *types of cognitive behavior* that might be crucial. Disagreements arise (Bates, 1979; Cromer, 1981; Reichle & Karlan, 1985) regarding attempts to correlate these specific behaviors (e.g., object permanence, means–end relations, imitation, causality) to success at demonstrating different communicative abilities.

Information about the interaction between the innate capacities of infants and the communicative environment provided by their caregivers has been adapted with considerable success to communication training with individuals with varying degrees and types of disabilities. This training includes necessary modifications to ensure chronologically age-appropriate extensions. Researched applications of these methods to individuals with profound disabilities, however, are still in their formative stages. Therefore, the data base on communication and language intervention efforts with these individuals is still sorely lacking. Although the major focus of this chapter is on approaches to communication intervention with individuals who are profoundly disabled, the reader should be cautioned that clinical proof of the efficiency and efficacy of many of these approaches *with this population* has not yet been demonstrated. However, given the success of these approaches with individuals with lesser degrees of disability, one would anticipate that successful applications or modifications can be rendered.

As Sternberg points out in Chapter 1, individuals who meet the criteria for inclusion into the category of profoundly disabled demonstrate substantial delays in the areas of motor and mobility development, activities of daily living, cognition, social and affective development, and communication. Even with this definition, Sternberg emphasizes that individuals who meet these criteria constitute a heterogeneous group with a wide range of capabilities and communicative needs. For some, communication goals might comprise awareness of contingent relationships between motor acts and environmental reinforcement. For others, goals might include the use of words, pictures, or signs to request items needed to complete a task.

It is both frustrating and gratifying that the following discussion is by no means complete. It is frustrating because those providing services to individuals with profound disabilities need access to the widest variety of resources available to effectively meet the communicative needs of the individuals whom they serve. An overriding problem is that individuals with profound disabilities are somewhat new to the communication–language arena in terms of both research and practice (Sternberg & McNerney, 1988). Given that the data base is thereby limited, the available resources are not as comprehensive as they should be. It is gratifying, however, to see that the field has become more attuned to the communicative needs of this population; with this emphasis, the body of literature and appropriate research-to-practice directives continue to grow.

Another positive trend has been the movement toward integrating communication training into all aspects of the individual's life. This has provided opportunities to greatly expand the community of communication facilitators to include speech–language clinicians, teachers, parents, siblings, and peers. Roles have been redefined and refined so that the focus is no longer on who should provide the "service" but rather on the anticipated communicative outcomes of the facilitative effort. What is first required, however, is an understanding of the theory, rationale, or philosophy underlying intervention strategies; this will hopefully provide all facilitators with the foundation necessary to modify intervention strategies when necessary to meet the communicative needs of individuals with profound disabilities.

PHILOSOPHY OF INTERVENTION

The intervention strategies presented in this chapter reflect two trends that have emerged in the last 20 years. The first is the growing body of literature that has demonstrated that communication development in children both with and without disabilities occurs within the context of social interactions, and is best facilitated by adapting conversational strategies to teach communicative behaviors and language forms. The second trend has been the move toward functional, ecologically valid, and age-appropriate intervention goals.

Historically, communication intervention focused on teaching individuals with varying types and degrees of disabilities some form of symbolic communication, such as speech or sign language. Little consideration was given to how those skills might be used in the individual's natural environment (Alvares, Falor, & Smiley, 1991; Bryen & Joyce, 1985; Cirrin & Rowland, 1985; Goetz, Schuler, & Sailor, 1981). These attempts were largely unsuccessful for two reasons (Goetz et al., 1981). First, many individuals with profound disabilities possessed little or no potential to use symbolic communication. Second, targets were chosen with little regard for individuals' interests, preferences, or opportunities to use these targets in their natural environments.

The fundamental goal of any intervention program should be to improve the quality of life of the individual with profound disabilities (Sailor, Gee, Goetz, & Graham, 1988; Siegel-Causey & Downing, 1987). One tenet of quality of life can be operationalized as providing the individual the opportunity for maximum participation in natural environments. Sailor et al. (1988) provided examples:

> Measures of educational outcomes need to reflect more general "quality of life" measures, including preference, choice making, the ability to receive sensory input, the ability to remain awake and alert, and increased power and control over one's environment. (p. 90)

The American Speech-Language-Hearing Association (1992) has also emphasized these quality of life tenets, and has developed a "Bill of Rights" for students with severe or profound disabilities. It asserts that all individuals can benefit from intervention, and that all individuals have the right to make choices, demonstrate preferences, initiate interactions, and receive responses to communication attempts. What is also important is that the Bill of Rights stresses the concept that all persons should respect each individual's method of communication, regardless of whether that method is conventional.

Current best practices and the approaches to intervention advocated in this chapter can be characterized as an integration of developmental and functional approaches. The developmental perspective incorporates principles of communication development derived from studies of how infants and toddlers without disabilities progress through stages of communication development as a result of interactions with caregivers. The developmental model provides a sequence for the stages of development of communication skills and outlines requisite skills for progresssion to the use of later developing skills. The functional approach advocates that communication goals should be chronologically age appropriate, be useful in the individual's natural environment, and allow for maximum independence and control over one's environment. Using the functional approach, the intent of communication facilitation is to analyze the communicative demands required in naturalistic environments and attempt to develop communication goals that the individual can use to participate maximally in that environment.

ESTABLISHING INTENTIONAL COMMUNICATION

Infants are born with innate capacities for language development, which rely on the development of motor, social, cognitive, and sensory skills. These skills allow the infant to receive communication input through interactions, typically with adults. In the first 8 months of life, interactions are directed primarily by an adult. Infants develop social responses such as smiling, eye contact, and kicking in response to these interactions. The adult times his or her behavior to allow children to participate as though they were equal partners in directing the interaction. These routine sequences are characterized by mutual engagement between child and interactant, predictability, few linguistic and gestural elements, and turn-taking. As a result of these exchanges, the infant begins to understand that communication is based upon reciprocal exchanges (e.g., vocal, gestural) between adult and child. According to Rogers-Warren and Warren (1984), to participate in and benefit from interactions, children must exhibit four critical classes of behavior: attention to the environment, engagement with objects and people, responsiveness to caregiver communication, and signaling of communicative intentions.

Many individuals with profound disabilities have difficulty in participating in reciprocal interactions. Motor, sensory, and cognitive deficits, as well as parental attitudes, often interrupt normal flow of communicative exchanges. Unless individuals with profound disabilities experience synchronous and predictable relationships, communication development will likely be thwarted (Higginbotham & Yoder, 1982; Rogers-Warren & Warren, 1984; Siegel-Causey, Ernst, & Guess, 1988).

The first step in communication intervention with individuals with profound disabilities is to determine their ability to understand operant contingencies. Preintentional individuals need to understand that their behavior can cause changes in the type of sensory or social input they receive. The ability to understand operant contingencies has been demonstrated in newborn infants (Walton & Bower, 1991), as well as infants with profound disabilities (Dunst, Cuishing, & Vance, 1985). Dunst et al. demonstrated that six infants who were profoundly retarded and multiply handicapped could learn to operate a switch to activate a light display. Prior to the study, these children had not made developmental gains in a traditional intervention program in which they received noncontingent sensory stimulation.

Focusing on associating contingency awareness with communication, Sternberg and his colleagues demonstrated in a series of studies that both communication awareness and primitive signaling behaviors could be acquired by individuals with profound disabilities. Sternberg, Pegnatore, and Hill (1983) attempted to discover whether communication awareness behaviors could be acquired by four students with profound mental disabilities. None of these students had demonstrated communicative behaviors in the past. In this case, communication awareness responses were defined as a change in the state of the individual as a result of human interaction. Using techniques originally described by van Dijk (1965), the researchers assisted these students to develop various communication awareness behaviors that simultaneously indicated an understanding of contingent relationships. These techniques, termed resonance level programming, involved four basic components: (1) targeting a voluntarily committed motor behavior as a potential indicator of communication awareness; (2) assuming a position with the individual so that body-to-body physical contact was assured; (3) simultaneously committing whole body movements with the individual; and (4) monitoring changes in the targeted motor behavior in relation to the movement's occurring or not occurring.

Sternberg and Owens (1985) and Sternberg, McNerney, and Pegnatore (1987) studied the acquisition of primitive signals by individuals with profound mental retardation. None of the individuals in these studies had been observed to produce signaling behavior. Again, using the principles advocated by van Dijk (1965), individuals were exposed to coactive programming techniques (Sternberg, McNerney, & Pegnatore, 1985). Instead of requiring body-to-body contact as part of the method, only close physical proximity was necessary. The results of these studies indicated that individuals with profound disabilities could develop communicative signals to initiate coactive movement with another.

Wilcox, Kouri, and Caswell (1990) reported that children with cognitive, sensory, and/or motoric limitations often emit ambiguous signals that are difficult to read and use these signals inconsistently and infrequently. As a result, individuals interacting with children with profound disabilities may have different perceptions as to what the children understand and what they might be attempting to communicate. This inconsistency across communicative partners makes it difficult for individuals with profound disabilities to recognize contingent relationships between their behavior and the behaviors of others.

Wilcox et al. (1990) have used a team approach to train interactants to make contingent, appropriate, and consistent responses to both intentional and nonintentional communicative behaviors of infants with disabilities. The focus of training is to ensure consistency across interactants in the recognition of the child's signals and in the delivery of contingent responses. In their method, all members of the facilitation team are videotaped interacting with the infants. The team then meets to reach a consensus as to the meaning of any communicative signals the child might be using, to decide which motor acts will be reinforced, and to determine the type of contingent responses that will be provided. Members also select nonintentional or nondirected motor acts, such as eye contact, facial expression, oral motor behaviors, vocalizations, and body attitudes to which they will consistently respond. In choosing the motor acts that will be reinforced, the following guidelines are offered: (a) the behaviors must already be in the child's repertoire, (b) the behaviors selected must be ones for which there is the most agreement among the facilitation team, (c) abnormal movements are avoided as targets, and (d) self-injurious behaviors or behaviors that may be injurious to others are also avoided. In addition, contingencies are chosen that are conversationally appropriate. The consistency provided by this approach increases the number of opportunities for reciprocal communication exchanges and provides a foundation for further communicative development. This approach has the further advantage of including family members in the intervention process. It empowers the family as communication facilitators by validating their observations and making them active participants in their children's programming.

To summarize, the goal of intervention for the preintentional learner is to establish reciprocal communicative exchanges. This is best facilitated by providing consistent, contingent reinforcement to initial nondirected and nonintentional behavioral acts. Once individuals are able to participate in communicative exchanges, they may be able to benefit from training in more conventional communication skills.

It is important to consider, however, situations in which individuals with profound disabilities exhibit extremely limited behavioral repertoires. For these individuals, it becomes problematic to target a behavior for contingency awareness and management. Through recent research and intervention efforts dealing with behavior state and arousal (see Chapter 4), future intervention efforts may focus on physiologic changes (e.g., respiration rate, pulse rate) as potential targets. Using these targets, it is possible to conceive of communication awareness and signaling behaviors being acquired.

COMMUNICATION DEVELOPMENT IN THE INTENTIONAL COMMUNICATOR

Many individuals with profound disabilities have developed a system of intentional communication that may be refined through intervention. Once an individual realizes that he or she may have an effect on the environment, those skills may be expanded in three ways. The first way in which communication skills may be enhanced is to increase the number or conventionality of communicative forms used by the individual. Communicative forms can be defined as the means by which the individual communicates. These forms can include gestures, pictures, sign language, or speech. Some of these communicative signals may be easy to interpret, as when an individual who wants someone to open the door puts her hand on the door knob. The individual may have other consistent behaviors, however, that are not recognized by unfamiliar observers. One goal of intervention is to teach individuals to use communicative signals that may be readily understood by the greatest number of potential interactants.

The second way to enhance communication skills is to expand the individual's use of communicative intentions—that is, the effect that the speaker (communicator) intends for the signal to have on the listener. Intentions include requests for action, requests for objects, greeting, answering, naming, and social interaction. The use of communicative intentions for many individuals with profound disabilities has been limited to requesting (Cirrin & Rowland, 1985; McLean, McLean, Brady, & Etter, 1991; Ogletree, Wetherby, & Westling, 1992; Sternberg, 1991). However, communicative acts that can increase the opportunity for social interactions may enhance the individual's ability to function in a number of natural environments.

The third way to enhance communication skills, which is frequently ignored in intervention, is the use of conversational management techniques. These techniques, such as modification of a signal when the listener signals communication failure, helps the individual become a more effective communicator across a variety of communicative partners.

Communicative Forms and Augmentative and Alternative Communication

Ideas may be transmitted via many communicative forms, including gestures, sign language, printed words, and speech. Individuals who are profoundly disabled may be restricted in available communication forms due to motor, sensory, and/or cognitive limitations. For some, the forms of communication may be as elemental as changes in body tone or arousal level.

Forms differ primarily in their level of representation. For example, forms may be very abstract in relation to the surface structure of what they represent, known as the *referent* of the form. The spoken word "dog" is considered significantly more abstract than a photograph of a dog. In language, terms such as "beauty" are abstract because they do not have any concrete representation. "Big" and other adjectives are relational terms that, in and of themselves, mean nothing. When describing something else, however, they provide a basis for comparison. With children who are not disabled, nouns and verbs are the first to develop because they are the most salient and the least abstract. As mentioned previously, individuals with profound disabilities will likely experience significant problems with formal language systems, in part because of the level of abstraction that may be required. Therefore, a primary consideration when deciding which communicative forms to target should be the representational level of the targeted communicative behavior.

Augmentative and alternative communication (AAC) is a term that is frequently associated with the use of electronic communication devices. This is misleading, as any communicative form that is nonspeech (e.g., objects, gestures, pictures) is considered to be AAC. Most learners with profound disabilities must use some type of augmentative or alternative communication system because few are able to use spoken language as their primary mode of communication.

The advantages and limitations of communicative forms that may be used as AAC systems are discussed below. The forms are presented hierarchically from least representational to most representational.

Gestures

Gestures are typically considered the least representational communicative form because the referent is frequently observable in the immediate environment and may be part of the communicative act itself. For many individuals with profound disabilities, gestures may be the primary or sole means of communication. For others, use of gestures may be a prerequisite for the acquisition of more conventional communicative forms. A number of authors have provided descriptions and definitions of gestures, which have been or may be adapted for clinical use (Bates et al., 1977; Cirrin & Rowland, 1985; McLean, McLean, et al., 1991; Stillman & Williams, 1991; Stremmel-Campbell, Clark-Guida, & Johnson-Dorn, 1984).

McLean, McLean, et al. (1991) distinguished between *contact* and *distal* gestures in learners who are profoundly disabled, and this distinction has implications for intervention. Contact gestures are those that either make contact with or are made within 6 inches of the referent. Contact gestures include touching a bowl to request food or holding up a drink can to request that someone open it. Distal gestures are those made 6 inches or greater from the referent. Distal gestures include pointing to an airplane flying overhead or making a blowing gesture to request that someone blow up a balloon. Contact gestures appear to develop earlier and are more frequently in the repertoire of individuals with profound disabilities. Therefore, for the individual who is just beginning to use intentional communication, contact gestures should be targeted before distal gestures. For the learner who is already using contact gestures, intervention should focus on progression to distal gestures. Cirrin and Rowland (1985) also observed a hierarchy in gestural use and suggested that distal gestures, such as pointing, are later to develop.

Others (Sternberg, 1991; Sternberg & McNerney, 1988) have indicated that it is also important to delineate between those gestures that are *common or conventional* and those that are *natural*. Common gestures are those that anyone would likely understand (e.g., an arm-waving motion indicating "come here"). Natural gestures, on the other hand, are those that may be self-taught and understood by only a few. These gestures are rather idiosyncratic to the individual and are typically displayed when the individual is interacting with an object or person, or involved in certain activities. For the most part, these gestures tend to be of the *performative* or *depictive* variety (i.e., a motor behavior indicating what the person typically does with the object or person, or within the activity). Later, these natural gestures may become *referential*. In these cases, the gestures begin to physically describe the referent.

According to Sternberg and McNerney (1988), natural gestures may not be used initially by the individual for expressive communication purposes. Rather, an individual may exhibit the gesture as a form of "talking to oneself." They recommend that the facilitator structure the situation in such a way that the individual would be required to exhibit the gesture in an expressive manner. For example, if the individual were interacting with an object, that object might be taken away. Assuming that the individual has already exhibited a natural gesture for that object, the removal might cause the individual to exhibit the natural gesture as a request mode.

Sternberg and McNerney (1988) emphasized that natural gestures should be accepted and reinforced as expressive communicative forms prior to instituting a program to refine these gestures into more conventional forms. For example, using a paired-associate approach, if the individual consistently displayed the natural gesture within a communicative interchange, it would be appropriate to match this gesture with a more symbolic form.

Gestures have distinct advantages for individuals with profound disabilities. Gestures may be used to communicate about a wide range of topics and, because most people understand gestures, they allow the individual access to many communicative partners. Furthermore, fewer gross- and fine-motor skills are required when using gestures than when using many signs or speech. Also, unlike some other augmentative or alternative communication systems (e.g., picture books), the individual always has the system readily available.

Objects

Three-dimensional communicative symbols can also be used by individuals with profound disabilities. Beukelman and Mirenda (1992) indicated that a wide range of possibilities exists, although they cautioned against making a priori assumptions regarding what might be best for an individual user. Real objects and miniature objects can be used to represent activities. When an activity involves a referent that is large, partial objects might be appropriate. In addition, certain cases may necessitate the use of other tangible objects that have a more artificial connection to an activity (e.g., a piece of a placemat to represent lunch).

A number of researchers have described methods that incorporate objects into communicative routines. Rowland and Schweigert (1989, 1990) and Sternberg and McNerney (1988) suggested that objects could initially serve in an anticipatory role to activities that followed. In practice, the individual is directed to interact with an object that represents an activity prior to the individual's engaging in the activity itself. Based upon repetitions of this sequence, the individual comes to anticipate the activity from the object. Later, the individual can use the object to communicate about (e.g., request) the activity.

Pictures

Pictures can be defined as two-dimensional representations of concepts, and may be classified into photographs or drawings, with photographs being less representational than drawings (Mirenda & Locke, 1989). Pictures have the advantages of requiring little motor skill other than showing or pointing, and can be used with a large number of interactants. Disadvantages of pictures are that they interrupt the normal flow of communicative exchanges because the user needs to select the appropriate picture and then draw the listener's attention to the picture before communicating about the topic.

Furthermore, the individual is dependent upon having the pictures readily available. If pictures are nonportable and posted in one environment, the same pictures should be accessible in other natural environments. Finally, pictures are suited primarily to the expression of nouns; therefore, it may be difficult for individuals with profound disabilities to understand actions represented in a static, two-dimensional form.

Sign language

Sign language continues to be widely used as a target for intervention. Because it is less representational than spoken language, is visual, and requires less motor skill development than is required in speech, it is a form of language that is more readily understood and of potential use by some individuals with profound disabilities. Sign language, like gestural forms of communication, has the advantage of being readily available to the user, although its use requires greater motor and cognitive skill prerequisites than does use of gestures. Because sign language is highly representational, it does not confine the communicative topics to referents that are present in the environment. The main limitation of any sign language is that it is not understood by everybody, thus limiting the interactive partners available to the individual. Furthermore, an individual who does not have symbolic representation may learn only a few rudimentary signs. Knowing only a few signs should not, however, be an indication that sign is the optimal mode for the individual, or that sign should be trained to the exclusion of gestures.

The foremost consideration in the selection of targets for sign language training is functionality. Doherty (1985) provided additional guidelines for the selection of signs for training. Aside from the necessity that the individual possess adequate motor and visual skills coupled with cognitive ability for symbolic representation, consideration should be given to the ease of sign production. The simplest signs to learn are those that are two-handed and require contact between hands, that are symmetrical and produced in the user's visual field, that are reduplicated simple hand shapes resembling referents, and that express individual preferences.

Symbol systems

Several symbol systems have been used in communication training with individuals with disabilities. The systems might have some utility for certain individuals with profound disabilities, given that those individuals' functioning levels match the demands of the systems themselves. Some commonly used systems are Blissymbols (Bliss, 1965) and Rebus symbols (Clark, Davies, & Woodcock, 1974). These systems have the advantage of being less representational than written language. These systems are also flexible in that they provide means by which symbols can be combined to express more abstract concepts. For individuals with severe motor impairments who possess good representational ability and vision, these systems may provide an expressive communicative mode. These symbols must also be recognizable by those interacting with the system, which may be difficult for interactants unfamiliar with the system unless some voice output device is also included.

Speech

Generative and intelligible speech is likely the most difficult communicative form for individuals with profound disabilities to master. Few will use this form as their primary means of communication. Speech requires the cognitive skill of representation and places the greatest demands on fine-motor skills. Furthermore, programs to increase the speech intelligibility of individuals with profound disabilities have largely been unsuccessful due to the cognitive and linguistic knowledge required to benefit from speech interventions. Intelligible speech does have the advantage of allowing an individual to interact with many communicative partners across many communicative environments and, therefore, may be the least restrictive form of communication for some individuals.

Electronic devices

Advances in technology have allowed for the development of communicative devices that allow individuals, primarily those with motor impairments, access to sophisticated communication systems at ever-decreasing expense. Furthermore, these systems can be adapted to teach communications skills to individuals with disabilities (e.g., to teach operant contingencies). These systems, however, have the same limitations for individuals with profound disabilities as do other symbol systems. Primarily, they require symbolic communication abilities and, therefore, may not be useful for many individuals who do not display that level of cognitive competence.

Historically, individuals with profound disabilities were not considered candidates for electronic systems. It was believed that potential benefits of using electronic systems with these individuals were outweighed by the cost of the early devices. As technology has become more sophisticated and less expensive, however, some individuals with profound disabilities may be able to benefit from the use of an electronic communication system.

Romski and Sevcik (1993), who developed the System for Augmenting Language (SAL), have reported success in using a speech output device with learners who are severely disabled. They contend that five requisites are critical for a person to use SAL: (1) presence of receptive language skills, (2) extant nonsymbolic communication skills, (3) use of a speech output device, (4) naturalistic learning opportunities, and (5) available vocabulary. These requisites have implications for the use of electronic devices with individuals who are profoundly disabled. Specifically, Romski and Sevcik have highlighted the importance of using the device within naturalistic interactions, which mandates that both conversational partners use the device to communicate. Using this approach, the individual learns the situations in which the device may be used, the potential stigma of using an AAC system is lessened, and the individual is able to use the device to facilitate comprehension. Romski and Sevcik also pointed to the importance of using a device with speech output. They have concluded that using such a device facilitates interaction with speaking persons, and provides the individual with auditory symbols that can be paired with a referent, thereby enhancing language learning.

System selection, as well as training for the student and other interactants, is highly individualized. The design of the electronic device and programming for its use should be decided upon by all members of the facilitation team. The following considerations for system selection have been adapted from Mirenda, Iacono, and Williams (1990):

1. *Mobility* (positioning): The individual and his or her interactive partners must have ready access to the system. It is important to consider that the system will be used both to provide communicative input to the individual and as an expressive system.

2. *Manipulation:* The individual must possess the fine motor skills necessary to select communicative targets.

3. *Communication:* A range of communicative forms, intents, and conversational skills should be available to the individual through use of the device.

4. *Cognitive–Linguistic:* The user must possess the representational ability necessary to comprehend the symbols used. In addition, to use symbols intentionally, an individual must have an awareness of operational causality (Bates et al., 1977).

5. *Sensory–Perceptual:* The individual should possess the visual, auditory, and or tactual skills necessary to use the system effectively. That does not mean, however, that a voice output device would not be included on a system for a person who is deaf; the device should be accessible to interactive partners as well as the individual.

Forms targeted for intervention should also be functional. Selection of targeted forms should be based on the opportunities available for spontaneous use of that form. For example, teaching an individual a gesture for "stove" may not be practical if the individual is in an institutional setting where the food is prepared for him or her. Even if the individual is in a setting where a "stove" is available and he or she partially participates in cooking routines, a primary concern is whether the individual will have the opportunity to use the gesture outside of the kitchen. If the only time he or she refers to the item is when it is present in the environment, then it may not be necessary to make that item a communicative target. However, if the individual is proud of his or her cooking abilities and can use the gesture for "stove" to initiate conversations regarding these interests, then "stove" may be an appropriate communicative target.

For a comprehensive review of electronic communication devices, and other augmentative and alternative systems, the reader is referred to Beukelman and Mirenda (1992) and Reichle, York, and Sigafoos (1991).

Facilitated Communication

Recent interest has developed in the use of what is termed *facilitated communication* with certain individuals who are disabled. This approach uses adult facilitators to provide the individual with the physical guidance and social support necessary to use spelling devices that provide voice and/or coded (e.g., alphabetic) output. This process typically involves the implementation of a series of procedural steps (Biklen, Morton, Gold, Berrigan, & Swaminathan, 1992). The communicator is first taught, through hand-over-hand support, to use the index finger to point to or touch the keys of an output device. This support is then progressively changed and lessened (hand-over-wrist, hand-to-elbow, touch cues to elbow, etc.). Output tasks are usually structured at first (e.g., choice selections) and then proceed to unstructured varieties (e.g., open-ended questions).

Support has been generated for the use of this approach, especially with some individuals identified as autistic (Biklen, 1990, 1992; Biklen et al., 1992; Crossley, 1991; Crossley & Remington-Gurney, 1992; Schalow & Schalow, 1985). The approach, however, has not been without its critics (Calculator, 1992; Cummins & Prior, 1992; McLean, 1992; Wheeler, Jacobson, Paglieri, & Schwartz, 1993). Much of the criticism has involved issues regarding the proven validity of the facilitated communication approach. In most cases, this criticism has centered around the issue of whether the facilitator or student is actually communicating the message. There has been, therefore, a general call for additional research to provide the necessary validation (Donnellan, Sabin, & Majure, 1992; Silliman, 1992).

To this end, Calculator and Singer (1992) conducted a study in which facilitated communication was used to assess the accuracy of diagnostic information obtained from five students with various types of developmental disabilities. For the most part, expectations and educational programs provided for these students were rather inconsistent. This situation was based, in part, on diagnostic information that was either supported or rejected by teachers and caregivers. Using various types of control procedures, the researchers compared nonfacilitated to facilitated performance of these students on the *Peabody Picture Vocabulary Test–Revised* (PPVT-R) (Dunn & Dunn, 1981). Their findings indicated that the students' performance significantly increased as a result of the use of facilitated communication. What was also apparent was that these findings tended to be accepted by skeptics as proof of the efficacy of facilitated communication more than have facilitators' descriptions of various student outputs (e.g., consistent misspellings, innovative use of words) that have been used in past attempts to establish validity.

Wheeler et al. (1993) also conducted an experimental analysis of facilitated communication. Twelve individuals who were classified as autistic and nine facilitators participated in the study. Pictures of familiar objects were displayed to the individuals and their facilitators under three conditions: pictures shown only to the individual while facilitation was being provided, pictures shown to the individual only with no facilitation being provided, and pictures shown to both the individual and the facilitator with instances of the same and different pictures being presented simultaneously. The results of the study indicated that facilitation was not successful. In fact, the data seemed to indicate that facilitators tended to determine what the individual would eventually type. Wheeler et al. stressed the point that any instance of communication that is tendered through the use of facilitation must be validated through the use of other communicative modalities (e.g., sign, gesture) and/or collaboration from other, independent facilitators.

At first glance, it might seem absurd to consider the use of facilitated communication for individuals with profound disabilities given the cognitive, communicative, and motoric deficits typically found with this group (see Chapter 1). What is important to consider, however, is that the assessment practices to determine content or domain-specific deficits are far from being an exact science. Inaccurate assessments of functioning type and level are very possible, especially with those individuals who experience multiple disabilities (Crossley, 1992). If the implementation of facilitated communication proves to be successful with an individual labeled as profoundly disabled, it is almost certain that that label is inappropriate. Therefore, the applicability of facilitated communication to individuals with profound disabilities should be based on assessment of its implementation, rather than on preconceived notions or mind-sets regarding the literacy or communicative functioning level of these individuals. Our level of understanding of the communicative prowess of individuals with profound disabilities is, at best, lacking. Therefore, implementation of alternative procedures, especially in an area as crucial as communication, should be assessed as part of the normal determination of best practice (Donnellan et al., 1992; Kangas & Lloyd, 1988).

DEVELOPING AND EXPANDING COMMUNICATIVE INTENTS

A communicative *intent* is the effect the communication is intended to have on the listener. A communicative *function* is the actual effect of the communication. However, the two terms are frequently used interchangeably. Communicative forms cannot be separated from their intent when considering the communication behaviors of individuals with profound disabilities (Alvares et al., 1991). Many early communication training programs for children with severe or profound disabilities, however, focused only on artificial reinforcement of symbol acquisition as unrelated aspects of the full communicative act. Goetz et al. (1981) argued that the reason many operant models of teaching communicative forms failed was because they focused on production in isolation without natural consequences. Therefore, there were no elements of the environment that maintained the newly acquired skill. For example, the sign "jump" would be modeled for the individual, the individual would imitate the sign, and finally he or she would be given an edible reward. Consequently, the individual was neither able to establish the meaning of the sign nor able to use the sign as a way to control events in the environment.

Communicative intents fall into three broad categories as described by Bruner (1975). *Behavioral regulation* is an attempt to elicit or direct an overt act from the listener, and can involve an object. Intentions that fall into this category include requesting actions or objects and protesting. Intents that fall into the *social interaction* category are those that elicit affective behavior (e.g., smiling) from the listener in face-to-face situations, or those that are components of social conventions (e.g., gaining a listener's attention or providing a greeting). *Joint attention* acts are used to elicit or maintain the attention of another on a single referent. The only requirement on the part of the listener is attention to or acknowledgment of the speaker's referent. Such intentions include naming, commenting, copying, answering, and acknowledging. A number of instruments have been developed to document use of communicative intentions in individuals with communicative disabilities (Cirrin & Rowland, 1985; Coggins & Carpenter, 1981; Donnellan, Mirenda, Mesaros, & Fassbender, 1984; Stremmel-Campbell et al., 1984).

For individuals with profound disabilities, the primary communicative intents used are those related to behavioral regulation—that is, requesting objects, requesting action, and protesting (Cirrin & Rowland, 1985; McLean, McLean, et al., 1991; Sternberg, 1991; Stillman & Battle, 1984). Intentional communicators with profound disabilities typically use few or no social interaction or joint attention acts. The reasons for this are unclear. Some have speculated that individuals with profound disabilities are more inwardly directed, seeking to satisfy sensory rather than social needs (e.g., Stillman & Battle, 1984). Others have speculated that the ability to use joint attention acts is related to the ability to communicate at a distance. Therefore, some individuals with profound disabilities who must interact with the distant referent will be unable to use these intentions (McLean, McLean, et al., 1991). Still others argue that environmental causes, such as lack of reinforcement of joint attention acts due to poor quality or attitudes of caregivers, decreases the probability that the individual will use these acts (Calculator, 1985; McLean, McLean, et al., 1991). Because the motivation for communication is the expression of communicative intents, the communication facilitator will want to ascertain the type of intents an individual may need or want to express in determining the communicative form to be targeted for intervention. In addition, determining the motivation behind the use of the form will identify the potential reinforcement for its use. Many programs have taught communicative forms through using forms to request (e.g. Hunt, Goetz, Alwell, & Sailor, 1986; Romski, Sevcik, & Pate, 1988).

It remains unclear, however, if communication of other intents, particularly joint attention acts, can be expected or developed in individuals with profound disabilities. If form and function are inextricably tied together, and if intentions "drive" forms of communication (Sternberg, 1991), it is unlikely that such expansion of intents will be possible for these individuals. Only through further efforts at enhancing communication environments for individuals with profound disabilities (e.g., those requiring social-interactive and joint attention communicative behaviors) can the issue be resolved.

DEVELOPING COMMUNICATIVE COMPETENCE

The ability to participate in conversation requires more than the ability to use communicative forms to express communicative intents. Effective speakers must gain the listener's attention prior to the communicative act, initiate communication, respond to others, and modify their communication in response to communication failure. These are abilities required in using conversation within the context of interaction regardless of the communication mode used. In assessing current performance and targeting intervention goals, the practitioner should determine if the individual possesses these skills and, if he or she does not, provide opportunities to develop these skills.

One important aspect of communication is to ensure the attention of the listener. In the case of nonverbal communication, the person sending the communication signal needs to ensure that the listener is attending to the signal. This is generally accomplished through body orientation and eye contact. Some individuals with profound disabilities fail to make listener contact (e.g., eye contact) prior to using a communicative signal. A communication facilitator or partner should not respond to the signal until the individual establishes contact. This will also assist the individual to understand the importance of establishing joint attentional focus prior to communicating.

Communication repair is a skill that has been observed in nonverbal infants (Alvares, 1992; Golinkoff, 1986) as well as adults with profound disabilities (McLean, McLean, et al., 1991). Communication repair is the modification of the communication signal when the listener indicates there has been communication failure. The facilitator should occasionally feign communication breakdown to determine how an individual might respond in the event of communication failure, and provide models of how the message can be expressed using an alternative form. This technique can also be used to model new communicative forms for individuals. For example, if the individual reaches for some milk, the facilitator might use a questioning facial expression and model the sign for "milk," requesting confirmation from the individual that the milk was the desired object. This strategy is one that mothers use to teach language within an interactive context to their infants (Alvares, 1992).

Many individuals with profound disabilities are passive in the communication process. Because they are primarily responders, they are dependent on others for their communicative interactions. This limits their opportunities to use their communication skills. Several techniques, such as time delay techniques described by Halle (1982), have been used to promote initiation in individuals with profound disabilities. This technique will be discussed in greater detail in a later section.

COMMUNICATION ASSESSMENT FOR INDIVIDUALS WITH PROFOUND HANDICAPS

Communication assessment of individuals with profound disabilities should have two primary purposes: (1) the identification of communicative strengths and weaknesses of the individual and how he or she uses these skills to adapt to the environment, and (2) the identification of aspects of the environment that can be modified to facilitate communication development. This type of assessment requires both direct interaction with the individual and repeated, careful observation of the individual across various environments and interactants.

No standardized communication assessments exist for individuals with profound disabilities. Such assessments would be of little value in intervention as most standardized assessments are designed to determine the difference between an individual's performance and the performance of a peer group that is nondisabled (Peck, 1989). A more practical approach is to assess the individual's communicative strengths and weaknesses through systematic observation across communicative environments.

A device that is widely used in the assessment of communicative functioning of children with profound disabilities is the *Callier–Azusa Scale (H): Scales for Assessment of Communicative Abilities* (Stillman & Battle, 1985). Communication skills are evaluated in four domains: representational and symbolic development, receptive communication (i.e., the ability to respond to communication of others), development of intentional communication, and reciprocity (i.e., the ability to participate in communicative exchanges). Information is gathered through observation of students in instructional settings across several interactants and activities. The *Callier–Azusa Scale* assesses the communicative partner's ability to elicit the communication, as well as the child's ability to demonstrate those skills. Because the instrument is developmentally based, it provides goals for intervention, as well as a means by which to document developmental change in communicative competence. In addition, it provides measures of cognitive and social abilities related to communication development (Stillman & Battle, 1985).

Another device that has been designed for use for individuals with profound disabilities is the *Communication Programming Inventory* (CPI) (Sternberg, 1988). Four areas are assessed: cognition, receptive communication, expressive communication, and social/affective behaviors. Behaviors representative of each area are rated as to whether they occur naturally, are person or situation specific, do not occur at the present time, or cannot occur because of the presence of a condition that precludes their performance. Behaviors are also categorized in terms of developmental level of performance. Scoring protocols are established in which a communication facilitator is referred to a chart that summarizes an individual's performance in relation to readiness for interventions within a modified van Dijk approach. (For more in-depth information concerning the approaches suggested, the reader is referred to Sternberg & McNerney, 1988.)

Observation instruments have also been designed to assess the use of communicative intentions across interactants and across environments (Cirrin & Rowland, 1985; Coggins & Carpenter, 1981; Donnellan et al., 1984; Owens & Rogerson, 1988; Schuler, Peck, Willard, & Theimer, 1989; Stremmel-Campbell et al., 1984). Information is obtained through both observation of the individual and interview with significant interactants in the individual's life. Although most of these instruments are designed to be used "on-line," it is recommended that the individual doing the assessment videotape these interactions if possible.

The inventory described by Donnellan et al. (1984) is specifically designed to assess the communicative function of maladaptive behaviors, such as aggression, property destruction, and self-injurious behaviors. The authors contend that maladaptive behaviors often have communicative function and, by analyzing the communicative function of aberrant behavior, either a substitute behavior can be taught or the environment changed to decrease frustration leading to maladaptive behavior. In one case, they described an 18-year-old man who used self-injurious behaviors to gain attention. As an alternative means to initiate interactions, he was taught to signal for attention, sign "help," and indicate the aspect of the work with which he needed assistance. As a result, the individual's exhibition of self-injurious behavior decreased significantly.

Investigators have also developed procedures through which one can systematically elicit communicative intentions in disabled children (Wetherby & Prizant, 1989), as well as adults (McLean, McLean, et al., 1991) and children with profound mental retardation (Ogletree et al., 1992). These procedures provide opportunities in which behavior regulation acts can be elicited, as well as joint attention and social interaction acts. For example, Wetherby and Prizant provided opportunities for creating spectacles, such as the spilling of water, to encourage children to draw the adult's attention to the event, thereby demonstrating a joint attention act. Wetherby, Yonclas, and Bryan (1989) found that the use of communicative intents in preschoolers provided diagnostic information; for example, children identified as autistic used few joint attention acts. McLean, McLean, et al. (1991) provided standardized procedures by which communicative forms and intents, as well as other conversational skills, such as initiation and communication repair, could be elicited in adults with profound disabilities. Ogletree et al. employed 12 structured situations (e.g., eating a desired food in front of the individual but not offering any to him or her) and unstructured play situations to assess various aspects of intentional communication in children with profound mental retardation. These aspects included communicative function, communicative means (form), discourse structure (whether the communication was self-initiated or in response to another), and syllable shape (descriptions of vocalizations).

Cognitive Assessment

For children with profound disabilities, cognitive abilities exert a profound influence on communication and social abilities. Therefore, assessment of the individual's cognitive skills may provide important intervention information. As with communication, standardized tests of intelligence provide little clinically relevant information. The use of ordinal scales of assessment, however, appear to represent an appropriate method to assess cognitive skills (Dunst, 1980). Dunst adapted the *Ordinal Scales of Psychological Development* (Uzgiris & Hunt, 1975), which were based on Piagetian sensorimotor cognitive stages, for use with children with disabilities. These scales allow the practitioner to assess progress along a continuum rather than providing comparative performance data to peers. The emphasis is on a delineation of specific areas of strength and weakness. Because attainment of some sensorimotor stages is correlated with presymbolic and early symbolic communication (Bates et al., 1977), this information may be of particular significance for those facilitating communication skills development.

Assessing the Communicative Environment

Assessment and intervention procedures should always take into account the interactive role of the natural environment. These procedures that take place in the natural environment have three distinct advantages. First, focusing assessment and intervention efforts on natural environments is a move away from the traditional model of who is and who is not appropriate for access and participation in activities. Second, it allows for maximum participation across least restrictive environments (Mirenda et al., 1990). The environmental assessment approach, therefore, facilitates the movement of individuals with profound disabilities to less restrictive environments. The third advantage is that, when training takes place within natural environments, programming for generalization becomes easier and, in some cases, may be unnecessary.

Peck (1989) argued that the development of communicative competence in individuals with disabilities is a product of their adaptation to the environment. Therefore, it is essential to assess not only how individuals use the skills they have, but how the environment (including interactive partners) can be engineered to promote further communication development. Peck provided a number of guidelines for assessing characteristics of the environment.

The first area for assessment is *dyadic variables.* These include the assessment of partner responsiveness, complexity of communicative forms used by partners, adult compliance with preferences that are communicated, partner's familiarity with the individual, repair attempts, topic maintenance, and affective behavior. The second set of variables are *situational variables,* which include joint activity routines, opportunities to request assistance, opportunities for protesting, and opportunities for choice making. The third area of assessment, *setting variables,* comprises activities available, social climate, and communication partners available. By manipulating these environmental variables, such as increasing partner responsivity or providing more opportunities for choice making, the practitioner can facilitate communication development in individuals with profound disabilities.

Stillman and Williams (1990) developed an instrument with which teachers and other significant interactants may identify, describe, and analyze communicative forms and intentions used during interactions with students with profound disabilities. By analyzing the use of forms and intentions, teachers can identify behaviors that serve to establish and maintain reciprocal exchanges with their students. Using these procedures, interactions are videotaped, transcribed, and coded for communicative form and intention. The teacher identifies which forms are the most effective in providing information to the student, and those that are most effective in eliciting communication from the student. By analyzing the use of communicative intents, the teacher can establish the frequency with which students and teachers are engaging in different types of communicative acts. The authors also suggested that teachers count teacher and student communications per minute to determine if one partner is dominating the interaction. By using these analyses, teachers can determine the most effective means to engage students in mutual communicative exchanges.

Mirenda et al. (1990) somewhat expanded environmental assessment to include a number of other components. For example, they proposed that such assessment include evaluating the environment and activities of nondisabled age-matched peers; completing task analyses for peers and determining which aspects of the task the individual with disabilities may perform; and determining how an individual learner may most effectively participate in that environment.

For individuals who are capable of workplace inclusion, environmental assessment should likely focus on the communication demands of that environment. Communication skills required in vocational settings might include requesting assistance, requesting more materials, and interacting with co-workers during break periods. Van der Gaag (1988) developed a protocol through which one can evaluate an individual's ability to give information, respond to and ask questions, and describe events and feelings. In addition, the protocol gives direction to the evaluation of components of conversational skills, such as turn-taking behavior and topic maintenance. Although the protocol was designed to provide assessment directives on how language users with developmental disabilities communicate, the instrument could be modified for use with presymbolic communicators.

FACILITATING COMMUNICATION DEVELOPMENT WITHIN AN INTERACTIVE FRAMEWORK

Much of the foregoing discussion has emphasized the role of social interaction in the development of communication, and the importance of communication training within the natural environment. Several intervention models that have been developed incorporate these principles, and have been used successfully in facilitating communication development with individuals with profound disabilities. Although some of the intervention models discussed below have been designed to facilitate language acquisition in children with disabilities, they may be modified to be used to facilitate use of nonsymbolic communication. They can also be adapted to provide age-appropriate communication experiences for older individuals.

Ecological Communication Model and Developing Communicative Interactions

Like the Wilcox et al. (1990) program, the focus of intervention training for the ecological communication model (MacDonald & Gillette, 1985) and the Developing Communicative Interactions series (McLean, Sack, McLean, O'Connor, & Simmons, 1991) is to increase the responsivity of caregivers. Both approaches train caregivers to recognize communicative signals, within a conversational context, of preintentional and intentional individuals with profound disabilities. The ecological communication approach was designed to be used with young children and has been used with children with a wide range of communicative needs. This approach has been used successfully with preintentional children and with children with mild to moderate mental disabilities, multiple disabilities, autism, hearing impairments, learning disabilities, and specific language impairments (MacDonald & Carroll, 1992). The Developing Communicative Interactions series was designed to train caregivers of adults with disabilities to promote communication development through social interactions.

The goal of the ecological communication system approach is to establish reciprocal exchanges between the caregiver and the child. MacDonald and Gillette (1985) speculated that interactions between individuals and their caregivers are mismatched in terms of quality and quantity, and that this mismatch impedes communication development. Sources of communicative mismatch include (a) turn-taking that is too brief in duration, (b) turn-taking episodes totally controlled by the caregiver, and (c) turn-taking in which expectations of the caregiver are above the capabilities of the individual. The recommended interventions train caregivers to use progressively matched turn-taking, which includes both qualitative and quantitative elements. *Qualitative match* refers to the content of caregivers' communication, primarily with respect to their ability to communicate based on the child's attentional focus as well as the linguistic and nonlinguistic forms used by the caregiver and child. *Quantitative match* occurs when the caregiver and child are equal partners in the interaction, as measured by the frequency of communication turns exhibited by each partner.

In addition to its adaptability with a wide range of individuals, this approach has several other advantages. First, training occurs in the natural environment with the child's primary caregiver, thus increasing the time in which the child participates in communicative exchanges. Second, because the focus is on playing together rather than teaching language, communicative exchanges become highly rewarding for the caregiver. Finally, caregivers may be less intimidated when asked to play with a child, as opposed to teaching communication.

The Developing Communicative Interactions program is a series of videotapes with four training modules that help caregivers of adults with disabilities to recognize opportunities to facilitate communication development. The first module focuses on requisites for communication, such as establishing attentional focus and turn-taking. The second teaches interactants how to recognize verbal and nonverbal forms of communication. The third module introduces how one can enhance conversational skills, establish joint attention, match for level of symbolic representation, and check for comprehension and communication repair. The final module introduces communicative intentions and provides strategies for structuring the environment to promote communication.

The Transactional Approach

McLean and Snyder-McLean (1978) adopted as the cornerstone of their approach many of the tenets espoused by Bates (1976). In addition to what they see as a phase-to-phase development of communication skills, they emphasized the social-interactive qualities of communication. Also important is their contention that what an individual will eventually communicate about is based, for the most part, on his or her level of cognitive competence. *Transaction* involves how the individual can develop control over the environment using communicative, social-interactive, and cognitive skills.

In terms of preintentional communication, McLean and Snyder-McLean (1978) systematically refined and behaviorized the phases of early communication development. In their initial phase, a *reactive stage* leads to a *proactive stage*. In the former, the individual merely responds (reacts) to environmental stimuli using both voluntary (e.g., crying) and involuntary (e.g., reflex) behaviors. These reactions can "force" others to attend; however, the individual never actually intends for this to happen. In the proactive stage, the individual more directly wants to achieve a goal, but the intent does not seem to be planned. For example, the individual might be involved in a motor activity with another person (e.g., rocking together). Once the activity stops, the individual might begin a component of that activity. The other person may ascribe intent to the movement and begin the motor activity again. In this case, the actual motor activity had to be presented before the "intentional" response was generated.

In the second phase, a *primitive stage* progresses toward a *conventional stage.* In the primitive stage, the individual displays self-initiated communicative intent; the individual wants and does begin to communicate about something in particular. Unfortunately, there may still be a problem with how clear the intent is. For example, the individual may purposefully reach or cry out for another person. The person will definitely know that he or she is wanted, but will have to discover the specific thing that he or she is to provide or do. During the conventional stage, however, not only is purposeful communicative intent displayed, but the individual is much clearer concerning what he or she wants. For example, the individual might not only reach for the other person but also display a gesture or pointing motion to indicate exactly what he or she wants.

The transactional approach provides a framework for viewing the development of communication skills. By referring to behavioral exemplars that represent the interplay among social-interactive, communicative, and cognitive skills development, the facilitator can not only understand an individual's current type of communication functioning, but also outline a methodological approach for effecting communication skill change.

Incidental Learning and Mand–Model Training

Hart and Risley (1975) were among the first to develop means by which communication could be taught within natural environments. Their approach, called *incidental learning,* was a technique used to teach language based on children's spontaneous utterances. For example, if the child pointed to a picture of a duck, the adult would respond by saying, "Yes, that's a duck." This was different from traditional models of language intervention because the communication intervention was based on the child's attentional focus, and was conducted within the natural environment rather than teaching language in a noncontextual manner. Rogers-Warren and Warren (1980) modified the procedure using what they described as a *mand–model approach.* This procedure provided more direct cueing to the child to use language. Using the previous example, if the child pointed to the duck, the teacher would provide the prompt, "Yes, that's a duck; say 'duck.'" Like the incidental training approach, the mand–model approach provides a means by which language intervention may take place within a natural environment, use the child's attentional focus as the basis for language training, and provide systematic procedures such as cueing strategies and fading of prompts. To increase communicative opportunities, both models suggest that the environment be structured to increase communicative opportunities (e.g., placing toys out of children's reach so that they needed to request adult assistance to obtain a toy). Norris and Hoffman (1990) provided further suggestions as to how these techniques might be incorporated into play with objects.

Time Delay and Chain Interruption

A limitation of both the incidental learning and the mand–model techniques is that they rely on child-initiated communications upon which the communication facilitator must expand. These approaches are more effective with children who are already intentionally communicating than with those who communicate infrequently or are not showing intentional communications (Warren, Yoder, Wilcox, & Girolametto, 1991). Many individuals with profound disabilities initiate infrequently, thereby reducing the number of opportunities for the use of either technique and promoting dependence on another individual for communication interaction.

Halle (1982) argued that initiation would occur when the environment, rather than an interactant, provided a cue for the individual to communicate. Furthermore, generalization would be best facilitated across partners if communication was contingent upon environmental events rather than adult cueing, thereby increasing the individual's independence in the communication domain. Halle used *time delay* as a means by which to promote initiation. This approach was used in conjunction with the mand–model technique. For example, if a child wanted to go outside through a door that he or she was unable to open, the adult would stand by a door and wait for the child to make some type of signal. The adult cued the child as necessary, either by using physical assistance or modeling the correct response. After repeated trials, the adult would fade the prompt and simply pause until the child provided the targeted communicative behavior. The effectiveness of the approach was enhanced by the use of highly structured activities that were repeated frequently. By using such activities, the child learned the successive steps of an activity and could produce the communicative target that would lead to a contingent and predictable response from the adult.

Hunt et al. (1986) further refined the time delay technique into a procedure called *behavior chain interruption*. The foundation for this procedure is the incorporation of time delays into highly structured routines. This delay takes place at the point of maximum motivation, at which time the individual is most compelled to finish the routine. The facilitator withholds the item needed to complete the task, requiring the individual to use a symbol, such as a sign or a picture, to obtain the object needed to complete the routine. This approach has been demonstrated to be effective with individuals who communicate infrequently and, as Halle (1982) observed, can become a generalizable technique because the cue for communication is the pause itself.

Use of Peers

One purpose of movement to less restrictive environments is to allow an individual who is disabled to learn skills from peer models. Another is to provide individuals who are not disabled with opportunities for social interaction with peers who are disabled. One means by which peer interaction may be facilitated between individuals with and without disabilities is the use of peers in communication programming.

In determining how peers who are not disabled may be used in communication intervention, Paul (1985) suggested that assessment focus on three questions: Do peers provide appropriate models? Do peers provide sufficient opportunities for the child to interact? and Do peers provide opportunities for reinforcement of children's initiations? Because most of the approaches already discussed have used routines to facilitate communication, an appropriate means to encourage social interaction with peers is to incorporate them into communicative routines. For example, if an individual who is disabled needed a key to open the door to a room, the routine might be engineered so that the key was kept by the peer who was not disabled. Therefore, an interaction between the peers would be necessary so that the routine could be completed. Also, the peer without disabilities would need to be apprised of how to provide the appropriate communicative response.

Some research indicates that interactive models of *language* intervention with children with disabilities are beneficial in enhancing a child's use of but not developmental improvements in language (Tannock, Girolametto, & Siegel, 1992). Without a similar research thrust in the nonlinguistic area with individuals with profound disabilities, it is not possible to ascertain whether interactive emphases will prove as limited in their effects.

GENERALIZATION

Historically, speech and language services were delivered using a "pull-out" model in which communicative targets were taught outside of the natural environment and without natural contingencies. When using the pull-out model, it was necessary to specifically program for generalization so that the individual could use the skills outside of the therapy room. A naturalistic approach to intervention decreases the amount of programming that needs to be directly geared toward generalization.

Generalization of skills for individuals with profound disabilities should be directed toward increasing the opportunities for using communicative forms and intentions with an increasing number of partners and contexts. Generalization will be facilitated when communicative forms targeted for intervention are chosen so that they can be used with the greatest number of interactive partners in the greatest number of contexts. Therefore, generalization needs to be considered in initial intervention planning. The following discussion will present some ways in which generalization of skills may be included in this planning.

Across Contexts

One way to facilitate generalization across contexts is to target for intervention communicative forms that may be used in several contexts. Individuals with profound disabilities may be limited in the number of communicative forms, particularly symbolic forms, they may acquire. If the individual is capable of learning a few symbolic forms, forms should be chosen that can be used in many situations. For example, if an individual has demonstrated a gesture for "open" or learned the sign "open" in order to have another open a door, the gesture or sign should be taught in other contexts (e.g., requesting the bus driver to open the door of the school bus; requesting a caregiver at home to open the drawers of a dresser).

Across Interactants

Generalization and communication require that all significant interactants in an individual's life be involved in the assessment and intervention process. When many interactants in the individual's environment provide opportunities for communication, the individual's communicative competence will be enhanced. Again, the communicative forms targeted for intervention should take into account consideration of the number of individuals with whom the person will be able to interact. For example, generalization would be facilitated if an individual learned to point to request "juice" rather than sign "juice," because, although teachers in the classroom may understand some sign language, communicative partners in other environments may not. Therefore, focusing on a less symbolic system, such as gestures, has the advantage of providing flexibility across communicative partners.

Communicative intent is also a consideration when choosing communicative targets. As stated earlier, targets for augmentative and alternative communication have focused on requests to the exclusion of joint attention and social interaction intents. Targets should be chosen that mirror the individual's interests, for this will increase the likelihood of the individual's using the communicative form. However, by providing the individual with opportunities to use greetings and social amenities, the opportunities for interactions across partners increase substantially.

Partner Use of the Communication System

For an individual to recognize the contexts in which forms may be used, it is important for those interacting with the individual to consider those contexts as well. As stated earlier, research by Romski and Sevcik (1993) suggests that communication is enhanced when both partners use the communication system in naturalistic interactions. It merits repetition that these systems must provide means by which individuals can receive information as well as express themselves.

CONCLUSION

The preceding discussions have focused on methods that may be used to effect communicative change and development in individuals with profound disabilities. The unifying theoretical orientation of these approaches is that communication is a social act that develops within the context of conversation-like interactions between the person with profound disabilities and the significant individuals in his or her life. This perspective represents a shift from the traditional didactic paradigm in which language has been taught to individuals with disabilities. Rather, communication is viewed as a social activity between two individuals, with the more competent member of the dyad serving as a guide to facilitate the participation of the less capable member.

The available data base on communication interventions conducted with these individuals is truly insufficient to persuade one to adopt or reject any method for potential use. It is likely that a melding of components from many of these approaches will be necessary to effectively meet the communication needs of many individuals with profound disabilities. It is also likely that more creative communication interventions will be necessary for those individuals whose cognitive and/or motoric deficits prevent them from exhibiting the type of observable behaviors that have a clearer potential to be incorporated into a communication intervention program.

REFERENCES

Alvares, R. (1992). *Preverbal infants' responses to adult misunderstandings.* Unpublished doctoral dissertation, The University of Texas at Dallas, Richardson.

Alvares, R., Falor, I., & Smiley, L. (1991). Research on nonlinguistic communication functioning of individuals with severe or profound handicaps. In L. Sternberg (Ed.), *Functional communication: Analyzing the nonlinguistic skills of individuals with severe or profound handicaps* (pp. 18–37). New York: Springer-Verlag.

American Speech-Language-Hearing Association. (1992). Guidelines for meeting the communication needs of persons with severe disabilties. *ASHA, 34*(3, Suppl.), 1–8.

Bates, E. (1976). *Language and context: The acquisition of pragmatics.* New York: Academic Press.

Bates, E. (1979). *The emergence of symbols: Cognition and communication in infancy.* New York: Academic Press.

Bates, E., Benigni, L., Bretherton, I., Camaioni, L., & Volterra, V. (1977). From gesture to the first word: On cognitive and social prerequisites. In M. Lewis & L. Rosenblum (Eds.), *Interaction, conversation, and the development of language* (pp. 247–307). New York: Wiley.

Beukelman, D. R., & Mirenda, P. (1992). *Augmentative and alternative communication.* Baltimore: Brookes.

Biklen, D. (1990). Communication unbound: Autism and praxis. *Harvard Educational Review, 60,* 291–314.

Biklen, D. (1992). Typing to talk: Facilitated communication. *American Journal of Speech-Language Pathology, 1*(2), 15–17.

Biklen, D., Morton, M. W., Gold, D., Berrigan, C., & Swaminathan, S. (1992). Facilitated communication: Implications for individuals with autism. *Topics in Language Disorders, 12*(4), 1–28.

Bliss, C. K. (1965). *Semantography—Blissymbolics.* Sydney, Australia: Semantography Publications.

Bruner, J. (1975). The ontogenesis of speech acts. *Journal of Child Language, 1,* 1–19.

Bryen, D. N., & Joyce, D .G. (1985). Language intervention with the severely handicapped: A decade of research. *Journal of Special Education, 19,* 7–37.

Calculator, S. N. (1985). Describing and treating discourse problems in mentally retarded children: The myth of mental retardese. In D. N. Ripich & F. M. Spinelli (Eds.), *School discourse problems* (pp. 125–147). San Diego: College-Hill.

Calculator, S. N. (1992). Perhaps the emperor has clothes after all: A response to Biklen. *American Journal of Speech-Language Pathology, 1*(2), 18–20

Calculator, S. N., & Singer, K. M. (1992). Letter to the editor: Preliminary validation of facilitated communication. *Topics in Language Disorders, 13*(1), ix–xvi.

Cirrin, F. M., & Rowland, C. M. (1985). Communicative assessment of youths with severe/profound mental retardation. *Mental Retardation, 23*(2), 52–62.

Clark, C. R., Davies, C. O., & Woodcock, R. W. (1974). *Standard rebus glossary.* Circle Pines, MN: American Guidance Service.

Coggins, T., & Carpenter, R. (1981). The Communication Intention Inventory: A system for observing and coding children's early intentional communication. *Journal of Applied Psycholinguistics, 2,* 235–251.

Cromer, R. (1981). Reconceptualizing language acquisition and cognitive development. In R. Schiefelbusch & D. D. Bricker (Eds.), *Early language: Acquisition and intervention* (pp. 51–137). Baltimore: University Park Press.

Crossley, R. (1991). Facilitated communication training. *Communicating Together, 2*, 20–23.

Crossley, R. (1992). Getting the words out: Case studies in facilitated communication training. *Topics in Language Disorders, 12*(4), 46–59.

Crossley, R., & Remington-Gurney, J. (1992). Getting the words out: Facilitated communication training. *Topics in Language Disorders, 12*(4), 29–45.

Cummins, R., & Prior, M. (1992). Autism and assisted communication: A reply to Biklen. *Harvard Educational Review, 62*, 228–241.

Doherty, E. (1985). The effects of sign characteristics on sign acquisition and retention: An integrative review of the literature. *Augmentative and Alternative Communication, 1*, 108–121.

Donnellan, A., Mirenda, P., Mesaros, R., & Fassbender, L. (1984). Analyzing the communicative functions of aberrant behavior. *Journal of The Association for Persons with Severe Handicaps, 9*, 202–212.

Donnellan, A. M., Sabin, L. A., & Majure, L. A. (1992). Facilitated communication: Beyond the quandry to the questions. *Topics in Language Disorders, 12*(4), 69–82.

Dunn, L., & Dunn, I. (1981). *Manual for forms L and M of the Peabody Picture Vocabulary Test–Revised.* Circle Pines, MN: American Guidance Services.

Dunst, C. J. (1980). *A clinical and educational manual for use with the Uzgiris and Hunt Scales of Infant Psychological Development.* Austin, TX: PRO-ED.

Dunst, C. J., Cuishing, P. J., & Vance, S. D. (1985). Response-contingent learning in profoundly handicapped infants: A social systems perspective. *Analysis and Intervention in Developmental Disabilities, 5*, 33–47.

Goetz, L., Schuler, A., & Sailor, W. (1981). Functional competence as a factor in communication instruction. *Exceptional Education Quarterly, 2*, 51–61.

Golinkoff, R. M. (1986). "I beg your pardon?" The preverbal negotiation of failed messages. *Journal of Child Language, 13*, 455–476.

Halle, J. W. (1982). Teaching functional language to the handicapped: An integrative model of natural environment teaching techniques. *Journal of The Association for the Severely Handicapped, 7*, 29–37.

Hart, B., & Risley, T. (1975). Incidental teaching of language in preschool. *Journal of Applied Behavior Analysis, 8*, 411–420.

Higginbotham, J., & Yoder, D. E. (1982). Communication within natural conversational interaction: Implications for severe communicatively impaired persons. *Topics in Language Disorders, 2*(2), 1–19.

Hunt, P., Goetz, L., Alwell, M., & Sailor, W. (1986). Using an interrupted chain strategy to teach generalized communication responses. *Journal of The Association for Persons with Severe Handicaps, 11*, 196–204.

Kangas, K. A., & Lloyd, L. L. (1988). Early cognitive skills as pre-requisites to augmentative and alternative communication use. What are we waiting for? *Augmentative and Alternative Communication, 4*, 211–221.

Lobato, D., Barrera, R. D., & Feldman, R. S. (1981). Sensorimotor functioning and prelinguistic communication of severely and profoundly retarded individuals. *American Journal of Mental Deficiency, 85*, 489–496.

MacDonald, J., & Carroll, J. Y. (1992). A social partnership model for assessing early communication development: An intervention model for preconversational children. *Language, Speech, and Hearing Services in Schools, 23,* 113–124.

MacDonald, J. D., & Gillette, Y. (1985). *Conversations with children.* Columbus: The Nisonger Center, Ohio State University.

McLean, J. (1992). Facilitated communication: Some thoughts on Biklen's and Calculator's interaction. *American Journal of Speech-Language Pathology, 1,* 25–27.

McLean, J. E., McLean, L. S., Brady, N. C., & Etter, R. (1991). Communication profiles of two types of gestures using nonverbal persons with severe to profound mental retardation. *Journal of Speech and Hearing Research, 34,* 294–308.

McLean, J. E., Sack, S. H., McLean, L. S., O'Connor, A., & Simmons, S. J. (1991). *Developing communicative interactions.* Parsons: Bureau of Child Research, University of Kansas.

McLean, J. E., & Snyder-McLean, L. (1978). *A transactional approach to early language training.* Columbus, OH: Merrill.

Mirenda, P., Iacono, T., & Williams, R. (1990). Communication options for persons with severe and profound disabilities: State of the art and future directions. *Journal of The Association for Persons with Severe Handicaps, 15,* 3–21.

Mirenda, P., & Locke, P. (1989). A comparison of symbol transparency in nonspeaking persons with intellectual disabilities. *Journal of Speech and Hearing Disorders, 54,* 131–140.

Norris, J. A., & Hoffman, P. R. (1990). Language intervention in naturalistic environments. *Language, Speech and Hearing Services in Schools, 21*(2), 72–84.

Ogletree, B. T., Wetherby, A. M., & Westling, D. L. (1992). Profile of the prelinguistic intentional communicative behaviors of children with profound mental retardation. *American Journal on Mental Retardation, 97,* 186–196.

Owens, R. E., & Rogerson, B. S. (1988). Adults at the presymbolic level. In S. N. Calculator & J. L. Bedrosian (Eds.), *Communication assessment and intervention for adults with mental retardation* (pp. 189–238). Austin, TX: PRO-ED.

Paul, L. (1985). Programming peer support for functional language. In A. K. Rogers-Warren & S. F. Warren (Eds.), *Teaching functional language* (pp. 289–307). Austin, TX: PRO-ED.

Peck, C. A. (1989). Assessment of social communicative competence: Evaluating environments. *Seminars in Speech and Language, 10*(1), 1–15.

Reichle, J., & Karlan, G. (1985). The selection of an augmentative system in communication intervention: A critique of decision rules. *Journal of The Association for Persons with Severe Handicaps, 10,* 146–156.

Reichle, J., York, J., & Sigafoos, J. (1991). *Implementing augmentative and alternative communication.* Baltimore: Brookes.

Rogers-Warren, A., & Warren, S. (1980). Mands for verbalizations: Facilitating the display of newly trained language in children. *Behavior Modification, 4,* 361–382.

Rogers-Warren, A. K., & Warren, S. F. (1984). The social basis of language and communication in severely handicapped preschoolers. *Topics in Early Childhood Special Education, 4*(2), 57–72.

Romski, M., & Sevcik, R. (1993). Language learning through augmented means: The process and its products. In A. T. Kaiser & D. B. Gray (Eds.), *Enhancing children's communication: Research foundations for intervention* (Vol. 2, pp. 85–104). Baltimore: Brookes.

Romski, M., Sevcik, R., & Pate, J. (1988). Establishment of symbolic communication in persons with severe retardation. *Journal of Speech and Hearing Disorders, 53,* 94–107.

Rowland, C., & Schweigert, P. (1989). Tangible symbols: Symbolic communication for individuals with multisensory impairments. *Augmentative and Alternative Communication, 5,* 226–234.

Rowland, C., & Schweigert, P. (1990). *Tangible symbol systems: Symbolic communication for individuals with mutisensory impairments.* Tucson, AZ: Communication Skill Builders.

Sailor, W., Gee, K., Goetz, L., & Graham, N. (1988). Progress in students with the most severe disabilities: Is there any? *Journal of The Association for Persons with Severe Handicaps, 13,* 87–99.

Schalow, A. T., & Schalow, A. L. (1985). The endless search for help. In M. P. Brady & P. Gunther (Eds.), *Integrating moderately and severely handicapped learners: Strategies that work* (pp. 5–15). Springfield, IL: Thomas.

Schuler, A. L., Peck, C. A., Willard, C., & Theimer, K. (1989). An assessment of communicative means and functions through interview: Assessing the communicative capabilities of individuals with limited language. *Seminars in Speech and Language, 10*(1), 51–62.

Siegel-Causey, E., & Downing, J. (1987). Nonsymbolic communication development: Theoretical concepts and educational strategies. In L. Goetz, D. Guess, & K. Stremmel-Campbell (Eds.), *Innovative program design for individuals with dual sensory impairments* (pp. 15–48). Baltimore: Brookes.

Siegel-Causey, E., Ernst, B., & Guess, D. (1988). Non-symbolic communication in early interactional processes and implications for intervention. In M. Bullis & G. Fielding (Eds.), *Communication development in young children with deaf–blindess: Literature review* (pp. 69–122). Monmouth: Teaching Research Division, Oregon State System of Higher Education.

Silliman, E. R. (1992). Three perspectives of facilitated communication: Unexpected literacy, Clever Hans, or enigma. *Topics in Language Disorders, 12*(4), 60–68.

Sternberg, L. (1988). Communication programming inventory. In L. Sternberg (Ed.), *Educating students with severe or profound handicaps* (pp. 345–363). Austin, TX: PRO-ED.

Sternberg, L. (1991). The Sonoma research project: Discussion and conclusions. In L. Sternberg (Ed.), *Functional communication: Analyzing the nonlinguistic skills of individuals with severe or profound handicaps* (pp. 113–124). New York: Springer-Verlag.

Sternberg, L., & McNerney, C. D. (1988). Prelanguage communication instruction. In L. Sternberg (Ed.), *Educating students with severe or profound handicaps* (pp. 311–344). Austin, TX: PRO-ED.

Sternberg, L., McNerney, C. D., & Pegnatore, L. (1985). Developing co-active imitative behaviors with profoundly mentally handicapped students. *Education and Training of the Mentally Retarded, 20,* 260–267.

Sternberg, L., McNerney, C. D., & Pegnatore, L. (1987). Developing primitive signalling behavior of students with profound mental retardation. *Mental Retardation, 25,* 13–20.

Sternberg, L., & Owens, A. (1985). Establishing pre-language signalling behaviour with profoundly mentally handicapped students: A preliminary investigation. *Journal of Mental Deficiency Research, 29,* 81–93.

Sternberg, L., Pegnatore, L., & Hill, C. (1983). Establishing interactive communication behaviors with profoundly mentally handicapped students. *Journal of The Association for the Severely Handicapped, 8,* 39–46.

Stillman, R., & Battle, C. (1984). Developing prelanguage communication in the severely handicapped: An interpretation of the van Dijk method. *Seminars in Speech and Language, 5*(3), 159–169.

Stillman, R. D., & Battle, C. (1985). *Callier–Azusa Scale (H): Scales of Assessment of Communicative Abilities.* Dallas, TX: University of Texas at Dallas, Callier Center for Communication Disorders.

Stillman, R. D., & Williams, C. (1990). *Assessing forms and intentions of teacher communications.* Unpublished manuscript, Callier Center for Communication Disorders, The University of Texas at Dallas.

Stillman, R. D., & Williams, C. (1991). *Assessing teacher effects.* Unpublished manuscript, The University of Texas at Dallas, Richardson.

Stremmel-Campbell, K., Clark-Guida, J., & Johnson-Dorn, N. (1984). *Pre-language communication curriculum for children/youth with severe handicaps.* Monmouth, OR: Teaching Research.

Tannock, R., Girolametto, L., & Siegel, L. S. (1992). Language intervention with children who have developmental delays: Effects of an interactive approach. *American Journal on Mental Retardation, 97,* 145–160.

Uzgiris, I., & Hunt, J. (1975). *Assessment in infancy: Ordinal Scales of Psychological Development.* Urbana: University of Illinois Press.

van der Gaag, A .D. (1988). The development of a communication assessment procedure for use with adults with a mental handicap—An interim report. *British Journal of Mental Subnormality, 34,* 62–68.

van Dijk, J. (1965). The first steps of the deaf–blind child towards language. *Proceedings of the Conference on the Deaf–Blind, Refnes, Denmark.* Boston: Perkins School for the Blind.

Walton, G. E., & Bower, T. G. R. (1991). *Operant control of the single suck in newborns.* Paper presented at the International Conference on Infants Studies, Miami, FL.

Warren, S. F., Yoder, P. J., Wilcox, M. J., & Girolametto, L. (1991, November). Methods and models of prelinguistic intervention. Miniseminar presented at the Annual Meeting of the American Speech-Language-Hearing Association, Atlanta.

Wetherby, A., & Prizant, B. (1989). Expressions of communicative intents: Assessment guidelines. *Seminars in Speech and Language, 10*(1), 77–90.

Wetherby, A., Yonclas, D., & Bryan, A. (1989). Communicative profiles of children with handicaps: Implications for early identification. *Journal of Speech and Hearing Disorders, 54,* 148–158.

Wheeler, D. L., Jacobson, J. W., Paglieri, R. A., & Schwartz, A. A. (1993). An experimental assessment of facilitated communication. *Mental Retardation, 31,* 49–60.

Wilcox, M. J., Kouri, T. A., & Caswell, S. (1990). Partner sensitivity to communication behavior of young infants with developmental disabilities. *Journal of Speech and Hearing Disorders, 55,* 679–693.

Chapter 8

Special Health Care Needs

MARILYN MULLIGAN AULT, JANE P. RUES, and J. CAROLYN GRAFF

In this chapter, we describe the health care needs of children and youth with profound disabilities, discuss some of the training needs of their teachers and other service care providers, and present suggestions for implementing special health care procedures within an educational setting. The chapter is divided into two major sections. The first presents some general information and major issues related to meeting the needs of children with special health care needs outside a clinic or hospital setting. These broad areas include a description of the health care needs of students with profound disabilities, considerations for training the persons who will implement the health care procedures, ethical issues surrounding the implementation of health care procedures, biomedical and ergonomic considerations, and ways the educator can facilitate a family-centered approach to the care of children with special health care needs. The second section of the chapter identifies specific health care procedures that may be used with children and youth who have profound disabilities. These are clustered into categories of procedures that have a general application to all students with profound disabilities, those procedures with specialized application, and those procedures that may be present, but rarely, in a classroom.

GENERAL INFORMATION

Characteristics of Students with Profound Disabilities Who Have Special Health Care Needs

Special health care needs are clearly a significant characteristic of students with profound disabilities. Thompson and Guess (1989) found that, when teachers of students with profound disabilities were asked to describe their students, one of the four major characteristics that emerged was the presence of medically complex needs. The teachers additionally placed a great deal of importance on acquiring information and skills related to medical areas and valued periodic contacts with a wide range of health care professionals in order to adequately serve these students. The characteristic of having special health care needs, however, describes a wide range of conditions differentiated by varying etiologies and levels of severity and complexity. For example, students can be described by the number of special health care procedures they receive; the presence and frequency of acute illness and impaired health associated with the conditions requiring special health care procedures; the severity level and overall stability of the health condition; whether the health condition is degenerative and the student is dying; and the impact of the health condition on cognition, mobility, and management of self-care.

Despite the large number of varying health-related conditions, there is also a great deal of similarity among these students. It has been estimated that 15% of the issues surrounding the care of a child with chronic health disorders are specific to the condition while 85% of the issues are common to the general case of chronic health disorders (Hobbs, Perrin, & Ireys, 1985). The differences generally surround the actual health care procedures that need to be implemented and the progression of the health-related condition.

Two recent studies have included descriptions of the health history and status of children and youth with profound disabilities (Roberts, Siegel-Causey, Guess, & Rues, 1992; Siegel-Causey, Rues, Harty, Roberts, & Guess, 1991). Students identified by their teachers as having the most pronounced disabilities served as subjects in the studies. The first study provided subject descriptions in a number of areas, including motor impairment characteristics and medication usage (Siegel-Causey et al., 1991). Seventy-nine percent of these students were characterized as having a severe level of motor involvement, and all the students used wheelchairs for mobility. Ninety-one percent of the students were identified as having quadraplegia, a significant finding when compared with the prevalence of 19% overall for children in the United States with cerebral palsy (Menkes, 1985). Medication administration was the most common special health care procedure, with 88% of the students receiving medications at the time of the study, 84% for seizure disorders. Twenty-two percent of the students were receiving four or more medications, and each of the remainder of the students received one, two, or three medications.

The second study replicated some of the findings of the first study and provided additional descriptive data (Roberts et al., 1992). Eighty-six percent of the students in this study had one or more hospitalizations during the school-aged years, 69% were receiving medications, and 76% of the medications were anticonvulsants. Seventy-eight percent of the students were identified as having seizures, with 77% of these disorders considered uncontrolled.

This study also provided information on the health experiences and status of the students. One of the more significant findings was that 48% of the students presented with significant growth and weight retardation (e.g., weight and height below the fifth percentile). A growth indicator, such as inadequate weight or height, suggests the potential for serious problems in health, development, and the ability to interact and learn while in school (Ault, Guy, & Rues, 1992; McCamman & Rues, 1990). In addition, data indicated that 98% of the students required some form of assistance during mealtime, with the majority being totally dependent upon a caregiver and 17% receiving nutrients through a gastrostomy tube. Typical problems related to mealtimes included chewing difficulty, difficulty sucking and swallowing, and, to a lesser degree, chronic constipation, dehydration, gagging, choking, or aspiration (breathing of fluids or objects into the lungs). Finally, and most distressing, at least 16% of the students appeared to the teachers to be in pain during the school day.

These findings, as well as others, suggest that the presence of special health care needs is a predominant characteristic of students with profound disabilities (Lehr & Noonan, 1989; Logan, Alberto, Kana, & Waylor, 1991; Sobsey & Cox, 1991). These students require a variety of health care procedures varying in intensity, occurrence, and life-threatening nature throughout the school day.

Teacher Preparation Needs

Guidelines for receiving training and implementing health care procedures

The teaching staff should be trained in all aspects of emergency response to any potential health-related condition in the classroom. Typically, this includes cardiopulmonary resuscitation (CPR), first aid, and infection control. Teachers should also be trained in the routine implementation of any special health care procedure that is conducted in the classroom. Even if someone other than the teaching staff is designated as the responsible agent to normally implement the procedure, the staff should be capable of substituting and implementing the procedure on a routine basis.

State laws, through the Nurse Practice Act in each state, identify who is capable of implementing nursing procedures. States vary on their restrictiveness in allowing nurses to delegate the responsibility to non-nursing personnel. Most often, the implementation of special health care procedures is seen as the primary responsibility of the school nurse. The availability of school nurses in rural as well as urban areas, however, makes single-person implementation a virtual impossibility.

The school district or local administration will also have guidelines on their interpretation of the Nurse Practice Act. For example, the Nurse Practice Act of a particular state may allow nurses to delegate health-related procedures to non-nursing personnel with the proper training. The district, however, may limit those to noninvasive procedures. There is, unfortunately, no one way to identify who should be responsible for the implementation of a particular procedure in the classroom. Teachers have long been willing to implement those procedures that they felt were necessary to allow the student to attend school, even if they felt they should not have primary responsibility (Mulligan-Ault, Guess, Struth, & Thompson, 1988). It should be assumed that the routine implementation of special health care procedures will be the responsibility of the instructional staff. Arrangements should be made to have other persons within the school (e.g., the bus driver, secretary, or principal) also trained for response to emergency situations. The final team decision as to who will be routinely responsible is ultimately based on input from the school administration, health care professional, family, teacher, and related staff.

The adequate and timely training of all persons involved becomes the crucial element in the implementation of special health care procedures. Training should be conducted by a certified or qualified health care professional. The participants should be trained in the general case application of a special health care procedure, as well as the particular needs of the individual student. Training could begin with orientation, followed by demonstration, carrying out the procedure with support, and finally carrying out the procedure without support or with supervision by the school nurse or physician. A judgment should be made by the trainer as to the competence of the person being trained, with the requirement for routine reevaluation of the implementation of the procedure. An evaluation should also be made of the person carrying out training to ensure that he or she is adequately prepared to train within the parameters of his or her own professional practice, knowledge, and skills. For example, the school nurse will most likely be involved in training school staff in measures related to infection control, and will be involved in medication administration. For less frequent procedures, such as catheterization and suctioning, the school nurse should assist the teacher and family in consulting the appropriate health care provider. The nurse, along with other school staff, should be trained in the procedure and continue to receive ongoing supervision.

Figure 8.1 (Guidelines for the Provision for Special Health Care Procedures) lists minimal considerations necessary for the implementation of special health care procedures in the classroom (Overeem, 1991). The form is completed for each health care procedure and includes a detailed descrip-

GUIDELINES FOR THE PROVISION OF SPECIAL HEALTH CARE PROCEDURES

Name of the student _____ Birthdate _____ Date _____

Address _____

Phone number _____ Zip code _____

CLASSROOM-BASED GUIDELINES

1. We (I), the undersigned, who are the parents/guardians of _____,
   request that the following procedure be administered to our child during the school day:

   _____   _____
   (Signature of Parent or Guardian)   (Date)

2. Name of physician requesting specific procedure:

   _____   _____
   (Signature of Physician)   (Date)

3. Physician's approval/disapproval of procedure. Check one:

   _____ I have reviewed and approve the attached standardized procedure as written below.

   _____ I have reviewed and approved the attached standardized procedures as written
   below with the attached modification.

   _____ I do not approve of the school's standardized procedure and therefore have
   attached my alternate written recommendations.

4. The Procedure: _____

5. Guidelines for administration of the procedure: _____
   _____
   _____

6. Protocol for the specific procedure (make a check in the space provided if additional sheets
   are attached _____)
   _____
   _____

7. Precautions, possible reactions, and interventions: _____
   _____
   _____

8. Time schedule and/or indication for the procedure: _____
   _____

9. The procedure is to be continued as above until _____
   _____

Figure 8.1. Guidelines for the classroom provision of special health care procedures, including emergency medical release.

Figure 8.1. *Continued.*

10. Person to be trained for the specific procedure and date of training:

_____

Name   Position   Date

By whom: _____ _____

                    Name   Position/Title

Address _____

Phone _____

11. I have reviewed the statements above and find them acceptable in regard to the specific
    health care procedure for _____.

_____ Parent   Date _____

_____ Teacher   Date _____

_____ School Nurse Date _____

_____ Physician   Date _____

EMERGENCY MEDICAL RELEASE

It is understood that due care and concern for the welfare of the student will be given in every respect
by the staff. It is agreed, however, in the case of accident, injury, or illness of the student, that the
school's action will be limited to the following procedures:

1. Notify the person specified (legal guardian, parent, relative, etc.) on Public Information Form.

2. If needed, call 911 for Emergency Medical Transportation and contact the personal physician.

   Dr. _____ at _____.

   Phone _____ for emergency medical care.

3. Monitor the student's well-being until appropriate assistance arrives.

CHILD-SPECIFIC EMERGENCIES

IF YOU SEE THIS   DO THIS

_____   _____

_____   _____

_____   _____

_____   _____

Figure 8.1. *Continued.*

I, _____, understand and agree to the

contents of this emergency medical release. I also agree that this release will be effective from the

time of student's attendance at _____ until

student's termination from the program. I also understand that either party, at any time, may request

to reevaluate this Emergency Medical Release.

_____   _____
(Signature of Parent or Guardian)   (Date)

---

tion and schedule of implementation of the procedures, as well as documentation of persons responsible and their training. An emergency medical release component is included on the form for use, when appropriate, to deal with responses that are not routine in nature.

Body mechanics and ergonomics

It is imperative that prevention techniques be used to ensure that teachers or caregivers do not become disabled themselves as they provide continued physical care for students who are dependent. Primary prevention involves providing instruction to teachers or caregivers in lifting or postural techniques and ergonomic job design. The application of proper body mechanics is an essential aspect of any functional activity to protect oneself and to protect the student. The application of good body mechanics occurs when bending to pick up or lift a student, working with a student on the mat, or assisting a student up from the floor. Palmer and Toms (1992) specified general rules for maintaining good body mechanics. They include

1. Maintaining a normal relaxed curve in the lower back while flexing the hips, knees, and trunk.

2. Keeping the student or object being lifted as close to your body as possible.

3. Rotating or turning your body from the hips and feet, not from the trunk.

4. Moving slowly, avoiding twisting or jerking.

5. Assuming a wide stance, with feet shoulder-width apart and in a side-to-side position, or with the leading foot slightly ahead of

the other, to allow for proper shifting of body weight with the student.

Application of the above techniques allows school staff to use the strong thigh muscles, rather than the back muscles, when lifting and carrying a student. To lift and carry, providers should first squat; then stand to lift; and lift and carry heavy objects close to the body using muscles that pull shoulder blades together to lessen fatigue and avoid back strain (Killingsworth, 1976). Whenever possible, the rule is to work with the force of gravity by pushing, pulling, and lowering, rather than against the force of gravity by lifting (Brill & Kilts, 1980).

Ergonomics is the study of people in relation to their working environments. Effective job design, or ergonomics, seeks to minimize the health hazards of activities and postures related to employment (Mandell, Lipton, Bernstein, Kucera, & Kampner, 1989). Adequate workplace design and principles of energy conservation and work simplification should be introduced and practiced within classrooms for students with profound disabilities. Although educators readily adapt the environment daily to meet the above standards for students, they do not always apply the same principles for their own health and safety.

Occupational and physical therapists can be resources for the design of the educational environment, including proper equipment dimensions and placement. The design should incorporate principles of work simplification and reflect the relationship of the staff and students with the environment, as well as provide a functional and age-appropriate setting for students.

Involvement in medical and ethical dilemmas

When a student's health begins to deteriorate because of an underlying condition or a new disease or condition, the school staff, parents, or others must address how the student's education and educational program may need to be altered. Changes in the student's health may be expected by the student's parents and the physician, with information being shared with school staff. There may be instances, however, when degeneration occurs with no known reason, or is suspected although a definite diagnosis has not been made. School staff can then provide invaluable information about a student's behavior, responses, and performance that may well assist the physician in diagnosing a condition.

When a student's condition is degenerative, questions will be raised regarding the student's overall health and ability to remain in the classroom or participate in school. These questions may originate from the school staff, parents, or others. The school staff should participate as partners in support of the family as the needs of the individual student are met. It is also essential that school staff have opportunities to discuss their own feelings, particularly around the issues of pain and death. Often support systems are helpful within the school setting for teachers, as well as for other students and their families.

If a student's condition is expected to worsen or death is expected, four educationally related options are generally considered:

1. The student should continue attending school with educational programming focused on maintaining the student's present functioning level as long as possible.

2. Teaching should be geared toward assisting the student to develop skills that compensate for lost ability.

3. The student, family, school, and other students should be aided in dealing with the degenerative condition.

4. Assistance should be provided in lessening the likelihood of secondary complications, such as pain or additional impairment.

The option, or combination of options, selected will depend on the student's condition and ongoing changes. These recommendations are based on the assumption that it is important for the student's life to continue to be as normal as possible, and part of that life includes school (Holvoet & Helmstetter, 1989).

The teacher may be confronted with a situation in which the family and medical professionals involved have decided upon a limited response or no response as the student experiences life-threatening conditions. The teacher must respect the parents' decision whether to pursue a treatment, while being fully aware of and implementing the school district or agency policy on supporting no-response or limited-response options.

A family-centered approach to the provision of special health care needs

When serving a student with special health care needs, educators must not view health needs as separate from educational needs. All aspects of the student's life, including the family's perspectives and needs, should be included in all programming considerations (Shelton, Jeppson, & Johnson, 1992). This consideration of the "whole" student from the perspective of the school, home, and community provides a realization that health-related procedures and issues influence and are influenced by all aspects of the student's life.

A family-centered approach recognizes the parents as experts in the overall care of the student, particularly in carrying out activities to maintain and promote the student's health. Often they have been extensively trained in the implementation of special health care procedures, and the home was the first nonclinical setting in which these procedures were implemented. Careful communication and collaboration among family, school staff, and health professionals can result in easy-to-carry-out, safe health-related activities in the classroom. Using the parents' knowledge of their child's health, responses to health-related procedures, and previously tried but unsuccessful approaches to their child's health should be included in the development of the Individualized Education Program (IEP) or Individualized Family Service Plan (IFSP).

HEALTH CARE PROCEDURES FOR GENERAL APPLICATION

Cardiopulmonary Resuscitation

Cardiopulmonary resuscitation (CPR) is an emergency procedure used in life-threatening situations. CPR is not considered a procedure for routine implementation in the classroom, but a response to an emergency situation when breathing, or breathing and the heart, have stopped (Ault, Rues, & Graff, 1993).

Using CPR

CPR involves three basic rescue skills: opening the Airway, and restoring Breathing and Circulation—the ABCs of CPR. These skills should be carried out only by persons properly trained in CPR until more advanced life support can be made available (American Heart Association, 1993). Therefore, a person reading through the following description is *not* considered to be trained.

Opening the airway

The following description of CPR is for children from 1 to 8 years of age, or students whose size is that of a child. Procedures for persons over 8 years are the same as those for an adult (see American Heart Association, 1993). When it is suspected that breathing or the pulse has stopped, attempt to arouse the student. If unsuccessful, call out for help, then position the student in supine while supporting the head and neck. Open the airway by tilting the head and lifting the chin.

Restoring breathing

Determine whether the student is breathing by looking, listening, and feeling for a breath while holding the airway open (tilting the head and lifting the chin). If there is no breath, give the student two breaths into the mouth.

Restoring circulation

Determine whether a pulse is present by feeling for the carotid (neck) pulse while continuing to tilt the head and open the airway. If the pulse is absent, begin repeated compressions of the chest. Alternate five compressions with one breath for 5 cycles. Feel for the pulse, and if no pulse is felt, the cycle of five chest compressions and one breath is continued. If the pulse returns, check for spontaneous breathing. If there is no breathing, give one breath every 3 seconds. When the student begins breathing spontaneously, remain to monitor the breathing and pulse (American Heart Association, 1993).

Managing an obstructed airway

When the student is choking, identify if there is complete airway obstruction. If the student can speak or cough effectively, do not interfere with the student's own attempts to force out the object. If the student is unable to speak or cough, perform the Heimlich maneuver (see the following paragraph) until the object is forced out. The Heimlich maneuver can be conducted with the victim in the standing, sitting, or supine position.

Place the unconscious student on his or her back, support the head and neck, and look down into the mouth and airway for an object blocking the airway. If an object is seen, turn the student on his or her side and use fingers to remove the object. If unable to see and remove an object, attempt to breathe into the student. Give 6 to 10 upward thrusts over the abdomen (the Heimlich maneuver for an unconscious student lying on the floor). Repeat the cycle of looking for the object, opening the airway and breathing, and performing abdominal thrusts, until the student revives or emergency assistance arrives (American Heart Association, 1993).

Classroom applications

Difficulty with breathing is the most common medical emergency for children ("Standards and Guidelines," 1986). Although any individual may need CPR, students with profound disabilities tend to have additional characteristics that increase the possibility of cessation of breathing. Some of these characteristics include heart defects, seizure disorders, aspiration of fluids or objects, tracheostomies, or excess fluids in the mouth. For example, immature chewing and swallowing combined with abnormalities of the structure of the oral cavity may result in a student's being at a higher risk for choking on certain foods or saliva. The child is additionally at a higher risk for choking, when compared with an adult, because the child's airway is smaller and the cough is weaker (Harris, Baker, Smith, & Harris, 1984).

The majority of emergency situations requiring CPR for children are preventable. Special attention, therefore, must be paid to providing environments that are safe, with staff trained in appropriate positioning, handling, and mealtime skills ("Standards and Guidelines," 1986). Not all students with profound disabilities will experience cessation in breathing. It is crucial, however, that the staff of each classroom or instructional setting be prepared to meet a medical emergency. The teacher must specify who is CPR trained, indicate the location of the emergency equipment, and designate whom to call in an emergency for each of the student's instructional settings.

Additional resources

CPR must be attempted *only* by a person who is adequately trained. If a person who is trained in CPR does somehow injure the victim, that person is protected in a number of states by good samaritan laws that prevent a victim (or the victim's family) from filing a lawsuit against someone who attempted to perform a lifesaving technique (Batshaw & Perret, 1986). CPR and management of airway obstruction classes are conducted by the American Heart Association, local hospitals, and other local agencies. Standards and guidelines were updated at the 1985 National Conference on Cardiopulmonary Resuscitation and Emergency Cardiac Care.

First Aid

First aid involves providing immediate assistance to students who have been injured, or otherwise disabled, prior to arrival of or transportation to a health care professional (Thomas, 1985). The most frequent applications are in response to bites, stings, burns, fractures, lacerations, and abrasions that occur while the student is in school. Students with profound disabilities are as prone to these injuries as are their peers who are not disabled. Often, however, the teacher is not aware of a student's pain response, and such injuries may, unfortunately, go unnoticed and untreated for a period of time.

Classroom applications

Insect bites or stings can occur at almost any time. The reaction to the bite depends on the individual student's response as well as the particular insect. The student may have a reaction of pain accompanied by redness and swelling at the site of the sting or a systemic reaction resulting in anaphylaxis. Anaphylaxis is a condition that may be mild (including a slight fever, redness of skin, and itching) or severe [including difficulty breathing, violent coughing, cyanosis (bluish coloration of the skin), fever, changes in pulse, seizures, and collapse]. An anaphylaxis kit, containing epinephrine, should be available for all students having severe reactions to food or stinging insects. Most insect bites and stings, after the stinger has been removed, may be cleaned and application of an ice cube may help relieve pain temporarily (Schmitt, 1980). It is important, however, to determine whether the skin reaction is the result of an insect bite or the sign of a disease such as chicken pox. Consideration of the student's medical history, season of the year, and knowledge of the student's environment will provide additional information. Insects such as the mosquito, fly, gnat, flea, and hornet tend to bite exposed parts of the body, whereas body lice, scabies, and chiggers (mites) tend to establish themselves on areas of the body that are covered by clothing.

Human bites may occur accidentally or intentionally during classroom activities. Infection develops rapidly and extensively because of the variety of organisms present in the mouth and saliva. *Animal bites* require careful evaluation and determination of the need for rabies prophylaxis. Both types of bites require careful cleaning with soap and running water. The wound should also be left open to permit any drainage to occur and prevent the growth of certain harmful organisms (e.g., anaerobic organisms) that can survive in tissue and do not require oxygen to live.

Burns can occur as a result of scalds, electricity, flames, or improper positioning near heat sources. Dribbling ice water over the burned area lessens pain and cleanses the wound. Sterile gauze bandages dampened with cold water may be used to cover the burned areas. If sterile bandages are unavailable, a clean moistened cloth may be used to cover the wound. If large areas of a student's body are burned, run cool water over the burn to cool the area. Do not attempt to remove clothing, open any blisters, or apply any type of ointment. Transport the child for immediate medical attention (Schmitt, 1980).

Signs of a *bone fracture* include crookedness, shortening, or rotation of an extremity; pain or tenderness at the site of the fracture; or swelling and discoloration of the overlying skin because of bleeding around the fracture site. For many students with profound disabilities, fractures may occur as a result of positioning, improper range of motion, or falls because the student often lacks protective responses (Batshaw & Perret, 1986). Keep the area immobilized until assistance arrives and apply cool compresses to reduce swelling (Chow, Durand, Feldman, & Mills, 1984).

Abrasions or scrapes occur when there is loss of the surface of the skin, resulting in pinhead-sized openings with fluid or blood oozing. The area should be washed with soap and running water for about 5 minutes or swabbed with a mild nonirritating, antiseptic solution. Any dirt in the area should be flushed out with a normal saline solution (Foster, Hunsberger, & Anderson, 1989). Leave the wound exposed to the air, if possible, or cover loosely. Ointments are not necessary and alcohol or methiolate damage tissue (Schmitt, 1980).

A *laceration* refers to a wound that has a smooth or irregular tear of the skin and blood vessels. The area should be washed with soap and running water or a mild antiseptic. If suturing is required, it should occur within 6 hours of the injury to prevent scarring.

A *puncture wound* refers to the penetration of the skin with a sharp object, such as a nail, pencil, or tooth, causing a small hole in the skin. There is usually little bleeding; however, making the wound rebleed assists in cleansing. The area should be washed with soap and running water or a mild antiseptic solution, or soaked in warm water for 10 minutes. A tetanus booster is recommended if the student has not received one within 5 years (Schmitt, 1980).

If bleeding occurs as a result of a burn, laceration, or puncture wound, many school districts recommend that school staff wear gloves when having contact with blood or body fluids or secretions that may have blood in them. Concerns about transmission of human immunodeficiency virus (HIV), hepatitis B virus, and other organisms that may be present in the blood have resulted in changes in policies in school districts. Authorities have emphasized that any transmission of HIV and hepatitis B would most likely involve exposure of skin lesions or mucous membranes to blood and possibly to other bodily fluids of an infected person ("Education and Foster Care," 1985). Finally, any application of first aid procedures should be done only after thorough handwashing by the caregiver.

Additional resources

The Red Cross in local communities routinely offers courses in first aid. A local pediatrician and the local health departments may also recommend resources.

Medication Administration

The primary purpose of medication administration is to relieve symptoms, treat an existing disease, or promote health and prevent disease. Most students with profound disabilities receive medications several times during the school day. It is important to determine state and local education agency regulations regarding medication administration. The teacher will likely be involved in some way with medication administration, and in the identification of factors contributing to problems with medication administration and secondary effects of a variety of medications.

Before administering any medication, the school should have the parents' request or authorization to give a medication, the physician's written approval or request for administration of a medication (the prescription on the medication container may be an example), and secure storage for the medication (Gadow & Kane, 1983). The requirement of a physician's written approval may also apply for over-the-counter medications.

The method of medication administration depends on the student's ability to chew and swallow. Students who have difficulty retaining food or fluid in the mouth are usually held in a semi-reclining position; the smaller student can be held, whereas the larger student can remain in a wheelchair or chair (Whaley & Wong, 1987). When providing support, it is important to ensure a relaxed position to decrease the chances of choking. This may be achieved by ensuring the student's neck is flexed, the shoulders are rounded, and the student is in a slightly forward position. Carefully measure the medication and place it in the student's mouth from a spoon, plastic dropper, or plastic syringe minus the needle. Give the medication slowly to ease swallowing and avoid choking. For the student with tongue thrust, medications may need to be rescued from the student's lips or chin and readministered. If the student uses a suck to take in liquid, the medication can also be slowly pushed into the nipple while the student is sucking (Whaley & Wong, 1987). If the student is able to swallow a tablet, place the medication on the middle of the tongue and encourage swallowing with juice or water (Wagner, 1983). Because of the possibility of aspiration (pulling the tablet and/or secretions into the lungs), a whole tablet should not be given until the student is about 5 years old.

Classroom applications

Medication administration involves teachers and/or school staff in providing the student with the medication, monitoring for complications due to misadministration, and identifying side and interaction effects (Ault, Guy, Graff, & Paez, 1992; Graff, Ault, Guess, Taylor, & Thompson, 1990). The person administering the medication must adhere to the *"Five Rights" of medication administration:* the *right dose* of the *right medication* is given to the *right patient* at the *right time* by the *right route* (Wagner, 1983). Double-checking a medication each time it is given, or writing down routine procedures, can prevent a serious error. The teacher should also routinely document each medication administration.

Accuracy of administration and the side effects of medications are additional components of medication administration not easily controlled within the classroom. For a variety of reasons, the actual dosage prescribed by the physician or recommended by the manufacturer may not be the actual dosage received by the student. Factors such as choking, drooling, vomiting, or imprecise administration when the medication is mixed with food are among the many factors contributing to inaccurate dosages. An analysis of the actual dosage received by the student may shed some light on the overall effectiveness of the medications. Figure 8.2 presents one procedure for analyzing the administration procedures, as well as the side and interaction effects of medications (Ault, Guy, Graff, & Paez, 1992). The form is relatively simple to use and should be implemented during the process of assessment or evaluation conducted in the class. First, all the medications that the student is known to be receiving are listed. Information in Appendix 8A at the end of this chapter can be used as a reference. It provides an alphabetical list of common medications prescribed for students with profound disabilities, and lists drugs by the brand name (in bold), the chemical name (in regular type), the classification name (in italics), and the drug category (in parentheses). It also provides information on side and interactive effects of medications.

Second, medications are identified as either maintenance or episodic. A maintenance medication is received for years at a time to address a chronic condition, such as seizures or diabetes. An episodic medication is received for treatment of a short-term or acute condition, such as an infection, cold, or allergy. Third, a dosage analysis involves listing the prescribed dosage of the medication in the column entitled "Indicated Dosage" and all times the medication is actually given in the column entitled "Time Received." If a medication is prescribed to be given three times daily, the actual times that the medication is given are listed, even if different from three times. The final aspect of dosage analysis is entered in the column, "Full Dosage Received at Time Prescribed." In this column, the teacher estimates whether the student actually received the prescribed dosage. In summary, the form provides information on whether the student (a) may be receiving too much medication during certain times of the day because the scheduling of the administrations does not coincide with the prescription or (b) may not be receiving enough medication because of continual problems in oral-motor function.

In an effort to understand the effect of medications on the student's overall awareness levels and ability to engage the environment, the teacher should be aware of (a) the side effects of medications and (b) the interaction effects of a combination of medications. The portion of Figure 8.2 providing an analysis of the side effects of drugs is completed by listing all possible side effects of the medication in the far column under "Possible Side Effects with Full Dosage." If the drug being used is not included in Appendix 8A, the teacher should refer to the most recent *Physician's Desk Reference* for dosages and possible side effects. The teacher should circle any side effects the student

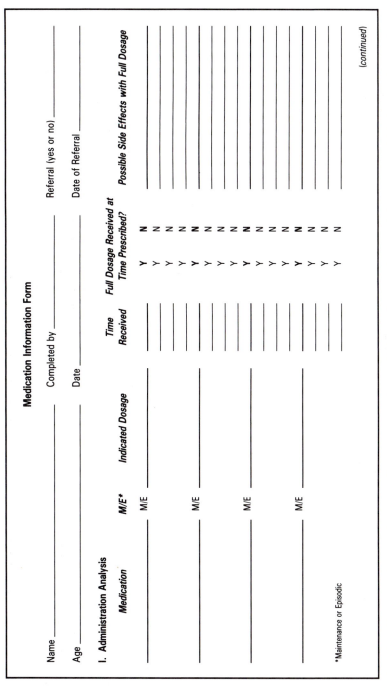

Figure 8.2. Medication information form. From "Medication Analysis" by M. M. Ault, B. Guy, J. C. Graff, and S. Paez, in *Project ABLE: Analyzing Behavior States in Learning Environments* (Project No. HO86D00013 by the Office of Special Education Programs, United States Department of Education), 1992, Lawrence: University of Kansas, Department of Special Education.

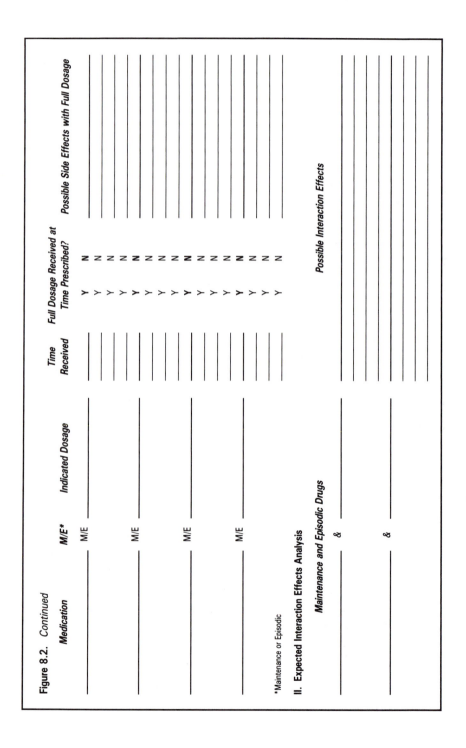

Figure 8.2. *Continued*

Medication	M/E*	Indicated Dosage	Time Received	Full Dosage Received at Time Prescribed?		Possible Side Effects with Full Dosage
_____	M/E	_____	_____	Y	N	_____
			_____	Y	N	_____
			_____	Y	N	_____
_____			_____	Y	N	_____
	M/E	_____	_____	Y	N	_____
			_____	Y	N	_____
			_____	Y	N	_____
_____			_____	Y	N	_____
	M/E	_____	_____	Y	N	_____
			_____	Y	N	_____
			_____	Y	N	_____
_____			_____	Y	N	_____
	M/E	_____	_____	Y	N	_____
			_____	Y	N	_____
			_____	Y	N	_____

*Maintenance or Episodic

II. Expected Interaction Effects Analysis

Maintenance and Episodic Drugs   *Possible Interaction Effects*

_____ & _____   _____

_____ & _____   _____

Figure 8.2. *Continued*

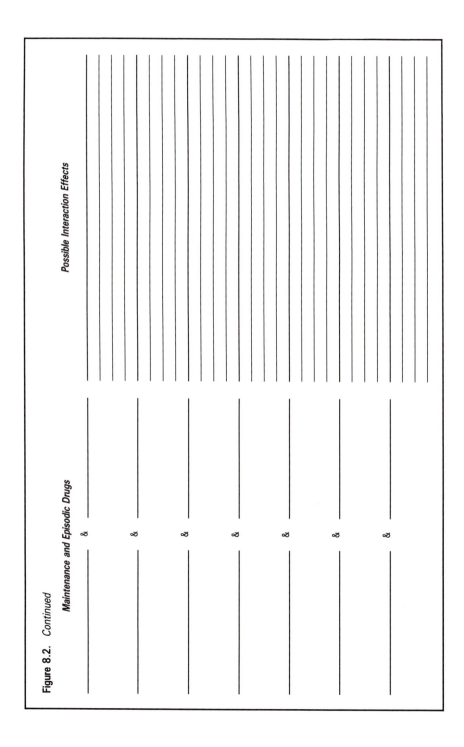

Maintenance and Episodic Drugs

Possible Interaction Effects

displays and inform the primary care provider through the family if these seem to significantly interfere with the student's overall level of functioning.

Often students with profound disabilities are served by multiple health care providers. These providers may be unaware of the range of medications the student is taking, including over-the-counter medications. Thus, the student may receive a combination of medications that interact in such a way as to depress the intended effect of one medication or to produce other side effects. To complete the "Expected Interaction Analysis" section of Figure 8.2, the teacher lists each possible combination of medications, both maintenance and episodic. Using the information provided in Appendix 8A, list possible interaction effects of the medications and specify any behaviors that the student displays.

With the completion of this analysis, the teacher has additional information on possible sources of, or factors contributing to, some of the student's learning characteristics. Problems resulting from the timing and administration of the medication, as well as side or interaction effects of medications, should be immediately identified and reviewed with the family and the school nurse.

Additional resources

Nurses in the school, the physician's office, public health department, or local hospital can provide assistance on methods of administration, side effects, and toxic effects of medications. The student's physician or pharmacist can be a resource for a medication log. The occupational and physical therapist can provide guidance on proper positioning for medication administration and advice on oral-motor problems hindering medication administration. School staff can find more information on administration of medication in a number of references (Ault, Guy, Graff, & Paez, 1992; Graff et al., 1990; King, Wieck, & Dyer 1983; Scipien, Barnard, Chard, Howe, & Phillips, 1986; Whaley & Wong, 1987).

Infection Control

Infections occur when organisms enter the body, find an environment that allows the organisms to grow, and potentially spread to other parts of the body or to other people. Infections are an almost expected part of childhood (Ault, Graff, & Rues, 1993). Children are susceptible to childhood infections (e.g., chicken pox, measles, mumps, colds). Students with profound disabilities may be particularly vulnerable to infections caused by bacteria, viruses, rickettsiae (e.g., bacteria transmitted by the bite of certain lice or ticks), fungi, and helminths (e.g., tapeworms). Once an infection is established, there is also a potential for transmission to others.

Infection control refers to efforts made by public health officials and schools first to prevent an infection and second to prevent the spread of an already established infection. The main infection control strategy is to ensure that children in schools are properly immunized. Immunizations are given because the body does not provide perfect protection from all diseases, and immunity does not occur unless the child has the disease or receives an immunization to stimulate production of antibodies. The process of immunization is begun prior to entry into schools for diphtheria, pertussis, and tetanus (DPT injection); polio (oral polio vaccine); and measles, mumps, and rubella or German measles (MMR injection). These immunizations are typically done on a schedule established by the Centers for Disease Control. In addition, a tuberculin (TB) test is given to determine whether a child has been exposed to tuberculosis. Haemophilus Influenzae (type B) is known to cause serious infections, such as meningitis, and immunization is especially recommended for infants and children attending day care centers (Andersen, Bale, Blackman, & Murph, 1986).

When an infection is present, consultation with the school nurse or health professional is needed to determine whether the child can remain in the classroom. Many infections are highly contagious and can be spread through various ways, depending on the area of the body that is home for the organism. These methods include contact with droplets that are sneezed into the air; contact with secretions from the body, such as saliva, mucus, urine, feces, or blood; or ingestion of the organisms in food.

Viruses that may present with no symptomatology include cytomegalovirus (CMV), herpes, and HIV. Prevention of the spread of these infections includes a clear understanding of how they are transmitted. For example, a child may have acquired CMV early in life, but the virus will leave the body through saliva or urine only at certain times. Wearing gloves whenever changing the child's diaper or feeding the child during periods of transmission may be recommended by school district policy. Because there is thought to be risk to an unborn fetus, many recommend that a pregnant staff person not work directly with the child with CMV. Current understanding is that HIV is not spread through common "household" contact, so staff persons need not be hesitant to include students with HIV infection in routine classroom activities.

Classroom applications

The most effective way to prevent the spread of infection in the classroom is for the instructional staff to use clean procedures, reducing the chance of sharing secretions across students. This requires staff to routinely wash their hands with running water and foaming soap. Proper handwashing (see Figure 8.3) must especially occur after contact with diapers and before handling of any food or liquid for each student. Clean procedures also involve washing items with running water before the items are shared. This is particularly necessary if items are mouthed; if saliva is present outside the mouth, on the hands or clothing; or if sneezing or coughing onto materials is common (Ault et al., 1993). The implementation of clean procedures requires a classroom equipped with a sink in an area designed for food preparation, and a separate sink in an area designed for toileting and handwashing.

Additional resources

Local health departments and local hospitals with departments responsible for infection control can provide additional information. Guidelines from the Centers for Disease Control and the American Academy of Pediatrics provide information about infectious diseases, signs and symptoms, methods of spread to others, and strategies for prevention.

HEALTH CARE PROCEDURES THAT HAVE SPECIALIZED APPLICATION

The procedures reviewed in this section have a high prevalence among students with profound disabilities. Teachers should be familiar with techniques to assess and monitor conditions, as well as implement the procedures when necessary. These procedures include seizure monitoring; growth monitoring, nutrition supplementation, and feeding management; teeth and gum care; skin care; and therapeutic physical management.

Seizure Monitoring

A seizure is a temporary change in behavior resulting from sudden, abnormal bursts of electrical activity in the brain, which may be limited to one area of the brain or may begin in one area and spread to other areas of the brain. Electrical disturbances limited to part of the brain result in a *partial seizure,* the stiffening or jerking of one arm or leg. Electrical disturbances affecting the entire brain result in a *generalized seizure.* This category includes grand mal or tonic–clonic seizures (Dreifuss, Gallagher, Leppik, & Rothner, 1983).

The monitoring of a student's seizures has been identified as one of the major health-related procedures performed by the classroom teacher

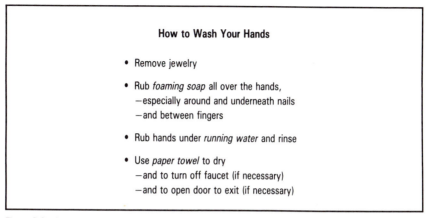

How to Wash Your Hands

- Remove jewelry

- Rub *foaming soap* all over the hands,
  - especially around and underneath nails
  - and between fingers

- Rub hands under *running water* and rinse

- Use *paper towel* to dry
  - and to turn off faucet (if necessary)
  - and to open door to exit (if necessary)

Figure 8.3. Instructions for thorough handwashing. Adapted from *What You Can Do to Stop Disease in Child Day Care Centers* by the Centers for Disease Control, 1985, Atlanta: Department of Health and Human Services. Obtain through your local or state department of health or write to Public Health Advisor, Center for Professional Health and Training, Centers for Disease Control, 1600 Clifton Road, Atlanta, GA 30333.

(Mulligan-Ault, Guess, Struth, & Thompson, 1988). Monitoring involves carefully observing and recording information about a student's seizures. These systematic observations, over time, help distinguish behaviors that are and are not related to the seizure, and help in communication with family and health care providers. Careful observation of the seizure will also help in determining appropriate techniques to use to physically protect the child during a seizure.

Monitoring a seizure

The following are general guidelines for what to do during and after a seizure (Ault et al., 1993; Graff et al., 1990):

1. Remain calm. Remember that no one can stop a seizure once it has started.

2. Stay with the student to monitor progress throughout the seizure.

3. Record events prior to the seizure on an appropriate form. Include, for example, the student's behaviors, activities preceding the seizure, changes in muscle tone, and the person(s) who first identified the seizure.

4. Place the student on the side or stomach so the tongue does not block the airway and the student does not choke on secretions.

5. *NOTHING* (fingers, objects, etc.) should be placed into the student's mouth as this could injure the student or produce vomiting.

6. Loosen tight clothing, especially around the neck and waist.

7. A student standing or sitting should be eased down to avoid a fall, even if the student is secured in adaptive equipment (e.g., wheelchair, standing frame, prone board). When possible, place a cushion or blanket under the student's head to prevent injury during jerking movements.

8. Do *not* give the student medications or anything to drink during the seizure.

9. Record the student's activity. Include, for example, the time the seizure began; the location on the body where the seizure began and any movement to other body parts; movements of the eyes (e.g., rolled back, to the right, to the left); any cessation in breathing; skin color (e.g., pale, blue, reddened in color); and time the seizure ended.

10. After the seizure is over, clean secretions from the mouth with a suction machine, bulb syringe, or hand wrapped in a handkerchief.

11. Monitor the student's breathing. *If breathing is absent, notify the emergency medical system and begin resuscitation efforts* (see the earlier section, "Cardiopulmonary Resuscitation").

12. Immediately talk to or interact with the student to determine the level of awareness (e.g., alert, drowsy, confused, unable to respond). Record this information.

13. Determine if there is any change in the student's ability to move.

14. Check for loss of control of urine and stool, and determine if the student sustained any injuries (e.g., bleeding from the mouth).

15. Make the student comfortable and quiet, allowing opportunities to sleep if indicated (a student may sleep for several hours after a seizure).

16. Record the length of the seizure (in seconds or minutes) and a description of what happened during the seizure. An "Anecdotal Record for the Student with Epilepsy" has been recommended by Prensky and Palkes (1982) for use by teachers in a classroom.

A series of consecutive seizures lasting longer than 10 to 15 minutes is generally referred to as *status epilepticus,* and may require immediate medical care (Dreifuss et al., 1983; Low, 1982).

Classroom applications

Adequate preparation for meeting the needs of students with seizure disorders requires that the school staff consult the family regarding the type of seizure the student has, as well as typical behaviors seen before, during, and after the seizure. Timely and comprehensive seizure monitoring requires ongoing family involvement. It is also important for school staff to be aware of any changes in behavior due to medication, particularly if the physician is in the process of evaluating the student's medication. An increase in the number of seizures per day or per week may indicate that the student is not receiving medication as prescribed, or that the student is in need of a change in medication as a result of a change in the student's metabolism or altered utilization of the medication (Low, 1982). Careful, accurate reporting of seizure activity to parents and/or health care providers will hopefully result in improved seizure management.

After obtaining the above information, the staff can prepare the school areas and routines accordingly. For example, the student producing large amounts of secretions during the seizure will need a suction machine or bulb syringe available in the classroom to remove secretions from the mouth. A student may also become somewhat drowsy after some fixed time period following administration of medication. In this instance, the teacher may need to plan for activities requiring less interaction and response from the student at that time.

The potential for injury to the student during a seizure is a concern for all school staff. A student whose seizures are not well controlled can experience a head injury as a result of a seizure-related fall. Such a student often wears a lightweight helmet to protect the head. The student must *never* be restrained during a seizure because of the possibility of breaking bones or tearing muscles or ligaments (of the child or the school staff) while the student is being held or restrained (Yard, 1980).

In addition, the school environment must be as safe as possible for students with seizures. Objects (e.g., furniture, equipment, toys) that could cause an injury should be portable and easy to remove during a student's seizure. Pathways and instructional environments should be wide and free of unnecessary objects (e.g., unused wheelchairs, storage boxes) to minimize the chance of injury during a fall.

Additional resources

The Epilepsy Foundation of America sponsors a wide variety of programs and activities for persons with epilepsy. The foundation also provides workshops and training for staff, and kits developed for educators working with students with epilepsy.

Growth Monitoring, Nutrition Supplementation, and Feeding Management

Feeding is one of the primary experiences in life. It is a universal event for children of all ages, from all cultures, and from all socioeconomic classes. The well-nourished child grows at an expected rate, is resistant to illness, and has the energy to take advantage of social and educational opportunities. It is estimated, however, that 35%–40% of children with chronic diseases or chronic disabling conditions develop feeding disorders that result in their being inadequately nourished. This incidence is higher for students with profound disabilities. If a student is not receiving adequate nutrition, or if the body is not appropriately utilizing the nutrients being received, then the student is not physiologically prepared to be active, awake, and interactive with persons or materials in the environment. To initiate appropriate intervention, the special educator must be aware of children at risk for nutrition problems and the simple screening methods used to identify these children.

Growth monitoring procedures

Monitoring the nutritional status of a student, as reflected by his or her growth, involves the use of a simple screening method. Trends revealed through repeated height and weight measurements can be used to detect growth abnormalities, monitor nutritional status, or evaluate the effects of nutritional or medical interventions.

Guidelines for monitoring growth (Ault, Guy, & Rues, 1992; see Figure 8.4) target three major areas that may be indicators of nutritional problems (McCamman & Rues, 1990). These include problems in overall growth, complications that may arise from the combined nutritional effect of the student's medications, and the conditions surrounding mealtime that may have implications for nutritional problems. Because persons with profound disabilities tend to grow at different rates than their normally developing peers, a growth chart, plotted for height by weight, should be used in conjunction with the more commonly used percentile charts for boys and girls that plot weight and height against age (e.g., see Figure 8.5).

Measuring weight, height, and length

Measures of growth involve an accurate and systematic recording and plotting of a student's weight against height or length. Even though these

Nutrition Information
Form

Name _____   Completed by _____

Date _____   Age _____

Special Considerations: _____
_____

I. _____ **At risk for growth problems.**
  *Refer if height for weight is less than the 5th or greater than the 95th percentile or if there is no weight gain over a nine month period.

  Date: _____   _____   _____   _____

  Height: ____/____%   ____/____%   ____/____%   ____/____%

  Weight: ____/____%   ____/____%   ____/____%   ____/____%

  Ht/Wt: _____%   _____%   _____%   _____%

II. _____ **At risk for medications compromising utilization of nutrients.**
  *Refer if the student is receiving two or more of the listed medications for nine months or more.

  _____ Analgesics (e.g. aspirin)   _____ Antacid
  _____ Phenobarbital   _____ Dilantin
  _____ Mineral oil   _____ Exlax
  _____ Prednisone   _____ Ritalin
  _____ Dexedrine   _____ Mellaril

III. _____ **At risk due to mealtime characteristics.**
  * Refer if two of the three characteristics apply.

  _____ Meal lasts longer than 40 minutes.

  _____ Student continuously displays difficulty with ingestion during or after the meal.

      _____ excessive crying, whining, or signs of discomfort

      _____ frequent gagging, coughing or choking

  _____ Meal consistently contains items from only two of the four food groups (meat, dairy, vegetables, fruit, grain) or contains less than suggested amounts of food for height (see attached guidelines).

Hydration Summary: _____   Date

Figure 8.4. Nutrition information form. From "Medication Analysis" by M. M. Ault, B. Guy, C. Graff, and S. Paez, in *Project ABLE: Analyzing Behavior States in Learning Environments* (Project No. HO86D00013 by the Office of Special Education Programs, United States Department of Education), 1992, Lawrence: University of Kansas, Department of Special Education.

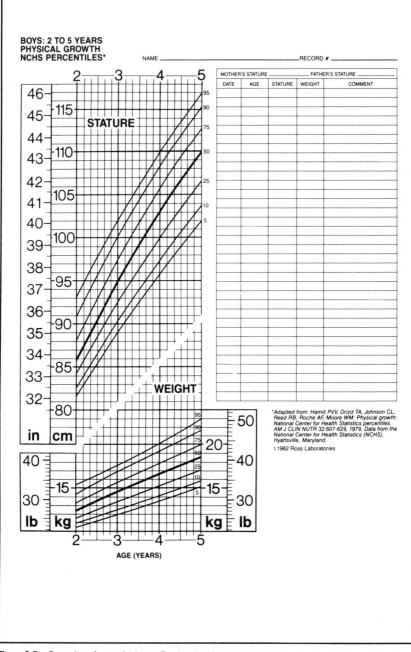

Figure 8.5. Examples of growth charts. Reprinted with permission of Ross Products Division, Abbott Laboratories, Columbus, OH 43216. © 1982 Ross Products Division, Abbott Laboratories.

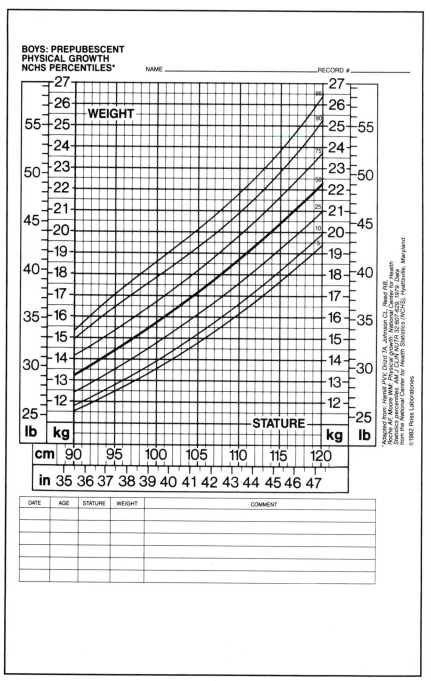

Figure 8.5. *Continued.*

are relatively simple procedures, errors occur with improper use of equipment and inadequate checks on measurements (McCamman & Rues, 1990).
To avoid major errors in weight measurements, the scale should be "zeroed"
before use, and measures should be repeated until they are within ¼ pound.
A measure of weight does not provide maximum information without corresponding measures of height or length. Measures may be taken from head
to toe with the student standing or lying down. A finger-tip to finger-tip measure may also be used. These measures also should be repeated until they
are within ¼ inch.

By making accurate measurements and plotting them on appropriate
growth charts, a visual representation of the student's growth status emerges.
Weight-by-height measurement compares a student with others of the same
size rather than age (McCamman & Rues, 1990). The curved lines on the
graph (Figure 8.5) indicate the percentile ranges for individuals of the same
height and weight. One can, therefore, determine a student's ranking for
height and weight in relationship to these percentile markings.

Nutrition supplementation as a result of medications

Medications may also affect the body's ability to utilize nutrients
(McCamman & Rues, 1990). If a child is being served by multiple physicians, or if the parent uses over-the-counter medications, the student may
be receiving a combination of medications that inhibit the utilization of vitamins and minerals by the body.

Different drugs produce different types of side effects. Some influence
food consumption by producing a change in taste sensation, and others can
cause a dry mouth, nausea, or a stomachache. These reactions may decrease
the amount of food a student will eat. Similarly, nonprescription medications
can also have some impact on the nutrition status of students. For example,
over-the-counter medications as simple as laxatives or aspirin can alter the
body's utilization of nutrients, as well as cause gastrointestinal irritations,
nausea, and heartburn (Crump, 1987). Referral to a nutritionist, or consultation with the primary health care provider through the parents and school
nurse, should be initiated if the student is receiving two or more of the listed
medications for a chronic (long-term) condition (see Appendix 8A).

Feeding management procedures

Many children with profound disabilities experience difficulty with feeding. This may be due to chronic health problems, early negative oral experiences (tube feedings, intubation, suctioning), neurological problems, fatigue
during meals due to poor nutrition, or a combination of these factors. The
teacher, trained as an observer of behavior, can play an important role in

monitoring the child's feeding abilities, eating behaviors, food intake, and preferences.

A mealtime that regularly exceeds 30–40 minutes may be an indication that the student is having difficulty with the eating process. Further assessment may be required for the student who experiences difficulty sucking or swallowing; frequent gagging, choking, or coughing; or excessive crying, whining, or signs of discomfort (e.g., vomiting or cramping) during or after the mealtime. These characteristics may be observed in children who are fed orally, by gastrostomy tube, or a combination of the two. Referral to a nutritionist or a feeding team, via the primary health care provider, should occur if these conditions consistently accompany mealtime for a long period of time. The teacher should immediately discuss any concerns about the student's well-being with the parents and/or school nurse whenever a problem is present, or if there is an abrupt change in the characteristics and quality of mealtime.

Recording the foods eaten at each meal and the child's responses to the various textures, tastes, and consistencies can provide the family and school with important information about preferences and differential oral-motor responses to various foods. Some students with profound disabilities will be tube fed or receive a combination of tube and oral feedings. For these youngsters, it will be important to monitor, over time, the amount and types of food ingested orally and/or through the tube.

Occasionally, a student will not receive enough food or enough variety to provide the range of vitamins and nutrients needed for growth. Recognizing that appetites fluctuate and that mealtime patterns may be inconsistent, a problem may be present when the mealtime continuously contains inadequate amounts or variety of food. If the amounts and variety of food seem to be inadequate over time, then the teacher should address this concern with the parents through the school nurse. It is a myth, however, that failure to thrive is a necessary part of having a disability. The reason for a child's weight or height being less than the 5th percentile is frequently because the child does not get enough calories. Simply increasing the amount of food to facilitate weight gain is often unsatisfactory due to impaired oral-motor function and/or effects of fatigue. As with certain medications, frequent illness or infection may decrease a child's appetite.

Several techniques can be tried to increase the number of calories a student intakes when not enough food is consumed to maintain an appropriate rate of growth. The addition of fats (a particularly concentrated source of calories), evaporated milk, wheat germ, or eggs into the preparation of foods increases the caloric and nutrient intake without requiring the student to eat more food. A regular meal pattern with two or three high-calorie snacks per day is also recommended to promote weight gain (McCamman & Rues, 1990).

Hydration

Adequate hydration is a complicated health issue that is often misunderstood, or even overlooked, as an educational consideration for students with profound disabilities. Water is present in all human tissue and is required for life as well as the efficient or adequate functioning of the body. If a person receives insufficient amounts of water, multiple systems in the body function less efficiently, causing problems in bowel, bladder, skin, and kidney functioning. The symptoms of dehydration, or inadequate amount of fluid ingested by the body, are very similar to characteristics already present with students having profound disabilities. Common symptoms of dehydration include drowsiness, loss of appetite, flushed skin, sunken eyes, and decreased skin turgor (fullness). Other symptoms are constipation, concentrated urine, and an increase in body temperature and pulse rate.

If students are showing signs of severe dehydration, the parents and primary care providers should be notified through the school health professional. Usually it will be determined that an increase in fluids is sufficient to address the problem. A student's consumption of liquids can be increased by (a) increasing the routine offering of small sips of fluids, (b) thickening liquids for students who have difficulty swallowing, and (c) increasing the amounts of solid foods that contain large percentages of fluids.

Classroom applications

Because growth is such a sensitive measure of health and development, recording and plotting a child's height and weight at the beginning, middle, and end of the school year will help monitor the student's health. A variety of charts are available for assessing the growth of children. The growth charts adapted from the National Center for Health Statistics (NCHS) (Hamill et al., 1979) can be used to assess the growth of most children and should be a permanent part of each child's record.

To determine if a child is underweight, overweight, or has short stature, the data gathered for a particular student is typically compared with standard data. Problematic are those youngsters who fall at either end of the continuum. Possible reasons for an underweight condition include improper nutrition due to poor caloric intake, chronic disease, dehydration, iron deficiency, infectious disease, or measurement error. Possible reasons for an overweight condition include higher caloric intake than the child's energy expenditure (common in Prader–Willi syndrome and Down syndrome), edema, and measurement error.

Yearly measures of growth should be made as a part of the overall assessment process. If the student appears at risk for developing nutritional problems, then quarterly growth measures are recommended. Students should be referred to a nutritionist if the following conditions occur: (a) height for weight is less than the 5th or greater than the 95th percentile when plotted on the growth charts for all ages; (b) the child is under 12 months of age and has not gained weight in 1 month; (c) a child between the ages of 1 and 2 years has not gained weight in 3 months; or (d) a youth, to 15 years of age, has not gained weight during the school year.

Additional resources

A registered dietitian can be contacted through a local hospital, a hospital clinic, county or state extension service, or state or local chapter of the Dietetic Association. The request should be for dietitians who work with children who have special health care needs and/or profound disabilities. In addition, the state's Services for Children with Special Health Care Needs and University Affiliated Programs can offer consultation and technical assistance for the development of nutrition services in schools. These agencies may also provide an interdisciplinary feeding clinic or assist in locating a clinic for evaluation and follow-up of children with complex, chronic feeding disorders.

Teeth and Gum Care

Components of teeth and gum care include oral hygiene, proper nutrition with good eating habits, and dental care. Many factors, such as an improperly formed jaw and teeth, lack of stimulation from chewing, inadequate cleaning of the teeth and gums, infrequent dental care, and the side effects of medications can result in unhealthy and malformed teeth and gums. Dental care involves regular visits to the dentist begun as early as 18 months of age.

Oral hygiene is the process of removing food debris and plaque from the teeth to prevent cavities. The most effective methods for preventing plaque buildup are brushing and flossing. Routine oral hygiene should begin as soon as teeth appear during infancy, and continue throughout life, two to three times per day.

Toothbrushing

The following procedure for toothbrushing is suggested by the American Dental Association:

1. Place the head of the toothbrush beside the teeth, with the bristle tips at a 45-degree angle against the gumline.

2. Move the brush back and forth in short strokes (half-a-tooth-wide) several times, using a gentle "scrubbing" motion.

3. Brush the outer surfaces of each tooth, upper and lower, keeping the bristles angled against the gumline.

4. Use the same method on the inside surfaces of all the teeth, still using short back-and-forth strokes.

5. Scrub the chewing surfaces of the teeth.

6. Clean the inside surfaces of the front teeth by tilting the brush vertically and making several gentle up-and-down strokes with the "toe" (the front part) of the brush.

7. Brush the tongue to help freshen the breath and clean the mouth by removing bacteria. (American Dental Association, 1984, p. 8)

Flossing

The American Dental Association has recommended the following procedure for flossing:

1. Break off about 18 inches of floss, and wind most of it around one of your middle fingers.

2. Wind the remaining floss around the same finger of the opposite hand. This finger will "take up" the floss as it becomes soiled.

3. Hold   e floss tightly (without slack) between the thumbs and forefingers, with about an inch of floss between them. Use a gentle sawing motion and guide the floss between the teeth. Never "snap" the floss into the gums.

4. When the floss reaches the gumline, curve it into a C-shape against one tooth. Gently slide it into the space between the gum and the tooth until resistance is felt.

5. Hold the floss tightly against the tooth. Gently scrape the side of the tooth, moving the floss away from the gum.

6. Repeat this method on the rest of the teeth, including the back side of the last tooth. (American Dental Association, 1984, p. 6)

Classroom applications

Students with profound disabilities are particularly in need of oral hygiene programs at school. Typically, these students are unable to clear debris from their mouths, by toothbrushing, rinsing, or oral-motor movements. Oral hygiene should focus on teaching students to participate in or tolerate brushing and flossing on a routine basis. Toothbrushing should be performed after meals and snacks, and flossing should be performed at least once a day at school. Gloves may be used when completing any oral hygiene procedure to protect both the students and the staff members.

Proper positioning is an important component of oral hygiene. If unable to sit, the student can be turned onto the side with the face along the edge of a pillow, and a towel and basin placed under the chin. If the student can sit, several positions are possible. The optimal position is for the adult to be positioned behind the student with the ability to reach around the student, supporting the student's chin while brushing the teeth with the other hand. A second position may be with the adult sitting in front of the student, providing oral-motor control and brushing assistance as needed. If biting is a problem when cleaning the teeth, an object, such as a padded tongue blade or a new, clean rubber door stopper, can be placed between the biting surfaces of the upper and lower jaw (Woelk, 1986). Toothbrushing can then be carried out with this device holding the mouth slightly open. If at all possible, brushing should be accomplished in the bathroom in front of a sink with both the student and the teacher looking in the mirror.

Additional resources

The American Dental Association provides information on care of teeth and gums. Information can be obtained from local dentists or from the Bureau of Health Education and Audiovisual Services, 211 East Chicago Avenue, Chicago, IL 60611. Information and assistance may be available from the local health department. Protocols have been developed for dentists and dental hygienists working with persons having herpes (McMechen & Wright, 1985) and with persons having acquired immune deficiency syndrome (AIDS) (Evans, 1986).

Skin Care

The most appropriate skin care treatment is prevention of skin breakdown and pressure sores. These sores heal slowly under the best of conditions and, once they have formed, all positioning strategies and programming for a student must be altered to accommodate for their treatment. Skin care is designed to maintain or regain healthy skin for the student.

Skin monitoring for healthy skin

To maintain healthy skin, it must remain clean and dry and the student should have proper nutrition, adequate activity, and a reduction throughout the day in periods of continuous pressure on specific parts of the body.

Staying clean and dry is a necessary requirement for healthy skin and particularly for skin that comes in contact with feces or urine. A skin care program should first include efforts to reduce or eliminate incontinence or establish toilet training procedures, provide catheterization, or establish frequent routines of checking and changing diapers and cleansing the skin to reduce prolonged exposure of the skin to feces or urine. This exposure can result in maceration (the softening of the skin), resulting in an increased risk for the development of sores.

Prevention of pressure sores requires relief from prolonged pressure while ensuring that the skin is clean, dry, and free of abrasions (Walker, 1971). Optimal levels of activity must be encouraged as part of a proactive skin care program. Inactivity can result in increased opportunities for the student to experience pressure on the skin surfaces. Pressure occurs when the skin and subcutaneous tissue are squeezed between an underlying bony prominence and a hard surface (e.g., a bed). Certain body parts sustain more weight when sitting and lying and are considered pressure areas (e.g., heels, bony prominence along the spinal column, buttocks). A position change should occur about every 20 minutes for students with severe physical disabilities to relieve continuous pressure and to increase blood circulation (Walker, 1971).

The student, whether active or inactive, may also experience pressure from braces, shoes, or sitting in a wheelchair. The same concerns about pressure resulting from inactivity applies to pressure resulting from ill-fitting equipment. The skin underneath braces and splints or wheelchair seats should be checked daily to identify persistent red spots. If the spots do not fade within 20 minutes after the pressure is relieved, the health care worker should be notified of ill-fitting equipment and the potential for the development of a pressure sore.

Walker (1971) recommended the maintenance of adequate nutrition and hydration as an additional strategy in the prevention of pressure sores. Adequate nutrition and hydration provide a layer of cushioning in the subcutaneous tissue, making the skin more resilient and less susceptible to the effects of continuous pressure or the invasion of bacteria.

A final aspect of prevention is the need to identify methods the student uses to communicate the presence of discomfort. Usually, uncomfortable pressure causes a person to move or adjust his or her position to relieve the discomfort. Many students with profound disabilities cannot move independently to relieve the discomfort. Educational staff need to be extremely sensitive to changes in mood or posturing as indicators that the student is in pain or uncomfortable.

Skin monitoring for unhealthy skin

Care to unhealthy skin focuses on treatment promoting a return to a healthy condition. This may involve heat lamps, dressings, and exposure to the air. Actual care of the unhealthy skin is prescribed by the student's physician or other health care professional, or endorsed by the health care worker in the school.

Classroom applications

The student's skin should be examined daily, with particular attention to portions of the body susceptible to the development of pressure sores. A rating scale for determining the potential for pressure sore formation has been developed by Gosnell (1972; see Figure 8.6). A low score indicates great susceptibility to developing pressure sores and a high score indicates reduced risk. This scale should be completed annually as part of the overall assessment and program development process.

A general health plan should be written for the student at risk for skin problems by the school health care worker or the primary care physician. The plan should address the need for routine position changes, cleansing, maintenance of nutrition, and use of lotions or oils on the skin.

Additional resources

Parents are a valuable resource for school staff when there are questions about the condition of the student's skin. The student's physician or health care professional working with the physician can provide assistance and direction on prevention and/or treatment of skin problems. The enterostomal therapist from a local hospital and the physical therapist in the school system can provide additional assistance.

Therapeutic Physical Management

Therapeutic physical management techniques focusing on improving health and maintaining movement capacity include postural drainage, joint range of motion, positioning, therapeutic handling, and relaxation (Fraser, Hensinger, & Phelps, 1987). Suggestions concerning positioning, therapeutic handling, and relaxation are given in Chapter 6.

Postural drainage

The ability of the student with profound disabilities to expand the lungs may be decreased because of generalized muscle weakness and/or weakness of the muscles associated with coughing. Alternately, a student may lack the muscle control or coordination necessary to cough effectively and clear fluid

RISK OF DEVELOPING PRESSURE SORES

Screening Form

Awareness Levels Score
4   Alert/active
3   Alert/inactive
2   Dazed/drowsy
1   Asleep

Continence Score
4   Fully controlled
3   Usually controlled
2   Minimally controlled
1   Absence of control

Activity/Movement Score
3   Moves self frequently in and out
    of positions
2   Adjusts self within positions
1   Little to no independent movement

Communication Ability Score
3   Symbolic
2   Gestures
1   Nonsymbolic

Mobility Score
5   Fully ambulatory
4   Minimally ambulatory
3   Fully mobile with a device
2   Minimally mobile with a device
1   Immobile

Nutrition Score
3   Good
2   Fair
1   Poor

Name _____ Completed by _____

Date

Score									
Awareness Level									
Communication Ability									
Continence									
Mobility									
Activity/Movement									
Nutrition									
Total									

Figure 8.6. Screening form for risk of developing pressure sores. Adapted from "An Assessment Tool to Identify Pressure Sores" by D. Gosnell, 1972, *Nursing Research, 22,* pp. 55–59.

from the lungs. The resulting decrease in lung expansion or inability to cough leads to an increased pooling or accumulation of secretions in the lungs.

Postural drainage is performed to promote the drainage and coughing up of secretions from the lungs. The student is placed in various positions to allow gravity to assist drainage of secretions from the lungs, the bronchi, and the trachea.

Joint range of motion

The amount of movement that occurs at a joint is the range of motion of the joint. The range of motion of joints is maintained in active persons by the movements and exercises that occur daily with walking, running, working, and playing. Many students with profound disabilities have restricted movement. The student may be able to move some or all joints through complete range of motion, but the joints the student is unable to move must be passively moved by another person. This movement is referred to as *passive range of motion*. Passive range of motion can be incorporated into positioning, transfer, and other educational activities requiring movement. This strategy provides multiple opportunities for passive movement throughout the day and is important to maintain the student's existing range of motion.

Classroom applications

Training by the appropriate health care professional is a prerequisite to conducting any of the above management techniques. Training must also address optimal positioning of the student; the frequency with which the procedure is performed; the student's tolerance for the procedure; and, if possible, methods to incorporate these procedures into educational activities and routines.

Additional resources

Occupational and physical therapists in the school can provide assistance and information about joint range of motion, positioning, and therapeutic handling. Manufacturers and distributors of equipment can provide information about the use of equipment and new or different equipment that can be more effective for the student. Physical and occupational therapists are likely to have names and addresses of manufacturers and distributors. Respiratory therapists and nurses, from a local hospital, can instruct school staff in techniques of postural drainage. The nurses working in the physician's office, a public health nurse, or clinical nursing specialist working with children can teach postural drainage techniques to school staff.

LOW-INCIDENCE HEALTH CARE PROCEDURES

The procedures reviewed in this section tend to be used less frequently than procedures discussed previously. Teachers should, however, be familiar with general issues surrounding their implementation and know where to go for assistance. These low-incidence procedures include respiratory care, elimination management, shunt management, and cast management.

Respiratory Care

Respiratory care includes those activities and procedures that assist the student in maintaining adequate levels of oxygen in the bloodstream. Typically, these procedures include tracheostomy care, suctioning, oxygen supplementation, and assisting in ventilation.

Tracheostomy care

A *tracheostomy* refers to an opening through the throat into the trachea to permit air movement in and out of the lungs. A hollow tube, called a tracheostomy tube, is placed in this opening and secured by ties around the student's neck. Breathing occurs through the tracheostomy tube rather than through the student's mouth and/or nose.

Care of the tracheostomy includes removal of secretions from the student's trachea, cleaning the tracheostomy tube, care of the skin around the tube, changing the tracheostomy ties, and changing the tracheostomy tube (Graff et al., 1990). Secretions are removed from the trachea using a suction catheter. This catheter is attached to connecting tubing attached to a suction machine. Gloves are worn by the person suctioning the student to assure that secretions do not come in contact with the skin of the person carrying out the suctioning. A student may cough secretions to the outer edge of the tracheostomy tube. In this instance, the secretions are wiped away with a clean tissue or removed with a bulb syringe. Care again is taken to make certain that secretions from the trachea do not come in contact with the trained person's skin.

Classroom applications

Tracheostomies are remaining in children for longer periods of time and, increasingly, school staff are working with students having a tracheostomy tube in place. Although the tracheostomy tube is usually changed at home, all school staff working with the student should know what to do in an emergency, such as when the tube is plugged with secretions or is accidentally removed. If the tube is blocked with secretions, air will not move in and out of the student's lungs. Therefore, the secretions or mucus plugging the tube should be removed immediately. The tracheostomy tube may accidentally come out and require replacement. An extra sterile tracheostomy tube should always be kept in the classroom or in a bag with the student's suction equipment. If a sterile tube is not available, the used tracheostomy tube can be reinserted. Because the tube is secured in place around the neck with ties, these ties should be checked periodically to make sure they are secure and holding the tracheostomy tube in place. These ties, usually changed at home, may become soiled and require changing at school.

The student's skin can become irritated if secretions remain on the skin around the tracheostomy tube or along the ties. The skin around the tube should be cleaned at least daily, and more often as needed. A small gauze dressing or bib is often worn around the tracheostomy tube to collect secretions coming out of the tube. If this becomes soiled during the school day, it should be changed. School staff should visually examine the skin around the tracheostomy tube for any redness or signs of irritation before placing a clean dressing or bib around the tube. School staff should wash their hands before and after tracheostomy care at a sink that is not used for food preparation. A person trained in removal of secretions from the tracheostomy tube and replacement of the tube should always be available to the student.

Extra supplies should be available in the classroom, and equipment, such as the suctioning machine, should be checked at the beginning of each day to assure it is functioning properly. In addition, school staff should be trained in cardiopulmonary resuscitation of the student with a tracheostomy, and arrangements for emergency medical services should be in place.

Additional resources

A nurse and/or respiratory therapist who has taught the student's parents may be the most likely resource person for school staff. Staff from an equipment company providing supplies, such as suction machines and suction catheters, may provide a supportive function to the school staff. The local emergency medical services team or local rescue unit can assist school staff in emergency situations and transportation for further care. An emergency plan should be in place with telephone numbers and specific steps to follow if an emergency arises.

Suctioning

Suctioning refers to the removal of secretions from the mouth, throat, or trachea to allow the respiratory tract to be as free as possible of secretions so air movement can occur. Suctioning in the school will most likely be done through the mouth; however, *nasopharyngeal suctioning* or suctioning through the nose may also be done.

Classroom applications

Suctioning is required when a student is unable to remove secretions from the respiratory tract effectively. Signs that a student is in need of suctioning include audible secretions, signs of obstruction (e.g., decreased air movement at the mouth, nose, or tracheostomy tube), or signs of oxygen deficiency (e.g., irritability, increased respiration rate, fatigue, pale color, increase in heart rate). A suction catheter is attached to a suction machine by a connecting tubing, and negative pressure results in the pulling of secretions through a catheter placed near the secretions. A bulb syringe may be used to remove secretions from the nose or mouth. Assisting a student into a side-lying position can allow secretions to move out of the student's mouth and become more visible and more easily suctioned.

Suctioning using the bulb syringe requires the trained person to expel secretions from the syringe onto several layers of disposable tissues before a second attempt is made to remove secretions. Secretions removed from the student's mouth, nose, or trachea should not come in contact with the skin of the person doing the suctioning. Careful handwashing before and after suctioning is essential.

Additional resources

Nurses in home health agencies, community health departments, or local hospitals, and respiratory therapists can provide additional information and/or assistance.

Oxygen administration

Oxygen is administered in an effort to increase the amount of oxygen in the air breathed by the student. Without this supplementation, the student may experience an inadequate level of oxygen in the body. Oxygen is given by various methods, which can include nasal catheter (a small plastic catheter placed into one nostril), nasal prongs (two small plastic prongs placed into each nostril), a face mask (plastic mask fitting over the mouth and nose), or a tracheostomy mask (small plastic mask fitting loosely over the tracheostomy tube). Nasal prongs are commonly used to administer oxygen and, of the options, may be least noticed by and most comfortable for the student.

Classroom applications

The oxygen-to-air rate is prescribed by the student's physician. The rate should not be changed unless ordered by the student's physician. For example, some students may require more oxygen during mealtimes or certain other activities.

The student may receive oxygen from a portable oxygen tank, and humidification may or may not be available. It is important to remember that oxygen without humidification can dry up secretions and the mucous membranes in the respiratory tract. Therefore, oxygen should not be administered without humidity over a prolonged period of time.

Because oxygen is highly combustible, it is essential to avoid using highly flammable substances when oxygen is administered. Open flames from cigarettes or candles, electrical equipment that might produce sparks, and any items that can produce static electricity should be avoided. Areas in which oxygen is in use should be identified with large, easy-to-read signs warning others of this potential hazard. Special considerations regarding potential hazards may need to be given to the transportation of the student who is receiving continuous oxygen.

Additional resources

Additional information can be obtained from home health care staff, nurses, respiratory therapists, and medical equipment supply companies. The student's home health care nurse, physician, or respiratory therapist can be a resource for school staff when concerns arise about the student's responses to oxygen administration.

Assisted ventilation

Students who are unable to breathe in or breathe out to ensure adequate oxygen supply to the body require assisted ventilation. Students who require assisted ventilation (a) may not breathe spontaneously and may rely completely on the ventilator, (b) may begin a breath that the ventilator completes, (c) may receive breaths at a preset rate but be unable to spontaneously begin breathing without the ventilator, or (d) may breathe against a constant pressure. Oxygen is often administered with assisted ventilation, and students requiring prolonged ventilatory assistance will most likely have a tracheostomy tube.

Classroom applications

Students requiring ventilatory assistance, and their parents as well, may be anxious as others become responsible for managing care in this critical area. School staff must feel confident and secure with the student and have a clear understanding of the procedures and plans to be followed if problems arise. Careful planning can lead to increased confidence on the part of school staff and less anxiety for parents and the student.

Additional resources

Nurses working with the student in the hospital setting, home health care staff, respiratory therapists, medical supply and equipment companies, and the student's physician can provide information necessary to develop a comprehensive plan for managing respiratory care.

Elimination

Elimination procedures include those activities designed to monitor and assist the student in removing waste from the body in a safe and clean manner. These include bowel and ostomy care and bladder catheterization.

Bowel care

Optimal and healthy bowel functioning is maintained through adequate dietary fiber and fluid intake, physical activity, and routine elimination in a supportive environment with facilitative positioning (Given & Simmons, 1979; Shaddix, 1986). When a student has inadequate fiber and fluid intake and limited mobility and independent movement, the result can be infrequent stools, hard and painful bowel movements, or an impacted colon.

Classroom applications

Strategies to increase the fiber intake include reducing the use of commercial baby food, which contains little fiber, and serving bran cereal during a meal or mixing unprocessed bran in food each day to supply additional fiber (Shaddix, 1986). A grinder or food processor can also be used with table foods to obtain the best texture while retaining fiber content.

Adequate fluid intake is also critical for proper bowel functioning. The selection and presentation of fluid must be frequent and conducive to the retention of the fluid. Shaddix (1986) suggested that water and unsweetened juice be presented routinely, and cautions against the use of sweetened juice in that it causes salivation, drooling, and the loss of fluid. Prune juice, a natural laxative, can be combined with other fruit juices to be more acceptable. Other liquids can be thickened with infant cereals, blended fruit, or unflavored gelatin (see the earlier section titled "Feeding Management Procedures").

Bowel elimination can be facilitated by a supportive environment, proper positioning, and an adjustment in the student's overall muscle tone. The setting for toileting should include elements that aid in the process of defecation. Defecation is typically facilitated when the student is in a squatting or flexed position, which helps in attaining appropriate muscle tone for defecation. Using this position after meals takes advantage of the *gastrocolic reflex,* naturally occurring contractions of the colon that often happen after meals. Students may require assistance from others to move into this position, with support from an adult or use of adaptive equipment. A side-lying position, with hips and knees flexed and shoulders forward, may also be used if the student cannot assume a sitting position. Daily, routine physical activity may also assist in promoting regular bowel functioning. Physical activity assists the movement of fecal material through the large intestine toward and through the rectum.

Because the student may not recognize the urge to defecate or the student may receive medications that alter the color, consistency, and frequency of bowel movements, school staff must be aware of the student's regular elimination pattern. They must also be sensitive to nonverbal indicators, such as characteristic posturing or expressions of discomfort or pain, to identify the need to proceed with toileting or potential problems in bowel functioning.

Any changes in bowel functioning, such as diarrhea or constipation, should be discussed with the student's primary care provider and parents. Any sign of diarrhea, or frequent runny stools within one school day, should be considered the result of a virus (usually highly contagious) and referral to the school nurse should be made immediately.

Additional resources

Referral to a dietitian by the student's physician or school nurse may be needed to discuss changes in fiber and/or water content of the student's diet. Physical and occupational therapists can provide assistance in proper positioning, oral-motor facilitation, and increased levels of activity.

Ostomy care

An *ostomy* is a surgically created opening into a hollow organ of the body. When the opening is created from the bowel or intestine and leads to the abdominal surface, the student will be able to eliminate feces from the bowel or intestine without using the rectum. A *colostomy* is an opening of some portion of the colon onto the abdomen. An *ileostomy* is an opening of some portion of the ileum (lower part of the small intestine) onto the abdomen. Feces pass through the opening and are collected in a small pouch or bag. The bag adheres tightly to the skin around this opening on the abdomen, which is called a *stoma*. Because there is no control over when feces will move into the pouch, feces may well collect in the pouch during the school day. This is especially true when the student has an ileostomy. In this case, the material passing through the stoma is liquid or a pasty consistency and contains digestive enzymes that can be very irritating to the skin. Ostomy care includes the procedures of collecting feces in an odor-free manner and keeping the skin around the ostomy healthy and free of irritation.

Pouches without adhesive must be placed on the skin after adhesive is already in place around the stoma. Pouches can be drainable, with an opening that allows for frequent emptying, or have a closed end, in which case they are discarded after one use (Broadwell, 1984). If possible, the student is positioned over the toilet seat and the pouch is opened and drained into the toilet. The emptying or changing of a bag should take place in an area that is private and allows the student to be in the best position possible. After the pouch is emptied, the inside of the pouch is rinsed and dried, and the pouch is closed and secured with an ostomy clamp or a rubber band.

If gas accumulates in the bag, the drainable pouch can be opened for gas to escape, and the closed-end pouch can be punctured with a pin, thereby releasing the gas. Tape is placed over pinholes to avoid leakage (Adams & Selekof, 1986). Odor may permeate the pouch and the student's clothing regardless of the method being used. Therefore, a pouch with a gas filter is recommended (Erickson, 1987).

The stoma and the skin around the stoma should be examined during each bag change for signs of irritation or redness. Skin around the stoma should have its natural color with no flaking or sweating. The stoma should be pink and moist like the inside cheek of the mouth, and discoloration should be reported to the school nurse. Because feces are a primary source of infection, proper handwashing should be carried out before and after this procedure, and at any time there is contact with feces. Gloves are typically worn during the changing procedure.

Classroom applications

Although the colostomy or ileostomy pouch is usually changed at home, it may require changing at school. The pouch may become loose, leak, accidentally be pulled off, or become full. In addition, the student may develop diarrhea or excess gas after eating certain foods, and the pouch may require emptying or changing. Extra supplies for changing the pouch, as well as additional changes of clothing, should remain at school at all times to meet the needs of the student. A procedure for periodically checking the pouch and skin should be incorporated into the toileting routine for the student. Understanding how to manage these problems and being prepared to manage them can allow the student to continue classroom activities with little interruption.

Additional resources

Information on colostomy or ileostomy care can be obtained from the United Ostomy Association, the American Cancer Society, suppliers of ostomy products, and the International Association for Enterostomal Therapy, 5000 Birch Street, Suite 400, Newport Beach, CA 92660.

Bladder catheterization

Students having defects of the spinal cord, such as *spina bifida* or *myelomeningocele,* may also have neurologic impairment of the bladder (*neurogenic bladder*), resulting in little or no control over bladder emptying. The bladder usually stretches as it fills with urine until it is full; then nerve signals cause it to contract and empty. Usually, a person can delay bladder emptying and control the occurrence of urination. A neurogenic bladder may overstretch or contract frequently or irregularly, resulting in constant dribbling or incomplete emptying. Catheterization is a procedure for facilitating the routine emptying of the bladder.

Clean intermittent catheterization (CIC) is the insertion of a catheter through the urethra (passageway between the bladder and the opening to the outside of the body) into the bladder. This is usually done every 3–4 hours during the day. The environmental area chosen to carry out this procedure should allow for privacy, as well as have a sink for proper cleansing before and after the procedure.

During catheterization, the student may sit on the toilet, stand, or lie down. The urine, if not emptied directly into the toilet, should be collected in a container. After the person implementing the catheterization has completed thorough handwashing, the area around the opening to the urethra is cleansed with a towelette or soap and water. For a male, the penis is cleansed using a circular motion moving outward from the tip. The female student's labia are separated and cleansed using one downward motion with each separate towelette or soapy cotton ball with each motion.

The catheter, lubricated with a water-soluble jelly for the male student, is inserted into the bladder an additional 1–3 inches and held in place once the urine begins to flow (Chapman, Hill, & Shurtleff, 1979). The catheter is gently removed after the urine flow has stopped. If urine begins to flow as the catheter is removed, the removal is stopped until the urine flow ceases. The skin is washed again to remove any urine and prevent odors. The catheter is washed with soapy water, rinsed and air dried, and returned to its carrying case.

Classroom applications

The student with neurogenic bladder has little or no control over the process of emptying the bladder and will need assistance in controlling release of urine during the school day. The student should be taught to participate in urinary catheterization as much as possible. This may include the student's washing his or her own hands, holding equipment, or whatever activities are appropriate (Taylor, 1990). Because a student may experience leakage when laughing, coughing, or sneezing, and may not achieve complete dryness, use of protective clothing is generally recommended. In addition, an extra set of clothing should be available at school.

Additional resources

Nurses in clinics and hospitals serving children with myelomeningocele and the student's urological specialist can provide information and guidance in this area. Videotapes, such as *Clean Intermittent Catheterizations* (University of Colorado School of Nursing, 1986), can be useful in training others to perform this procedure.

Shunt Care

Students with profound disabilities may have a condition known as hydrocephalus. Often, the student with hydrocephalus has a shunt, consisting of a valve or pump and tubing, draining excess fluid from the ventricles of the brain into other parts of the body. This fluid, called cerebrospinal fluid, is formed primarily in the ventricles of the brain. When excess amounts of fluid accumulate, the ventricles may enlarge, possibly resulting in enlargement of the head and brain damage. Surgical placement of a shunt allows fluid to leave the ventricles and move to the peritoneal cavity or the right upper chamber (atrium) of the heart. This prevents further enlargement of the head and additional damage to brain tissue. If the shunt becomes blocked or malfunctions, fluid begins to build up, creating increased pressure. Signs of increased intracranial pressure include headache, nausea, vomiting, double vision, blurred vision, irritability, restlessness, personality change, lethargy, drowsiness, and seizures (Bell & McCormick, 1978; Hausman, 1981; Madsen, 1986).

Classroom applications

To assure proper functioning of the shunt, careful observations are routinely made, with signs of complications immediately reported to parents and/or the student's primary care provider. School staff should continuously be aware of deviations from the student's usual behavior, level of activities, and responses (Graff et al., 1990).

Additional resources

The student's physician (pediatrician, family physician, neurologist, neurosurgeon) and nurses working with children having neurologic disorders can provide additional information. The student's parents can provide information about the student's usual behaviors and about behaviors that can be expected when the shunt is not functioning properly.

Cast Management

Students with profound disabilities may require a cast after a fracture or while recovering from a variety of surgical procedures. Cast care is the ongoing process of protecting the cast from damage and monitoring the cast so it continues to support and protect the affected part of the body.

Classroom applications

To properly manage and care for a cast, school staff should know the purpose of the cast, whether the cast is new or has been in place for a period of time, the type of cast material used, activities that are appropriate for the student, and activities that are not allowed. Cast care includes protecting and cleaning the cast, assisting the student with a cast during toileting activities, checking the condition of the skin around and underneath the cast, and checking for the continued correct positioning of the cast. Damaged casts need attention to ensure that the student's body part that is to be immobilized is not injured. If injury does occur, school staff should report this immediately to the student's parents and physician.

Students with casts who are not capable of walking or moving around with some independence will require assistance in periodic repositioning. This is done to prevent excessive pressure on areas beneath the cast. Students who move about frequently, however, can cause skin irritation as the skin rubs against the cast. Constant pressure over an area can initially result in pain, but eventually pain stops as the skin sloughs off following prolonged pressure. A student who is unable to communicate discomfort or pain may indicate the presence of a problem by being irritable, fussy, or crying more than usual. If a change in behavior occurs with no apparent reason, it must be assumed that the problem may be with the cast (Hilt & Schmidt, 1975).

If a cast is too tight, circulation to the affected area can be impaired. Checking the student's circulation includes checking the student's fingers or toes of the arm or leg for color, temperature, presence of any swelling, and capillary filling. Sensation to touch and movement should also be routinely evaluated to determine if the cast is too tight. Signs that teachers should watch for include pale to white color of fingers or toes, fingers or toes cool or cold to the touch, sluggish capillary filling, swelling of fingers or toes, numbness or tingling, or decrease or absence of sensation or in movement of fingers or toes. With the presence of any one of the above, the school nurse should be notified immediately.

Swelling of the casted area can result in decreased circulation to the affected area. If circulation is not restored, damage to muscle tissue and nerves in the area can occur (Rang, 1983). Indications of pressure buildup beneath the cast include greater than usual pain, decreased or absent movement of toes or fingers of casted arm or leg, pain on stretching the toes or fingers, and decreased sensation to touch. The student's physician must be notified immediately so pressure can be released.

Additional resources

Information and guidance can be obtained from the student's orthopedic surgeon or physician applying the student's cast. The physical therapist and nurses in the local community health department, hospital, or home health agency may also provide useful information on cast care.

CONCLUSION

Students with profound disabilities require an integrated service delivery model to have their special health care needs met. A key issue relates to how non–medically trained school personnel should deal with students' complex health needs. The information that has been provided in this chapter should be looked upon as just that: information. One cannot fully understand and provide for the special health care needs of students without in-depth initial and continuous training by qualified individuals. Preneed planning by parents and professionals from the school, related services agencies, and the community can help to ensure that written protocols, delegation of duties, appropriate management systems, and training are provided to facilitate the process of meeting these special needs of students with profound disabilities.

Side and Interaction Effects of Common Medications

Side Effects of Medications Common to Students with Severe or Profound Disabilities (Listed Alphabetically)

> **Please Note:** The listing of possible side effects is *not comprehensive*. Only those side effects that were observable and might impact nutrition or behavior were selected. A devastating side effect of Depakene, for example, is liver damage. Although this side effect would eventually affect behavior, it was not listed as a side effect because the actual symptoms would not manifest themselves until the liver damage was in an advanced stage.

Medications
[**Brand name;** Chemical name
Classification (Category)] | **Possible Side Effects**

Medications [Brand name; Chemical name Classification (Category)]	Possible Side Effects
Aldactone; *Spironolactone* (Diuretic)	[M]Confusion; irregular heartbeat; nervousness; numbness or tingling in hands, feet, or lips; unusual tiredness or weakness; [R]shortness of breath, skin rash or itching
Alkets; Magnesium Oxide *Antacid* (Gastric Medication)	[M]Diarrhea or laxative effect; [R]mild constipation, stomach cramps, nausea, vomiting

Note: Differences in frequency of occurrence of side effects are indicated by a letter preceding the correspondent symptom(s) or sign(s). **M** = more frequent; **L** = less frequent; **R** = rare; **U** = unknown.

Alupent; Metaproterenol
Antiasthma/Bronchodilator
(Respiratory Tract Medication)

Chest discomfort or pain, dizziness or lightheadedness, fast heartbeat, headache, nausea, vomiting, unusual anxiety, nervousness, restlessness, severe weakness

Amoxil; *Amoxicillin* (Antibiotic)

^{M}Abdominal or stomach cramps, severe watery diarrhea, fever, increased thirst, increased weight loss, nausea, vomiting, unusual tiredness or weakness, skin rash, hives, or itching

Ascorbic Acid/Vitamin C

Prolonged use of high doses of ascorbic acid may result in urinary tract stones formation and, thus, side or lower back pain

Aspirin; *Salicylates* (Analgesic)

^{M}Nausea, vomiting, stomach pain; $^{L/R}$vomiting of blood, shortness of breath, skin rash, hives or itching, unusual tiredness or weakness

Augmentin; *Amoxicillin*
(Antibiotic)

^{M}Abdominal or stomach cramps; watery and severe diarrhea; fever; increased thirst; increased weight loss; nausea; vomiting; unusual tiredness or weakness; skin rash, hives, or itching; wheezing

Bactrim; *Sulfonamide*
(Antibiotic)

^{M}Itching, skin rash; ^{L}aching of joint and muscles; difficulty in swallowing; fever; sore throat; redness, blistering, peeling, or loosening of skin; unusual tiredness or weakness; ^{R}blood in urine, lower back pain, pain or burning while urinating, swelling of front part of neck

Beclovent; Adrenocorticoid
Antiasthmatic (Respiratory
Tract Medication)

^{M}Creamy-white, curd-like patches inside mouth (oral candidiasis); ^{R}difficulty in swallowing (monilial esopha-

Note: Differences in frequency of occurrence of side effects are indicated by a letter preceding the correspondent symptom(s) or sign(s). **M** = more frequent; **L** = less frequent; **R** = rare; **U** = unknown.

gitis), skin rash, shortness of breath (bronchospasm); [U]acne or other skin problems; back or rib pain; bloody or black tarry stools; chest pain; chills; cough; ear congestion or pain; fever; head congestion; hoarseness or other voice changes; nasal congestion; runny nose; sneezing, sore throat; decreased or blurred vision; eye pain, redness, or tearing; frequent urination or increased thirst; fullness or rounding out of the face; hives; itching of skin; unusual weight gain (edema); increased susceptibility to infections; unusual tiredness or weakness; muscle weakness; nausea or vomiting; stomach pain or burning

Beconase; Adrenocorticoid *Anti-inflammatory* (Respiratory Tract Medication)

[M]Unusual increase in sneezing, burning, dryness or other irritation inside the nose; [L]bloody mucus or unexplained nosebleeds, crusting inside nose, sore throat; [R]shortness of breath, troubled breathing in chest, wheezing, skin rash or hives, swelling on face (signs of chronic overdose: fullness or rounding of the face)

Benadryl; Diphenhydramine *Antitussive* (Respiratory Tract Medication)

[L/R]Sore throat, fever, unusual tiredness or weakness

Chronulac; Lactulose *Laxative* (Gastric Medication)

[R]Confusion, irregular heartbeat, muscle cramps, unusual tiredness or weakness, dizziness or lightheadedness

Colace; Docusate *Laxative* (Gastric Medication)

[R]Asthma, skin rash or itching, esophageal blockage, intestinal impaction, confusion, irregular heartbeat, muscle cramps, unusual tiredness or weakness

---

Note: Differences in frequency of occurrence of side effects are indicated by a letter preceding the correspondent symptom(s) or sign(s). **M** = more frequent; **L** = less frequent; **R** = rare; **U** = unknown.

Cortisporin Ophthalmic;
Hydrocortisone (Antibiotic)

No relevant observable side effect

DDAVP; *Desmopressin*
(Antidiuretic)

R(dose-related) confusion, drowsiness, continuing headache, problem with urination, seizures, weight gain (water retention); L/R(Dose-related) abdominal or stomach cramps; flushing or redness of skin; pain in the vulva; runny or stuffy nose; pain, redness, or swelling at site of injection

Depakene; *Valproic Acid*
(Anticonvulsant)

Nausea, vomiting, cramping, swelling of face, tiredness, weakness, lack of coordination, easily bruised, gastroenteritis, ataxia, tremor, confusion, apathy, nystagmus

Dexedrine; Dextroamphetamine
Amphetamine (CNS Stimulant)

Decreased growth, nausea, dizziness, drowsiness

Diamox; Acetazolamide
Carbonic Anhydrase Inhibitor
(Anticonvulsant)

Thirst, anorexia, increased urine output, drowsiness, abdominal cramping

Digoxin; Digitalis
Antiarrhythmic
(Cardiovascular Medication)

Nausea, vomiting, irregular heartbeat, loss of appetite, abdominal pain, diarrhea, weakness, headache

Dilantin; Phenytoin *Hydontoin*
(Anticonvulsant)

Gingivival hyperplasia; uncontrolled movements, confusion, dizziness, ataxia, drowsiness, constipation, anorexia, nausea, vomiting

Ducolax; Bisacodyl *Laxative*
(Gastric Medication)

No relevant observable side effect

Ex-Lax; Phenolphthalein
Laxative (Gastric Medication)

Abdominal cramping

Note: Differences in frequency of occurrence of side effects are indicated by a letter preceding the correspondent symptom(s) or sign(s). **M** = more frequent; **L** = less frequent; **R** = rare; **U** = unknown.

Folic Acid	No relevant observable side effect
Feosol; Ferrous Sulfate (Iron Supplement)	[M]Abdominal or stomach pain, cramping, soreness, nausea, vomiting; [L/R]chest or throat pain especially when swallowing; stools containing blood, fresh or digested; constipation, darkened urine, diarrhea; heartburn
Glyrol; Glycerin (Diuretic)	No relevant observable side effect
Klonopin; Clonazepam *Benzodiazepine* (Anticonvulsant)	No relevant observable side effect
Lasix; Furosemide (Diuretic)	[L]Unusual tiredness or weakness, nausea or vomiting, muscle cramps or pain, mood or mental changes, irregular heartbeats, increased thirst, dryness of mouth
Levoxine; Levothyroxine *Thyroid Modifier* (Hormone)	[R]Severe headache, skin rash or hives
Maalox; Aluminum and Magnesium *Antacid* (Gastric Medication)	[M]Mood or mental changes, swelling of wrists or ankles, constipation, unusual loss of weight, unusual tiredness or weakness
Mebaral; Mephobarbital *Barbiturate* (Anticonvulsant)	[L]Confusion, mental depression, excitement; [R]bleeding sores on lips, sore throat, fever, tiredness
Mellaril; Thioridazine *Phenothiazine* (Sedative/ Hypnotic–Antipsychotic)	[M]Blurred vision; [L]chewing movements, lip smacking or puckering, puffing of checks, rapid or worm-like movements of tongue, uncontrolled movements of arms and legs, difficult urination; [R]difficult breathing, fast heartbeat, fever, increased sweating, loss of bladder control, muscle stiffness, seizures,

Note: Differences in frequency of occurrence of side effects are indicated by a letter preceding the correspondent symptom(s) or sign(s). **M** = more frequent; **L** = less frequent; **R** = rare; **U** = unknown.

unusual tiredness or weakness, unusual pale skin

Metaprel; Metaproterenol
Antiasthma/Bronchodilator
(Respiratory Tract Medication)

MSevere chest discomfort or pain; dizziness or lightheadedness; fast heartbeat; headache; severe nausea or vomiting; severe trembling; unusual anxiety, nervousness, or restlessness; blurred vision, unusual paleness and coldness of skin; weakness

Minipress; Prazosin
Antihypertensive
(Cardiovascular Medication)

LChest pain, dizziness, faint, shortness of breath, weight gain (water retention), swelling of feet or lower legs; Rinability to control urination, numbness or tingling of hands or feet

Mylicon; Simethicone
Antiflatulent (Gastric
Medication)

No relevant observable side effect

Mysoline; *Primidone*
(Anticonvulsant)

LUnusual excitement or restlessness; Rhives, skin rash, swelling of eyelids, wheezing or tightness in chest, unusual tiredness or weakness

Neosporin Ophthalmic;
Neomycin (Antibiotic)

MItching, rash, redness, swelling, or other sign of irritation not present before therapy; Lburning or stinging

Opticrom; Cromolyn
Antiallergenic
(Ophthalmic agent)

REye irritation not present before therapy including styes, severe swelling of conjunctiva

Pepcid; Famotidine *Antiulcer Agent* (Gastric Medication)

RFast or pounding heartbeat, fever, swelling of eyelids, tightness in chest, unusual bleeding or bruising, unusual severe tiredness or weakness

Note: Differences in frequency of occurrence of side effects are indicated by a letter preceding the correspondent symptom(s) or sign(s). **M** = more frequent; **L** = less frequent; **R** = rare; **U** = unknown.

Peri-Colace; Casanthranol
Laxative (Gastric Medication)

[R]Asthma, skin rash, itching, esophageal blockage, intestinal impaction

Phenobarbital *Barbiturate*
(Anticonvulsant)

[L]Confusion, unusual excitement; [R]weight loss, bleeding sores on lips, chest pain, skin rash, sore throat, fever

Poly-Vi-Flor; plus fluoride
Multivitamin combination
(Vitamin)

[R]Skin rash; sores in the mouth and on the lips; constipation; loss of appetite, nausea, or vomiting; pain and aching bones; stiffness; weight loss

Prednisone *Glucocorticoid*
(Antiinflammatory)

[L]Decreased or blurred vision, decreased growth, frequent urination, increased thirst; [R]hallucinations, skin rash or hives, burning or pain at place of injection, mental depression or other mood or mental changes

Proventil; Albuterol *Adrenergic*
Bronchodilator (Respiratory
Tract Medication)

[M]Fast heartbeat; [L]coughing or other bronchial irritation, difficult or painful urination, dizziness or lightheadedness, drowsiness, dryness or irritation of mouth or throat, headache; [R]chest discomfort or pain, increase in wheezing or difficulty in breathing; [U]hallucinations; irregular heartbeat; mood or mental changes; flushing or redness of face or skin; nausea or vomiting; severe trembling; unusual anxiety, nervousness, or restlessness

Reglan; Metoclopramide
Antiemetic (Gastric Medication)

[R](Signs of overdose) confusion, drowsiness; muscle spasms especially of jaw, neck, and back; shuffling walk, tic-like movements of the face and head, trembling or shaking of hands

---

Note: Differences in frequency of occurrence of side effects are indicated by a letter preceding the correspondent symptom(s) or sign(s). **M** = more frequent; **L** = less frequent; **R** = rare; **U** = unknown.

Riopan Plus; Simethicone and Magaldrate *Antacid* (Gastric Medication)

[M]Loss of appetite, muscle weakness, unusual loss of weight, continuous feeling of discomfort, diarrhea or laxative effect; [L]stomach cramps, vomiting, nausea

Ritalin; *Methylphenidate Adrenergic* (CNS Stimulant)

[M]Fast heartbeat; [L]chest pain, uncontrolled movements of the body, bruising, fever, joint pain, skin rash or hives, [R]blurred vision, convulsions, sore throat, fever, unusual tiredness or weakness

Slo-Bid; Theophylline *Bronchodilator* (Respiratory Tract Medication)

[L]Heartburn, vomiting; [R]skin rash or hives, chest pain, dizziness, fast breathing, flushing, headache, pounding heartbeat, chill, fever, pain or swelling at site of injection

Synthroid; Levothyroxine *Thyroid Modifier* (Hormone)

[R]Severe headache, skin rash or hives

Tagamet; Cimetidine *Antacid* (Gastric Medication)

[R]Sore throat, fever, unusual bleeding or bruising, unusual tiredness or weakness

Tegretol; *Carbamazepine* (Anticonvulsant)

[M]Blurred vision or double vision, confusion, agitation, headache, increase in seizure frequency, nausea, vomiting, unusual drowsiness or weakness; [L]behavioral changes, hives, itching or skin rash; [R]chest pain, fainting, troubled breathing, continuous back-and-forth eye movements, trembling, uncontrolled body movements, visual hallucinations

Tetracyn; *Tetracycline* (Antibiotic)

[M]Cramps or burning of the stomach, diarrhea, sore mouth or tongue, itching of rectal or genital areas, nausea, vomiting

---

Note: Differences in frequency of occurrence of side effects are indicated by a letter preceding the correspondent symptom(s) or sign(s). **M** = more frequent; **L** = less frequent; **R** = rare; **U** = unknown.

Theo-Dur; Theophylline
Antiasthmatic/Bronchodilator
(Respiratory Tract Medication)

[L]Heartburn, vomiting; [R]skin rash or hives

Tranxene; Clorazepate
Benzodiazepine (Sedative/
Hypnotic–Anticonvulsant)

[L]Confusion, mental depression; [R]trouble sleeping, unusual excitement, nervousness or irritability, skin rash, itching

Tylenol; *Acetaminophen*
(Analgesic)

[R]Difficult or painful urination, sudden increase in amount of urine, skin rash, hives or itching, unexplained sore throat and fever, unusual tiredness or weakness

Valium; Diazepam
Benzodiazepine
(Sedative/Hypnotic)

[L]Confusion, mental depression, blurred vision, constipation, dizziness or lightheadedness, dryness of mouth or increase in thirst, headache, increased bronchial secretions or watering of mouth, nausea or vomiting, problems with urination, slurred speech

Ventolin; Albuterol
Adrenergic Bronchodilator
(Respiratory Tract Medication)

[M]Fast heartbeat; [L]coughing or other bronchial irritation, difficult or painful urination, dizziness or lightheadedness, drowsiness, dryness or irritation of mouth or throat, headache; [R]chest discomfort or pain, increase in wheezing or difficulty in breathing; [U]irregular heartbeat; mood or mental changes; hallucinations; nausea or vomiting; unusual anxiety, nervousness, or restlessness

Vitamin A

Acute overdose signs: bleeding from gums or sore mouth, confusion or unusual excitement, diarrhea, dizziness or drowsiness, double vision, severe headache, severe irritability, peeling of skin (especially lips and palms), seizures, severe vomiting

Note: Differences in frequency of occurrence of side effects are indicated by a letter preceding the correspondent symptom(s) or sign(s). **M** = more frequent; **L** = less frequent; **R** = rare; **U** = unknown.

Vitamin B1; Thiamin *Vitamin B* (Vitamin)	[R]Skin rash or itching, wheezing
Vitamin B6; Pyridoxine *Vitamin B* (Vitamin)	No relevant observable side effect
Vitamin D	No relevant observable side effect
Zarontin; Ethosuximide *Succinimide* (Anticonvulsant)	[M]Headache, hiccups, loss of appetite, nausea and vomiting, stomach cramps; [L]dizziness, drowsiness, irritability, tiredness

Note: Differences in frequency of occurrence of side effects are indicated by a letter preceding the correspondent symptom(s) or sign(s). **M** = more frequent; **L** = less frequent; **R** = rare; **U** = unknown.

From "Medication Analysis" by M. M. Ault, B. Guy, J. C. Graff, and S. Paez, in *Project ABLE: Analyzing Behavior States in Learning Environments* (Project No. HO86D00013 by the Office of Special Education Programs, United States Department of Education), 1992, Lawrence: University of Kansas, Department of Special Education.

Expected Interaction Effects of Common Medications

Medications	Expected Interaction Effects
Depakene and Phenobarbital	Increased CNS depression caused by increased blood concentration of Phenobarbital, decreased effect of Depakene with possible increase in seizure frequency
Dilantin and Aluminum Magnesium	Reduced seizure-depressing effect of Dilantin, resulting in possible increase in frequency of seizures
Dilantin and Antidepressants	Reduced seizure threshold (i.e., possible increase in seizure frequency)
Dilantin and Bactrim	Increased depressive result of Dilantin; increase in dizziness
Dilantin and Calcium	Decreased seizure-depressing effect of Dilantin by 20%

Dilantin and Calcium Carbonate	Reduced seizure-depressing effect of Dilantin (i.e., possible increase in seizure frequency)
Dilantin and Depakene	Decreased seizure-depressing effect of Dilantin (i.e., possible increase in seizure frequency)
Dilantin and Enteral Nutritional Formulas	May reduce the seizure-depressing effect of Dilantin (i.e., possible increase in seizure frequency)
Dilantin and Folic Acid	Decreased seizure-depressing effect of Dilantin (i.e., possible increase in seizure frequency)
Dilantin and Phenobarbital	Variable and unpredictable effect of both
Dilantin and Tylenol	Possible liver damage (no observable signs)
Dilantin and Vitamin D	Decreased effect of Vitamin D or inhibition of the contribution of the vitamin to bone development, may result in fragile bones (no observable signs)
Librium/Valium and Antacids	Delayed absorption and therapeutic effect of Librium/Valium
Phenobarbital and Antidepressants	Decreased therapeutic effect of antidepressant
Phenobarbital and Haloperidol	May cause a change in the pattern and/or frequency of seizures
Phenobarbital and Tegretol	Decreased serum concentration of either one (i.e., possible increase in seizure frequency)
Phenobarbital and Tylenol	Decreased effect of barbiturate, either sedating or activating

Phenobarbital and Vitamin C	Decreased effect of barbiturate (i.e., possible increase in seizure frequency)
	Decreased absorption of Vitamin C resulting in increased requirements, which may result in susceptibility to respiratory infections
Phenobarbital and Vitamin D	Decreased effect of Vitamin D or inhibition of the contribution of the vitamin to bone development, which may result in fragile bones
Tegretol and Antidepressants	Decreased anticonvulsant effect of Tegretol (i.e., possible increase in seizure frequency)
Tegretol and Depakene	Decreased serum concentration of both (i.e., possible increase in seizure frequency)
Tegretol and Librium/Valium	Increased effect of both, with possible enhancement of undesirable side effects
Tegretol and Tagamet	Increased plasma concentration of Tegretol, with possible enhancement of undesirable side effects
Tegretol and Tylenol	Increased risk of liver damage (but no observable signs)
	Decreased therapeutic effect of Tylenol

From "Medication Analysis" by M. M. Ault, B. Guy, J. C. Graff, and S. Paez, in *Project ABLE: Analyzing Behavior States in Learning Environments* (Project No. HO86D00013 by the Office of Special Education Programs, United States Department of Education), 1992, Lawrence: University of Kansas, Department of Special Education.

REFERENCES

Adams, D. A., & Selekof, J. L. (1986). Children with ostomies: Comprehensive care planning. *Pediatric Nursing, 12*, 429–433.

American Dental Association. (1984). *Cleaning your teeth and gums.* Chicago: Bureau of Health Education and Audiovisual Services.

American Heart Association. (1993). *Heartsaver guide: A student handbook for cardiopulmonary resuscitation and first aid for choking.* Dallas, TX: Author.

Andersen, R. D., Bale, J. F., Blackman, J. A., & Murph, J. R. (1986). *Infections in children: A sourcebook for educators and child care providers.* Rockville, MD: Aspen.

Ault, M. M., Guy, B., Graff, J. C., & Paez, S. (1992). Medication analysis. In B. Guy, M. M. Ault, & D. Guess (Eds.), *Project ABLE: Analyzing behavior states in learning environments.* Lawrence: University of Kansas, Department of Special Education.

Ault, M. M., Guy, B., & Rues, J. P. (1992). Nutrition analysis. In B. Guy, M. M. Ault, & D. Guess (Eds.), *Project ABLE: Analyzing behavior state in learning environments.* Lawrence: University of Kansas, Department of Special Education.

Ault, M. M., Graff, J. C., & Rues, J. P. (1993). Special health care and teaching. In M. Snell (Ed.), *Systematic instruction of persons with severe disabilities* (pp. 215–247). Columbus, OH: Merrill.

Batshaw, M. L., & Perret, Y. M. (1986). *Children with handicaps* (2nd ed.). Baltimore: Brookes.

Bell, W. E., & McCormick, W. F. (1978). *Increased intracranial pressure in children: Diagnosis and treatment* (2nd ed.). Philadelphia: Saunders.

Brill, E. L. & Kilts, D. F. (1980). *Foundations for nursing.* New York: Appleton-Century-Crofts.

Broadwell, D. C. (1984). Study guide for ostomy products. *Journal of Enterostomal Therapy, 11*(2), 74–76.

Centers for Disease Control. (1985). *What can you do to stop disease in child day care centers.* Atlanta: Department of Health and Human Services.

Chapman, W., Hill, M., & Shurtleff, D. B. (1979). *Management of the neurogenic bowel and bladder.* Oak Brook, IL: Eterna Press.

Chow, M. J., Durand, B. A., Feldman, M. N., & Mills, M. A. (1984). *Handbook of pediatric primary care.* New York: Wiley.

Crump, M. (1987). *Nutrition and feeding of the handicapped child.* Boston: College-Hill.

Dreifuss, F. E., Gallagher, B. B., Leppik, I. E., & Rothner, D. (1983). Keeping epilepsy under control. *Patient Care, 17,* 107–149.

Education and foster care of children infected with human T-lymphotropic virus type III/lymphadenopathy-associated virus. (1985). *Morbid Mortal Weekly Report, 34*(34), 517–520.

Erickson, P. J. (1987). Ostomies: The art of pouching. *Nursing Clinics of North America, 22*(2), 311–320.

Evans, B. E. (1986). AIDS–dental considerations: A 1986 update. *New York State Dental Journal, 52*(9), 40–48.

Foster, R. L. R., Hunsberger, M. M., & Anderson, J. J. (1989). *Family-centered nursing care of children.* Philadelphia: Saunders.

Fraser, B. A., Hesinger, R. N., & Phelps, J. A. (1987). *Physical management of multiple handicaps.* Baltimore: Brookes.

Gadow, K. D., & Kane, K. M. (1983). Administration of medication by school personnel. *The Journal of School Health, 53,* 178–183.

Given, B. A., & Simmons, S. J. (1979). *Gastroenterology in clinical nursing.* St. Louis: Mosby.

Gosnell, D. (1972). An assessment tool to identify pressure sores. *Nursing Research, 22,* 55–59.

Graff, J. C., Ault, M. M., Guess, D., Taylor, M., & Thompson, B. (1990). *Health care for students with disabilities.* Baltimore: Brookes.

Hamill, P. V. V., Drizd, T. A., Johnson, C. L., Reed, R. B., Roche, A. F., & Moore, W. M. (1979). Physical growth: National Center for Health Statistics percentiles. *American Journal of Clinical Nutrition, 32,* 607–629.

Harris, C. S., Baker, S. P., Smith, G. A., & Harris, R. M. (1984). Childhood asphyxiation by food. *Journal of the American Medical Association, 251,* 2231–2235.

Hausman, K. A. (1981). Nursing care of the patient with hydrocephalus. *Journal of Neurosurgical Nursing, 13,* 326–332.

Hilt, N. E., & Schmidt, E. W. (1975). *Pediatric orthopedic nursing.* St. Louis: Mosby.

Hobbs, N., Perrin, J. M., & Ireys, H. T. (1985). *Chronically ill children and their families.* San Francisco: Jossey-Bass.

Holvoet, J. F., & Helmstetter, E. (1989). *Medical problems of students with special needs: A guide for educators.* Boston: College-Hill.

Killingsworth, A. (1976). *Basic physical disability procedures.* Oakland, CA: CAL-FYL Press.

King, E. M., Wieck, L., & Dyer, M. (1983). *Pediatric nursing procedures.* Philadelphia: Lippincott.

Lehr, D. H., & Noonan, M. J. (1989). Issues in the education of students with complex health care needs. In F. Brown & D. H. Lehr (Eds.), *Persons with profound disabilities: Issues and practices* (pp. 139–160). Baltimore: Brookes.

Logan, K., Alberto, P., Kana, K., & Waylor, T. (1991). *Who are students with profound disabilities? A data based description.* Paper presented at The Association for Persons with Severe Handicaps National Convention, Washington, DC.

Low, N. L. (1982). Seizure disorders in children. In J. A. Downey & N. L. Low (Eds.), *The child with disabling illness: Principles of rehabilitation* (pp. 121–144). New York: Raven Press.

Madsen, M. A. (1986). Emergency department management of ventriculo–peritoneal cerebrospinal fluid shunts. *Annals of Emergency Medicine, 15,* 1130–1343.

Mandell, P., Lipton, M. H., Bernstein, J., Kucera, G. J., & Kampner, J. A. (1989). *Low back pain.* New Jersey: Slack.

McCamman, S., & Rues, J. (1990). Nutrition monitoring and supplementation. In J. C. Graff, M. M. Ault, D. Guess, M. Taylor, & B. Thompson (Eds.), *Health care for students with disabilities: An illustrated medical guide for the classroom* (pp. 79–118). Baltimore: Brookes.

McMechen, D. L., & Wright, D. M. (1985). A protocol for the management of patients with herpetic infections. *Dental Hygiene, 59,* 546–548.

Menkes, J. H. (1985). *Text book of child neurology* (3rd ed.). Philadelphia: Lea & Febiger.

Mulligan-Ault, M., Guess, D., Struth, L., & Thompson, B. (1988). The implementation of health related procedures in classrooms for students with severe multiple impairments. *Journal of The Association for Persons with Severe Handicaps, 13,* 100–109.

Overeem, L. (1991). *Classroom based guidelines for the provision of special health care procedures.* Unpublished master's project, University of Kansas, Department of Special Education, Lawrence.

Palmer, M. L., & Toms, J. E. (1992). *Manual for functional training.* Philadelphia: F. A. Davis.

Prensky, A. L., & Palkes, H. S. (1982). *Care of the neurologically handicapped child.* New York: Oxford University Press.

Rang, M. (1983). *Children's fractures* (2nd ed.). Philadelphia: Lippincott.

Roberts, S., Siegel-Causey, E., Guess, D., & Rues, J. P. (1992). *Etiological and medical characteristics of students with profound disabilities.* Unpublished manuscript, University of Kansas, Department of Special Education, Lawrence.

Schmitt, B. D. (1980). *Pediatric telephone advice: Guidelines for the health care provider on telephone triage and office management of common childhood symptoms.* Boston: Little, Brown.

Scipien, G. M., Barnard, M. U., Chard, M. A., Howe, J., & Phillips, P. J. (Eds.). (1986). *Comprehensive pediatric nursing.* New York: McGraw-Hill.

Shaddix, T. (1986). *Meal planning for the childhood years: Nutritional care for the child with developmental disabilities.* Birmingham: United Cerebral Palsy of Greater Birmingham.

Shelton, T. L., Jeppson, E. S., & Johnson, B. H. (1992). *Family centered care for children with special health care needs.* Bethesda, MD: Association for the Care of Children's Health.

Siegel-Causey, E., Rues, J. P., Harty, J., Roberts, S., & Guess, D. (1991). *Analysis of medical and educational characteristics for students with profound, multiple disabilities.* Unpublished manuscript, University of Kansas, Department of Special Education, Lawrence.

Sobsey, D., & Cox, A. W. (1991). Integrating health care and educational programs. In F. P. Orelove & D. Sobsey (Eds.), *Educating children with multiple disabilities: A transdisciplinary approach* (2nd ed., pp. 155–186). Baltimore: Brookes.

Standards and Guidelines for Cardiopulmonary Resuscitation (CPR) and Emergency Cardiac Care (ECC). (1986). *The Journal of the American Medical Association, 255*(21), 2905–2989.

Taylor, M. (1990). Clean intermittent catheterization. In J. C. Graff, M. Mulligan Ault, D. Guess, M. Taylor, & B. Thompson (Eds.), *Health care for students with disabilities* (pp. 241–252). Baltimore: Brookes.

Thomas, C. L. (1985). *Taber's cyclopedic medical dictionary.* Philadelphia: F. A. Davis.

Thompson, B., & Guess, D. (1989). Students who experience the most profound multiply handicapping conditions: Teacher perceptions. In F. Brown & D. Lehr (Eds.), *Persons with profound disabilities: Issues and practices* (pp. 3–43). Baltimore: Brookes.

University of Colorado School of Nursing. (1986). *Clean intermittent catheterization* (Videotape and user's manual). Lawrence, KS: Learner Managed Designs.

Wagner, M. (Ed.). (1983). *Nurse's reference library—Drugs.* Springhouse, PA: Intermed Communications.

Walker, K. A. (1971). *Pressure sores: Prevention and treatment.* London: Butterworth.

Whaley, L. F., & Wong, D. L. (1987). *Nursing care of infants and children.* St. Louis: Mosby.

Woelk, C. G. (1986). The mentally retarded and his family. In G. M. Scipien, M. U. Barnard, M. A. Chard, J. Howe, & P. J. Phillips (Eds.), *Comprehensive pediatric nursing* (pp. 639–666). New York: McGraw-Hill.

Yard, G. J. (1980). Managing seizures in mainstream education. *The Journal for Special Educators, 17*(1), 52–56.

Chapter 9

Components of
Instructional Technology

PAUL A. ALBERTO, WILLIAM SHARPTON,
LES STERNBERG, and TONI WAYLOR-BOWEN

Students with profound disabilities pose serious challenges to those responsible for providing them with educational services. The issue of educability surfaces periodically; however, both legal mandates (e.g., the Individuals with Disabilities Education Act) and the paucity of available research outlining "fail-proof" instructional approaches for those who are profoundly disabled mitigate against this becoming an overriding concern. What is important is to consider the current status of instructional approaches applied to or designed for these students, and to provide some direction for future research.

Two major trends have defined past and current instructional efforts with students with profound disabilities. Initially, suggested practices involved incorporating early infant or preschool program elements into educational approaches regardless of the age of the student. A developmental content emphasis defined much of what was applied to students with profound disabilities; this was assumed to be appropriate because of the perceived cognitive "infancy" of the population. More recently, the trend has been to use techniques that have proven to be appropriate for students with moderate to severe levels of disability, with the emphasis on a more functional approach to program design and delivery. What has become apparent, however, is that students with profound disabilities do not easily fit into any single mold of application. This has as much to do with heterogeneous levels of functioning as with the inconsistent nature of the students' responses to various instructional methods (Collins, Gast, Wolery, Holcombe, & Leatherby, 1991; Guess et al., 1988; Reid, Phillips, & Green, 1991).

The following overview specifies aspects of an instructional technology that represent current best practice *ideas* for many students who are profoundly disabled. The reader is cautioned again, however, that a research base in support of a comprehensive range of approaches is currently not available for students with profound disabilities.

INSTRUCTIONAL COMPONENTS

While the content of an educational program is operationalized through a curriculum design, the implementation of the curriculum is dependent on the use of an effective instructional technology. For students with profound disabilities, the foundation upon which an effective instructional technology should rest includes the following:

- An understanding of learning theory (e.g., principles of reinforcement) and the relationship of instruction to the levels of learning or response competence (acquisition, fluency, and generalization).

- An affirmation that all students with profound disabilities, regardless of their presenting needs or perceived level of functioning, should be taught to participate at least partially in a wide range of school and nonschool activities and environments, resulting in the student's being perceived as a valuable and contributing member of society (Baumgart et al., 1982).

- Instruction that requires the active engagement and interactions of students, rather than passive receipt of instruction and care.

- Planning that coordinates the scheduling of individual and group instruction for each class member, and the scheduling of the various professionals considered part of the essential educational team (e.g., physical, occupational, and speech–language therapists).

- Assurance that, to the maximum extent possible, instructional materials and tasks are functional, age-appropriate, and socially validated (Brown et al., 1979; Reid et al., 1985) (see Table 9.1 for examples of nonfunctional materials and activities).

- Selection of appropriate community settings for generalized learning.

- Consistency of instruction and contingencies across various instructional personnel, including parents.

TABLE 9.1. Examples of Nonfunctional Materials and Activities

Domain	Functional Task	Nonfunctional Because of Material	Nonfunctional Because of Activity
Domestic/Self-Help	Student puts arms through coat held by teacher prior to community-based instruction	Student puts arms through holes in sleeveless practice vest	Student identifies pictures of children putting on coats
Leisure	Student uses switch-activated tape player	Adolescent plays with switch-activated dancing bear	Student is guided in putting pegs in a pegboard
Community	Student takes items from store shelves and puts them in shopping cart	Student bags toy "food" in classroom vocational area	Student watches video of appropriate bus-riding behavior
Vocational	Student tears plastic off bagged items in stockroom of department store	Student sorts plastic toy nuts and bolts into slots on a form board	Student "listens" to a story about community helpers

Adapted from "Providing a More Appropriate Education for Severely Handicapped Persons: Increasing and Validating Functional Classroom Tasks" by D. Reid et al., 1985, *Journal of Applied Behavior Analysis, 18,* p. 292. Copyright 1985 by the Society for the Experimental Analysis of Behavior, Inc. Adapted by permission.

- Instructional grouping such that there is a mix of levels of functioning and physical disability.

- The ongoing use of an accurate and useful system of documenting learning.

A Trial as the Basic Unit of Instruction

A *trial* is an instance of instruction or an opportunity for performance by the student. Operationalized, a trial has three components as illustrated in Figure 9.1: the *behavior* itself (B); the *antecedent,* or the event(s) that immediately precede(s) the behavior (A); and the *consequence,* or the event(s) that immediately follow(s) the behavior (C). For the purpose of skill instruction, "behavior" in this case refers to *operant* behavior. Operant behavior is voluntary, as opposed to involuntary or reflexive behavior (*respondent* behavior). Operant behaviors include activities such as communicating, eating, walking, object manipulation, and attending to a task. Antecedents to a behavior include those arrangements that facilitate student performance: the instructional setting, instructional materials, verbal or nonverbal instructions, and

A **Antecedent**	B **Behavior**	C **Consequences**
Setting Materials Instruction Collateral events Task analysis		Reinforcement Correction

Figure 9.1. Components of an instructional trial.

task analysis. Consequences of a behavior during skill instruction include those arranged by the teacher, as well as those that occur naturally as a result of performance of the behavior. Reinforcement and correction are the primary forms of consequences.

Reinforcement during the trial

Reinforcement serves two major purposes in the instructional process. First, it provides a motivator for student performance. The student is motivated to comply with the instructional cue to obtain the reinforcing item or event being offered. If the item or event is truly a reinforcer, it will increase the future rate and/or probability of the student's producing the behavior. If the item or event does not have this effect, it may be only a one-time satisfying occurrence (reward), but one that is not a useful instructional tool over time.

The second purpose of reinforcement, and one that is especially relevant for students with profound disabilities, is to train the understanding of cause and effect. The student learns that the response he or she makes (*cause*) results in the reinforcer (*effect*). For the student to make this connection, the delivery of the reinforcer must immediately follow the requested behavior (or, at times, occur during the behavior), and its delivery must be contingent upon performance of the behavior. This understanding is the underpinning of the instructional interaction between a teacher and a student. The student is, in effect, learning the process of learning.

Our purpose in this chapter is not to provide a full review of reinforcement theory; however, several critical points need to be remembered. The greater the level of a student's disability, the more difficult reinforcer identification becomes. With many students with profound disabilities, identifying reinforcers will likely challenge a teacher's creativity and problem-solving skills. It is important to remember, however, that every student is reinforced by something. Also, there is no one item or event that will reinforce every student. Students with profound disabilities may make choices (e.g., playing with certain toys), show preferences (e.g., food items), or actively seek out opportunities to obtain certain events (e.g., pressing a switch to turn on a tape recorder). These consequences, however, may not necessarily act as reinforcers for performance of other behaviors (Guess et al., 1988; Haywood, Meyers, & Switzky, 1982; Landesman-Dwyer & Sackett, 1978; Reid et al., 1991).

In the event that a reinforcer is determined to increase the occurrence or rate of a behavior, the teacher must be aware that, once the student has become satiated on that specific reinforcer, responding and its accuracy will decrease. This is not a function of an inability to learn, but a function of the student's satiation on the reinforcer. If possible, it is important to identify a number of potential reinforcers for the student; this will allow the teacher some flexibility and, at the same time, decrease the probability of satiation.

If primary reinforcers (e.g., edibles) are initially selected for use, it is appropriate to plan for a transition to the use of secondary reinforcers (e.g., preferred activities). Typically, this is accomplished through a pairing of primary and secondary reinforcers. It must be remembered that, in teaching students with profound disabilities, the ultimate goal is for the student to be motivated by reinforcement that naturally occurs due to performing a behavior. Therefore, activities that have naturally occurring reinforcing consequences should be included in instruction. For example, when teaching the student to ask for a cup (e.g., by pointing to the object), there should be some juice in the cup so the student may experience the reinforcing result of using the cup appropriately.

Finally, it is important to attempt to reduce the number of reinforcers that are systematically being provided to a student. Such thinning of the schedules of reinforcement delivery will hopefully assist a student to accept delayed gratification for increasing amounts of performance. It will also establish a more normalized type of reinforcing environment.

Correction during a trial

When the student's attempt at behavior performance is not correct, it should not be reinforced. Rather, it should be corrected by the teacher in such a manner that the student experiences the correct performance and its resulting reinforcement. For many students with profound disabilities, this correction often requires that the teacher put the student through the requested behavior in a "hand-over-hand" manner. There are several variations of correction procedures. Following are two examples.

The first procedure is recommended when the student is being trained on a single step of a task analysis (Wuerch & Voeltz, 1982):

1. Immediately interrupt the student's incorrect response.

2. Repeat the instructional cue paired with the activity cue that preceded the incorrect response.

3. Give whatever additional assistance is necessary to ensure a correct response by the student.

4. Immediately reinforce the correct response.

5. Repeat the procedure, this time fading the additional assistance, to provide additional practice on the missed step.

6. If the student meets the performance criterion for the step, continue on to the next step.

The following procedure is recommended when the student is being trained concurrently on a number of steps of a task analysis (e.g., in vocational training procedures; Bellamy, Horner, & Inman, 1979):

1. Immediately interrupt the student's incorrect response.

2. Go back two steps in the task analysis and give the appropriate instructional cue for that step.

3. Have the student repeat the two steps and the missed step, providing enough assistance to ensure correct responses on all three steps.

4. Reinforce each correct (assisted and unassisted) response.

5. Repeat the procedure to provide additional practice on the missed step.

6. Proceed to the next step in the task analysis.

Trial management

In the past, it was assumed that trials should be arranged such that an instance of a given behavior was presented repeatedly in the belief that isolated, repeated presentations were more likely to result in the acquisition of a new behavior. Such an arrangement of trials is known as *massed trials* presentation. It may be represented as A-A-A-A-A-A. For example, a cup is placed in front of the student, and 10 repetitions are presented of "Michael, give me cup." Such trial management, however, has proven to be inefficient when measured by the number of trials needed to reach the criterion, and by the crucial and problematic concern for generalization of learning (Mulligan, Lacy, & Guess, 1982).

An alternative management is *distributed trials* presentation (Ault, 1988; Brown, Holvoet, Guess, & Mulligan, 1980; Mulligan, Guess, Holvoet, & Brown, 1980; Sailor & Guess, 1983). Distributed trial presentation interposes time and / or a related interaction with the material between each repetition of a particular trial. Such an arrangement of trials may be within a teaching session (*intrasession* trial distribution) or between sessions (*intersession* trial distribution). Distributed trials can be represented as follows: A-B-C-D A-B-C-D A-B-C-D.

Within a session, distributed trials may be conducted such that, when the student is presented in the cafeteria with an array of functionally related instructional materials, such as a cup, dish, and spoon, the following distribution of trials might occur (Holvoet, Brown, & Helmstetter, 1980):

A: "Point to cup" (requires receptive vocabulary skill).

B: "Hand me cup" (requires compliance and social interaction skills).

C: "What is this?" (requires expressive verbal or nonverbal vocabulary skill).

D: "Show me what you do with cup" (requires functional use skill).

For another student presenting a different array of skills, a distribution might occur as follows:

A: Visual scan of materials array (requires scanning skill).

B: "Pick up the cup" (requires grasp and hold).

C: "Drink from the cup" (requires functional use skill).

D: "Put cup on table" (requires place and release).

If instruction is designed to teach functional grasp and hold, and the intent is to use an intersession distribution, instructional trials would take place during scheduled activities of the day whenever the student would be required to use these behaviors (e.g., grasping and holding a towel to dry hands during a hygiene activity, during a domestic activity, and after a snack; using a switch to activate a tape player). In such an arrangement, the trials are separated by time and are designed to promote generalization.

Prompting

When instructing a new behavior, an immediate problem will occur after delivery of the instructional cue for performance if the student does not respond. This is to be expected when asking a student to perform a response that is not part of his or her behavior repertoire. Skinner (1968) referred to this as the "problem of the first instance." This first instance must be occasioned so that it can be reinforced to increase the probability of continued performance, so that an incorrect response can be corrected, or so that an approximation of the response can be shaped. First instances of a new behavior can be effected by teacher assistance known as *prompting*.

A prompt may be placed in relation to different components of a trial. Various *antecedent prompts* can augment the antecedent event(s), and various *response prompts* can be paired with the instructional cue to assist response performance. Multiple options are available, and a number of investigations have been directed toward determining the effectiveness of separate response classes as well as comparisons of the efficacy of both prompt classes (Adams, Matlock, & Tallon, 1981; Billingsley & Romer, 1983; Day, 1987; Doyle, Wolery, Ault, & Gast, 1988; Farmer, Gast, Wolery, & Winterling, 1991; Wolery, Ault, & Doyle, 1992).

Antecedent prompts

Antecedent prompts are alterations of, or additions to, the instructional material to focus student attention on the natural cue(s) for making correct responses. There are a number of categories of antecedent prompts, including relevant feature prompts, proximity prompts, context prompts, errorless prompts, and modeling.

Relevant feature prompts are those by which the teacher "cues" the feature of the task materials on which the student should focus to make the correct response. Use of this procedure teaches the student to distinguish the features that define a correct response. The teacher may use various means, such as color, size, and shape, to focus or prompt the student's attention by highlighting the relevant feature. For example, if the student is being instructed to discriminate a spoon from a fork, the relevant feature of the spoon is the bowl portion, and of the fork, the tines. In teaching this discrimination, these are the places the antecedent prompt should be placed, instead of the handle (e.g., the bowl and tines could be of different colors). In teaching a student how to put on a sweater or T-shirt, the prompt for determining front from back should be placed on the label at the back (e.g., a brightly colored ribbon). A typical scenario in the use of relevant feature prompts, as with all prompts, is to eventually fade them so that the natural cue (e.g., the label of a shirt) will indicate to the student what behavior to exhibit.

Proximity prompts are employed by varying the placement of materials on the instructional plane (Lovass, 1981). If the student is being taught the spoon–fork discrimination (with fork the correct response), during initial training trials, the two materials might be placed on the table such that the fork is immediately in front of the student, with the spoon several inches above it. Over trials, the distance between the two materials would be reduced until they were finally presented in parallel fashion.

Context prompting is presentation of instructional materials in an array as similar as possible to that in the natural setting. For example, if the student is being taught "fork," the array within which the student should learn to select the fork is one containing a fork, spoon, and knife (e.g., a utensil tray in a cafeteria, as this is the array from which he or she must select the item in the natural environment).

Errorless prompts are exaggerated, external, and basically irrelevant cues that dramatically draw the student's attention to the correct response. For example, in the spoon–fork discrimination ("fork" being the correct response), a large sheet of colored paper might be placed under the fork as trials are conducted. Once the student stabilized correct responding, the size of the errorless cue would be reduced over successive trials or sessions until it was removed altogether.

A *modeling prompt* is when another individual, such as a teacher or peer, demonstrates the behavior to allow for student imitation. For example, the student might watch the teacher put toothpaste on a brush and then be asked to imitate the process. For modeling to be effective, a teacher should follow some basic guidelines (Baer, Peterson, & Sherman, 1967; Bandura, 1969; Parton, 1976). First, one must gain the student's attention before presenting the model. The instructional cue for student imitation should be a simple generalizable cue, such as a gestural or verbal "Do this." During modeling, the student must have a clear view of the demonstration, and must be made aware of the position of any materials and how they are applied or handled. The pace of the demonstration should be such that the student can clearly discriminate the order and interdependence of each step. When initially modeling a series of actions, the individual should keep the length or complexity short and simple; extensions may be added as successful imitations occur. Finally, when directionality of the response is important, both the teacher and the student should face the same direction.

Effective antecedent prompting is characterized by the following guidelines:

- Prompts should focus students' attention on the natural cue, not distract from it.

- Prompts should be as weak as possible. The use of strong prompts when weak ones will do is inefficient and may unnecessarily prolong instruction.

- Prompts should be faded as rapidly as possible. Continuing to prompt longer than necessary may result in artificial dependence on the prompt rather than on natural cues. Abrupt removal of prompts, however, may result in termination of the desired behavior. Fading is conducted by progressively and systematically providing less frequent intrusive or intense prompts over the course of instruction.

- Unplanned prompts should be avoided. A teacher may be unaware that students are being prompted by facial expression or focal inflection (Alberto & Troutman, 1990). Consider the example of a teacher involved in teaching a student to select a fork. The teacher may be unaware that his or her facial expression, as the student's hand approaches the correct or incorrect utensil, may be prompting the student's correct selection rather than the shape of the utensil.

Response prompts

Response prompts are types of assistance for actual behavior performance. They require the teacher to assist the student in the act of producing the response. There are at least five types of response prompts: full physical prompts, partial physical prompts, model prompts, gesture prompts, and verbal prompts.

Full physical prompts provide total guidance to the student. The teacher actually puts the student through the entire behavior, thereby providing assistance for each movement necessary for successful performance. A *partial physical prompt* is physical assistance to initiate or provide direction for performance. As soon as the teacher feels the student engaging in the response, the assistance is terminated. A *model prompt* is a response prompt when its purpose is to occasion coactive imitation by the student. The procedure is implemented to increase a student's ability to imitate a response when given a concurrent (continuing) model presentation, and has been shown to be particularly useful with students with profound disabilities (Sternberg, McNerney, & Pegnatore, 1985; Sternberg & Owens, 1985). A *gesture prompt* is a gesture to signal response initiation, as in pointing to or tapping the target instructional material(s). A *verbal prompt* is assistance provided beyond the initial verbal instruction (e.g., *encouragement* ["You are doing fine." "Keep going."]; *hints* ["You put it on your foot."]; or *questions* ["How do you turn on the radio?"]), which further stimulates student consideration and interest, or provides information for student initiation and performance of the response.

Systematic use of response prompts

To provide consistent assistance to students, a systematic use of response prompts should be employed. Guidelines for their systematic use have been proposed for both single prompts and coordinated use of various prompts, when it is necessary. One systematic use of a single response prompt is known as the *time delay procedure.* The systematic use of multiple response prompts may be seen in the *system of maximum prompts,* the *system of least prompts,* and *graduated guidance.*

Systematic use of a single prompt

When a teacher works with a student to instruct a skill, he or she may give an instruction such as "Michael, pull up your pants," and then wait for the student to perform the response. After waiting, if the student does not respond, the teacher should help him perform the task. The time delay procedure is an approach to systematizing the amount of time the teacher waits before providing assistance (Snell & Gast, 1981). The use of a time delay procedure with students with profound disabilities can be seen in studies by Collins et al. (1991) and McCuller and Salzberg (1984).

If the skill being taught is completely new to the student, the teacher may begin the instructional session at a *zero-second delay:* The teacher gives the instruction and the prompt simultaneously. In that way, the student learns to associate the verbal instruction and the nature of the response called for. After several repetitions at zero-second delay, or simultaneous presentation, the teacher begins to give the student time to respond before he or she administers any prompt. The teacher then systematically increases the length of delay between the verbal instruction and the assistance. This is known as *progressive time delay.*

As illustrated in Table 9.2, a typical strategy is for the teacher to increase the time delay by 1-second intervals. The length of delay is increased once the student shows a pattern of anticipating the prompt (i.e., is correctly performing the behavior during the delay time, thereby no longer requiring the prompt). Indeed, the goal of the procedure is for the student to perform the correct response in the absence of a response prompt. Alternatively, the teacher may employ *constant time delay.* This format differs from progressive time delay in that, instead of using increasing increments of time between the antecedent and the response, the teacher moves directly from a zero-second delay to a fixed duration (e.g., 4-second delay).

Doyle et al. (1988) found that progressive time delay was more effective than constant time delay. Billingsley and Romer (1983) suggested that time delay is as effective as, and may be more efficient than, the use of some multiple prompting strategies. However, Collins et al. (1991) suggested that responses by students with profound disabilities may be inconsistent and that further research is needed on the application of time delay procedures to these students.

TABLE 9.2.   Sequence of Components of a Time Delay Procedure: Use of a Single Prompt

Antecedent	Delay (in seconds)	Prompt	Response	Consequence
Verbal cue of "pick up cup" or "pick it up" (for students at nonsymbolic level of communication, teacher may pair the verbal cue with a nonsymbolic cue, e.g., a touch cue of tapping the top of the student's hand)	0 0.5 1 2 3 4	Full physical guidance to pick up cup	Student picks up cup	a. Natural reinforcer: student drinks milk b. Teacher praise

Adapted from "Applying Time Delay Procedure to the Instruction of the Severely Handicapped" by M. Snell and D. Gast, 1981, *Journal of The Association for the Severely Handicapped, 6,* pp. 3–14. Copyright 1981 by Association for Persons with Severe Handicaps. Adapted by permission.

Systematic use of multiple prompts

To use the *system of maximum prompts,* the teacher begins by providing the student with the most assistance possible. Gradually, the amount of assistance is reduced. The amount or intrusiveness of the prompt is faded as the student's independence increases over sessions. As seen in Figure 9.2, instruction begins with a full physical prompt where the teacher physically assists the student through the entire response while restating the instruction. The teacher performs the task hand-in-hand with the student, providing errorless practice. After one or more sessions of full guidance, the teacher reduces the amount of assistance by employing a partial physical prompt. After sessions in which the student can successfully respond with a partial physical prompt, the teacher reduces his or her level of assistance to the use of a less controlling prompt, such as a gesture or verbal instruction. The goal is for the student to perform the response without any assistance when given an instructional cue. The use of a system of maximum prompts procedure with students with profound disabilities may be seen in studies by Reese and Snell (1991) and Westling, Ferrell, and Swenson (1982). Sternberg, Ritchey, Pegnatore, Wills, and Hill (1986) applied the system within a curricular format.

The *system of least prompts* operates from the opposite perspective. Instead of beginning instruction with the greatest amount of assistance, the teacher begins by providing the student with the least amount of assistance necessary. The student is provided the opportunity to perform at his or her highest level of independence on each occasion before assistance is increased within a trial (Doyle et al., 1988). The use of system of least prompts procedures with students with profound disabilities may be seen in studies by Pancsofar and Bates (1985) and Giangreco (1982).

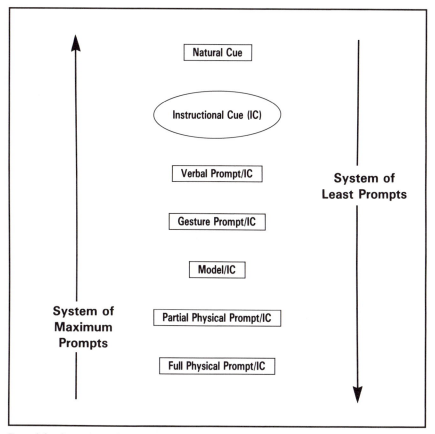

Figure 9.2. Components of the system of maximum prompts and least prompts.

Instruction begins with a presentation of the materials and a request for the response. If the response is not initiated after 3 to 5 seconds, the teacher increases the amount of assistance in a sequential manner (e.g., from providing only the instructional cue to providing the cue plus a gesture simultaneously). If the increased prompt is still insufficient to occasion the response, the level of assistance is increased to a partial physical prompt, and so on, until the response is made by the student or until the teacher makes use of the most assistance possible, a full physical prompt. At each subsequent request (trial) for the response, the teacher again begins at the instructional cue and progressively increases assistance as needed.

Response prompting systems are most often used in teaching activities that require a motor movement, such as dressing, vocational tasks, play tasks, and other tasks that involve material manipulation (as in sorting by size or color) or material selection to indicate receptive language skills.

Although the two prompting systems have common elements, there are several practical differences in their application. As noted, when using the system of maximum prompts, each teaching session is conducted at one assistance level, but in subsequent sessions the assistance level is decreased. In the system of least prompts, each opportunity for performance (trial) begins at the level of instructional cue, regardless of how much assistance was required on the previous trial. As maximum prompts initially provide greater physical assistance by the teacher, they are thought to be most appropriate for use during the acquisition stage of learning. Decreasing assistance provides more intensive instruction at an earlier point in time, thereby minimizing errors and reducing time between the instructional cue and the student response (Schoen, 1986). The least prompts procedure is thought most useful at higher levels of learning, such as fluency and generalization (Csapo, 1981).

Graduated guidance, or constant contact, provides an amount of physical contact by the teacher that is necessary for the student to correctly complete a response (Foxx, 1981). The amount of physical assistance given can be adjusted throughout the trial depending on the student's performance. The use of a graduated guidance strategy has been found to be effective for students with profound disabilities in a number of skill areas, especially motor skill development (Reid et al., 1991).

There are three components of graduated guidance. The first is *full graduated guidance.* During this procedure, the teacher keeps his or her hands in full contact with the student's hands. The teacher puts the student through the entire behavior until the student offers no resistance to the movement, or begins to initiate the movement on his or her own. At this point, *partial graduated guidance* is offered. This may be done in one of two ways. The full contact by the teacher may be moved up the student's arm, to the wrist, then the elbow, then the upper arm, and finally to the shoulder. In the second method of partial graduated guidance, the teacher uses only his or her thumb and forefinger on the student's hand or wrist to assist in movement (Foxx, 1981). Again, guidance is given by the teacher when resistance to movement is felt. In both methods, the student begins to take more responsibility for the actions. If the action is not initiated by the student, if resistance is felt, or if an incorrect action is started, the teacher may return to full graduated guidance.

Once the student is reliably performing the behavior with the least amount of partial graduated guidance, the teacher may use *shadowing.* With this procedure, the teacher does not touch the student. Rather, the teacher keeps his or her hand within an inch of the student's hand throughout the trial until the behavior is completed. Therefore, if assistance is needed, it can be easily provided. As the student continues to perform the behavior, the teacher may move further away, thereby allowing for more independent movement.

With any response prompting system, the goal of instruction is for the student to comply with the instructional cue when presented by the teacher. Such a goal, however, can result in a student who still relies on the teacher for initiation and/or correction of his or her performance. Although response to a teacher-delivered cue may be appropriate in certain situations, such as the classroom or community, it does not provide sufficient independence for adolescents or adults. True independence is the ability to respond to cues that occur naturally in the environment that signal the student to perform a particular behavior or that indicate that a behavior is being performed incorrectly. For many students with profound handicaps, however, the extent of educators' current knowledge of instruction is such that the students may be unable to perform certain behaviors or series of behaviors independent of additional cueing. One solution is the use of *partial participation* (Baumgart et al., 1982; Ferguson & Baumgart, 1991). Many students with profound disabilities will be unable to perform specific steps of a task. Using the principle of partial participation, a student would be encouraged to participate in the display of the step(s) in any manner in which he or she is capable. The full demonstration of the step and overall task, however, would be accomplished by the teacher. The teachers might use full physical guidance with the student, or perform the remaining components of the task. For many students with profound disabilities, partial participation will not involve an actual display of a motor component of the step(s), but rather basic developmental skills associated with the step(s). For a comprehensive description of possible options, the reader is referred to Chapter 10.

General Instructional Formatting

The precision of trial management is incorporated within various methodological formats. One set of formats is used for instructing single-step behaviors, such as labeling functional objects or learning which restroom to use. Another set is used for learning multiple-step behaviors, such as self-help activities.

Formats for single-step behaviors

Formats for single-step behaviors include at least the following procedures: match-to-sample, sort-to-sample, simple discrimination learning, and shaping.

Match-to-sample

The match-to-sample format is used to teach the ability to select, from a variety of items, one that matches a sample item. The teacher is in effect saying, "Here is one of these; find another." The teacher provides a model or "instance" of the item (correct choice) and an array consisting of an instance and one or more "noninstances" (incorrect choices) from which to select one similar to the model. The sequence of increasing complexity of a selection array is illustrated in Table 9.3. The ability to match an item to a given sample is a useful skill in a number of settings, including home (selecting utensils for eating), leisure (choosing an item with which to play), and community (selecting items in a grocery store) settings.

Sort-to-sample

The sort-to-sample format is used to teach a student to sort an array of items into categories when two models are presented. The first step is sorting by dimensions in which the student sorts by the "likeness" of dimensional features, such as color, size, and shape. Initially, the determination is based on a *single-dimensional difference*. For example, socks or cups identical in all respects except color might be sorted. The next step is sorting with *multiple-dimensional differences*. Multiple-dimension sorting involves such items as toys and articles of clothing. Sorting may then progress to categories such as function of objects (e.g., sorting objects one wears vs. things one eats; or things found in the kitchen vs. things found in the bathroom).

For both match-to-sample and sort-to-sample tasks, one begins with real objects before using pictures or some other form of representation. Klein and Stafford (1978) stated that classification competence is enhanced by experience with concrete, familiar materials before the use of symbolic materials.

Simple discrimination learning

Simple discrimination learning is used to teach differential selection of two items without an exemplar, such as correctly selecting a fork when

TABLE 9.3. Sequence of Instruction for the Match-to-Sample Format

Fork	(Model)	The array consists of a single, identical choice.
Fork	(Instance)	
Fork	(Model)	The array consists of an identical match and a grossly dissimilar choice.
Fork	Bowl	
(Instance)	(Noninstance)	
	Fork	The array consists of an identical match and two alternative selections.
Fork	Bowl	Spoon

requested or when needed. On another level, discrimination learning is said to occur when a student can tell whether two objects (e.g., socks and cups) are the same or different.

During initial stages of discrimination learning, the relevant dimension should vary while the irrelevant dimensions remain constant (Zeaman & House, 1979). In a case such as discriminating forks and spoons, or cups and bowls, the relevant feature that varies is form. Therefore, when teaching the spoon–fork or cup–bowl discrimination, only form should vary while all other dimensions, such as size and color, should not. Progress to higher level learning occurs when sets of items can be correctly identified even though they vary in multiple dimensions, such as size, color, and position (Gagne & Briggs, 1979). The student has learned that a cup is a cup despite variations in color and/or size.

The tendency of some students to respond to only one component of a training procedure suggests that antecedent prompts of the relevant feature prompt variety should be employed in discrimination learning. Such prompts will tend to ensure that the student is focusing on the appropriate natural cue for responding once the prompt is faded, as opposed to a response prompt that does not directly focus student attention to dimensions of the instructional material (Schriebman, 1975; Wolfe & Cuvo, 1978).

Figure 9.3 provides a simplified example of the progression from basic discrimination to generalized concept using "towel" as the example. Step 1 is the basic discrimination, in which the only thing varied is the relevant dimension of size; color and shape are held constant. In Steps 2 and 3, size *and* color are varied. In Steps 4 and 5, the task is generalized to a concept applicable across dimensional differences, complexities, and materials.

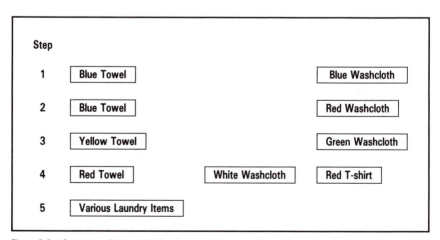

Figure 9.3. Sequence of instruction for discrimination learning.

Shaping

Shaping is instruction of a behavior by reinforcing successive approximations of the target behavior. It is assumed that the student has made or is capable of making some attempt at performing the behavior. Shaping molds a change or extension of the attempted topography of the response. By accepting small incremental steps, and assuring mastery of each approximation before moving on to the next, each step becomes the foundation upon which a more sophisticated response is established.

Many skills are acquired through shaping. Walking, imitation, reaching, and grasping are examples of complex skills that started from simpler, easier forms of behavior that were built upon until more extensive, complex performances developed. For typical children, certain skills, such as learning to walk, are learned through accidental or natural selection of the successive approximations. Shaping, as an instructional procedure with students with profound disabilities, must be thoughtfully planned.

Shaping is a linear procedure. It always moves from current capability toward the target behavior. Performance criteria are shifted so as to drive this advancing capability. Criteria for step advancement may be qualitative (e.g., improved use of gestures) or quantitative (e.g., working for increasing periods of time or at a faster rate). As the steps move from easier to harder, one never progresses to a harder requirement until the easier has been mastered.

Shaping is a systematic procedure. The steps for shaping for a teaching procedure include (1) identifying the objective; (2) identifying the incremental steps; (3) determining the student's current level of ability; (4) teaching to the first criterion, providing the student with reinforcement and correction until mastery of the initial targeted step; (5) teaching each successive step until the student can successfully perform the total objective; and (6) terminating reinforcement of previous accomplishments once the student has moved to succeeding steps.

When employing the shaping procedure, one must bear in mind that, if the approximations are too small, the procedure may be needlessly time-consuming, inefficient, and boring to the student. If they are too large, instruction will be just as frustrating to the student as if he or she had been initially presented with the requirement of performing the original objective. If the teacher finds that some of the steps are indeed too large, he or she should return to the step of the student's last successful performance and advance again, but at smaller increments.

Formats for multiple-step behaviors

Formats for *multiple-step behaviors* include three variations of *chaining*. Much of what we teach students makes use of skills or behaviors in various combinations or series to achieve new ends. These skills are related by their usefulness in obtaining new objectives. When sequenced, these related skills are known as *chains*.

Chains may allow a complex behavior, such as toothbrushing, or a series of activities, such as moving from the classroom to the bathroom and back again. Teaching how to form and make use of chains of behaviors is known as *chaining*. The components of a chain may be individual behaviors already in a student's repertoire, or a combination of established and new behaviors. The various steps or components of a chain of a complex behavior are taught in a sequence. The variations in sequencing are known as *forward chaining, backward chaining,* and *total task* or *whole task programming.*

One way of approaching the teaching of a chained performance is to teach the first link in the chain and then each step in its natural order of succession. This is known as *forward chaining.* If the objective is to teach a student how to put on a sock, the teacher begins by identifying the sequential steps in putting on a sock as follows: (1) pick up sock, (2) lift foot, (3) insert thumbs at opening, (4) separate and open hole, (5) insert toe, (6) pull to heel, and (7) pull over heel and up to ankle. In forward chaining, the teacher instructs the student how to do Step 1 until the student demonstrates acquisition. The student then is instructed in the performance of Step 2 (with Step 1 expected to occur). Once acquisition of Step 2 is demonstrated, the teacher moves on to Step 3 (with Steps 1 and 2 expected to occur). This progression continues in succession until the student can perform all the steps in a coordinated series resulting in the ultimate objective of putting on the sock. As a rule, steps beyond those focused on for instruction should be "walked through" with the student. This gives the student an opportunity to continuously view the targeted behavior in its entirety. This process has been referred to as "progressive chaining" (Sternberg et al., 1986).

An alternate choice is *backward chaining.* In this case, instruction begins with the last step in the chain and proceeds in reverse order until the student can perform all the steps in succession. In the case of teaching the student to put on a sock, the teacher first performs Steps 1 through 6 and requires the student to perform only Step 7, the last step. Instruction proceeds on Step 7. Once the student demonstrates acquisition of Step 7, the teacher performs Steps 1 through 5 and requires student performance of Steps 7 and 6 (with instruction of Step 6 only, and expectation of performance on Step 7). The teacher continues in this reverse order until the student shows acquisition of the entire chain. Such instruction continues in reverse order until the student is finally presented with only the sock and must independently perform all the necessary steps. In Table 9.4, an example is given to compare procedural steps of the same task taught through forward and backward chaining.

TABLE 9.4. Examples of Forward and Backward Chaining Sequencing

	Environment:	Home (domestic/self-help)
	Subenvironment:	Bathroom
	Activity:	Washing face

Forward Teaching Order		*Backward Teaching Order*
1.	Carry grooming items (in basket) to sink	14.
2.	Get washcloth out of basket	13.
3.	Get pump soap out of basket	12.
4.	Turn on water	11.
5.	Pump soap onto washcloth	10.
6.	Place washcloth under water	9.
7.	Ring out washcloth	8.
8.	Wash face	7.
9.	Place washcloth under water	6.
10.	Ring out washcloth	5.
11.	Rinse face	4.
12.	Put pump soap into basket	3.
13.	Put washcloth in basket	2.
14.	Carry grooming items (in basket) back to storage place	1.

Adapted from Community-Based Curriculum: Instructional Strategies for Students with Severe Handicaps (2nd ed., p. 82) by M. Falvey, 1989, Baltimore: Brookes. Copyright 1989 by Paul H. Brookes, P.O. Box 10624, Baltimore, MD 21285-0624. Adapted by permission.

Spooner and Spooner (1984) suggested a procedural modification of backward chaining they called *backward chaining with leap-aheads*. In this modification, the student is presented with a completed assembly except for the last step. If that step is completed with minimal or no assistance from the teacher, several steps are skipped and a step farther up the chain is selected for training. Although not every step in the chain is trained, each step must be performed correctly before the terminal criterion is met. The leap-ahead procedure is reported to speed up learning significantly.

A final variation of chaining is *total task programming*. In this approach, the student begins with the first step, but every step in the sequence is trained on every trial until the student performs the whole task to a predetermined criterion (Bellamy et al., 1979; Gold, 1976). A trial is defined as an opportunity to perform the entire chain, not only a single step or subset of steps of the chain. At the beginning of each trial, the student is given the instructional cue for performance of the entire chain. As the student begins with the first step, he or she is encouraged to continue with the succeeding steps.

As the student confronts a step he or she cannot perform, the teacher provides assistance through that step. For each trial, the teacher records the number of steps the student performed independently and the number that required assistance. Bellamy et al. (1979) suggested that difficult steps be taught in isolation until an accuracy rate of 80% is achieved, at which point the responses may be chained together. This approach seems to include a reasonable use of massed trials for difficult steps.

In a review of various chaining options, Spooner and Spooner (1984) concluded, "In the final analysis, it may be that different learners do better with different procedures, and that when different tasks are used (e.g., dressing vs. vocational) different results are obtainable" (p. 123).

Task Analysis

All chaining formats just discussed are conducted within the framework of a *task analysis*. Task analysis involves preparing three components: the objective, the steps of the task sequence, and identification of the prerequisite skills.

The *instructional objective* is derived from the information gathered through functional, behavioral, and ecological assessments (Browder, 1987; Brown et al., 1979; Falvey, 1989). The objective should contain an operational definition of the behavior to be taught, the conditions under which it will be taught (e.g., materials, cues, setting), and the criterion required for acceptable performance.

The *component steps* are arranged in an ordinal listing required to accomplish the target behavior. The detail required in this listing should be determined by the student's ability level (Crist, Walls, & Haught, 1984; Gold, 1980). One student may learn to wash hands through a 10-step process, whereas another may need a 30-step process. There should be only enough steps to allow efficient and systematic teaching. Often, a teacher will analyze a task to such a fine degree that unimportant or nonfunctional steps are included (Cuvo, Jacobi, & Sipko, 1981). If the student has special difficulty in successfully performing a step, the step can be further analyzed (Falvey, 1986). For example, a step that states "dusts end table" may be broken down into the following steps: (1) places hand in dustmit, (2) waits for teacher to spray table with cleaning solution, (3) moves dustmit from middle to one edge of table, (4) moves to another side of table, (5) moves dustmit from middle to edge of table, and (6) repeats steps until all cleaning solution is removed.

Prerequisite skills can usually be identified by examining the first three or four steps of the task analysis and asking whether they can be performed without other skills already being in the student's repertoire. One must be very careful when identifying prerequisites to instruction. With students with profound disabilities, identification of prerequisite skills may result in never embarking on instruction, as teachers are continually diverted to instruction of prerequisites. Rather, the teacher must think of the student's "task engagement capability" and be alert to "alternative performance strategies" to enable task instruction and performance (Wilcox & Bellamy, 1982). A student might use two hands on either end of a knife to cut butter, use special equipment or a prosthetic device (e.g., a special knife) that accommodates the student's limited range of motion, or partially participate in the activity (e.g., signal a peer to cut the butter).

Fluency and Generalization

The focus to this point has been to ensure that the student can accurately perform a new behavior. This is the level of learning, or competence, known as *acquisition.* This is not the point at which instruction should end, as behaviors must be performed accurately and in a functionally reasonable amount of time. Consider the student who takes 5 minutes to put on a coat or 15 seconds to reply to a social greeting. After acquisition instruction, fluency instruction is designed to decrease duration (as in time to put on a coat), increase duration (as time on task), and/or decrease latency (as in replying to a greeting) (Liberty, Haring, & Martin, 1981). *Fluency instruction,* being based on a time criterion, necessitates that the teacher alter a performance criterion by setting a time limit; that is, for the student's behavior to result in reinforcement, the behavior must be performed accurately within a time limit. White and Haring (1980) suggested that fluency of performance may be a better indicator of a student's ability to maintain, generalize, or apply a newly acquired skill than accuracy of performance alone.

Generalization refers to the performance of previously learned behaviors in new situations, in new settings, in response to new people, in response to new requests (instructional cues), or with new materials (e.g., different garments). One methodology for generalization programming is *general case instruction* (Horner, McDonnell, & Bellamy, 1986; Horner, Sprague, & Wilcox, 1982), a strategy for teaching skills that will be performed across people, places, and materials, or the efficient teaching of students to perform in nontrained situations. A general case has been taught when, after instruction on some tasks in a particular class, any task in that class can be performed correctly (Becker & Engelmann, 1978). General case instruction begins by examining the environment in which the student may be expected to perform the behavior to identify the range of variations that may be reasonably expected. For example, it may be appropriate to teach some students to make item selections in all grocery stores in their city, regardless of product arrangements and checkout operations. For other students, this goal may be unrealistic, and instruction might focus on only those stores in a particular neighborhood. In either case, two representative groups of examples of various stores are analyzed. To minimize errors in generalized settings, positive and negative training examples should be included in the general case (Horner, Eberhard, & Sheehan, 1986). One set of examples is used for direct instruction; the other set is used to probe generalization of the target activity to nontrained situations systematically, thus ensuring maintenance of the ability to perform the behavior.

As an example, Williams and Horner (1984) provided the following steps for applying general case instruction to street crossing:

1. Define the instructional universe (specifying all streets the student will be expected to cross after training).

2. Select the streets that will be trained and those that will serve as untrained probes (include streets that have features present in the student's instructional universe, such as stop signs and street lights).

3. Conduct the training, and collect the data reflecting the student's performance.

4. Modify the instruction based on an analysis of the "error patterns."

5. Train street crossing under exceptional traffic conditions (e.g., emergency vehicles with sirens, malfunctioning traffic signals).

6. Determine when to stop training based on verification of the student's performance on nontrained streets.

Group Instruction

A key element to efficient and effective instructional programming in public school classes for students with profound disabilities is instruction in other than the clinical one-to-one student–teacher ratio. There now exists evidence that students with severe disabilities can benefit and learn in instructional arrangements that use larger student–teacher ratios, at rates comparable to or better than on-to-one instruction (Favell, Favell, & McGimsey, 1978; Kohl, Wilcox, & Karlan, 1978; Oliver, 1983; Storm & Willis, 1978; Westling et al., 1982). As a result of their review of the research on group instruction, Reid and Favell (1984) concluded, "The published research leaves virtually no doubt that useful skills can be taught to these individuals using a group format" (p. 175). Group instruction also provides opportunities for "a) increased control of motivational variables; b) opportunities to facilitate observational learning, peer interaction, and peer communication; and c) generalization of skills" (Brown et al., 1980, p. 353).

Students are often not automatically capable of participating as group members. A variety of procedures can be used for preparing students for group instruction. One such procedure was suggested by Koegel and Rincover (1974; Rincover & Koegel, 1977). They took the members of a class and initially instructed each student in a one-to-one ratio. Each was taught on a one-to-one basis to familiarize him or her with the following instructional process: "I am going to ask you to do something, you are expected to do it, and I will reinforce you." A general class of activity, such as imitation, was the focus of instruction.

Once the students reached the criterion level of accuracy, they were grouped into a two-to-one ratio. The instructional content remained imitation, although a different sample of imitative behaviors was taught. The content matter remained the same because the focus of instruction was not the content (i.e., imitation capability) but the ability to be an attentive and active group member. Again, once the students reached a criterion of accuracy, they were reformed into a group with a three-to-one ratio. For reasons of management, three is the suggested maximum size for a group with targeted instructional goals. Reinforcement is suggested to start on a continuous reinforcement schedule of one reinforcement for each correct response, and be thinned as the group size increases. Reinforcement is delivered to students for appropriate behaviors expected of a group member (e.g., attending, waiting turn, staying in seat).

Alternatively, Sobsey, McLarney, Missall, and Murphy (1985) suggested that the initial formation of group instruction occur such that the students are in close proximity at a table, but each is initially working on different instructional tasks with different instructional materials. As such, the teacher does a trial distribution with one student and then rotates to the next.

Although instruction may start with what is essentially one-to-one instruction in close proximity, this is not yet "group" instruction. It is critical to progress beyond merely one-to-one instruction with students placed in close proximity at a table. To assist in this progress, Brown et al. (1980) and Sobsey et al. (1985) suggested two variations on management of content for group instruction. These variations included teaching the same program to each group member. In such a case, the goal of instruction and the ensuing distribution of trials are identical for each group member. For example, each group member would engage in the following distribution of trials: (1) point to hairbrush, (2) verbalize "brush," and (3) brush hair (Brown et al., 1980).

A second approach is to use different programs with the same theme (Sobsey et al., 1985). In this case, group members may be working on different skills or different levels of the same skill, but the members are unified in that they are all being instructed with and interacting with the same materials. This approach is illustrated in Figure 9.4.

Data Collection

An instructional session may be structured so that it contains a predetermined number of trials (usually 10 to 20) without regard to how long it will take to complete them, or a predetermined number of minutes (usually 10 to 20) within which a varying number of trials may occur. Generally, the first approach is used during the acquisition phase of instruction, and the second in a higher level of response competence (fluency and generalization). With the first approach, trial-by-trial data recording is usually employed;

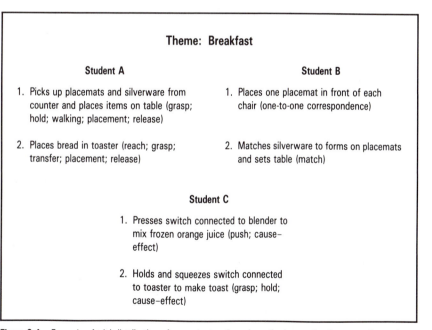

Figure 9.4. Example of trial distribution of group instruction where the instructional program for each student is different, but the theme is the same. Adapted from "Group Instruction: Theory and Application to Students with Severe Handicaps" by R. Sobsey, P. McLarney, P. Missall, and G. Murphy, 1985, paper presented at the 12th Annual Conference of the Association for Persons with Severe Handicaps, Boston. Reprinted by permission.

a data notation is recorded for each trial in which the student engages. With the second approach, a probe approach to data collection is usually employed. After the predetermined number of minutes of instruction, a sample of the behavior is tested (probed), and the result of this performance is recorded as the data for the session.

Two basic forms of data can be taken during instruction. One is *dichotomous data*. When using dichotomous data, the teacher records only whether the student performed the requested behavior correctly or incorrectly. One form of data sheet that can be used for dichotomous data collection is presented in Figure 9.5 and is a variation of one by Saunders and Koplik (1975). It may be used as follows:

1. Circle the trial number that corresponds to a correct response.
2. Slash (/) through the trial number that corresponds to an incorrect response.

Following each instructional session,

1. Total the number of correct trials (those circled).
2. Place a square around the corresponding number in the session column that corresponds to the number of correct trials.
3. To graph directly on the data sheet, connect the squared numbers across the sessions to yield a learning curve.

To collect dichotomous data when using a task analysis with the total task program format, the data sheet in Figure 9.6 may be used (Bellamy et al., 1979). The far left column is for listing antecedents to be provided. The other columns are for describing the steps of the chain. Each trial consists of an opportunity for the student to perform the entire chain of steps. For each trial, the teacher records the accuracy of the student's performance of each step using the same circle and slash procedure described above. This format also allows for graphing directly on the data sheet. The number corresponding to the number of correctly performed steps is indicated by a square, and the squares are connected across trials.

The other form of data collection indicates the instruction required for the student to perform the requested behavior. It is used when the teacher is employing a system of response prompting. Figure 9.7 presents such a data sheet (Alberto & Schofield, 1979). It depicts 20 sessions, each containing 10 trials. For each trial, the teacher can indicate the type of assistance that was necessary to enable the student to perform the response. Following each trial, the trial number is marked on the row corresponding to the type of assistance provided (e.g., a signal). This data sheet may also serve as a

Adaptation of Dichotomous Data Sheet

Name: _____

Task: _____

Criterion: _____

DATE:

10	10	10	10	10	10	10	10	10	10	10	10	10	10	10	10	10	10	10	10	10	10	10	10	10
9	9	9	9	9	9	9	9	9	9	9	9	9	9	9	9	9	9	9	9	9	9	9	9	9
8	8	8	8	8	8	8	8	8	8	8	8	8	8	8	8	8	8	8	8	8	8	8	8	8
7	7	7	7	7	7	7	7	7	7	7	7	7	7	7	7	7	7	7	7	7	7	7	7	7
6	6	6	6	6	6	6	6	6	6	6	6	6	6	6	6	6	6	6	6	6	6	6	6	6
5	5	5	5	5	5	5	5	5	5	5	5	5	5	5	5	5	5	5	5	5	5	5	5	5
4	4	4	4	4	4	4	4	4	4	4	4	4	4	4	4	4	4	4	4	4	4	4	4	4
3	3	3	3	3	3	3	3	3	3	3	3	3	3	3	3	3	3	3	3	3	3	3	3	3
2	2	2	2	2	2	2	2	2	2	2	2	2	2	2	2	2	2	2	2	2	2	2	2	2
1	1	1	1	1	1	1	1	1	1	1	1	1	1	1	1	1	1	1	1	1	1	1	1	1
0	0	0	0	0	0	0	0	0	0	0	0	0	0	0	0	0	0	0	0	0	0	0	0	0

Comments:

DATE:

10	10	10	10	10	10	10	10	10	10	10	10	10	10	10	10	10	10	10	10	10	10	10	10	10
9	9	9	9	9	9	9	9	9	9	9	9	9	9	9	9	9	9	9	9	9	9	9	9	9
8	8	8	8	8	8	8	8	8	8	8	8	8	8	8	8	8	8	8	8	8	8	8	8	8
7	7	7	7	7	7	7	7	7	7	7	7	7	7	7	7	7	7	7	7	7	7	7	7	7
6	6	6	6	6	6	6	6	6	6	6	6	6	6	6	6	6	6	6	6	6	6	6	6	6
5	5	5	5	5	5	5	5	5	5	5	5	5	5	5	5	5	5	5	5	5	5	5	5	5
4	4	4	4	4	4	4	4	4	4	4	4	4	4	4	4	4	4	4	4	4	4	4	4	4
3	3	3	3	3	3	3	3	3	3	3	3	3	3	3	3	3	3	3	3	3	3	3	3	3
2	2	2	2	2	2	2	2	2	2	2	2	2	2	2	2	2	2	2	2	2	2	2	2	2
1	1	1	1	1	1	1	1	1	1	1	1	1	1	1	1	1	1	1	1	1	1	1	1	1
0	0	0	0	0	0	0	0	0	0	0	0	0	0	0	0	0	0	0	0	0	0	0	0	0

Comments:

Figure 9.5. Adaptation of dichotomous data sheet. Adapted from "A Multi-Purpose Data Sheet for Recording and Graphing in the Classroom" by R. Saunders and K. Koplik, 1975, *AAESPH Review, 1*, p. 1. Copyright 1975 by The Association for Persons with Severe Handicaps. Adapted by permission.

Data Sheet for Chain Instruction (Task Analysis)

SD	RESPONSE																				
25.	_____	25	25	25	25	25	25	25	25	25	25	25	25	25	25	25	25	25	25	25	25
24.	_____	24	24	24	24	24	24	24	24	24	24	24	24	24	24	24	24	24	24	24	24
23.	_____	23	23	23	23	23	23	23	23	23	23	23	23	23	23	23	23	23	23	23	23
22.	_____	22	22	22	22	22	22	22	22	22	22	22	22	22	22	22	22	22	22	22	22
21.	_____	21	21	21	21	21	21	21	21	21	21	21	21	21	21	21	21	21	21	21	21
20.	_____	20	20	20	20	20	20	20	20	20	20	20	20	20	20	20	20	20	20	20	20
19.	_____	19	19	19	19	19	19	19	19	19	19	19	19	19	19	19	19	19	19	19	19
18.	_____	18	18	18	18	18	18	18	18	18	18	18	18	18	18	18	18	18	18	18	18
17.	_____	17	17	17	17	17	17	17	17	17	17	17	17	17	17	17	17	17	17	17	17
16.	_____	16	16	16	16	16	16	16	16	16	16	16	16	16	16	16	16	16	16	16	16
15.	_____	15	15	15	15	15	15	15	15	15	15	15	15	15	15	15	15	15	15	15	15
14.	_____	14	14	14	14	14	14	14	14	14	14	14	14	14	14	14	14	14	14	14	14
13.	_____	13	13	13	13	13	13	13	13	13	13	13	13	13	13	13	13	13	13	13	13
12.	_____	12	12	12	12	12	12	12	12	12	12	12	12	12	12	12	12	12	12	12	12
11.	_____	11	11	11	11	11	11	11	11	11	11	11	11	11	11	11	11	11	11	11	11
10.	_____	10	10	10	10	10	10	10	10	10	10	10	10	10	10	10	10	10	10	10	10
9.	_____	9	9	9	9	9	9	9	9	9	9	9	9	9	9	9	9	9	9	9	9
8.	_____	8	8	8	8	8	8	8	8	8	8	8	8	8	8	8	8	8	8	8	8
7.	_____	7	7	7	7	7	7	7	7	7	7	7	7	7	7	7	7	7	7	7	7
6.	_____	6	6	6	6	6	6	6	6	6	6	6	6	6	6	6	6	6	6	6	6
5.	_____	5	5	5	5	5	5	5	5	5	5	5	5	5	5	5	5	5	5	5	5
4.	_____	4	4	4	4	4	4	4	4	4	4	4	4	4	4	4	4	4	4	4	4
3.	_____	3	3	3	3	3	3	3	3	3	3	3	3	3	3	3	3	3	3	3	3
2.	_____	2	2	2	2	2	2	2	2	2	2	2	2	2	2	2	2	2	2	2	2
1.	_____	1	1	1	1	1	1	1	1	1	1	1	1	1	1	1	1	1	1	1	1

Figure 9.6. Data sheet for chain instruction (task analysis). From *Vocational Habilitation of Severely Retarded Adults: A Direct Service Technology* (p. 75) by G. T. Bellamy, R. Horner, and D. Inman, 1979, Austin, TX: PRO-ED. Copyright 1979 by PRO-ED, Inc. Reprinted by permission.

Data Sheet that Indicates Response Prompting

NAME: ______________________ MONTH: ____________

GOAL: ______________________

CRITERION: ______________________

COMMENTS: ______________________

	V.CUE	1 2 3 4 5 6 7 8 9 10	1 2 3 4 5 6 7 8 9 10	1 2 3 4 5 6 7 8 9 10	1 2 3 4 5 6 7 8 9 10	1 2 3 4 5 6 7 8 9 10
	SIGNAL	1 2 3 4 5 6 7 8 9 10	1 2 3 4 5 6 7 8 9 10	1 2 3 4 5 6 7 8 9 10	1 2 3 4 5 6 7 8 9 10	1 2 3 4 5 6 7 8 9 10
	MODEL	1 2 3 4 5 6 7 8 9 10	1 2 3 4 5 6 7 8 9 10	1 2 3 4 5 6 7 8 9 10	1 2 3 4 5 6 7 8 9 10	1 2 3 4 5 6 7 8 9 10
	PARTIAL	1 2 3 4 5 6 7 8 9 10	1 2 3 4 5 6 7 8 9 10	1 2 3 4 5 6 7 8 9 10	1 2 3 4 5 6 7 8 9 10	1 2 3 4 5 6 7 8 9 10
TRIALS	FULL	1 2 3 4 5 6 7 8 9 10	1 2 3 4 5 6 7 8 9 10	1 2 3 4 5 6 7 8 9 10	1 2 3 4 5 6 7 8 9 10	1 2 3 4 5 6 7 8 9 10
	INCORR	1 2 3 4 5 6 7 8 9 10	1 2 3 4 5 6 7 8 9 10	1 2 3 4 5 6 7 8 9 10	1 2 3 4 5 6 7 8 9 10	1 2 3 4 5 6 7 8 9 10
	V.CUE	1 2 3 4 5 6 7 8 9 10	1 2 3 4 5 6 7 8 9 10	1 2 3 4 5 6 7 8 9 10	1 2 3 4 5 6 7 8 9 10	1 2 3 4 5 6 7 8 9 10
	SIGNAL	1 2 3 4 5 6 7 8 9 10	1 2 3 4 5 6 7 8 9 10	1 2 3 4 5 6 7 8 9 10	1 2 3 4 5 6 7 8 9 10	1 2 3 4 5 6 7 8 9 10
	MODEL	1 2 3 4 5 6 7 8 9 10	1 2 3 4 5 6 7 8 9 10	1 2 3 4 5 6 7 8 9 10	1 2 3 4 5 6 7 8 9 10	1 2 3 4 5 6 7 8 9 10
	PARTIAL	1 2 3 4 5 6 7 8 9 10	1 2 3 4 5 6 7 8 9 10	1 2 3 4 5 6 7 8 9 10	1 2 3 4 5 6 7 8 9 10	1 2 3 4 5 6 7 8 9 10
	FULL	1 2 3 4 5 6 7 8 9 10	1 2 3 4 5 6 7 8 9 10	1 2 3 4 5 6 7 8 9 10	1 2 3 4 5 6 7 8 9 10	1 2 3 4 5 6 7 8 9 10
	INCORR	1 2 3 4 5 6 7 8 9 10	1 2 3 4 5 6 7 8 9 10	1 2 3 4 5 6 7 8 9 10	1 2 3 4 5 6 7 8 9 10	1 2 3 4 5 6 7 8 9 10
	V.CUE	1 2 3 4 5 6 7 8 9 10	1 2 3 4 5 6 7 8 9 10	1 2 3 4 5 6 7 8 9 10	1 2 3 4 5 6 7 8 9 10	1 2 3 4 5 6 7 8 9 10
	SIGNAL	1 2 3 4 5 6 7 8 9 10	1 2 3 4 5 6 7 8 9 10	1 2 3 4 5 6 7 8 9 10	1 2 3 4 5 6 7 8 9 10	1 2 3 4 5 6 7 8 9 10
	MODEL	1 2 3 4 5 6 7 8 9 10	1 2 3 4 5 6 7 8 9 10	1 2 3 4 5 6 7 8 9 10	1 2 3 4 5 6 7 8 9 10	1 2 3 4 5 6 7 8 9 10
	PARTIAL	1 2 3 4 5 6 7 8 9 10	1 2 3 4 5 6 7 8 9 10	1 2 3 4 5 6 7 8 9 10	1 2 3 4 5 6 7 8 9 10	1 2 3 4 5 6 7 8 9 10
	FULL	1 2 3 4 5 6 7 8 9 10	1 2 3 4 5 6 7 8 9 10	1 2 3 4 5 6 7 8 9 10	1 2 3 4 5 6 7 8 9 10	1 2 3 4 5 6 7 8 9 10
	INCORR	1 2 3 4 5 6 7 8 9 10	1 2 3 4 5 6 7 8 9 10	1 2 3 4 5 6 7 8 9 10	1 2 3 4 5 6 7 8 9 10	1 2 3 4 5 6 7 8 9 10
	V.CUE	1 2 3 4 5 6 7 8 9 10	1 2 3 4 5 6 7 8 9 10	1 2 3 4 5 6 7 8 9 10	1 2 3 4 5 6 7 8 9 10	1 2 3 4 5 6 7 8 9 10
	SIGNAL	1 2 3 4 5 6 7 8 9 10	1 2 3 4 5 6 7 8 9 10	1 2 3 4 5 6 7 8 9 10	1 2 3 4 5 6 7 8 9 10	1 2 3 4 5 6 7 8 9 10
	MODEL	1 2 3 4 5 6 7 8 9 10	1 2 3 4 5 6 7 8 9 10	1 2 3 4 5 6 7 8 9 10	1 2 3 4 5 6 7 8 9 10	1 2 3 4 5 6 7 8 9 10
	PARTIAL	1 2 3 4 5 6 7 8 9 10	1 2 3 4 5 6 7 8 9 10	1 2 3 4 5 6 7 8 9 10	1 2 3 4 5 6 7 8 9 10	1 2 3 4 5 6 7 8 9 10
	FULL	1 2 3 4 5 6 7 8 9 10	1 2 3 4 5 6 7 8 9 10	1 2 3 4 5 6 7 8 9 10	1 2 3 4 5 6 7 8 9 10	1 2 3 4 5 6 7 8 9 10
	INCORR	1 2 3 4 5 6 7 8 9 10	1 2 3 4 5 6 7 8 9 10	1 2 3 4 5 6 7 8 9 10	1 2 3 4 5 6 7 8 9 10	1 2 3 4 5 6 7 8 9 10

Figure 9.7. Data sheet that indicates response prompting. V.CUE = verbal cue; SIGNAL = gesture prompt; MODEL = modeling prompt; PARTIAL = partial physical prompt; FULL = full physical prompt; INCORR = incorrect response. From "An Instructional Interaction Pattern for the Severely Handicapped" by P. Alberto and P. Schofield, 1979, *Teaching Exceptional Children, 12,* p. 19. Copyright 1979 by Council for Exceptional Children. Reprinted by permission.

performance graph if the marked trial numbers are connected within and across sessions, thus yielding a curve that displays the increasing independence of the student to perform the response.

The three data sheets presented are examples of some that have proven useful for teachers; however, they are only models. Teachers may adapt these examples or design a different data sheet they find easy to use and that provides the information required. Otherwise, data collection will be a cumbersome and neglected exercise. Data collection is a vital component of effective instructional programming for students with profound disabilities. Systematic review of program data allows the instructor to note the presence, absence, and rate of student progress. One strategy proposed for assisting in the evaluation is *trend analysis* or the *quarter-intersect method* (White & Liberty, 1976). As seen in Figure 9.8, evaluation is based on the trend of the acquisition curve developed from median values of the data when graphed. Such

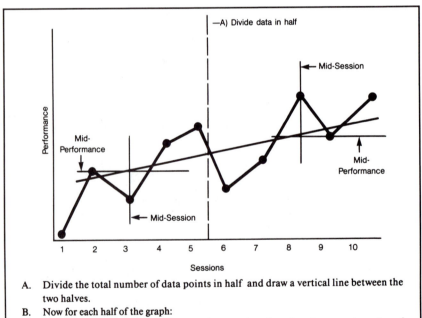

A. Divide the total number of data points in half and draw a vertical line between the two halves.
B. Now for each half of the graph:
1. Find the mid-session point (the session or point where there is an equal number of sessions on both sides), and draw a vertical line.
2. Find the mid-performance point (the data point that has an equal number of data points above and below it) and draw a horizontal line.
C. Connect the intersections of these points on both halves of the graph.

Figure 9.8. Constructing a trend line. From "Components of Instructional Technology" by P. A. Alberto and W. Sharpton in *Educating Students with Severe or Profound Handicaps* (2nd ed., p. 214) by L. Sternberg (Ed.), 1988, Austin, TX: PRO-ED. Copyright 1988 by PRO-ED, Inc. Reprinted by permission.

an analysis of trend lines can provide (a) an indication of the direction of behavior change in the past and (b) a prediction of the direction of behavior change in the future. The development of a such a prediction allows the teacher to consider the effectiveness and efficiency of the instructional program. When problems in an instructional program are indicated by the data, the teacher should review the major elements of instruction presented in this chapter to target the component in need of revision, whether it is the task selected, the materials used, the management of instructional trials, or the general methods format employed.

CONCLUSION

The major purpose of this chapter has been to provide a framework for understanding the complexities involved in instruction of students with profound disabilities. As mentioned previously, the extant data base indicating what type of instructional technology should be used with students who are profoundly disabled is sorely lacking. At the present time, we can only suggest approaches or components that appear to hold the most promise. Regardless, all tendered instructional technology should be effectively embedded in an overall curriculum design. The next chapter presents information on curriculum designs and development processes that are appropriate for use with these students. It also provides information on how some of the specific instructional technologies that have been tendered should be modified to meet the expressed needs of students who are profoundly disabled.

NOTE: This chapter is adapted from "Components of Instructional Technology" by P. A. Alberto and W. Sharpton in *Educating Students with Severe or Profound Handicaps* (2nd ed.) pp. 185–218 by L. Sternberg (Ed.), 1988. Austin, TX: PRO-ED. Adapted by permission.

REFERENCES

Adams, G., Matlock, B., & Tallon, R. (1981). Analysis of social praise given during the correction procedure of skill training. *American Journal of Mental Deficiency, 85,* 652–654.

Alberto, P., & Schofield, P. (1979). An instructional interaction pattern for the severely handicapped. *Teaching Exceptional Children, 12,* 16–19.

Alberto, P., & Troutman, A. (1990). *Applied behavior analysis for teachers.* Columbus, OH: Merrill.

Ault, M. M. (1988). Curriculum development. In L. Sternberg (Ed.), *Educating students with severe or profound handicaps* (pp. 219–265). Austin, TX: PRO-ED.

Baer, D., Peterson, R., & Sherman, J. (1967). The development of imitation by reinforcing behavioral similarity to a model. *Journal of the Experimental Analysis of Behavior, 10,* 405–416.

Bandura, A. (1969). *Principles of behavior modification.* New York: Holt, Rinehart and Winston.

Baumgart, D., Brown, L., Pumpian, I., Nisbet, J., Ford, A., Sweet, M., Messina, R., & Schroeder, J. (1982). Principle of partial participation and individualized adaptations in educational programs for severely handicapped students. *Journal of The Association for the Severely Handicapped, 7,* 17–27.

Becker, W., & Engelmann, S. (1978). Systems for basic instruction: Theory and applications. In A. Catania & T. Brigham (Eds.), *Handbook of applied behavior analysis: Social and instructional progress* (pp. 325–377). New York: Irvington.

Bellamy, G. T., Horner, R., & Inman, D. (1979). *Vocational habilitation of severely retarded adults: A direct service technology.* Austin, TX: PRO-ED.

Billingsley, F., & Romer, L. (1983). Response prompting and the transfer of stimulus control: Methods, research, and a conceptual framework. *Journal of The Association for the Severely Handicapped, 8,* 3–12.

Browder, D. M. (1987). *Assessment of individuals with severe handicaps: An applied behavior approach to life skills assessment.* Baltimore: Brookes.

Brown, F., Holvoet, J., Guess, D., & Mulligan, M. (1980). The individualized curriculum sequencing model: III. Small group instruction. *Journal of The Association for the Severely Handicapped, 5,* 352–367.

Brown, L., Branston, M. B., Hamre-Nietupski, S., Pumpian, I., Certo, N., & Gruenewald, L. (1979). A strategy for developing chronological age-appropriate and functional curricular content for severely handicapped adolescents and young adults. *Journal of Special Education, 13,* 81–90.

Collins, B. D., Gast, D. L., Wolery, M., Holcombe, A., & Leatherby, J. G. (1991). Using constant time-delay to teach self-feeding to young students with severe/profound handicaps: Evidence of limited effectiveness. *Journal of Developmental and Physical Disabilities, 3,* 157–179.

Crist, K., Walls, R., & Haught, P. (1984). Degrees of specificity in task analysis. *American Journal of Mental Deficiency, 89,* 67–74.

Csapo, M. (1981). Comparison of two prompting procedures to increase response fluency among severely handicapped learners. *Journal of The Association for the Severely Handicapped, 6,* 39–47.

Cuvo, A., Jacobi, L., & Sipko, R. (1981). Teaching laundry skills to mentally retarded students. *Education and Training of the Mentally Retarded, 16,* 54–64.

Day, H. M. (1987). Comparison of two prompting procedures to facilitate skill acquisition among severely mentally retarded adolescents. *American Journal of Mental Deficiency, 91*(4), 366–372.

Doyle, P., Wolery, M., Ault, M., & Gast, D. L. (1988). System of least prompts: A literature review of procedural parameters. *Journal of The Association for Persons with Severe Handicaps, 13,* 28–40.

Falvey, M. (1989). *Community-based curriculum: Instructional strategies for students with severe handicaps* (2nd ed.). Baltimore: Brookes.

Farmer, J. A., Gast, D. L., Wolery, M., & Winterling, V. (1991). Small group instruction for students with severe handicaps: A study of observational learning. *Education and Treatment in Mental Retardation, 26,* 190–201.

Favell, J., Favell, J., & McGimsey, J. (1978). Relative effectiveness and efficiency of group vs. individualized training of severely retarded groups. *American Journal of Mental Deficiency, 83,* 104–109.

Ferguson, D. L., & Baumgart, D. (1991). Partial participation revisited. *Journal of The Association for Persons with Severe Disabilities, 16,* 218–227.

Foxx, R. M. (1981). *Effective behavioral programming: Graduated guidance and backward chaining.* Champaign, IL: Research Press.

Gagne, R., & Briggs, L. (1979). *Principles of instructional design.* New York: Holt, Rinehart and Winston.

Giangreco, M. (1982). Teaching imitation to a profoundly delayed learner through functional tasks. *Education and Training of the Mentally Retarded, 17,* 164–167.

Gold, M. (1976). Task analysis of a complex assembly task by the retarded blind. *Exceptional Children, 43,* 78–84.

Gold, M. (1980). *Try another way: Training manual.* Champaign, IL: Research Press.

Guess, D., Mulligan-Ault, M., Roberts, S., Struth, J., Siegel-Causey, E., Thompson, B., Bronicki, G. J., & Guy, B. (1988). Implications of biobehavioral states for the education and treatment of students with the most profoundly handicapping conditions. *Journal of The Association for Persons with Severe Handicaps, 13,* 163–175.

Haywood, H., Meyers, C., & Switzky, H. (1982). Mental retardation. *Annual Review in Psychology, 33,* 309–342.

Holvoet, J., Brown, F., & Helmstetter, E. (1980). *Writing functional group sequences using the ICS curriculum sequencing model.* Paper presented at the 7th Annual Conference of The Association for Persons with Severe Handicaps, San Francisco.

Horner, R., Eberhard, J., & Sheehan, M. (1986). Teaching generalized table bussing: The importance of negative teaching examples. *Behavior Modification, 10,* 457–471.

Horner, R., McDonnell, J., & Bellamy, G. T. (1986). Teaching generalized skills: General case instruction in simulation and community settings. In R. Horner, L. Meyer, & H. D. Fredericks (Eds.), *Education of learners with severe handicaps: Exemplary service strategies* (pp. 289–314). Baltimore: Brookes.

Horner, R., Sprague, J., & Wilcox, B. (1982). Constructing general case programs for community activities. In B. Wilcox & G. T. Bellamy (Eds.), *Design of high school programs for severely handicapped students* (pp. 61–98). Baltimore: Brookes.

Klein, N., & Stafford, P. (1978). The acquisition of classification skills by trainable mentally retarded children. *Education and Training of the Mentally Retarded, 13,* 272–277.

Koegel, R., & Rincover, A. (1974). Treatment of psychotic children in a classroom environment: Learning in a large group. *Journal of Applied Behavior Analysis, 7,* 45–59.

Kohl, F., Wilcox, B., & Karlan, G. (1978). Effects of training conditions on the generalization of manual signs with moderately handicapped students. *Education and Training of the Mentally Retarded, 13,* 327–331.

Landesman-Dwyer, S., & Sackett, G. (1978). Behavioral changes in non-ambulatory, profoundly mentally retarded individuals. In C. Meyers (Ed.), *Quality of life in severely and profoundly mentally retarded people: Research foundations for improvement* (pp. 55–141). Washington, DC: American Association on Mental Deficiency.

Liberty, K., Haring, N., & Martin, M. (1981). Teaching new skills to the severely handicapped. *Journal of The Association for the Severely Handicapped, 6,* 5–13.

Lovass, O. I. (1981). *Teaching developmentally disabled children: The Me Book.* Austin, TX: PRO-ED.

McCuller, W., & Salzberg, C. (1984). Generalized action–object verbal instruction-following by profoundly mentally retarded adults. *American Journal of Mental Deficiency, 88,* 442–445.

Mulligan, M., Guess, D., Holvoet, J., & Brown, F. (1980). The individualized curriculum sequencing model: I. Implications from research on massed, distributed, or spaced trial training. *Journal of The Association for the Severely Handicapped, 5,* 325–336.

Mulligan, M., Lacy, L., & Guess, D. (1982). Effects of massed, distributed, and spaced trial sequencing on severely handicapped students' performance. *Journal of The Association for Persons with Severe Handicaps, 7,* 48–61.

Oliver, P. (1983). Effects of teaching different tasks in group versus individual training formats with severely handicapped individuals. *Journal of The Association for the Severely Handicapped, 8,* 79–91.

Pancsofar, E., & Bates, P. (1985). The impact of the acquisition of successive training exemplars on generalization. *Journal of The Association for Persons with Severe Handicaps, 10,* 95–104.

Parton, D. (1976). Learning to imitate in infancy. *Child Development, 47,* 14–31.

Reese, G., & Snell, M. (1991). Putting and removing coats and jackets: The acquisition and maintenance of skills by children with severe multiple disabilities. *Education and Training in Mental Retardation, 26,* 398–410.

Reid, D., & Favell, J. (1984). Group instruction with persons who have severe disabilities: A critical review. *Journal of The Association for Persons with Severe Handicaps, 9,* 167–177.

Reid, D., Parsons, M., McCarn, J., Green, C., Phillips, J., & Schepis, J. (1985). Providing a more appropriate education for severely handicapped persons: Increasing and validating functional classroom tasks. *Journal of Applied Behavior Analysis, 18,* 289–301.

Reid, D. H., Phillips, J. F., & Green, C. W. (1991). Teaching persons with profound multiple handicaps: A review of the effects of behavioral research. *Journal of Applied Behavior Analysis, 24,* 319–336.

Rincover, A., & Koegel, R. (1977). Classroom treatment of autistic children: Individualizing instruction in a group. *Journal of Abnormal Child Psychology, 5,* 113–125.

Sailor, W., & Guess, D. (1983). *Severely handicapped students: An instructional design.* Boston: Houghton Mifflin.

Saunders, R., & Koplik, K. (1975). A multi-purpose data sheet for recording and graphing in the classroom. *AAESPH Review, 1,* 1.

Schoen, S. (1986). Assistance procedures to facilitate the transfer of stimulus control: Review and analysis. *Education and Training of the Mentally Retarded, 21,* 62–74.

Schriebman, L. (1975). Effects of within-stimulus and extra-stimulus prompting on discrimination learning in autistic children. *Journal of Applied Behavior Analysis, 8,* 91–112.

Skinner, B. F. (1968). *The technology of teaching.* New York: Appleton-Century-Crofts.

Snell, M., & Gast, D. (1981). Applying time delay procedure to the instruction of the severely handicapped. *Journal of The Association for the Severely Handicapped, 6*(3), 3–14.

Sobsey, D., McLarney, P., Missall, P., & Murphy, G. (1985). *Group instruction: Theory and application to students with severe handicaps.* Paper presented at the 12th Annual Conference of The Association for Persons with Severe Handicaps, Boston.

Spooner, F., & Spooner, D. (1984). A review of chaining techniques: Implications for future research and practice. *Education and Training of the Mentally Retarded, 19,* 114–124.

Sternberg, L., McNerney, C., & Pegnatore, L. (1985). Developing co-active imitative behaviors with profoundly mentally handicapped students. *Education and Training of the Mentally Retarded, 5,* 260–268.

Sternberg, L., & Owens, A. (1985). Establishing prelanguage signalling behavior with profoundly mentally handicapped students: A preliminary investigation. *Journal of Mental Deficiency Research, 29,* 81–93.

Sternberg, L., Ritchey, H., Pegnatore, L., Wills, L., & Hill, C. (1986). *A curriculum for profoundly handicapped students.* Austin, TX: PRO-ED.

Storm, R., & Willis, J. (1978). Small-group training as an alternative to individual programs for profoundly retarded persons. *American Journal of Mental Deficiency, 83,* 283–288.

Westling, D., Ferrell, K., & Swenson, K. (1982). Intra-classroom comparison of two arrangements for teaching profoundly mentally retarded children. *American Journal of Mental Deficiency, 86,* 601–688.

White, O., & Haring, N. (1980). *Exceptional teaching.* Columbus, OH: Merrill.

White, O., & Liberty, K. (1976). Evaluation and measurement. In N. Haring & R. Schiefelbusch (Eds.), *Teaching special children* (pp. 31–71). New York: McGraw-Hill.

Wilcox, B., & Bellamy, G. T. (1982). *Design of high school programs for severely handicapped students.* Baltimore: Brookes.

Williams, J., & Horner, R. (1984). *General case street crossing instructional package.* Unpublished manuscript, University of Oregon, Eugene.

Wolery, M., Ault, M. J., & Doyle, P. M. (1992). *Teaching students with moderate and severe disabilities: Use of response prompting strategies.* White Plains, NY: Longman.

Wolfe, V., & Cuvo, A. (1978). Effects of within-stimulus and extra-stimulus prompting on letter discrimination by mentally retarded persons. *American Journal of Mental Deficiency, 83,* 297–303.

Wuerch, B., & Voeltz, L. (1982). *Longitudinal leisure skills for severely handicapped learners.* Baltimore: Brookes.

Zeaman, D., & House, B. (1979). A review of attention theory. In N. R. Ellis (Ed.), *Handbook of mental deficiency* (pp. 63–120). Hillsdale, NJ: Erlbaum.

Chapter 10

Curriculum Development and Instructional Design for Students with Profound Disabilities

KENT R. LOGAN, PAUL A. ALBERTO, THOMAS G. KANA, and TONI WAYLOR-BOWEN

I n this chapter, we outline a process for designing appropriate curriculum, conducting educational assessments, and developing instructional objectives for students with profound disabilities. We also specify an instructional framework that educators may use to assist students to acquire these objectives. We describe four major areas that impact the design process and instructional framework: the cognitive and physical characteristics of students that affect curriculum planning, activity-based curricula and adaptations for use with students with profound disabilities, assessment procedures for selecting appropriate activities for instruction, and assessment procedures for developing and writing appropriate instructional objectives.

CHARACTERISTICS OF STUDENTS WITH PROFOUND DISABILITIES

As described in Chapter 1, students with profound disabilities are a heterogeneous group. This group includes a range of students, from those who are minimally responsive to external stimuli and who have no voluntary control over their extremities, to those who are ambulatory and have cognitive skills such as matching, sorting, and symbolic communication. Regardless of the level of their skills, however, students with profound disabilities will always need caregivers to attend to their basic health, hygiene, and safety needs. Educational outcomes for these students will be increased levels of partial participation rather than independent performance of a given activity (Ferguson & Baumgart, 1991).

According to Logan, Alberto, Kana, and Waylor (1992), appropriate educational planning must take into consideration the multiple cognitive, physical, alertness, behavioral, sensory, mobility, medical, and age characteristics of the students. These characteristics affect how the student may partially participate in any given activity. Table 10.1 displays three functioning levels for each characteristic. The three levels for physical disabilities, vision, hearing, mobility status, and age should be self-explanatory. The levels for cognitive functioning, behavior interference with instruction, alertness, and health need additional explanation.

In defining minimal and functional cognitive responses to the environment, students with profound disabilities are described as not following traditional stimulus control instructional procedures. In essence, they exhibit a lack of response to these instructional procedures (Guess et al., 1988; Haywood, Meyers, & Switzky, 1982; Landesman-Dwyer & Sackett, 1978). At the instructional prompting level, these students have inconsistent responses to stimulus control procedures, such as time delay (Collins, Gast, Wolery, Holcombe, & Leatherby, 1991). In addition, these students may show preferences, make choices, or activate switches to obtain preferred stimulus events. These preferences, however, do not function consistently as generalized reinforcers (Reid, Phillips, & Green, 1991). For example, a student may activate a switch to turn on a radio, but access to the radio does not serve as a consistent reinforcer for picking up or looking at one of two objects to indicate a choice between stimulus items.

Levels of behavioral interference with instruction and health status are operationalized based on the amount of time the teacher spends managing a student's behavior or health care needs. As these descriptions are based on educational considerations, the amount of time a teacher engages in management of the behavior is a more relevant descriptor than the actual severity of the behavior or health care need itself. Within the characteristic of alertness to environmental stimuli, students are described as being in one of the three alertness levels (i.e., asleep, agitated, awake) if they were in that level more than 50% of their school day.

The primary characteristics most relevant to instructional planning are levels of cognitive functioning and physical disability. Although other characteristics have been described, they do not impact instructional planning within the conceptual framework we are discussing. They may affect other aspects of educational planning. For example, chronological age determines the age appropriateness of the activity and materials. Health status may affect environments in which the student can safely function or length of time engaged

TABLE 10.1. Definitions of Characteristics of Students with Profound Disabilities

Cognitive Functioning	Physical Disability	Alertness to the Environment
Minimal Cognitive Responses Students who are alert to the environment but do not show recognition of significant persons, do not use familiar stimuli except in a stereotypic manner, do not show anticipation of upcoming events or steps in a chain, and do not respond to traditional stimulus control instructional procedures. Includes students who do not orient to environmental stimuli, or respond at a purely reflexive level.	*Restricted Use of Extremities* Students who demonstrate no functional use of arms or legs except the ability to activate a head, hand, arm, leg, or body switch when correctly positioned. Students who may engage in gross arm movements, but exhibit no fine-motor control.	*Asleep* Students who are either asleep or, if they are awake, give no behavioral indications that they are visually, auditorily, or motorically attending to environmental stimuli. Includes the "biobehavioral states" of asleep–inactive, asleep–active, drowsy, daze, chronic seizure (Guess et al., 1991).
Functional Cognitive Responses Students who do recognize significant person, do use familiar stimuli in a functional manner, and do anticipate events or upcoming steps in a chain. Students who do not follow traditional stimulus control instructional procedures.	*Partial Use of Extremities* Students who demonstrate functional use of arms and hands. This includes the ability to hold a spoon or cup, manipulate large and small items in a functional manner, and partially participate in dressing and hygiene tasks. These skills may be performed with adaptations.	*Agitated* Students who engage in constant stereotypic, self-injurious, and/or crying behaviors, which greatly restrict their attention to stimulus items. Includes the "biobehavioral states" of awake–active/self-stimulatory and crying/agitated (Guess et al., 1991).
Higher Cognitive Responses Students who are labeled profoundly disabled based on IQ test scores but who demonstrate or have emerging the following cognitive and communicative behaviors: matching, imitation, one-to-one correspondence, expressive symbolic communication systems of more than three symbols, and receptive comprehension as evidenced by symbolic instruction following behaviors. Includes students who do follow traditional stimulus control instructional procedures.	*Unrestricted Use of Extremities* Students who are ambulatory and engage in a range of gross- and fine-motor tasks.	*Awake* Students who are awake and attending to environmental stimuli at one of the three levels described under cognitive functioning. Includes the "biobehavioral states" of awake active–alert and awake inactive–alert (Guess et al., 1991).

(continued)

TABLE 10.1. *Continued*

Behavior Interference	Vision Impairment	Hearing Impairment
Severe Interference Students who engage in challenging, stereotypic, or other undesirable behaviors regardless of the teacher's engaging in systematic instruction within the context of a functional curriculum. Students require close teacher proximity and even physical control. Management and redirection of the behavior take 10 or more minutes and require the teacher to stop teaching other students. Behaviors occur five or more times per day.	*Blind* Students who may detect light and dark or motion, but have no pattern or form discrimination, no evidence of eye–hand coordination, and no visual exploration of the environment.	*Deaf* Students who neither startle in response to nor orient to sound.
Moderate Interference Students who, if given systematic instruction within the context of a functional curriculum, do not require additional teacher proximity or physical control. Students engage in undesired behavior if the teacher fails to maintain appropriate instructional or curricular control. Management and redirection of the behavior take less than 10 minutes. Teacher does not typically have to stop teaching other students. Behaviors occur less than five times per day.	*Impaired* Students who have functional vision as evidenced by eye–hand coordination and visual exploration of the environment. There is a visual impairment as diagnosed through a medical evaluation or functional evaluation resulting in a need to make adaptations to the instructional environment.	*Impaired* Students who have functional hearing as evidenced by orientation to sound either with or without aids. There is a hearing impairment, as diagnosed through a medical or audiological evaluation or through a functional evaluation, resulting in a need to make adaptations to the instructional environment.
Occasional Interference Students who engage in occasional undesired behaviors that require a few minutes of teacher verbal or physical intervention. Behaviors occur less than five times per day, and the teacher rarely has to stop teaching other students. Includes students who have no undesired behaviors.	*Normal* Students who demonstrate no visual impairments as functionally identified by staff or testing by an eye care professional which require the teacher to make adaptations to the instructional environment.	*Normal* Students who demonstrate no hearing impairments—as diagnosed functionally by staff or through medical or audiological evaluation—that require the teacher to make adaptations to the instructional environment.

(continued)

TABLE 10.1. *Continued*

Mobility Level	Health Status	Chronological Age
Attendant	*Chronic*	*Elementary*
Students who must be pushed in wheelchairs, carried, or physically assisted by another person from location to location.	Students who regularly require emergency medical care, either through a nurse's intervention or emergency service, need nurse monitoring of their health because it is too complex for teachers to evaluate, and/or need more than 1 hour of adult physical health care on an individual basis during a school day. Tube feeding is not considered a medical procedure. Seizure activity must be medically monitored due to its life-threatening nature. Student health care needs interrupt the teacher's schedule on a daily basis, taking him or her away from instruction of students for longer than 10 minutes.	Students who are ages 5 through 12.
Limited	*Routine*	*Middle*
Students who push their own wheelchair, use a walker, or roll or scoot in school or home environments. They cannot move self independently in community settings.	Students who require physical health care procedures, such as postural drainage, suctioning, catheterization, etc., but whose needs can be accommodated as part of a teacher schedule and take less than 1 hour. Procedures do not interrupt other instructional activities on a daily basis. Seizures may occur several times per day, but they require only a few minutes of teacher monitoring and are not normally life threatening.	Students who are ages 12 through 15.
Self	*Occasional*	*High*
Students who walk, use a walker independently, or move self in wheelchair not only in home and school environments, but also in the community.	Students who may require regular dispensing of medication. They may also have colds or intestinal dysfunctions occurring on widely scattered days. These students may also have occasional seizures which do not take more than a few moments of teacher time to monitor and evaluate and are not normally life threatening.	Students who are ages 16 through 22.

in activities. Student mobility may affect how long it takes a teacher to move students from one location to another or the number of students that may be involved in community-based instruction. Vision and hearing impairments affect how stimuli are presented to students, as well as safety concerns in various environments. Behavioral interference with instruction may affect grouping arrangements, staffing ratios, and selection of certain activities and/or environments. Alertness levels may affect time of day for instruction, length of the instructional session, and scheduling of instruction based on student receptivity to learning.

Cognitive functioning characteristics are important because they determine students' responses to traditional stimulus control instructional procedures and reinforcement strategies. Problems with responses are probably due to developmental ceilings on cognitive development stemming from organic dysfunctions (see Chapter 3). As indicated previously, responses of students with profound disabilities are often inconsistent, thereby making the teaching process extremely challenging. The presence of a physical disability is important because it affects how students can interact motorically with materials. This, in turn, impacts their level of independent participation in functional activities.

Both cognitive functioning and physical disability characteristics affect the development of adaptations and alternative performance strategies (Baumgart et al., 1982). Based on these two characteristics, seven characteristics clusters emerge as relevant to educational planning for students with profound disabilities. These clusters and a description of one student representing each cluster are contained in Table 10.2.

ACTIVITY-BASED CURRICULA AND ADAPTATIONS FOR STUDENTS WITH PROFOUND DISABILITIES

The activity-based model was first described for students with severe disabilities as the Individualized Curriculum Sequencing (ICS) model (Sailor & Guess, 1983). In this model, all instructional objectives for the student are taught within the context of a functional activity rather than in isolation. This instructional format makes use of effective instructional strategies, such as distributed practice (Mulligan, Lacy, & Guess, 1982); planning for generalization (Horner, McDonnell, & Bellamy, 1986); and natural cues, corrections, and reinforcers (Ford & Mirenda, 1984). For example, and in application to those with profound disabilities, a student might be taught a basic motor response, such as reach and grasp, within the context of shopping, snack preparation, or switch activation rather than in drill format sitting

TABLE 10.2. Characteristics Clusters of Students with Profound Disabilities

Cluster	*Student Description*
1. Students with minimal cognitive responses combined with restricted use of their extremities.	Calvin is an 11-year-old, nonambulatory student. Use of arms and legs is limited to gross-motor movements that are slow and often accompanied by tremors. Head and trunk control is also difficult to maintain, and he spends most of his time in his adapted wheelchair, in tumble form chairs, or a beanbag chair. He is often congested and drools. Although vision and hearing are thought to be normal, he does not respond to most sounds, including verbalization, and does not fixate on most items or look at people except while being fed. He does not demonstrate awareness of cause and effect and has little interaction with people or objects. Without appropriate stimulation, he will sleep at least 4 hours a day, even though he is not given medication. He cries, turns his head, or falls asleep to protest participation in activities. He has no other communicative behaviors.
2. Students with minimal cognitive responses with either partial or unrestricted use of their extremities.	Tom is a 14-year-old ambulatory student with functional use of his hands. He has no safety awareness and will wander away if not supervised. He has seizures 12–18 times per day. He is awake during the day but is occasionally sleepy due to medication. He wears diapers. He feeds himself with a spoon and with his fingers and drinks from a cup. However, he does not grasp and hold other objects except to engage in stereotypic behaviors with them. He focuses only on food, but will make occasional eye contact with staff. He demonstrates no recognition of other people but will smile occasionally at his mother. He demonstrates no understanding of routines or anticipation of upcoming steps in a task.
3. Students with functional cognitive responses combined with restricted use of their extremities.	Sally is a nonambulatory 9-year-old girl. She can move her right arm from midline to the edge of her lap tray. She focuses on people and smiles in response to verbalizations from them. She will look at objects but does not use her vision to make choices between objects. She does not look at one of two objects named by the teacher. She has lung congestion and must be placed over a wedge three times a day for postural drainage. A careful program of oral hygiene is also accomplished twice a day. She needs oral–motor facilitation prior to being fed and needs chin control for chewing and drinking from a cup. She is awake–alert all day and enjoys being with other people.
4. Students with functional cognitive responses combined with partial or unrestricted use of their extremities.	Melanie is a 16-year-old ambulatory student with functional use of her hands. She has visual impairments, but appears to see well directly to the front. This does not affect her ambulation and she can find small food items with ease.

(continued)

TABLE 10.2.   *Continued*

Cluster	Student Description
	She can eat and dress herself with only minimal assistance. She is toilet trained to an established schedule and has only occasional accidents. Melanie requires constant supervision since she will eat almost any object (pica). She engages in head banging, and sucks her fingers when frustrated or not engaged in other activities. She prefers to sit and at times complains through general vocal noises. She responds inconsistently to food reinforcement. Although Melanie seems to have some recognition of familiar environments, she shows little evidence of discriminating between people. She does show some anticipation of succeeding steps when engaged in familiar activities.
5. Students with higher cognitive responses combined with restricted use of their extremities.	Jerry is a 13-year-old nonambulatory student. He can move his right arm and hand enough to activate and release a pressure switch mounted on his lap tray. He uses his vision to make choices by looking at objects and pictures. He has a clear yes–no head shake and responds appropriately to questions. If asked if two items are the same, he can shake his head yes or no correctly. He uses his right hand to activate a loop tape with five messages on it. He is totally dependent on caregivers for eating, dressing, and toileting. He does not wear diapers and will answer yes or no when asked if he needs to go to the bathroom. He indicates his need to use the bathroom by using a specific vocalization. He laughs appropriately at humorous events and enjoys being with people.
6. Students with higher cognitive responses combined with partial or unrestricted use of their extremities.	Rashad is a 7-year-old ambulatory student with functional use of his hands. He has no medical problems. He wears glasses (when he brings them to school). He is awake–alert throughout the school day. Although he still wears diapers, he is on an hourly toileting schedule. When told, he can go to the bathroom, and pull down his pants and diaper. He partially assists in dressing. He indicates the need to go to the bathroom approximately three times per week. He understands simple commands and requests such as "come here," "go to," and "stop." His means of expressive communication consists of a few simple gestures and facial expressions. He can match five noun pictures to their objects and use them for communication in responding to questions. He can match socks by color (white, black, red). He feeds himself, given continuous verbal prompting, and can complete each task in his hygiene routine (cannot judge water temperature). When on a tricycle or plastic skates, he makes no attempt at movement

(continued)

TABLE 10.2. *Continued*

Cluster	Student Description
	without verbal and some physical prompting. He demonstrates no curiosity or interest in toys. He will listen to music on a tape recorder for up to 15 minutes. He goes into the kindergarten class three times per week during storytime. He sits among the children but makes no attempt at social interaction and ignores attempts by the kindergartners.
7. Students with minimal cognitive responses combined with *both* restricted use of their extremities and either asleep/agitated levels or chronic/routine health care needs.	Linda is an 8-year-old girl with no voluntary control over her body except for limited head turning. She is visually impaired but does focus occasionally on another person. She sleeps over half the day and has three to eight crying spells per day. She has irregular breathing, has chronic respiratory distress, and requires oxygen intermittently. She has a severe scoliosis, an ulcerated gastrointestinal tube opening, and sensitive skin that is subject to pressure sores and diaper rash.

around a table in the classroom. The reader is referred to Chapter 9 for a more complete discussion of options for formatting instruction.

The ICS model has been extended for use with many students with profound disabilities and validated through a series of research studies and classroom implementations (Gee, Graham, Sailor, & Goetz, in press; Green, Canipe, Way, & Reid, 1986; Sailor, Gee, Goetz, & Graham, 1988; Snell, Lewis, & Houghton, 1989). This extension of activity-based curriculum especially applies to students in Characteristics Clusters 1–6 (Table 10.2). These students comprise the vast majority of those classified as profoundly disabled. Students in Characteristics Cluster 7 appear to comprise between 8% and 12% of the population (Logan et al., 1992). An alternative curriculum model and educational outcome measures for this latter cluster of students are proposed later in this chapter.

The extension of the activity-based model includes some reconceptualization of how students with profound disabilities partially participate in functional activities in integrated settings. However, the basic format of activity-based instruction is retained. Instructional objectives are taught within the context of functional, age-appropriate activities in integrated settings.

Conceptual Format for Partial Participation in Activities

Curriculum development for students with profound handicaps has as its primary goal identifying and developing skills to increase partial participation in functional activities in home, school, and community environments. Partial participation affirms that students with profound disabilities can learn critical skills within the context of a wide variety of functional activities that occur in integrated settings. This learning of critical skills occurs even though the student may not be able to learn enough skills in the activity to perform it independently.

The extension of activity-based instruction for students with profound disabilities necessitates defining partial participation across three levels within the activity: (a) tasks within the activity, (b) steps within each task, and (c) basic developmental skills that comprise each step. Table 10.3 illustrates this framework for the activity of "doing the laundry," and Table 10.4 illustrates this framework for the activity of "hygiene."

Students with profound disabilities may have organic and developmental limitations that affect the level of their partial participation, but some type of active partial participation in meaningful activities is always possible. These activities provide not only the vehicle for instruction, but also the context for social relationships. These relationships provide meaning and quality of life not only for these students, but also for their caregivers and others who interact with them (Dunst, Cuishing, & Vance, 1985; Evans & Scotti, 1989).

Activities are the global routines in which a person engages during the day in various environments (e.g., doing the laundry, hygiene). Each activity comprises multiple *tasks*. Different people may describe the tasks that make

TABLE 10.3. Activity Description for Doing the Laundry

Tasks: For doing laundry	Steps: For operating the machine	Basic Developmental Skills: For setting amount of time for machine to run
Gather dirty clothes	Open the lid	Fixate on dial while completing other skills
Sort clothes	Distribute heavy items in machine	
Operate washing machine	Distribute light items in machine	Reach for dial
Operate dryer	Add detergent	Grasp the dial
Fold clothes	Set amount of time for machine	Hold the dial
Hang clothes	to run	Turn dial to setting
Put clothes away	Close lid	Release the dial
	Set water level	
	Set temperature level	
	Set appropriate cycle	
	Turn on machine	

TABLE 10.4. Activity Description for Hygiene

Tasks: For hygiene activity	Steps: For washing hands	Basic Developmental Skills: For turning on water
Brush teeth	Approach sink	Anticipate need to turn on water
Wash hands	Turn on water	Focus on faucet
Brush hair	Adjust water temperature	Understand cause–effect that faucet turns on water
Take a bath	Pick up soap	Reach for faucet
Take a shower	Soap hands	Grasp faucet
Wash face	Put away soap	Hold faucet
Clean fingernails	Rub hands to clean	Turn faucet
Clip fingernails	Rinse hands	Release faucet
Put on deodorant	Turn off water	
Shave	Dry hands	
Menstrual care	Leave sink area	

up an activity in slightly different ways. Whatever description is used, the task selected for instruction is typically broken down into *steps* for instruction. This series of steps is called a task analysis. Steps in the task analysis are typically broken down based on motor actions (action verbs). Teaching through the use of task analyses has proven to be a powerful instructional tool (Snell & Zirpoli, 1988). As with task selection and breakdown, the number of steps in the task analysis may vary from person to person, but the conceptual framework remains the same.

At a more refined level of analysis, each step in the task can be described as being made up of *basic developmental skills*. These are skills that typically emerge in children during the first 2 years of normal development. These developmental skills are usually specified by developmental domain: fine-motor, gross-motor, vision and hearing, communication, social, and play. Within the fine-motor domain, examples include reach, pincer grasp, hold, twist, and turn. Vision includes focus, fixate, scan, and track (Sternberg, Ritchey, Pegnatore, Wills, & Hill, 1986). As a rule, it takes completion of two or more basic developmental skills to complete a step in a task analysis.

Partial participation at any of these three levels may need to be facilitated through adaptations and alternative performance strategies. If these are needed, persons without disabilities must often make them. These include adaptations to the environment, social attitudes, materials, rules, or the child (see Baumgart et al., 1982, for a complete discussion of appropriate adaptations). Table 10.5 specifies the level of partial participation that would be expected of students in different characteristics clusters.

Partial participation at the task level

Some students with profound disabilities are able to learn tasks within an activity. These students are typically found in Characteristics Cluster 6. For example, a student may learn to collect dirty laundry and carry it to the laundry room. Another student may learn to wash her hands.

Rationale for approach

After being taught a complete task, students are able to be independent in that task. This reduces the burden of caregiving on the part of the parent or friend. For many students with profound disabilities, adaptations must be made in the task to allow for independent completion. For example, the handles on the laundry basket may need to be expanded or padded. Also, the first step in the task analysis may have to be prompted. For example, students may not be 100% independent in that they may not know *when* to do the laundry. Once told, however, they can then collect the laundry from clothes hampers in the house and carry it to the laundry area. The caregiver must still load, set, and turn on the washing machine. As can be seen, this level of partial participation allows the student to work cooperatively with someone else, thus allowing for social interactions.

Partial participation at the step level

As indicated above, steps in a task analysis comprise motor actions. Opening the lid to a washing machine involves muscle action. Placing clothes in the machine also is a motor behavior. Completing these motor actions implies that the functional effect of the step is attained; that is, the washing machine lid is open rather than closed, and the clothes are in the machine rather than still in the basket. In general, students will need some level of voluntary arm and hand control to complete these motor steps. This type of partial participation, therefore, is typical for students in Characteristics Cluster 4, although some students in Characteristics Cluster 2 will partially participate in this manner.

Learning one or more steps in the task analysis can be further described in three ways: learning only one step, learning two or more nonsequential steps, and learning two or more sequential steps. At the most basic level, some students may learn only one step in the task. For example, a student may learn to roll the dice in a board game, open the washing machine lid,

TABLE 10.5. Student Characteristics Clusters Related to Level of Partial Participation

Characteristics Cluster	Level of Partial Participation
1	Basic developmental skills
2	Basic developmental skills for most students
	Skill step(s) for some students
3	Basic developmental skills
4	Skill step(s) for most students
	Basic developmental skills for some students
5	Basic developmental skills indicative of higher cognitive levels
6	Tasks for most students
	Skill step(s) for some students
7	Basic developmental skills with alternative educational outcomes

lift a glass to his or her lips, turn on the tape player, or push a bowling ball down an adapted ramp.

Other students may learn several steps in the task, but not steps that occur in a row. For example, in handwashing, the student may learn to turn on the water and then, after the adult has washed the student's hands, to turn off the water. A student may learn to pick up the toothbrush and then to put it in his or her mouth after the teacher has put toothpaste on it.

Many students with profound disabilities have adequate motor skills, and can complete steps in a chain independently. However, they must be prompted to complete a step after they have independently performed the preceding step (see Chapter 9). For example, a student may be able to open the microwave door, take the container out of the microwave, close the door, and carry the container to the table. The student, however, may open the door and then stop. Once verbally or gesturally prompted, he or she then takes the container out, but again stops. If prompted, the student then closes the door. If prompted again, he or she carries the container to the table. For these students, the ability to complete sequential steps in the task analysis becomes the primary objective. Teaching the student to complete two or more of these steps without prompts would be an appropriate target for instruction.

Rationale for approach

Students who have the motor ability to complete a step in the task analysis no longer need to rely on the caregiver or friend to do that step for them. Students who can pull up their pants no longer need the caregiver to stoop down and do it for them. Students who can scoop and bring food to their mouths no longer need one-to-one feeding assistance. Students who can turn on the radio can access a leisure skill by themselves without having to wait passively for another person to pay attention to them. The more steps students can do, the more actively they can participate in and control their own lives. Completing even a single step provides behaviors that lead to positive interactions with and positive reinforcement from other people.

Partial participation at the basic developmental skill level

At the most basic level, instruction focuses on teaching the student a basic developmental skill within the context of a specific step in the task (Gee et al., in press). These skills are both the developmental building blocks for higher level skills and skills that can have a functional effect in their own right (Sternberg et al., 1986). This level of partial participation is applicable to students in Characteristics Clusters 1, 3, and 5 and to most students in Characteristics Cluster 2, even though they have the motor ability to participate at the *step* level.

These basic developmental skills (BDSs) are the core of the curriculum process for the majority of students with profound disabilities. A listing of core BDSs is contained in Table 10.6. This list was developed through extensive literature review and classroom intervention and instruction (Logan et al., 1992).

The distinction between mastering a step or steps in a chain and mastering a basic developmental motor skill within the given step can be confusing.

TABLE 10.6. Core Basic Developmental Skills Listed by Developmental Domain

Developmental Domain	Basic Developmental Skills
Sensory	Focus, fixate, accommodate, converge, track, shift gaze, scan, track, detect sound, orient to sound
Motor	Control head, bear weight, cooperate in body movement, sit, change position in wheelchair, pull to stand, stand, have endurance, reach, grasp, hold, place, release, transfer, push, pull, twist, turn, roll, crawl, creep, cruise, walk, climb stairs, descend stairs, transfer in/out of wheelchair, be self-mobile in wheelchair
Social	Accept, calm, attend, acknowledge, show, interchange, initiate, explore, take turns, share
Cognitive	Change behavior when stimulated, attend, follow guided action, anticipate, demonstrate cause–effect, discriminate, make choice, make one-to-one correspondence, imitate, match, sort
Communication	Protest or reject, request attention to self, request object or action, request more, vocalize, make movement cues, make object cues, make touch cues, make gesture cues, use communication board, use manual sign, verbalize, follow directions

In general, it takes motor ability to complete a step in the task analysis. Completing a step leads to obtaining the functional effect of the step. For example, during a dressing task, at the BDS level, a student might be taught to reach, grasp, and hold his pants. He might not, however, be able to pull them up. The teacher would then provide hand-over-hand assistance to complete the step. But at the step level, the student would be taught to actually pull up his pants, thereby achieving the functional effect of the step. Using washing hands as another example, the student might be taught to reach and grasp the soap at the BDS level. At the step level, the student would be taught to actually pick up the soap.

Rationale for approach

The BDSs targeted for instruction are selected for five reasons. First, their mastery should lead to increased sensory, motor, social, cognitive, and communicative participation in the activities. This increased partial participation provides the student with choice and control over the environment, increases motor and sensory functioning, and provides access to social interaction with others. These increases have also been documented to have positive effects on caregivers, who then provide more opportunity to their children (Dunst et al., 1985). For example, a student might learn to activate a switch to turn on a favorite toy at school. The parents then could set up switches for the student at home to activate the radio, television, or blender. Another student may learn to hold onto a grocery cart during community-based instruction, and the parent then could take the student shopping.

A second reason for targeting certain BDSs is that mastery of these skills decreases the amount of time or effort caregivers must spend in caregiving activities. If a child learns to hold his or her mouth open during toothbrushing, the parent can more easily and thoroughly brush the child's teeth (Snell et al., 1989). If a child learns to hold his or her head at midline, then the father can more efficiently hold the cup for the child to drink.

Third, instruction on these BDSs increases the alertness levels of students and facilitates increased interaction with other people and objects in the environment (Belfiore, 1990; Green, Canipe, Gardner, & Reid, 1990). This increased alertness and participation in interactions improves the quality of life outcomes for students with profound disabilities (Borthwick-Duffy, 1990).

Fourth, mastery of these BDSs may enable the student to move into higher levels of partial participation, as these skills are the building blocks for completing steps in the chain. In many cases, however, learning and generalizing the BDSs are the primary objectives for students with severe motoric impairments.

Fifth, these BDSs occur across most activities in which students typically engage. Reach and grasp is a basic component of almost all motor skills.

Scanning from one item to another is the basic component in visual exploration of the environment and choice making. The teaching of the same BDS across multiple activities is also the foundation in training for generalization (Horner et al., 1986).

Defining Type of Partial Participation Within the Basic Developmental Skill Level

Most students with profound disabilities partially participate in activities at the BDS level using skills from one or more sensory, motor, cognitive, communicative, or social domains (Gee et al., in press). These areas typically follow the developmental domains from birth through 24 months (Sternberg et al., 1986). There is considerable overlap among the skills from these different domains, and boundaries between them may not always be clear. One person may describe an objective as social participation, whereas another may describe it as communicative. Therefore, the definitions of the types of partial participation that follow are given only as a general conceptual framework.

Sensory participation

In this type of partial participation, students learn to use their eyes and ears within the context of the activity. This participation can vary by degree. At a basic degree, students may open their eyes only when spoken to. At more advanced degrees, students may look at another person and smile or use their eyes to look from item to item in order to make a choice.

Motor participation

In this type of partial participation, students learn to use their bodies to manipulate objects and people in the environment. At a basic degree, students may reach in the direction of an object. At more advanced degrees, students may grasp an item and move it for play purposes or to obtain the functional effect of the item (e.g., holding a toothbrush while brushing teeth).

Mobility participation

In this type of partial participation, students learn to move from one location to another independently. At a basic degree, students may learn to roll over to access desired objects or be close to another person. At more advanced degrees, students may learn to use a walker to get to the bathroom or move their wheelchairs up to the table.

Cognitive participation

In this type of partial participation, students learn that their motor participation has an effect on *objects* in the environment. At a basic degree, students may learn to open their mouths when the caregiver touches their lips with a spoon full of food. At a higher degree, students may learn to activate a switch to turn on the radio. At the most advanced degree, students can learn relationships among objects, such as one-to-one correspondence or matching.

Communicative participation

In this type of partial participation, students learn that their sensory or motor participation has an effect on *other people.* At a basic degree, students learn that smiling leads to continued interaction with another person, or that raising an arm tells another person they want an activity to continue. At a more advanced degree, students learn that focusing on or pointing to an object tells another person they want the object.

Social participation

In this type of partial participation, students learn to engage in sensory, motor, mobility, or communicative behaviors that indicate the desire for, or continued pleasure in, interacting with another person. At a basic degree, students learn that eye contact with another person keeps that person communicating with them. At more advanced degrees, students may learn to activate a loop tape to ask another person for conversation.

Summary

In the activity-based model, teaching of instructional objectives always occurs within the context of an activity. The focus for the instructional objective can be at any of the three levels discussed above. The students may learn to complete a hygiene *task,* such as washing their hands, but need assistance in brushing teeth and hair. Alternatively, students with partially restricted physical abilities may complete only the *steps* of rubbing their hands together after the soap has been placed on them, and rinsing their hands while the caregiver returns the soap to the soap tray and turns off the water. Students with restricted use of their hands and limited vision may learn only the *basic developmental skills* of focusing on and reaching for and grasping the soap but need assistance in applying the soap to their hands. Students with minimal cognitive responses may learn only to look in the direction of the towel (anticipation) while the teacher reaches and grasps the towel and dries their hands.

ASSESSMENT FOR SELECTING ACTIVITIES FOR INSTRUCTION

The first step in designing an appropriate curriculum is to select the activities for instruction. The ideas for activities come from family interviews and ecological assessments of the school and the community. Family interviews are necessary because the family has primary caregiving responsibilities for the student in the current environment. Given the long-term dependency needs of the child, the family also has primary responsibility for the student in most future environments. School ecological assessments are important because school is the current location for most of the 6 hours of instruction the student receives. Selecting specific environments in the community is important because it highlights environments for instruction deemed important by the family, and for future environments in which students will participate in post–school settings.

Determining Valued Activities, Tasks, and Environments Through Family Assessment

Activities are clusters of tasks that result in functional outcomes. The value of an activity is a subjective judgment made by the student's family. This determination is often based upon the necessity or regularity of the activity, the enjoyment or reinforcement received by the family member, or enjoyment demonstrated by the student or attributed to the student by a family member. The expected outcomes from a family interview include the following:

1. A specificaton of current family activities in which the student is included.

2. A description of the extent of the student's participation in the activities.

3. A delineation of the family members with whom the student interacts in each activity.

4. The number and variety of environments in which the student participates.

5. A specification of the future activities and environments in which the family would value the student's participation.

6. A description of activities in which other family members participate that could be adapted to include the student.

The family interview should be conducted using a two-stage process. First, a list of family members should be developed. All questions for the interview should be provided on a written form and reviewed with these individuals. Family members would be expected to fill out the form following private family discussion and evaluation. Second, after the written responses are returned, a staff member should arrange a follow-up interview, during which time responses can be expanded and more fully described.

Following is a list of tasks that must be completed.

1. *List each activity or task in which the student is currently engaged.* Ask family members to list, in order, each activity in which the youngster is engaged from the time the family awakes until they go to sleep. It will be most helpful to have this information provided for each day of the week. However, asking the family to provide this information for weekdays in general, and separately for the weekend, will suffice as an initial response. For weekdays, information should include the regularly occurring morning activity for preparing to go to school, mealtimes, after-school leisure activities, evening activities such as television watching and playing with parents and siblings, and going to bed. For weekends, information should be provided about family activities in which the student is included when most or all family members are at home. These may include going to church and Sunday school, eating meals out, and visiting extended family members. As the staff begins looking at a broader scope of content, a similar analysis should focus on summer activities, such as going to the pool, lake, beach, sporting events, picnics, and camping trips.

2. *List who is engaged in each activity or task with the student.* Request that the person(s) engaged in each activity with the student be identified. Be sure to include those who are not members of the immediate family, such as extended relatives, babysitters, neighbors, and neighborhood children. During the follow-up interview, ask family members to describe what they do and what the youngster does in each activity. In addition, it is important to ask the following questions:

- Why is this person engaged in the activity with the student?

- What does this person enjoy about doing this activity with the student?

- Who initiates the activity? Does the student initiate any?

- If the student does, how do you know he or she is initiating it?

Answers to these questions will provide information concerning what it is the person finds reinforcing about doing the activity with the youngster and the extent of the student's current social network. These answers will also allow for a discussion and evaluation with the family of who else can become socially involved with the student.

3. *List the environments and subenvironments in which the activity or task takes place.* Write down the rooms or other locations (yard, car, neighbor or extended family homes, community) where the activities take place. The interviewer should note whether the activities are brought to the student or the student is taken to the place of occurrence. This provides an indication of the number of environments in which the student is involved. Identifying these environments will allow for an analysis of natural cues and consequences available for instruction.

4. *List the materials being used in each activity.* For each activity in which the student is engaged, ask the family to list the materials involved. The interviewer should note how much contact or interaction with the material the student has. This information will allow for determination of the natural materials that should be included within school instruction. In addition, it permits an assessment and discussion of age appropriateness and adaptations currently in use, or that could be developed, to increase student interaction with the materials.

5. *List time parameters.* List the approximate time an activity begins and ends. Family members, not the interviewer, should provide and set time blocks. The interviewer should try to obtain responses to the following questions, which will assist staff in targeting instructional objectives:

- Is an activity, due to lack of training, taking too long and, therefore, causing resentment or other problems with the flow of the family schedule?

- Are certain activities taking so long as to have the effect of isolating the parent from other family activities, family members, or personal hobbies?

- Are there long periods of down time in a student's schedule that could potentially cause behavior problems?

6. *List the activities or tasks in which other family members are engaged at these times and where they occur.* The goal is to determine those activities in which the student is not included that may be targeted for his or her future inclusion. For example, if the student is playing on the floor with stuffed toys while the sibling is playing video games, it may be possible to teach the student to partially participate in playing a video game with the sibling. This partial participation extends the student's range of social interactions and activities.

7. *Identify those parts of activities or tasks in which the student does not participate that, if participation were possible, would be helpful to the*

family member(s). This information provides an indication about the student's current level of partial participation, and possible instructional objectives to increase that level of participation in critical activities. The interviewer should ask questions such as the following:

- What is very difficult for you to accomplish with your youngster now (e.g., bathing, dressing, physical health procedures, eating)?

- What could your youngster learn to do during that activity that would make it easier for you to complete the activity?

- What could your youngster learn to do in any given activity that would make your or your other children's day easier to manage?

8. *Identify activities or tasks in which the student does not engage but in which the family would like him or her to be included.* The family is asked to provide information about objectives that go beyond the student's current functioning. The goal is to determine where the family wants instruction to go from here, how instruction can help the family provide more opportunities for the child, how instruction can expand student inclusion into current activities, and how the student's involvement in the family social network can be enhanced. These activities often include environments within the community and can, therefore, be used as critical components for community-based instructional programs. At this juncture, the interviewer should be trying to determine additional information, such as

- What are the student's strengths?

- Which of these strengths can be expanded into additional activities?

- What does the student do that the family members view as "good" (e.g., fun, skillful)?

- What activities does the student seem to enjoy doing?

- How does the family determine that the student is enjoying an activity?

- What times during the day do parents need additional assistance (e.g., when cooking, after dinner)?

Conducting an Ecological Analysis of the School and Community

At the same time that the family interview process is taking place, a further analysis should be made of the school and community environment. The process is called an *ecological analysis,* and first involves the identification of relevant *environments* (Snell & Grigg, 1988); that is, those locations in which students currently function and those in which they may be expected to function in the future. These include both current and future school locations (i.e., elementary, junior, and senior high schools). In the later grades, when the child is an adolescent, future environments are determined by the student's transition committee as they target those locations in which he or she will live and recreate following graduation (see Chapter 13). In community settings, these environments include places the family currently takes the student, and those to which they would like to take him or her if certain changes in the student's behavior were to come about. These would include the grocery and convenience stores, clothing stores, restaurants, swimming pools, and parks.

Environments selected should be those that have importance to the student's current and future quality of life. For these students, these locations would be ones that provide the student with the opportunity to learn and live in integrated locations, and to extend their social networks. Therefore, environments selected should provide opportunities for interaction with nondisabled individuals, especially nondisabled peers. This means increasing the number of locations within the regular school campus in which these students participate, and the number of locations in the community in which family members are willing and comfortable to take them.

The second step in an ecological analysis is to divide environments into *subenvironments.* In the school, teachers have traditionally taken students to a variety of subenvironments, including the cafeteria, library, playground, office, bathrooms (integrated and segregated), home living suite, clinic, teachers' lounge, school building and grounds, and the immediate neighborhood. Educators should make efforts to integrate students into other subenvironments in order to provide increased contact with nondisabled peers and to conduct functional instruction. These include the gym, home economics lab, shop classes, and regular education classes. In the community, typical subenvironments include aisles of grocery or clothing stores, cashier locations, tables or booths at restaurants, seating areas at bowling alleys, and swingsets or picnic tables at parks.

The third step is to determine what *activities* within these subenvironments can currently be used or developed for use for active student involvement. It is important to determine if there is a match between the student's assessed instructional needs and these activities within the subenvironments. Identification of appropriate activities takes observation and creativity. This process for community settings has been discussed extensively by Falvey (1989). The ecological assessment process for the school has not been as extensively discussed. Therefore, an example of a school activity selection process is described in Table 10.7.

TABLE 10.7. Activity Analysis of School Subenvironments

Subenvironment	What Peers Currently Do that Students Could Do	Activities Others Do that Students Could Do	Teacher-Created Activities
Cafeteria	Eat with peers Clean cafeteria Bus dishes	Prepare trays Hand out milk Collect lunch tickets Collect money Sell ice cream Wash and stack dishes	Pass out napkins Pass out silverware Pour Wrap silverware in napkins
Library	Participate in storytime Check out books, records, tapes, filmstrips Browse magazines Socialize	Shelve books Dust books and shelves Arrange chairs Insert cards in books Magnetize and demagnetize books Stamp date Vacuum (carpet sweeper)	Water plants Clean windows Clean TV screen
Playground	Play with peers Learn to use equipment	Pick up trash Rake	Plant flowers Collect equipment Pass out equipment
Office	Take messages to office staff Interact socially	Collect attendance sheets Collect lunch money Photocopy Put messages in box Collate Dust	Staple and collate Stuff envelopes Deliver mail to teachers from their boxes
Bathrooms	Wash hands Comb and fix hair Toileting	Fill paper towels Fill soap dispenser Replace toilet paper Mop Empty wastepaper basket	Clean mirrors
Clinic	Take medication Socialize with nurse–volunteer	Clean Strip and make bed Wash linens Stock supplies	Roll ace bandages
Building and grounds		Rake Collect trash on grounds Clean windows Empty trash cans Plant Weed	Collect pencils to sharpen Recycle (include cans from all classes) Buy materials when on community-based instruction

(continued)

TABLE 10.7. *Continued*

Subenvironment	What Peers Currently Do that Students Could Do	Activities Others Do that Students Could Do	Teacher-Created Activities
Home economics or home living	Cook Clean Do laundry Socialize	Perform custodial cleaning chores Launder cafeteria items Load and unload dishwasher	Prepare snacks Prepare lunches for community-based instruction outings or field trips
Music class or band	Stack and carry instruments Play music	Clean music stands Arrange music stands	Pass out music folders Put records back in jackets Put cassette tapes in holders
Art class	Paint Clay sculpture Draw Glue Cut	Pass out supplies Collect supplies Clean brushes Clean tables Sweep floor Arrange supplies on shelves	Hang things on bulletin boards Stir paint Fill paint, glue, and water bottles
Gym	Participate in Sports Exercise/warm-ups Aerobics Attend pep rally	Clean bleachers Sweep floor Clean equipment	Collect equipment Pass out equipment
Regular education classroom	Participate in Unit activities Storytime Hands-on learning activities (e.g., nature) Field trips Assemblies Lunch Recreation/leisure/play Attend art, music, etc. Socialize		Participate in tutoring by peers Partially participate in various activities

ASSESSMENT FOR DEVELOPING INSTRUCTIONAL OBJECTIVES

The next major step in designing an appropriate curriculum is to assess student functioning within selected activities. This task includes the assessment of the *level* and *type* of partial participation. In addition, instructional objectives based on this assessment must be integrated (matrixed) across the activities.

Rationale for Assessment of Level and Type of Partial Participation for Instructional Objectives

Assessment of instructional objectives always occurs within the context of the activities selected. This is done for three reasons. First, the activities are the avenue for participation with persons without disabilities. Second, teaching the same basic developmental skills or similar steps in a task across multiple activities promotes generalization. Third, students with profound disabilities often demonstrate inconsistent responding to reinforcers. Therefore, motivation for participation must typically be intrinsic to the activity, materials, or persons engaging in the activity with the student.

Assessment can occur across any of the three *levels* of partial participation discussed above: assessment to decide which task(s) to teach, assessment to decide which step(s) to teach, and assessment to decide which basic developmental skill(s) to teach. If assessment occurs at the BDS level, the teacher must also assess which *type* of partial participation to emphasize within each activity: sensory, motor, mobility, cognitive, communicative, or social.

Assessment for Determining Basic Developmental Skills for Instruction

Most students with profound disabilities partially participate at the basic developmental skill level. This is due primarily to the presence of a physical disability and/or cognitive deficit. Students from Characteristics Clusters 1, 2, 3, and 5 are typical candidates for this level of partial participation. The purpose of assessment is to target basic developmental skills that will increase students' (a) competence in motor, cognitive, or sensory components of the task; (b) ability to control their environment and make choices; (c) levels of communicative or social interaction with other persons engaging in the task; and (d) enjoyment in participating in the activity.

Assessment to determine the level or type of partial participation comprises seven steps:

1. Observe the student in targeted activities and record performance.

2. Discuss the student's performance with caregivers, family members, previous teachers, related services personnel, nondisabled peers, and adults at school, and revise conclusions if necessary.

3. Develop and prioritize instructional objectives from your observations.

4. Write instructional objectives.

5. Develop an instructional matrix integrating the instructional objectives and the activities.

6. Select an instructional strategy to teach the objectives.

7. Develop a data collection process to monitor student performance.

Observe the student

Students with profound disabilities have inconsistent responses to objects and people, both within and across activities. Therefore, the teacher must teach and observe the student across materials, people, environments, and times of the day. This teaching and observation typically takes 2 to 3 weeks. The teacher should systematically prompt the student through the steps in the activity (see Chapter 9 for prompt and prompt sequence options).

Figure 10.1 illustrates an assessment sheet for 23 BDSs. Using this type of device, the teacher records the student's response on each BDS for the steps in the task. This assessment is not done step-by-step for each task, as that would be too time-consuming. Rather, the teacher reviews the student's general responses across the steps in the task for each activity. In this case, the type of response is specified in the "Response" column of the assessment form and is based on the definitions that follow:

- *Generalized (G).* If the skill is performed independently (with no teacher prompts) across two or more tasks about 80% of the time, the teacher records a "G." Independent performance is also credited if an adaptation has been made. In the comments section, the teacher should note in which tasks the student performs the skill.

- *Specific (S).* If the skill is performed independently in only one task about 80% of the time, the teacher records an "S." In the space provided for comments, the teacher should record for which task the student performs the skill.

- *Inconsistent (IN).* If the skill is independently performed less than 80% of the time, the teacher should record an "IN." The teacher should also note whether the skill is inconsistently performed across two or more tasks (ING) or only one task (INS). Again, the teacher should note the level of inconsistency and in which task or tasks the skill is inconsistently performed.

- *Prompted (P).* If the student performs the skill across two or more tasks if given a prompt less than hand-over-hand (verbal, gestural, model, etc.), then the teacher should record a "P." If the student

Asessing Basic Developmental Skills

Student	Response	Comments/Notes
A. VISION		
1. Focus and fixate		
2. Accommodate/converge		
3. Track		
4. Shift gaze		
5. Scan		
B. AUDITORY		
6. Detect		
7. Orient		
C. MOTOR BODY CONTROL		
8. Head control		
9. Weight bearing		
10. Cooperative body movement		
11. Sitting		
12. Self-position change in wheelchair		
13. Pull to stand		
14. Standing		
15. Endurance		
D. FINE-MOTOR MANIPULATION		
16. Reach		
17. Grasp		
18. Hold		
19. Placement		
20. Release		
21. Transfer		
22. Push		
23. Pull		

Figure 10.1. Assessment form for basic developmental skills.

performs the skill with the prompt in only one task, a "PS" should be recorded. The teacher should note what prompt occasions the skill and in which tasks the prompted skill is performed.

- *Full Physical Guidance (F).* The teacher should mark an "F" if he or she must provide hand-over-hand assistance for the student to perform the skill. The teacher should also note if he or she must provide full physical guidance in all tasks (FG) or only in a specific task (FS). For the latter case, the teacher should record which task requires full guidance. The teacher should also note if more physical control is necessary in some tasks than in others. The use of more control may indicate that the student is "protesting" participation in that task. Some BDSs, such as focusing, are difficult if not impossible to prompt with full physical guidance.

- *Not applicable (N).* If staff believe that the student does not have the motoric or sensory abilities to learn the skill, then the teacher should record an "N." This should be used with caution and restricted to the motor and sensory domains. It should also be based on medical or well-documented experiential evidence.

Discuss the student's response with others

As described above, students with profound disabilities perform skills inconsistently. It may be that the student consistently or inconsistently displays a BDS for various steps in a sequence for a parent or peer but not for the teacher. The teacher should review observational data with parents, siblings, previous teachers, nondisabled peers, related services personnel, and any other adults with whom the student has contact. It is important to note and discuss any differences between those observations and reports from others. These differences provide valuable information as to whether the student has learned a skill but may not have generalized it to other people, materials, or environments.

Prioritize skills for instruction

After the assessment is completed, the teacher and caregivers should prioritize 8 to 16 BDSs for instructional objectives. Various factors (see Table 10.8) should be considered in this process. These factors are not necessarily hierarchical.

Write instructional objectives

As previously noted, basic developmental skills are conceptually organized by developmental curricular domains. However, instruction in these skills should occur across age-appropriate activities identified within traditional functional domains (e.g., domestic, recreation and leisure, community, and vocational). The instructional objective becomes the format that blends together the developmental and functional curriculum concepts. As with all

TABLE 10.8. Prioritizing Basic Developmental Skills Within a Step for Instruction

1. Motor skills that increase competence in motor steps of the task, that provide range of motion and stretching, and that prevent muscle and structural deterioration.

2. Skills that increase the student's social and communicative interactions with others (choice making, expressing preferences).

3. Skills that, if mastered, would decrease the amount of time and effort caregivers spend in health, hygiene, transfer, and mobility tasks.

4. Skills that occur across multiple activities and environments, especially community environments.

5. Skills that, if mastered, would lead to increased participation in activities engaged in by family members or peers without disabilities in which the student does not presently participate.

6. Skills that are *inconsistently* performed across materials, people, or environments. The inconsistent performance may indicate a difficulty with motivation, generalization, or maintenance rather than acquisition.

7. Skills that are performed with prompts that are less than full physical guidance. This prompted performance may indicate that the student is beginning to learn the skill.

8. Skills that may be functionally equivalent to undesired behaviors.

9. Skills that, if mastered, would increase the perception of competence by persons without disabilities.

10. Skills for which sufficient time, materials, and access to appropriate environments can be allocated so that the skills can be taught.

instructional objectives, conditions, behaviorial terms, criteria for mastery, and generalization should be included. Criteria for mastery may include *acquisition* (initial learning of the skill), *fluency* (how quickly or efficiently the student does the skill), *generalization* (performance of the skill across multiple people, materials, or locations), or *maintenance* (can the student continue to do the skill over time). Criteria may also include decreases in level of prompt needed, latency between cue and prompt, or independent performance. Objectives are typically written to reflect the performance of the BDS across multiple functional activities. Illustrations of sample objectives in which only basic developmental skills are stressed can be seen for Student A in Table 10.9. (Students B and C, who are introduced in the figure, are discussed in later sections.)

Develop an instructional matrix

The objectives written after assessment typically cover more than one developmental domain and are taught across multiple activities. For example, during a snack activity, the student may have a cognitive or communicative objective (choose which food to eat), a visual objective (focus on the spoon), a motor objective (reach and grasp the spoon), an eating objective (chewing with rotary action), and a social objective (waiting his or her turn for the pudding). During a laundry activity, the student may have some of

TABLE 10.9. Sample Short-Term Objectives

Student A: Each objective at a basic developmental skills level

- Les will turn his head to the side at which a teacher or peer is talking for 80% of the trials for 5 consecutive days.
- Les will relax the part of his body the teacher touches and stay relaxed while she moves that body part to complete a task for four tasks for 5 consecutive days.
- Les will fixate on the spoon being brought from the plate to his mouth during snack and lunch on 80% of the opportunities given to him for 5 consecutive days.
- During three activities (leisure time, snack preparation, can crushing), Les will move his arm to pull a switch when given the touch cue "pull" (teacher touches his elbow) for 80% of the trials for each activity for 5 consecutive days.

Student B: One objective at a step level and one at a basic developmental skill level

- Given three situations on a daily basis (after morning snack, prior to lunch, after vocational cleaning) when the task of washing her hands is required, Cindy will perform the steps of "turning" on the water, "placing" her hands under running water, and "reaching" for a towel to dry her hands, all at the gestural prompt level, for four of five opportunities for each step, over 5 consecutive days.
- Given situations in the classroom and community when Cindy is moving away more than 5 feet from the appropriate place, she will respond by stopping and remaining in place to teacher or adult verbal directions of "stop," "wait," or "no" within a 5-second period for each command, on 8 of 10 consecutive opportunities.

Student C: One objective at a total task level

- Given five opportunities per day, Frank will complete all steps in his dressing task analysis, with only verbal assistance, on 75% of the opportunities given to him for 3 consecutive weeks.

---

the same objectives: a cognitive or communicative objective (choose to do the wash or to dry), a visual objective (focus on the item to be picked up), and a motor objective (reach and grasp the laundry item). The student may also have more than one objective from the same developmental domain.

Given that students are typically instructed in multiple objectives across multiple activities throughout the day, it is important to provide some systematic organization to these efforts. This is done through the use of a *matrix*. In the matrix, the activities are usually listed across the top. The objectives are listed on the left side of the form. For each activity, the teacher notes in the corresponding space which objectives are targeted for instruction within that activity. The instructional matrix for Student A is contained in Figure 10.2. The matrix serves as both a schedule and a visual reminder of the objectives targeted for instruction. If the space is used to record the student's performance, it can also serve as a data collection sheet. Clarity on which skills are targeted for which steps and in which activities is crucial. Without this clarity, teachers run the risk of merely putting students through the activities with limited or no instructional focus.

Objective	Arrival	Can Crushing	Snack Prep	Hygiene	CBI	Hygiene	Lunch	Leisure	Room Clean-up	Hygiene	Departure
1. Focus on object	X	X	X	X	X	X	X	X	X	X	X
2. Detect sound	X	X	X	X	X	X	X	X	X	X	X
3. Cooperative body movement	X		X	X		X	X			X	X
4. Pull		X	X					X			
5. Attend	X	X	X	X	X	X	X	X	X	X	X
6. Make eye contact	X	X	X	X	X	X	X	X	X	X	X
7. Receptive communication–touch		X	X					X			
8. Shape head turn			X	X		X	X	X		X	

Figure 10.2. Instructional matrix for Student A. CBI = community-based instruction. *X indicates that the objective is targeted for instruction within that activity.

Select an instructional strategy

For each objective, the teacher must select an instructional strategy. These strategies include both prompting and reinforcement procedures (see Chapter 9).

Select a data collection form

Although the matrix can also function as a data collection sheet, teachers may prefer to use a separate data collection sheet for each activity or objective. A sample data sheet for Student A is provided in Figure 10.3. The reader is referred to Chapter 9 for a discussion of data collection options.

Assessment for Determining the Step or Steps for Instruction

Many students with profound disabilities have adequate motor skills to learn to independently perform a complete step or steps in the task. These students typically have adequate use of their arms and hands and can interact motorically with objects. These students are primarily from Characteristics Clusters 4 and 2, with a few from Characteristics Cluster 6. They usually have generalized responses across all or most basic developmental skills when assessed at the BDS level. If an inconsistent motor response is found, it usually is a function of motivation or lack of generalization rather than ability. Students may also have mastered the BDSs for a given step, but they fail to appropriately sequence and perform those skills within a given step.

The purpose of assessment at the step level is threefold: to target specific skill steps, which if mastered, will increase the student's level of independent functioning in completing or engaging in the task; to provide information on how to decrease the amount of caregiving time that will be necessary; and to develop ideas on how to increase the student's interactions with nondisabled peers. Through the assessment process, the teacher can target a single step, nonsequential steps in the chain, or two or more sequential steps in the chain for instruction. This process is basically the same as a "discrepancy analysis" (Ford & Mirenda, 1984) used with students with severe disabilities. An operational sequence similar to the one suggested for specifying basic developmental skills should be used in this assessment process.

Observe the student

The teacher should write or use an existing general task analysis for each task. In observing and prompting a student through the steps in a sequence,

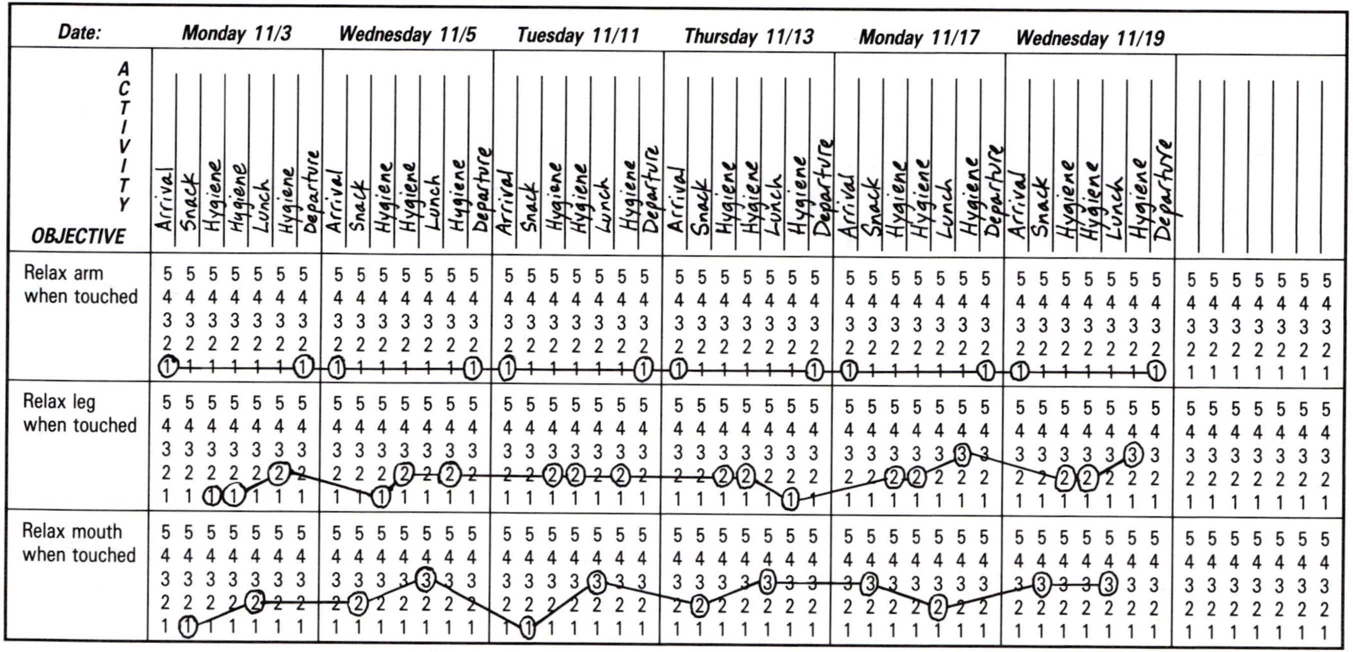

1 = Full physical guidance
2 = Partial physical guidance
3 = Gestural prompt
4 = Verbal prompt
5 = Independent performance

Figure 10.3. Sample data sheet for Student A. *Graph interpretation:* On Monday, the teacher recorded a full physical guidance prompt once during arrival and once during departure for the basic developmental skill of "relax arm when touched." The teacher did not take data on that skill for the other activities. For the basic developmental skill of "relax leg when touched," the teacher recorded full physical guidance for the first and second hygiene activities and partial assistance for the third hygiene activity. She did not record data for that skill for the other activities. For the basic developmental skill of "relax mouth when touched," the teacher recorded full physical guidance for the snack activity and partial physical guidance for lunch. The teacher recorded this data point for the first trial of the activity.

the teacher should record the student's response for each step using the following descriptions:

- *Independent Performance (I).* If the step is performed independently (with no teacher prompts) about 80% of the time, the teacher records an "I." Independent performance is also credited if an adaptation has been made.

- *Inconsistent Independent Performance (IN).* If the step is independently performed less than approximately 80% of the time, the teacher should record an "IN." The teacher should note whether the inconsistency varies by time of day or from day to day, or is correlated with other medication or alertness variability.

- *Prompted (P).* If the student performs the step if given a prompt less than full physical guidance (hand-over-hand), the teacher should record a "P." The teacher should note which prompt enables the student to complete the step and should record "PIN" if the prompt inconsistently enables the student to perform the step.

- *Full Physical Guidance (F).* The teacher should mark an "F" if he or she must provide hand-over-hand assistance for the student to complete the step. The teacher should also note if he or she must provide more physical control on this step than other steps used in other tasks. The use of more control may indicate that the student is "protesting" participation in that step.

- *Between-Step Prompt (SP).* The teacher should also note if the student can complete the step once a prompt is given for the student to initiate the step. It was noted above that many students with profound disabilities do not perform steps in a row for a given task even though they have the motor ability to do so. Finding sequential steps that the student can independently perform is a high priority for instruction.

Discuss the student's performance with others

The teacher should review his or her discrepancy analysis with the caregivers, previous teachers, and related services personnel in the school. These informants should report the student's performance for each step across the five performance levels (I, IN, P, F, SP). Differences in the informants' reports of the student's performance, as compared with the teacher's, should be noted as this gives valuable information as to acquisition and generalization of the steps in the task analysis. As with BDS assessment, each informant's report should be considered reliable.

Prioritize steps or sequences of steps

The step(s) targeted for instruction are typically specific to each task because they are based on different task analyses. Prioritizing step(s) targeted for instruction within each activity should be based on nine criteria (see Table 10.10). As with the priority criteria for establishing BDSs, these criteria are not necessarily hierarchical. We suggest targeting from three to eight steps per task. Examples of prioritized step objectives for Student B (introduced in Table 10.9) are contained in Table 10.11.

Write instructional objectives

For students at the step level, instructional objectives are typically written more like objectives for students with severe disabilities. The difference is that the objective is written to indicate mastery of some, but not all, of the steps in the task. Even though these students display higher level motor skills, it is still not anticipated that they will independently perform all the steps in the task. Objectives can be written to reflect acquisition, fluency, generalization, or maintenance of the step. In addition, criteria may reflect a less intrusive prompt or reduced latency in performing the step. An example of a combination of one step and one basic developmental skill objective for Student B can be found in Table 10.9 (see section below titled "Students with Objectives from Both BDS and Step Levels").

The objectives to master steps in a task are not typically matrixed as with BDSs because they are specific to certain tasks. However, the activity

---

TABLE 10.10.   Prioritizing Motor Step(s) Within a Task for Instruction

1. Steps in which the student's performance is independent but inconsistent.
2. Steps that the student can complete with a prompt of less than full physical guidance.
3. Steps that, if mastered, would decrease the amount or intensity of caregiving time.
4. Steps whose functional effects are seen as valued by persons without disabilities and that, if mastered, would lead to perceptions of increased competence and greater inclusion in integrated activities.
5. Sequential steps in the task analysis that the student can complete independently if prompted to begin the step.
6. Steps that are critical to obtaining the functional effect of the task.
7. Steps that are motorically similar across multiple tasks (i.e., opening the refrigerator door; opening the microwave door; opening the car door; wiping the lunch table; wiping the lap tray; clearing the table after lunch, after a vocational task, or after playing a game with a nondisabled peer).
8. Steps that can be independently performed if an adaptation is made.
9. Steps for which sufficient time, materials, and access to appropriate environments can be allocated so that the steps can be taught.

TABLE 10.11. Priority Objectives for Student B and Student C

Student B (at the independent level unless indicated otherwise)

1. Hang coat on hook upon arrival in the morning (with gestural prompts).
2. Push button to start a tape recorder and share music experience with a peer during leisure time.
3. Hold various objects for the duration of their functional use (brush, deodorant, Chapstick, hand lotion, tissues).
4. Remain standing for the course of vocational and domestic activities (sweeping, wiping tables, can crushing, laundry, shopping).
5. Complete three steps in washing and drying hands before and after various activities (with verbal prompts).
6. Enter restroom, pull down pants, and sit on toilet.
7. Respond to one-word teacher commands: "stop," "wait," "no."
8. Indicate anticipation by starting the next motor component of the tasks of making toast and mixing a drink for a snack.

Student C (at the independent level)

1. Dress self for art and after toileting.
2. Wash hands.
3. Brush teeth.
4. Feed self.
5. Ride tricycle.
6. Roller skate.
7. Select music and activate tape recorder.
8. Make choice during snack, lunch, and art through use of picture cards.

schedule for the day is still used to structure the instructional flow according to natural sequences.

Select an instructional strategy

For each step targeted for instruction, the teacher should select an appropriate instructional strategy. These strategies include both prompting and reinforcement procedures (see Chapter 9).

Select a data collection form

As with all instruction, teachers should record student performance data. For each task within a scheduled activity for which the student has objectives, the teacher has a separate data sheet noting the steps targeted for instruction. An example of a data sheet reflecting targeted step(s) for instruction for Student B is provided in Figure 10.4. The reader is referred to Chapter 9 for a discussion of data collection options.

P L A C E & D A T E	M 8/18	M 10/19	L 10/19	L 10/20	Vo 10/21	M 10/21								
OBJECTIVE: *Washing Hands*														

STEPS:

grasp handle and turn on water

I	I	I	I	I	I	I	I	I	I	I	I	I	I
V	V	V	V	V	V	V	V	V	V	V	V	V	V
G	G	G	(G)—(G)—(G)			G	G	G	G	G	G	G	G
P	(P)—(P)		P	P	P	P	P	P	P	P	P	P	P
(F)	F	F	F	F	F	F	F	F	F	F	F	F	F

place hands under running water

I	I	I	I	I	I	I	I	I	I	I	I	I	I
V	V	V	V	V	V	V	V	V	V	V	V	V	V
G	(G)	G	G	(G)	G	G	G	G	G	G	G	G	G
P	P	(P)—(P)		P	(P)	P	P	P	P	P	P	P	P
(F)	F	F	F	F	F	F	F	F	F	F	F	F	F

reach for paper towel

I	I	I	I	I	I	I	I	I	I	I	I	I	I
V	V	V	V	(V)	V	V	V	V	V	V	V	V	V
G	G	(G)—(G)		G	(G)	G	G	G	G	G	G	G	G
(P)—(P)		P	P	P	P	P	P	P	P	P	P	P	P
F	F	F	F	F	F	F	F	F	F	F	F	F	F

F = Full physical guidance	I = Independent performance
P = Partial physical guidance	M = Morning snack
G = Gestural prompt	L = Lunch
V = Verbal prompt	Vo = Vocational activity

Figure 10.4. Sample data sheet for Student B. *Graph interpretation:* On 10/18 during morning snack, the teacher recorded a full physical guidance prompt for the step of "grasp handle and turn on water." On 10/19 during morning snack, she recorded a partial physical guidance prompt for the same step for both morning snack and lunch. On 10/20, she recorded a gestural prompt for that step during lunch. On 10/21, she recorded a gestural prompt for that step during both the snack and the vocational activity.

Students with Objectives from Both BDS and Step Levels

Many students with profound disabilities will have objectives at both BDS and step levels. In these cases, a matrix should be developed for objectives from the BDS level and separate task analytic data sheets for the targeted step(s). This dual level of partial participation often occurs with students who have skill steps targeted for instruction in eating and hygiene tasks, such as scooping or flushing a toilet, which do not occur across multiple activities. However, they still have basic developmental skills, such as reach and grasp or focus, which occur not only during those eating and hygiene routines, but also across other activities. These students most typically are in Characteristics Clusters 2 and 4 and have functional use of their arms and hands.

Assessment for Determining Tasks Within Activities for Instruction

All students in Characteristics Cluster 6 and some students in Characteristics Cluster 4 may be able to learn a complete task within an activity. For example, these students may learn to wash their hands, not only the steps of turning on the water and soaping their hands. They may learn to put on their pants, not only pull them up. It may be necessary to make adaptations in how these students complete the task independently. For example, they may be independent in putting on sweatpants, but not in putting on jeans due to the difficulty of hooking the belt. They may be able to pour juice from a container into a glass, but only when using a certain type of container.

The important point to remember is that these students may learn to complete all the steps in the task if adaptations are made. Therefore, all steps in the task are targeted for instruction and/or adaptation. For these students, task selection following a standard ecological assessment (Snell & Grigg, 1988) is the critical dimension of the curriculum process.

Conduct an ecological inventory

An ecological inventory should be completed based on procedures developed for use with students with severe disabilities. This involves delineating environments, subenvironments, and activities within each subenvironment.

Prioritize tasks

Once the activities are selected, tasks within them should be listed. Teachers and parents should then prioritize tasks for instruction based on nine criteria (Table 10.12). Once again, these criteria are not hierarchical. Prioritized tasks for Student C (introduced in Table 10.9) are contained in Table 10.11.

TABLE 10.12. Prioritizing Tasks Within Activities for Instruction

1. Tasks selected as critical by the caregiver. Mastery of these tasks will typically lead to decreases in caregiving time.

2. Tasks deemed important by the teacher for functioning in current and future environments.

3. Tasks that will bring the student into interaction with nondisabled persons and are viewed as valuable by persons without disabilities. Mastery of these tasks will lead to the perception of increased competence.

4. Tasks that will serve as sources of positive reinforcement to replace undesired behaviors that presently secure reinforcement.

5. Tasks needed to function independently as an adult in normalized community environments.

6. Tasks for which sufficient time, materials, and access to appropriate environments can be allocated so that the tasks can be taught.

7. Tasks that are age appropriate.

8. Tasks that the student prefers.

9. If independently completing the task involves safety concerns, then teachers must decide if the task can be taught to a criterion that ensures that the student will not suffer an injury in performing the task.

Conduct a discrepancy analysis

The purpose of a discrepancy analysis is to target the steps in the task that need instruction so that the student can complete the task. This analysis sets the stage for a decision-making process in which one determines whether to teach a step or make an adaptation in the step. For each step, the teacher should record the student's response using the same abbreviations described under the section titled "Assessment for Determining the Step or Steps for Instruction." As with assessment for the BDS and step levels, the teacher should discuss the student's response with others and note any differences in student performance for the steps in the task analysis.

Make adaptations and develop alternative performance strategies

Many students with profound disabilities can be task independent if adaptations are made. Because the outcome is for the student to be independent, adaptations should always be considered and implemented. If appropriate, they can be faded later. Most adaptations for students with profound disabilities, however, are permanent. One way to tell if an adaptation is needed is to analyze student performance data. If the student is making no progress on one step while he or she is making progress on others, then an adaptation for that step should be considered. Based on previous experience, caregivers or previous teachers may know that the student had never mastered a similar step on other tasks. In that case, also, an adaptation should be considered. If the student has a documented physical or sensory disability that would prevent mastery of the step, an adaptation should also be made.

Write instructional objectives

Objectives for these students are written across functional domains, reflect mastery of the task, and are similar to objectives for students with severe disabilities. Generalization is addressed by specifying where and when the activity takes place. The activity schedule for the day is still used to structure the instructional flow. For each scheduled activity, the student will have a task targeted for instruction (refer to Table 10.9 for a description of a sample objective written at the task level for Student C).

Select an instructional strategy

For each task targeted for instruction, the teacher should select an appropriate instructional strategy. This includes both prompting and reinforcement strategies (see Chapter 9).

Select a data collection form

Once again, teachers should record student performance data. An example of a data sheet reflecting anticipation of task mastery for Student C is provided in Figure 10.5.

Students with Objectives from Both Step and Task Levels

A few students with profound disabilities will have objectives at the step and task levels. If that is the case, a task analytic sheet targeting the step(s) for instruction will be used for the step objectives and a complete task analytic data sheet will be used for the task level objectives.

STUDENTS FOR WHOM ACTIVITY-BASED CURRICULUM AND INSTRUCTION IS PROBLEMATIC

Within the category of students with profound disabilities, there appears to be some for whom the downward extension of functional, activity-based curriculum is problematic (Logan et al., 1992). Appropriateness of a functional curriculum for some students with profound disabilities has also been questioned by Guess (1989). These students can all be described as having minimal cognitive responses, restricted use of their extremities in combination with either asleep or agitated alertness levels (see Chapter 4), and/or chronic or

Objective: Dressing

STEPS	9/14	9/17	9/21	9/24	9/26	10/1	10/5	10/8	10/12	10/15	10/19	10/22	10/26	10/29	11/2
15.															
14.															
13.															
12.															
11.															
10.															
9.															
8.															
7.															
6.															
5. Buckle belt	P	P	G	P	P	G	G	G	G	P	G	G	P	G	G
4. Zip	F	P	F	F	F	P	P	F	F	P	F	P	P	P	P
3. Place shirt in pants	F	F	F	F	P	F	P	F	F	F	P	F	F	F	F
2. Stand up and pull pants to waist	P	P	P	G	G	G	P	G	G	G	I	G	G	I	G
1. Bend and grasp pants top	G	G	P	G	P	G	V	I	G	I	I	I	I	I	I
DATES =															

F = Full physical guidance   V = Verbal prompt
P = Partial physical guidance   I = Independent performance
G = Gestural prompt

Figure 10.5. Sample data sheet for Student C. *Graph interpretation:* On 9/14, the teacher recorded the following prompts for the steps in the task analysis that were being taught: Gestural for "bend and grasp pants top"; partial physical guidance for "stand up and pull pants to waist"; full physical guidance for "place shirt in pants"; full physical guidance for "zip"; and partial physical guidance for "buckle belt." Over time, the student made progress for the step of "bend and grasp pants top" until able to perform that step independently. However, limited progress was made on Step 3 ("place shirt in pants") as only a few less intrusive prompts were given over the 2-month period.

routine health care needs (see Chapter 8). In addition to this combination of multiple disabilities, several behavioral descriptions can be made about these students that can assist teachers in differentiating these students from other students with profound disabilities for whom activity-based curriculum is appropriate.

First, these are students whose alertness levels do not significantly improve with appropriate stimulation via systematic instruction within age-appropriate activities. Second, these students' partial participation in functional activities can be achieved only through intensive and continual hand-over-hand instruction. In spite of this intensive and systematic full guidance, these students demonstrate little or no change in affect that would indicate enjoyment in the task or awareness that they are partially participating. Third, their acquisition of basic developmental skills within the activity-based curriculum appears to be minimal or nonexistent. Fourth, these students require high levels of teacher time for maintenance of their health care, nutritional, and structural positioning needs. Fifth, teachers have reported that these students require high levels of nurturing, calming, and touching or holding (Thompson & Guess, 1989). Sixth, because these students typically have internal control over their alertness (Guess et al., 1988), their receptivity to instruction is determined by their internal schedule and not by the teacher's activity schedule. Therefore, teachers must be alert and ready to provide contingent stimulation based on the child's alertness and receptivity rather than a predetermined schedule.

This type of intensive, physical, emotional, and one-to-one instructional demand on the teacher leads to difficulties in implementing activity-based curriculum. It is difficult to provide instruction to these students in heterogeneous groups and engage them in community- and activity-based formats without such approaches adversely affecting the instructional time for other students in the group. Unfortunately, the usual result is that a small, homogeneous class is established for students with complex and multiple disabilities. This classroom model is not considered optimal, but it appears to be a reality in many systems due to staffing restrictions, budgetary constraints, and health and safety considerations. Under no circumstances, however, should these classes be in segregated environments. These students still can profit from planned and continual social interactions with students without disabilities. Our belief is that a decision to include a student in Characteristics Cluster 7 and to develop an alternative curriculum approach should be made *only after* the student's inclusion in activity-based curriculum has failed to show positive student outcomes.

Establishing an Alternative Curriculum Framework

Even though these students have shown minimal or nonexistent progress under an activity-based curriculum, the proposed, alternative curriculum structure should still have components of systematic instruction. First, the intervention should be active. In other words, the teacher should still expect some type of response from the student. Second, the intervention should be contingency based. The teacher should try to teach students that their behaviors have an effect on other people and objects in the environment. Therefore, an instructional paradigm favoring active, contingency-based programming over passive, sensory stimulation programs is an absolute necessity (Utley, Duncan, Strain, & Scanlon, 1983).

A third component of the alternative curriculum framework is the use of systematic and data-based interventions. A data-based program should include not only the specific configuration of the student's response, but a specification of the following: the type of intervention attempted; the location, materials, people, and time of day; the frequency, duration, and intensity of the intervention; and the amount of systematic, contingency-based instruction provided. Anecdotal records should also be maintained. Without a correlation among teaching variables, situational variables, and student performance, interventions that do have an effect may not be noted.

Components of an active, contingency-based curriculum

The components of the alternative curriculum are built around the four primary needs of these students. These needs are not necessarily hierarchical. Usually, the balance across these four needs will fluctuate daily.

Organic health care needs

These students typically have a variety of nutritional, respiratory, gastrointestinal, seizure and medication, cardiac, and body temperature control needs (see Chapter 8). Many of these are life-threatening, and most are time-consuming for teachers to monitor and attend to. Many of these needs, such as nutrition, suctioning, breathing treatments, and medication, can be scheduled as an integral part of the instructional day. As such, they should be used as opportunities to develop contingency awareness.

Structural needs

Structural needs are centered around the positioning needs of these students. All of these students have postural dysfunctions. Their positions must be continually changed to prevent further bone, joint, muscle, and skin deterioration (see Chapter 8). These students must also be correctly positioned to facilitate both voluntary motor control and sensory input. As with organic health care needs, positioning needs can typically be met on a scheduled basis and contingent stimulation can be provided to the student in all positions. In addition, students can always be positioned in proximity to one another, to nondisabled peers, or other staff members.

Social-emotional needs

Many of these students appear to require large amounts of caregiving time from teachers. Some of this time is related to the health needs of these students. Students who are in respiratory distress, having seizures or gastrointestinal disturbance, or apparently experiencing physical discomfort, elicit and typically require caregiving behaviors from teachers, such as holding, rocking, touching, and calming vocalizations. Because these teacher responses are based on variable student behaviors, the time and duration of these teacher behaviors are also highly variable and may be looked upon as disruptive to scheduled instruction with students. However, by focusing on contingency awareness and contingency building activities during these interactions, positive outcomes may be achieved.

Cognitive, sensory, and communication development

In spite of the minimal cognitive responses displayed by these students and the consuming demands for their organic, structural, and social-emotional needs, these students should be provided with contingency-based interventions that attempt to increase their alertness to the environment, and their interaction with people and objects. These interactions should be planned to increase, generalize, or maintain the following: an understanding of cause and effect; the ability to express wants and needs, choice making, and control over the environment; social responses, such as eye contact and smiling in response to interactions with other people; and enjoyment in participation in activities (this includes avoidance of negative stimulation). A series of activities should be developed and scheduled to provide this contingent stimulation. The majority of these activities can be designed so that a minimum of two students are participating in the activity.

Activity selection

If possible, activity selection should follow the parameters previously discussed, with a focus on family interviews and school ecological assessment. However, many of these activities are not motivating or reinforcing to these students, so teachers must be creative in developing simple, short activities that may not appear as functional as seen in other classrooms. These activities should be based on observed student preference, hypothetical student preference based on interviews and previous experience, or motor and sensory needs of the student.

Activities centered around switch operation for cause and effect are often selected for these students. If possible, the item activated should be multisensory. These items include the standard array of battery-operated toys, vibrators, televisions, radios, tape recorders, and computer programs.

Movement-based activities are another option. These activities have two different purposes. The first is development of motor skills and includes range of motion exercises; vestibular stimulation; and proprioceptive, protective, and balance reactions. The second is acquisition of cause–effect behaviors and early communication (Sternberg, Pegnatore, & Hill, 1983). These include such behaviors as rocking, swinging, and bouncing.

Recreation and leisure activities with nondisabled peers should also be planned. The teacher should encourage the student's partial participation in activities in which the nondisabled peers are engaging, such as video game playing, wheelchair relay races, sand and water play, and art.

When possible, all activities except hygiene should be done with non-disabled peers and in multiple environments, including community and regular education settings. These locations and interactions should be determined by the student's health, physical state, and behavioral responses to those people and settings, rather than by preset teacher or staff beliefs.

Selecting instructional objectives

Educational outcomes for these students will be different from the simple acquisition of basic developmental skills or skill steps as described earlier. These outcomes include small degrees of change in basic developmental skills, such as focusing, smiling, and behavior change when stimulated. Specific exemplars might be (a) changing behavior when stimulated, (b) focusing on objects and people, (c) orienting to sounds, (d) indicating the desire for con-tinuance of an activity (recurrence or more), (e) smiling in response to verbal interaction, (f) acknowledging the presence of another person, (g) developing cause–effect behaviors, and (h) making choices in reaction to stimulus input.

Additional educational outcomes for these students have been described by Evans and Scotti (1989). They include changes in affect indicating enjoy-ment in partial participation, changes in alertness levels, increases in num-ber of locations and activities where instruction occurs, increases in the types of materials and people with which and whom they interact, changes in oppor-tunities provided by caregivers as a result of improvements in alertness or contingency responses by students, increases in the amount of time engaged in contingent stimulation, increased functional effect of behaviors, and increased complexity of behaviors in which they are engaged. These types of changes, rather than student responses, are usually targeted for data col-lection as a matter of teacher routine.

Building an Integrated Curriculum Across the Needs of the Student

The four need areas described above are all theoretically equal and teachers should try to seek a balance across them. Given the health, structural, and social–emotional needs of these students, their need for cognitive–communicative–social development is easily overlooked. Teachers must carefully and consistently plan and implement contingency-based activities with their students and not become only physical and emotional care providers. The balance for these students across the four need areas is difficult to attain and is easily interrupted by the health and social–emotional needs of the students. Nevertheless, teachers should plan for the balance. Table 10.13 presents examples of instructional objectives for Student D. The BDSs and teacher monitoring objectives could be listed on a matrix similar to the one displayed in Figure 10.2. These would then cut across the various activities that would be specified.

Almost all interactions with the student can combine two or more of the areas described above. Examples of blending activities from two areas include feeding (health) and sidelying (structural); postural drainage (health) and switch activation (cognitive); and rocking (social–emotional) and lap sitting (structural). Examples of combinations of activities from three areas are "more" (cognitive), rocking chair (social–emotional), and lap sitting (structural); tumble form (structural), focus (cognitive), and feeding (health); and postural drainage (health), over a wedge (structural), and switch activation (cognitive). Examples of combining activities from all four areas are postural drainage (health), wedge (structural), switch activation (cognitive), and patting on the back (social–emotional); tube feeding (health), sidelying (structural), focus (cognitive), and calming vocalizations (social–emotional); and

---

TABLE 10.13. Instructional Objectives for Student D

Active basic developmental skills

1. Orient to sound through head turn.
2. Focus on objects during multisensory activities.
3. Vocalize to signal "more."
4. Smile in response to social, auditory, visual, and/or tactile input.
5. Activate a switch to obtain desired stimulation.

Teacher monitoring objectives

6. Chart changes in alertness levels in response to activity and time of day.
7. Maintain upright alignment in kneel position for 20 minutes per day.
8. Maintain range of motion program daily.
9. Maintain optimal positioning schedule throughout the day while engaged in activities (side-lying, prone over a wedge, wheelchair sitting, lap sitting, straddling over a bolster while supported by staff, sitting in tumble form).
10. Monitor respiratory levels.
11. Tube feed two times per day.

orient to sound (cognitive), feeding (health), tumble form (structural), and calming vocalizations (social–emotional).

Scheduling

All four curriculum areas must be addressed in the schedule. The following process is suggested.

1. *Develop and plan activities for cognitive development.* These activities should be as age appropriate and contextual (functional) as possible. It is suggested that activities for cognitive development be done first as this is the most easily overlooked curriculum area for these students. These activities should be scheduled into 15-minute blocks. Some of these activities will be scheduled around times when related services personnel are present (e.g., speech-language therapists, vision or hearing teachers, adaptive physical education staff). This schedule may also change over time as these personnel rearrange their schedules. Most cognitive activities can be done with two or more students. If true group instruction is not possible, the students should be kept in close proximity to one another, with a staff member interacting with one student at a time.

2. *Develop structural positioning schedule.* Optimal positions should be determined for each activity planned for the student. The physical therapist should be consulted for input on type and number of positions and frequency for changing positions. Because all students will likely require multiple positions, an appropriate correspondence between an activity and a given position can usually be developed.

3. *Develop health care needs schedule.* These activities center around eating, diapering, postural drainage, breathing treatments, catheterization, range of motion, and suctioning. The nurse should be consulted for all health care procedures. Some of these procedures will be done by the teacher with supervision from the nurse. Other procedures will be done by the nurse, physical therapist, or occupational therapist. When possible, the positions required for these activities should be integrated with the schedule for the structural needs of the student. As described above, the possibility of integrating cognitive development activities with health care needs should also be considered.

4. *Schedule time for social and emotional support.* Many of these needs cannot be scheduled. They typically arise from the health and structural needs of the students. All teachers, however, can plan a balance between active stimulation and less stressful, more caregiving times. Teachers should also plan to attend to the nurturing needs of their students during transition times by taking an extra moment or two to hold or touch a student in a reassuring manner. All teachers will learn the ebb and flow of their students'

emotional lives. This will be of assistance in designing a plan for preventive caregiving.

5. *Live with schedule breakdowns.* By definition and self-selection, these students set their own schedules. Various medical and organic dysfunctions, such as diarrhea or respiratory distress, do occur. Throughout the continual rearrangements of the schedule necessitated by the students, the teachers must keep alert to losing the curricular balance, and seek to regain the balance as quickly as possible.

Summary

Students in Characteristics Cluster 7 provide the ultimate challenge to educators. Their apparent noninstructional needs, such as health care, structural, and social–emotional support, often overshadow their instructional needs in sensory, motoric, cognitive, and communicative development. These students' level of partial participation in activities, the teacher effort needed to provide the continual hand-over-hand instruction necessary for that partial participation, and the students' minimal response to that partial participation all challenge educators to find activities that appear stimulating and motivating to these students and that enhance their enjoyment of life.

CONCLUSION

A comprehensive curriculum design for students with profound disabilities is a multistep process that calls for creativity on the part of the teacher and a commitment to including the family in the design. The curriculum model of choice for almost all students labeled profoundly disabled is an adaptation of an activity-based curriculum in which the adaptations focus on refining how students can increase their partial participation in a more active manner.

Students with profound disabilities are a very heterogeneous group. Regardless of the severity of their multiple instructional needs, these students can learn critical skills that will improve their quality of life. These critical skills should always be taught within the context of integrated instructional environments where the students can regularly interact with persons without disabilities. This interaction not only can improve the quality of life and educational outcomes for students with profound disabilities, but also can enrich the lives of persons without disabilities.

ACKNOWLEDGMENT

Development of this chapter was supported in part by Federal Grant No. H086P9001 from the Office of Special Education and Rehabilitation Services (OSERS). The opinions expressed in this chapter are those of the authors, and no official endorsement by any agency should in inferred.

REFERENCES

Baumgart, D., Brown, L., Pumpian, I., Nisbet, J., Ford, A., Sweet, M., Messina, R., & Schroeder, J. (1982). Principle of partial participation and individualized adaptations in educational programs for severely handicapped students. *Journal of The Association for Persons with Severe Handicaps, 7,* 17–27.

Belfliore, P. (1990, December). *The impact of setting on the behavior of persons with profound disabilities.* Paper presented at the meeting of The Association for Persons with Severe Handicaps, Chicago.

Borthwick-Duffy, S. A. (1990). Quality of life of persons with severe or profound mental retardation. In R. L. Schalock & M. J. Begab (Eds.), *Quality of life: Perspectives and issues* (pp. 177–190). Washington, DC: American Association on Mental Retardation.

Collins, B. D., Gast, D. L., Wolery, M., Holcombe, A., & Leatherby, J. G. (1991). Using constant time-delay to teach self-feeding to young students with severe/profound handicaps: Evidence of limited effectiveness. *Journal of Developmental and Physical Disabilities, 3,* 157–179.

Dunst, C., Cuishing, C., & Vance, S. (1985). Response contingent learning in profoundly handicapped infants: A social system perspective. *Analysis and Intervention in Developmental Disabilities, 5,* 33–47.

Evans, I. M., & Scotti, J. R. (1989). Defining meaningful outcomes for persons with profound disabilities. In F. Brown & D. H. Lehr (Eds.), *Persons with profound disabilities: Issues and perspectives* (pp. 83–108). Baltimore: Brookes.

Falvey, M. A. (1989). *Community based instruction* (2nd ed.). Baltimore: Brookes.

Ferguson, D. L., & Baumgart, D. (1991). Partial participation revisited. *Journal of The Association for Persons with Severe Disabilities, 16,* 218–227.

Ford, A., & Mirenda, P. (1984). Community instruction: A natural cues and correction decision model. *Journal of The Association for Persons with Severe Handicaps, 9,* 77–87.

Gee, K., Graham, N., Sailor, W., & Goetz, L. (in press). Use of integrated, regular school and community settings as primary contexts for skill instruction of students with severe, multiple disabilities. *Behavior Modification.*

Green, C., Canipe, V., Gardner, S., & Reid, D. (1990). *A behavior analysis of the (non)existence of biobehavioral states among persons with profound multiple handicaps.* Paper presented at the meeting of The Association for Persons with Severe Handicaps, Chicago.

Green, C. W., Canipe, V. S., Way, P. J., & Reid, D. H. (1986). Improving the functional utility and effectiveness of classroom services for students with profound multiple handicaps. *Journal of The Association for Persons with Severe Handicaps, 11,* 62–170.

Guess, D. (1989). Foreward. In F. Brown & D. Lehr (Eds.), *Persons with profound disabilities: Issues and practices* (pp. ix–xi). Baltimore: Brookes.

Guess, D., Mulligan-Ault, M., Roberts, S., Struth, J., Siegel-Causey, E., Thompson, B., Bronicki, G. J., & Guy, B. (1988). Implications of biobehavioral states for the education and treatment of students with the most profoundly handicapping conditions. *Journal of The Association for Persons with Severe Handicaps, 13,* 163–175.

Guess, D., Roberts, S., Siegel-Causey, E., Mulligan-Ault, M., Guy, B., Thompson, B., Rues, J., & Siegel-Causey, D. (1991). *Investigations into the state behaviors of students with severe and profound handicapping conditions.* Lawrence: University of Kansas.

Haywood, H., Meyers, C., & Switzky, H. (1982). Mental retardation. *Annual Review in Psychology, 33,* 309–342.

Horner, R. H., McDonnell, J. J., & Bellamy, G. T. (1986). Teaching generalized skills: General case instruction in simulation and community settings. In R. H. Horner, L. H. Meyer, & H. D. Fredericks (Eds.), *Education of learners with severe handicaps: Exemplary service strategies* (pp. 289–314). Baltimore: Brookes.

Landesman-Dwyer, S., & Sackett, G. (1978). Behavioral changes in nonambulatory profoundly mentally retarded individuals. In C. E. Meyers (Ed.), *Quality of life in severely and profoundly mentally retarded people: Research foundations for improvement* (pp. 55–144). Washington, DC: American Association on Mental Deficiency.

Logan, K., Alberto, P., Kana, T., & Waylor, T. (1992). *Characteristics of students with profound disabilities and their relationship to curriculum planning* (Project Report OSEP No. 086P9001). Atlanta: Department of Special Education, Georgia State University.

Mulligan, M., Lacy, L., & Guess, D. (1982). Effects of massed, distributed, and spaced trial sequencing on severely handicapped students' performance. *Journal of The Association for Persons with Severe Handicaps, 7,* 48–61.

Reid, D. H., Phillips, J. F., & Green, C. W. (1991). Teaching persons with profound multiple handicaps: A review of the effects of behavioral research. *Journal of Applied Behavior Analysis, 24,* 319–336.

Sailor, W., Gee, K., Goetz, L., & Graham, N. (1988). Progress in educating students with the most severe disabilities: Is there any? *Journal of The Association for Persons with Severe Handicaps, 13,* 87–99.

Sailor, W., & Guess, D. (1983). *Handicapped students: An instructional design.* Boston: Houghton Mifflin.

Saunders, R. R., & Spradlin, J. E. (1991). A supported routines approach to active treatment for enhancing independence, competence, and self-worth. *Behavioral Residential Treatment, 6,* 11–37.

Snell, M. E., & Grigg, N. C. (1988). Instructional assessment and curriculum development. In M. E. Snell (Ed.), *Systematic instruction of persons with severe handicaps* (pp. 64–109). Columbus, OH: Merrill.

Snell, M. E., Lewis, A. P., & Houghton, A. (1989). Acquisition and maintenance of toothbrushing skills by students with cerebral palsy and mental retardation. *Journal of The Association for Persons with Severe Handicaps, 14,* 216–226.

Snell, M. E., & Zirpoli, T. J. (1988). Intervention strategies. In M. E. Snell (Ed.), *Systematic instruction of persons with severe handicaps* (pp. 110–150). Columbus: Merrill.

Sternberg, L. (Ed.). (1988). *Educating students with severe or profound handicaps* (2nd ed.). Austin, TX: PRO-ED.

Sternberg, L., Pegnatore, L., & Hill, C. (1983). Establishing interactive communication behaviors with profoundly mentally handicapped students. *Journal of The Association for Persons with Severe Handicaps, 8,* 39–46.

Sternberg, L., Ritchey, H., Pegnatore, L., Wills, L., & Hill, C. (1986). *A curriculum for profoundly handicapped students.* Austin, TX: PRO-ED.

Thompson, B., & Guess, D. (1989). Students who experience the most profound disabilities: Teacher perspective. In F. Brown & D. H. Lehr (Eds.), *Persons with profound disabilities: Issues and practice* (pp. 3–42). Baltimore: Brookes.

Utley, B., Duncan, D., Strain, P., & Scanlon, K. (1983). Effects of contingent and noncontingent vision stimulation on visual fixation in multiply handicapped children. *Journal of The Association for Persons with Severe Handicaps, 8,* 29–42.

Part III

Specific Applications

Chapter 11

Early Intervention with Infants, Toddlers, and Preschoolers with Profound Disabilities

KATHRYN A. HARING and DAVID L. LOVETT

Never have efforts to provide comprehensive special services for very young children with disabilities been more systematically pursued than at the present time. Directives now include the inclusion of families as a predominant focus, and state departments of health and education are working to implement federal public laws requiring the downward extension of the Individuals with Disabilities Education Act (IDEA). Free appropriate services are now mandated for children from birth to 6 years old who are at risk for developing disabilities, as well as for their families. The myriad issues surrounding provision of family-centered, transdisciplinary early intervention are forcing special service personnel to question many previously accepted guiding principles. No longer can special education professionals simply assume they know what is best for young children with disabilities and their families. Professionals are now required by law to listen to what parents are saying about their child and the family's strengths and needs. This family focus has startled some professionals who previously defined their roles as experts as telling families what they needed. In addition, the transdisciplinary requirements of early intervention have redefined how professionals representing many different disciplines relate to one another. The purpose of this chapter is to discuss how these and other issues surrounding early childhood special services can be addressed when serving families and their young children with pervasive disabilities.

We begin the chapter with a discussion of transdisciplinary early intervention in terms of team membership, comparison to other teaming models, and components of effective transdisciplinary services. We then discuss family involvement and focus on issues and concerns related to the effect of families on the development of young children with profound disabilities. We then provide coverage of such topics as effective interventions, the manner in which professionals interact with families, the development of the Individualized Family Service Plan (IFSP) and Individualized Education Program (IEP), and components of exemplary early childhood education programs.

This chapter concentrates on program planning across life domains, including strategies to enhance the development and participation of young children with profound disabilities in care routines, mobility, communication, social development, and play. Emphasis is placed on imbedding the concepts of inclusion and normalization into early childhood intervention. In addition, consideration of critical transition periods and actions is stressed (e.g., from neonatal intensive care units [NICUs] to home or community-based programs; from early intervention [birth to age 3] services to preschool special education [ages 3 to 6]).

TRANSDISCIPLINARY TEAMING

Due to the complex and interactive nature of multiple debilitating conditions that hinder young children with profound disabilities, a team including professionals from many disciplines should be created to plan for and deliver services (Orelove & Sobsey, 1992). Without sufficient planning and dedication, multidisciplinary coordination and communication may be ineffective. Early intervention may occur in a number of environments, including NICUs, family homes, and day care centers, as well as private nonprofit and public preschool settings. With this large variety of possible settings, and with the many professionals working in those environments, the potential for inadequate multidisciplinary case management is great. Thus, a systematic process to ensure the establishment of a cohesive and coordinated team is critical.

Team members who provide services can include special educators; regular educators; child development specialists; family members; paraprofessionals; providers of therapies, such as physical, occupational, and communication; psychologists; social workers; administrators; specialists in vision, hearing, orientation, and mobility; nutritionists and dietitians; nurses; physicians; and numerous other medical and nonmedical specialists. Obviously, coordination must be considered mandatory. Each person on the team has his or her own set of skills, expertise, or technical knowledge and is likely to be using discipline-specific vocabulary. Therefore, steps must be taken to ensure adequate communication among professionals. Public law requires that a case manager be assigned to the family of each individual served through special education funds to coordinate communication and services provided by these team members. The person designated to manage special services may be referred to as a *resource coordinator* (RC). The RC serves as the single point of contact for the parents and, at the same time, coordinates and facilitates the delivery of services. The RC works with all team members to ensure that families receive the services they need.

Multidisciplinary Team

The multidisciplinary team model (Hart, 1977; McCormick & Goldman, 1979) is an example of early efforts to serve individuals with profound disabilities through the involvement of professionals from many disciplines. The major disadvantage of the multidisciplinary model is that professionals may work in isolation from one another. The potential for ineffective or duplicated services is greatly increased when professionals attempt to alleviate a young child's motor, sensory, or communication impairments as if each professional were providing a separate, highly specialized function (Orelove & Sobsey, 1992). Multidisciplinary assessments may result in complicated, uncoordinated, and competing recommendations from each professional involved, thus hindering educational planning and actual program implementation.

Interdisciplinary Model

A more refined model of teaming, the interdisciplinary team, is characterized by increased communication and planning among professionals. Program implementation, however, can still take place in isolation (Garland, McGonigel, Frank, & Buck, 1989). The interdisciplinary model still allows for related services to be provided in a nonintegrated fashion. For example, the therapist may take the child into a separate room for direct one-on-one therapy. Even if therapy is performed in a natural setting (e.g., a classroom or home), there is no assurance that therapy activities will be incorporated into naturally occurring routines of care or instruction. Numerous problems are associated with isolated (nonintegrated) related services (Giangreco, York, & Rainforth, 1989; York, Rainforth, & Giangreco, 1990). For instance, therapy may be nonfunctional; that is, it may not be designed and implemented to help the child gain control over the environment. In addition, isolated services may miss opportunities for helping parents and other professionals develop an understanding of how they can integrate appropriate instructional or therapeutic methods into their activities with the child. Although limited research on the efficacy of isolated, direct therapies exists, common sense dictates that this is not an efficacious approach for serving young children with profound disabilities. Due to the high cost of related services, and the limited personnel with pediatric expertise available to provide direct service, the interdisciplinary model is not recommended.

Transdisciplinary Model

The transdisciplinary team model generates wide appeal and has been adapted as the model of choice for serving individuals with multiple disabilities (Dunn, 1991). This model relies on an indirect therapy approach. In other words, therapists act as consultants to other members of the team. For example, the physical therapist may make recommendations to the RC regarding handling of the child during dressing. Although direct assessment and therapy may still be necessary and are not precluded by this model, they are no longer the primary vehicle for related service provision.

The value of a transdisciplinary team approach in early intervention for children with profound disabilities is readily apparent. With this model, all team members collaborate to conduct a comprehensive developmental assessment, all are fully active participants in the team, program planning is based on family priorities, regular team meetings become vehicles for sharing knowledge across disciplinary boundaries, and a primary service provider is assigned to each family to efficiently implement the coordinated service plan.

The provision of transdisciplinary related services to young children with profound disabilities can be difficult. It requires individual team members to engage in role release. Effective professionals on transdisciplinary teams must make extraordinary efforts to demystify their discipline-specific knowledge. This requires communicating in functional, understandable language so that team members without specific technical training (e.g., parents, paraprofessionals, educators, social workers) can apply knowledge from various disciplines to family-focused early intervention. For example, the physical, occupational, or motor therapist may determine that the child is hypotonic and needs to strengthen head and trunk control, weight bearing, and crossing midline. This is extremely valuable information that should be incorporated into all aspects of the child's daily living routines. However, the people who are in most frequent contact with the child (i.e., members of the family system and early interventionists) may lack the knowledge necessary to incorporate this information into their caregiving and instructional activities. The motor therapist's role, then, is to demonstrate the how, when, where, and why of developing motor skills without the use of vocabulary that might be confusing to caregivers (e.g., hypertonic–hypotonic, abductor–adductor, proximal–distal, prone–supine).

It is benefical for therapists, therefore, to speak a common, "understandable" language. For example, it would be wise for these specialists to explain to the team using language such as the following: "This baby is floppy. A good way to handle her is like this. Let's see Mom try this technique. Good, that's the way to keep her head in the middle while giving her body support. Look, now she has free use of her hands. Do you think you can open the refrigerator while holding her this way?" To communicate in such basic language, the specialist must be secure and trust that the rest of the team knows that he or she knows the technical terminology (i.e., the discipline-specific content knowledge). Demonstrating how their knowledge can be used to ensure that the young child receives appropriate services throughout the day is a challenge to all related services personnel. By releasing some of their role responsibilities through the sharing of knowledge, these personnel increase their impact and expand intervention services.

In transdisciplinary teaming, all members are challenged to share their discipline or experientially based knowledge. For example, in providing appropriate services for young children who have profound visual and auditory disabilities, a number of comprehensive tasks must be performed (Michael & Paul, 1991). The vision specialist must be able to incorporate findings from various devices (e.g., a visually evoked response test) into activities that will stimulate the use of functional vision. These activities should seem like play to the young child and involve lights, color, and movement. The audiologist may use information obtained from a sensitivity prediction acoustic reflex, an auditory brainstem response, and a behavior observation audiometric test. From these findings, novel and entertaining activities should be devised to motivate the child to orient and attend to sound and vibration. The speech–language therapist should also assess to what degree the child is communicating with caregivers and interventionists, and how nonintentional behaviors might be shaped into functional communication.

Primary caregivers will have valuable information to share, including medical history, scheduling needs, and preferred stimulation. It is important to remember that mothers are the experts about their children. The primary caregivers have likely learned all the medical and health-related activities needed to support the life of their young children with profound disabilities. They can train the team in how to suction, clear the tracheostomy tube, tube feed, attach and read monitors, and respond to medical emergencies. The concerns associated with sustaining the lives of infants, toddlers, and preschoolers with profound disabilities fall largely on the primary caregivers. Therefore, it is important that they be highly respected team members, and that they be given frequent and warm social validation from professionals.

Special educators may be responsible for writing medical routines and helping other members take data necessary to make important team decisions (e.g., occurrences of seizures, behavioral influences of medication). The special educators will also help team members to use various instructional methodologies and reinforcement strategies, and to establish social contingencies in their interactions with young children and their families.

The value of a smoothly functioning transdisciplinary team should be readily apparent. This type of teaming can effectively ensure that the specific knowledge provided by members is valued, and its application beneficial to the identified child. The developmental potential of youngsters who are profoundly involved is maximized because the interactions they experience are infused with integrated learning goals from various disciplines. These interactions involve such concerns as correct positioning for comfort and movement, clear communication with sensitivity to contingent responses, maximizing sensory input, and instruction through play and care routines. Effective transdisciplinary teaming is a dynamic process that requires professionals to continually evaluate their provision of services and team participation to meet the ever-changing needs of the child and family.

FAMILY INVOLVEMENT

At no other point in the life span of individuals with profound disabilities must family involvement be emphasized to the degree that it is in early childhood. The earliest and, in many cases, most crucial social exchanges and learning opportunities for the young child are found within the family or home environment. From birth, babies are active and socially responsive, and their learning is largely social in nature (Lewis, 1984). In the earliest years, babies develop an awareness of objects and people, awareness of cause–effect relationships, coordination of actions, and primary social relationships or attachments to their major caregivers. Although young children with profound disabilities demonstrate these abilities to a lesser degree, we must assume that development, although staggered, is continuous in this population. Services should be designed with this assumption in mind.

It is important to stress that infants and young children learn predominantly from socially reciprocal relationships that exist in interactions with their families. Parents, siblings, caregivers, friends, and extended family members all provide crucial opportunities for learning. It is important that early intervention providers reinforce family members and friends for interacting with the young child who is profoundly disabled. It is also helpful to construct simple reciprocal games for adults and children to play with the identified youngster.

Siblings are often overlooked in the provision of family services. They can be a critical part of home-based early intervention. Siblings provide excellent language and play models, but it is often necessary to point out to young siblings the communicative attempts from the child with profound disabilities. When family members feel that their presence and involvement is acknowledged and enjoyed by the individual who is profoundly disabled, the likelihood of improved interaction is increased.

Early social relationship ties are linked to social-emotional development in later years (Ainsworth, 1973). As childhood progresses from infancy to toddlerhood to the preschool stage, the child becomes increasingly able to separate from the parent or primary caregiver and engage in interactions with peers and other individuals in the environment. Children with profound disabilities may not readily relate to unfamiliar persons; however, if the quality of interaction with primary caregivers is consistently high, and unfamiliar persons are taught how to communicate effectively with the child, some degree of separation and increased engagement with others can occur (Ogletree, Wetherby, & Westling, 1992). It is critical, therefore, that service providers emphasize early learning within the context of the family, particularly during infancy. Early intervention services that fail to support child–family interactions, or exclude family members from participation, run the risk of not only being ineffective in facilitating the child's development, but possibly producing negative effects. For example, if service providers fail to help parents understand the communicative intent of their child's behavior, the child may decrease the number of attempts to communicate with the parents.

A review of the literature by Silber (1989) addresses the dimensions of family life that are important to the child's early development. These dimensions include (a) an attentive attachment figure who is warm and responsive; (b) use of consistent disciplinary standards with appropriate parental explanation and affect; (c) an organized, stimulating environment; (d) encouragement of learning through questioning and cueing that responds to the child; (e) parent expectation of the child's competence; (f) harmonious parents, encouraging siblings, and absence of family conflict; and (g) a positive relationship of the family to the outside environment, which includes access to community services and the extended family.

The importance of the family is recognized in the shift away from early childhood services that are exclusively oriented toward child change to more family-focused approaches (Bailey et al., 1986; Dunst, 1985). This shift in focus is reflected in Public Law (PL) 99-457 (1986), Part H (Education of the Handicapped Act Amendments of 1986), through the options for including family services in the IFSP. The development of the IFSP is viewed as a *process* rather than a product, with the formation of collaborative partnerships with families being the primary goal.

Although the degree and type of family involvement and input in the education–intervention process may change somewhat during the preschool years, the concept of family involvement must be maintained. Even though preschool-aged children spend more time engaged with peers and separated from their family members, their primary learning environment remains the family, and their primary learning opportunities are focused on social interactions.

Families of young children with profound disabilities represent an interconnected and dynamic system. Recently, the clinical literature on family systems (e.g., Minuchin, 1974; Olson et al., 1983) has been applied to the formation of a framework for serving families of individuals with special needs (Turnbull, Summers, & Brotherson, 1984; Turnbull & Turnbull, 1986). The view of the family through family systems theory emphasizes the interrelatedness of all family members. The focus is on the entire family as it defines itself rather than on a particular member, such as the child with a profound disability. This focus translates into new approaches in home-based delivery of early childhood services in which the primary caregivers are empowered and receive continuous positive regard. Emphasis now is placed on supporting and strengthening families through the recognition of each family's own strengths and resources (Dunst, 1985; Dunst, Trivette, & Cross, 1986), and services increasingly reflect a family-centered or family-driven system for goal setting (Bailey et al., 1986).

Early intervention, preschool special education, and child care services must be adaptive to support the wide range of needs experienced by families of children with profound disabilities. In addition to direct interventions and educational programs for children, early childhood services may provide information to families, family support groups and/or counseling, parent education, and assistance in activating community resources or networks. Programs must be flexible, provide a wide range of service options, and deliver services in a respectful and culturally sensitive manner (Lynch & Hanson, 1992). The population of the United States is dynamic, and recent demographic changes reflect an ever-increasing diversity of citizens. These factors increase the need for professional personnel to become more sensitive and knowledgeable about a range of cultures, and to deliver services in a manner that is respectful and supportive of this diversity (Hanson, Lynch, & Wayman, 1990).

Kaiser and Hemmeter (1989) cautioned against a total needs-based approach to family intervention and offered a more value-based approach as an alternative. They postulated four value elements to be considered in designing family-focused early interventions. The four element questions to be asked in the development of family interventions are as follows:

1. *Does the intervention enhance community?* The approach should encourage integration of children with profound disabilities and their families into normalized environments where children without disabilities are found. Early interventionists should determine whether a targeted goal enhances the child's potential for social inclusion and whether it is a goal that will be naturally reinforced in the community in which the child is living. The assumption is, therefore, that other children without disabilities will also be asked to execute the targeted behavior(s).

2. *Does the intervention strengthen the family?* This question focuses on whether the intervention can be used to muster the resources necessary to provide a nurturing, supportive environment for the child. Service providers should explore ways to incorporate as many family members and significant others as possible into the program goals, while ensuring that the goals will effectively extend interaction with each member of the child's interaction group.

3. *Does the intervention enable parents to do their jobs well?* Early intervention should not add additional stress to families' lives. Professionals should share responsibilities with the families to ensure that the child receives appropriate services. As with most principles of early intervention, this is easier to say than to implement. When professionals set up goals that cannot be worked on within the natural context of family activities, the family members may not be able to follow through. Expecting parents to provide half an hour of therapy a day is not realistic for most families. However, parents can be encouraged to use a time delay procedure in every care and play routine to prompt their child to initiate an action.

4. *Does the intervention enhance individual development and protect the rights of individual family members?* The emphasis is on protecting each family member from abuse and neglect while providing opportunities to grow for all.

Clearly, the literature in early intervention identifies the family as the strongest mediating factor in child development. A healthy family system is viewed as the primary causative agent to enhance the opportunity for more healthy child development. Current practice is attempting to incorporate this perspective into improved methods for determining family priorities and ensuring family involvement in program planning and implementation for children with profound disabilities (Haring, Lovett, & Kliene, 1992).

EFFECTIVE INTERVENTIONS

Hanson and Haring (1992) identified six characteristics of effective early interventions. The overriding characteristic is *individualization*. Whether the focus of service is on the needs of the child, the family, or both, the plan and methods of intervention must be individually designed with family input. It must be remembered that all children and families are unique, and services should be designed to address those special qualities.

A second characteristic of effective early intervention is a *focus on the social context of development*. Intervention strategies should be designed to foster the child's social growth. In early years, parent (family)–child interactions are emphasized, whereas in later years, peer interactions may have greater importance. Effective programs should be designed to provide positive social interactions. This can be achieved through educating parents and significant others about the communicative intent of the child's behaviors and by reinforcing appropriate interactions between the child and his or her peers.

A third characteristic is the *recognition of the child as an active learner involved in experiential learning*. This mandates that environments be created that provide the child with opportunities to learn by having some impact on the environment. As the child learns that certain behaviors (e.g., requesting juice) can enhance control over the environment, and if the environment (especially family members) is responsive to those behaviors (e.g., providing juice), the child is more likely to display those behaviors.

Fourth, *areas of development should be seen as interrelated;* that is, intervention goals should be developed with the recognition of the relationships between developmental areas. For example, a child may communicate through gestures. For that child, therefore, motor development should be seen as an integral part of the development of language. The individualized plan should be created with an emphasis on the development of communication skills associated with motor skills. In this case, the physical therapist and the speech–language therapist would work together to facilitate the use of these skills to enhance communication.

The fifth characteristic of effective early interventions is that *goals, although often based on developmental milestones, must also be functional*. Because young children with profound disabilities experience uneven development, an overemphasis on developmental milestones may force caregivers to ignore functional skills that could help the child achieve more positive interactions with the environment.

Skills that may be functional for a child or family should be based on individual characteristics. The final characteristic of effective early interventions, therefore, is that these *interventions must be family driven*. The interventions should support and strengthen the family, enabling them to access and use resources as desired. It is also critical that these interventions be consistent with the values held by the family.

Curricular Models

Lehr (1989) discussed various models that have been used as a basis for the development of curricula to serve young children with the most severe disabilities. She cited several reasons why the *normal developmental model* was an inappropriate curricular foundation for these children. These reasons included the differences in skill development among children with pervasive disabilities, inappropriate skill selection, isolated skill instruction, and the difficulty in translating information based on developmental assessments into curricular objectives.

Another model described by Lehr (1989) is the *functional curriculum model*. Although this model has advantages in helping to identify appropriate objectives that may be required in future environments, it may not be appropriate to apply to very young children. Most of the research on this model has focused on older children and the skills they will need to be more independent in the future. It may be difficult to identify which skills the very young child will need in long-term future environments. One may encounter this problem even when attempting to predict which skills will be valuable in the very next environment the child will enter. For example, attempting to determine which skills a 2-year-old will need to develop to be prepared for a preschool setting may be difficult because of the uncertain and uneven skill development the child may display. In addition, children with profound disabilities will always need special support of some type. Therefore, it may be difficult to predict what degree or type of support an individual might need in the future. It is likely that many of these problems could be alleviated through an effective transdisciplinary approach in which service providers from anticipated future environments work with current service providers to develop the objectives most valuable to the child and family.

Due to problems with existing curricular models, Lehr (1989) proposed using a set of four continua in determining curricular goals: *dependence–independence, no participation–full participation, difficult to care for–easy to care for,* and *unpleasant–pleasant.* Goals would be selected to help young children progress along these continua. The use of these continua could provide the transdisciplinary team with a valuable perspective to help identify goals that will enhance the young child's quality of life. In addition, goals selected according to these continua would likely enhance the child's interaction with others and the environment.

Inclusive Services

A guiding principle to appropriate interventions for young children with profound disabilities is the importance of normalized inclusive services. Historically, children with pervasive needs have been removed from home and community activities and provided special services in isolated locations. These segregated settings hinder the development of relationships between young children with disabilities and their nondisabled peers. This may impede the development of social skills because children with disabilities have no peer models to interact with and imitate. In a comprehensive review of the literature, Odom and McEvoy (1988) found support for serving young children with disabilities in integrated environments. Strain (1990) concluded that parents strongly desire to have their children develop friendships with more typical children, integrated services generally are superior to segregated services, social skill development is very important and enhanced in integrated programs, staff must facilitate quality social interactions, and normally developing children derive positive developmental and attitudinal outcomes as a result of integrated experiences. Because most young children work on similar goals (e.g., communication, self-help, social interaction), at no other stage of life can meaningful integration of individuals with profound disabilities be achieved so easily and fully as during early childhood. Therefore, whenever possible, all young children with profound disabilities should be served in inclusive settings.

Although it is difficult to collect data on the attitudes held by very young children without disabilities toward their peers who are profoundly disabled, a number of assumptions pertinent to early inclusion experiences can be drawn. It is assumed that very young children look toward significant adults and older peers when forming early attitudes. If important role models demonstrate clear and consistent messages about the positive value of differently abled or culturally diverse individuals, they can have a significant impact on the developing value systems of youngsters. Additionally, if parents of children who are not disabled are exposed to inclusive preschool environments that include children with profound disabilities, they may never question inclusion models during school-aged educational services. Indeed, when faced with a public school classroom setting that does not evidence full inclusion, they may wonder aloud "Why not?" It is conceivable that such parents will have grown to value the collaborative and prosocial attitudes their children gained from inclusive preschool programs. Hopefully, their children would have formed valuable friendships with others of diverse ability levels, and wish the bonds to continue. Such experiences could be the foundation for maintaining friendships outside of the program and in neighborhood settings.

PROFESSIONAL ROLES AND RESPONSIBILITIES

Professional Relationships with Families

In many early intervention programs, the RC serves as the primary point of contact and communication. The strength of this type of service model is in coordination, so that young children who are disabled and their family members have opportunities to become familiar and bond with all of the various service providers. For young children experiencing profound disabilities, familiarity with service providers is essential to the development of early communication skills. Through repeated contacts with the child, the service providers can develop an understanding of the favored communication methods of the child, and respond in a positive manner to enhance social reciprocity. As the child becomes more familiar with each service provider, rapport will reinforce communicative and social interaction behaviors. Service providers can encourage these behaviors and help the family members support these positive early interactions.

The majority of infant and toddler (birth to age 3) programs are home based. This places special education professionals in unique roles and provides them opportunities to learn extremely intimate, personal information about family functioning. Access to this type of information and opportunities for frequent observations can enhance the relationship between professionals and family members by promoting better understanding, communication, and acceptance. With the development of this special relationship, professionals must assume a responsibility to protect the privacy of families they serve. It is critical, therefore, that a sense of trust develop between professionals and families.

A fairly global characteristic of infants and toddlers with profound disabilities is that they exhibit differences in early interactions that can negatively impact the development of relationships and parent–child communication (Siegel-Causey & Ernst, 1989). Parents may not believe that their child who is profoundly disabled is capable of interacting with them because the perceived severity of the disability does not "fit" with their concept of interaction. The parents themselves may be experiencing problems interacting due to the stress of having a young child with profound disabilities. The combination of a child with serious communication difficulties and parents undergoing the substantial stresses associated with caring for a child with such pervasive needs may result in extreme communication difficulties, not only between parents and children but with significant others as well. Parents of newborn infants who have experienced profound disabilities are often reeling from a health crisis, such as a dramatic interruption of the normal prenatal gestation or birth process. They may be experiencing extreme anxiety regarding the child's survival and future development. It is also useful to bear in mind that families have very individual needs in terms of how much information they want and what information they can actually process or understand. People in crisis may not be able to "hear" (understand or accept) some of the information professionals are providing. The most important skills a home-based service provider needs to possess are the abilities to listen and observe.

Young children with profound disabilities have typically experienced long-term hospitalization and medical complications that may have severely interrupted parent–child bonding. Parents of children in NICUs are not necessarily encouraged to participate in care routines, and may not feel competent in nourishing and nurturing their infants. The disrupted attachment that is likely after a perinatal health crisis greatly reduces the opportunities parents have to establish an early working communication system with their infant (Kent-Udolf, 1984).

Numerous researchers have studied interactions of infants and toddlers with disabilities and their primary caregivers. In general, results indicate that caregivers exhibit less positive affect and enjoy interactions less with youngsters from birth through 2 years of age who are disabled than with nondisabled children (Barnard, Bee, & Hammond, 1984; Crnic, Ragozin, Greenberg, Robinson, & Basham, 1983). Other studies indicate reduced maternal involvement and interaction after 2 years of age for preschoolers who are disabled (Bricker & Carlson, 1981; Kogan, Tyler, & Turner, 1974; Tyler & Kogan, 1977). Although many problems can inhibit the establishment of a nurtural relationship with children with profound disabilities (Siegel-Causey & Ernst, 1989), developing this type of relationship between families and children should be the most critical goal of early intervention. Service providers may have to directly model nurtural, reciprocal relationships with infants, and encourage family members to develop communicative rapport.

Cultural Sensitivity

One of the major personnel preparation issues facing early childhood special education is the lack of cultural and lingual diversity in the students attracted to direct service roles (Lynch & Hanson, 1992). Current prevalence figures indicate that 6% to 7%, or approximately 240,000 low birthweight infants ($\leq 2,500$ grams), are born each year in the United States. Of these births, up to 2% are classified as very low birthweight ($\leq 1,500$ grams). The incidence rates for children with low and very low birthweights are twice as high in non-white populations, and these rates have remained stable for the past 20–25 years (Bennett & Guralnick, 1992). Technologically enhanced neonatal intensive care has dramatically reduced mortality and increased the prevalence of biologically vulnerable infants and toddlers in the general population. Follow-up data indicate that improved survival may be accompanied by persistent health and/or neurodevelopmental impairments (Bennett, 1987). A small portion of these neonates will be profoundly disabled as a result of their circumstances of birth. Half will be released from the NICU to families whose cultural, ethnic, or linguistic backgrounds are divergent from mainstream U.S. society. Lack of background compatibility between early interventionists and the families they serve can be a major deterrent to the efficacy of home-based, family-focused early intervention. It is critical, therefore, that service providers are prepared to be culturally sensitive to individual family systems. It is equally important that students from culturally diverse backgrounds be recruited into and retained in early intervention personnel preparation programs. This will provide more personnel who can establish positive relationships with a diverse group of families. In addition, paraprofessionals from traditionally underrepresented groups can be instrumental in communicating with and providing support to culturally diverse families.

The concept of cultural sensitivity must, however, be expanded beyond ethnic and racial considerations. Socioeconomic status and environment-specific concerns must also be addressed. Research being conducted in rural environments (Haring et al., 1992) has demonstrated that there is a culture of isolation in rural poverty that may be more overwhelming than that described in ethnic or racial terms. But the critical guiding principles for sensitivity must remain the same: to allow families to explain how their cultural heritage influences child-rearing practices and to not overgeneralize by stereotyping any family.

Sensitivity to a family's preconceived notion of human exceptionalities is a critical characteristic for effective home interventionists. Families are often willing to share their stories with professionals who are sensitive and who listen. It is important to take the time to observe how families are living, and listen to their descriptions of life experience with their young child who is profoundly involved before formal intervention plans are developed. The rapport and trust that this develops initially in parent–professional contacts will greatly enhance early intervention services because families will feel truly involved and valued.

PROGRAM PLANNING

A number of program planning processes have been developed in attempts to improve the life-styles of persons with profound disabilities. Examples of these include *Personal Futures Planning* (PFP) (Mount, 1987; Mount & Zwernik, 1988) and *McGill Action Planning System* (MAPS) (Vandercook, York, & Forest, 1989). *The Lifestyle Development Process* (LDP) (Malette et al., 1992), a recent innovation in program planning, incorporates critical aspects of PFP and MAPS into a comprehensive model. Within the LDP approach, stakeholders are provided assistance in articulating a vision of the targeted individual's life in the community. The individual is involved in the process as much as possible, as are friends, neighbors, and service providers, in helping family members carefully analyze current conditions weighed against desired outcomes. During the first step of the process, critical information is obtained, including background and history; schedules of current activities; descriptions of present program placement and social–friendship networks; behavioral deficits and excesses and interventions used to deal with each; and skills and attitudes of the primary caregiver. A careful analysis of the targeted individual's daily and weekly schedules is then compared with that of individuals of the same gender, similar age, and similar cultural background who are not disabled. Discrepancies between the two schedules are used to help to define need areas for intervention.

In regard to program planning for children from birth to age 3, and plans that focus on children of preschool age and older, a description of an early intervention process is necessary. The process described here is one presently used by the state of Oklahoma. Called SoonerStart, it is a network of intervention programs that are housed regionally in 16 health departments throughout the state. Each regional office is directed by an RC who is responsible for managing administrative, fiscal, personnel, data collection, and policy issues. Infants with profound disabilities are typically referred for early intervention services through transition programs from hospitals with level-three or tertiary NICUs (those that handle the sickest and smallest babies). Infants with more mild central nervous system damage, or who move from out of state, are less likely to receive immediate referral for early intervention services. Table 11.1 describes the process families go through to receive early intervention services.

Individualized Family Service Plan

The first consideration in developing an IFSP is that parents will probably not be familiar with the concept or specifics of an IFSP. Parents may be extremely anxious when meeting with early interventionists for the first time. Parents of infants and toddlers who are profoundly disabled have typically been through extreme trauma. The information that parents received in the hospital may not have included a projection of what level of future development they could reasonably anticipate as a result of early interven-

TABLE 11.1. The SoonerStart Process

Step	Action
1. Referral	Referral is received by the regional coordinator, who assigns a resource coordinator to work with the family.
2. Initial Contact	The resource coordinator contacts the family to make an initial home visit.
3. Clinical Intake	The resource coordinator notifies appropriate early intervention contact person. Clinical intake and developmental–health screenings are conducted as needed. This may be on a team visit and is followed by staffing to determine appropriate evaluation team members.
4. Transdisciplinary Evaluation	Appropriate transdisciplinary evaluation team members evaluate the identified child for eligibility purposes and assess for individual needs. The team may include, but not be limited to, nurse; speech–language, child development–child guidance, or special education specialist; physical or occupational therapist; psychologist; and nutritionist.
5. Transdisciplinary Staffing	The primary purpose of this meeting is to determine eligibility and needs for sevice provision. The staffing will include the parents, resource coordinator, appropriate evaluation team members, and service providers.
6. Individualized Family Service Plan (IFSP)	The purpose of the IFSP meeting is to develop the coordinated plan of service for the child and family based on identified needs. The primary and consulting service providers are selected and services are scheduled. The resource coordinator records the plan of service on the IFSP form.
7. Service Provision	Services as outlined on the IFSP are provided by designated team members. The resource coordinator monitors service provision and the changing child and/or family needs.
8. IFSP Reviews	IFSPs are reviewed every 6 months, or more often if needed. The resource coordinator coordinates the review process.
9. Transition Evaluation and IFSP	The resource coordinator works with the family, service provider team, and potential sources for future services for the child. Families, with assistance from staff, visit potential sites for future placements. The process of transition to appropriate preschool services is initiated 6–12 months prior to the child's third birthday.
10. Initiation of Preschool Services and Individualized Education Program (IEP)	The resource coordinator, early intervention service providers, and parents meet to develop the IEP. The resource coordinator monitors the transition and initiation of preschool services and is available to parents and preschool service providers for consultation as needed.

tion. The parents and extended family members will need to be provided with basic information about what comprises early intervention. They will need to know the roles and functions of persons from many disciplines and how these services should be provided. Parents cannot be expected to assume full membership in a transdisciplinary team if they do not understand what each discipline is and what professionals within those disciplines should be providing.

Many times professionals prematurely ask parents what their goals are for their child and what they expect in terms of special services. Parents are asked to make choices when they may not even know what the options are. Therefore, it is extremely important that parents are first apprised of what the transdisciplinary team model involves. They should be made familiar and comfortable with the concepts behind transdisciplinary services. It is necessary for parents to understand that therapy goals are being incorporated into all professional and interpersonal interactions with their child, for parents tend to value direct therapy (Haring, Staub, & Farron-Davis, 1990). They may fear that their child will not be receiving needed therapy or related services due to the indirect nature of transdisciplinary service provision. Again, this fear can be alleviated when parents (or primary caregivers), as full members of the team, understand therapy goals and know how to maximize development by infusing goals into daily living contexts. It is the responsibility of professionals to monitor carefully what parents are understanding and whether the indirect therapy approach is effective. The case manager or RC, together with parents, decide when direct therapy or additional consultation from other professionals is needed.

In most states, special educators, in the role of resource coordinators, are primarily responsible for assisting the transdisciplinary team in the development of the IFSP. When convening the team for assessment and program development, it is important to discuss each member's philosophical base for providing services. This will help build collaborative relationships and decrease misunderstandings. When facilitating this discussion, the RC is responsible for assuring that each team member understands the process and the goals of the meeting. The RC may need to translate technical vocabulary, use exemplars to aid less sophisticated team members in conceptual understanding, and provide frequent cueing or probing to elicit responses from family members.

It is critical to remember that effective early intervention gives family members needed information and the power to use new knowledge to make decisions for their young child with profound disabilities. In providing this information, service providers are giving families the specialists' assumptions concerning the extent of the child's disability and probable future. Thus, a clear understanding of each service provider's personal life philosophy or world view is critical in early intervention. If a service provider says something like "This is what I think is wrong with your child" while presenting results of diagnostic tests and evaluation instruments, the parents may feel that the specialist is holding out a stick with which to hit them. On the other hand, the service provider can hold out a carrot by saying "This is how early intervention can help." When describing how the child's development is or will be severely delayed by the extent of his or her disabilities, specialists must make sure that families are not too devastated to reach for the carrot. In the case of families whose child is profoundly disabled, the carrot is hope.

Haring et al. (1992) indicated that some parents perceive their child who has survived NICU as a miracle. These positive perceptions should be supported. Early interventionists need to help parents preserve hope that their child can do better, while giving them realistic tools and resources for facilitation. It is not fair for service providers to tell parents that they can make the child "normal." It may not even be realistic to promise that the child's functional skills can be significantly improved. Service providers can, however, help parents identify alternative strategies for coping with their loss of "the perfect baby." Specialists can also show families ways to assist their child to help compensate for sensory, motor, and cognitive impairments. Service providers can help families, caregivers, and other professionals learn not to value a child based on the child's presumed abilities, and to help people understand that a person is not less valuable because he or she is less able.

It is important to understand what the valued outcomes of the IFSP are in order to write the goals or plan the program. Not agreeing as a transdisciplinary team on what are realistic goals and how outcomes will be measured makes the program plan a meaningless document that exists only to satisfy regulations. One of the major limitations in the efficacy data on early intervention is due to the problem of poorly defined outcome goals and measures (A. Kaiser, personal communication, July 22, 1992). When developing the IFSP for a youngster who is profoundly disabled, goals should be clearly delineated and measurable. Goals at this level can, but do not have to, involve child change. The only mandatory child change goal that each plan must specify is one describing how the child communicates, and how caregivers and professionals will respond consistently and contingently to increase communication skills or repertoires. The goal to increase the child's intentional communication skills should be incorporated within all other goals. Other important child change goals include planning for the child to actively participate as much as possible in care routines, enhancing mobility, and social development.

Helping family members and caregivers articulate their goals for a young child with profound disabilities typically involves some type of interview process. Unfortunately, structured interviews or questionnaires tend to elicit superficial information (Haring et al., 1992). This is particularly problematic for families of various cultures and languages. Again, listening and observing are critical skills of professionals to ensure that parents are truly involved in IFSP development. Some professionals may argue that this level of personal attention is too time-consuming, given the large numbers of children and families in need and the limited resources available for providing service. However, if this early stage of rapport development is skipped, the early intervention services that families do receive will be jeopardized. It is important to recall that the young child in home-based early intervention services may receive only 1 hour a week of direct special service. Service providers are relying on the primary caregivers to provide meaningful interactions, quality instruction, and experiences infused with complex child–family development goals during the remaining 167 hours in the week. If these caregivers do not perceive the importance of their role in facilitating the child's development, 1 hour a week of early intervention cannot be expected to produce significant child or family change.

Individualized Education Program

The guiding principles followed in the creation of the IFSP are also critical in the development of the IEP. That is, the focus should be on the needs of the child, with strong family involvement addressed through a transdisciplinary team approach. A primary difference is the emphasis on child change in the development of the IEP. There is also increased emphasis on systematic instruction to meet the needs of the child. These services are typically provided in preschools with somewhat less focus on home-based intervention.

Due to the change in service setting, it is imperative that the initial IEP address the smooth transition from early intervention (birth to age 3) to preschool (ages 3–5) services. Therefore, the receiving service providers should be part of the IEP team and help identify the goals and services necessary to meet the child's needs.

EXEMPLARY EARLY CHILDHOOD SPECIAL EDUCATION

Clearly, the development of an IFSP is qualitatively different from writing the traditional IEP. Gathering appropriate information from families is an important first step in the process. We have discussed why family priorities should be the basis of program planning, and how culturally sensitive methods for determining priorities should be implemented. We move now to a discussion of exemplary practices necessary for the development of high-quality early childhood special education (ECSE) programs. This term is customarily used to encompass early intervention services for children from birth to age 3 and preschool services for children 3 through 5 years of age.

Researchers and service providers are showing great interest in what constitutes best practice in programs serving children under 6 years of age who are disabled or at risk. It is apparent that guidelines describing basic tenets to ensure program quality are needed. Unfortunately, in the past, research to determine the most effective practices has not preceded practice in this area (Westlake & Kaiser, 1991).

McDonnell and Hardman (1988) reviewed the literature and identified six characteristics of exemplary ECSE programs. These programs tended to be (1) integrated, (2) comprehensive, (3) normalized, (4) adaptable, (5) peer and family referenced, and (6) outcome based. The authors defined *integration* as grouping together children with and without disabilities for instructional or social activities. They further specified that service sites outside the family home should be generic, and that systematic contact with nonhandicapped children should be arranged. *Comprehensive programs* included assessment, planning, instructional programming, service coordination, and evaluation; a transdisciplinary approach; theoretically and procedurally well-defined models; and direct instruction. A *normalized program* was described as one that supported the parents' role, was age appropriate, promoted generalization, encouraged self-initiation, and avoided artificial reinforcement or the use of aversive techniques. *Adaptable services* were those that supported a variety of family structures; were flexible, noncategorical, and individualized; and emphasized functionality of response as well as formative evaluations for programmatic changes. *Peer- and family-referenced services* included parents as full partners; considered family routines when enhancing child skill development; and referenced the curriculum to individual child, family, peer, and community concerns. *Outcome-based programs* were those that emphasized information pertaining to what each child would accomplish as a result of inclusion in a program, rather than what specific services were provided.

As described previously, major principles provide a foundation for exemplary ECSE services for children with profound disabilities and their families. They are the necessity and importance of family involvement; transdisciplinary coordination of services with transition supports between service delivery systems; a developmental as well as a functional life skills–based curriculum; and normalization and integrated opportunities for young children and their families.

Early Intervention Versus Preschool Emphases

To more adequately define best practices for programs serving young children, Hanson and Haring (1992) conducted a survey of early childhood educators, researchers, and other professionals serving childen with severe disabilities. The survey was designed to determine the perceptions of these individuals of the importance of a large number of variables associated with services for young children with disabilities in early intervention or preschool programs. It was anticipated that differences between priorities for these two levels of programs would be found. In addition, the study attempted to determine qualities of equal importance for both program groups. The findings of the study are discussed in the following sections.

Family involvement

A large majority of the survey items concerning family involvement were identified as features most critical to programs serving children from birth to age 3. Only one item, which related to the sensitivity of the program to different cultures, ethnicities, and values, was determined to be a higher priority for children in preschool programs. Data indicated that most respondents deemed it was more important in early intervention programs for the family to have available a primary liaison for coordinating services from various agencies. Hanson and Haring (1992) posited that this perception was most probably due to the fact that many children in the younger group need intense medical interventions. This situation would likely overwhelm families with immediate adjustment issues, and leave them minimal energy for seeking and organizing special services. The primary liaison (e.g., the resource coordinator), therefore, must be knowledgeable about existing agencies and programs, possess skills related to how systems operate, and know how to get systems to serve children with profound disabilities. These responsibilities have interesting implications for how service providers *intend* to serve families. For example, there is a critical difference between programs that are family centered as opposed to family focused. In family-centered services, families receive only what they request. This model is based on the assumption that families will follow through with only those early intervention activities for which they perceive a need. The major weakness in this approach is that it depends on a high degree of family sophistication and knowledge. Simply put, families need to first know what is available in order to know what they can request. One intent of the transdisciplinary approach is to make sure parents understand what each discipline or agency should be providing.

Respondents also considered the need for a vast array of family support services important for children in early intervention programs. The message appears to be that early, family-focused services are crucial if families are to be sustained as the strongest mediating influence on early child development. In addition, family involvement in team planning and service delivery was judged to be of substantially more importance for the younger age group. This appears to indicate that parent involvement in programs for infants and toddlers was perceived as more crucial to program success than in preschool programs. On an overall basis, then, the data supported the contention that the major goals of early intervention programs are to understand and support families, to enhance the parent–child bond, and to establish frequent, effective communication between the home and program.

Intervention and curriculum goals

Far fewer items in the intervention and curriculum goals category were determined to be of higher priority for infants and toddlers than for preschoolers. Of these items, several were developmentally oriented, reflecting the importance professionals place on a developmental model for programs serving the youngest children. The fact that fewer best practices involving intervention and curriculum goals were thought to be significantly more important for the infant and toddler population may indicate that people are less clear about what is best practice within this category for the younger age group (Hanson & Haring, 1992).

One curriculum-related goal setting practice for which no significant differences were found between age groups is worthy of note. Apparently, it is equally important for infants and toddlers and for preschoolers that IFSP and IEP goals and objectives include performance in natural environments (e.g., the home and other age-appropriate environments). This was viewed as an important fundamental principle that should not vary across age groups.

A number of best practices were considered to be of greater priority for preschoolers. These included an emphasis on viewing the child as an active learner, focusing on the whole child, providing comprehensive instructional objectives that could be implemented by different service providers, utilizing task analyses of functional goals, emphasizing social interaction and communicative competence, and providing for generalization. It appears that respondents considered a systematic, behavioral approach to be more necessary within a preschool program. The fact that concepts such as functionality, generalization, and consistency were stressed further indicates that respondents supported the idea that learning should not take place in isolation.

Integration and normalization

The concepts of integration and normalization underlie a critical principle of early childhood special education. However, they are rarely dealt with in isolation. Normalization (Wolfensberger, 1972) implies that children who are or are at risk for becoming disabled be served where children of similar ages who are not disabled are being served. For infants and toddlers, this is the home or day care setting. The concept of integration detailed in the least restrictive environment requirements of PL 94-142 (1975) and PL 99-457 (1986) stipulates that, whenever possible, children with disabilities should be provided educational services with children who are developing in a typical manner.

There were only six best practice survey items that dealt directly with the concepts of integration and normalization. Principles related to services being provided in integrated settings, emphases on integrated play activities, and the need for programs to be offered in integrated facilities were perceived as more important for preschool-aged children. This may reflect respondents' views that integration is a more discernible concept for this age group.

Interdisciplinary/interagency coordination of services with transition supports between service delivery systems

Two survey items reflected best practices that were identified as more pertinent in early intervention programs. They related to the need for communication and coordination between and among agencies serving the child and family. Two other items were judged to be more salient in services to preschool-aged children. These items emphasized the need for integration and a focus on functioning within current and future environments. The interdisciplinary nature of early childhood special education services, then, appears to be considered equally important for infants and preschoolers.

Additional program characteristics

Other characteristics of programs serving young children with disabilities were also investigated through the survey method. These included concerns related to assessment, administration, staff training, staff-to-child ratios, physical plant and environmental settings, and philosophy.

Considered equally vital for infants and toddlers and for preschoolers were the need for an adequate financial base for program operations and an environment that was contingent on and responsive to all children's needs. Clearly, these are fundamental to any quality program, regardless of the age of student served.

One item of primary concern for infants and toddlers related to the need for the provision of adequate health and safety standards (e.g., childproof environment, diapering procedures, food service procedures). Two items concerned with properly identifying very young children in need of special services were also categorized as more vital for the birth to 3-year-old group. Although the debate continues (Bricker, Bailey, & Bruder, 1984; White, Bush, & Casto, 1985), most early interventionists believe that the earlier in life services are provided, the more effective they will be. That belief necessitates rigorous child-find and diagnostic activities.

Results indicated that more items describing program characteristics were considered to be of higher priority for preschool-aged children. A number of items concerning the environment were rated to be much more important for preschoolers (e.g., the need for specialized equipment, an environment that encourages interactive play). Once again, these findings are in line with previous results related to professionals' perceptions of the increased need for active involvement and systematic instructional programs for preschool-aged students.

The way in which a special education program for preschoolers should operate was also more clearly defined by survey respondents. The following program characteristics were classified as significantly more essential for preschoolers than for infants and toddlers: (a) a current schedule describing, in a comprehensive manner, what each child is doing in the program; (b) continuous evaluation of overall program operations; (c) a systematic procedure for training and monitoring staff; (d) criterion-referenced assessment to form a basis for curriculum planning; (e) the use of developmentally appropriate and nonbiased assessments for children; and (f) a program that meets all legal and regulatory requirements for the state and locality. These findings indicated that professionals believed that preschoolers require a more structured environment than do infants and toddlers.

CONCLUSION

In this chapter, various issues and concerns regarding early childhood services for young children with pervasive needs were discussed. Emphasis was placed on developing comprehensive, transdisciplinary, and family-focused services. In some areas appropriate practices are well defined, whereas in others research is needed to determine what is appropriate.

Early special education services can be delivered in a variety of natural settings, such as homes, hospitals, day care centers, or preschools. This greatly extends opportunities for interactions between children with and without disabilities. The early interventionist should be able to organize play groups in which more able children are encouraged to provide models for language and social development. The early intervention service providers can also model their skills in this area so that other adults are more likely to provide social inclusion for children with disabilities. Beyond child assessment, special service providers need to analyze integrated environments and assist in adapting them if specific equipment or communication devices are necessary.

In established programs that are not designed specifically for children with disabilities, special service providers may have to overcome administrative or attitudinal barriers to inclusion. The physical and emotional environment must be prepared for the identified child and family. Preparations include talking with staff, parents, and enrolled children about human differences in general, as well as the benefits of inclusion for all children. Prior training for staff and peers who are nondisabled, concerning the specific equipment or communication needs of the targeted child, may also be necessary.

The practice of bringing nondisabled children into programs serving primarily children with disabilities is common. Given the shortage of quality preschools, it is not difficult to identify parents willing to enroll their children in these settings. This is not the preferred inclusion setting, however, because it reinforces the concept that separate classrooms or facilities for people with disabilities are acceptable.

Team teaching in preschools has been demonstrated to be an effective practice. This involves the merging of special and regular preschool classes with staff members sharing teaching responsibilities. This practice conveniently increases the skill levels and knowledge areas of both special and regular teachers. With the identified shortages in trained early childhood special services personnel, this model provides an opportunity for extant special educators to gain the necessary skills and knowledge needed to work with very young children. In addition, trained special educators could share their expertise in behavior management, individualization, and direct instruction with the regular teacher.

In this chapter, we emphasized that service providers cannot work in isolation with young children who experience pervasive needs. These children's families and their support networks are the most critical components of early intervention. No paid provider can equal the love and commitment family members bring to the relationship with their child. Early childhood special education is responsible for meeting the needs of families as well as the needs of identified youngsters. Again, a primary role of special service providers is to strengthen family systems, helping family members articulate their needs and desires.

We emphasized in this chapter the conceptual framework and goals of transdisciplinary teaming, curricular models, and inclusive services. These are the technical aspects—the mechanics—of early childhood special education. There is more than science to this discipline, however. Gifted professionals must assist parents to articulate their vision, maintain hope, and rejoice in the miracle of life. The early interventionist must become an artist, and help focus and potentiate each family's dream for their child, regardless of the intensity and endurance of the child's needs.

REFERENCES

Ainsworth, M. D. S. (1973). The development of infant–mother attachment. In B. Caldwell & H. Ricciuti (Eds.), *Review of child development research* (Vol. 3, pp. 1–94). Chicago: University of Chicago Press.

INFANTS, TODDLERS, AND PRESCHOOLERS

Bailey, D. B., Simeonsson, R. J., Winton, P. J. Huntington, G. S., Comfort, M., Isbell, P., O'Donnell, P., & Helm, J. M. (1986). Family-focused intervention: A functional model for planning, implementing, and evaluating individualized family services in early intervention. *Journal of the Division for Early Childhood, 10,* 156–171.

Barnard, K., Bee, H. L., & Hammond, M. A. (1984). Developmental changes in maternal interactions with term and preterm infants. *Infant Behavior and Development, 7,* 101–113.

Bennett, F. C. (1987). The effectiveness of early intervention for infants at increased biological risk. In M. J. Guralnick & F. C. Bennett (Eds.), *The effectiveness of early intervention for at-risk and handicapped children* (pp. 79–112). Orlando, FL: Academic Press.

Bennett, F. C., & Guralnick M. J. (1992). Promoting development and integration of infants experiencing neonatal intensive care. In K. A. Haring, D. L. Lovett, & N. G. Haring (Eds.), *Integrated lifecycle services for persons with disabilities* (pp. 198–219). New York: Springer-Verlag.

Bricker, D., Bailey, E., & Bruder, M. (1984). The efficacy of early intervention and the handicapped infant: A wise or wasted resource. *Advances in developmental and behavorial pediatrics.* In M. Wolraich and D. K. Routh (Eds.), Volume 5, pp. 373–423. Greenwich, CT: JAI Press.

Bricker, D. D., & Carlson, L. (1981). Issues in early language intervention. In R. L. Schiefelbusch & D. D. Bricker (Eds.), *Early language: Acquisition and intervention* (Vol. 6, pp. 477–515). Baltimore: University Park Press.

Crnic, K. A., Ragozin, A. S., Greenberg, M. T., Robinson, N. M., & Basham, R. B. (1983). Social interaction and developmental competence of preterm and full-term infants during the first year of life. *Child Development, 54,* 1190–1210.

Dunn, W. (1991). Integrated related services. In L. H. Meyer, C. A. Peck, & L. Brown (Eds.), *Critical issues in the lives of people with severe disabilities* (pp. 353–377). Baltimore: Brookes.

Dunst, C. J. (1985). Rethinking early intervention. *Analysis and Intervention in Developmental Disabilities, 5,* 165–201.

Dunst, C. J., Trivette, C. M., & Cross, A. (1986). Roles and support networks of mothers of handicapped children. In R. Fewell & P. Vadasy (Eds.), *Families of handicapped children: Needs and supports across the life span* (pp. 167–192). Austin, TX: PRO-ED.

Garland, C., McGonigel, M., Frank, A., & Buck, D. (1989). *The transdiciplinary model of service delivery.* Lightfoot, VA: Child Development Resources.

Giangreco, M. F., York, J., & Rainforth, B. (1989). Providing related services to learners with severe handicaps in educational settings: Pursuing the least restrictive option. *Pediatric Physical Therapy, 1*(2), 55–63.

Hanson, M. J., & Haring, K. A. (1992). Community-based early childhood service practices. In K. A. Haring, D. L. Lovett, & N. G. Haring (Eds.), *Integrated lifestyle services for persons with disabilities* (pp. 220–245). New York: Springer-Verlag.

Hanson, M. J., Lynch, E. W., & Wayman, K. I. (1990). Honoring the cultural diversity of families when gathering data. *Topics in Early Childhood Special Education, 10*(1), 112–131.

Haring, K. A., Lovett, D. L., & Kliene, P. (1992). *The impact of federal legislation on family systems theory: Year two continuation report.* Unpublished manuscript, University of Oklahoma, Norman.

Haring, K. A., Staub, D., & Farron-Davis, F. (1990). *Level two data summary report.* Unpublished manuscript, California Research Institute, San Francisco State University, San Francisco.

Hart, V. (1977). The use of many disciplines with the severely and profoundly handicapped. In E. Sontag, J. Smith, & N. Certo (Eds.), *Educational programming for the severely and profoundly handicapped* (pp. 391–396). Reston, VA: Council for Exceptional Children.

Kaiser, A. P., & Hemmeter, M. L. (1989). Value-based approaches to family intervention. *Topics in Early Childhood Special Education, 8*(4), 72–86.

Kent-Udolf, L. (1984). Current therapy of communication disorders: Programming language. In W. Perkins (Ed.), *Language handicaps in children* (pp. 15–25). New York: Thieme-Stratton.

Kogan, K., Tyler, N., & Turner, P. (1974). The process of interpersonal adaptations between mothers and their cerebral palsied children. *Developmental Medicine and Child Neurology, 16,* 518–527.

Lehr, D. (1989). Educational programming for young children with the most severe disabilities. In F. Brown & D. H. Lehr (Eds.), *Persons with profound disabilities: Issues and practices* (pp. 213–237). Baltimore: Brookes.

Lewis, M. (1984). Developmental principles and their implications for at-risk and handicapped infants. In M. J. Hanson (Ed.), *Atypical infant development* (pp. 3–24). Austin, TX: PRO-ED.

Lynch, E. W., & Hanson, M. J. (1992). *Developing cross-cultural competence: A guide for working with young children and their families.* Baltimore: Brookes.

Malette, P., Mirenda, P., Kandborg, T., Jones, P., Bunz, T., & Rogow, S. (1992). Applications of a lifestyle development process for persons with severe intellectual disabilities: A case study report. *Journal of The Association for Persons with Severe Handicaps, 17,* 179–191.

McCormick, L., & Goldman, R. (1979). The transdisciplinary model: Implications for service delivery and personnel preparation for the severely and profoundly handicapped. *AAESPH Review, 4*(2), 151–161.

McDonnell, A., & Hardman, M. (1988). A synthesis of "best practice" guidelines for early childhood services. *Journal of the Division for Early Childhood, 12,* 328–341.

Michael, M. G., & Paul, P. V. (1991). Early intervention for infants with deaf–blindness. *Exceptional Children, 57,* 200–210.

Minuchin, S. (1974). *Families and family therapy.* Cambridge, MA: Harvard University Press.

Mount, B. (1987). *Personal futures planning: Finding directions for change.* Unpublished doctoral dissertation, University of Georgia, Athens.

Mount, B., & Zwernik, K. (1988). *It's never too early, it's never too late* (Publication No. 421-88-109). St. Paul, MN: Metropolitan Council.

Odom, S. L., & McEvoy, M. A. (1988). Integration of young children with handicaps and normally developing children. In S. L. Odom and M. B. Karnes (Eds.), *Early intervention for infants and children with handicaps* (pp. 241–268). Baltimore: Brookes.

Ogletree, B. T., Wetherby, A. M., & Westling, D. L. (1992). Profile of the prelinguistic intentional communicative behaviors of children with profound mental retardation. *American Journal on Mental Retardation, 97*(2), 186–196.

Olson, D. H., McCubbin, H. I., Barnes, H., Larsen, A., Muxen, M., & Wilson, M. (1983). *Families: What makes them work?* Beverly Hills, CA: Sage.

Orelove, F. P., & Sobsey, D. (1992). *Educating children with multiple disabilities: A transdisciplinary approach* (2nd ed.). Baltimore: Brookes.

Public Law 94-142. (1975). *Education for All Handicapped Children Act of 1975*, 20 U.S.C., Secs. 1401–1461.

Public Law 99-457. (1986). *Education of the Handicapped Act Amendments of 1986*, 20 U.S.C., 676.

Siegel-Causey, E., & Ernst, B. (1989). Theoretical orientation and research in nonsymbolic development. In E. Siegel-Causey & D. Guess (Eds.), *Enhancing nonsymbolic communication interactions among learners with severe disabilities* (pp. 15–51). Baltimore: Brookes.

Silber, S. (1989). Family influences on early development. *Topics in Early Childhood Special Education, 8*(4), 1–23.

Strain, P. A. (1990). LRE for preschool children with handicaps: What we know, what we should be doing. *Journal of Early Intervention, 14*(4), 291–296.

Turnbull, A. P., Summers, J. A., & Brotherson, M. J. (1984). *Working with families with disabled members: A family systems approach.* Lawrence: University of Kansas, Kansas University Affiliated Facility.

Turnbull, A. P., & Turnbull, H. R. (1986). *Families, professionals, and exceptionality: A special partnership.* Columbus, OH: Merrill.

Tyler, N. B., & Kogan, K. L. (1977). Reduction of stress between mothers and their handicapped children. *The American Journal of Occupational Therapy, 31*, 151–155.

Vandercook, T., York, J., & Forest, M. (1989). The McGill Action Planning System (MAPS): A strategy for building the vision. *Journal of The Association for Persons with Severe Handicaps, 14*, 202–215.

Westlake, C. R., & Kaiser, A. P. (1991). Early childhood services for children with severe disabilities: Research, values, policy, and practice. In L. H. Meyer, C. P. Peck, & L. Brown (Eds.), *Critical issues in the lives of people with severe disabilities* (pp. 429–458). Baltimore: Brookes.

White, K., Bush, D., & Casto, G. (1985). Learning from reviews of early intervention. *Journal of Special Education, 19*, 417–428.

Wolfensberger, W. (1972). *Normalization: The principle of normalization in human services.* Toronto, Canada: National Institute on Mental Retardation.

York, J., Rainforth, B., & Giangreco, M. F. (1990). Transdisciplinary teamwork and integrated therapy: Clarifying the misconceptions. *Pediatric Physical Therapy, 2*(2), 73–79.

Chapter 12

Curriculum and Instruction for Elementary-Aged Students with Profound Disabilities

PAUL A. ALBERTO, KENT R. LOGAN,
TONI WAYLOR-BOWEN, and THOMAS G. KANA

In Chapter 10, we discussed various aspects of an effective curriculum design for students with profound disabilities. We recommended that an activity-based curricular approach be emphasized, including its component analyses of basic developmental skills (BDSs), steps, and tasks. In this chapter, we discuss the application of this design and components to elementary-aged students who are profoundly disabled.

ACTIVITY-BASED CURRICULA: GOALS AND TENETS

An activity-based curriculum for elementary-aged students with profound disabilities addresses three learning goals: increased performance, increased social interaction, and expanded social networks and environments. Within an activity-based curriculum, specific performance targets are considered to be the acquisition of basic developmental skills, task steps, and/or whole tasks. Application of these performance targets is always considered within the context of functional activities because learning at all three performance levels is more efficient, especially for BDSs, when embedded within the context of functional activities (Gee, Goetz, Graham, & Lee, 1987). It has also been demonstrated that students are more motivated when performance is used in such an applied manner (Goetz & Gee, 1987). For example, a student may learn to push in an isolated and nonfunctional manner by practicing over and over moving a block across a wheelchair lap tray. In contrast, the student can learn the same skill by pushing into a tub during cleanup the blocks with which he or she played during leisure time. When a student learns and performs BDSs and/or steps within the context of a functional activity, the result is a functional effect.

Acquisition of BDSs and/or steps can be viewed within single functional activities. It is just as important, however, to demonstrate application of BDSs and/or steps to multiple functional activities across the day. Teaching across the day involves changing the materials used, the settings, and possibly the instructor. These changes facilitate maintenance and generalization (Goetz & Gee, 1987). Teaching with such distributed and spaced opportunities (trials) is more effective than teaching a skill in a massed trial fashion (i.e., repeating the skill over and over within a single session) (Mulligan, Lacy, & Guess, 1982; see Chapter 9). For example, the student may learn to *push* blocks off a wheelchair tray during cleanup, *push* a microswitch to turn on a tape player during the class leisure period, and *push* dirty cans into a water tub during recycling. Again, the functional effect of the action may be learned and, at the same time, serve as a reinforcer. When the switch is pushed, desired music is heard from a tape player; when the can is pushed, it drops into soapy water so that it may be cleaned.

As a student acquires BDSs, steps, and/or tasks through direct instruction, related performance is also affected. This is often termed *corollary learning*. One type of corollary learning is increased control over one's environment. In that activity-based curriculum has as its emphasis the active involvement of the student, such involvement can increase students' competence in being active and directive in performing portions of activities. Students may learn that their actions have an effect on their surroundings, that they can make choices, and how to initiate behaviors and interactions (Brown, Helmstetter, & Guess, 1986; Sternberg, McNerney, & Pegnatore, 1985). This corollary learning is not achieved when the student is a passive receiver–participant in class activities.

Increased social interaction also requires an active student role in learning. Actively involved students become more awake and alert, thus increasing their potential to interact with persons and objects in the environment (McWilliam, Trivette, & Dunst, 1985). Increasing the amount of time in which the student is actively engaged in activities allows for increases in the overall number, diversity, and complexity of performance. It also provides opportunities for increasing the number and types of environments in which performance can take place (Evans & Scotti, 1989).

Increased performance competence by the elementary student in social, communication, play, and mobility skills can bring concurrent increases in the quality, number, and variety of interactions with others in the student's social network (e.g., peers, adults, family members). For example, learning skills such as looking and vocalizing when spoken to can elicit enjoyment in others, and increase subsequent attentiveness and responsiveness to the student. These have been referred to as *second-order effects* (Dunst, Cuishing, & Vance, 1985). Second-order effects may also be of help to teachers and caregivers in allowing them more time for their own responsibilities and interests (Dunst et al., 1985). For example, a student may learn to occupy himself or herself with a favorite toy for a period of time at home, or to initiate and engage with a sibling. This may leave a parent free to perform household tasks. While in the community, a student may learn to hold a grocery basket instead of continually grabbing items off the shelves. For the parent, this may mean that the student can be taken to the grocery store instead of being left at home with a babysitter. For the student, it may mean that trips to the store are more likely, thereby giving that student more opportunities for maintenance and generalization of the skill. This may also increase the number of environments into which he or she is taken. In the classroom, improvement in performance objectives allows the teacher more time to work with other students or to work with all the students in other activities. The teacher may also be able to place the student with other groups of students, allowing for still more and different social interactions.

CURRICULUM DOMAINS

For elementary-aged students with profound disabilities, the three learning goals described should be dealt with within three learning domains: domestic, leisure, and community. The domestic domain contains activities that are concerned with personal and residential care. The purpose for emphasizing activities within this domain is to afford the student increased participation in critical activities and tasks that relate to the development of traditional self-help skills. The leisure domain relates to individual and group play activities within the school, home, and community. A primary focus within the play area is the development of social interaction and communication skills. The community domain provides the opportunity for students to generalize school-based learning into community settings that are less structured and have different performance variables. This allows both the student and the teacher to confront community performance standards, natural cues, reinforcement, and correction. In the following sections, we provide examples of activities and instruction within each of these domains.

Domestic Domain

For elementary-aged students, the focus of instruction in the domestic domain is on *critical activities*. Critical activities are defined as those that are necessary in everyday life and that, if the student is unable to complete them independently, must be done for the student by a caregiver (Brown et al., 1983). These are activities and tasks such as eating, toileting, dressing, and washing. The first goal of instruction is to improve performance within the context of such critical activities.

With increased student participation in domestic activities, several corollary learning and second-order effects will likely occur:

1. *Increase in student control over the environment.* As a result of participation in these activities, the student's personal dignity is enhanced as he or she can perform certain intimate tasks for himself or herself.

2. *Encounters with environments, such as alternative living arrangements and social meeting places, that will require the ability to participate in personal care activities* (Brown et al., 1983). Meeting the performance objectives during the elementary school years can have a direct impact on the number of environments students may eventually access.

3. *Reduction in student dependence on the caregiver* (Dunst et al., 1985). Through increases in student performance, there is a concomitant decrease in the amount of time necessary for the caregiver to provide the student assistance in completing the activity.

4. *Increase in health and cleanliness from increased participation in hygiene tasks.* Performance objectives that lead to a healthier environment for the student, as well as for those around the student, are important for classroom health management.

5. *Increase in social interaction.* As students participate in personal care activities, the quality of their appearance and hygiene also increases. These changes may lead to increases in social interactions, as physical elements that may have stigmatized the students are reduced.

Increased participation in residential care activities (maintenance of the home and school environments) extends the number of environments in which the student may participate. Residential care activities may take place in the home, classroom, or other areas of the school building. Participation in each of these environments may lead to generalization of performance objectives. Activities at the elementary level lay the foundation for secondary experiences in community residential sites in preparation for transition to postschool alternative living arrangements (Sternlicht, 1978; see Chapter 13).

Examples of activities, tasks, steps, and basic developmental skills

Personal and residential care activities can be broken down into their component tasks, steps, and BDSs. The following are examples of how each may be structured for instruction within specified activities.

Personal care

Personal care activities include those activities related to toileting, grooming, dressing, eating, and hygiene or first aid (Table 12.1). Activities can be subdivided to accommodate the learning needs of individual students.

Focusing on the *activity* of grooming and the *task* of toothbrushing, a task analysis might result in eight steps: (1) gather necessary materials, (2) turn on water, (3) rinse toothbrush, (4) put toothpaste on toothbrush, (5) brush teeth, (6) rinse mouth and toothbrush, (7) turn off water, and (8) return materials. A targeted *step* of the task analysis might be turning on the water using a single grasp and pulling the handle forward. Within this step, a *basic developmental skill* might be targeted, such as pulling (fine motor) the water faucet handle forward to turn on the water.

Depending on the student's functioning level, he or she may partially participate at the task level by independent performance of any one or more

TABLE 12.1. Activities Associated with Personal Care

Toileting	Grooming	Dressing	Eating	Hygiene or First Aid
Following toileting schedule	Face washing	Dressing and undressing	Use of utensils	Keeping hand and objects out of mouth
Locating bathroom	Handwashing	Hanging clothes on hook or hanger	Use of cup	Blowing nose
Toileting routine (undressing, sitting on toilet, dressing, handwashing)	Toothbrushing	Folding clothes	Chewing	Accepting medications
	Combing or brushing hair		Swallowing	
	Deodorant use	Opening and closing Velcro fasteners	Sucking	
Indicating accidents			Wiping mouth	
			Signaling for empty and/or finished	

of the steps, partially participate at the step level (e.g., by holding the toothbrush while the teacher puts on the toothpaste), or partially participate at the basic developmental skill level (e.g., by opening his or her mouth when he or she sees the toothbrush).

Residential care

Residential care activities include those activities related to food preparation, home cleaning, classroom cleaning, and performing cleaning tasks within the school building (Table 12.2).

Using the *activity* of home living and the *task* of dusting as examples, a task analysis might result in the following six steps: (1) locate dustmitt, (2) place on hand, (3) place mitt surface on end table, (4) make sweeping motions with mitt over entire table, (5) repeat until each end table is dusted, and (6) return materials. A *step* for this task might be dusting the end table by making a sweeping motion with a dustmitt. A *basic developmental skill* might be targeted for instruction within this step, such as pushing (fine motor) the dustmitt with the hand along the corner of the end table.

Depending on functioning level, the student might partially participate at the task level by independent performance of any one or more of the steps in the task, partially participate at the step level (e.g., by moving the dustmitt after a peer has sprayed the end table with furniture polish), or partially participate at the basic developmental skill level (e.g., by holding the dustmitt while the teacher moves the student's hand in a sweeping motion).

General implementation suggestions

It is important that both personal and residential care activities take place in locations where they would naturally occur. These locations may be found in many different environments, both within the school itself and in the community. For example, grooming activities can take place in the bathroom connected to the classroom, a bathroom in the school building, or the bathroom in a local store.

Along with the natural location for activities, the natural time and sequence of activities should also be taken into account. Natural time refers to the time of day that the activities and/or tasks would routinely be performed. Natural sequence refers to the order in which the tasks would routinely be performed within an activity. For example, the natural times in which a personal care activity should be scheduled would be when the student arrives in the morning, after snack and lunch, before going into the community, and before going home. Within those times, several natural sequences may occur. These may include handwashing after a toileting activity, and before and after a snack, or a toy pickup task after play.

TABLE 12.2. Activities Associated with Residential Care

Food Preparation	Home	Classroom	In School
Gathering materials	Clothes washing	Picking up toys	Can crushing
Adapted use of appliances	Bedmaking	Putting chairs under table	Delivering office messages (with peers)
Washing or drying dishes	Vacuuming	Wiping tables and/or desks	Cleaning other classrooms, media center, and/or cafeteria
Cleanup	Dusting	Wiping boards	
	Watering plants	Cleaning sinks	
	Cleaning sinks	Cleaning and straightening lockers and/or cubbies	Collecting and sharpening pencils for peers
	Wiping countertops and/or tables		

Activities should accommodate students with various needs. For example, when arranging morning snack, it is important to ensure that students who are tube-fed have something to do throughout the activity. If they are fed prior to snack time, they can operate the toaster as do other students, assist in pouring beverages, or pass out napkins. If they are fed at the same time, they should be close to the table and involved communicatively and socially. Students with physical limitations may often be included within activities with the use of alternative performance strategies (Wilcox & Bellamy, 1982). For example, a basic microswitch will allow a student to operate the blender when making juice drinks. Switching from bar soap to a pump dispenser may allow a student to participate more fully in his or her own handwashing.

Because instruction and performance take place within natural activities, "natural" materials should also be used. Not all materials, however, can be used directly by young children. Teacher assessment determines if adaptations in materials need to be made in order to allow a student some participation in an activity in which there was none previously, or for the student to become more independent and/or fluent in his or her performance. For example, a student with limited use of his or her hands might not be able to hold a typical spoon. He or she may, however, be able to make a scooping motion and open his or her mouth when a spoon is presented. The spoon, therefore, may require an adapted handle to increase independent feeding. If the student is already using a spoon with a built-up handle but is still unable to eat with it, it might be made more effective by bending the scoop end toward the student's mouth, thereby making an existing adaptation more efficient. Occupational and physical therapists should be asked to assist in evaluating and designing new adaptations and/or changes in current adaptations of materials.

Certain student-directed activities can become routine for the teacher and inadvertently exclude student learning. Administering medication to students is one example. This activity can often be accomplished rather easily by the teacher or paraprofessional, but it can also provide important learning opportunities for the student. Therefore, a task sequence should be prepared for this activity as for all others. The student can learn to cooperate and partially participate by learning to track the pill and open his or her mouth, grasp a pill from the teacher's hand, or hold the liquid dispenser with the teacher. This inclusion through partial participation should extend to other critical skills, such as hip movement during diaper changes and grasping pants after toileting.

For personal care activities, it is especially important to confer with parents. They have been engaged in these activities with their child for years before he or she started school. They will likely have established personal care routines that should be considered for use in school. If, after appropriate consultation, the teacher develops an alternative approach, all caregivers need to accept this alternative so the student is learning only one sequence.

Leisure Domain

As in the domestic domain, the primary focus of the leisure domain is acquisition and application of basic developmental skills, steps, and/or tasks. Performance objectives taught in the leisure domain should directly increase the competence of students in their use of toys, equipment, and other leisure materials. Play is also a natural setting for the development of communication and social skills (Pellegrini & Galda, 1990; Sachs, 1984).

Structured play provides a reason to communicate and a setting for social interactions. A leisure activity may be an individual activity or may be designed to include other class members, peers who are nondisabled, and/or adults. Therefore, both individual and group use of items should be targeted as objectives. Increases in individual competence in toy or equipment use, communication, and social skills relate to several corollary and second order effects, as follows:

1. *Increase in the type and number of social interactions in which the student participates.* The student can move from playing individually, to cooperating with another student in a game, to participating in a large group. Opportunities can progress from those structured by the teacher, to play with siblings, to play during school recess and with neighborhood peers.

2. *Increase in choice-making skills development.* As the student becomes more familiar with toys, play equipment, and materials,

and more competent in their use, he or she may begin making choices. Choice making can also extend into control of the social environment. As a student's social skills increase, he or she may begin to choose not to play alone, but rather to cooperate in interactions with a playmate. After a number of interactions have occurred, the student may also start to choose among playmates.

3. *Decrease in the amount of dependence on the teacher or caregiver to occupy the student's time.* As the student becomes more competent in play and leisure activities alone and with others, the teacher or caregiver is given more time for other duties. This may, in turn, lead to a more positive perception of the child, and reduce the stress of caring for children with profound disabilities.

As the number and type of social interactions increase for students who are profoundly disabled, there are more opportunities for communicative and cognitive skills to develop (Siegel-Causey & Guess, 1985, 1987). Given the degree of disability of these students, social and communication exchanges may be difficult to see and/or interpret. The challenge for the teacher is recognition and interpretation of communication signals. If the student's repeated attempts to elicit a causal effect are missed or ignored, the teacher may have to assume increasing responsibility in initiating and controlling interchanges (Siegel-Causey & Downing, 1987; see Chapter 7). This would result in lessening students' skill development and influence on their environment.

Examples of activities, tasks, steps, and basic developmental skills

The following are examples of goals for basic developmental skills, steps, and tasks, and of how they might fit into activities in three leisure domain activities: play with toys and materials, play with equipment, and social interaction and group play (see Table 12.3).

Play with toys and materials

Toys and materials are items such as dolls, animals, paints, and manipulative items (e.g., a plastic Slinky). Teachers should attempt to teach students an appropriate way in which to play and interact with toys (e.g., push the car across the lap tray to another student as opposed to placing the car in the mouth). Parents should be asked what toys the student likes to play with at home, as well as how they are played with and with whom. Toy play can occur alone (e.g., holding and squeezing a ball to get a sound) and in a group (e.g., passing a ball to a classmate). If play occurs in groups, the teacher can take advantage of that context to work on specific social-interactive and

TABLE 12.3. Leisure Domain Activities and Materials

Play with toys and materials

dolls	puzzles
plastic Slinky	musical instruments
animals	bean bags
blocks	Zube tubes
cars	paints
Nerf balls	battery-operated toys (microswitch use)
clay	sound-activated toys
Ooze	body heat–activated toys
puppets	motion-activated toys
bubbles	crayons

painting with pudding, shaving cream, whipped cream, cake icing (materials used may be applied directly with hands or with brushes, sponges, deodorant rollers)

water play with small plastic figures, whistles, balls, floating toys, pouring implements (can also use beans, styrofoam peanuts, or sand in place of water)

Play with equipment

television	Big Wheels
video cassette recorder	scooter boards
computer games	rocking horses and chairs
tape recorders	small trampolines
walkmans	playground equipment
record players	plastic skates
radios	fans
keyboards	

Games for social interaction and group play

"Flippin Flapjacks"	Duck–Duck Goose
"Ants in the Pants"	Ring Around the Rosey
"Cootie"	"Animal Dominos"
"Don't Spill the Beans"	Hot Potato

communication skills (e.g., acknowledgments, interchanges, initiations, turn-taking, sharing), as well as instruction in the use of the toy(s). While group play that requires the cooperation of students is being learned, students may also learn to play individually within a group context (*parallel play*). Sand, water, and beans can provide different media for the use of toys. Battery-operated toys have the advantage of being adaptable for use with microswitches.

For the *activity* of playing with dolls, there are a variety of possible tasks, including (a) locating doll(s) and play area, (b) feeding the doll lunch, (c) washing the doll and combing its hair, (d) changing the doll, (e) rocking the doll, (f) putting the doll to bed, and (g) cleaning up materials.

An example of a *task* might be giving the doll a bottle for lunch. A possible task analysis for feeding the doll might result in seven steps: (1) locating the doll and bottle, (2) filling the bottle with "formula" (water from sink), (3) grasping the doll and holding it with one arm, (4) grasping the bottle with the opposite hand, (5) placing the end of the bottle in the doll's mouth, (6) feeding the doll until the formula is gone, and (7) cleaning up the materials.

An example of a targeted *step* might be grasping the bottle with one hand and placing the end of the bottle in the doll's mouth. A number of *basic developmental skills* may be targeted for instruction within the step, and might include *attending* (cognition) to the doll by looking at it while the doll is being fed and *signaling* (expressive communication) to summon the teacher or peer when the student is finished feeding the doll.

A student might partially participate at the task level by feeding the doll as part of the overall activity of playing with dolls. He or she may partially participate at the step level by grasping the doll with one arm and holding it in his or her lap while the teacher or peer feeds the doll the bottle. At the basic developmental skill level, the student might partially participate by attending, as demonstrated by moving his or her body toward the doll in order to help feed it.

Playing with equipment

Equipment includes items such as televisions, tape recorders, tricycles, and playground equipment. The use of electronic equipment has as its emphasis fine-motor skills, whereas the larger toys and playground equipment typically require gross-motor skills. Gross-motor play need not involve direct contact with equipment. For example, a student might dance or do aerobics by swinging his or her arms when a record is played. Gross-motor play also includes running and searching games, such as hide-and-seek, which may not involve the use of any equipment. As with toy play, playing with equipment can be done individually (e.g., playing the keyboard alone) and in groups (e.g., playing the keyboard with a friend).

For the *activity* of operating a tape player, there may be a number of tasks: (a) finding the area and materials, (b) choosing what to play, (c) loading and turning on a tape recorder, (d) listening to the tape, and (e) unloading and turning off the tape recorder.

An example of a *task* might be loading and turning on a tape recorder. The task analysis might be as follows: (1) locate tape recorder, (2) open lid of tape recorder, (3) grasp tape with hand, (4) place tape in recorder, (5) close door, and (6) locate and push the start button. A targeted *step* might be placing the tape in the recorder. A *basic developmental skill* might be targeted for the step, such as *orienting* (auditory) through a head turn to the sound of the tape door closing.

Students might partially participate at the task level by learning to perform steps independently as part of the overall activity of listening to music (e.g., locating and pushing the start button). They may partially participate in one or more of the steps (e.g., grasping the tape prior to its placement into the tape recorder). At the basic developmental skill level, a student might partially participate by indicating which tape he or she would like to continue to hear by producing a communicative signal (expressive communication), such as a smile or vocalization.

Social interaction and group play

Social interactions with others can take place during almost all activities. They can, therefore, be specifically structured and taught within activities. Leisure activities such as group games are an especially good context in which to practice these skills, which are, by their very nature, interactive. Games such as "Don't Spill the Beans" and Hot Potato can be used and adapted as activities for students with profound disabilities (e.g., some portion may be performed by the student). Other games (e.g., Duck–Duck Goose) may not involve the direct use of equipment, but are equally valuable as an interactive context.

For the *activity* of playing a group game, such as "Don't Spill the Beans," there are a number of possible tasks, including (a) locating and retrieving the game, (b) unpacking and setting up the game, (c) taking turns playing the game, (d) repeating turns or completing the game, and (e) cleaning up and replacing materials.

An example of a *task* might be playing when it is one's turn to play. A task analysis for turn-taking in this game might result in seven steps: (1) wait for turn to come; (2) locate and grasp bean; (3) find opening for pants; (4) put hand with bean over opening; (5) drop in bean; (6) if pants spill, collect beans; and (7) wait for next turn.

A targeted instructional *step* for the student might be placing his or her hand with the bean over the pants and releasing the bean. A number of *basic developmental skills* may be targeted for instruction within this step, including *showing* (social) the bean to one's peers once it is within his or her grasp and/or *anticipating* (cognition) his or her turn by holding out a hand when shown a bean.

A student might partially participate at the task level by learning to take a turn as part of the overall activity of playing the game. He or she might partially participate at the step level by reaching for a bean and holding it in his or her hand. At the basic developmental skill level, a student may partially participate by pushing (motor) all the spilled beans to each of his or her classmates after the beans have spilled out of the pants.

General implementation suggestions

Prior to teaching play skills, one should consider the materials to be used. Toys, materials, and equipment should be age appropriate; that is, matched to the chronological age of the student and peers. In addition, the size and adaptability of items should be considered in relation to the physical characteristics of the students (e.g., Is the item too big? Can a microswitch be used?). Students with sensory disabilities may prefer toys that are sensorially attractive (e.g., can make noise, have flashing bright lights). Toys are also available that are activated by methods other than a switch (e.g., through heat, sound, movement).

Caregivers can be asked to send in toys from home. Direct instruction with these toys can then take place in the classroom. These learned skills can then be of value in both the classroom and the home environment. Prior to ordering toys, teachers can show catalogs to caregivers, who can provide information concerning student preferences. Physical and occupational therapists should be consulted concerning the roles that specific toys may have in the development of movement skills, and physical constraints that may make the selection of some toys inappropriate. These professionals also have valuable knowledge on student-specific adaptations for materials.

Skills should be selected so that both group and individual leisure activities are addressed. Play with peers is an appropriate and normalizing activity. Group leisure activities are important in that "rules" for interaction (e.g., waiting and responding, turn-taking, sharing) may be learned. Games and other play activities are a good context in which to use peer tutors. Tutors can often suggest adaptations, ideas, and methods for incorporating students into leisure activities that the teacher may not have yet considered. Individual play skills should not be ignored, however, in that they are also important in allowing a student to be actively involved in an appropriate manner by himself or herself.

Activities for practicing communication and social skills may occur spontaneously or may need to be arranged by the teacher. For example, a game of catch with a Nerf ball requires another participant. If the student prefers to squeeze the ball, the teacher may require that the student communicate with a peer to obtain a turn with the ball. These types of interactions, therefore, can be structured and taught around objects such as toys. It is important to build these types of experiences into the overall curriculum design, in that increases in student performance levels may bring interaction and attention from family members, other adults, nondisabled peers, and classmates in various environments.

Students should have various types of balanced play opportunities. They should engage in activities that require small-item manipulation (toys, tape recorders, water play) and use of larger equipment (tricycles, scooters, trampolines); emphasize small-muscle use (building blocks) and large-muscle experiences (aerobics, playground equipment); expose students to rules of toy use or interaction (catch) and those that allow exploration (art); require play alone and play with others; and emphasize play in and out of the classroom. To provide this range of activities, it may be necessary to schedule more than one play period per day. For young children, this should not be considered wasted or free time. In each activity, there are specific basic developmental skills or steps to be learned, as well as communication and social skills.

The teacher should remember that the main idea behind leisure activities is for the student to experience intrinsic enjoyment and motivation (Wolery & Bailey, 1989). The teacher should be aware of signs of positive affect from the student, such as smiling, vocalizations, and body movements toward the materials and/or playmates. If the student seems not to enjoy the activity, it is probably best to try another one.

Community Domain

As with students with moderate and severe disabilities, the basis of instruction in the community domain for students with profound disabilities is a community-referenced curriculum taught in appropriate community settings. Curriculum content should be derived in part from an ecological analysis of relevant community settings, and instruction should take place in those settings.

Community-based instruction for elementary-aged students with profound disabilities should provide varied opportunities for practice of basic developmental skills, steps, and/or tasks within functional, age-appropriate activities. This opportunity should be provided in various integrated environments in which the student can associate with individuals who are not disabled. It is expected that these instructional opportunities will result in outcomes that demonstrate both increased independence through partial participation and beneficial effects for caregivers (Evans & Scotti, 1989).

The goals of instruction in the community domain include the following:

1. *Student application of basic developmental skills, steps, and/or tasks.* The community provides the opportunity for generalized practice in nonschool environments of skills initially learned in school (e.g., generalizing from the school cafeteria to community eateries). Instruction across community settings provides opportunities for distributed and spaced practice, which enhances long-term learning and habit formation.

2. *Analysis of the generalization of skills acquired.* Being in the community provides the opportunity to analyze the generalization of students' communication and mobility systems in order to make modifications or adaptations necessary for functional use outside the school building. Unless these systems are used in the com-

munity, their functional effectiveness outside the school cannot be judged.

3. *Increased opportunities for students to become aware of, participate in, and become accustomed to the demands of a variety of community environments.* Students should learn to accommodate to varied environmental conditions (e.g., noise levels, activity levels, size of locations, crowds). Changes in the location of instruction also assist in maintaining alertness levels of the students (Belfliore, 1990).

4. *Positive effect of student learning on caregivers.* Parents may be reluctant to take students into the community because of their behaviors (e.g., vocal control; touching self, others, and items; drooling). Instruction in the community provides the teacher the opportunity to take students into various environments in order to analyze functional reasons for inappropriate behavior. The teacher can then try various strategies for behavior reduction similar to what is done in classroom analyses of behavior (see Chapter 5). Successful, community-based strategies can then be shared with caregivers so they can be encouraged to take the children into community environments.

As stated above, community-based instruction provides the educator with opportunities to discover the status and potential limitations of a student's current communication and mobility skills. For example, the functionality of a student's communication system can be judged by determining answers to questions such as (a) Does the student make generalized use of the system? (b) Does the system provide for effective communication in the community with individuals who are not disabled? (c) Can individuals who are not disabled quickly learn the system in order to provide two-way communication, or is the system so idiosyncratic that it needs an adaptation for use in the community or constant assistance through the use of a third party?

In relation to a student's mobility system, additional questions should be asked: (a) Can the student use the system across various contours (e.g., concrete, grass, gravel, up–down grades, entrances and exits, stairways, elevators, escalators)? (b) If necessary, can another person manage the mobility system across various contours? (c) Can the student (or assistant) negotiate barriers (curbs, puddles, curb cuts)? (d) Can the student move easily along store aisles? (e) Can the student move while holding things? (f) Is an acceptable classroom system not appropriate for use in the community (e.g., the student can get out of a chair and body roll to the toy shelf; however, this is not deemed appropriate in the community setting)?

Being in the community may also bring to the teacher's attention certain behaviors that occur at tolerable levels in the classroom but do not meet community acceptance standards. For example, in the classroom, a student may engage in low-level vocalizations that may be ignored because they do not interrupt instruction. In the community, however, such levels may bring unwanted attention to the student. Being in the community may also occasion behaviors from the student that are not encountered in school. Community-based instruction provides the opportunity to analyze inappropriate behaviors and develop management strategies.

Community experiences can also result in a more positive view of the student's capabilities as appropriate behaviors are observed. For example, a student might show limited head control most of the day in class. When in a community setting, however, head control is improved. Determining why there is this difference points to changes that must be made in the classroom to support this behavior.

Examples of activities, tasks, steps, and basic developmental skills

In most instances, community settings for elementary-aged students include three general categories: eateries, stores, and play–leisure sites (see Table 12.4).

Eateries

Various types of places to eat provide the opportunity to generalize performance objectives that might have been taught in the classroom during snack time and in the school cafeteria (e.g., focusing and accommodating on spoon or sandwich as it approaches mouth; reaching for and grasping of utensils, cups, and sandwiches; chewing and swallowing; communicative indication for next bite; locating seat).

Using the example *activity* of eating at McDonalds, there may be a number of tasks, including (1) entering and going to the counter, (2) ordering,

TABLE 12.4. Community Environments

Category	Examples
Eateries	Fast food restaurants, cafeteria-style restaurants, food courts, vendors, vending machines
Stores	Large grocery stores, convenience stores, department stores (e.g., Kmart, Wal★Mart), individual stores (clothing, sports, music, pet, greeting card, toy, hardware, pharmacy, book, laundromat)
Play–Leisure	City parks, playscapes and playgrounds, arcades, miniature golf, skating rinks, swimming pools, bowling alleys, lakes and ponds, libraries

(3) paying for one's food, (4) taking the order to a table, (5) eating, (6) disposing of trash, and (7) exiting (restroom use may be an added task).

An instructional *task* may be carrying one's tray from the counter to the table where classmates are sitting and placing the tray on the table. A task analysis might result in five steps: (1) grasp and lift tray, (2) hold tray while walking, (3) locate empty seat where companions are seated, (4) place tray on table, and (5) sit down at table. A targeted *step* for the task might be carrying the tray from the counter to a table, with *basic developmental skills* being the use of a *bilateral grasp* (fine motor) for tray carrying and *orienting* (auditory) to a teacher's voice (where the teacher is standing next to the table that the student should approach).

Depending on the student's functioning level, he or she may partially participate at the task level by independent performance of any one or more of the steps, partially participate at the step level by holding the tray while someone pushes his or her wheelchair, or participate at the basic developmental skills level by turning his or her head toward the sound of the teacher's voice.

Stores

The specific store selected as the site for instruction on any given day does not impact directly on the selection of tasks and skills, because opportunities for similar tasks and skills will occur across all stores. The overall range of store sites, however, should be diverse because each will have differing motivational and sensory experiences.

For the *activity* of shopping at Kmart, there may be five key tasks: (1) entering the store, (2) getting a shopping cart, (3) selecting items, (4) paying at the register, and (5) exiting the store. An example of a *task* might be taking items off a shelf and placing them in the shopping cart. A task analysis might result in the following steps: (1) focus on item; (2) reach, grasp, lift, and hold item; (3) transport item to cart; and (4) place and release item into cart. A targeted *step* might be placing and releasing items into the shopping cart. A number of *basic developmental skills* could be recommended for instruction, including *orienting* (vision) by turning one's head toward the cart in which an item is to be placed and *releasing* (fine motor) items into the cart when touched on one's hand.

Based upon functioning level, the student might partially participate at the task level by independent performance of any one or more of the steps; partially participate at the step level by releasing the item into the hand of a classmate, who would then deposit the item into the cart; or participate at the basic developmental skills level by smiling when he or she has a firm grasp of the item on the shelf.

Play–leisure sites

Neighborhoods provide numerous settings in which students may practice play and leisure skills, as well as learn how to engage in those skills across settings. Parks, playgrounds, and playscapes provide the opportunity to engage in objectives targeted by the physical therapist which involve large-muscle motor goals, ambulation on various surfaces (e.g., concrete, grass, up–down grades), and social skills (e.g., sharing, turn-taking, use of play materials).

For the *activity* of sandbox play, possible tasks include (a) filling pails, (b) emptying pails, (c) using toys in the sand, (d) digging holes, and (e) building things. An example of a *task* might be placing a shovel into the sand, and lifting and placing some dirt into a pail until it is full. A task analysis for filling a pail with sand might result in the following six steps: (1) locate pail and shovel, (2) lift shovel, (3) place shovel into sand, (4) scoop sand, (5) place sand into pail, and (6) repeat until pail is full. A targeted *step* might be placing a shovel in the sand and lifting the shovel. A number of *basic developmental skills* could apply to this step, including *reaching* and *grasping* (fine motor) the handle of a shovel, and *focusing* and *fixating* (vision) on the pail.

Depending on the functioning level of the student, he or she might partially participate at the task level by independent performance of any one or more of the steps; partially participate at the step level by holding the shovel and receiving assistance with placing it in the sand and lifting it; or participate at the basic developmental skills level by smiling as each shovel-full of sand is deposited in the pail.

General implementation suggestions

Community-based instruction is not a field trip. There is a clear and educationally important distinction between the two. Although both have a place within an educational program, they serve different purposes.

Field trips are typically for fun. They are exposure experiences without a lesson plan and without targeted instructional objectives. Field trip locations are not community sites to which one goes regularly. Although skills can be practiced in these locations, the infrequency of visits to the location does not make them appropriate for other than probe data.

Community-based instruction, on the other hand, is not simply an exposure activity. Nor is it an episodic teaching strategy. Community-based instruction is individualized instruction that employs the same systematic instructional procedures used in the classroom, with added emphasis on assisting students to attend to natural cues, corrections, and reinforcers (Ford & Mirenda, 1984). Lesson plans are prepared and data are collected in coordination with in-class instruction. Community-based instructional sessions should occur on a regularly scheduled basis, typically 2–4 hours per week for elementary-aged students who are profoundly disabled.

In that the community is treated as an extension of the instructional setting, it is important to develop a plan for these efforts. Active student participation must be ensured in each setting and planned in advance. This planning includes knowing what is targeted for instruction, in which activities, for each student, and in each location. It also means knowing when data are being collected on each student's performance. It is important to have a purpose for where the students are going. For example, the purpose for going to a store is usually to purchase something; therefore, the behavior of buying something should normally be targeted (Ferguson & Baumgart, 1991).

For efficient management of instruction and time while in the community, students should be grouped in a heterogeneous manner. This strategy mandates that the group represent student differences in prompt-level requirements, cognitive capabilities, and/or physical performance capabilities. Students in wheelchairs can hold small baskets in their laps while ambulatory students push their chairs. More capable students can guide the carts and point to items on the shelf or put them on another student's lap tray. Students functioning at a lower level can also put things in the cart and then remove them at the checkout counter. In addition, it is important to include a mix of *closed-end activities* (those whose function is completed when out in the community; e.g., eating in a restaurant, playing in a park, visiting a pet store, getting a haircut) and *continued activities* (those that are completed back in school or at home; e.g., shopping for arts and crafts materials used at school, buying popcorn or pudding to prepare for snack).

Sites selected for community-based instruction should include a wide range of locations, varied sizes of facilities (e.g., free-standing shops, strip malls, enclosed malls), limited access to public facilities, and locations that present varying types and levels of stimulation. The characteristics of these locations should be known in advance (e.g., visual and auditory stimulation, busy and slack times). Preplanning avoids down time, which may lead to inappropriate behavior because the students have nothing to do (Brown et al., 1983). As part of this planning, the educator should note such additional characteristics as wheelchair access, toileting access, and presence or absence of changing tables. As part of the preparation for community-based instruction, a final checklist should be made, which includes reminders related to data sheets, medications, toileting schedules, shopping lists, money, emergency phone numbers, and the need for communication boards.

During initial community-based instruction, each trip should be to only one site per session. As students' endurance, attention, and creative use of environments increase, so should the number of instructional locations per session. Session chains should be expanded to two and three sites by the time the student is in upper elementary grades. When planning multisite sessions, it is important to emphasize the natural sequence of activities (e.g., shopping, then eating at the food court). Finally, instruction in the community also provides the teacher with the opportunity to practice and generalize his or her instructional skills, such as practice for physical handling of students, investigation of safety requirements and dealing with emergencies and accidents, recognition of natural cues and consequences, and assessing the adequacy of task analyses.

SCHEDULING

Implementing a functional curriculum for elementary-aged students with profound disabilities involves developing a number of activities for each domain in which a student can acquire and apply basic developmental skills, steps, and/or tasks. Part of the implementation process requires the use of a schedule of activities both for the class as a whole and for each student in the class. A schedule that is based on activities and students' needs allows the teacher to manage content within the activities, students' performance, time, and other personnel who come into contact with the students.

Developing a schedule in which each student's educational objectives are embedded into identified instructional activities should help to ensure the following:

1. That all students are participating in instructional activities throughout the school day. Developing and implementing a student-based activity schedule reduces down time in the classroom, as gaps within and between activities are minimized.

2. That students are receiving the opportunity to participate in a variety of instructional environments. As activities are planned and put into a schedule, more environments in which these activities can take place become apparent.

3. That each student's basic needs are being met. These basic needs include toileting, position change, and receipt of medications and physical and/or health care procedures that must occur on a regular basis (e.g., tube-feeding, percussion therapy).

4. That those students who are given instruction from auxiliary personnel are receiving that instruction. A schedule in which activities are planned allows for instruction by auxiliary personnel to take place within the same functional activities in which the class is participating.

5. That others who work with the students can follow through with instruction. A schedule of activities and instruction, both for the class and for individual students, should be clearly posted and explained so that it may be used by everyone who has contact with the students. These people include paraprofessionals and others who have frequent contact with the students, as well as volunteers and substitute teachers who have infrequent contact.

6. That the maximum opportunity for learning is being provided. Students with profound disabilities learn mostly through habit formation. Therefore, opportunities presented for learning must be frequent and consistent. Activities should be scheduled to take place repeatedly over the school day and consistently throughout the school week.

7. That students can participate in the natural sequence of a daily routine. Throughout both the school and the nonschool day, students without disabilities must complete a number of activities. Each activity follows a natural sequence, such as getting ready for school before the bus comes and doing homework before going to bed. Each classroom activity also has a natural sequence of tasks. Incorporating such natural sequences within the schedule of activities on a regular basis gives the student with profound disabilities the opportunity to anticipate the next task or activity in the sequence.

8. That both individual and group formats of instruction are provided (Farmer, Gast, Wolery, & Winterling, 1991; Reid & Favell, 1984). Group instruction within activities is important for several reasons. First, it allows for a number of students to be instructed at the same time, giving the teacher a more efficient method of instructing all the students. Second, it allows for all students to participate in activities scheduled throughout the day. For example, while the teacher is working with a group of three students in one area of the room, the paraprofessional can work with a group of three in another area, thereby having all students actively engaged. Finally, participating in group instruction gives the students the opportunity to develop social and communicative skills with peers who are both disabled and not disabled. Although individualized instruction must still be addressed, especially for the initial acquisition of performance objectives, both individualized and group instruction can be achieved through the proper planning of a schedule.

Preparing a Schedule

Preparing both a class activity and a student schedule can be achieved in four basic steps: (1) blocking out inflexible times, (2) blocking out times that must be negotiated with others, (3) sequencing activities in remaining time blocks, and (4) matrixing student performance objectives by activity (Wilcox & Bellamy, 1982; see Chapter 10). At the elementary level, the amount of time that should be scheduled for each activity is approximately 30 minutes. This period includes 20 minutes for the activity itself and 10 minutes for transition into and out of the activity (gathering materials, incidental toileting, changes in positioning, putting away materials, going to other environments). It should be noted that this time period is merely a rule of thumb and may be changed. Once the schedule is implemented, it may be seen that students need more time to complete the activity or more time in transition. That time should be added to the period, and some activities may need to be rearranged. As the students become more proficient in the activities, the time needed to complete them may be shortened. In this case, more activities can be added to the schedule. When activities occur in different environments, time periods may be combined so that excessive movement can be avoided. For example, longer time periods can be given to community-based trips and activities done in the home living room.

Blocking out inflexible times

Within the school day, the teacher has little or no control over a number of time blocks. These include times that are determined by the principal as part of the school schedule (e.g., arrival, dismissal, lunch, assemblies) or by other teachers who have contact with the students (e.g., art and music classes). Because these times are basically non-negotiable, they should be entered into the schedule first.

Negotiated times for activities

Activities that should be placed in the activity schedule next are those over which the teacher has some control but which must fit with others' schedules. These are activities that, once within the schedules, will not be subject to frequent change. These time blocks include community-based instruction, instruction or services by auxiliary personnel, integration, peer tutoring activities, and activities that occur in other parts of the school building.

Scheduling for community-based instruction must take into account the schedule of others both in the community and in the classroom. Unless community sites are within walking distance, public transportation schedules and availability of school transportation will affect the times at which community-based instruction can take place. Factors in the classroom that may affect the time of day or amount of time for community-based instruction include the grouping of students, the number of personnel available to go into the community, the number of personnel who must stay to work with students who remain in the classroom, and the students' endurance levels and health concerns. These factors may affect not only the time of day (or days of the week) in which community-based instruction may take place but also the length of the trip.

A second scheduling negotiation involves other professionals, such as the occupational therapist, physical therapist, and speech–language pathologist. Each of these individuals has individualized caseloads and schedules. A joint review of IEPs will identify which students in the class are to receive the various services. The goal when negotiating with each professional is to avoid a daily schedule's being subjected to constant interruptions as various individual students are pulled out for isolated therapy. If necessary, these professionals should be made aware of the best practice of conducting therapy in the classroom and community while students are engaged in learning activities (Beukelman & Mirenda, 1992; Cusick, 1991; Rainforth & York, 1987). This will enable the various therapists to design programs based on actual activity demands and student performance.

Activities that incorporate peers who are not disabled may also be subject to schedules with which the teacher must negotiate. For example, some schools may have academic periods in which all regular education students must be in their home classrooms. Individual teachers of students without disabilities may have blocks of times in which they will not allow students to visit other classrooms. Likewise, teachers often have times in which they would be more willing either to incorporate students with disabilities into their classrooms (e.g., storytime, work on a unit project) or to have peer tutors visit other classrooms.

Other environments within the school building, and activities that take place in them, may be subject to schedules. The use of certain areas, such as the teachers' lounge or cafeteria, may have constraints at specific times during the day. Other activities may need to be completed by a certain time as requested by the principal, school secretary, or janitorial staff. For example, the school secretary may request that all classroom attendance forms be collected and returned to the office by 10:00 A.M. Therefore, this activity must be scheduled so that the time restriction can be met.

Sequencing activities in remaining time blocks

After completing the first two steps in preparing a schedule, there are blocks of time in which no activities have been planned. Classroom and other school-based activities can be scheduled within these blocks. These activities include snack, toileting, grooming, dressing, classroom care, office duties, and leisure activities. Whereas some of these activities have the advantage of being very flexible (i.e., they can be incorporated into the schedule at almost any time during the day), other activities should be scheduled during times at which they would naturally occur. This order of occurrence may be based on the way peers who are nondisabled structure their school day. The order may also be based on the sequences of activities that occur in other environments, such as the home and workplace. For example, peers who are nondisabled usually use the school restroom for engaging in grooming activities in the morning, after lunch, and before going home. Therefore, grooming activities may be scheduled for students with profound disabilities after their snack in the morning, after lunch, and before they leave the school building. At home or at work, the area in which an activity is performed is typically cleaned after that activity (e.g., washing dishes after meals, picking up toys after they have been played with, cleaning up the desk at the end of the work day). Therefore, it would be appropriate for students who are profoundly disabled to be engaged in cleaning tasks after such activities as snack, leisure times, and preparing to leave school for home.

After this step, the teacher should develop a daily schedule in which activities occur throughout the day in a number of different environments (see Table 12.5). This schedule becomes the basis upon which individual student and class schedules are completed.

Matrixing student performance objectives by activity

Each student in the class should be instructed on at least one performance objective in each activity during the day. To ensure that each student is participating, individualized schedules should be prepared. Group instruction should be included in activities; therefore, a class activity schedule will also have to be developed. Both schedules are compiled by designating within each activity the objective that the student, either individually or as part of a group, is to perform.

As described in Chapter 10, a matrix can adequately serve as the communication device for schedules. The first step in designing a matrix is to list the activities and the times they are to be done across the top of the matrix. The performance objectives for the student should be listed vertically on the left. These may be basic developmental skills, steps, or tasks. A grid can then be made so that there is a block for each objective under each activity. Within this block, a note should be made regarding when the objective is to be included within the activity. Tables 12.6, 12.7, and 12.8 illustrate schedule matrices for elementary-aged students who are performing at the basic developmental skill, step, and task levels, respectively.

TABLE 12.5. Preliminary Daily Schedule

Time	Monday	Tuesday	Wednesday	Thursday	Friday
8:00–8:30	Arrival and toileting	Same as Monday	Same as Monday	Same as Monday	Same as Monday
8:30–9:00	Collecting attendance (Group 1) Food preparation (Group 2) Snack (All) (Speech)	Same as Monday	Same as Monday	Same as Monday	Same as Monday
9:00–9:30	Toileting and grooming	Same as Monday	Same as Monday	Same as Monday	Same as Monday
9:30–10:00	Play with equipment	Arts and crafts	Play with equipment	Arts and crafts	Play with equipment
10:00–10:30	Clean home living room (Group 1) Clean teachers' lounge (Group 2)	Clean home living room (Group 2) Clean teachers' lounge (Group 1) (Physical Therapy)	Community-based instruction	Clean home living room (Group 1) Clean teachers' lounge (Group 2) (Physical Therapy)	Clean home living room (Group 2) Clean teachers' lounge (Group 1)
10:30–11:00	Storytime with kindergarten class (Group 1) Can crushing (Group 2)	Storytime with kindergarten class (Group 2) Can crushing (Group 1)	Community-based instruction	Storytime with kindergarten class (Group 1) Can crushing (Group 2)	Storytime with kindergarten class (Group 2) Can crushing (Group 1)

(continued)

TABLE 12.5. *Continued*

Time	Monday	Tuesday	Wednesday	Thursday	Friday
11:00–12:00	Lunch	Lunch	Lunch	Lunch	Lunch
12:00–12:30	Toileting and grooming	Same as Monday	Same as Monday	Same as Monday	Same as Monday
12:30–1:00	Music	Physical education	Music	Physical education	Music
1:00–1:30	Group games with peers	Same as Monday	Same as Monday	Same as Monday	Same as Monday
1:30–2:00	Clean classroom (Group 1) Deliver teacher messages (Group 2)	Clean classroom (Group 2) Deliver teacher messages (Group 1)	Clean classroom (Group 1) Deliver teacher messages (Group 2)	Clean classroom (Group 2) Deliver teacher messages (Group 1)	Clean classroom (Group 1) Deliver teacher messages (Group 2)
2:00–2:30	Toileting and grooming	Same as Monday	Same as Monday	Same as Monday	Same as Monday
2:30–3:00	Departure	Same as Monday	Same as Monday	Same as Monday	Same as Monday

When matrixing objectives by activities, it is important that each objective has a number of activities in which it can be incorporated, and each activity has at least one objective to be completed. At times, opportunities to complete performance may be overlooked. On the other hand, some opportunities may need to be created. For example, transitions into and out of activities offer times in which communication, mobility, and social skills may be performed. The teacher may add additional steps that are not a part of the normal occurrence of the activity, but within which objectives can be met. For instance, additional natural opportunities to practice objectives associated with dressing can be provided during art or water play, when smocks and shirts can be put on, or during gym or outside play, when shorts and sneakers can be put on.

After listing the objectives to be met, and the activities in which these objectives are to be placed, each student should have an individualized schedule that shows a profile of his or her day. From these individual schedules, a class activity matrix can be generated. For each activity during the day, each student's performance objective for that activity is recorded. Based on these objectives, groups can be arranged in which students from different levels work together. As there may be more than one group working on activities in the same time period, the person who is to work with the group is also specified on the matrix. Additional information that may be on the class activity schedule includes (a) positioning of students, (b) schedule of auxiliary personnel, (c) times and type of data to be collected, (d) names of peers without disabilities who are to work with the group, and (e) special anecdotal notes about the students and/or their performance within the activity (see Table 12.9).

When schedules are completed, they should be posted, explained to those who work with the students, and open to review. As the students progress through the school year and teachers and others who are in the classroom become more proficient in moving from one activity to another, the schedule may be changed to allow further opportunities for instruction in a larger number of activities and environments.

CONCLUSION

Instructional outcomes for elementary-aged students with profound disabilities should directly impact the student and his or her family. Instruction for these students should result in more interactive and less restrictive life-styles. These life-style changes will likely result in a variety of outcomes. Family members and educators will begin to view the student as being more capable because he or she will have developed an increased number of skills, thereby

TABLE 12.6. Activity Schedule with Two Examples for Student on Basic Developmental Skills Level

	8:00–8:30	8:30–9:00	9:00–9:30	9:30–10:00	10:00–10:30 CBI	10:30–11:00 CBI
Objective	Arrival and toileting	Collect attendance ——— Food prep	Toileting and grooming	Play with equipment ——— Arts and crafts	Clean home living room ——— Clean teachers' lounge	Storytime with kindergarten ——— Can crushing
1. Cause and effect		Smile at peers when collecting attendance		Vocalize when tape is turned on		Smile at peers ——— Knock can into water
2. Bilateral hold				Hold basket in which grooming materials are placed	Hold basket in which cleaning materials or messages are placed	

CBI = community-based instruction.

enabling him or her to participate in a wider range of functional and valued activities. The social network for students will be enhanced because they will have developed more social and communication skills that provide reinforcement for them, their family members, and peers. As a result of strategies derived from the functional analysis of inappropriate behaviors and the generalization of skills, the student will be taken into an increased number of environments by both teachers and family members. Stimulation provided by these environments can impact the students' arousal levels as participation is encouraged in functional activities. Finally, through the assistance of school professionals, family members should find caregiving activities easier and less time-consuming.

Curriculum for elementary-aged students with profound disabilities should focus on the acquisition and application of basic developmental skills, steps, and tasks embedded within functional activities. Through the use of systematic instructional procedures, increased participation in self-care activities, increased social interaction, and development of effective communication and mobility systems should result (see Chapter 10). All students with profound disabilities, including those with the greatest cognitive, physical, and medical involvement, should be actively engaged in instruction, as opposed to being only passive recipients of care.

11:00–12:00 CBI	12:00–12:30	12:30–1:00	1:00–1:30	1:30–2:00	2:00–2:30	2:30–3:00
Lunch	Toileting and grooming	Music _____ Physical education	Group games with peers	Deliver messages _____ Clean classrooms	Toileting and grooming	Departure
			Smile at peers	Smile at peers when delivering messages		
Hold food tray in lap while moving to table	Hold basket in which grooming materials are placed				Hold basket in which grooming materials are placed	

TABLE 12.7. Activity Schedule with Two Examples for Student on Step Level

	8:00–8:30	8:30–9:00	9:00–9:30	9:30–10:00	10:00–10:30 CBI	10:30–11:00 CBI
	Arrival and toileting	Collect attendance ___ Food prep	Toileting and grooming	Play with equipment ___ Arts and crafts	Clean home living room ___ Clean teachers' lounge	Can crushing ___ Storytime with kindergarten
Objective						
1. Grasp and pull			___ Turn on water for food prep	Turn on water for toothbrushing	Turn on water to water plants ___	Turn on water to wash cans ___
2. Hold, place, and release		Put bookbag into cubbyhole ___	Hold attendance form and put in large basket	___ Hold, place and release paint jar	Hold, place and release sheets to make up bed ___	

CBI = community-based instruction.

11:00–12:00 CBI	12:00–12:30	12:30–1:00	1:00–1:30	1:30–2:00	2:00–2:30	2:30–3:00
Lunch	Toileting and grooming	Music _____ Physical education	Group games with peers	Deliver messages _____ Clean classrooms	Toileting and grooming	Departure
	Turn on water for toothbrushing					
			Hold, place, and release dice when playing a board game			

TABLE 12.8.   Activity Schedule with Two Examples for Student on Task Level

	8:00–8:30	8:30–9:00	9:00–9:30	9:30–10:00	10:00–10:30 CBI	10:30–11:00 CBI
	Arrival and toileting	Collect attendance ———— Food prep	Toileting and grooming	Play with equipment ———— Arts and crafts	Clean home living room ———— Clean teachers' lounge	Can crushing ———— Storytime with kindergarten
Objective						
1. Load pail with sand					During CBI at the playscape	
2. Vacuum floors					Vacuum floors in home living room ———— Vacuum floors in teachers' lounge	

CBI = community-based instruction.

11:00–12:00 CBI	12:00–12:30	12:30–1:00	1:00–1:30	1:30–2:00	2:00–2:30	2:30–3:00
Lunch	Toileting and grooming	Music _____ Physical education	Group games with peers	Deliver messages _____ Clean classrooms	Toileting and grooming	Departure
			With peers on playground			
				Vacuum floors in classroom		

TABLE 12.9. Class Schedule for All Students During the 10:00–10:30 Time Period

	Monday	Tuesday	Wednesday	Thursday	Friday
10:00–10:30	Group 1—with Paraprofessional	Group 2—with Paraprofessional	CBI—with Teacher and Paraprofessional	Group 1—with Paraprofessional	Group 2—with Paraprofessional
Clean home living room Dust	Elvis—Vacuum floors with verbal prompts —Dust furniture with verbal prompts (using dustmitt)	Rhonda—Hold basket with materials —Dust furniture with full physical prompts (using duster) (Physical Therapy)	*Playscape* Elvis—Put sand into and fill bucket with partial physical prompts	Same as Monday (Physical Therapy)	Same as Monday
Water plants Vacuum Make bed Clean windows Clean mirrors	Beth—Make bed with partial physical prompts —Turn on water independently, water plants (hold plants under water) with partial physical prompts	Andy—Dust furniture with partial physical prompts (using dustmitt) —Make bed with partial physical prompts	Beth—Hold onto chain of swing —Swing with partial physical prompts (paraprofessional push)	Same as Monday	Same as Monday
	Dan—Make bed with partial physical prompts —Dust furniture with partial physical prompts (using dustmitt)	Michael—Make bed with partial physical prompts —Water plants with verbal prompts (using watering can)	Dan—Use bilateral hold on sides of sliding board when pushed with full physical prompts	Same as Monday	

(continued)

TABLE 12.9. *Continued*

	Monday	Tuesday	Wednesday	Thursday	Friday
	Group 2—with Teacher	Group 1—with Teacher		Group 2—with Teacher	Group 1—with Teacher
Clean teacher's lounge ___ Dust	Rhonda—Hold basket with materials —Hold messages to be put on board	Elvis—Vacuum floors with verbal prompts —Clean sink with verbal prompts	Rhonda—Hold onto chains and swing in adaptive swing with partial physical prompts (paraprofessional push)	Same as Monday	Same as Monday
Vacuum Put messages on board Water plants	Andy—Dust furniture with partial physical prompts (using dustmitt) —Clean counter with partial physical prompts (using rag)	Beth—Dust furniture with physical prompts (using dustmitt)	Andy—Bounce ball (hold and release) to another student with physical prompts	Same as Monday	Same as Monday
Clean counters Clean sink	Michael—Dust furniture with partial physical prompts (using dustmitt) —Wipe sink with verbal prompts (using rag)	Dan—Clean counter with partial physical prompts (using rag) (Physical Therapy)	Michael—Hold sand bucket for another student to fill, then pour out sand when full, with verbal prompts	Same as Monday (Physical Therapy)	Same as Monday

CBI = community-based instruction.

ACKNOWLEDGMENTS

Development of this chapter was supported in part by Federal Grant No. H086P9001 from the Office of Special Education and Rehabilitation Services of the United States Department of Education. The opinions expressed in this chapter are those of the authors, and no official endorsement by any agency should be inferred.

REFERENCES

Belfliore, P. (1990). *The impact of setting on the behavior of persons with profound disabilities.* Unpublished manuscript.

Beukelman, D., & Mirenda, P. (1992). *Augmentative and alternative communication: Management of severe communication disorders in children and adults.* Baltimore: Brookes.

Brown, F., Helmstetter, E., & Guess, D. (1986). *Current best practices with students with profound disabilities: Are there any?* Unpublished manuscript.

Brown, L., Ford, A., Nisbet, J., Sweet, M., Donnellan, A., & Gruenewald, L. (1983). Opportunities available when severely handicapped students attend chronological-age appropriate regular schools. *The Journal of The Association for Persons with Severe Handicaps, 8,* 16–24.

Cusick, B. (1991). Therapeutic management of sensorimotor and physical disabilities. In J. Bigge (Ed.), *Teaching individuals with physical and multiple disabilities* (3rd ed.). New York: Macmillan.

Dunst, C., Cuishing, P., & Vance, S. (1985). Response-contingent learning in profoundly handicapped infants: A social systems perspective. *Analysis and Intervention in Developmental Disabilities, 5,* 33–37.

Evans, I., & Scotti, J. (1989). Defining meaningful outcomes for persons with profound disabilities. In F. Brown & D. Lehr (Eds.), *Persons with profound disabilities: Issues and practices* (pp. 83–107). Baltimore: Brookes.

Farmer, J. A., Gast, D. L., Wolery, M., & Winterling, V. (1991). Small group instruction for students with severe handicaps: A study of observational learning. *Education and Treatment in Mental Retardation, 26,* 190–201.

Ford, A., & Mirenda, P. (1984). Community instruction: A natural cues and correction decision model. *Journal of The Association for Persons with Severe Handicaps, 9,* 79–88.

Ferguson, D., & Baumgart, D. (1991). Partial participation revisited. *Journal of The Association for Persons with Severe Handicaps, 16,* 218–227.

Gee, K., Goetz, L., Graham, N., & Lee, M. (1987). *Establishing generalized use of residual vision through instruction in natural contexts.* Unpublished manuscript.

Goetz, L., & Gee, K. (1987). Teaching visual attention in functional contexts: Acquisition and generalization of complex visual motor skills. *Journal of Visual Impairment and Blindness, 1,* 115–117.

McWilliam, R., Trivette, C., & Dunst, C. (1985). Behavior engagement as a measure of the efficacy of early intervention. *Analysis and Intervention in Developmental Disabilities, 5,* 59–71.

Mulligan, M., Lacy, L., & Guess, D. (1982). Effects of massed, distributed and spaced trial sequencing on severely handicapped students' performance. *Journal of The Association for the Severely Handicapped, 7,* 48–62.

Pellegrini, A., & Galda, L. (1990). Children's play, language, and early literacy. *Topics in Language Disorders, 10,* 76–88.

Rainforth, B., & York, J. (1987). Integrating related services in community instruction. *Journal of The Association for Persons with Severe Handicaps, 12,* 190–198.

Reid, D., & Favell, J. E. (1984). Group instruction with persons who have severe disabilities: A critical review. *Journal of The Association for Persons with Severe Handicaps, 9,* 167–177.

Sachs, J. (1984). Children's play and communication development. In R. Schiefelbusch & J. Pickar (Eds.), *The acquisition of communicative competence* (pp. 109–140). Baltimore: University Park Press.

Siegel-Causey, E., & Downing, J. (1987). Nonsymbolic communication development: Theoretical concepts and educational strategies. In L. Goetz, D. Guess, & K. Stremel-Campbell (Eds.), *Innovative program design for individuals with dual sensory impairments* (pp. 15–48). Baltimore: Brookes.

Siegel-Causey, E., & Guess, D. (1985). Early development of prelinguistic communication. In M. Bullis (Ed.), *Communication development in young children with deaf–blindness: Literature review I* (pp. 61–77). Monmouth, OR: Teaching Research.

Siegel-Causey, E., & Guess, D. (1987). Elements of nonsymbolic communication and early interactional processes. In M. Bullis (Ed.), *Communication development in young children with deaf–blindness: Literature review III.* Monmouth, OR: Teaching Research.

Sternberg, L., McNerney, C., & Pegnatore, L. (1985). Developing co-active behaviors with profoundly mentally handicapped students. *Education and Training of the Mentally Retarded, 20,* 260–267.

Sternlicht, M. (1978). Variables affecting foster care placement of institutionalized retarded residents. *Mental Retardation, 16,* 25–28.

Wilcox, B., & Bellamy, G. (1982). *Design of high school programs for severely handicapped students.* Baltimore: Brookes.

Wolery, M., & Bailey, D. (1989). Assessing play skills. In D. Bailey & M. Wolery (Eds.), *Assessing infants and preschoolers with handicaps* (pp. 428–446). Columbus, OH: Merrill.

Chapter 13

Instructional and Curricular Approaches for Adolescents with Profound Disabilities

DAVID L. LOVETT, THOMAS B. PIERCE, and KATHRYN A. HARING

As all children reach adolescence, their educational programs should be modified to meet individual needs and abilities, while preparing them for a future that is often difficult to predict. The necessity of altering curricula is no less imperative for adolescents with profound disabilities. With only a few years remaining in the public schools, it is critical that instruction focus on skills that can assist the individual to become more interactive with the environment and to achieve an acceptable level of interdependence with others. Support services and resources needed to achieve these goals in current and future settings should be identified. Professionals working with these students must be knowledgeable about the student's strengths and weaknesses as they relate to the demands of current settings as well as of future environments.

In this chapter, we provide information on how to design and implement educational programs for adolescents with profound disabilities. We emphasize an individualized program approach with a focus on current and future needs, as well as skill development addressing increased independence, control over the environment, improved social interactions, and enhanced communication. In addition, support structures that are necessary to help students achieve progress are discussed. These supports may include instruction, prostheses, or environmental modifications, including the education of significant others, peers, and co-workers.

A major portion of the chapter is devoted to the development of appropriate curricula that are functional for the individual; designed with natural environments in mind; and based on the environmental domains of community, job, home and family, and recreation and leisure. Also included is a discussion of planning for the future of students as they transition to adult life. In this section, an emphasis is placed on ensuring that support mechanisms are established to help each individual lead as fulfilling an adult life as possible.

The last major section of the chapter addresses issues concerning integration, personal dignity, and choice making. Each of these areas is addressed as it pertains to the development of an appropriate educational program designed to meet needs of individuals with profound disabilities.

CURRICULUM DEVELOPMENT

Curriculum development for adolescents with profound disabilities has grown in depth and scope since the passage of Public Law (PL) 94-142, the Education for All Handicapped Children Act of 1975. No longer is the concept of a custodial existence the accepted form of service. Instructional goals have changed in response to the reduction of large institutions and increased emphasis on serving people with profound disabilities in the community.

Over the past decade, educators, parents, and researchers have suggested the use of various instructional approaches for those with profound disabilities. In the past, much instruction focused on the instructional technology of skill development. More recently, emphasis has been placed on the meaningfulness of such learning: Meaningfulness should be based not on the efficacy of instructional techniques but on the usefulness of the learned behaviors. Instructional objectives should be selected based on their relevance to the life of the individual. For example, teaching a student how to grasp objects may have little meaning, but grasping a switch to indicate a preference may be very important.

Approaches to Curriculum Development

In part because people with profound disabilities experience pervasive needs, curricula have been developed from a "bottom–up" approach. Teachers have used criterion-referenced assessments and task analysis strategies to identify and teach skills. Because the needs of this group appear to be so global, many teachers have found comfort in basing instruction on developmental milestones. Developmental instruments that have been created for people with more severe disabilities have provided teachers with initial instructional points. Unfortunately, developmental guides may increase the tendency to teach skills outside of natural environments, as well as to focus on skills that are neither age appropriate nor functional.

Although attempts have been made to teach students with disabilities functional and age-appropriate skills, much of the focus has been on the instructional process rather than on instructional objectives. Emphasis has been on enhancing strategies for teaching people with disabilities, rather than on making an impact on the lives of the people receiving instruction. Examples include training people with profound disabilities to respond to meaningless stimuli, such as reacting to squeaking rubber duck toys or turning to lights, and misguided attempts at sensory integration, such as running students' hands through pebbles or rubbing their skin with lotion. Service providers have been frustrated by the pointlessness inherent in instructional programs of this type, but have been offered limited alternatives. Currently, however, there is greater potential for using environmentally-based strategies to assist individuals with profound disabilities to participate more fully in the community.

Guiding Principles for Curricula Development

Functional curricula

It is of utmost importance that the activities included in educational curricula be functional for the individual. The skills or responses identified as target goals of the educational program should be useful and provide the individual with greater control over the environment (Wehman, Moon, Everson, Wood, & Barcus, 1988). Functional behaviors have been defined as behaviors that would have to be performed by someone else if not performed by the student (Brown et al., 1984). Concern regarding functional skills should focus not only on the student's current environments (e.g., school or home) but also on skills that may be useful for the individual in future settings (e.g., vocational settings, group homes). This functional curriculum design is based on an ecological approach in which environments are analyzed to determine activities and skills that might be used across life domains and multiple settings. Information can be gathered from a variety of sources to determine the most functional skills used in these environments. Methods to obtain this information are addressed later in this chapter.

Because instruction based on functional curricula is intended to prepare students for future environments and to enhance their participation in present ones, a functional curriculum provides instruction on skills that are useful now as well as those that will prove functional in the future. Brown et al. (1985) pointed out, however, that all goals need not be "functional" in the strictest sense. These authors suggested that goals be selected based on affirmative responses to the following questions:

1. Are the number of environments in which the student participates increased (e.g., a recreation and leisure skill that is useful in many situations)?

2. Is the goal chronologically age appropriate (e.g., selecting clothing similar to those of peers without disabilities)?

3. Will the student have the opportunity to practice the skill in other environments (e.g., using a microwave oven at school as well as at home)?

4. Is the skill required in adulthood (e.g., using a stall toilet)?

5. Is the behavior preferred by the student (i.e., the student was able to make a choice)?

6. Is the skill preferred by the student's parents or guardians (i.e., they had input in selecting the skill)?

7. Does the skill enhance the student's physical well-being (e.g., therapeutic recreation skills that enhance several aspects of an individual's life)?

8. Does the skill enhance the student's social contacts (e.g., communication skills)?

9. Is there a high probability of acquisition of the skill (e.g., considering whether the student can learn to dress himself or herself, or whether limb movements would be a more realistic goal)?

10. Does the skill enhance the student's status (e.g., learning to communicate when one needs to use the toilet rather than remaining on a toileting schedule)?

Brown et al. (1985) stressed that skills should not be selected if they (a) do not represent some credible dimension of the areas listed above, (b) rarely lead to instruction in natural environments, or (c) are not meaningful to the student.

A functional curriculum should include goals and objectives that prepare students for successful adjustment in school, in environments outside of school, and in environments in which they are likely to work, live, and recreate as adults. Therefore, appropriate functional curriculum domains include vocational and employment, residential and home living, community living, and recreation and leisure skills. In addition, social–affect and communication–language skills should be emphasized across all environments. It must be kept in mind that not all domains should be emphasized equally for all students. For example, it may be unrealistic to assume that some students with profound disabilities will ever be meaningfully employed even with extensive support. An appropriate educational program for such students may focus to a large extent on the communication domain and relatively little on vocational and employment skill development.

One method to determine an appropriate functional curriculum is to ascertain the potential future environments for the individual, and the skills needed in those settings that will facilitate positive outcomes. Brown, Nietupski, and Hamre-Nietupski (1976) proposed the *criterion of ultimate functioning* as a guideline for developing curricula. This principle is based on the concept that students with more severe disabilities are likely to learn fewer skills and take more time to acquire those skills than are other students. Targeted skills, therefore, should be meaningful and functional. This means that the criteria for selection of instructional goals and objectives should relate to those environments where the student is likely to reside and work. The teacher, for example, could ask the staff of a community group home what they deem as desirable skills for adults with profound disabilities. An instructional program to address those skills could then be designed, thereby preparing the student for a life in a potential future environment.

Age-appropriate education

An age-appropriate emphasis is consistent with a functional curriculum approach. Instructional objectives should be similar to tasks in which same-age peers without disabilities would be engaged. For example, learning to wind a musical toy would not be age appropriate for an adolescent; however, learning to turn on a radio using a switch would be. In addition to being functional, age-appropriate skills have the potential for increasing the opportunities for social interaction with peers without disabilities. For example, social interaction between adolescents is more likely to occur when one adolescent is listening to a radio rather than playing with a child's toy. It must be emphasized that the individual's dignity is paramount, not only in respect to the person, but also for the moral development of those who come in contact with individuals with profound disabilities.

Partial participation

Some students with profound disabilities may be so limited in their capacity to acquire skills that learning truly "functional" behaviors may become problematic (i.e., they will continue to be dependent on others for basic care and other needs). These students may *partially participate* in functional activities contributing to their own independence (Baumgart et al., 1982; Ferguson & Baumgart, 1991; see Chapter 10). For example, a student may not be able to perform the functional skills needed to dress himself or herself, but may be able to demonstrate partial assistance through whatever movement or basic developmental skill he or she is able to exhibit (e.g., selecting clothing appropriate for the weather, indicating preferences of clothing).

Even though the concept of partial participation may help instructors identify objectives, some authors have recently questioned the application of partial participation to students with profound disabilities (Sailor, Gee, Goetz, & Graham, 1988). Helmstetter (1990) suggested that the concept of partial participation be extended to include *passive participation.* He emphasized that, although an ecological approach to curriculum development may be appropriate for students with profound disabilities, greater dependence on technological adaptations and assessment of the communicative intent of students' behaviors should be stressed. It is reasonable to assume that technological advances and further research into instructional strategies will yield new and innovative ways to increase the potential of students with profound disabilities to perform tasks that previously would have been considered impossible.

In a recent discussion of the frustrations service providers experience when implementing partial participation for individuals with the most severe disabilities, common errors in implementation have been identified (Ferguson & Baumgart, 1991). The major limitation in partial participation of students who have few voluntary or volitional behaviors is the often passive nature of their inclusion in normative social or task routines. Ferguson and Baumgart (1991) described this level of participation as mere presence during an activity in which others are actively engaged. Indeed, with many individuals with profound disabilities, measuring levels of engagement is difficult (Guess et al., 1988; see Chapter 4). It is crucial to emphasize assessment of state and arousal variables if service providers are to determine engagement types and levels. Exploratory research that manipulates setting variables on arousal is a needed natural extension of present research looking at the biobehavioral states of persons with profound disabilities. Measuring subtle changes in alertness and awareness of and orientation to activities in self-contained special education settings, as compared with inclusive classroom environments, could provide further empirical support to partial participation as a concept.

The second error pattern in partial participation that Ferguson and Baumgart (1991) identified occurs when service providers fail to consider a full range of variables when selecting activities for involvement of adolescents with profound disabilities. Errors of this type occur when service providers seek the most convenient solution to complex program scheduling decisions. For example, problems of generalization may occur when providing a student with dual sensory impairments orientation and mobility training in the neighborhood immediately accessible to the high school when the curbs and traffic patterns are vastly different from those of the home neighborhood. Ferguson and Baumgart cautioned:

> While any components taken alone might be appropriate for a student to learn, the error lies in not considering the student's current and potential skill repertoire, the student's preferences, long-term learning needs, family priorities, reactions of peers, and other socially validated, community-referenced guidelines. (p. 220)

Service providers often fail to consistently apply the principles of age-appropriate, functional, and relevant social contexts that scaffold partial participation. This tendency, called *piecemeal participation,* has been identified as another implementation error (Ferguson & Baumgart, 1991). The development of quality secondary programs for adolescents with profound disabilities presents unique challenges to service providers. The competing priorities of special service providers, regular classroom teachers, transportation systems, families, and community members can be overwhelming. As a result, students' programs can be fragmented across community and classroom settings. Examples include programs in which meaningful community-based activities take place on a sporadic, field trip–style frequency, and daily classroom routines include long periods when students are presented objects they cannot manipulate or are provided with largely ignored taped music.

Ferguson and Baumgart (1991) concluded their discussion of partial participation with excellent observations on ways to avoid missed opportunities for participation. They observed that well-intentioned efforts toward building independent functioning can impede meaningful interaction. This is particularly pertinent when considering levels of participation for adolescents with profound disabilities for whom an independent adult life-style cannot be reasonably anticipated. Adolescence is an appropriate time to carefully analyze critical skills in order to balance autonomy and interdependence. Thinking through each of the following six considerations can minimize missed participation:

1. Is this student likely to have a person present for this activity either because of disabilities that cannot be remediated or accommodated, or because of some lifestyle preference?

2. What abilities can this student practice in each component of this activity?

3. How can this practice be maximized through all activity components?

4. If we maximize practice in this way, what skills might be developed that could expand this student's participation?

5. How can we maximize image, helping the student to appear, and perhaps feel, less dependent and more competent?

6. How can we expand this student's cooperative and supportive relationships with others in this, and similar, settings and activities? (Ferguson & Baumgart, 1991, p. 226)

Community-based instruction

Falvey (1989), among others, emphasized that due to the difficulties many students with disabilities have in transferring learned skills from one environment to another, skills should be taught in environments where they will be used. Therefore, community-based instruction, as well as community-referenced instruction, should be an integral part of programs for students with profound disabilities.

Community-referenced instruction may involve both school-based and community-based instruction. With school-based training, students practice skills in school immediately prior to community-based instruction (e.g., the student practices communicating the choice of a soft drink from a vending machine just prior to going to use an actual vending machine in the community; Brown et al., 1983). The time lapse between school-based and community-based instruction should be minimized. Many writers (e.g., Falvey, 1989; Wehman et al., 1988) have stressed that students should not be denied community-based instruction because of poor performance of skills taught in school (e.g., not allowing a student to work on crossing streets because he or she is unable to distinguish "Walk" and "Don't Walk" on cards resembling street signs). Subsequently, many recommend that all students should receive direct instruction in the community (Brown et al., 1983; Patton, Cronin, Polloway, Hutchison, & Robinson, 1989).

School personnel should address a number of issues concerning the implementation of community-based services (Falvey, 1989; Wehman et al., 1988). First, personnel should establish policies that specify procedures for various potential happenings, including what to do in emergencies, who is responsible for students' safety, and what to do if students become lost. Second, staff should obtain informed consent from parents or guardians before instructing students in the community. Third, school districts should provide insurance for accidents or injuries. Fourth, students should be educated in their home schools (and in their home communities) to reduce transportation time and to make instruction more functional for their experiences in their communities. Fifth, instruction should be consistent and ongoing as opposed to a field trip approach to community-based learning. Sixth, instruction should involve individual or small heterogeneous groups of students to maintain as natural a proportion as possible of people with disabilities to those without disabilities, and to help ensure appropriate individualized instruction. For example, it is difficult logistically to access the community if more than one student is in a wheelchair or is mobility impaired due to limited sensory input. Pairing students who can walk with limited assistance with those who cannot encourages natural peer supports.

A number of barriers to community-based instruction have been cited (Wehman et al., 1988). These include transportation problems, liability concerns, personnel assignment issues, scheduling difficulties, misunderstanding of the roles of different agencies involved, and funding problems. Most of these barriers can be diminished through effective communication. The funding issue, however, often requires considerable creativity. One potential and convenient solution to limited funding for community-based instruction involves developing a shopping service for high school staff, faculty, peers, and parents. Weekly newspaper advertising enclosures with coupons can be effectively used as curricular material for students who can match with assistance. Participants who wish to use the service identify needed items and provide money plus a small handling charge to purchase these items. Planning periods are established in which students are assisted in matching coupon-to-sample item activities. Once in the store, they again can be assisted to match the coupon to the actual item and then participate in making a purchase. The money earned from handling charges can aid in funding other community-based activities. In terms of transportation, most communities have a low- or no-cost van service or lift-equipped public transportation that can be used. In rural communities, creative transportation problem solving can include using church buses or community members to assist with transportation difficulties. The shopping service can be expanded to include laundry, housekeeping, and errand or delivery services to generate additional funds. These meaningful activities provide instructional opportunities as well as income for community-based programs.

Additional staff is frequently required to make community-based instruction a reality for students who are profoundly disabled. In secondary schools across the nation, peers provide an excellent and no-cost natural support. Many high school students without disabilities have time in their schedules to spend a study hall or elective period as an instructional assistant. Murray-Seegert (1989) completed a qualitative study of how low-achieving high school students were used as peer tutors in an urban school district. Some of these students were having significant academic difficulties and some had been ejected from classes. Not only were they successful in efforts with the students who experienced profound disabilities, but they in turn benefited greatly from their associations. If special education teachers have problems recruiting students, school counselors and other school staff might be of assistance in identifying and recruiting peer helpers.

One barrier to community-based instruction for students with profound disabilities involves the medical problems some of these students experience. It is critical, therefore, that educators weigh the benefits of community-based instruction with the limitations that critical medical problems pose for the student. Most adolescents with medically complex needs can access the community when adequate care is taken to ensure the presence of needed medical technology and trained personnel to accompany them. The dignity of risk principle may be applied here. For example, people in the final stages of acquired immune deficiency syndrome (AIDS) can enter the community freely with no increased danger to themselves or others. Critical illness should not be used as a reasonable justification for isolation or segregation.

Over the past decade, the community-based instruction model has gained popularity for those with moderate and severe disabilities (Brown et al., 1983; Falvey, 1989; Snell & Browder, 1986). However, virtually no research base exists on the effectiveness of teaching skills to adolescents with profound disabilities in the community. Therefore, much of the research that is used to justify community-based teaching methods, strategies, and curricula for this population is founded upon research directed toward those who are not as severely involved. It may be some time before research that truly addresses meaningful community-based instruction for adolescents with profound disabilities is conducted. If future research suggests that these students are unable to successfully learn skills in the community, some fear that such findings might be used as a rationalization to limit their community access. What is needed, therefore, is a research agenda that is based on an a priori assumption: that the only *acceptable* environment within which interventions should be implemented and researched is one that is inclusive. Again, biobehavioral state research offers promise in this research agenda. For many adolescents with profound disabilities, a major benefit of community-based instruction may be the increase in state of alertness or functional orientation (attending) that it affords them. Questions regarding efficacy can be answered empirically through experimental designs that vary the community-based settings of instructional activities, the positioning of adolescents with profound disabilities, and the interactions of surrounding staff or community members.

DOMAIN-SPECIFIC INSTRUCTIONAL STRATEGIES

With the recent emphasis on transition planning for adult community living (Halpern, 1985) and the world of work (Wehman et al., 1988), a rethinking of the curricula has occurred. The new emphasis has been to develop curricula based on environmental domains rather than traditional curricular domains (e.g., self-help, expressive–receptive language, gross motor). Environmental domains typically include community, vocational, home and family, and recreation and leisure. This approach uses the natural environment as the setting in which meaningful learning will occur. For example, a student may need to learn how to bear weight on his or her legs. A traditional approach would be for the student to attend physical therapy and be placed in a standing table, while the physical therapist assesses the amount of time the student is able to bear weight. Using the domain-based approach, however, this traditional gross-motor activity could be taught in an environment that will produce a more meaningful outcome. The student could bear weight, with appropriate assistance, from a sitting to standing position at the grocery store. The student could stand to reach an item on a shelf that is needed to prepare lunch that will be made later in the day, or stand with assistance while his or her wheelchair is folded for transport.

Utilizing community or regular education environments provides continual opportunities to incorporate a myriad of skills that teachers in traditional school classrooms may have taught in isolation. The difference is that the domain approach stresses where these skills occur rather than the mere mastery of the skill. It is also an approach that limits skills to be taught. If the skill is not useful in coping with the demands of multiple settings, it is not considered an appropriate focus for instruction.

For adolescents with profound disabilities, there may be very little meaningful knowledge about the outside world that can be learned within the classroom. The domain approach assumes that generalization of learned skills will be preprogrammed, thus eliminating the difficulty in transferring learned skills to appropriate environments. It has been well documented that people with mental retardation have great difficulty in generalizing information across environments, people, materials, and cues (Haring, 1988). The domain approach can help to alleviate this problem.

As a member of the instructional team, the teacher's role becomes that of explorer. The teacher must determine where the adolescent with profound disabilities should be learning new skills. Some teachers feel initial discomfort with projecting the future needs of their students. It is necessary, however, to work through this discomfort and not cling to the security of a self-contained environment or one that does not allow for immediate transfer and generalization possibilities.

Determining appropriate environments in which skills should be taught requires investigation. Interviewing parents, observing the local community, and understanding the services and options available for the student in the community are only some of the ways in which information can be gathered prior to developing and implementing a meaningful plan. Especially at the secondary level, with limited time for schooling, gathering environmental information is critical.

Information Gathering

As PL 101-476, the Individuals with Disabilities Education Act (IDEA) (1990), is implemented and transition planning becomes a reality for all adolescents who are disabled, the secondary teacher becomes instructor, detective, prophet, and orchestrater of services. Planning for the future for someone with profound disabilities may be overwhelming, but using a team process in fact finding pursuits will prove of great benefit. The following considerations will assist teams in developing a meaningful plan for adolescents with profound disabilities.

1. *Determine what services (residential, vocational, recreation and leisure, social services, case management) are available in the community to people with profound disabilities.* For veteran teachers, this may seem effortless, as they may be very familiar with services available in the community. Even the veteran teacher, however, will need to continually update knowledge of community services. For those without this information and experiential base, the job may be more challenging. Some possible starting points may be to contact the state Developmental Disabilities Planning Council or the state Office of Protection and Advocacy. Another source of information may be local or state parent or professional organizations, such as the Arc (previously the Association for Retarded Citizens) or other advocacy groups. In that paraprofessionals are significantly more likely to reside in the school community and share the linguistic, cultural, or ethnic identities of the students (Haring, Saren, Lovett, & Shelton, 1992), they can be an invaluable aid to identifying business owners or community members amenable to providing assistance in community access for adolescents with profound disabilities.

A more difficult but very rewarding task is for the educator to directly explore the community. Driving around the student's community can help determine the availability of accessible housing, employment options, and transportation systems. Perhaps the most important questions will be asked of the student's parents: Where do they see their child in 5 or 10 years? What is it they would like the child to learn? Where do they see their child living after school? Parents can also be a great resource. A word of caution, however, is in order. Some parents have not really thought about future planning for their child, and sensitivity should be exercised when asking questions concerning the future of their son or daughter.

If it is determined that services are nonexistent or substandard, the task becomes even more challenging: developing, improving, or increasing the available service options. The educator may not see this as a responsibility, but, as in all other aspects of services provision, educators must be integrally involved in the process. It must be remembered that, if there are not appropriate environments in which students can exercise their skills, then school time spent learning those skills may be wasted.

To facilitate nonduplication of efforts, it may be helpful to compile community access information by individual school site. A transition task force, at either the school or the district level, can be created to help facilitate this information gathering. Teachers can use this information to assist them in preparing Individualized Transition Plans (ITPs). Once information about available service options is collected, a resource manual can be compiled for future use by team members.

2. *Determine what providers in these service settings believe are critical skills for meaningful participation in their service.* The educator should talk to employers, service providers, social services agencies, apartment managers, and community leaders. A teacher may not be adequately preparing students for the world that awaits them unless there is an awareness of what the world expects. It is important to be both sensitive to the concerns and needs of service providers and positive about the abilities of people with disabilities. In today's litigious society, some community members may be somewhat reluctant to speak candidly if asked "Will you hire someone with a disability?" or "Will you allow access and involvement for these students?" What is important to learn is what range and types of possibilities exist. One may also want to use the interview as a time to educate a potential provider about people with disabilities.

It then becomes important to determine specifics regarding access and involvement. What are the behaviors that the community member deems required? What is the community member's attitude toward people with disabilities? What are some of the social systems that exist within the access and involvement site? Would the community member like additional information? Could the teacher or students come to the site to observe? It is important to remember that the manner in which information is requested will influence the way it is provided.

Service providers should be asked if there are entrance or exit criteria for their service. For example, a local group home may accept only those who are ambulatory and who take care of all their personal hygiene needs. In this case, one may confront a skills restriction "wall." Some students may never become ambulatory or be able to independently toilet themselves. The issue, then, becomes whether access based upon skill restrictions can be modified. Although it might be reasonable to expect that agencies will change their restrictions based upon possible accusations of potential discrimination (e.g., in relation to PL 101-336, the Americans with Disabilities Act [ADA]), legal constraints may interfere with a timely resolution. One may also try to teach these prerequisite skills to the student in the final years of high school. Unfortunately, success may not be forthcoming. What needs to be done is for the educational system to have ongoing involvement with service agencies beginning with the time the student with profound disabilities enters school. It does not make sense to initiate contact with adult service agencies when the student is of adolescent age. This involvement should entail information sharing as well as collaborative efforts toward systemic change. For example, it may be discovered that access restrictions that are currently in place are based upon inaccurate assumptions, including those describing personnel training needs and costs. Through collaboration and cooperation, changes can be wrought. This collaboration should include all interested parties, from parents to those who provide community services. As important as it is to initiate reasonable service agency changes, it is equally worthwhile to prepare parents for the reality of adult services and the situations that are likely to be confronted (e.g., education services are based upon entitlement, whereas adult services are not). In addition, the earlier that these collaborations occur, the higher the probability that waiting time for adult services can be diminished.

Cooperation can be difficult to obtain if administrators of adult services do not have formal agreements with the public schools. Although local agreements are possible, Wehman and his colleagues (1988) suggested that a state-level, top–down cooperation model is effective for assuring administrative support. Briefly, the top–down approach encourages interagency agreements to be adopted at the state level. After these agreements are in place, they can be reinforced by local districts, individual schools, and local agency representatives.

3. *Develop lists of skills grouped according to whether they are required, desirable, or unnecessary.* In each of these lists of skills, a tentative prioritized plan of instruction develops. Close scrutiny should be placed on those skills that are required. As discussed above, there may be times in which a required skill may be for the convenience of the service agency rather than an absolute necessity. A teacher may soon learn that there are skills that have been taught in the past that may not be meaningful for life outside of school. Although such skills may have value in the world of "learning," they may have little practical application to the world outside. For example, the student who has been trained in sorting shapes by color may never be able to use this skill if there are no options for this skill use in the local community.

For those skills in the desirable group, which will likely be many, further information gathering is necessary. The types of questioning that team members use regarding desirable skills will usually determine whether the skill is highly desirable or somewhat desirable. This latter group of skills may be seen as important; however, they are prioritized lower than those in the highly desirable category. Typically, skills that cannot be useful in several environments, discrete skills that are very specific to a particular stimulus, and skills that are specific to a professional discipline may be desirable, but not the top priority of the team.

Finally, those skills that are not necessary are given very low priority. These skills may include those that are not community referenced or that do not result in functional outcomes. Only skills that allow individuals with profound disabilities to have enhanced control over their environment, or assist them in maintaining a healthy interdependence with others, are appropriate.

The information gathered above can now be used to design the student's curriculum. Once skills are prioritized, the team breaks them down by environments, subenvironments, activities, and movements and activities across functional domains of community, recreation and leisure, vocational, and home and family. In most respects, this effort will follow the curriculum design concepts discussed in Chapter 10.

Table 13.1 provides some specific examples of domain-based environments, subenvironments, and activities for adolescents with profound disabilities.

Environments

The key question regarding environments is where will instruction take place? The home and family domain environments include the student's house, group home, or a relative's house. In this particular category, an environment is always a place.

Subenvironments

The subenvironments are also places, and include the specific parts of the environment. Examples of subenvironments in the home and family domain might include the various rooms of the house (e.g., kitchen, bathroom, bedroom), as well as areas that surround the house (e.g., backyard, swimming pool, garage).

Activities

Unlike environments and subenvironments, activities include the specific events or teaching situations that can occur in the subenvironments. Again, using the home and family domain, activities might include gardening in the backyard, using appliances in the kitchen, or making up the bed.

Tasks

After the activities are delineated, these can be broken down into teachable units or tasks. For example, in the environment *home,* the subenviron-

TABLE 13.1.   Examples of a Domain-Based Curriculum

Home and Family

Kitchen	Bedroom	Bathroom
Preparing meals	Dressing	Washing hair
Using kitchen appliances	Making bed	Washing hands
Cleaning dishes	Listening to music	Transferring to toilet
Eating meals	Putting clothes away	Shaving

Recreation and Leisure

Community Center	Video Arcade	Movie Theater
Swimming	Paying for tokens	Buying ticket
Dressing	Choosing game	Buying snack
Using exercise equipment	Playing game	Finding seat
Going to specialty clubs	Watching others play game	Using bathroom

Community

Restaurants (Fast Food)	Public Transportation	Grocery Store
Ordering	Using bus	Maneuvering aisles
Bringing food to table	Using taxi	Locating items
Eating	Paying for transportation	Purchasing
Cleaning up	Boarding/unboarding	Requesting help

Vocational

Job Specific	Job Preparation	Skill Development
Housekeeping	Following routine	Communicating needs
Food service	Requesting help	Production rates
Assembly	Increasing on-task time	Task completion
Quality control	Showing preferences	Using equipment

ment *backyard,* and the activity *gardening,* the required skills to complete a gardening task in the backyard would be delineated for a student. A task analysis for "watering the garden" might be required. As indicated in Chapter 10, there may be skills involved in that task that a student will be unable to accomplish. Alternative instructional strategies will likely involve partial participation, and the focus may be on skills (steps) of the task or on basic developmental skills that are not motor aspects of the task itself (Baumgart et al., 1982; Ferguson & Baumgart, 1991).

4.   *Develop a method of assessment to determine at what level the student performs each of the required and desirable skills.* An assessment of particular skills will yield information about the ability the person has with respect to that skill. Sometimes this is referred to as a *discrepancy analysis* (Orelove & Sobsey, 1991). A discrepancy analysis is the process of determining the skills necessary for exhibiting a behavior, the level of adequate

performance, and the nearness of the student's behavior to that standard of performance. For example, by observing the task of toothbrushing and determining how well students can brush their teeth, one can determine what parts of the task need addressing through instructional procedures. Focus should be on functional information that identifies the student's strengths and needs. What are the student's current abilities? What does the student need to learn to become proficient at the skill? If there are skills that the student may not be able to master, because of medical or physical reasons, can adaptations be created? If the skill is necessary, at what level can the person partially participate?

After the discrepancy analysis is completed, the assessment can be discussed at the ITP or Individualized Education Program (IEP) meeting. Once agreement is met at the meeting, strategies for instruction can be developed; these can be incorporated into the transition plan. In this way, agreement between all service providers can be reached, and may facilitate communication and preparation for future service delivery. The implementation of this type of functional–ecological assessment allows for a direct connection to recommended interventions (Browder, 1991; Evans, Brown, Weed, Spry, & Owen, 1987). It also is perceived by teachers as an effective, alternative approach to other assessment procedures that rely on standardized or criterion-referenced measures that do not take into account the environments within which skills are to be taught (Downing & Perino, 1992).

5. *Develop a transdisciplinary approach and formulate the plan of instruction.* Transdisciplinary planning has become an important avenue for facilitating communication among team members who represent various constituencies. Orelove and Sobsey (1991) presented a comprehensive review of the strengths and weaknesses of this approach. Implementation of a transdisciplinary model provides for an open discussion of a student's strengths and needs. It requires that professionals be willing to leave their egos and titles outside the door. The team develops a plan that is based on priorities, rather than on disciplinary biases. For example, the team may determine that the student needs skill development in the recreation and leisure domain. The team then determines how each member can address instruction on recreation and leisure skills through his or her particular discipline focus. This is a very different procedure from asking, for example, What does the student need in physical therapy?

Membership at the transdisciplinary meeting should include all individuals who have knowledge about the student as well as those who will be directly providing services. If there is a particular community setting that will be frequently used, it is appropriate to invite people from that setting. For example, if instruction is provided frequently in a local grocery store, what better person to have present than the grocer? In this way, a working relationship with the grocer can be developed. He or she can develop an understanding of the purpose of the program, see the potential customer, and may be more willing to make reasonable accommodations for the individual in the store.

In addition to the transdisciplinary involvement of professionals, parents should play a critical role in the development of the plan. For secondary students, the cessation of school services is imminent and provides increased motivation to maximize remaining instructional opportunities. The termination of school services may cause concern and stress for parents. Steps must be taken to alleviate some of this concern by providing adequate services and planning. The steps that have been discussed thus far are designed to create a secondary plan that projects to the future through an analysis of present skill discrepancies.

Perhaps the most important persons to have present at team meetings are the students. Often students do not participate in meetings because staff feel their communication skills are too limited. A team that perceives adolescents with profound disabilities as unable to understand the discussion are not likely to enhance the students' community participation. Although many adolescents with profound disabilities may appear incapable of communicating effectively with the team about their educational program, this is no reason to exclude them from the meeting.

Through the team process, specific teaching strategies can be identified. The team should review past teaching strategies to evaluate their effectiveness. It is important to remember that a teaching method that cannot be used in public is probably not a valuable instructional strategy. Teaching people functional skills in the community using appropriate methods can have the added benefit of maintaining a student's personal dignity, as well as providing functional skills.

Specific Domain-Based Instructional Activities

Integral to all special education activities is the compilation of skills as articulated by the team. The IEP team is the local authority on what an individual experiences over the next year. Particularly for students with profound disabilities, the set-in-stone curriculum is not appropriate. Some school districts may have a curriculum for students with mental retardation upon which goals and objectives have been formulated. Typically, these "cookbook" curricula do not address the specific needs of adolescents with profound disabilities and do not provide a focus on the impending cessation of formalized education that these students will experience.

The examples of domains and accompanying activities in Table 13.1 provide suggestions for functional curriculum development. Involvement in these types of activities can be used as a springboard for teams to develop functional skills leading toward meaningful participation in the community. Many of the activities will likely require adaptations or augmentations for completion. As indicated previously, many students may be unable to complete any of the component skills for these activities. In these cases, the team should determine whether the skill remains a priority, the strategy used is effective, additional adaptations are needed for the individual to successfully participate in the skill, or a focus on partial participation through basic developmental skills is necessary.

TRANSITION PLANNING AND IMPLEMENTATION

A number of issues regarding transition planning and implementation are generally recognized (Richards, Lovett, & Gaylord-Ross, 1992). Many of these issues may be categorized according to the following areas: parent and consumer issues, interagency collaboration issues, and individual transitioning issues.

Parent and Consumer Issues

Parents and students are obviously those most affected by the success or failure of transition programs. It is paramount, therefore, that they participate in the transition process to the fullest extent possible. Turnbull and Turnbull (1988) suggested several areas in which families and schools may improve efforts to increase the chance of successful transitions. First, students and families should be encouraged to increase personal decision making. Participation in the development of IEPs and ITPs is one excellent way to increase the opportunities for personal decision making. Second, families should be encouraged to consider and plan for the future. Parents and, where appropriate, students with profound difficulties should be provided with opportunities to discuss the future, both formally (e.g., during IEP or ITP meetings) and informally. Third, parents should be encouraged to help their sons or daughters develop friendships with nondisabled peers. By providing integrated educational settings, the schools may encourage and enhance this possibility. Such friendships not only may help the adolescent with a profound disability learn how to interact more appropriately but also may encourage individuals without disabilities to accept and even advocate for the inclusion of people with disabilities in community and work environments. Turnbull and Turnbull also noted that, as assistive technology improves, parents and students will need support in learning to acquire and use the assistive devices. Schools and other service providers can be instrumental not only in developing these devices on an individual basis but also in increasing affordability and availability.

Wehman et al. (1988) identified several responsibilities that parents and families can assume in the actual transition process. These include (a) attending ITP meetings; (b) providing input to the team concerning the family's and student's needs and the responsibilities family members are willing to assume; (c) advocating for an ITP that ensures community integration and decreases the student's dependence on the family and adult service providers; (d) focusing the team's planning on family and student needs; (e) requesting information about services, programs, and issues that the family will need to address (e.g., residential options, financial planning, recreation and leisure opportunities); and (f) providing additional training in the home and community that complements school-based interventions. Professionals should be aware of and sensitive to the family's needs and desires; however, transition team members must be prepared to provide the best possible services regardless of the level of parental involvement (Wehman et al., 1988).

Interagency Collaboration Issues

Hasazi and Clark (1988) noted that local interagency agreements are excellent mechanisms for promoting cooperation among schools and adult service providers. Participants in these agreements might include personnel from special and vocational education, vocational rehabilitation, developmental disabilities councils or services, and employment and training agencies. Such agreements should specify what services are provided by each agency; a means for identifying local needs, in terms of both services needed and the extent of services; provisions for developing a plan to meet those needs; ways to identify, locate, and contact individuals who may need services; provisions for cross-agency inservice to enhance understanding of each agency's roles and responsibilities; and a means for measuring, evaluating, and modifying services provided under the agreement.

Individual Transitioning Issues

At the heart of the transition process is the individual transition team and the ITP itself. The IDEA mandates that transition planning be implemented when the student reaches age 16. Most authorities agree that transition planning for students should begin no later than when they enter high school, or at least 4 years before they are to leave school. The planning, however, may begin much earlier. Typically, the more severe a person's disability, the earlier a transition team should be formulated. This is particularly important if community resources are limited and the need for extensive services is obvious.

The individual transition team

The responsibility of the individual transition team is to develop and implement an individual transition plan. During the initial stages of transition planning, special education staff, family members, and the student may be the only participants. However, before the student leaves school, personnel from developmental disabilities and other agencies may also be included on the individual transition team.

A member of the school community will usually assume the role of initial transition coordinator at the team's inception. For example, a special education teacher often initiates contact with appropriate personnel and the family to inform them of the team's purpose. Ultimately, however, the parent or guardian may assume the role of transition coordinator (Wehman et al., 1988). The initial transition team meeting and subsequent meetings may be conducted in conjunction with the annual IEP meeting. Annual meetings may be sufficient until the final year of school, when the team may need to meet more frequently to ensure that goals and objectives are being met. Wehman et al. (1988) stressed that a final "exit" meeting should be held to ensure that the transition of responsibility from school to adult service personnel is smooth and timely, and does not result in an interruption or delay in services.

The individual transition plan

The ITP typically specifies, as does the IEP, present levels of performance, goals, objectives, timelines, and persons responsible for specific objectives and activities. The ITP is typically considered supplemental to the IEP. Some components that should be included in an ITP for a student with profound disabilities are (a) skills needed in home and family, recreation and leisure, community, and vocational domains; (b) required support services both before and after leaving school; (c) successful instructional methods or activities; (d) possible options for future services; (e) names of persons and/or agencies involved in the plan; and (f) timelines for completion of instruction or services.

Wehman et al. (1988) stressed that only those weaknesses that interfere with successful postschool adjustment ought to be addressed as part of the ITP. The authors also recommended that ITP objectives be delineated as either educational or administrative; that is, objectives may be related to employment or community living adjustment, or they may be identified as objectives to be met by school or agency personnel or parents or guardians (e.g., conducting an assessment of necessary skills in the preferred residential option).

Because the concept of ITPs is relatively new, no single standardized format has been generally accepted (Strickland & Turnbull, 1990; Wehman et al., 1988). An example of an ITP can be seen in Table 13.2. It addresses the supports that an individual might need when entering adulthood, the current strengths and weaknesses of the individual, persons and agencies responsible for providing support, and implementation and review dates.

EDUCATIONAL SERVICE ISSUES

A number of crucial educational service issues face adolescents with profound disabilities. Although these issues invariably affect *all* individuals with disabilities, it is often in later school years when their effects become most notable.

Integration

Over the past decade, there has been a great amount of discussion surrounding the issues of integration of people with disabilities. These discussions have often centered around the appropriate place in which learning and instruction should occur. Is the appropriate placement for students with disabilities in a full-time regular class, or in a regular class for part of the time and a special (segregated) class for part of the time? These issues have stimulated great debate within the professional community. This debate focuses on inclusion versus integration models. In its truest form, inclusion assumes that all students are full-time students in the regular classroom. Integration assumes that, for some time during the day, there is possibility for segregation of students.

In what environment do adolescents with profound disabilities learn best? Based on the extant literature, this question is impossible to answer. The research community cannot articulate the appropriate placement other than through a philosophical argument. However, the setting in which an adolescent receives services is particularly challenging to the integration–inclusion debate.

We have discussed at great lengths the need for a community-based functional curriculum. It is very difficult to include adolescents with profound disabilities in full-time regular class placements when they are learning skills in the community. On the other hand, very few secondary students who are not disabled are schooled in the natural environment. If students with profound disabilities are spending a great deal of their time at the grocery store or at a domestic site, they have little opportunity to interact with their same-

TABLE 13.2. Example of an Individualized Transition Plan

Supports Needed[a]	Current Level (Strengths/Needs)	Responsibilities	Person/Agency	Date Begun/ Reviewed
		Community		
Shopping	Reaches for items/has difficulty in selecting foods to buy	Supervise in shopping	Warby/Group Home Haney/Teacher[b]	5-92/11-93
Facilities	Enjoys swimming pool	Enroll in swimming program	Higgins/Parks & Rec. Haney/Teacher[b]	5-92/11-93
	Enjoys music	Attend community concerts	Warby/Group Home	5-92/11-93
		Residential		
Living arrangement	Needs supervised living	Visit group home Determine entrance criteria	Parents Warby/Group Home	6-92/12-93
		Visit supported living Determine entrance criteria	Parents Warby/Group Home	6-92/12-93
		Apply for admission	Parents Warby/Group Home	7-92/12-93
	Attends daily living skills program	Continue program	Haney/Teacher[b]	5-92/11-93
		Financial and Legal		
Financial	Needs supervision for all personal finances	Identify financial guardian	Rhu/Advocacy office Parents	5-92/11-93
		Obtain information on and apply for all eligible government supports	Howe/Social Security Office Haney/Teacher[b] Parents	5-92/11-93

(continued)

TABLE 13.2. *Continued*

Supports Needed[a]	Current Level (Strengths/Needs)	Responsibilities	Person/Agency	Date Begun/ Reviewed
		Financial and Legal *(cont.)*		
Legal	Needs public guardian	Identify guardian	Rhu/Advocacy office Parents	5-92/11-93
		Review procedure with parents	Rhu/Advocacy office	5-92/11-93
		Provide information to student	Rhu/Advocacy office Parents	6-92/11-93
		Vocational and Employment		
Supported employment	Can maintain sustained activity	Locate supported employment programs	Haney/Teacher[b] Boone/Voc. Rehab.	5-92/11-93
Vocational training	Attends daily vocational education program at school	Continue program	Haney/Teacher[b]	5-92/11-93
	Needs placement and experience in community employment sites	Identify possible community employment sites	Haney/Teacher[b]	7-92/11-93

[a]For space limitations, these are only a sampling of possible supports. [b]As long as the individual remains in school.

aged peers who are not disabled. The dilemma is obvious. Community-referenced practice can remove the student from the integrated school setting.

Students aged 18 years or older are not with the majority of their same-aged peers if they are spending most of the school day at a high school. Therefore, providing community-based instruction for students with profound disabilities who are 18 years or older would not appear to be inappropriate. For younger students, however, there should be consideration of a balance between the need for contact with peers of similar chronological age and the need for integration in the community at large. Again, the involvement of family members is required to balance the school-based versus community-based instructional time. Some families provide sufficient community-referenced experiences for their offspring with profound disabilities within the natural routines of family life. With these involved families, coordination between families and schools can further enhance community instructional benefits.

Many have suggested that structuring interactions that lead to friendships between people with profound disabilities and their peers who are not disabled increases understanding and tolerance, while building appropriate concepts of community (Haring, Lovett, & Haring, 1992). Insightful experiences with people with disabilities can prove helpful in developing meaningful relationships, providing age-appropriate models, and shaping a more informed society. With adequate support, adolescents who are profoundly disabled can benefit from regular high school class placement. Early inclusionary practices have included placing them into nonacademic classes, such as physical education or shop. Current practice has expanded meaningful inclusion to a wider variety of high school courses. The critical determinants of success, however, are the acceptance of the regular educator and the consultative skill of the special educator. Adolescents with profound disabilities can likely participate in many courses, given appropriate inclusionary methods.

It should seem obvious that secondary education is not the time to begin inclusionary education. Secondary education is typically geared toward preparation for adulthood. At first glance, it seems somewhat ludicrous to place a student with profound disabilities into a high school French class when there is a need for this student to develop functional skills to be used in the community. However, if an old friend is in the class and the course is activity based, this could be an appropriate inclusionary setting. An individual with profound disabilities has an entire adult life to experience the community, but he or she is age appropriate for high school courses for only 4 years. Any opportunity for successful inclusion should be seized.

Personal Dignity

Our society is based on the equality of its citizens. However, helping the general public to view individuals with profound disabilities as equal members of society continues to be a difficult undertaking. Indeed, this is a problem within the special education community as well. It seems ironic that many special educators argue for inclusion of people with disabilities but retreat when this includes those with profound disabilities. This may be due to the fact that inclusion does not mean mere placement in an integrated environment. Inclusion means that each individual is *meaningfully* included in the environment. Respecting personal dignity is a critical aspect of inclusion. If personal dignity is not ensured, inclusion is not appropriate or at least not appropriately implemented. The development of a sense of self-dignity also can be a major benefit of meaningful inclusion. Through appropriate inclusion, people with profound disabilities may feel they are perceived as having some value in the eyes of others.

The mere discussion of the need for personal dignity suggests that adolescents with profound disabilities are not afforded the same rights, privileges, and freedoms as others. However, developing a sense of dignity may not be possible if others do not perceive these individuals in a dignified fashion. Most people with disabilities have been gradually afforded an opportunity to develop a sense of dignity, in part because of legislation and a society that has become more tolerant. Most people with profound disabilities, however, continue to occupy a space that is isolated from others within the society.

Choice

The freedom to make choices enhances one's personal dignity. When given the opportunity to make choices, individuals can exert greater control over their environment. In making choices, an individual becomes a decision maker and, therefore, a person due respect. For adolescents with profound disabilities, choice may be the major vehicle in achieving respect. Having choices can increase a sense of personal dignity and improve positive interactions with others. To make true choices, however, a person must be informed of the options that can be chosen. Adolescents with profound disabilities may need to experience the options before a truly informed choice is possible. For example, asking people whether they would prefer to live in an institution or in a group home may not be a matter of choice if they have experienced living in only one environment.

Appropriate educational programs should incorporate instruction to teach the skills necessary for choice making. For many students, this teaching can be enhanced through systematic instructional methods, such as modeling and reinforcement techniques. These programs should focus on learning through experience to increase the repertoire of choice-making skills that students possess. The programs should also emphasize the development of communication skills that will enhance choice-making abilities.

For individuals with profound disabilities, there is great confusion with respect to choice-making skills. Can informed choices be made? Are choices coerced? Are choice-making abilities limited by teachers who do not offer choices? Do teaching strategies prohibit choice making? Until further research is conducted and improved practices implemented, the arguments surrounding meaningful choice making among people with profound disabilities will continue. One rule of thumb, however, is to assume that the student is able to make choices; therefore, opportunities for choice should follow.

Choice and personal dignity relate to value. Perhaps no other group of individuals is perceived as having less value than those with profound disabilities. For example, they may be the only people who are routinely segregated in schools. If there is any integration, it is usually in some type of experimental unit, exemplary program, or a research setting that cannot easily allow for transfer into practice. They may be the only people who are denied access to appropriate community housing because their needs cannot be met by the existing service delivery system. They may be the only people who do not have the opportunity to learn about personal autonomy and choices. They may be the only people who are taught in a fashion that accentuates their differences rather than their similarities. It is the responsibility of service providers, therefore, to assist adolescents with profound disabilities to develop skills that will enhance their interaction with the environment. It is also the responsibility of team members to educate others that adolescents with profound disabilities have the right to receive the respect that is due all citizens.

CONCLUSION

The primary focus of this chapter was to provide an information base on how to develop and implement appropriate educational programs for adolescents who are profoundly disabled. Many of these individuals may lack functional skills not because of the presence of a disability, but because of inappropriate teaching emphases and the use of nonfunctional curricula. An emphasis on a domain-specific, community-referenced approach will likely address many of the educational problems that have existed for this group of students. It matters little if persons with profound disabilities are able to use technology, communicate needs in the classroom, or even be accommodated in the regular classroom, if what they learned in school will be nonfunctional in the environments they will encounter as adults.

REFERENCES

Baumgart, D., Brown, L., Pumpian, I., Nisbet, J., Ford, A., Sweet, M., Messina, R., & Schroeder, J. (1982). Principle of partial participation and individualized adaptations in educational programs for severely handicapped students. *Journal of The Association for the Severely Handicapped, 7,* 17–27.

Browder, D. (1991). *Assessment of individuals with severe handicaps: An applied behavior approach to life skills assessment* (2nd ed.). Baltimore: Brookes.

Brown, L., Nietupski, J., & Hamre-Nietupski, S. (1976). Criterion of ultimate functioning. In M. A. Thomas (Ed.), *Hey! Don't forget about me!* (pp. 2–15). Reston, VA: Council for Exceptional Children.

Brown, L., Nisbet, J., Ford, A., Sweet, M., Shiraga, B., York, J., & Loomis, R. (1983). *The critical need for nonschool instruction in educational programs for severely handicapped students.* Madison: University of Wisconsin and Madison Metropolitan School District.

Brown, L., Shiraga, B., Rogan, P., York, J., Zanella, K., McCarthy, E., Loomis, R., & VanDeventer, P. (1985). *The "why" question in educational programs for students who are severely intellectually disabled.* Madison: University of Wisconsin and Madison Metropolitan School District.

Brown, L., Sweet, M., Shiraga, B., York, J., Zanella, K., & Rogan, P. (1984). *Functional skills in programs for students with severe handicaps.* Madison: University of Wisconsin and Madison Metropolitan School District.

Downing, J., & Perino, D. M. (1992). Functional versus standardized assessment procedures: Implications for educational programming. *Mental Retardation, 30,* 289–295.

Evans, I., Brown, F., Weed, K., Spry, K., & Owen, V. (1987). The assessment of functional competence: A behavioral approach to the evaluation of programs for children with disabilities. In R. Prinz (Ed.), *Advances in behavioral assessment of children and families* (Vol. 3, pp. 93–121). Greenwich, CT: JAI Press.

Falvey, M. A. (1989). *Community-based instruction: Instructional strategies for students with severe handicaps* (2nd ed.). Baltimore: Brookes.

Ferguson, D., & Baumgart, D. (1991). Partial participation revisited. *The Journal of The Association for Persons with Severe Handicaps, 16*(4), 218–227.

Guess, D., Mulligan-Ault, M., Roberts, S., Struth, J., Siegel-Causey, E., Thompson, B., Bronicki, G. J., & Guy, B. (1988). Implications of biobehavioral states for the education and treatment of students with the most profoundly handicapped conditions. *The Journal of The Association for Persons with Severe Handicaps, 13,* 163–174.

Halpern, A. S. (1985). Transition: A look at the foundation. *Exceptional Children, 51,* 479–483.

Haring, K. A., Lovett, D. L., & Haring, N. G. (Eds.). (1992). *Integrated life cycle services for persons with disabilities.* New York: Springer-Verlag.

Haring, K. A., Saren, D., Lovett, D. L., & Shelton, M. (1992). A study of the demographic and attitudinal differences between paraprofessionals and teachers in self-contained special education classrooms. *Journal of Developmental and Physical Disabilities,* 4(1), 51–70.

Haring, N. G. (1988). *Generalization for students with severe handicaps: Strategies and solutions.* Seattle: University of Washington Press.

Hasazi, S. B., & Clark, G. M. (1988). Vocational preparation for high school students labeled mentally retarded: Employment as a graduation goal. *Mental Retardation, 26,* 343–349.

Helmstetter, D. (1990). Curriculum for school-aged students: The ecological model. In F. Brown & D. H. Lehr (Eds.), *Persons with profound disabilities: Issues and practices* (pp. 239–263). Baltimore: Brookes.

Murray-Seegert, C. (1989). *Nasty girls, thugs, and humans like us: Social relations between severely disabled and nondisabled students in high school.* Baltimore: Brookes.

Orelove, F. P. & Sobsey, D. (1991). *Educating children with multiple disabilities: A transdisciplinary approach* (2nd ed.). Baltimore: Brookes.

Patton, J. R., Cronin, M. E., Polloway, E. A., Hutchison, D., & Robinson, G. (1989). Curricular considerations: A life skills orientation. In G. A. Robinson, J. R. Patton, E. A. Polloway, & L. R. Sargent (Eds.), *Best practices in mild mental disabilities* (pp. 21–37). Reston, VA: Council for Exceptional Children.

Public Law 94-142. (1975). *Education for All Handicapped Children Act,* 20 U.S.C. secs. 1401–1461.

Public Law 101-336. (1990). *The Americans with Disabilities Act of 1990,* 42 U.S.C., 12101.

Public Law 101-476. (1990). *Individuals with Disabilities Education Act,* 20 U.S.C., Chapter 33.

Richards, S. B., Lovett, D. L., & Gaylord-Ross, R. (1992). Integrated services for adolescents with disabilities. In K. A. Haring, D. L. Lovett, & N. G. Haring (Eds.), *Integrated lifecycle services for persons with disabilities* (pp. 246–280). New York: Springer-Verlag.

Sailor, W., Gee, K., Goetz, L., & Graham, N. (1988). Progress in educating students with the most severe disabilities: Is there any? *Journal of The Association for Persons with Severe Handicaps, 13,* 87–99.

Snell, M., & Browder, D. (1986). Community-referenced instruction: Research and issues. *Journal of The Association for Persons with Severe Handicaps, 11,* 1–11.

Strickland, B. B., & Turnbull, A. P. (1990). *Developing and implementing individualized education programs* (3rd ed.). Columbus, OH: Merrill.

Turnbull, A. P., & Turnbull, H. R. (1988). Toward great expectations for vocational opportunities: Family–professional partnerships. *Mental Retardation, 26,* 337–342.

Wehman, P., Moon, M. S., Everson, J. M., Wood, W., & Barcus, J. M. (1988). *Transition from school to work.* Baltimore: Brookes.

Chapter 14

Support Needs and Strategies for Adults with Profound Disabilities

NANCY BRAWNER-JONES

To be imprisoned in one's body is dreadful. To be confined in an institution for the profoundly retarded does not crush you in the same way. It just removes all hope. (Crossley & McDonald, 1980, p. viii)

For the past 20 years, creating community inclusion has been touted as the goal for policy and practice for people who are disabled. For the vast majority of adults with profound disabilities in our nation, however, the hope mentioned by Crossley and McDonald has remained elusive. This elusiveness is due, in large part, to the lack of comprehensive information about those adults referred to as having profound disabilities. The lack of information has resulted in diminished levels of expectations for these individuals. Legislation and programs have been designed for those persons with *the most severe disabilities*. Experience shows, however, that those who are considered persons with profound disabilities are not the people finding success and adequate support from the legislative and programmatic advances intended for them. Persons with profound disabilities are those whom Forest and Pearpoint (1992) called the "yes buts" and "what about" people in society—those people who have not been successfully supported as full members of communities. When attempts are made to identify appropriate services or methods of instruction for people with profound disabilities, discussions often take the form of exclusionary messages, such as "But what about Myra" or "Yes, but that method has not been successful with Ricardo." In these instances, the failure to provide an adequate match is all too often attributed to the actual or perceived presence of a profound disability of the person in question rather than a lack of skill and/or creativity on the part of the service provider.

West and Parent (1992) stated that people who "fall between the cracks" in the human service systems are those whose "preferences and needs do not 'fit' the available options" (p. 51). Needs of individuals with profound disabilities are often intense and diverse. Therefore, when their needs do not coincide with services designed for other groups of people (or those designed for some ill-defined, stereotypic group), the inevitable "yes but" and "what about" barriers deny full membership and participation in the community. These barriers will not be overcome until adults with profound disabilities are better understood. As a part of this understanding, it is important to acknowledge that characteristics and needs for all people differ with age. Persons with profound disabilities are no exception.

PROVIDING AN ADEQUATE DEFINITION

Attempts to define the group of people who are known as adults with profound disabilities have taken two directions. The definition provided in Chapter 1, when extended to adults, is based upon degree of disability, a point on a continuum. Another major direction taken in forming a group definition of adults with profound disabilities has been one that emphasizes inability, incapacity, and little or no expectation for growth and development. This is in direct comparison to definitions of persons with milder degrees of disability, which describe expectations of ability, capacities, and potential for development (Sharpton & West, 1992). Descriptions such as "unlikely to achieve any measure of productivity . . . unable to enter into relationships . . . total dependency on family or support agencies . . . potential limited to self-help skills . . . require lifelong supervised care. . ." (Sharpton & West, 1992, p. 16) perpetuate the myth of the "eternal child" and do not allow for considerations of the adult qualities, capacities, and needs of people with profound disabilities. Whereas the first definition provides a group framework, emphasis is on depiction of the individual within the group. On the other hand, the latter definitional paradigm seeks to establish adults with profound disabilities within a homogeneous group.

Holvoet (1989) defended the need for a homogeneous group definition of persons with profound disabilities. She made the point that, without homogeneity, any attempts to improve an individual's condition would likely have to be considered experimental. The lack of a widely accepted homogeneous definition is only one of the issues that has spawned a scattered approach to research focusing on the lives of persons with profound disabilities. Holvoet likened the approach of research in the area of profound disabilities to a jigsaw puzzle, where a myriad of individuals are attempting to fit pieces together in a puzzle whose entirety has never been seen.

On the other hand, West and Parent (1992) cautioned against efforts to establish homogeneity for persons with profound disabilities. Homogeneous definitions may defeat the long-range purpose of providing the best services and supports to match the needs of adults with profound disabilities. West and Parent warned that attempting to meet needs of groups of individuals assumes a commonality of abilities, desires, and limitations. The necessary individual focus may, therefore, be lost.

Regardless of whether one presupposes some type of homogeneity among persons with profound disabilities or maintains the position that the individual needs of people should be considered only within a heterogeneous framework, the only reasonable solution appears to be the adoption of the transdisciplinary approach (Albano, 1983; Giangreco, York, & Rainforth, 1989; Lyon & Lyon, 1980; Orelove & Sobsey, 1991; Sears, 1981; Woodruff & McGonigel, 1988). This approach can effectively serve to clarify definitions, identify needed services and interventions, and develop appropriate methods for delivery supports. Sources of important information are so diverse that families and professionals must work together, overcoming barriers to role release, to develop, assimilate, and apply research to the betterment of the lives of adults with profound disabilities. Without such a transdisciplinary effort, service providers will not be able to create supports that afford persons with profound disabilities the opportunity to achieve the dignified adult life-styles that they deserve.

HISTORY OF SERVICE SYSTEMS

A pervasive theme in the study of services for adults with profound disabilities is one of limitations. This includes limitations of what is known about adults with profound disabilities.

Limitations on Information

In the past, very few people born with profound disabilities survived to adulthood. Chronic medical conditions are more prevalent for people with profound disabilities than for any other group of people (Brawner-Jones, in press; Hill, Bruininks, & Lakin, 1983; McDonald, 1985; Rowitz, 1988). Only in recent years has medical science made the advances that allow many people with profound disabilities to survive to adulthood; however, those medical advances have not served to increase the level of expectations. The medical professionals who save and sustain the lives of persons with profound disabilities often establish limited expectations for their future quality of life (Weir, 1984). Unfortunately, such expectations lead to predictions that follow people throughout their lives, and serve to limit their perceived potential and possibilities. The danger in this practice was identified by Sternberg (1988), who encouraged the review of many of the past quality of life prognoses made for people with less severe degrees of disability. The limiting prognoses made by medical professionals for the quality of life for these individuals have been contradicted by the success many individuals with severe disabilities have experienced in recent years when given the supports necessary to achieve improved quality of life (Lusthaus, 1985; Rynders, 1982).

Another reason for the limitations in the knowledge base about adults with profound disabilities is the tendency in the past to mesh information about persons with severe and profound disabilities. This has been true in studies of residential and vocational services, instructional technology, and other areas that are a part of the adult life of people with profound disabilities. Bates (1989) illustrated the problem in relation to vocational training. Although many studies purport to include individuals with profound disabilities in community vocational training endeavors, very few actually include individuals with multiple disabilities or involve them in integrated settings.

Limitations in Services

Historically, adults with profound disabilities have experienced inadequate support through the service delivery system. Limitations have existed in the types, quantity, and quality of those supports. Until the last two decades, people with profound disabilities who survived to adulthood lived in very segregated settings. The options for individuals consisted of the homes of their family, where they were "family secrets," or institutions in which they were kept with minimal efforts toward habilitation or the development of supports that might enhance their quality of life.

In the distant past, family members with disabilities lived at home and were the responsibility of the family. Only when poverty threatened a family's ability to support a family member with disabilities did the community intercede. This often took the form of removing the person with profound disabilities from the family, either by physical transfer to other communities or through isolation in the community with other devalued citizens (Ferguson, 1988).

By the end of the colonial period, almshouses and workhouses had been established to hide away from society persons with disabilities. Unfortunately, such strategies are still in use today. Individuals with profound disabilities are typically those who continue to reside in publicly supported institutional settings in the United States. Blatt (1987) described a situation in which the limited expectations proposed by the medical model are supported in reality for adults with profound disabilities living in institutional settings. He described these institutions as being more about "psychological killing than psychological living" (p. 168). Although the original names (e.g., "hospital for the incurable") have changed, the lack of expectations for growth have been resistant to change. Blatt described the institutions of the past as places where persons with no expectation for growth were kept to die away from family and neighbors, and to spare the living from the sight of literal or psychological death. He proposed that the segregation that still exists for persons with profound disabilities is a permutation of antiquated concepts and attitudes.

Consideration of employment and training of any kind for persons with profound disabilities was almost out of the question until the last 20 years. *Wyatt v. Stickney* (1972) challenged the perpetuation of provision of custodial care as the only support for people with profound disabilities. In this case, Judge Frank M. Johnson ruled that several deficiencies were present at Partlow State Hospital, a residential facility in Alabama where persons with profound disabilities resided. One of the significant deficiencies was the lack of individual habilitation plans. The right to habilitation was further strengthened by the Supreme Court ruling in *Romeo v. Youngberg* (1982) which affirmed that persons with profound disabilities have a right to more than food, shelter, and medical care (Ellis, 1982; Turnbull, 1982; Westling, 1986). The right to habilitation acknowledged that *all people* are educable. Directly as a result of this litigation, significant efforts in recent years have focused on strategies for teaching persons with profound disabilities.

The same perception that adults with profound disabilities are not able to learn also has served as an excuse for a lack of habilitation in vocational programs. Until the late 1980s, people with severe or profound disabilities were excluded from vocational training programs due to a perceived lack of potential benefit from such involvement (Bates, 1989; Bellamy, Horner, & Inman, 1979; Wehman, Renzaglia, & Bates, 1985).

THE REALITIES OF PRESENT SERVICE OPTIONS

The right to habilitation effectively brought to an end a legislative and practical filtering system in which adults with profound disabilities were the ones continually filtered out. For school-aged children with profound disabilities, the zero exclusion policy, upheld most recently in *Timmy W. v. Rochester, New Hampshire School District* (1989), supports the same nonexclusion principle for habilitation services for adults with profound disabilities. The court in *Timmy W.* referred to the finding in *Board of Education of Hendrick*

Hudson Central School District v. Rowley. The presiding judge explained that "while the Act does not require a school to maximize a child's potential for learning, it does provide a 'basic floor of opportunity' for the handicapped [sic]" (p. 46). The court in *Timmy W.* went on to state that "Nowhere does the Court imply that such a 'floor' contains a trap door for the severely handicapped [sic]" (p. 46). The assurance of no trap door is, therefore, now offered for adults with profound disabilities. However, yet establishing an enforced acknowledgment of the rights of adults with profound disabilities, and demanding that habilitation be available for those adults, is still a far cry from honoring the basic values that are held dear by the community supporting people with disabilities. These include normalization, inclusion, social role valorization, and lives characterized by dignity, personal fulfillment, and equal opportunity. These are values espoused for *all* people.

Service providers are obviously at a new starting point for providing the support and respect that adults with profound disabilities have always deserved. The basic values must be kept in mind as service providers learn the best way to provide supports to adults in the communities. As with all learning processes, however, it will take time and patience to determine what is best practice for adults with profound disabilities. Such learning will best be achieved through a marriage of research and values (Snell, 1991).

Residential Service Options

Despite the increased flexibility that has evolved in the system of community support, there is still little known about the efficacy of various types of residential settings and supports for individuals with profound disabilities. Brown, Davis, Richards, and Kelly (1989) conducted an extensive literature review that encompassed over 190 data-based articles on the community living settings of people with disabilities. Their review revealed that few studies specifically addressed people with profound disabilities but instead included this population within a broader range of disabilities (e.g., severe and profound, moderate through profound). Only a few studies took place in integrated home environments (Brown et al., 1989; Brown, Helmstetter, & Guess, 1986; Lakin, Hill, & Bruininks, 1988; Lakin, Hill, White, & Wright, 1988; Landesman & Vietze, 1987). National data on living environments of people with disabilities are difficult to determine because of the extreme variance among states regarding residential services and their orientations toward community placements (Lakin, Hill, & Bruininks, 1988).

National data, 10 years after the deinstitutionalization movement began, revealed that most (60.5%) residents of public and private facilities for persons with developmental disabilities experienced severe or profound mental retardation. Even though people with profound disabilities are finding success moving into community-based placements (10% of the population in group environments with six or fewer housemates and specialized foster homes), the largest proportion of persons still left in institutional settings are those with multiple disabilities, including profound mental retardation (Best-Sigford, Bruininks, Lakin, Hill, & Heal, 1982; Lakin, Hill, & Bruininks, 1988; Scheerenberger, 1982).

Adults with profound disabilities fare worse than children with profound disabilities in the move to community-based services. Of those persons remaining in institutional settings, the majority are adults. In addition, the median age at which persons with profound disabilities are admitted to residential care is rapidly increasing (Lakin, Hill, Hauber, & Bruininks, 1982). This has been attributed to changes in delivery of support to children and families, which have allowed families to remain together for longer periods of time.

At the point when supports available only to children (i.e., educational services through public school entitlement programs) are lost due to the "aging out" of young adults with profound disabilities, some families may view institutional settings as the only option because they perceive that society has not and cannot provide sufficient support for residential alternatives in less restrictive settings (Biklen & Knoll, 1987). However, Borthwick-Duffy, Eyman, and White (1987) suggested that the deinstitutionalization and community residential support data describe a community support system that has absorbed some adults with profound mental retardation. Therefore, the system today can be characterized as providing services to a more heterogeneous group of persons with disabilities than was the case in previous years.

The studies of community living supports for people with disabilities have brought about change to some previously held beliefs. One important realization is that the size of where a person lives is not the best measure of adequacy of support or degree of membership in the community. It is recognized that those variables necessary for valued participation in the community are more likely to be present in smaller, more homelike settings. Small size, however, is no guarantee that the necessary supports will be present. Evans and Scotti (1989) attributed the move to family-sized homes from institutions to the desire to provide social structures that allow for the creation of desirable expectations. Particularly important is the expectation that people living in homes will *all* take part in daily duties that contribute to the general good of people living in the home. This is in opposition to the expectation traditionally found in institutions where adults with profound disabilities reside—that is, that professional people are viewed as total care providers, and individuals with profound disabilities as receivers of services. As long as the structure of any residential program is oriented toward these expectations, normalization can never be reached.

Taylor (1987) described a situation in which deinstitutionalization efforts often resulted in "transinstitutionalization." Rather than being provided the supports to live in homes as members of the community at large, adults with profound disabilities are being moved to units constructed on the grounds of state institutions (referred to as "community residences") or transferred from large public institutions to small, but just as segregated, private ones, including nursing homes. Therefore, regardless of the smaller size of the facility, segregation and isolation continue.

Supports in Residential Settings

Brown et al. (1989) suggested that the atmosphere of a person's particular living arrangement depends, to a large degree, upon the philosophy of the organization that is providing the services. The outcomes for adults with profound disabilities rely heavily on the service providers' adherence to what is emerging as best practice in provision of residential supports. Many suggest that providing adequate supports in homes in the community will entail a complete revamping of the systems that now exist to embrace new values (Nisbet, Clark, & Covert, 1991; Smull & Bellamy, 1991). The new vision is based on what has been learned from research and intervention efforts of the last 20 years. This knowledge is summarized in the following paragraphs:

1.   All individuals, regardless of the degree of disability, can have their needs met in the community. Where a person lives can no longer be based upon a continuum of "readiness slots" into which a person is placed based upon a generic assessment of needs associated with a certain disability label. The shift must be to what Bellamy and Horner (1988) have described as "persons with disabilities living where they want, for as long as they want, with the ongoing support needed to sustain that choice" (p. 506). This shift will avoid the prior tendency of placing a group of individuals with the same level of disability or support needs into one facility. For example, in the past, there was a tendency to homogeneously group several people with behavioral challenges or several adults who need intensive medical support in order to reduce the higher cost that results from intensive staffing patterns. This strategy has proven to be disastrous in that the individuals, each of whom may need three or four staff to be available during a crisis, can cause the staff to become burned out more quickly than in a living arrangement in which adults with less intensive needs are balanced with those who require more attention (Brown et al., 1989). The focus on individual support needs in whatever setting is chosen will preclude the equating of certain levels or types of support being germane to a particular setting. This will allow for the move from congregate settings to individual supports in the community.

2.   Recidivism and refusal of services based on lack of skills can no longer be allowed from those providing supports to adults with profound dis-

abilities. Studies of why people fail in the community and return to institutional settings identify a safety net syndrome. As long as the institution remains an option into which one can fall based upon failure to adjust, encouragement may not be provided for individualizing and intensifying supports in community living options. Entry skill requirements keep adults with profound disabilities from acquiring the supports they need to live adult lives in the community. In a study of families with members who are adults with profound disabilities, one sister spoke of her adult brother's limited skills as a barrier to his acquisition of supports to allow him to live in the community in a home of his own:

> There are group homes around but he can't go there because they have to take care of themselves and things like that and he can't. . . . There aren't any options. After a while they just got tired of trying to dig things up. It sounds cruel and people just look at me. But, I wish he could just go to sleep and not wake up. That would be better than a nursing home and the folks could have a little while with just each other. (Brawner-Jones, 1987, p. 27)

This quote exemplifies the point of acquiesence that can be reached by families with adults with profound disabilities if supports are denied them due to entry-level skill requirements.

Smull and Bellamy (1991) have emphasized that the way to avoid recidivism and barriers to supports is through establishment of access to regular environments through legal and legislative action, and increased efforts to establish ongoing supports that allow all individuals, including those with profound disabilities, to participate successfully in community settings.

Although reasons for recidivism have often been couched in terms such as "resident adjustment," closely related to this adjustment are the attitude and competency of support personnel. Sutter, Mayeda, Yee, and Yanagi (1981) found that people maintaining their home in the community had more success when support personnel were tolerant of maladaptive behaviors and were experienced in providing supports.

3. Choice must be available for adults with profound disabilities. This choice must be in how supports are delivered as well as settings in which they occur. The history of residential services for adults with profound disabilities is replete with examples of people having things done to them or for them and rarely with them. Adults in need of support often find themselves in a constant state of disability "boot camp" in which they have to respond to or accept the constantly changing demands of numerous caretakers. Brown (1991) validated the existence of this situation when she explained that behavior programs are too often designed to teach adults with profound disabilities to comply with a schedule of activities, regardless of the individual's willingness to participate in these activities.

Inconsistency in compliance expectations for adults with disabilities is due to a number of reasons, including staffing patterns in facilities that involve a large number of people who provide support with different expectations, changing staff patterns due to high turnover in personnel, and the lack of respect for choice in the way supports are provided for adults.

Inability to make choices is often given as the reason for not allowing adults with profound disabilities to have a say in how they are supported in their homes. Meyer (1991) purported that this practice is perpetuated because it effectively provides a rationalization for not changing anything. Williams (1991) proposed, however, that all individuals with disabilities possess the abilities to communicate with others and indicate preferences. These abilities can effectively be used to provide some type of control over one's life. The means necessary to enhance these abilities, therefore, should never be denied to individuals with profound disabilities.

Allowing choice can entirely change the relationship between adults with profound disabilities and those persons who support them. Giving adults choices in their life-style allows support people to develop a different interest in the individual that was likely not present when that person was seen as incapable of making choices (Evans & Scotti, 1989). The interest that develops as a result of allowing adults with profound disabilities to make choices or initiate a routine leads to respect for the adult. It also assists others in viewing the individual as in control and as one who is making decisions about his or her life. The caregiver has now been transformed into the role of care assistant. This is much closer to a parallel, equal relationship than a relationship of hierarchical power (Downie, 1985; Downie & Telfer, 1980; Evans & Scotti, 1989; Holvoet, 1989). A true home can exist only when relationships based on trust and respect are allowed to develop between people with profound disabilities and the people who provide support for them.

4.   An inadequate number of qualified people are available to provide supports for adults with profound disabilities in the places they live. A quick look through the help wanted section of any newspaper in cities where a large number of people reside will reveal a number of requests for personnel to provide supports to people with disabilities.

Since the beginning of the residential support system, there has always been concern with the recruitment and retention of personnel to provide the high-quality supports for people with disabilities that are critical to their success in the community (Baker, Seltzer, & Seltzer, 1977; Bruininks, Kudla, Wieck, & Hauber, 1980; Burchard & Thousand, 1988; McCord, 1981; O'Connor, 1976; Schalock, 1985). Presently, many community residential programs are unable to attract staff at current salary rates. As a result, there are few vacancies in existing programs and families have little hope that their adult family members will ever move from long waiting lists into situations in which they are adequately supported in the community (New York Office of Mental Retardation and Developmental Disabilities, 1987; Smull & Bellamy, 1991; Smull, Sachs, Cahn, & Feder, 1988).

Experienced support personnel are a rare commodity. A study by Lakin, Bruininks, and Hill (1982) revealed that the staff separation rate for small community residences was 87% annually. It is difficult to develop the long-term interpersonal relationships, nurturing, and understanding that are important to developing a sense of community when the people who provide support for success disappear frequently. However, longevity of support personnel employment is not necessarily a guarantee of adequately trained people providing quality services. In a national sample of residential settings, Lakin et al. found that people who left support positions were as likely to be exceptional employees as they were to be poor ones.

Employees who support adults with profound disabilities over long periods of time often experience high interpersonal stress leading to burnout. Burnout is a phenomenon of emotional distancing and detachment from people who are being supported. This condition can be related to sparse staffing patterns and the emotional and physical stresses of the job, and often becomes a coping mechanism for dealing with intense pressures. People experiencing burnout do not always leave their position, but the relationship between the supporter and the people being supported can deteriorate due to objectification and dehumanization of the persons being supported (Burchard & Thousand, 1988; Freudenberger, 1975; Maslach, 1976).

The achievement of community inclusion for adults with profound disabilities in the future will be dependent on reform in the provision of support in the community. Reform must address a number of variables in regard to training and maintenance of support personnel. Reforms should focus on the following:

1. Support for adults with profound disabilities in the community must shift to natural supports whenever possible. Public services must augment, not supplant, those efforts of persons who are informally supporting a person's life-style choices (Forest & Lusthaus, 1988; Froland, Pancoast, Chapman, & Kimboko, 1981; Nisbet & Callahan, 1987; Smull & Bellamy, 1991).

2. People providing support, both paid professionals and persons providing natural supports, must be provided the training that they need to effectively provide needed services. Training must be provided to preservice personnel, as well as ongoing training to those who continue to support people in the community. Research has shown that personnel training results in improved attitudes, increased appropriate interactions between support

personnel and persons being supported, and job satisfaction (Schinke & Wong, 1977).

3. Inadequacy of salaries and staffing patterns must be addressed. Pay for direct care staff positions in residential settings tends to be very low, often little more than minimum wage; however, the demands from people providing supports for adults with profound disabilities can be great. The lack of balance between performance demands and compensation is attributed to much of the high turnover in personnel that occurs in residential support systems. Improving this situation will require legislative action to appropriate more funding to support adults in community living options.

4. Another requirement for change will be using limited resources in creative ways. Lakin (1988) suggested lowering administrative costs and transferring savings to direct care support personnel, identifying mixes of direct wages and fringe benefits that allow employees to select from a menu of possible fringes, modifying scheduling of support personnel around level of demand for support, and increasing use of natural supports to reduce demand on paid support staff.

5. Training and support must be provided in a manner that honors respect, both for people with disabilities and for persons providing support. Respect is essential for adults with profound disabilities to be successfully included in the community. Equitable relationships cannot develop without respect among the people in the relationship. Therefore, only persons who have respect for the needs and contributions of adults with profound disabilities should be providing support.

6. Persons providing support must be assured that they are valued. This display of respect must come from management of agencies, family members, and the persons receiving support.

Vocational Options

Prior to the passage of PL 99-506, The Developmental Disabilities Act of 1984, adults with profound disabilities were excluded from consideration for vocational training. This exclusion has been attributed to a perceived lack of potential to benefit from such efforts (Bates, 1989; Bellamy et al., 1979; Wehman et al., 1985). The law defined supported employment as "competitive work in an integrated work setting for individuals who, because of their handicaps, need ongoing support services to perform that work" (*Federal Register,* 1987, p. 30546). Even with the law's nonexclusion policy, however, research shows that the vast majority of persons with profound disabilities are still not being meaningfully employed or benefiting from employment services (Kiernan, McGaughey, & Schalock, 1986; Kregel & Wehman, 1989; Rusch, Chadsey-Rusch, & Johnson, 1991). Individuals with profound disabilities are likely to experience exclusion after formal schooling is terminated. Many are relegated to nonvocational day activity programs without any consideration of options for employment in the community. More often than not, this translates into even more limitations in community involvement. It should not be surprising that institutionalization becomes a probable result (Bates, 1989).

Professionals, advocates, and consumers have not reached consensus regarding whether people with profound disabilities should work. However, two issues that must be addressed to clarify the issue are agreement on the definition of "work" and commitment to the idea that adults with profound disabilities must be allowed choice in all areas of life, including employment.

In the broad sense, work can be defined as "continued physical or mental exertion or activity directed to some purpose or end" (Landau & Bogus, 1975, p. 853). This definition can describe a wide range of activities, from work in integrated settings for competitive wages to moving an eyebrow to communicate readiness for being assisted to eat. With a definition that encompasses such a wide range of purposeful activity, one would be hard-pressed to identify any adult who is not capable of work. Acknowledging that any purposeful activity in which one engages requires work allows for respect for the efforts displayed by adults with profound disabilities. Respect for individual's work efforts cannot be gained if limitations are placed on what an individual is allowed to do by persons providing support.

It has been argued that United States society is one that can clearly afford to excuse individuals who are profoundly disabled from performing work that can be performed by others (Evans & Scotti, 1989). It has even been questioned whether it is ethical to expect those persons with the most severe disabilities to perform work. These arguments have been most prevalent in relation to those people with combinations of disabilities that often preclude them from working for pay outside of the home in community employment situations (Bates, 1989; Hill & Morton, 1988). However, those identifying arguments for exclusion from paid work still acknowledge that it should be possible to attain a dignified life-style even though it does not include paid employment. This argument recognizes the expanded definition of work by making the point that work, such as recreational and self-help behavior, should occupy at least a part of one's day.

The option of not working for wages in inclusive environments must be the choice of the individual with profound disabilities, not an option of exclusion imposed by persons making choices for them. The option to work in the community allows people in the community to see individuals who are profoundly disabled performing in socially valued roles. In addition, it allows those employees with profound disabilities in the community access to the benefits of employment that go beyond wages. These benefits include social connections, enhanced feelings of self-worth, and respect of persons supporting the adults in the community (Falvey, 1986; Wolfensberger, 1983).

Meaningful community participation must include the option to work in the community, if that is the desire of the adult with profound disabilities. Present practices in supported employment do not always allow this option. Traditional marketing strategies in supported employment have included promises to employers of work-ready, dependable employees who will not require additional supervisory support. When additional supervisory support is deemed necessary, promises have been made to the effect that production of employees will meet the quantity and quality of production of workers without disabilities. These promises, although appealing to employers, have served to exclude adults with profound disabilities who may require intense support for an infinite amount of time to be successful in employment in the community. Marketing strategies of this nature also perpetuate a value system that rejects individuals who are not as productive or independent as others. Until supported employment practices acknowledge that adults with profound disabilities may never meet those standards, discrimination against people with disabilities who are not as productive or independent as others will continue to exist (Bates, 1989; Ferguson & Ferguson, 1986).

Restructuring of the system that supports people in employment settings is necessary if adults with the most profound disabilities are to be included. An initial reform that must occur is change in vocational curriculum offered during the public school years. If young adults are to leave school to lives of inclusion in the community, their school experience must include vocational training that results in job placement and support before transition from school. This lessens the chances of exclusion from adult supports based on the assumption of inability to work in the community.

Another necessary reform is change in supported employment practices to provide the intense and ongoing supports necessary for some adults with profound disabilities to be successful in work environments. This change must begin with a cessation of the practice of presenting all potential employees as work ready and/or capable of working at standards expected of workers without disabilities. The value and worth of the individual must be emphasized to potential employers. In addition, adequate supports must be provided for the employee to experience the level of success that his or her potential will allow. Thus, the present concepts of support must be expanded. For example, sensory deficits and constraints in movement of many individuals require adaptations that are sometimes beyond the expertise of persons traditionally providing support. This change will necessitate expansion of the training of support personnel and inclusion of persons from disciplines not traditionally included in supported employment systems. The development of these adaptations to meet the unique needs of the employee with profound disabilities often poses challenges best addressed by *rehabilitation engineers.* These professionals have begun to be used as consultants in vocational programs. Their role, however, must be expanded to full membership in transdisciplinary teams that provide support; this will allow their expertise to be utilized in job analysis, development of modifications, and assistive technology. The inclusion of other professionals with diverse expertise must also be considered to make all possible efforts to avoid exclusion of persons who desire to work.

The manner in which adults with profound disabilities are educated and trained is another area for consideration for reform. When the onus for failure to learn is taken from the learner and focused back on the teacher–trainer, it becomes clear that present practices may not be providing adequate learning opportunities for adults with profound disabilities. This is true across all adult environments and is not limited to employment.

Education and Training

United States society is just beginning to comprehend the unique learning needs of adults with profound disabilities. It is a given that inclusion in the community requires acquisition of skills to interact in community settings. The evolution of educational technology in the next decade will be a major factor in determining the degree to which adults with profound disabilities realize their inclusion in the community. Blatt (1987) and Sternberg (1988) are among those who have dismissed the concept of educability as a pertinent issue. Baer (1981), in speaking of children with the most severe disabilities, stated "there is no way to affirm at the level of fact that some children cannot be taught effectively; and there is no way to affirm at the level of fact that all children can be taught effectively" (p. 97). The same is true for adults. Service providers must, therefore, move forward with the assumption that *all* people can learn at some level.

What little is known about effective teaching for adults with profound disabilities has basically evolved from two sources: behavior research with animals and successful interventions with various subpopulations of individuals who are disabled. Researchers in the area of behavior management gained much of what is now known by demonstrating that what had previously been explored in animal laboratories could be applied to human behavior. Many of the early investigations with humans involved persons with profound disabilities. Unfortunately, the research was not done with the purpose of developing instructional techniques uniquely designed for subjects in these studies, but to demonstrate the generalization of principles of learning to humans (see Chapter 5). Often the measured outcome of these research efforts was increasing the rate of some simple motor response or the use of a conditioned reflex to respond to a stimulus. The efforts were typically used to further demonstrate the classical conditioning paradigm, not to shape these responses into usable activities for the people involved in the studies (Evans & Scotti, 1989). These studies supported the hypothesis that behavior of people with profound disabilities could be shaped, and served to dispel the notion that people with the most severe disabilities were incapable of learning even simple contingencies (Rice, 1968). Unfortunately, despite the growth in optimism for persons with profound disabilities, the results of this research did not lead to outcomes that directly impacted the lives of the persons who were involved in the studies. Meyer (1991) warned of perpetuating the demonstration of experimental control at the expense of developing goals regarding meaningful outcomes for individuals who are subjects in various research studies:

> Surely it would not require 30 more years of continuing to teach simple operant responses to persons with all conceivable combinations of disabilities before we could move on to teaching more meaningful skills and behaviors and demonstrating their use in the real world. (p. 635)

Many professionals purport that there are no qualitative differences in disabling conditions. From this follows the reasoning that "the standards, expectations, and criteria that have emerged in the field for persons who are 'moderately' and 'severely' handicapped apply perhaps equally to those who are the most profoundly disabled" (Evans & Scotti, 1989, p. 84). There is, however, an inherent danger in embracing what is known about effective instructional technology with one subpopulation of people and applying it to another group with the expectation for the same outcomes. Errors from the past should warn of these dangers. Examples include the watered-down regular education curriculum that was used as an attempt to educate young people with moderate and severe disabilities, and the misguided attempts to apply the "train them and leave them" approach of successful vocational training with persons with mild disabilities to adults with more severe disabilities. The failure of persons with more severe disabilities to achieve in these attempts provided the impetus to develop specific educational curricula and technology that were more effective for these learners.

As previously stated, adults with profound disabilities are an extremely heterogeneous group of people with a wide variety of neurologic and other organic deficits. This fact must be acknowledged before effective instructional technology can be fully developed. Evans and Scotti (1989) suggested that an interesting outcome of research with people with profound disabilities is that they do not follow the exact same "laws" of conditioning that intact, nonorganically damaged persons follow. . . . The professional must be aware that persons with profound disabilities may require extensive shaping and training procedures, that acquisition curves are likely to be atypical and that such phenomena as "spontaneous extinction" may occur (Landesman-Dwyer & Sackett, 1978; Rice & McDaniel, 1966). (p. 86)

Service providers must remain cognizant of these differences, therefore, when attempting to apply or adapt instructional technology proven to be effective with other groups of adults to those who are profoundly disabled. They must likewise avoid assumptions that the same or similar techniques will be as effective.

Addressing the specific needs of persons with profound disabilities

Researchers and service providers are just beginning to understand the unique needs of adults with profound disabilities in relation to community inclusion. Two characteristics that many of these adults have in common have been recurring foci for research to date. These research efforts have been in the areas of motor functioning and behavior described as excessive and/or inappropriate.

Many adults with profound disabilities have few, if any, identified motor responses that can be used to effect their inclusion in the rhythm of daily life in the community. Technology is now at a point, however, that even the most minute movement can be used to allow persons with limited repertoires of motor function to participate in the activities of the community. Computers and other environmental controls can be accessed with the simplest eye movement. Research in this area in the next decade will allow individuals opportunities that could only be dreamed of in years past.

Another area of motor function that has received emphasis in research efforts is endurance. Many adults with profound disabilities do not exhibit functional levels of endurance. The aerobic status of people varies greatly, from those individuals who are ambulatory to those who are nonambulatory and spend most of their lives in their beds (Evans & Scotti, 1989). Research has demonstrated that endurance can be increased through exercise as simple as trunk, head, and arm movements, to something as demanding as riding an exercise bicycle. In addition to the aerobic benefits and improvements in muscle tone and strength that result from these activities, the acquisition of these skills affords participants options for inclusion in activities in their communities (Burch, Clegg, & Bailey, 1987; Dewson & Whiteley, 1987; Evans & Scotti, 1989; Weber & Thaeler, 1987).

Many adults with profound disabilities have had excessive and/or inappropriate behavior identified as excuses for their segregation from the mainstream of the community. Behavior research that values adults with profound disabilities is progressing with respectful timidity. A definition of behavior as excessive or inappropriate is often determined by social values. Therefore, unless the behavior in which a person engages is causing harm to the individual or other persons, great care must be employed to assure that the behavior is not being extinguished or modified if it serves a purpose for the person involved, regardless of whether or not one is emphasizing a "positive" change technology (Lovett, 1991).

Determining the function of behavior perceived as inappropriate by others is the essential first step in making a decision on whether a behavior should be altered to make it more acceptable to society. Evans and Scotti (1989) warned that, for persons with profound disabilities who often have limited repertoires of behavior, a focus must always be on positive, alternative behaviors. For example, extinguishing behaviors can remove a person's only manner to communicate that something is wrong in his or her environment, unless positive alternatives can be taught to serve the same function.

A research focus on the dignity of persons

Researchers must always consider whether reduction of excessive or inappropriate behavior leads to greater social opportunities and inclusion in the mainstream of community life. A delicate balance must be maintained between changing the behavior of adults with profound disabilities and changing the attitudes of society regarding acceptance of behaviors that are not the norm. Research in the areas of behavioral change and best practice instructional technology must be based on the assumption that dignity of adults with profound disabilities will be respected. Honoring the individual can avoid triviality in research and assure that research efforts are focused on the skills needed by individuals to improve their quality of life. Assurance of this research focus means that efforts will be socially valid and have relevance to the social situation and environment of participants (Kazdin, 1980; Sharpton & Alberto, 1988). Voeltz and Evans (1983) proposed that future efforts in research must determine validity for four aspects of interventions to ensure that the dignity of persons with disabilities is being respected. Service providers must determine whether what they do as practitioners actually accounts for the changes made with adult participants in these efforts (*internal validity*), whether the practitioners are doing what they actually proposed to do in relation to those interventions (*educational integrity*), and whether the behaviors acquired as a function of the interventions are truly beneficial to the participants (*empirical validity*) and valued by significant others (*social validity*).

Informed consent is another vehicle through which the dignity of individuals involved in studies should be assured. The purpose of informed consent is to respect the person's status as a human being by guaranteeing that he or she has the right of choice. However, the issue of consent is clouded for adults with profound disabilities because they may be less able than persons without disabilities or people with less significant degrees of disability to express a desire to stop participating in a study (Holvoet, 1989). A number of ethicists and researchers (Cleland, 1979; Holvoet, 1989; Kane, Robbins, & Stanley, 1982; Lowe & Alexander, 1981) purported that informed consent is not the only way to ensure that a subject's personhood is respected. In fact, following procedures of informed consent might preclude the possibility of an individual's participating in what could be effective education or training. Holvoet (1989) took this position based on her observation that, if during a study, a person with profound disabilities exhibited what appeared to be behaviors indicative of dissatisfaction (e.g., crying, tantrumming, self-abuse), these behaviors might be a normal part of the participant's repertoire and be typical responses to the technique being used. She further proposed that, if a person's rights were being protected by an advocate, and the advocate was unaware that the participant's behavioral repertoire included such behaviors, the advocate might have the person with profound disabilities released from the study on the basis of discomfort or unhappiness that actually had no basis in fact. Holvoet (1989) suggested, therefore, that if research is to be conducted with people with profound disabilities, informed consent must become more than a mere procedural step.

Beyond establishing validity of research, the dignity of persons with profound disabilities must be respected through the acknowledgment that remediation of individual deficits to "normalcy" is unreasonable for these adults. Sharpton and Alberto (1988) posited that independence is an unreasonable expectation for people identified as profoundly disabled. They suggested that participation, contribution, and satisfaction are often more noteworthy outcomes to expect. Researchers should honor acquisition of these outcomes in ongoing efforts. This shift in expected outcomes will avoid the cloak of competence effect that Meyer (1991) described as limiting the intervention efforts for persons with profound disabilities. She also warned that the results of research must be balanced with efforts in other areas (e.g., economic, political, and social considerations) to provide adults with profound disabilities opportunities for inclusion in the community. The need for balance between research and development of public policy has also been emphasized by Baumeister (1981), who viewed research as only one means to indicate what should be done.

The efforts to date for developing instructional technology and supports for adults with profound disabilities provide the basis for future growth. Service providers must respect what has been learned from animal research, studies involving persons with lesser degrees of disability, and limited studies specific to adults with profound disabilities. The information that has been gained from these efforts must be meshed with the values that honor the unique needs of adults with profound disabilities, protect the dignity of these individuals, and balance the errors of the past with needs for future development to include individuals in the community.

A research focus on respecting choice

Future development in instructional technology must include respect for the choices of adults with profound disabilities, maintenance of equilibrium with the needs for decision making of individuals with profound disabilities and those of their support providers, and balance between expansion of opportunities to utilize existing repertoires of behavior with development of new behaviors. Valuing an individual implies that there is respect for that individual. An attitude of respect for adults who are profoundly disabled requires a recognition that these individuals may have values that differ significantly from those of professionals and others who provide supports for them (Downie, 1985; Downie & Telfer, 1980; Holvoet, 1989). This implies that adults with profound disabilities should be provided choices in what they do and how they do it.

Choice is essential to maximizing an individual's inclusion in the flow of community life. Allowing the respect that provides choice for adults with profound disabilities is certainly not a given in the support systems that exist today. Adults with profound disabilities are often expected to comply with the choices made for them: where they live, with whom they live, if they will be allowed and supported to work, and if they will be included in activities in the community. Choices as basic as when to bathe or what to eat are often under the control of others. Disallowing choice denies adults with profound disabilities options and controls in their lives. Sternberg (1988) stated,

> It is certainly not unexpected that other individuals, in effect, will totally control the lives of persons with severe or profound handicaps. Although many might consider this "outer" or "other" control as in the best interests of the person with severe or profound handicaps, in many respects it may simply serve as a barrier to more meaningful and functional progress. (p. 480)

Adults with profound disabilities should not be expected to make great progress in attaining skills and becoming more independent unless they understand that they have some semblance of control over their lives (Guess, Benson, & Siegel-Causey, 1985). Programs that provide support to adults with profound disabilities are beginning to acknowledge the vital part that choice plays in their lives. One example of this shift in values is reflected in the evaluation standards adopted by progressive programs. Many are now basing standards for program evaluation on opportunities for choice and control over life-style, rather than other quality of life indicators (Brown, 1991; Meyer & Evans, 1989; O'Brien, 1987).

Denial of choice contributes to the negative perception of adults with profound disabilities. Meyer and Evans (1989) attributed many of the most serious behavior problems exhibited by persons with disabilities to issues of control. Furthermore, Seligman (1975) described the *learned helplessness* that is produced for many adults with profound disabilities. Denial of choice keeps adults in a position of having all aspects of their lives determined through an outer locus of control, thereby denying the person the opportunity to internalize control, which is essential to learning and growth.

The ability to make choices is not innate. Individuals who have had all aspects of their lives controlled by others have never had the opportunity to learn how to make choices. This skill must be taught. Guess et al. (1985) delineated three interrelated concepts that determine an individual's ability to make choices. The first is whether a person has a liking or preference for something. The second is whether the person actually has a choice in obtaining what he or she prefers. The third is whether the individual is aware that options concerning choice are available. Establishing these three concepts as a part of best practice leads to individuals' learning to make good choices. For adults to learn this skill, they must be provided experience with the process of decision making, with viable alternatives and the consequences of decisions.

As vital as choices are regarding what a person wants to do, so are choices related to nonparticipation. It is important for adults with profound disabilities to have the option to choose not to participate in activities, and to choose not to comply with decisons made by others who attempt to dictate their life-style. Honoring the choice of nonparticipation is vital to respect for persons as individuals. Brown (1991) suggested that support providers establish schedules that reflect personal freedom and allow a person to refuse participation, to escape from activities, and to just say "no." Even though support personnel may design schedules, the adult with disabilities should be able to control, as much as possible, events in his or her life. The person should have the freedom to refuse or escape participation in any or all parts of the daily routine. Respect for the adult with profound disabilities demands that the person have the freedom to participate in a way that reflects his or her wishes, and not in an arbitrary sequence of events meaningful only to others.

Choice of nonparticipation is not always the most convenient for support personnel but is essential for respecting the autonomy of the individual. West and Parent (1992) described the inconvenience that the choice of nonparticipation may present when related to keeping or resigning a job. In many cases, this may represent the most problematic situation, when providers are compelled to maintain placements regardless of the level of satisfaction experienced by the supported individual. Most people have the opportunity for choice of nonparticipation in their lives, and this should be no different for adults with profound disabilities.

Research on balancing needs

Holvoet (1989) suggested that the current focus on social validity in research, training, and provision of support might be shifting to emphasis on outcomes meaningful to persons in the lives of individuals with profound disabilities, rather than the individuals themselves. Persons who provide support for adults with profound disabilities can experience great physical and emotional stress. Making all the decisions for the persons they support can contribute to that stress by maintaining an imbalance in the relationship. Evans and Scotti (1989) described a very simple decision that could be made by an adult with profound disabilities that would, at the same time, allow him or her to have some control in a relationship with support providers— that is, the initiation of a toileting routine. Even if the adult with profound disabilities depends on support for all components of actual toileting, the initiation of the activity, through a hand signal or activation of a buzzer with a switch, places the person with disabilities in control of the activity. This transfers ownership of the routine from support personnel to the adult with disabilities.

Decisions that may potentially threaten life or safety might need to be joint decisions. Sharpton and West (1992) suggested that there may be situations in which independent choice making is not feasible or safe. In these instances, they suggested that partial participation in the decision-making process be supported to avoid exclusion of persons from the decisions that control their lives.

Research on balancing current and expected behaviors

Another balance that is important when considering training and support for adults with profound disabilities is that between existing skills (behaviors) that a person may possess and development of new behaviors. State of the art for instructional technology for adults with profound disabilities is not at a point that service providers can afford to ignore behaviors or skills that a person already possesses to establish new skills. At the present time, service providers are not able to teach efficiently enough and, at the same time, sacrifice the skills that are already a part of the repertoire of individuals. A behavior such as clenching a spoon with one's teeth may be an individual's only way to indicate that he or she has had enough to eat. Until that person can be given another option through training, the behavior should not be a target for elimination.

Meyer (1991) proposed that, with the shift to support models, individuals should be taught as many new (useful) skills as possible. However, the design of support systems should allow for "filling in" for the absence of any critical skills to ensure participation for the individuals. The concept of partial participation is critical to adults with profound disabilities. However, as already discussed in several prior chapters, it cannot be approached with the attitude that all steps of a task analysis of a desired activity can be achieved at a level of independence.

Behaviors that a person possesses should be expanded in the number of purposes they serve within a variety of activities. The skill of pushing a button to call an attendant can be used in other activities, such as choosing a movie to attend with a friend, changing the channels with the remote control to watch a television program of choice, or stopping the conveyer belt in an employment situation. Other supports may be needed to complete the whole activity in any of these situations; however, the person's opportunities are being expanded as new behaviors and skills are blended with ones previously possessed.

CONCLUSION

The future for adults with profound disabilities depends on the efforts of researchers, educators, support providers, policymakers, and other persons who care for and about them. Our position at this point in history is reflective of the words of Martin Luther King, which I recently saw posted on the office door of a colleague:

> Cowardice asks the question, is it safe?
> Expediency asks the question, is it politic?
> Vanity asks the question, is it popular?
> But, conscience asks the question, is it right?
> And there comes a time when one must take a position that is neither safe,
>   nor politic, nor popular.
> But, one must take it because their conscience tells that it is right.

Adults with profound disabilities have been ignored and segregated from society for too long. Providing them the supports that are necessary for participation as members of the community is "right," whether or not it is safe, politic, or popular.

REFERENCES

Albano, M. L. (1983). *Transdisciplinary teaming in special education: A case study.* Unpublished doctoral dissertation, University of Illinois at Urbana–Champaign.
Baer, D. M. (1981). A hung jury and a Scottish verdict: "Not proven." *Analysis and Intervention in Developmental Disabilities, 1,* 91–98.

Baker, B. L., Seltzer, G. B., & Seltzer, M. M. (1977). *As close as possible: Community residences for retarded adults.* Boston: Little Brown.

Bates, P. (1989). Vocational training for persons with profound disabilities. In F. Brown & D. Lehr (Eds.), *Persons with profound disabilities: Issues and practices* (pp. 265–294). Baltimore: Brookes.

Baumeister, A. A. (1981). Mental retardation policy and research: The unfulfilled promise. *American Journal of Mental Deficiency, 85,* 445–456.

Bellamy, G. T., & Horner, R. H. (1988). Beyond high school: Residential and employment options after high school. In M. E. Snell (Ed.), *Systematic instruction of the moderately and severely handicapped* (3rd ed., pp. 491–510). Columbus, OH: Merrill.

Bellamy, G. T., Horner, R. H., & Inman, D. P. (1979). *Vocational habilitation of severely retarded adults: A direct service technology.* Baltimore: University Park Press.

Best-Sigford, B., Bruininks, R., Lakin, K., Hill, B., & Heal, L. (1982). Residence release patterns in a national sample of public residential facilities. *American Journal of Mental Deficiency, 87,* 130–140.

Biklen, D., & Knoll, J. (1987). In S. J. Taylor, D. Biklen, & J. Knoll (Eds.), *Community integration for people with severe disabilities* (pp. 184–201). New York: Teachers College Press.

Blatt, B. (1987). *The conquest of mental retardation.* Austin, TX: PRO-ED.

Borthwick-Duffy, S., Eyman, R., & White, J. (1987). Client characteristics and residential placement patterns. *American Journal of Mental Deficiency, 92,* 24–30.

Brawner-Jones, N. G. (in press). Special concerns for students with chronic medical conditions and severe mental retardation during the transition years. In J. A. Mulick & R. F. Antanock (Eds.), *Transitions in mental retardation* (Vol. 5). Norwood, NJ: Ablex.

Brown, F. (1991). Creative daily scheduling: A nonintrusive approach to challenging behaviors in community residences. *The Journal of The Association for Persons with Severe Handicaps, 16,* 75–84.

Brown, F., Davis, R., Richards, M., & Kelly, K. (1989). Residential services for adults with profound disabilities. In F. Brown & D. Lehr (Eds.), *Persons with profound disabilities: Issues and practices* (pp. 295–332). Baltimore: Brookes.

Brown, F., Helmstetter, E., & Guess, D. (1986). *Current best practices with students with profound disabilities: Are there any?* Unpublished manuscript, Institute of Professional Practice, New Haven, CT.

Bruininks, R. H., Kudla, M., Wieck, C. A., & Hauber, F. A. (1980). Management problems in community residential facilities. *Mental Retardation, 18,* 123–130.

Burch, M. R., Clegg, J. C., & Bailey, J. S. (1987). Automated contingent reinforcement of correct posture. *Research in Developmental Disabilities, 8,* 15–20.

Burchard, S. N., & Thousand, J. (1988). Staff and manager competencies. In M. Janicki, M. Krauss, & M. Seltzer (Eds.), *Community residences for persons with developmental disabilities: Here to stay* (pp. 251–267). Baltimore: Brookes.

Cleland, C. (1979). *The profoundly mentally retarded.* Englewood Cliffs, NJ: Prentice-Hall.

Crossley, R., & McDonald, A. (1980). *Annie's coming out.* New York: Penguin.

Dewson, M. R. J., & Whiteley, J. H. (1987). Sensory reinforcement of head turning with nonambulatory, profoundly mentally retarded persons. *Research in Developmental Disabilities, 8,* 413–426.

Downie, R. S. (1985). Ambivalence of attitude toward the mentally retarded. In R. S. Laura & A. F. Ashman (Eds.), *Moral issues in mental retardation* (pp. 29–42). Dover, NH: Croom Helm.

Downie, R. S., & Telfer, E. (1980). *Caring and curing: A philosophy of medicine and social work.* London: Methuen.

Ellis, J. W. (1982). The Supreme Court and institutions: A comment on Youngberg vs. Romeo. *Mental Retardation, 20,* 197–200.

Evans, I. M., & Scotti, J. R. (1989). Defining meaningful outcomes for persons with profound disabilities. In F. Brown & D. Lehr (Eds.), *Persons with profound disabilities: Issues and practices* (pp. 83–107). Baltimore: Brookes.

Falvey, M. (1986). *Community-based curriculum integration strategies for students with severe handicaps.* Baltimore: Brookes.

Federal Register. (1984). Developmental Disabilities Act of 1984, Report #98-1074, September 25, 102(11)(F).

Ferguson, D. L., & Ferguson, P. M. (1986). The new victors: A progressive policy analysis for work reform for people with very severe handicaps. *Mental Retardation, 24,* 331–338.

Ferguson, P. M. (1988). *Abandoned to their fate: A history of social policy and practice toward severely retarded people in America, 1820–1920.* Unpublished doctoral dissertation, Syracuse University, Syracuse, NY.

Forest, M., & Lusthaus, E. (1988). *The kaleidoscope: Each belongs—Quality education for all.* Unpublished manuscript, Frontier College, Toronto, Canada.

Forest, M., & Pearpoint, J. (1992). The "butwhatabout" kids. In J. Pearpoint, M. Forest, & J. Snow (Eds.), *The inclusion papers: Strategies to make inclusion work* (pp. 18–27). Toronto, Canada: Inclusion Press.

Freudenberger, H. J. (1975). The staff burn-out syndrome in alternative institutions. *Psychotherapy: Theory, Research, and Practice, 12,* 73–82.

Froland, C., Pancoast, D., Chapman, N., & Kimboko, P. (1981). *Helping networks and human services.* Beverly Hills, CA: Sage.

Giangreco, M. F., York, J., & Rainforth, B. (1989). Providing related services to learners with severe handicaps in educational settings: Pursuing the least restrictive option. *Pediatric Physical Therapy, 1*(2), 55–63.

Guess, D., Benson, H. A., & Siegel-Causey, E. (1985). Concepts and issues related to choice-making and autonomy among persons with severe disabilities. *Journal of The Association for Persons with Severe Handicaps, 10,* 79–86.

Hill, B. K., Bruininks, R. H., & Lakin, K. C. (1983). Characteristics of mentally retarded people in residential facilities. *Health and Social Work, 8,* 85–96.

Hill, J. W., & Morton, M. V. (1988). Transition programming: Improving vocational outcomes. In L. Sternberg (Ed.), *Educating students with severe or profound handicaps* (2nd ed., pp. 439–471). Austin, TX: PRO-ED.

Holvoet, J. F. (1989). Research on persons labeled profoundly retarded: Issues and ideas. In F. Brown & D. Lehr (Eds.), *Persons with profound disabilities: Issues and practices* (pp. 61–82). Baltimore: Brookes.

Kane, J. M., Robbins, L. L., & Stanley, B. (1982). Psychiatric research. In R. A. Greenwald, M. K. Ryan, & J. E. Mulvihill (Eds.), *Human subjects research: A handbook for institutional review boards* (pp. 193–205). New York: Plenum Press.

Kazdin, A. E. (1980). *Behavior modification in applied settings* (2nd ed.). Homewood, IL: Dorsey Press.

Kiernan, W. E., McGaughey, M. J., & Schalock, R. L. (1986). *National employment survey for adults with developmental disabilities* (Tech. Rep.). Boston: Boston Children's Hospital, The Developmental Evaluation Clinic.

Kregel, J., & Wehman, P. (1989). Supported employment: Promises deferred for persons with severe handicaps. *Journal of The Association for Persons with Severe Handicaps, 14,* 293–303.

Lakin, K. C. (1988). Strategies for promoting the stability of direct care staff. In M. Janicki, M. Krauss, & M. Seltzer (Eds.), *Community residences for persons with developmental disabilities: Here to stay* (pp. 231–239). Baltimore: Brookes.

Lakin, K. C., Bruininks, R. H., & Hill, B. K. (1982). *Factors related to job stability of direct-care facilities for mentally retarded people.* Minneapolis: University of Minnesota, Department of Psychoeducational Studies.

Lakin, K. C., Hill, B. K., & Bruininks, R. H. (1988). Trends and issues in the growth of community residential services. In M. Janicki, M. Krauss, & M. Seltzer (Eds.), *Community residences for persons with developmental disabilities: Here to stay* (pp. 25–45). Baltimore: Brookes.

Lakin, K. C., Hill, B. K., Hauber, F. A., & Bruininks, R. H. (1982). Changes in age at first admission to residential care of mentally retarded people. *Mental Retardation, 20,* 216–219.

Lakin, K. C., Hill, B. K., White, C. C., & Wright, E. A. (1988). *Longitudinal change and interstate variability in the size of residential facilities for persons with mental retardation.* Minneapolis: University of Minnesota, Center for Residential and Community Services.

Landau, S., & Bogus, R. (Eds.). (1975). *The Doubleday dictionary for home, school, and office.* Garden City, NY: Doubleday.

Landesman, S., & Vietze, P. (Eds.). (1987). *Living environments and mental retardation.* Washington, DC: American Association on Mental Deficiency.

Landesman-Dwyer, S., & Sackett, G. P. (1978). Behavioral changes in nonambulatory profoundly mentally retarded individuals. In C. E. Meyers (Ed.), *Quality of life in severely and profoundly retarded people: Research foundations for improvement* (pp. 55–144). Washington, DC: American Association on Mental Deficiency.

Lovett, H. (1991). Empowerment and choices. In L. H. Meyer, C. A. Peck, & L. Brown (Eds.), *Critical issues in the lives of people with severe disabilities* (pp. 625–629). Baltimore: Brookes.

Lowe, C. U., & Alexander, D. F. (1981). Informed consent and the rights of research subject. In H. Wechsler, R. Lamont-Havers, & G. Cahill, Jr. (Eds.), *The social context of medical research* (pp. 97–126). Cambridge, MS: Ballinger.

Lusthaus, E. (1985). "Euthanasia" of persons with severe handicaps: Refuting the rationalizations. *Journal of The Association for Persons with Severe Handicaps, 10,* 87–94.

Lyon, S., & Lyon, G. (1980). Team functioning and staff development: A role release approach to providing integrated educational services for severely handicapped students. *Journal of The Association for the Severely Handicapped, 5,* 250–263.

Maslach, C. (1976, September). Burned-out. *Human Behavior, 5,* 16–22.

McCord, W. T. (1981). Community residences: The staffing. In J. Wortis (Ed.), *Mental retardation and developmental disabilities* (Vol. 12, pp. 111–128). New York: Brunner/Mazel.

McDonald, E. P. (1985). Medical needs of severely developmentally disabled persons residing in the community. *American Journal of Mental Deficiency, 90,* 171–176.

Meyer, L. H. (1991). Advocacy, research, and typical practices: A call for the reductions of discrepancies between what is and what ought to be, and how to get there. In L. H. Meyer, C. A. Peck, & L. Brown (Eds.), *Critical issues in the lives of people with severe disabilities* (pp. 629–650). Baltimore: Brookes.

Meyer, L. H., & Evans, I. M. (1989). *Nonaversive intervention for behavior problems: A manual for home and community.* Baltimore: Brookes.

New York Office of Mental Retardation and Developmental Disabilities. (1987). *Future of the workforce: Report of the panel on the future of the workforce serving persons with developmental disabilities.* Albany, NY: Author.

Nisbet, J., & Callahan, M. (1987). Achieving success in integrated workplaces: Critical elements in assisting persons with severe disabilities. In S. J. Taylor, D. Biklen, & J. Knoll (Eds.), *Community integration for people with severe disabilities* (pp. 184–201). New York: Teachers College Press.

Nisbet, J., Clark, M., & Covert, S. (1991). Living it up! An analysis of research on community living. In L. H. Meyer, C. A. Peck, & L. Brown (Eds.), *Critical issues in the lives of people with severe disabilities* (pp. 115–145). Baltimore: Brookes.

O'Brien, J. (1987). A guide to life-style planning: Using the Activities Catalog to integrate services and natural support systems. In B. Wilcox & G. T. Bellamy (Eds.), *A comprehensive guide to the Activities Catalog: An alternative curriculum for youth and adults with severe disabilities* (pp. 175–189). Baltimore: Brookes.

O'Connor, G. O. (1976). *Home is a good place: A national perspective of community residential facilities for developmentally disabled persons.* Washington DC: American Association on Mental Deficiency.

Orelove, F. P., & Sobsey, D. (1991). *Educating children with multiple disabilities: A transdisciplinary approach* (2nd ed.). Baltimore: Brookes.

Public Law 99-506. (1984). The Developmental Disabilities Act of 1984.

Rice, H. K. (1968). Operant behavior in vegetative patients: III. Methodological considerations. *Psychological Record, 18,* 297–302.

Rice, H. K., & McDaniel, M. W. (1966). Operant behavior in vegetative patients. *Psychological Record, 16,* 279–281.

Romeo v. Youngberg, 457 v.s. 307 (1982).

Rowitz, L. (1988). Health care issues in community residential settings. In M. Janicki, M. Krauss, & M. Seltzer (Eds.), *Community residences for persons with developmental disabilities: Here to stay* (pp. 203–217). Baltimore: Brookes.

Rusch, F. R., Chadsey-Rusch, J., & Johnson, J. R. (1991). Supported employment: Emerging opportunities for employment integration. In L. H. Meyer, C. A. Peck, & L. Brown (Eds.), *Critical issues in the lives of people with severe disabilities* (pp. 145–171). Baltimore: Brookes.

Rynders, J. (1982). Research on promoting learning in children with Down's syndrome. In S. Pueschel & J. Rynders (Eds.), *Down's syndrome: Advances in biomedicine and the behavioral sciences* (pp. 389–451). Cambridge, MA: Ware Press.

Schalock, R. L. (1985). Comprehensive community services: A plea for interagency collaboration. In R. H. Bruininks & K. C. Lakin (Eds.), *Living and learning in the least restrictive environment* (pp. 37–64). Baltimore: Brookes.

Scheerenberger, R. (1982). Public residential services, 1981: Status and trends. *Mental Retardation, 20,* 210–215.

Schinke, S. P., & Wong, S. E. (1977). Evaluation of staff training in group homes serving mentally retarded adults: Community placement and program success. *American Journal of Mental Deficiency, 85,* 130–136.

Sears, C. J. (1981). The transdisciplinary approach: A process for compliance with Public Law 94-142. *Journal of The Association for the Severely Handicapped, 6*(1), 22–29.

Seligman, M. (1975). *Helplessness: On depression, development, and death.* San Francisco: W. H. Freeman.

Sharpton, W. R., & Alberto, P. A. (1988). Transition programming: Independent living skills development. In L. Sternberg (Ed.), *Educating students with severe or profound handicaps* (2nd ed., pp. 401–438). Austin, TX: PRO-ED.

Sharpton, W. R., & West, M. (1992). Severe and profound mental retardation. In P. J. McLaughlin & P. Wehman (Eds.), *Developmental disabilities: A handbook for best practices* (pp. 16–29). Stoneham, MA: Andover Medical Publishers.

Smull, M. W., & Bellamy, G. T. (1991). Community services for adults with disabilities: Policy challenges in the emerging support paradigm. In L. H. Meyer, C. A. Peck, & L. Brown (Eds.), *Critical issues in the lives of people with severe disabilities* (pp. 527–537). Baltimore: Brookes.

Smull, M. W., Sachs, M. L., Cahn, L. E., & Feder, S. (1988). *Service requests: An overview.* Baltimore: University of Maryland at Baltimore, Applied Research and Evaluation Unit.

Snell, M. E. (1991). Forward. In H. Meyer, C. A. Peck, & L. Brown (Eds.), *Critical issues in the lives of people with severe disabilities* (pp. xv–xxi). Baltimore: Brookes.

Sternberg, L. (1988). Future educational concerns: Crucial questions. In L. Sternberg (Ed.), *Educating students with severe or profound handicaps* (2nd ed., pp. 475–482). Austin, TX: PRO-ED.

Sutter, P., Mayeda, T., Yee, S., & Yanagi, G. (1981). Community placement success based on client behavior preferences of care-providers. *Mental Retardation, 19,* 117–120.

Taylor, S. J. (1987). Introduction. In S. J. Taylor, D. Biklen, & J. Knoll (Eds.), *Community integration for people with severe disabilities* (pp. xv–xx). New York: Teachers College Press.

Timothy W. vs. Rochester, New Hampshire School District (1989).

Turnbull, H. R. (1982). Youngberg vs. Romeo: An essay. *Journal of The Association for the Severely Handicapped, 7*(3), 3–6.

Voeltz, L. M., & Evans, I. M. (1983). Educational validity: Procedures to evaluate outcomes in programs for severely handicapped learners. *Journal of The Association for the Severely Handicapped, 8*(1), 3–15.

Weber, D. B., & Thaeler, D. (1987). *Daily exercise: Is it possible for profoundly mentally retarded individuals?* Paper presented at the annual convention of the Association for Behavior Analysis, Nashville, TN.

Wehman, P., Renzaglia, A., & Bates, P. (1985). *Functional living skills for moderately and severely handicapped individuals.* Austin, TX: PRO-ED.

Weir, R. (1984). *Selective nontreatment of handicapped newborns: Moral dilemmas in neonatal medicine.* Ontario, Canada: Oxford University Press.

West, M. D., & Parent, W. S. (1992). Consumer choice and empowerment in supported employment services: Issues and strategies. *Journal of The Association for Persons with Severe Handicaps, 17,* 47–52.

Westling, D. L. (1986). *Introduction to mental retardation.* Englewood Cliffs, NJ: Prentice-Hall.

Williams, R. (1991). Choices, communication, and control—A call for expanding them in the lives of people with severe disabilities. In L. H. Meyer, C. A. Peck, & L. Brown (Eds.), *Critical issues in the lives of people with severe disabilities* (pp. 543–544). Baltimore: Brookes.

Wolfensberger, W. (1983). Social role valorization: A proposed new term for the principle of normalization. *Mental Retardation, 21,* 234–239.

Woodruff, G., & McGonigel, M. J. (1988). Early intervention team approaches: The transdisciplinary model. In J. B. Jordan, J. J. Gallagher, P. L. Hutinger, & M. B. Karnes (Eds.), *Early childhood special education: Birth to three* (pp. 164–181). Reston, VA: Council for Exceptional Children.

Wyatt v. Stickney, 34 F. Supp. 373, 387 (M.D. Ala. 1972), aff'd subnom, *Wyatt v. Aderholt,* 503 F.2d 1305 (5th Cir. 1974).

Contributors

Paul A. Alberto
Department of Special Education
Georgia State University
Atlanta, Georgia

Robin Alvares
Department of Communicative
  Disorders
Northern Illinois University
DeKalb, Illinois

Marilyn Mulligan Ault
Department of Special Education
University of Kansas
Lawrence, Kansas

Nancy Brawner-Jones
Department of Special Education
University of Maine at Orono
Orono, Maine

David L. Coulter
Division of Pediatric Neurology
Boston University School of
  Medicine
Boston, Massachusetts

J. Carolyn Graff
Childrens Rehabilitation Unit
University of Kansas Medical
  Center
Kansas City, Kansas

Kathryn A. Haring
Department of Educational
  Psychology
University of Oklahoma
Norman, Oklahoma

Thomas G. Kana
Gwinnett County Board of
  Education
Oakland Center
Lawrenceville, Georgia

Kent R. Logan
Gwinnett County Board of
  Education
Oakland Center
Lawrenceville, Georgia

David L. Lovett
Department of Educational
  Psychology
University of Oklahoma
Norman, Oklahoma

Thomas B. Pierce
Department of Special Education
University of Nevada–Las Vegas
Las Vegas, Nevada

Stephen Richards
Department of Educational
  Psychology
University of Oklahoma
Norman, Oklahoma

Jane P. Rues
Occupational Therapy
Rockhurst College
Kansas City, Missouri

William Sharpton
Department of Special Education
University of New Orleans
New Orleans, Louisiana

Les Sternberg
Department of Curriculum and
  Instruction
Iowa State University
Ames, Iowa

Ronald L. Taylor
Department of Exceptional
  Student Education
Florida Atlantic University
Boca Raton, Florida

Bonnie L. Utley
Special Education
University of Pittsburgh
Pittsburgh, Pennsylvania

Toni Waylor-Bowen
Department of Special Education
Georgia State University
Atlanta, Georgia

Lucille Zeph
Department of Special Education
University of Maine
Orono, Maine

Author Index

Subject Index